Colorado's

Incredible Backcountry Trails

Sneffels Highline Trail (page 361)

WARNING:
HIKING INVOLVES RISK!

Hiking is a sport, not a pastime, and like all sports it involves an element of risk. There have been several instances in recent years of people suffering injury while hiking in Colorado's backcountry and then filing a lawsuit against a person or organization that gave them information about the hike. This is a disturbing trend with serious implications for everyone involved in the sport.

The author and publisher of this book will not assume responsibility for any mishap that may occur as a result of information present or not present in this book. It is assumed that anyone attempting any of the hikes described in the following pages is already aware of the potential risks, has made all the necessary preparations, and has had sufficient experience to assume responsibility for himself.

Furthermore, while the author has done his best to assure that the information herein presented is accurate, he cannot guarantee its accuracy. Hikers using the information in this book should make allowance for the possibility that it may not be correct.

Colorado's
Incredible Backcountry Trails

Text and Photography
by
David Day

Mount Massive (page 220)

Rincon Publishing Company
1913 North Skyline Drive
Orem, Utah 84097
www.UtahTrails.com

Library of Congress Control Number: 2008938073
ISBN: 978-0-9660858-4-6

Other books by David Day:

Malaysia in Colour (1979)
Singapore, Gateway to the Far East (1986)
Java, Island of Antiquities (1988)
Malaysia, Gemstone of Southeast Asia (1990)
Thailand and the Kingdoms of Siam (1991)
Utah's Favorite Hiking Trails (1998)
Utah's Favorite Hiking Trails, 2nd Edition (2002)
Canyonlands National Park, Favorite Jeep Roads and Hiking Trails (2004)
Utah's Incredible Backcountry Trails (2006)

Printed by Art Printing Works, Kuala Lumpur, Malaysia

Published by:

Rincon Publishing Company
1913 North Skyline Drive
Orem, Utah 84097

(801) 377-7657
www.UtahTrails.com

For Lorena,

Without whose help
this book would have been finished
two years earlier.

Contents

Southern Colorado

Western Colorado

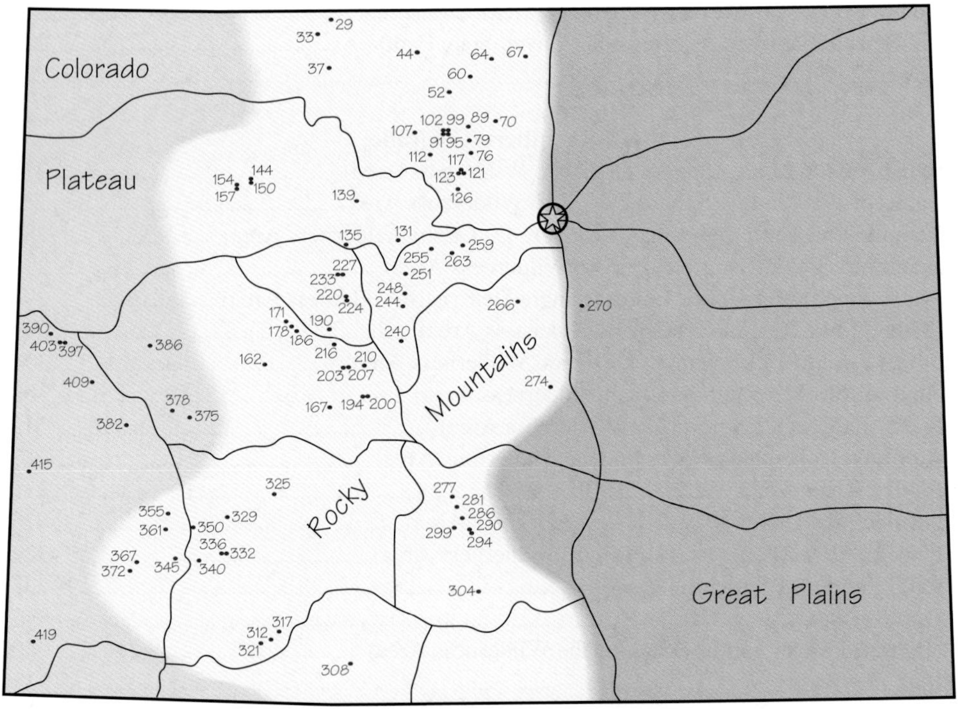

Trailhead Locations

Turn to the indicated page numbers for complete descriptions of the trails.

Preface

My first introduction to Colorado's backcountry came in the mountains above Georgetown, as a summer worker on the Cabin Creek Hydroelectric Project in 1965. Although that job only lasted for a few months it marked the beginning of a life-long love affair with the Colorado Rockies, and I have since returned dozens of times. My treks into the mountains of Colorado have always left me filled with wonder at the beauty and serenity I find there.

For a long time I dreamed of someday writing a book about my experiences in Colorado's mountains, but it wasn't until 1998 that I finally started committing my thoughts to paper. Initially I expected the book to be finished in a year or two, but as I began I quickly came to realize that words alone would not be enough. I needed photographs—hundreds of them—to convey the wonderment I have experienced on the trails in Colorado. So it was that I began the task of revisiting Colorado's backcountry, this time with a backpack full of camera equipment.

Although there is no shortage of good subject matter in Colorado, photographing it is not always easy. The biggest obstacle is the weather. Foul weather can often produce dramatic images but in general it is much easier to get good pictures when the sun is shining and the sky is blue. My trips into the mountains are always made with the expectation of good weather, but conditions can change rapidly in Colorado. Even when the morning sky is clear the afternoons are usually overcast, and afternoon thundershowers are common. It takes time to get good photographs, and a few hours in the morning are often not enough; consequently many of the hikes described here had to be done two or three times before good photographs could be obtained.

Each one of the hikes included in this book has some attraction that, for me, makes it a special outdoor experience. That is not to say, however, that they are all equally enjoyable; some of them deserve special mention. Recognizing this I have made an attempt to rate each trail with one to five stars, according to how much I personally enjoy that hike. A rating of five stars means that particular hike is, in my opinion, one of the ten most enjoyable and memorable hikes in the state.

Finally, I would like to say that there are thousands of miles of hiking trails in Colorado—enough for a lifetime of exploration—and even as this book goes to press I am still finding new trails I would have liked to include. I think I have covered most of the state's best hikes, but some will have to wait for a future edition. If any of you have any comments on the trails I have included or perhaps should have included I would like very much to hear from you.

May there always be wild places for us to explore!

David Day
davidday@utahtrails.com

Introduction

Climb the mountains and get their good tidings.
Nature's peace will flow into you as sunshine flows into trees.
The winds will blow their own freshness into you and the storms their energy,
while care will drop off like autumn leaves.

John Muir

Colorado's greatest attraction is her majestic mountains. From the Wyoming border south to New Mexico an almost unbroken chain of princely summits runs down the center of the state, neatly dividing the eastern plain from the western plateau. This mountainous parapet is actually a small part of the 3,000-mile Rocky Mountain Cordillera that runs almost the entire length of North America and forms the geologic backbone of the continent. Only 300 miles of the range are located in Colorado, yet this small segment is very special. Many would say that the Colorado Rockies are the most interesting and scenically beautiful mountains in North American. Colorado's mountains are far enough south to enjoy relatively long summers yet far enough north to benefit from a heavy winter snow pack. And although they are old enough to have produced the soil necessary to support expansive meadows and alpine tundras, the mountains are also young enough to retain the high, jagged peaks that so inspire us all.

Along with the countless pristine lakes, raging waterfalls and serene alpine meadows

Willow Lake (page 299)

that adorn Colorado's mountains it is worth noting that there are 55 peaks in the state more than 14,000 feet high. This number is particularly significant when one realizes that there are only 113 such summits in the whole of North America. Equally important is the easy accessibility of the Colorado Rockies. Thousands of miles of developed trails thread their way through Colorado's mountains and canyons, giving ordinary people an unparalleled opportunity to discover for themselves the wonders they hold. Most of the state's 55 fabled fourteeners are accessible by trail, while hundreds of other less strenuous paths lead to high mountain passes, historic mining camps, hanging lakes, hot springs, cascading waterfalls, and other mountain wonders.

Besides the Rocky Mountains, Colorado also contains two other major geologic provinces: the Great Plains Province in the eastern part of the state, and the Colorado Plateau Province in the west. The Great Plains Province is an immense sweep of undulating prairie, dotted with huge farms and ranches, that extends for 500 miles east of the Rocky Mountains. Although this vast flatland accounts for nearly a third of Colorado's total land area and is vital to the state's economy, it has little geologic diversity and few hiking trails. Pawnee National Grassland, in the northeastern corner of the state, contains a few short trails that are of interest because of the amazing diversity of bird species that live there. Another notable trail in eastern Colorado is the historic Santa Fe Trail. This trail was originally established in 1821 as a trading route between Missouri and New Mexico, and a portion of it traverses the southeast corner of Colorado near the town of La Junta. The Santa Fe Trail was designated a national historic trail by Congress in 1987, and today it is still possible to hike some parts of it. In general, however, most hiking enthusiasts will find the treeless, semiarid plains of eastern Colorado to be flat and uninteresting.

Of more interest than the Great Plains Province is the Colorado Plateau Province that lies on the western side of the state. This region is famous for its deep redrock canyons, its desert buttes and its natural arches, and it contains many interesting trails. In addition to its geologic attractions, the Colorado Plateau is an archeological wonderland. 700 years ago this was home to the Anasazi Indians, and today the relics of their prehistoric culture can still be seen in hundreds of canyons across the plateau. The best of their artifacts can be found in the recently designated Canyons of the Ancients National Monument and in Mesa Verde National Park.

Goose Creek Trail (page 266)

Geology

Colorado's incredible scenery is, in large part, the result of a series of geologic events that began a very long time ago. Lets go back about 200 million years ago to the beginning of the Jurassic Period when much of Colorado was swampland with mud flats that bordered a shallow western inland sea. This was 100 million years after an earlier geologic event, called the Colorado Orogeny, that resulted in the creation of the Ancestral Rocky Mountains in central Colorado. By the time of the Jurassic Period these earlier mountains were almost completely eroded away, and today most of the evidence of their prior existence is buried deep underground. We don't know what caused the Colorado Orogeny 300 million years ago, but scientists now point to this event as an early sign of a weakness in the center of the North American tectonic plate.

The beginning of the Jurassic Period is significant, because it was about that time that the North American plate broke free from Europe and began drifting westward. As the continent drifted it slid over the top of the Pacific plate and the land was pushed up. By about 100 million year ago the North American plate had moved some 1500 miles west, causing the land to wrinkle and buckle from the resulting stress. The collision with the Pacific plate produced a series of long north-south wrinkles and folds that first appeared in California, then Utah, and finally in Colorado. The North American plate continued to drift westward at an estimated speed of about one inch per year, and by 75 million years ago the resulting stress from the collision had initiated an intense period of mountain building in the west that we now call the Laramide Orogeny.

Willow Creek Falls (page 299)

The Laramide Orogeny continued for some 30 million years, and it was this geologic event that produced the present day Rocky Mountains. By about 45 million years ago this mountain building episode was complete, and a long period of calm began in Colorado. With the exception of some volcanism along the western side of the mountains, the land was relatively stable, and for the next 20 million years the major force shaping the land was erosion. The highest peaks were worn down until there was

Sloan Lake, American Basin (page 336)

probably no summit in Colorado higher than 9,000 feet above sea level. The lower areas on the east and west sides of the state were gradually covered with hundreds of feet of sediment washed down from the mountains.

Then began what is commonly known as the Miocene-Pliocene Uplift. This uplifting of the land went on from about 28 million years ago until 5 million years ago, ultimately causing almost the entire state to rise some 5000 feet. The dramatic uplifting virtually guaranteed that today all of the state's major rivers, the Rio Grande, the Colorado, the Plat, and the Arkansas, originate in Colorado and flow out into adjacent states. Only one narrow sliver of land in the southern part of the state was not affected by the uplift. This area, sandwiched between the Sangre de Cristo Mountains and the San Juan Range is today known as the San Luis Valley.

The eastern third of Colorado belongs to the Great Plains Province, a geologic province that extends eastward from the Rocky Mountains all the way to the Missouri and Mississippi Rivers. This is a broad, flat, almost featureless region that has remained remarkably geologically stable for 200 million years. Although eastern Colorado was pushed up several thousand feet during the Miocene-Pliocene Uplift, the Laramide Orogeny period of mountain building did not extend into the eastern plains. Nor is there any record of significant volcanic activity in the area. As a result, the eastern part of Colorado lacks the geological diversity that makes the rest of the state so unique.

The west side of Colorado belongs to the Colorado Plateau Province. This desert province of sedimentary rock stretches for 300 miles westward from the Colorado Rockies into Utah, Arizona, and New Mexico. It is an ancient circular-shaped accumulation of sedimentary rock that has remained structurally stable for at least 500 million years, and today the geologic record of the Colorado Plateau is preserved in the

Pollock Canyon Trail (page 390)

layers of sediment in astonishing detail. Hundreds of layers of sedimentary rock are chronologically stacked and arranged like the tattered pages of a very old history book, and the story they tell is the story of the earth. This region has on occasion been a lush tropical swamp, a dry Sahara-like desert, an expansive mud flat, and the bottom of a shallow sea. The details of each episode are all there, waiting to be read and interpreted with the tools of modern science.

Before the Miocene-Pliocene Uplift some parts of the West were periodically flooded by a broad, shallow inland sea that sometimes extended all the way from Mexico to the Arctic Ocean. The Colorado Plateau was greatly affected by the presence of this sea; at times the region was entirely submerged with water, and at other times it was turned into a gigantic mud flat. About 28 million years ago, however, forces inside the earth began pushing Colorado and the surrounding states upward, causing the inland sea to disappear. This uplift continued for some 20 million years, eventually causing most of the Colorado Plateau to gain 5000 feet of elevation. It was this uplift that gave rise to the great river that today drains most of the region: the Colorado River.

For the past 20 million years the Colorado River and its tributaries have been carving and etching out an incredible array of canyons and ravines into the soft sandstone, mudstone, and shale of the Colorado Plateau. Furthermore, because this is an arid region that receives an average of only ten inches of rain annually, there is little vegetation to cover the river's amazing handiwork. The geology of the land lies bare for all to see, and the result is some of the most dramatic and geologically interesting scenery in the United States.

History

On a cold December day in 1888 a Colorado rancher named Richard Wetherill and his brother-in-law, Charles Mason, were riding along the rim of a canyon in the southwestern corner of Colorado when they made a fantastic discovery. There, on the other side of the canyon, were the remains of what appeared to be an ancient city. The structure consisted of about 150 rooms, all made of sandstone, set in the back of a huge alcove just below the rim of the canyon. Needless to say the men were tremendously excited over their discovery, and for Wetherill this was a life changing event. He would spend the rest of his life exploring and discovering other ruins in the area and learning about the ancient people who built them, a people we now call the Anasazi Indians. He named his first discovery the "Cliff Palace", and it remains today the largest known cliff dwelling in North America. It is also a centerpiece of Colorado's Mesa Verde National Park, a park dedicated to the preservation of the prehistoric Anasazi culture.

The Anasazi are the most recent of a long line of prehistoric Americans that occupied Colorado and the adjacent states at least as early as 8000 B.C. The earliest of these peoples lived in nomadic hunter-gatherer societies and left behind little evidence of their existence, but around the time of Christ the Anasazi began to learn the secrets of agriculture and live in more permanent dwellings. Corn, introduced by other Indians living in Mexico, was probably their first crop. Following their discovery of agriculture they began farming extensively and lived near their fields in large subterranean pit houses.

The years between 700 and 1300 A.D. mark a time of increasing technological skill in building above-ground stone houses, first on the canyon rims and later in alcoves in the canyon walls. Their most famous structures, including those in Mesa Verde National Park, were built during the last 150 years of this period. It appears that these cliff dwellings had a defensive purpose, but it is not known who their enemies might have been. The Anasazi culture ended about 700 years ago when, for reasons that are not completely understood, they abandoned their impressive settlements and moved on. We can't be sure where they went, but today there is strong evidence that the modern Pueblo Indians living in Arizona and New Mexico are descendents of the Anasazi.

The more recent Native American inhabitants of Colorado include members of the Arapaho, Cheyenne, and Comanche tribes that subsisted by hunting buffalo on the state's eastern plains, and the Utes, who lived in the mountainous central and western parts of the state. The Ute Indians grew to become the largest single tribe, and they were often in conflict with white men during the great westward migrations of the

Anasazi ruins in Sand Canyon (page 419)

1800s. Their land was coveted by the pioneer settlers, and many treaties were made and broken during that unfortunate time. Today about 3,500 Utes still live in Colorado; they remain the states largest contingent of Native Americans.

The first Europeans to enter Colorado were probably members of a Spanish expedition lead by the infamous Francisco Vasquez de Coronado in 1541. It was not until the 1700s, however, that significant numbers of European explores, primarily from France and Spain, began coming into the state. The French explorers were generally interested in trapping and trading with the local Indians, while the Spanish were usually more interested in fortune hunting and spreading the word of God. Ultimately the southern part of Colorado came to be regarded as a territory of Spain, while France laid claim to the northern part.

Northern Colorado became a territory of the United States in 1803, when Thomas Jefferson negotiated the famous Louisiana Purchase with France. It wasn't until 45 years later, however that the southern part of the state was added to the American territories. It reverted from Spanish to Mexican control after the Mexican War of Independence, and finally became an American territory at the culmination of the Mexican-American War in 1848. At last the stage was set for the formation of the Colorado Territory and eventual statehood.

South Saint Vrain Creek (page 123)

The country's attention turned to Colorado in a big way in 1858. Gold was discovered in that year near what is now Denver. Word spread quickly, and soon a flood of prospectors were streaming in from the east. Within two more years gold was found in the mountains west of Denver, and the rush was firmly established. Following the second strike Congress moved to pass a bill that defined the Territory of Colorado and established a territorial government. The influx of fortune seekers accelerated in the 1870s with the arrival of the railroad in the territory, and in 1876 Colorado became the 38th state to join the Union.

The good times continued on throughout the 1880s and the Colorado

Old miner's shack near Browns Pass (page 194)

mountains swarmed with mining camps. Gold and especially silver were king, and dozens of tiny communities sprang up in the most remote places imaginable–wherever there was a hint of the precious metals. Immensely lucrative discoveries of silver ore were made at Georgetown, Aspen and Leadville, and Denver became the main supply point and social hub for the frenzy of activity. Every prospector's dream was to build an elaborate house in Denver and impress his friends with lavish parties after he had made his fortune in the mountains west of the high rolling city.

But the good times could not last forever. The American market eventually became flooded with silver, and by the mid-1890s the price of an ounce of silver had dropped to less than half of its value 15 years earlier. One by one the mines closed and by the turn of the century nearly all of the once booming mining camps were completely deserted. The mining industry in Colorado did enjoy a brief resurgence during World Wars One and Two, but there will never be a time quite like the wild heyday years of the 1870s and 80s. Those two decades will always find a special place in Colorado's history books.

Wildlife

One of the great joys of hiking in the Colorado Rockies is the opportunity it provides to see life in the wild. Don't expect to encounter a large animal every time you venture into the wilderness, but if you go often into the mountains you are certain to see lots of deer and at least an occasional bighorn sheep, mountain goat, moose, or elk. Mountain lions and black bears are also present in fair numbers but they are shy animals and rarely seen by hikers. Bears, unfortunately, are great scavengers, and they are more likely to be seen around campgrounds near garbage dumps than anywhere else. If you see one in the wild it will probably be at a lower elevation where there is abundant food such as service berries, choke cherries, nuts, and grubs. Mountain lions are extremely shy animals and usually stay far away from people. The exception is an

Mountain goats on Electric Peak, page 186)

animal that, for whatever reason, has lost its ability to hunt in the wild. Every few years in Colorado someone is attacked by a wayward mountain lion; sadly, the victims are usually small children.

Colorado's Rocky Mountain bighorn sheep seem to prefer the terrain at or near timberline, and that is where they are usually found. They prefer a habitat dominated by grass and low shrubs, with rock outcroppings nearby for possible escape from enemies. Mountain goats can sometimes be seen on the slopes of Colorado's highest summits, but it is unusual to get close to one. Moose can occasionally be seen in swampy areas near lakes and marshes. Most of the moose sightings are females; consider yourself lucky if you should happen to spot a bull moose. Deer are everywhere in the forests of Colorado, but the elk seem to prefer grazing in dry open meadows where the forage is good. Foxes also abound. They are very intelligent animals, not above stealing food from a deserted campsite, and if you see a fox it is probably because he saw you first and his curiosity got the best of him.

When hiking above timberline you will seldom be out of site of a fat, bushy-tailed, yellow-bellied marmot. These handsome animals love the rock-strewn terrain above timberline, where they dig protective burrows under the boulders for winter hibernation. During late summer you can see them all across the tundra, peering over the tops of boulders and gazing lazily at the hikers trudging up the alpine trails. There are so few predators at these elevations that the marmots often seem to have no fear of people. Also living in the same environment are the delightful pikas–little rabbit-like mammals that scamper over the rocks emitting shrill squeals to warn their neighbors of your approach. Picas are unusual animals because in spite of the harsh environment in which they live they do not hibernate in winter. During the summer they collect and store enough grass to keep them alive when their world is covered with snow.

Yellow-bellied marmot in Glacier Gorge (page 99)

Pica on Mount Audubon (page 117)

The most exciting of the animals you are likely to see in the plateau country of western Colorado are desert bighorn sheep. These are a different species from the Rocky Mountain bighorn sheep–better adapted to the hot, arid terrain west of the mountains. They are usually found in the sandstone canyons of the Colorado Plateau. The desert bighorns must have been avidly hunted by the prehistoric Anasazi Indians that once lived in southwestern Colorado because they are featured in many ancient petroglyphs throughout the area.

The other animals you are likely to see a lot of in western Colorado are jackrabbits, coyotes, and mule deer. Mountain lions are also found in the canyons, but like their mountain dwelling cousins they are very shy and it is extremely rare to see one. They generally feed on the mule deer and bighorn sheep. On the open range above the canyons you might be lucky enough to see a herd of pronghorn antelope. The pronghorns can run up to 60 miles per hour, the fastest of any animal in North America, and it is a real treat to watch a herd of them bounding graceful across the land. They too are shy animals, however, and not often seen.

Pronghorn antelope are more often encountered on the grass-covered plains of eastern Colorado, where they once numbered in the millions. Like the Great Plains bison, these magnificent animals were once hunted almost to extinction, but today, thankfully, the population of pronghorns is rising and the species is no longer endangered.

There was once also a significant population of grizzly bears and wolves throughout Colorado, but now they are gone. The last wolves in Colorado were killed before 1940, and the last grizzly bear was killed in 1979. Today eastern Colorado is probably best known as a habitat for birds. During certain parts of the year the grasslands are home to hundreds of migratory bird species, and predators like the ferruginous hawk and the golden eagle feast on an abundant supply of prairie dogs and field mice.

Desert bighorn sheep in Dominguez Canyon (page 409)

Tips for Hikers

Now he walks in quiet solitude the forests and the streams
Seeking grace in every step he takes.
His sight has turned inside himself to try and understand
The serenity of a clear blue mountain lake.

John Denver, *Rocky Mountain High*

Most of us relish our experiences in the natural world; we seem to be drawn by some primordial instinct away from our man-made abodes to the roots of our existence. Colorado's wilderness is a treasured gift for those who seek the grace and serenity of nature's wild places, where one can escape, if only temporarily, back to the dominion of God's original creation.

But all is not bliss in Colorado's wild places. Before you venture away from the safety and comfort of your home you should pause to consider the tribulations that may confront you. With some forethought and preparation most of the rigors of backcountry travel can be successfully dealt with, but a hike or backpacking trip into the wilds can quickly become a very unpleasant experience for the unprepared. Colorado's high country can be particularly unforgiving for the uninitiated, so it is essential to spend adequate time planning and preparing before venturing into the mountains. Question yourself: How long is the trail? How much climbing is required? Is the route well marked? How long will I be gone? How much water will I need? What kind of weather might I encounter? What kind

photo by Bob Vanderwalker

Upper Mohawk Lake (page 251)

Mount Democrat (page 244)

of clothing should I wear? Make the entire trip in your mind before you actually start, checking to see that you have packed what you will need for each phase of the journey. And plan for worse case unanticipated events, such as bad weather and medical emergencies.

Access

The first thing to consider in planning a hike is how to get to the trailhead. An ordinary car is all you need most of the time, but occasionally a good four-wheel-drive vehicle can come in very handy. In some cases you can avoid the necessity of a 4WD by walking or riding a mountain bike for the last few miles to the trailhead, and sometimes, if the roads are dry, a 2WD with high clearance will do nicely. There are only a few hikes in this book that you absolutely cannot do without a 4WD vehicle, but several more for which 4WD would be very useful. Furthermore, most of the hikes described here require at least some travel on dirt roads, and after a heavy rain even a good road can occasionally become a 4WD road.

Quite often a hike does not end at the same trailhead where it started, and in these cases you will need a plan for getting back to where your vehicle is parked. Again, a bicycle often fills the bill nicely but sometimes the roads are just too rough or too steep for bike travel. If you are hiking with a group of people the best way to handle this situation is to take two cars and leave one at the ending trailhead. Since I do a lot of hiking alone I often solve this problem by taking along a small motorcycle strapped to a platform on the back of my SUV.

Finally, let me point out that there are a few items you should always carry in your car when driving to remote trailheads:

- several gallons of water
- a tow strap
- a good spare tire
- a tire pump
- a few basic tools
- jumper cables

I also like to carry an extra fully charged car battery with me when I am driving on rough roads. Most people don't realize how fragile the lead plates inside a battery are,

Longs Peak (page 89)

but they can be easily bent or broken on a rough road causing the battery to short out and become useless. Dead batteries are even more common on rough mountain roads than flat tires.

Weather

Colorado's weather deserves special mention. If you are hiking in the plateau country of western Colorado the weather is usually quite predictable: hot and dry. But if you are planning a trip into the mountains it isn't quite that straightforward. The weather in the mountains can change very quickly and, regardless of what the weatherman might have said, you should prepare for the worst. Rain gear should be an essential part of your equipment, and if you intend to sleep in the mountains you will absolutely need a tent. Also be sure to take along sufficient clothing to keep you warm in the event of a drop in temperature.

A frequent pattern in the mountains is cloudless, windless mornings followed by scattered thunder showers in the afternoon. Morning in the Colorado Rockies is sure to make you delight in being alive. The meadows are glittering with beads of dew, the birds and the deer are out searching for food, the lakes are mirror smooth, and the sky is a gorgeous blue. Try to do most of your hiking in the morning, starting at dawn. So imperative is an early start that the most serious hikers do all of their driving the day before the hike, and spend the night at or near the trailhead. By about 10:00 a.m. the magic is almost gone, and by noon the sky will typically no longer be cloudless. Usually the mountains are overcast by early afternoon, and for several reasons you should try not to be on the summits beyond that time. The vistas loose their beauty, the temperature drops, the wind increases, and, most important, there arises a danger of getting struck by lightening. The exposed summit of a Colorado peak is a very dangerous place to be during a thunderstorm; someone is killed in Colorado by lightening nearly every summer.

The most unpredictable Colorado weather occurs in late summer from about the middle of July until the middle of September. The sun beating down on the plains of eastern Colorado during these last days of summer produces huge afternoon masses of hot air that rise into the upper atmosphere. This sets up a convection current that pulls in air from the west, across the Colorado Plateau and up into the mountains. As the wind blows across the Continental Divide it cools, and if the humidity is sufficient the result is an afternoon thundershower.

This effect is not as pronounced early in the summer, but unfortunately at that time hikers are confronted with another problem: unmelted winter snow. The snow doesn't fully melt in Colorado until July, so it is difficult to walk the highest trails before that time. The summer thunderstorms are generally finished by October, but by that time the lazy days of summer are finished and the cold is starting to set in. There are only a few days of ideal conditions each summer in the Colorado mountains, but if you are lucky enough to be out on one of those days you can expect a truly memorable experience.

Red Cloud Peak (page 332)

Clothing

Adequate clothing is crucial for any successful backcountry experience, but most of the rules are just common sense. The most important item of clothing on a hike is, of course, your foot wear. Your shoes must be comfortable and durable and they must give your feet the protection they need. Sneakers are acceptable on some of the easier trails, but many of the trails in Colorado are very rocky and on these trails boots are the only practical thing to wear.

When planning your hike be sure to find out if it will be necessary to wade across any streams. If so, you should wear some sort of wettable shoes. Walking for long distances with wet feet can cause blisters, but on hikes that require a lot of wading there may be no other alternative. Some hikers carry an extra pair of shoes in their pack for use around the camp or for wading streams, but for me it is more important to keep my weight down. Carrying extra socks, however, is a very good idea. It is important to keep your feet as clean and dry as possible, and a clean pair of socks each day will go a long way toward preventing blisters.

Walking generates a lot of body heat, especially if you are climbing. So you will probably want to wear jackets and sweaters that you can easily take off and put back on. Most hikers prefer to wear several layers of

Hallett Peak (page 91)

clothing rather than a single jacket, but on long trips the weight of additional sweaters and shirts can add up fast.

In my opinion shorts are impractical in most hiking situations. Your legs need protection from brush, from insects, and from the sun. If there is any doubt about what the trail conditions are going to be like, always opt for long pants. I also prefer to wear a long sleeved cotton shirt, even in summer, just for the protection it offers. Never go hiking without a hat. In hot weather it protects you from the sun and in cold weather it keeps your head warm. The most practical kind of headgear is a cheap, wide rimmed, foldable, canvas hat.

A special mention should be made about the hazards of skin cancer in Colorado. Since exposure to the sun is the largest single cause of skin cancer, hikers should choose clothing that will minimize their exposure and use a high SPF sunscreen lotion on those parts of the body that cannot be covered. The need for sunblock is obvious on the hot desert trails of western Colorado, but it is also important on the cooler mountain trails. Bear in mind that at high elevations there is less atmosphere to filter out the harmful ultraviolet rays.

Finally, when planning a trip into the mountains don't forget to include rain gear on your equipment list. Afternoon rain in the mountains of Colorado is very common. Even if the morning sky is clear blue you can almost always expect a high probability of scattered afternoon showers. Furthermore, the temperature can drop precipitously in the mountains and wet cloths don't do a very good job of conserving precious body heat.

Drinking water

The availability of water is one of the most important items to consider when planning a hike. Water is necessary for almost all of our body functions, and we cannot survive for more than a few days without it. In Colorado's mountains you will usually be able to get plenty of water along the trail, but in the dry desert country of western Colorado there is little water to be found.

On most of those trails you will have to carry all of your water with you. To make matters worse our bodies need a great deal more water in hot desert climates than they need in the cooler mountains. If you are out for an entire day under the August sun in western Colorado's desert country you will need to consume at least a gallon of water to stay healthy.

Another problem unique to desert hiking is insufficient salt retention. Sweating and drinking large amounts of water quickly leaches salt out of the body, and the nervous system does not work very well without salt. The first sign of salt deficiency is fatigue. You may think your exhaustion is simply the result of being out of shape, but a salt deficiency is often part of the problem. If you increase your intake of sodium and potassium while you are in the desert you will find that you have a lot more energy.

Finding water is much less of a problem in the mountains than in the desert, and it is seldom necessary to pack in all of the water you need. Collecting water along the way, however, poses yet another problem: making sure the water you find is safe to drink. There is always a possibility getting sick from ingesting contaminated water.

Opinions vary widely on the subject of when water is safe to drink. If you listen to the rangers in our national parks you will come away with the opinion that untreated water is never safe to drink. Yet I have known people who routinely drink from desert potholes, filled with tadpoles and mosquito larva, with no ill effects. Some people use inexpensive halogen tablets to treat their water in the backcountry, and others, claiming that the pills cause cancer, insist on carrying expensive filter pumps with them wherever they go. Again, common sense is the key. No one can guarantee that you will never get sick, but there is no need to be paranoid about the possibility. With a little common sense the risk can be minimized significantly.

First, it is important to remember where

Quandary Peak Trail (page 248)

the germs that carry human disease come from. Generally, they are carried by other humans and animals that associate with humans, i.e. cows, sheep, horses, pigs, cats, dogs, etc. Beaver should also be included in the list, since they have been known to carry the microbes that are responsible for giardia. Second, bear in mind that most microbes can't swim very far; hence they are only likely to be found downstream from the contamination point. Untreated spring water can be consumed with very little risk, but you should always treat the water you get from ponds and lakes. On rare occasions, especially near mines or mine tailings, you may come across water that is contaminated with poisonous minerals. This is generally not a problem, since the taste of contaminated water is usually so bad no one would want to drink it anyway. But if you are in doubt check for insects or frogs living in the water. If the water is lifeless and has a peculiar taste, don't drink it under any circumstances.

There are three commonly used ways of treating water to kill or remove microbes: halogen tablets, boiling, or filtering. Using halogen (iodine or chlorine) tablets is the most convenient and inexpensive method. As stated earlier, some studies indicate that prolonged use of these tablets can cause cancer, but for short term use the risk is infinitesimal. If you are boiling the water, be sure to boil it for at least several minutes. Above 8,000 feet you should boil it for a full five minutes, since at higher elevations water boils at a lower temperature. If you don't mind spending the extra money and carrying a little extra weight, filter pumps are probably the best way to purify your drinking water.

Finally let me say that in my opinion the danger in drinking untreated water in the wild has been vastly overstated. Even if you drink indiscriminately, the chances are good that you won't get sick. And in most circumstances even if you do get sick it will not be a life threatening illness. On

East Inlet, near Verna Lake (page 112)

the other hand dehydration can easily lead to a life threatening situation, especially in desert areas. If you are threatened with dehydration a muddy pool of untreated water could well save your life.

Minimum Impact

There was a time in the West when there were so few people using the backcountry that human impact was not a problem. That is no longer the case. The detrimental effects of man on the environment are becoming increasingly obvious, and it is up to each one of us to minimize them as best we can.

Probably the greatest amount of environmental destruction by hikers and backpackers is caused from incidents involving campfires. Many acres of prime forest land in the West have been destroyed by people who were careless with their fires. But fires adversely affect the environment even when they are carefully tended. The ugly marks from fires built in arid areas can last for years, and in places where wood is scarce campers often ravage the land for firewood, burning everything in sight. A much better solution is to carry a small camp stove. They are inexpensive, convenient, and weigh only a pound or two. Furthermore, open fires are now illegal in many of our national parks and forests. A small camp stove should be an integral part of every backpacker's standard equipment.

Another area of concern is garbage. There is nothing more disheartening to a nature lover than to walk through a pristine wilderness area that has been littered with trash. The slogan "pack it in, pack it out" is a good one to follow. Some organic material, such as unwanted food or body wastes can be buried, but only if it is deposited at least six inches below the surface and covered with well packed dirt. But do not bury your toilet paper. Furthermore, nothing should be buried near a lake or in a stream bed where it might pollute the surface water.

One of Colorado's greatest treasures is the incredible prehistoric cliff dwellings that were left behind by the Anasazi Indians some 700 years ago in the southwestern corner of the state. It is impossible to describe the thrill of discovering one of these archeological gems far from any road in a wild desert canyon. Yet through the years these ancient artifacts have received a great deal of abuse. Most of the damage was inflicted many years ago, but even today the ancient relics of the past are still being abused. If you visit one of these ruins remember that they are very fragile and can be easily damaged. Do not walk over them or climb on them. And do not remove any pottery shards, corn cobs, or other objects from the sites. Treat them just as you would treat an exhibit in a museum, because that is exactly what they are.

Pear Creek (page 76)

Maps

There is no substitute for a good map of the area in which you are hiking. The maps provided in this book should be sufficient to complete the described hikes, but if possible you should take along a more detailed map of the area you plan to visit. Part of the joy of hiking is exploring and taking side trips on your own that may not have been part of the original plan, and it is much easier to do this if you have a good map with you. Also, it is sometimes useful to know exactly where you are on the trail. A good map will help you plot your course with greater accuracy.

The best topographic maps available are the 7.5 minute series, published by the United States Geological Survey. They are large scale (about 2⅝ inches per mile, with contour lines at 40 foot intervals), and they are widely available in ranger stations, national park visitor centers, and stores that sell camping supplies. Unfortunately, many of the 7.5 minute USGS maps do not accurately depict the trail locations. The best trail maps are produced by National Geographic/Trails Illustrated, of Evergreen, Colorado. Most of the Trails Illustrated maps are only about 1/2 to 1/4 the scale of the detailed 7.5 minute maps, but they do give much more information about the hiking trails and trailheads.

You will find your map much more useful if you also carry a compass and a watch. The watch will help you estimate how far you have gone since the last landmark (most people walk about 2 miles per hour on level ground). When using your compass to determine a direction, bear in mind that the magnetic declination throughout Colorado is generally about 15 degrees east. In other words, your compass needle will always point 15 degrees east of the direction of true north.

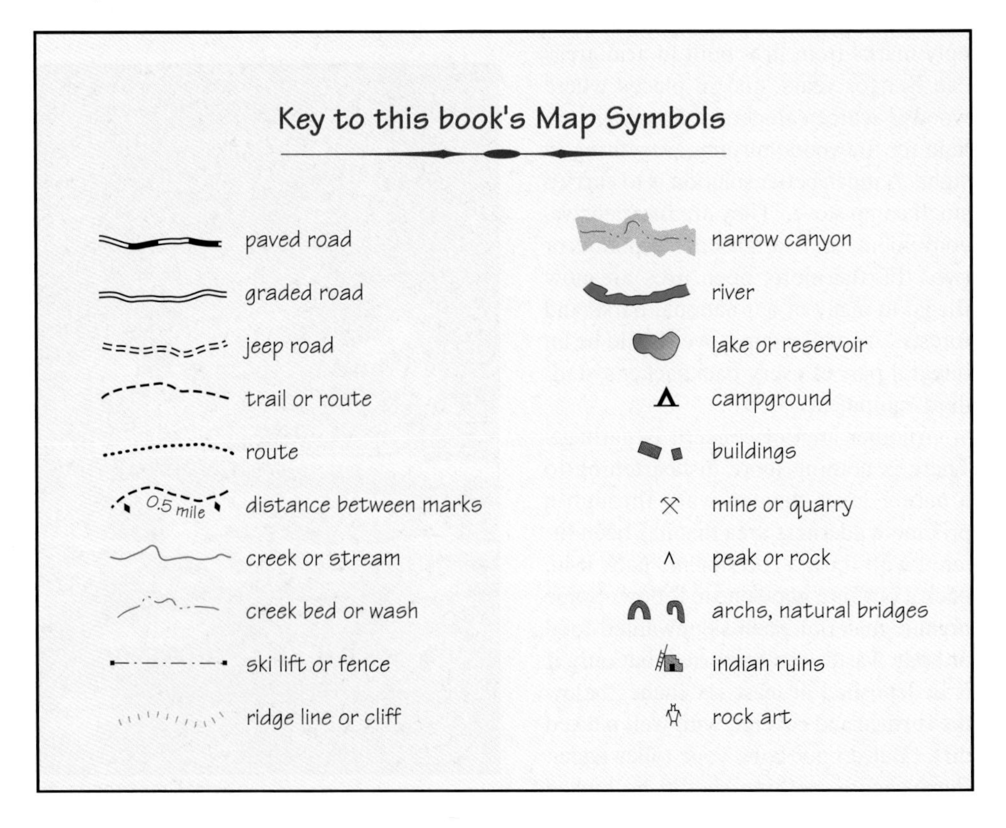

Big Creek Falls

★★ **day hike**

Distance:	4.8 miles (round trip)
Walking time:	2 1/2 hours
Elevations:	220 ft. gain/loss Seven Lakes Trailhead (start): 9,010 ft. Big Creek Falls: 9,220 ft.
Trail:	Easy, well marked trail
Season:	Summer through late fall. The trail is usually covered with snow from late November through May. Big Creek Lakes Campground is closed each year from December 2 until June 14.
Vicinity:	Near the Wyoming border north of Walden
Maps:	Pearl, Davis Peak (*USGS*) Hahns Peak, Steamboat Lake (*Trails Illustrated, #116*)
Information:	http://colorado.utahtrails.com/bigcreekfalls.html www.fs.fed.us/r2/mbr/ *(Routt National Forest)* phone: (970) 723-8204 *(Parks Ranger District)*

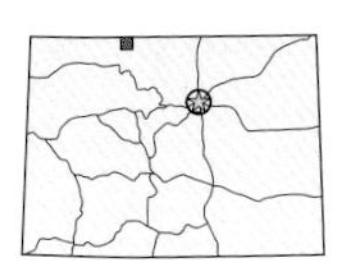

Drive north from Walden on Highway 125 for 9 miles to the farming community of Cowdrey. As you enter Cowdrey you will see a sign marking the road to Big Creek Lakes on the left (County Road 6). Turn west here and follow the signs for the next 25 miles to Big Creek Lake. When you arrive at Big Creek Lake you will come to a T junction. Turn right here and continue along the west shore of the lake for another 0.7 miles. The road ends at the trailhead.

The first 1.3 miles of this hike are along the Red Elephant Nature Trail, named after a prominent peak four miles south of Big Creek Lake in the Mount Zirkel Wilderness Area. Red Elephant Mountain is clearly visible from Upper Big Creek Lake at the end of the nature trail. A Forest Service pamphlet, available at the trailhead, describes the fauna and flora along the trail at 25 numbered stops.

From the trailhead the path proceeds in a southerly direction along the west side of Big Creek Lake. This mile-long lake is the second largest natural lake in Colorado, and at 9,000 feet above sea level it is surrounded

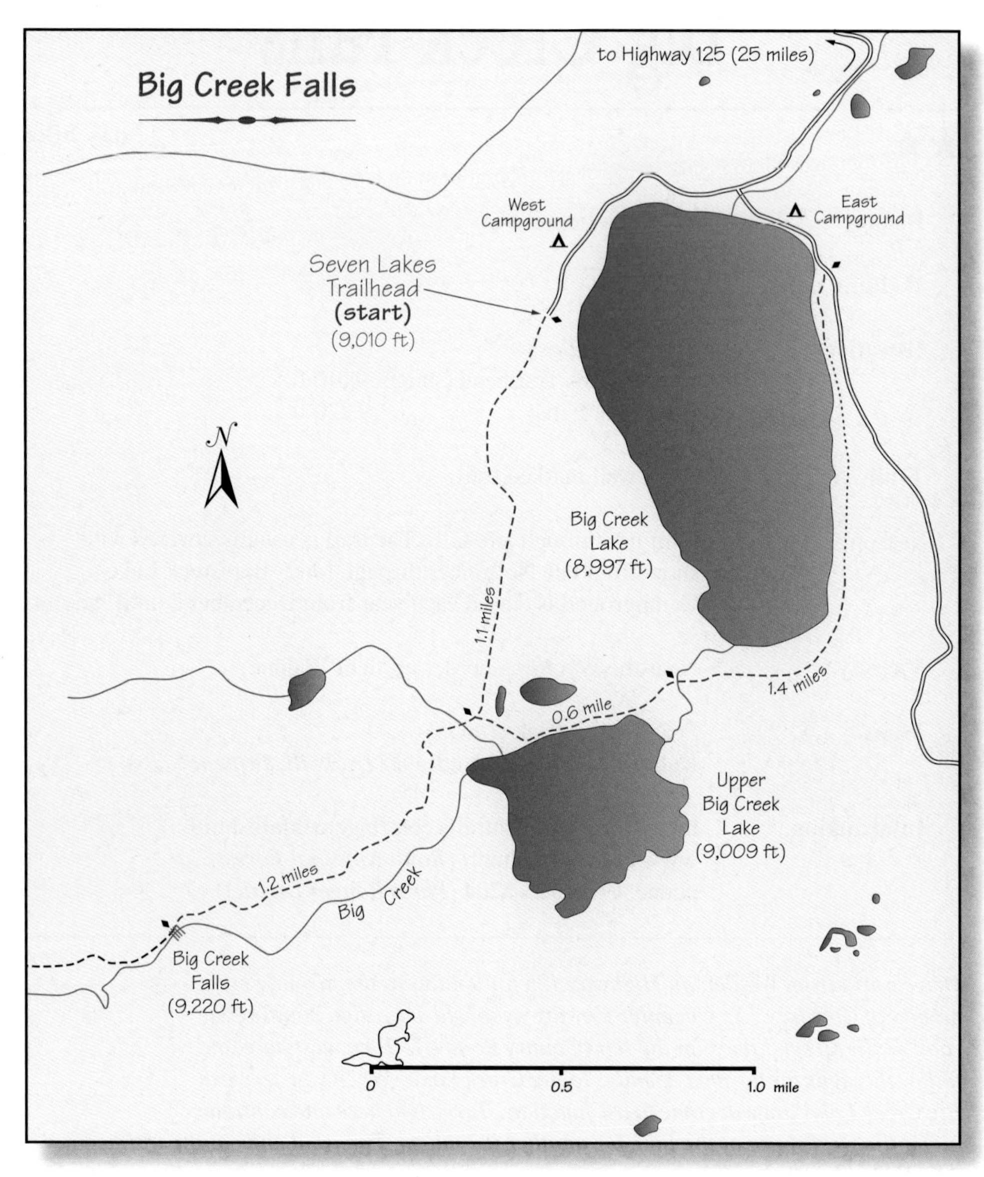

by a dense forest of Engelmann spruce and subalpine fir. The lake is very scenic and understandably popular with fisherman. Unfortunately the shore of the lake is often swampy, and to avoid marshes the Red Elephant Trail veers far inland from the shore so views of the water are not something you can expect. Nevertheless, this part of the hike is an extremely pleasant walk under a dense conifer canopy along a path that is almost perfectly level.

After 1.1 miles you will come to a trail junction where a sign points the way to Big Creek Falls on the right. Before continuing, however, you should turn left to complete the nature trail. It ends just 250 yards further on the north shore of Upper Big Creek Lake. The upper lake, while not as big as the lower

Red Elephant Nature Trail

lake, is still 0.4 mile in diameter. It is also surrounded by timber with a nice view of Red Elephant Mountain above its southern shore. There are no roads to the upper lake, however, so you won't see any boats here.

Turning west at the junction, the trail parallels Big Creek for the next 1.2 miles before finally arriving at Big Creek Falls. For almost the entire distance the path never approaches closer than 100 yards from the creek, so there is little indication of what lies ahead. But at the last minute the trail turns to intersect the creek at the bottom of the falls giving you a glorious view of the plunging cascade. The drop is only about 40 feet, but there is a considerable volume of water in the creek and the setting couldn't be more picturesque. The creek flows east at this point, so the best time to see the falls is in the morning around 10:00 a.m.

The trail does not end at Big Creek Falls, but continues on into the Mount Zirkel Wilderness Area for many more miles. Some people choose to walk another 3.2 miles to the headwaters of Big Creek where the Seven Lakes are located. After seeing the Big Creek Lakes, however, the Seven Lakes are bound to disappoint. The largest of the Seven Lakes is only about 100 yards wide by 350 yards long, and the rest of the lakes are little more than shallow puddles in a marshy meadow.

A better way to extend this hike would be to return to the trailhead via a long forgotten trail that follows the east side of Big Creek Lake. Many of the older maps show this trail, but it has not been maintained for years and much of it is now completely overgrown. Nevertheless, some parts of the route are quite interesting. Returning to the Seven Lakes Trailhead via the east side of Big Creek Lake will add 0.9 mile to the total length of this hike. Also, if you don't have two cars you will need to walk an additional 1.0 mile along the road to get from

Upper Big Creek Lake

the northeast side of the lake back to the northwest side where the starting trailhead is located.

To get on this old trail you must return to the end of the Red Elephant Natural Trail on the north side of Upper Big Creek Lake. From there just continue eastward along the faint trail that follows the north side of the lake. Soon the trail enters a marsh where the path was once elevated by a series of boardwalks. The old boardwalks are still there, but they are too dilapidated to do much good now so plan on getting your feet wet. After 0.4 mile the old trail comes to the section of Big Creek that flows between the upper and lower lakes. There was once a bridge across the creek at this point, but now the only option is to ford the stream. It is an easy ford if you have a good walking stick; the creek is about 20 feet wide here and the water is seldom more than 18 inches deep.

A good trail continues on the east side of the stream for a while, but after a few minutes it starts getting faint and soon it disappears altogether. The path passes through an old abandoned Forest Service campground on the southeast side of Big Creek Lake, and shortly after that you will be left to find your own way through the woods. Occasional glimpses of the lake through the trees make it tempting to search for a route near the shore as you proceed north, but unfortunately the shoreline is very swampy in this area. You will find it easier to walk along the edge of the forest just east of the marsh.

As you approach the northeast side of the lake the walking gets much easier, and soon you will be back on a real trail. The path passes the ruins of an old fishing lodge, then a few more recently constructed cabins, and finally you will come to the campground on the eastern shore. From there it is a 20-minute walk along the road back to the starting trailhead.

Big Creek Falls

Gilpin Lake Loop

★★★★

Mount Zirkel Wilderness Area
day hike

Distance:	9.8 miles (loop)
Walking time:	6 3/4 hours
Elevations:	2,300 ft. gain/loss Slavonia Trailhead (start): 8,480 ft. Gilpin Lake: 10,338 ft. Gilpin Ridge: 10,780 ft. Gold Creek Lake: 9,555 ft.
Trail:	Well marked and well maintained
Season:	Midsummer through mid-fall. The higher parts of the trail are usually covered with snow from mid-November through early July.
Vicinity:	Near Steamboat Springs
Maps:	Mount Zirkel (*USGS*) Hahns Peak (*Trails Illustrated, #116*)
Information:	http://colorado.utahtrails.com/gilpinlake.html www.fs.fed.us/r2/mbr/ *(Routt National Forest)* phone: (970) 879-1870 *(Hahns Peak/Bears Ears Ranger District)*

Drive west from Steamboat Springs for two miles on Highway 40, then turn north on County Road 129 toward the Steamboat Springs Airport. Continue on this road for 20 miles until you come to Seedhouse Road (Forest Road 400), then turn east and continue for another 14 miles. The Slavonia Trailhead and parking area are located at the end of the Seedhouse Road.

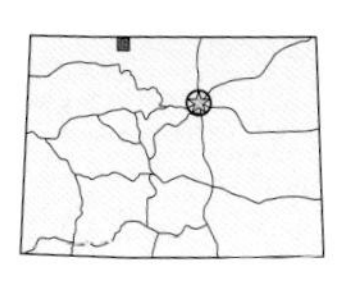

This loop hike can be walked in either direction, but if it is being done as a day hike I recommend you walk around the loop in a clockwise direction. That way you will have a better chance to see Gilpin Lake before the usual afternoon clouds roll in; Gilpin Lake is located in an extraordinarily scenic area.

In the first few miles the trail passes by several clearings in the forest where a surprisingly large number of tall trees have been uprooted and blown over. The fallen trees are the result of the Routt Divide Blowdown, a freak windstorm in 1997 that still has sci-

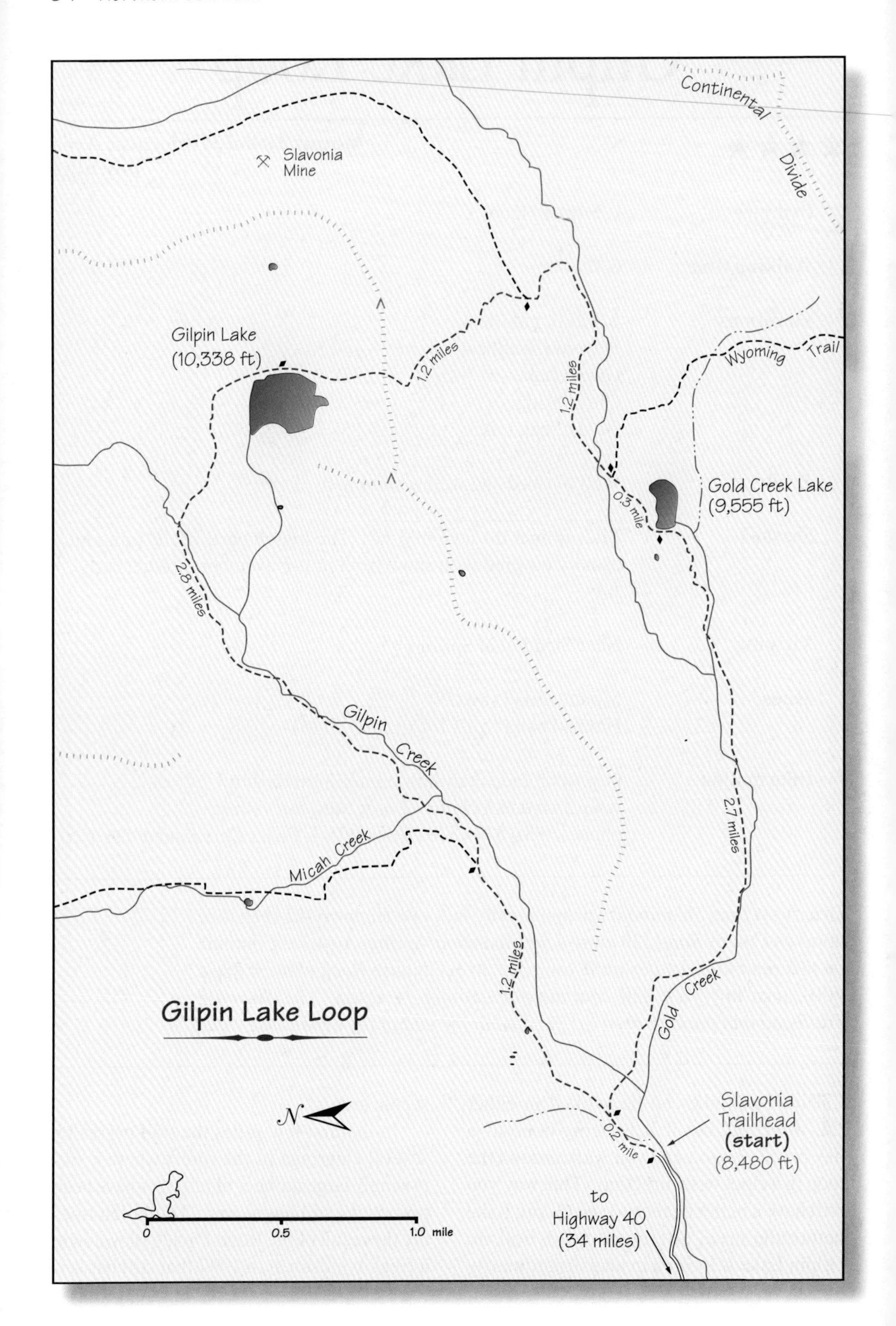

Continental Divide
Slavonia Mine
Gilpin Lake
(10,338 ft)
1.2 miles
1.2 miles
Wyoming Trail
Gold Creek Lake
(9,555 ft)
0.3 mile
2.8 miles
Gilpin Creek
Micah Creek
2.7 miles
1.2 miles
Gold Creek
Gilpin Lake Loop
N
Slavonia Trailhead
(start)
(8,480 ft)
0.2 mile
to
Highway 40
(34 miles)
0
0.5
1.0 mile

Gilpin Lake Trail

entists scratching their heads in amazement. It happened in the early morning hours of October 25. A blizzard had been raging along the entire Front Range for the previous two days, and there was heavy snowfall from Wyoming to New Mexico. The mountain tops were experiencing temperatures well below zero with wind chill temperatures as low as -60 degrees F. Then between 4:00 and 10:00 a.m. a high-altitude wind stream with a velocity estimated to be in excess of 120 miles per hour dipped down to the western side of the Continental Divide and hit the ground with devastating force. Before the wind had abated some four million trees were down along a band 4 miles wide and 30 miles long. The Routt Divide Blowdown of 1997 was the largest recorded blowdown that has ever occurred in the Rocky Mountains.

From the trailhead the path climbs gently upward through an aspen forest for 0.2 mile to a junction where you must bear left toward Gilpin Lake. The trail on the right is the Gold Creek Trail that you will be following on the return portion of the hike. From the Gold Creek Trail junction the path continues a long, gentle climb along the north side of Gilpin Creek. You will seldom be close enough to the creek to see the water, but the sounds of the cascading stream will remind you of its presence.

1.2 miles from the trailhead you will pass the Mica Basin Trail on your left, and from that point the path follows closer to the shore of Gilpin Creek. Finally, about an hour's walk beyond the junction with the Mica Basin Trail, the path comes to a relatively flat area where Gilpin Creek flows through a grassy meadow. Here the trail turns southeast, crosses the creek, and begins climbing in earnest for the last 0.8 mile to Gilpin Lake.

Gilpin Lake looks like it was taken from

Waterfall below Gold Creek Lake

a picture postcard. An 11,000-foot ridge rises above the lake to the south and west, but the elevation of the lake itself is only 10,338 feet—far enough below timber line for tall spruce trees to grow right to the water's edge. The trail follows the lake's eastern shore, and if you are there in the morning you can get some gorgeous photographs of the rocky ridge above the opposite shore.

From Gilpin Lake the trail climbs upward through several switchbacks into a pass that lies directly south of the lake. This is the most strenuous part of the hike, but it lasts only 0.3 mile. When you reach the top of the pass you will be 440 feet above the lake, and your reward will be another impressive view of Gilpin. The summit of this pass marks the highest point on the hike.

From the pass the trail meanders down the southern slope of Gilpin Ridge for 1.0 mile to a large glacial valley that students of geology will find interesting. The western end of the valley was dammed long ago by a large glacial moraine, and the bowl behind the moraine was almost certainly filled with water at one time. Now the long, swampy valley is drained by a small unnamed creek that breeches the natural dam and eventually runs into Gold Creek. When the trail reaches the valley it turns to follow the creek through the breech in the moraine; then, 0.8 mile later, it crosses the small stream and drops down to the northern shore of Gold Creek Lake.

From Gold Creek Lake the trail follows Gold Creek 2.6 miles back to the Gilpin Lake Trail junction near Slavonia Trailhead. The path crosses Gold Creek twice, and not long after the second crossing you will see a delightful waterfall on the left side of the trail. Finally the trail veers away from Gold Creek to a large foot bridge across Gilpin Creek, and 0.2 mile later it meets the junction with the Gilpin Lake Trail. You must turn left here for the last 0.2 mile back to the trailhead.

Gilpin Lake

Wyoming Trail

Mount Zirkel Wilderness Area
shuttle car required
3-day hike

Distance:	21.4 miles (plus 29 miles by car)
Walking time:	day 1: 6 3/4 hours day 2: 5 hours day 3: 3 1/4 hours
Elevations:	2,950 ft. gain, 4,300 ft. loss Buffalo Pass Trailhead (start): 10,300 ft. Luna Lake: 10,482 ft. Slide Lake: 10,540 ft. Rainbow Lake: 9,854 ft. Rainbow Lake Trailhead: 8,750 ft.
Trail:	Mostly well marked and well maintained
Season:	Midsummer through mid-fall. The higher parts of the trail are usually covered with snow from mid-November through early July.
Vicinity:	Near Steamboat Springs
Maps:	Buffalo Pass, Mount Ethel, Pitchpine Mountain (*USGS*) Clark, Buffalo Pass (*Trails Illustrated, #117*)
Information:	http://colorado.utahtrails.com/wyomingtrail.html www.fs.fed.us/r2/mbr/ *(Routt National Forest)* phone: (970) 879-1870 *(Hahns Peak/Bears Ears Ranger District)* or (970) 723-8204 *(Parks Ranger District)*

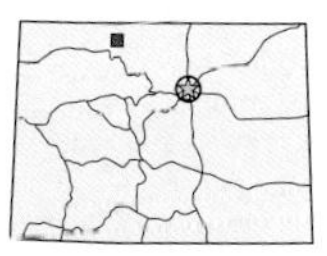

First drive to the town of Walden on Highway 14 between Fort Collins and Steamboat Springs. Continue west out of Walden on Highway 14 for 0.7 mile until you see a sign on the right that says "Lake John and Delaney Butte State Wildlife Areas", then turn right onto County Road 12W and drive west toward the mountains. After 5.0 miles you will come to a junction where you must bear left onto County Road 18. Continue west on Road 18 for another 4.7 miles to the junction with County Road 5 and turn left. After 1.8 miles Road 5 becomes County Road 22, which you must follow for the last 7.2 miles to the trailhead. Road 22 ends at the Rainbow Lake Trailhead where the hike ends and where you must leave a shuttle car.

To reach Buffalo Pass where the hike begins you must backtrack on County Road 22 for 7.2 miles and turn south on County Road 5. After 8.5 miles Road 5 comes to County Road 24, where you must turn right and follow the signs for the last 13.1 miles to Buffalo Pass. Shortly after passing Summit Lake at the top of the pass you will come to a parking area on the left. The trailhead is clearly marked by a sign on the north side of the parking area.

You can also reach the Buffalo Pass Trailhead from Steamboat Springs via County Roads 36 and 38 and Forest Road 60. Drive north from downtown Steamboat on 7th Street and follow the well-signed route for 13.5 miles the trailhead.

For the first 12 miles this interesting hike follows the Wyoming Trail north along the crest of the Continental Divide. Then, after passing just 280 feet below the summit of Mount Ethel, it turns east to descend past the Slide and Rainbow Lakes. Rainbow Lake is particularly impressive: at nearly 100 acres in size, it is the largest lake in the Mount Zirkel Wilderness Area.

Although the total amount of elevation gain for this hike is nearly 3,000 feet, it is not particularly strenuous. Most of the gain is realized along the 12-mile segment of trail that follows the Continental Divide where, although there is a great deal of up and down, none of the grades are particularly steep. I would classify the hike as long but relatively easy, with plenty of rewards to justify your effort. The trail passes six very scenic lakes, and the variety of landscapes range from pristine alpine tundra to dense conifer forest.

Day 1 (8.7 miles)

From Buffalo Pass the trail begins by climbing gradually through a wide meadow of grass and wildflowers with small groves of weathered spruce and subalpine fir scattered intermittently across the landscape. The elevation of the trailhead is not particularly high, about 10,300 feet, and at this altitude one would expect a much more luxuriant

Unnamed pond straddling the Continental Divide on the Wyoming Trail

Luna Lake

forest. But the area north of Buffalo Pass receives some of the heaviest winter snowfall in Colorado, and few seedling trees can survive under these conditions. Notice how the trees only grow in small, dense groves, where the older trees can give the saplings some protection from the severe winter weather. Sometimes the groves are arranged in long bands, perpendicular to the prevailing westerly winds with the young trees on the leeward side. A single tree in the open meadow would have a difficult time surviving the harsh winters.

The trail climbs about 450 feet over the first 1.4 miles, and then looses 200 feet over the following 0.6 miles—a good introduction for what you can expect over the next ten miles. If you got off to a late start you will find many good campsites along the way, but the first really great place to camp is beside a large pond 3.4 miles from the trailhead that straddles the top of the Continental Divide. This pond is a popular watering hole for deer, and you will likely see some if you are there in the early evening.

Older maps show a jeep road following the Divide to this pond, and as you walk you may occasionally catch glimpses of the road. It is never far from the trail; the trail even follows it in a few places. But the road has not been used by vehicles at least since the Mount Zirkel Wilderness Area was designated in 1964, and it is rapidly being reclaimed by the vegetation.

The trail crosses the 11,000-foot elevation line 0.9 mile after leaving the pond, and from that point you will begin to notice two changes in the environment. First, this elevation is very close to timber line, and the spruce and subalpine fir are very close to their limits of survival. They rarely grow more than 10 feet tall, and their twisted, knurled appearance bears little resemblance to the stately trees in the lower forest. Second, the terrain north of this point is very irregular, and the trail begins to meander more in an effort to avoid the steep places. The topology in this area is particularly rugged

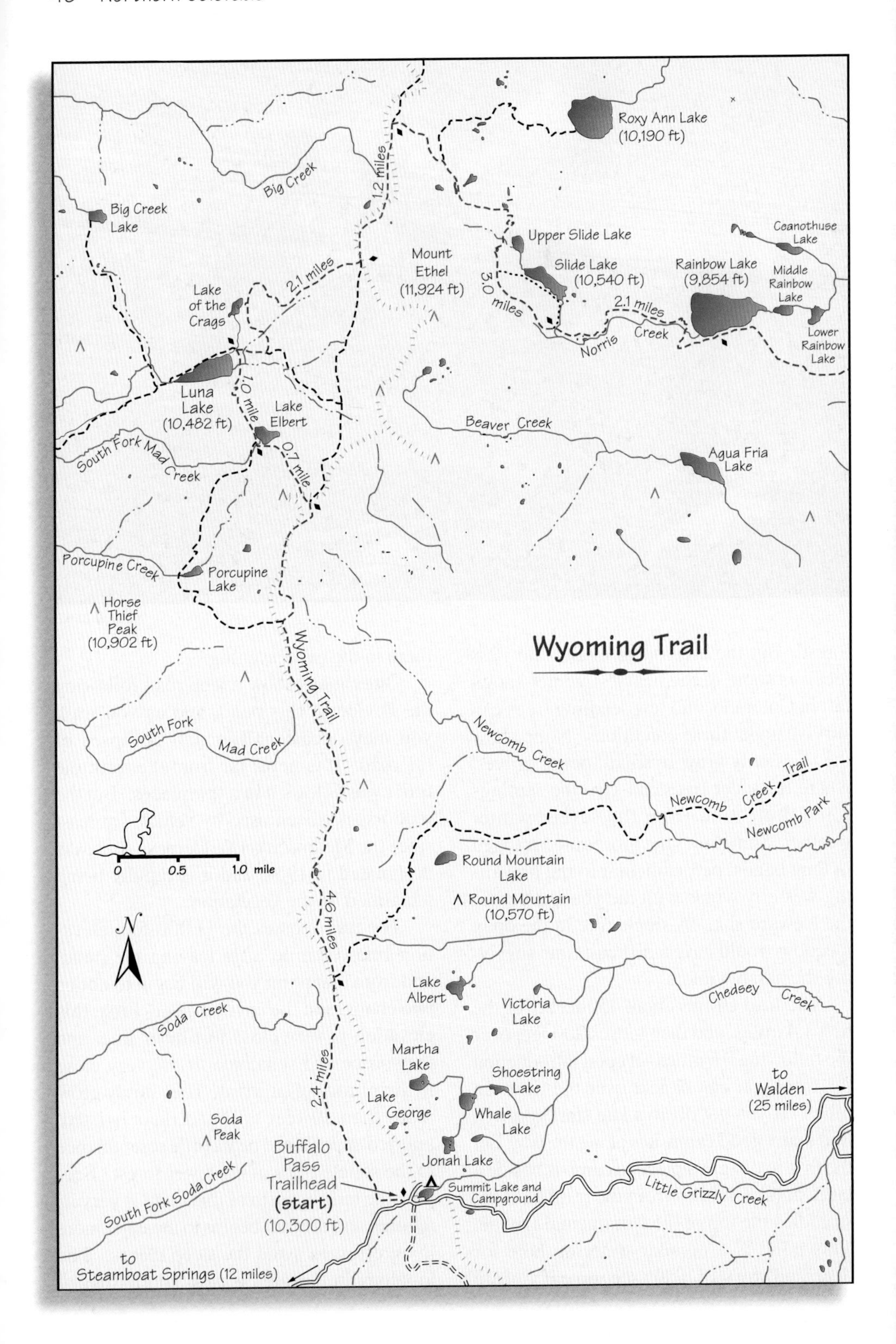

Wyoming Trail
Roxy Ann Lake
(10,190 ft)
Big Creek
1.2 miles
Big Creek
Lake
Upper Slide Lake
Slide Lake
(10,540 ft)
Rainbow Lake
(9,854 ft)
Ceanothuse
Lake
Middle
Rainbow
Lake
Lower
Rainbow
Lake
Mount
Ethel
(11,924 ft)
3.0 miles
2.1 miles
Norris
Creek
2.1 miles
Lake
of the
Crags
Luna
Lake
(10,482 ft)
1.0 mile
Lake
Elbert
0.7 mile
Beaver Creek
Agua Fria
Lake
South Fork Mad Creek
Porcupine Creek
Porcupine
Lake
Horse
Thief
Peak
(10,902 ft)
Wyoming Trail
South Fork
Mad Creek
Newcomb Creek
Newcomb Creek Trail
Newcomb Park
0
0.5
1.0 mile
N
Round Mountain
Lake
Round Mountain
(10,570 ft)
4.6 miles
Lake
Albert
Victoria
Lake
Chedsey Creek
Soda Creek
Martha
Lake
Shoestring
Lake
to
Walden
(25 miles)
2.4 miles
Lake
George
Whale
Lake
Soda
Peak
Buffalo
Pass
Trailhead
(start)
(10,300 ft)
Jonah Lake
Summit Lake and
Campground
Little Grizzly Creek
South Fork Soda Creek
to
Steamboat Springs (12 miles)

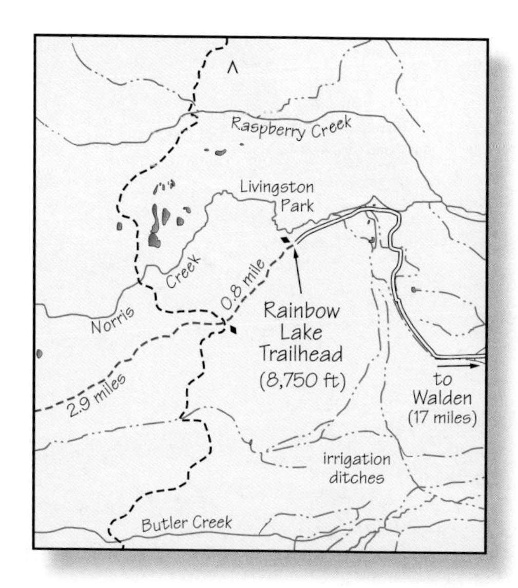

on the eastern side of the Divide, and with the absence of tall trees you will be treated to a number of great vistas to the northeast. Mount Ethel (11,924 ft.), the highest point along this section of the Divide, lies four miles to the north; it will come into view a half-hour after leaving the pond.

3.6 miles after leaving the pond you will come to a sign marking the departure of the Luna Lake Trail on the left. I suggest you leave the Wyoming Trail at this point and take the better-used trail below the west side of the Divide to the lake. Luna Lake is the highlight of this detour, but the route also passes Lake Elbert and Lake of the Crags. From Luna Lake you can return to the Continental Divide on the Crags Trail, which joins the Wyoming Trail 2.3 miles further north. If you choose not to take the detour to Luna Lake and continue straight along the Wyoming Trail you will save 1.5 miles of walking and 400 feet of elevation gain, but you will also miss the opportunity to see some gorgeous country.

Lake Elbert will come into view just a hundred yards after leaving the Wyoming Trail, and 0.7 mile later you will be standing beside it. The trail follows the southwest side of Elbert for 0.2 mile, and then leaves in a northerly direction toward Luna Lake. After 10 minutes you will come to the lip of a large bowl nearly a mile across, and in the bottom of the depression, 300 feet below the rim, lies one of the prettiest lakes in the Zirkel Wilderness.

Luna Lake is where you should plan to spend the night; you will find the best camp sites above the northwestern shore of the lake. After you have descended into the bowl continue following the trail across a large meadow, then when you come to the junction with the Crags Trail turn left and walk along the north shore of the lake until you find a suitable site. Bear in mind, however, that the Forest Service requires you to camp at least 200 feet from the water.

Day 2 (6.6 miles)

The best way to get back to the Wyoming Trail from Luna Lake is on the Crags Trail, a well-marked path that leaves from the

The Wyoming Trail

Lake of the Crags

northeast side of the lake. This route will also allow you to see the Lake of the Crags along the way. The Lake of the Crags is a much smaller and shallower lake than Luna, but still worth a visit. It lies in a long, narrow basin 370 feet above Luna Lake.

From the Lake of the Crags the trail continues to climb another 700 feet before finally reaching the crest of the Divide 1.3 miles later. Here you will see a sign marking the junction with the Wyoming Trail, where you must turn left. The elevation of this trail junction in 11,570 feet; it is the highest point on this hike. The summit of Mount Ethel is clearly visible 0.8 miles to the southeast, and if you are in the mood for a climb to the top it is an easy walk up the peak's flat northwest slope. The summit is only 350 feet above the junction.

Back on the Wyoming Trail you must continue north along the Continental Divide for 1.2 miles to a low saddle where there is another sign marking the Rainbow Lake Trail. The large lake you can see east of the ridge is Roxy Ann Lake. Roxy Ann lies in a heavily timbered bowl almost 1,200 feet below the Divide. There is a nearby trail to the lake and the fishing is reported to be good, but the two-mile hike back out of Roxy Ann is steep and tiring.

After leaving the Continental Divide the Rainbow Lake Trail first looses about 200 feet of elevation, and then turns south following the contour toward the eastern side of Mount Ethel. This part of the trail is covered with grass and may be hard to follow, but it is marked by a series of widely spaced stone monuments.

As you walk through this flat, grassy area watch for a 9-foot sign post that marks the junction with the Roxy Ann Lake Trail. Unfortunately the post no longer has a sign on it, and to make matters worse the trail to Roxy Ann is more distinct than the Rainbow Lake Trail. Bear right at the post and continue in a southerly direction; if you suddenly find yourself going downhill to the north you are on the wrong trail.

For the next 0.7 mile the Rainbow Lake Trail looses very little elevation as it passes several ponds with gorgeous views of Mount Ethel, then it enters a series of long switchbacks that take it down to the western side of Upper Slide Lake. Upper Slide Lake has some nice campsites, and there are also many lovely places to stop in the meadowland below the lake. But if time and weather permit I suggest you continue on to Lower Slide Lake where you will find the most interesting campsites.

Beyond Upper Slide Lake the trail continues its gradual descent through a pastoral, grassy area below the eastern flank of Mount Ethel. Then, 1.1 miles after leaving the upper lake the trail crosses a small creek that drains Lower Slide Lake. You will recognize the drainage because the water flows sheet-like down a smooth granite face above the left side of the trail. It is this water slide that gave Slide Lake its name. In order to reach Lower Slide Lake you must leave the main trail at this point and follow a series of stone cairns upward along the west side of the water slide. After you have climbed about 200 feet you will arrive at the southern end of the lake. Slide lake is a long narrow lake, about 150 yards wide and 0.4 miles long. There are several excellent campsites above the lake's southern shore.

Day 3 (6.1 miles)

Below Slide Lake the forest becomes denser and the trees taller as the trail continues to loose altitude. The next point of interest is Rainbow Lake, 2.1 miles and 680 feet below Slide. The trail first encounters Rainbow on its western side and then veers away to the south to avoid a swampy area. According to older maps the trail never returns to the lakeshore, but actually the trail does come back to follow the southern edge of the lake for most of its length. As you walk along the lake you will probably be astounded at Rainbow's size. It is 0.6 mile long and 0.3 mile wide—huge for a natural, un-dammed lake at this elevation. It is also in pristine condition, with tall spruce and subalpine fir trees growing right to the water's edge. Rainbow Lake is particularly photogenic when viewed from the eastern end with Mount Ethel rising behind it.

Two smaller lakes, Middle Rainbow and Lower Rainbow, can be reached by walking down the drainage on the east side of Rainbow Lake. There is a crude, hiker-made trail to the smaller lakes, occasionally used by fishermen, but the main attraction is definitely Rainbow Lake itself.

The trail from Rainbow Lake back to the trailhead is a rather uneventful 2.5 miles. Soon after crossing the Mount Zirkel Wilderness Area boundary you will pass the Grizzly Helena Trail, a motorcycle trail that runs north and south along the bottom of the range. Then, 0.8 mile later, you will arrive at the Rainbow Lake Trailhead.

Rainbow Lake below Mount Ethel

Rawah Lakes

★★★★

Rawah Wilderness Area
3-day hike

Distance:	23.7 miles (loop)
Walking time:	day 1: 7 hours day 2: 6¼ hours day 3: 4¼ hours
Elevations:	3,610 ft. gain/loss West Branch Trailhead: 8,580 ft. Twin Crater Lakes: 11,047 ft. Grassy Pass: 11,220 ft. Rawah Lake No. 3 10,873 ft. Camp Lake: 10,510 ft.
Trail:	Generally well marked and well maintained
Season:	Midsummer through mid-fall. The higher parts of the trail are usually covered with snow from November through late June.
Vicinity:	West of Fort Collins, near Cameron Pass
Maps:	Boston Peak, Rawah Lakes (*USGS*) Poudre River (*Trails Illustrated, #112*)
Information:	http://colorado.utahtrails.com/rawahlakes.html http://www.fs.fed.us/arnf/ *(Roosevelt National Forest)* phone: (970) 498-1375 *(Canyon Lakes Ranger District)*

Drive west from Fort Collins on Highway 14. Check your odometer as you pass the junction with Highway 287 (Teds Place) and continue driving east for 48.5 miles. Just before arriving at Chambers you will see a sign marking the Laramie River Road. Turn right here and continue north for 6.8 miles, past the Tunnel Campground, to the West Branch Trailhead.

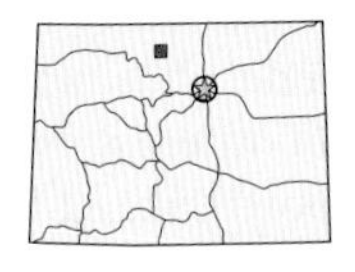

The Rawah Wilderness Area has long been recognized as one of Colorado's special places. A portion of it was classified as a protected area by the Forest Service as far back as 1927, and with the passage of the Wilderness Act in 1964 it became one of America's very first officially designated wilderness areas. This hike will take you into an area known as the Lakes District that lies in the rugged southern half of the

Rawah Wilderness. More than two dozen lakes adorn the eastern slopes of the Medicine Bow Mountains in the Lakes District. The loop hike described here visits no fewer than ten of them, all of which are regularly stocked with brook, rainbow, and cutthroat trout.

Day 1 (7.3 miles)

The trail first heads south along the road for 200 feet, then turns west for a few hundred yards along the north side of a small canal. Soon you will come to a footbridge where the trail crosses the canal and enters the woods in a southerly direction. After a few minutes you will begin to hear the sounds of rushing water as the trail approaches the West Branch of the Laramie River. Then, shortly after passing a spur trail to the Tunnel Campground, the path turns west to follow the north side of the West Branch.

The trail continues to follow the West Branch of the Laramie River for the next 3.1 miles, occasionally approaching the water's edge but more often staying high above the shore. After 2.1 miles you will come to a junction where the Camp Lake Trail departs from the West Branch Trail. This junction marks the beginning of the Rawah Lakes Loop, and the second half of the hike will be down the Camp Lake Trail to this point. For now, however, you should bear left and continue following the West Branch Trail.

After leaving the Camp Lake Trail junction the terrain becomes noticeably flatter, and the walk through the forest of spruce and subalpine fir is really quite pleasant. Within 0.7 mile the West Branch of the Laramie is joined by the North Fork of the river, and in another 0.3 mile the trail comes to a primitive log bridge across the North Fork. Many a tired backpacker has stopped for the night in this area. There are several fine camping spots nearby, but the area has been heavily

Twin Crater Lakes Basin

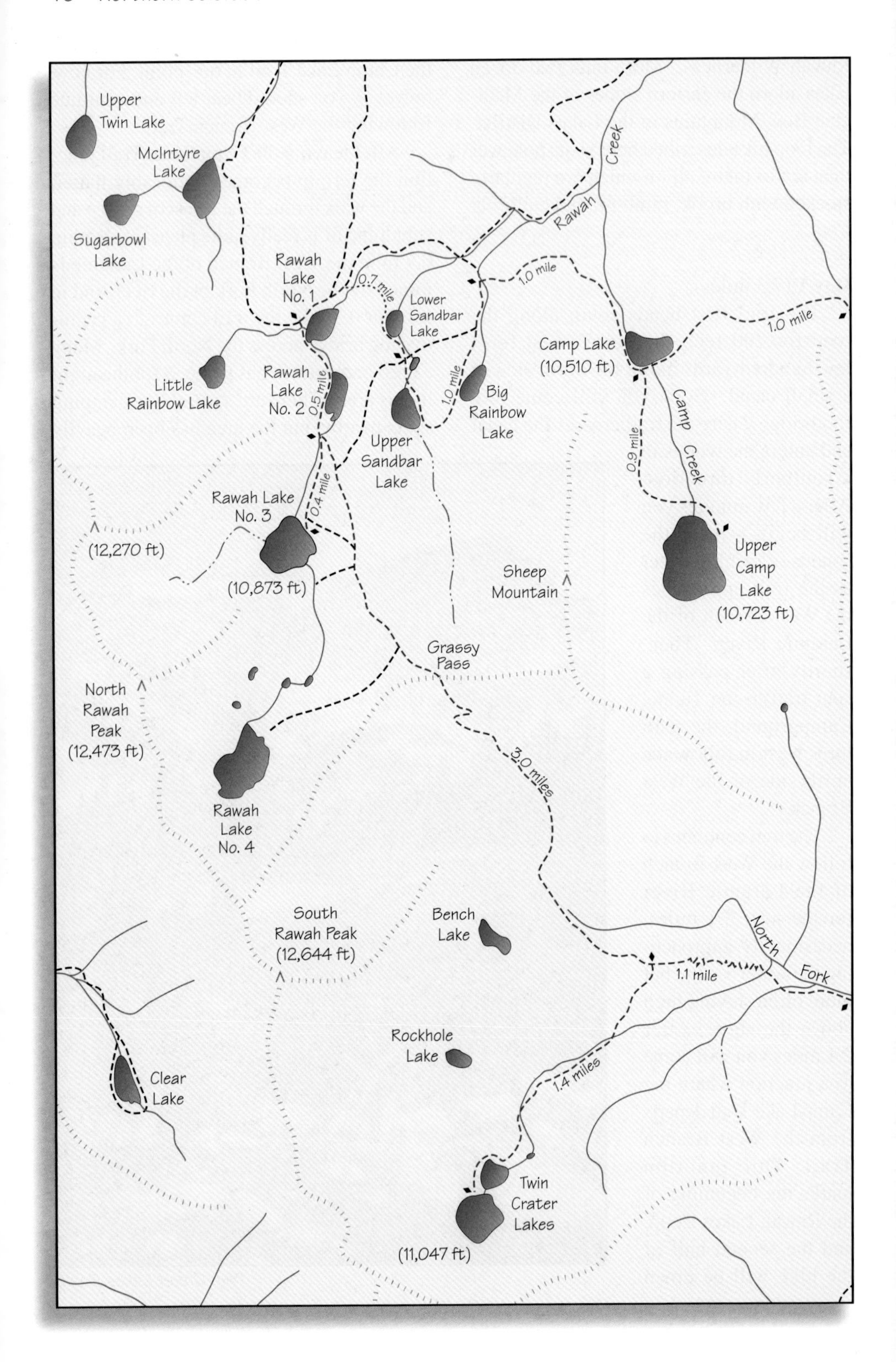
Upper Twin Lake
McIntyre Lake
Sugarbowl Lake
Rawah Lake No. 1
0.7 mile
Lower Sandbar Lake
1.0 mile
Rawah Creek
Camp Lake (10,510 ft)
1.0 mile
Little Rainbow Lake
Rawah Lake No. 2
0.5 mile
1.0 mile
Big Rainbow Lake
Upper Sandbar Lake
Camp Creek
0.9 mile
Rawah Lake No. 3
0.4 mile
(12,270 ft)
(10,873 ft)
Sheep Mountain
Upper Camp Lake (10,723 ft)
Grassy Pass
North Rawah Peak (12,473 ft)
3.0 miles
Rawah Lake No. 4
South Rawah Peak (12,644 ft)
Bench Lake
North Fork
1.1 mile
Rockhole Lake
1.4 miles
Clear Lake
Twin Crater Lakes
(11,047 ft)

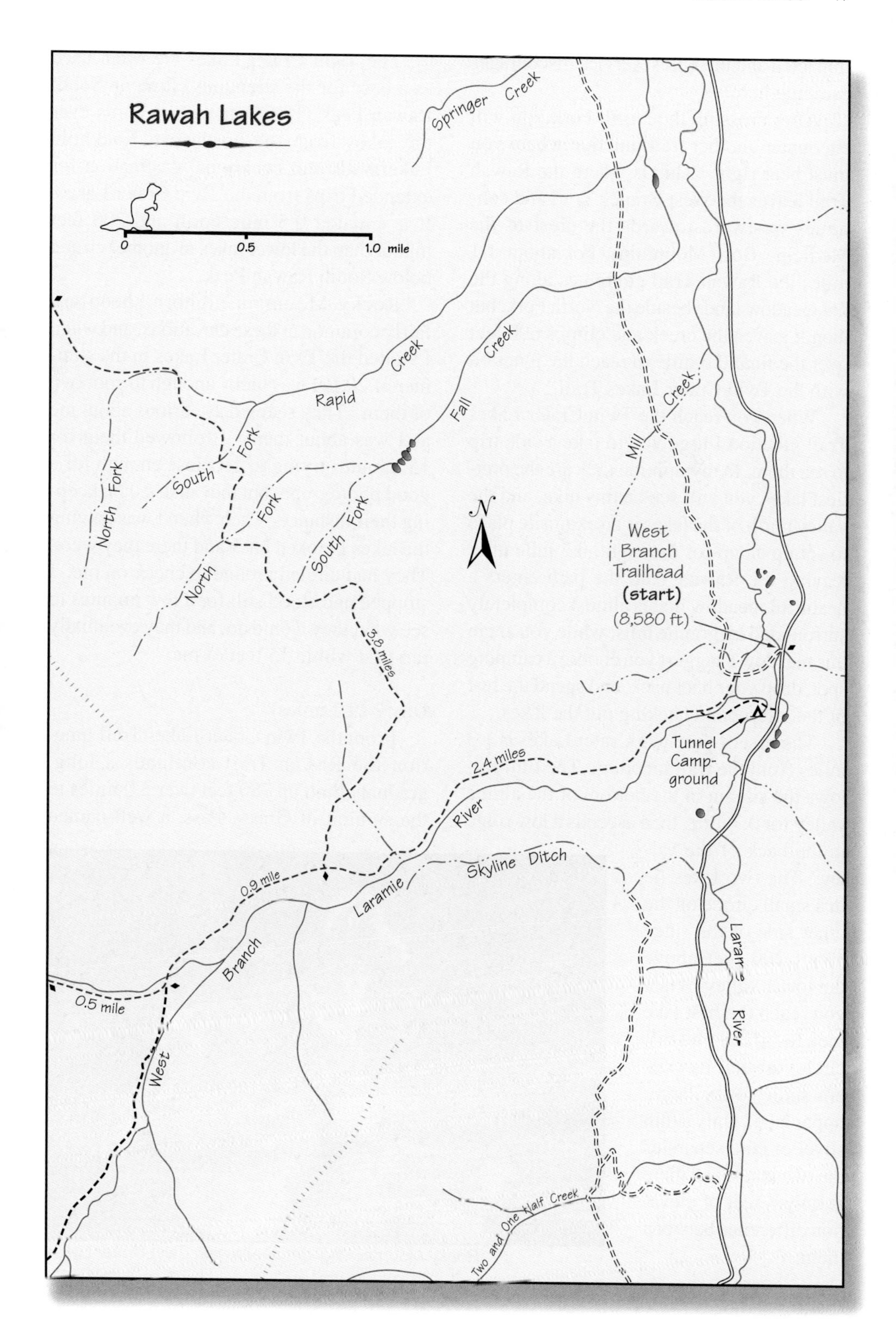

Rawah Lakes
0
0.5
1.0 mile
Springer Creek
Rapid Creek
Fall Creek
Mill Creek
South Fork
North Fork
North Fork
South Fork
West Branch Trailhead
(start)
(8,580 ft)
Tunnel Campground
3.8 miles
2.4 miles
0.9 mile
0.5 mile
River
Laramie
Skyline Ditch
Branch
West
Laramie River
Two and One Half Creek
N

impacted and the Forest service discourages camping here.

After crossing the North Fork you will encounter another trail junction where you must bear right. This is where the Rawah Trail leaves the West Branch Trail and continues westward towards the crest of the Medicine Bow Mountains. For about 1.1 miles the Rawah Trail continues along the flat meadow lands beside the North Fork, but then it leaves the creek and climbs 600 feet over the final 0.6 mile to reach the junction with the Twin Crater Lakes Trail.

When you reach the Twin Crater Lakes Trail junction I urge you to take a side trip to see them. In my opinion they are the prettiest lakes you will see on this hike, and the valley north of the lakes is an exquisite place to set up camp for the night. 0.3 mile after leaving the Rawah Trail the path enters a beautiful meadow that is almost completely surrounded by granite hills; while you are in this meadow I suggest you choose a camping spot, drop your backpack, and spend the rest of the afternoon checking out the lakes.

The first of the Twin Crater Lakes is 1.3 miles from the trail junction. The trail follows the stream in the bottom of the alpine valley for 0.7 mile, then ascends a low ridge in the back of the valley. The two lakes lie in a small cirque on the other side of the ridge about 200 feet above the lower valley. When you reach the first lake look for a faint trail that circles around its eastern shore to the larger upper lake. Only a thin sliver of land separates the two lakes, and there is only 4 feet of elevation difference between them.

The Twin Crater Lakes are often used as a base for the strenuous climb up South Rawah Peak (12,644 ft.) which lords over the lakes from the northwest. Rockhole Lake is also an occasional destination for extended trips from the Twin Crater Lakes. It is situated 0.5 mile north and 200 feet higher than the lower lakes in another cirque below South Rawah Peak.

Rocky Mountain bighorn sheep are fairly common at these elevations, and when I visited the Twin Crater Lakes in the summer of 2001 I was lucky enough to spot two of them. They seemed as curious about me as I was about them. I followed them for 15 minutes trying to get close enough for a good photograph, but they insisted on keeping their distance. Then when I was leaving the lakes I looked back and there they were. They had circled around to check on me. I stopped and stood still for a few minutes to see what they would do, and they eventually ran past within 15 feet of me.

Day 2 (9.2 miles)

From the Twin Crater Lakes Trail junction the Rawah Trail continues a long, gradual climb up 780 feet over 2.0 miles to the summit of Grassy Pass, a well-named

Rocky Mountain bighorn sheep near Twin Crater Lakes

alpine pass that sits right on the edge of timberline. North and South Rawah Peaks rise abruptly to the west, proudly watching over the rolling grasslands of the alpine tundra like proud parents at a children's park. Although you can't see it from the trail, Rawah Lake No. 4 lies midway between the two peaks 0.7 mile away and 254 feet higher. A faint, unmarked trail to the lake departs from the main trail about 0.2 mile below the north side of the pass.

Pond near summit of Grassy Pass

The four Rawah Lakes lie along a straight line on the west side of Grassy Pass, and the hike described here passes by three of them. The first lake you can see from the trail is Rawah Lake No. 3. The trail passes above its east side about 15 minutes north of the pass. The trail is situated 120 feet above the lake, but there are two short spur trails that lead down to its shore. When you reach the north end of Lake No. 3 you will come to a junction where you must bear right to see the other Rawah Lakes. The trail descends a short distance down to the bottom of the drainage and follows it northward for another 0.2 mile to Lake No. 2. (If you wish, you can turn south and walk back up the drainage a few hundred yards for a closer look at Lake No. 3.)

Lake No. 2 is only about half the size of Lake No. 3, but it is nevertheless very pretty, with large spruce trees growing right to the water's edge. Continue along the trail and 200 yards beyond Lake No. 2 you will come to Lake No. 1, which is very similar in size and appearance to Lake No. 2. You will also pass another trail junction where the path to McIntyre Lake branches off to the west.

If you stay on the Rawah Trail for another 1.0 mile beyond the McIntyre Lake Trail you will come to the Camp Lake Trail which will allow you to complete the loop back to the trailhead. However if you do this you will miss three other nearby lakes: Upper and Lower Sandbar Lakes and Big Rainbow Lake. As an alternative, I suggest you cut across country from the north end of Rawah Lake No. 1 to Lower Sandbar Lake and then follow the Sandbar Lakes Trail to the Camp Lake Trail. This route is about

Rawah Lake No. 1

0.7 mile longer, but the three other lakes are worth seeing.

Lower Sandbar Lake is only a ten-minute walk from Rawah Lake No. 1. To get there you should stay on the trail for about 200 yards past the northern end of Rawah Lake No. 1, and then leave the path in an easterly direction. You will have to ford Rawah Creek, but that is no problem. The creek is usually only 6 feet wide. Once you are on the other side of the creek head straight into the forest and begin following the contour of the land around to the southeast. It is easier to walk in the trees above the meadow, but Lower Sandbar Lake is almost exactly the same elevation as Rawah No. 1 so try not to gain too much altitude. If you follow the contour you will make a gradual turn to the right and approach Lower Sandbar while walking southeast. If you bear too much to the east you will run into the stream that drains Lower Sandbar, and if you bear too much to the south you will intersect the trail below the lake. Either way, you can't really get lost.

Once you reach Lower Sandbar Lake look for the trail on its west side. Follow the trail in a southerly direction and within 0.3 mile you will be on the eastern shore of Upper Sandbar. Both of the Sandbar Lakes are rather shallow; hence they are not the best lakes in the area for fishing. But Upper Sandbar Lake in particular is just the sort of place that moose love, and there is often one of the large animals in the lake. They seem to enjoy lazing about in the tall reeds on the west side, and they don't appear to have any fear of people.

After leaving Upper Sandbar Lake the trail bends around to the north and arrives at Big Rainbow Lake less than ten minutes later. It then follows the drainage down from the north end of Big Rainbow for another 0.3 mile to the junction with Camp Lake Trail. Once you get on the Camp Lake Trail it will take you about 20 minutes to walk to

Camp Lake.

Camp Lake is probably the most popular lake in the area. It is not the most scenic lake you will see on this hike, but nevertheless it is quite pretty. It is also situated at a more comfortable elevation than most of the other lakes and there are a number of good camping sites nearby. I suggest you pick a spot away from the lake and set up camp for the night. Upper Camp Lake is also an option if Camp Lake is too crowded. But wherever you decide to camp, you should take the short walk to see Upper Camp Lake before ending your day.

Upper Camp Lake is an easy 20-minute walk from the lower lake with only 200 feet of elevation gain, and your reward will make it well worth the effort to see it. The upper lake is the largest lake in this area, and it is nestled in a beautiful little valley just east of Sheep Mountain. The trail to the upper lake is easy to find; it is marked by a sign on the south side of Camp Lake.

Day 3 (7.2 miles)

The walk from Camp Lake back to the West Branch Trail is 4.8 miles long. The trail proceeds eastward from the lake across a flat meadowland for 0.8 mile, then turns south through a low saddle between two hills. On the east side of the saddle the trail begins following an old abandoned ditch that was dug years ago to channel more water to Fort Collins. Farmers in Wyoming contested Colorado's claim to the water rights, however, and after many years of litigation the ditch project was abandoned. The trail follows the ditch for 2.0 miles, and as you walk you will probably be stunned to see the amount of wasted effort that was invested in to the project.

Finally, 1.3 miles before reaching the West Branch Trail, the route leaves the ditch and turns sharply downward over a steep, rocky section of trail to the junction. From there you must retrace your steps the last 2.4 miles back to the trailhead.

Camp Lake

Cache la Poudre River

Comanche Peak Wilderness Area
day hike

Distance: 11.8 miles (one way)
(plus 13.2 miles by car from Big South Trailhead)

Walking time: 7 hours

Elevations: 1,900 ft. loss, 300 ft. gain
Corral Creek Trailhead (start): 10,040 ft.
Big South Trailhead: 8,440 ft.

Trail: The trail is Easy and well marked, but you will need to ford the river near Peterson Lake.

Season: Late summer through mid-fall. This hike requires a ford across the Cache la Poudre River. The river is usually too high to ford comfortably before August, but a shorter hike along the upper part of the river is possible earlier in the summer. The shorter hike ends at Peterson Lake just before the trail crosses the river.

Vicinity: West of Fort Collins

Maps: Chambers Lake, Boston Peak (*USGS*)
Poudre River (*Trails Illustrated, #112*)

Information: http://colorado.utahtrails.com/poudreriver.html
http://www.fs.fed.us/arnf/ *(Roosevelt National Forest)*
phone: (970) 498-1375 *(Canyon Lakes Ranger District)*

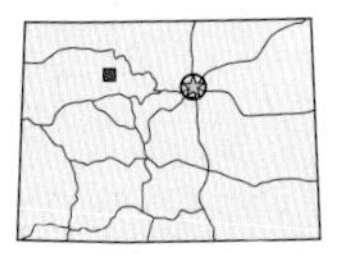

The Big South Trail along the Cache la Poudre River can be accessed from three different trailheads: the Big South Trailhead on Highway 14, the Peterson Lake Trailhead above Peterson Lake, and the Corral Creek Trailhead on Long Draw Road. The hike described here begins at the Corral Creek Trailhead and ends at the Big South Trailhead; however it is also possible to end the hike at the Peterson Lake Trailhead.

The Big South Trailhead is located west of Fort Collins on Highway 14. Check your odometer as you pass the junction with Highway 287, 10 miles out of Fort Collins, and continue driving west for another 44 miles. You will see a sign marking the Big South Trailhead and parking area on the left side of the road just before you come to the bridge crossing the Cache la Poudre River.

In order to reach the Corral Creek Trailhead continue west on Highway 14 for another 4.8 miles from the Big South Trailhead to Long Draw Road. Turn left on Long Draw Road and drive south for 8.4 miles to the Corral Creek Ranger Station. The Corral Creek Trailhead and parking area is on your left, 200 feet east of the ranger station.

To reach the Peterson Lake Trailhead you must backtrack 4.9 miles north of the Corral Creek Ranger Station on Long Draw Road. There you will see a sign marking the Peterson Lake Road. Turn east here and drive 1.8 miles to the end of the lake, where the 2WD road ends. Continuing east on the 4WD road for another 0.3 mile will bring you to the Peterson Lake Trailhead.

The Cache la Poudre River is, by many accounts, the most scenic river in Colorado. In 1973 the U.S. Congress added it to its official list of America's Wild and Scenic Rivers, and even today it remains the only waterway in the state to enjoy this status. Because of its federal designation the river has also enjoyed certain legal protections; consequently it still retains much of its original pristine charm. The Cache la Poudre is currently the only river in Colorado's Front Range that is still free-flowing and undammed along its entire 70-mile length. After this hike I think you will agree it is a jewel worth saving.

Cache la Poudre River

There is an interesting story about how the Cache la Poudre River got its name. In the Fall of 1836 a wagon train of French fur trappers became snowbound on the shore of the river while trying to make there way into southern Wyoming. The wagons were stuck for over a week, but by lightening the loads they were finally able to proceed. A portion of the supplies, including several hundred pounds of gunpowder, was carefully buried in a large pit, enabling the wagons to ford the river and continue into Wyoming. The trappers returned the following spring to reclaim their supplies, but from that time forward the stream came to be know as the Cache la Poudre River, which in the French language means "hiding place of the powder".

Today most of the Cache la Poudre is paralleled by Highway 14 west of Fort Collins, but the first 20 miles of its course is through

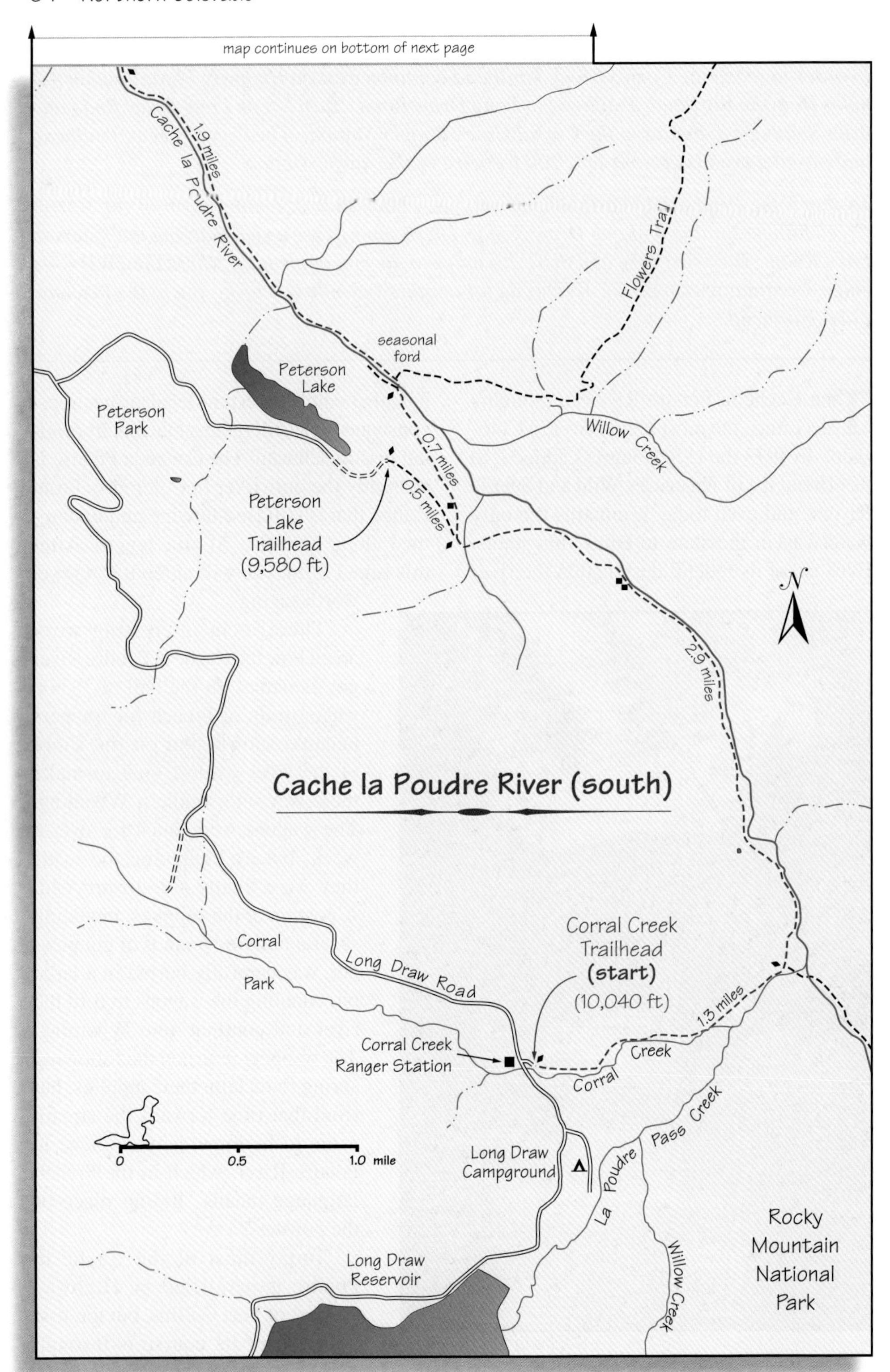

map continues on bottom of next page
Cache la Poudre River (south)
Cache la Poudre River
1.9 miles
Flowers Trail
seasonal ford
Peterson Lake
Peterson Park
Willow Creek
0.7 miles
0.5 miles
Peterson Lake Trailhead (9,580 ft)
2.9 miles
N
Corral Park
Long Draw Road
Corral Creek Trailhead (start) (10,040 ft)
1.3 miles
Corral Creek Ranger Station
Corral Creek
Pass Creek
0
0.5
1.0 mile
Long Draw Campground
La Poudre
Willow Creek
Rocky Mountain National Park
Long Draw Reservoir

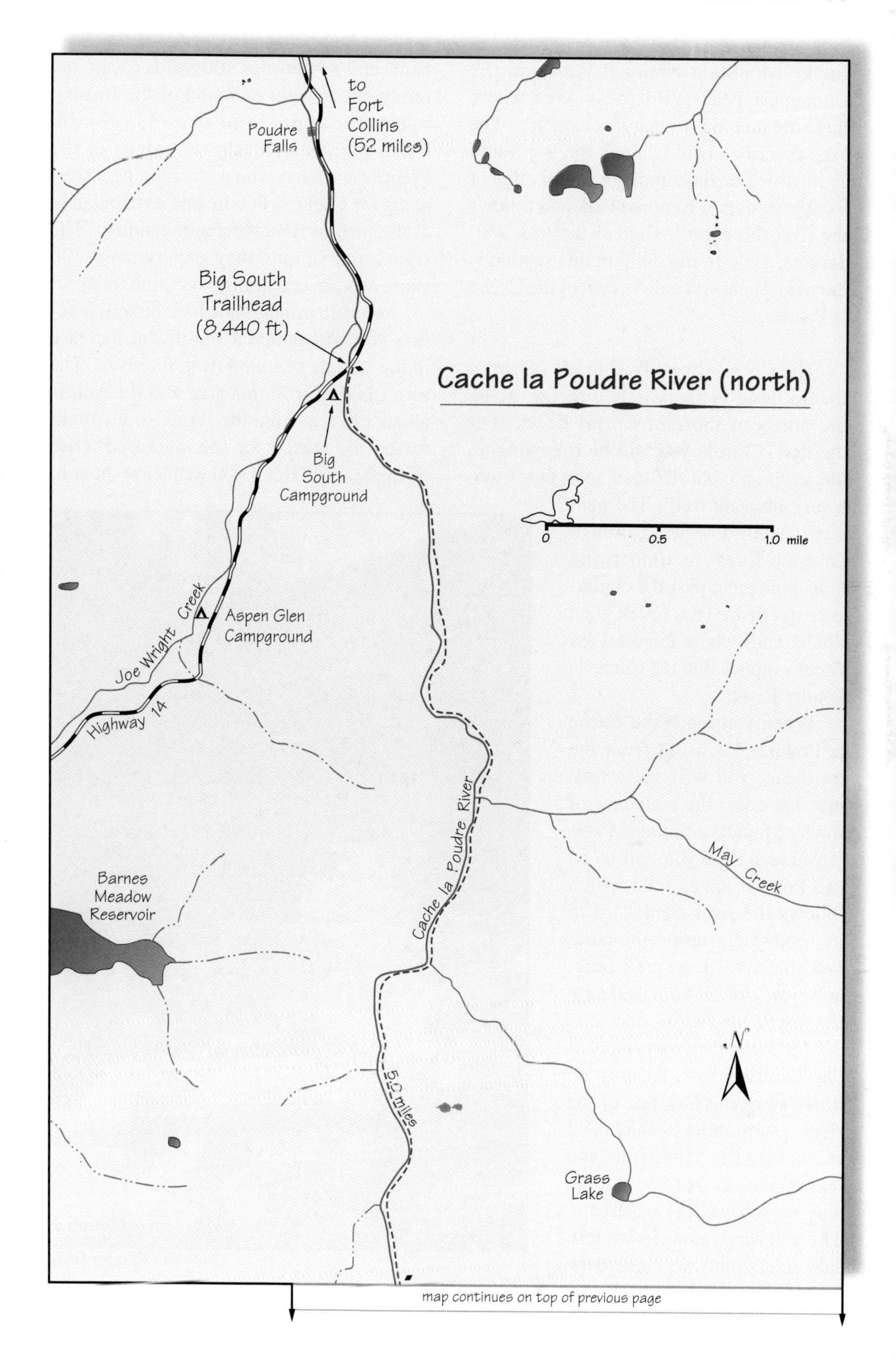
to
Fort
Collins
(52 miles)
Poudre
Falls
Big South
Trailhead
(8,440 ft)
Cache la Poudre River (north)
Big
South
Campground
0
0.5
1.0 mile
Aspen Glen
Campground
Joe Wright Creek
Highway 14
Cache la Poudre River
May
Creek
Barnes
Meadow
Reservoir
N
5.0 miles
Grass
Lake
map continues on top of previous page

Rocky Mountain National Park and the Comanche Peak Wilderness Area where there are no roads to mar its character. The hike described here is along the Big South Trail which begins on the northern edge of Rocky Mountain National Park and follows the river through the Comanche Peak Wilderness Area. In my opinion this section is the wildest, most scenic stretch of the Cache la Poudre.

The Corral Creek Trail heads out from the trailhead in an easterly direction along the northern shore of Corral Creek. For the first 0.3 mile you will be following an old jeep road, but the road soon fades into a very pleasant trail. The path winds gently downward through an open forest of limber and lodgepole pine, past the confluence of Poudre Pass Creek, then finally ends where Poudre Pass Creek empties into the Cache la Poudre River.

When you reach the Cache la Poudre, 1.3 miles from the trailhead, you will see a trail junction near the boundary of Rocky Mountain National Park. If you turn right you will be on the Poudre River trail which follows the river southward to its headwaters inside the park. For the hike described here, however, you must turn left onto the Big South Trail.

Although the headwaters of the Cache la Poudre are only ten miles away, the flow rate of the river is substantial by the time it reaches the Big South Trail, and it continues to increase noticeably as you walk downstream. The trail winds along its western side, sometimes very close to the bank and sometimes 100 yards away, but rarely out of sight or sound of the rushing water. The setting is pristine. As you walk try to put yourself into the minds of the French fur traders who were trapping beaver along the Cache la Poudre and its tributaries at the turn of the nineteenth century. The sights and sounds they experienced 200 years ago are essentially the same today.

About 20 minutes north of the trail junction you will notice a significant increase in the volume of sound from the river. The forest is denser in this area and the trail is about 100 feet from the shore, so it is hard to see the reason for the increased noise from the trail. But if you will leave the trail

Cache la Poudre River

at this point and walk through the trees to the water's edge you will be treated to the first of two spectacular cascades. Here the rushing water is confronted with a number of large boulders and other irregularities in the streambed, and it must draw upon all its energy to get around the obstacles. Like a trapped animal it roars and lunges, as if trying to intimidate its adversary. Then, having found a weakness, it pours through the barrier with unstoppable force.

0.7 mile beyond the first waterfall you will come to the second. This time the fall is about 200 feet from the trail so, again, you must leave the path when you hear an increase in the noise level. The second cascade is caused by a constriction in the riverbed that forces the entire flow to direct itself through an opening in the rock that is only four feet wide. At the bottom of the fall there is a large pool of relatively calm, deep water that must be a popular hangout for a few wise old trout. The Big South Trail is a favorite of backcountry fisherman, and I am sure many lines have been dropped into this pool.

Big South Trail

From the second cascade the trail continues northward, sometimes climbing 100 feet up the west side of the canyon, but ultimately returning to the river. 1.1 mile after leaving the second waterfall the path passes within two feet of the remains of two old log cabins that were built years ago on the shore of the river. Then soon after leaving the cabins it turns west, away from the river, and climbs out of the valley toward Peterson Lake.

Fifteen minutes after leaving the Cache la Poudre the trail crosses another small drainage and comes to a junction where the Peterson Lake Trail departs. If you don't want to ford the river you must bear left at this point towards Peterson Lake. Soon it will become apparent that the spur trail is following an old wagon or jeep road, but the road has not been used for at least 10-20 years—the roadbed is filled with trees, some of which are six inches in diameter. Finally, 15 minutes from the junction with the Big South Trail, the hike ends at the Peterson Lake Trailhead.

Continuing north from the Peterson Lake Trail junction along the Big South Trail you will soon come to the remains of two more cabins that appear to have been built in the late 1800s or early 1900s. From there the trail begins a gradual descent, and within 15 minutes you will once again arrive at the river. If you look carefully at the point where the trail reaches the water you can still see the footings on each side of the river where a footbridge used to be, but unfortunately the bridge was washed out by a flood in the early 1990s. All that is left now are two piles of stones and a couple of small logs; if you want to continue you must find a place to ford to the other side. Look for a smaller trail that continues downstream for another 100 yards to the place where most people make the ford. The stream is about 30 feet wide at this point and usually not more than 2 feet deep. But the current can be swift, and the bottom is covered with large, slippery rocks, so be careful.

Big South Trail

Timing is critical in fording the Cache la Poudre. The river normally has its peak flow around June 10, but this can vary from year to year. By August the flow rate is generally down to about 30% of its peak flow–low enough to allow a safe ford. Some strong, long-legged individuals attempt earlier crossings, but personally I would not even consider fording the river before mid-July. In any case you should carry a river bag as part of your gear and put your critical items in it during the crossing. If you fall into the water on the way across you will be thankful for a dry change of cloths when you reach the other side. Another point to consider: the Long Draw Reservoir empties into the Cache la Poudre River just above Corral Creek Trailhead, and occasional releases of water into the river by the reservoir operators can cause the water level of the river to rise dramatically and unexpectedly. Such dramatic changes are rare, especially in late summer, but they are not unknown. Please do not attempt to ford the river if it appears unsafe.

Find a strong stick, at least 8-10 feet long with a pointed end, and position it on your downstream side as you walk. Dig the pointed end into the river bottom and hold it at a 45-degree angle to the bottom, so that it forms a tripod with your legs. Only one leg of the tripod should be moved at a time, and only while the other two legs are securely pinned to the bottom. Unfasten the waste strap on your backpack while your are fording, so you can easily get out of it should you fall. But don't take off your shoes. The bottom is very irregular and the current bangs your feet against the rocks as you move, so you will need the protection of your boots. Finally, take your time and look up occasionally to reorient yourself. If you stare at the water too long it will begin to feel like you are the one that is moving and the river is standing still, and this can cause you to loose your balance.

The first time I did this hike I was alone.

It was mid-July, and the ford was a little more difficult than I had expected. It took me a full ten minutes to get across and I almost stumbled at least once, but when I reached the other side, changed my socks, and started down the trail again I felt like I had found the Garden of Eden. The air was so still, the vegetation on the forest floor was so green, and the sun was glinting softly through the mist below a canopy of pines. Ahead of me I knew all of the fishermen were at least five miles away near the Big South Trailhead. And behind me, well surely no one else would be crazy enough to make the ford I had just done. My solitude was secure. The river and the distance were protecting me from the confusion of the outside world. And, at least for the moment, I was in the most serene place in the universe. Heaven itself was my own private domain.

The terrain near the ford is quite flat, and for 1.5 miles the trail meanders through the well shaded woods, occasionally approaching the river and then veering away again. If you are not in a hurry the Big South Trail provides a fine opportunity for an overnight hike, especially if you are a fisherman. The forest service has established a number of backcountry campsites along the eastern side of the Cache la Poudre River, and asks that you camp only in these designated sites. In all there are 16 of them, spaced roughly at half-mile intervals with the first one being just north of the ford. The camps are all clearly marked with small signs along the trail.

After 1.9 miles the canyon becomes so narrow that the trail is forced to climb to a plateau above the ravine, and the following 1.2 miles are filled with exciting views of the raging torrent below you. Frothy water rushing ever downward—continually searching for the low ground at the end of the valley. The canyon remains narrow for the next 1.5 miles, but then the east bank becomes somewhat flatter allowing the trail to return briefly to the river.

The last 3.4 miles of the hike is punctuated with a lot of up and down, as the trail climbs to avoid the narrow sections of the river and then comes back down again when the opportunity presents itself. As you approach the end, however, the trail seems to stick more to the water's edge regardless of the narrow canyon. This is also the area where you are likely to see many fishermen. Finally, 6.9 miles beyond the point where the trail crosses from the west to the east side of the river, you will come out of the trees to the parking area beside Highway 14.

Big South Trail

Emmaline Lake

★★

Comanche Peak Wilderness Area
day hike

Distance: 10.6 miles (round trip)

Walking time: 7 hours

Elevations: 1,940 ft. gain/loss

Emmaline Lake Trailhead (start):	9,060 ft.
Cirque Meadow:	9,800 ft.
Emmaline Lake:	11,000 ft.

Trail: Well marked, well maintained

Season: Midsummer through mid-fall. The higher parts of the trail are usually covered with snow from November through early July.

Vicinity: Poudre Valley, near Fort Collins

Maps: Comanche Peak, Pingree Park (*USGS*)
Poudre River (*Trails Illustrated, #112*)

Information: http://colorado.utahtrails.com/emmalinelake.html
http://www.fs.fed.us/r2/arnf/ (*Roosevelt National Forest*)
phone: (970) 295-6700 (*Canyon Lakes Ranger District*)

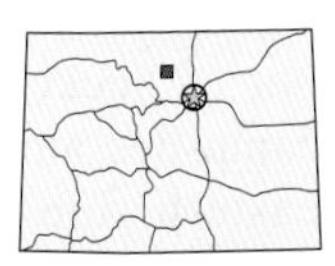

Drive north of Fort Collins on Highway 287 for 10 miles until you reach Highway 14; then turn west and follow Highway 14 into the Poudre River Valley. 26 miles after leaving Highway 287 you will come to the Pingree Park Road, a graded gravel road that departs on the south side of the highway. Turn here and continue south, following the signs to Pingree Park. 15.4 miles after leaving the pavement you will see a sign directing you to Tom Bennett Campground and Sky Ranch on the right. Turn right here and drive for the last 0.3 mile, past the campground, until you see a large sign that says Emmaline Lake and Mummy Pass Trailhead. The actual trailhead is another 0.5 mile along a smaller road that heads west from the sign. The last half-mile is quite rough, however, so if you are not driving a high-clearance vehicle you may want park at the sign and walk the last 0.5 mile.

Emmaline Lake is one of those scenic alpine jewels that make hiking in Colorado so enjoyable. It is set in a deep mountain cirque on the northern side of the Mummy Range. The lake lies 1,700 feet below the summit of Comanche Peak, the highest point

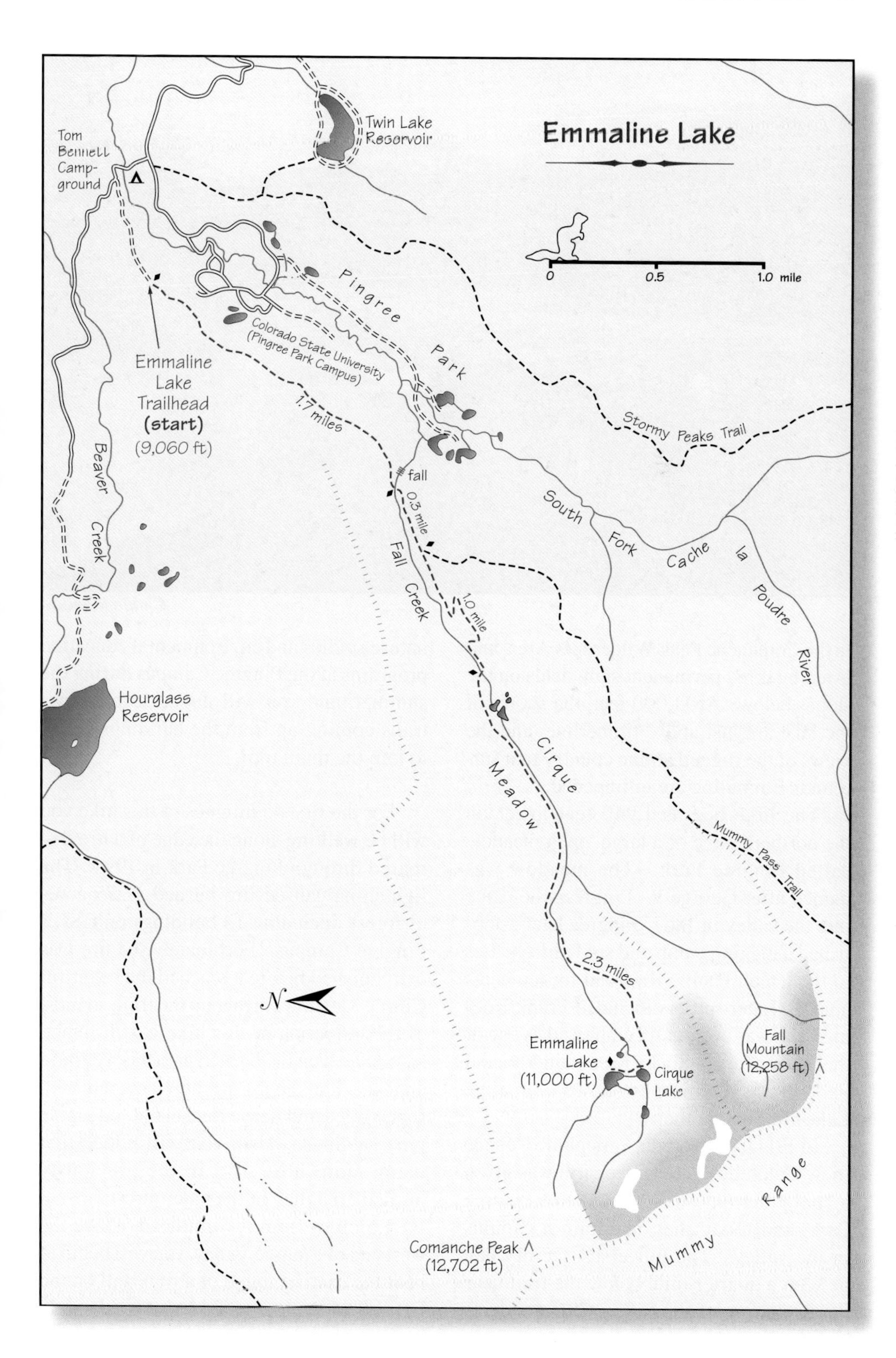

Emmaline Lake
0
0.5
1.0 mile
Twin Lake Reservoir
Tom Bennett Campground
Pingree Park
Colorado State University (Pingree Park Campus)
Emmaline Lake Trailhead (start) (9,060 ft)
1.7 miles
fall
0.3 mile
1.0 mile
2.3 miles
Stormy Peaks Trail
South Fork Cache la Poudre River
Beaver Creek
Fall Creek
Hourglass Reservoir
Cirque Meadow
Mummy Pass Trail
N
Emmaline Lake (11,000 ft)
Cirque Lake
Fall Mountain (12,258 ft)
Comanche Peak (12,702 ft)
Mummy Range

Cirque Meadow

in the Comanche Peak Wilderness Area, and is fed by three permanent snowfields on the slopes below. At 11,000 feet, the shores of the lake are just above timberline, and the views of the rugged alpine country that surrounds Emmaline are unimpeded.

The hike begins 1,940 feet lower on the northern edge of a large, open meadow called Pingree Park. The meadow was named after George W. Pingree who came into the valley in 1867. Pingree later established a logging camp and sold railroad ties to the Union Pacific Railroad for ten cents apiece. Later settlers included Frank Koenig, who was eventually employed as one of the first rangers in Rocky Mountain National Park. It was Koenig who named Emmaline Lake after his mother.

In 1914 the Colorado Agriculture College (now Colorado State University) was given a land grant that included most of Pingree Park, and today they maintain a campus in the valley. The university facility can be seen a quarter-mile below the trail near the beginning of the hike. CSU conducts nature studies and environmental education programs at the Pingree Campus during the summer, and you will notice several spur trails coming up from the buildings below to join the main trail.

For the first 45 minutes of this hike you will be walking along the edge of a fire that roared through Pingree Park in 1994. The lightening-caused fire burned 1,275 acres of forest, including 13 buildings on CSU's Pingree Campus. Fortunately the fire was extinguished before it reached the beautiful Cirque Meadow further up the trail, so most of the attraction of this hike is still intact. Actually, even the burned area has a certain appeal. The slopes are now covered with aspen trees and dense thickets of lodgepole pine saplings. Also, you will notice that many more birds live in the previously burned area than in the older forest.

1.6 miles from the trailhead, above the west end of Pingree Valley, you will begin to hear the roaring sound of a waterfall on the left side of the trail. The forest is relatively dense here so it is hard to see where all the racket is coming from, but occasionally you can catch a glimpse of the water below the trail. Then, a few minutes beyond the cascade the trail breaks out into a small clearing where a crude log bridge takes you to the south side of Fall Creek. The trail continues on the south side of the creek for the next 1.3 miles to Cirque Meadow.

By now you will have surely noticed that you are walking on an old jeep road. The road has not been used for many years and the vegetation is slowly reclaiming its sides, but it is nonetheless a road. The road goes as far as Cirque Meadow before ending near an old unused gaging station.

Cirque Meadow is one of the highlights of this hike. The trail first enters the eastern side of the meadow and then crosses Fall Creek again on a footbridge before continuing along the north side of the meadow. The view is especially pretty early in the morning when the mountain ridge behind the grassy flat is in direct sunlight. The snowfields above Emmaline Lake form a perfect backdrop for the flower-covered meadow. There are several campsites on both sides of the meadow for anyone wishing to spend more time in the area.

Soon after crossing Fall Creek the trail passes an immense pile of old rough-cut lumber, probably the remnants of an old lumber mill from the last century. Beyond the lumber pile the trail becomes much narrower, and within a few minutes you will see a sign marking the boundary of the Comanche Peak Wilderness Area.

Over the next mile after entering the wilderness area the trail passes four primitive campsites that have been developed and marked by the Forest Service, but soon after campsite 4 you will see a sign that says "No Camping Beyond This Point". Wilderness managers do not like people to camp at the higher altitudes because the growing season is so short and the ground cover is so easily damaged. It can take many decades for the alpine tundra to revegetate itself.

As the trail approaches timberline it crosses again to the south side of Fall Creek and soon enters a field of large granite boulders. The route is marked only by cairns in this area and in one or two places it may be difficult to follow, but within a few hundred yards the trail becomes obvious again. Over the last 0.7 mile the trail veers to the south and then bends back to the north again to cross Fall Creek for the fourth time just below Cirque Lake.

Cirque Lake is almost the twin of Emmaline Lake. It is located just to the south of the larger lake, 200 yards distant and 50 feet lower in elevation. Many people think they have arrived at Emmaline when they first see Cirque Lake, but if you continue along the lower lake's eastern shore for another 3 or 4 minutes you will arrive at your final destination. There, elegantly situated beneath the towering Comanche Peak with white snowfields reaching down the slopes toward its western shore, is the picture-perfect alpine tarn that Frank Koenig named after his mother 90 years ago.

Emmaline Lake

Mount McConnel

Cache La Poudre Wilderness Area
day hike

Distance: 4.2 miles (loop)

Walking time: 3 hours

Elevations: 1,350 ft. gain/loss
Kreutzer Trailhead (start): 6,660 ft.
Kreutzer Trail Junction: 7,320 ft.
Mount McConnel: 8,010 ft.

Trail: Excellent, well-marked trail

Season: Summer, Spring, and Fall. There is usually snow on Mount McConnel from late November through March, but this hike is often attempted in spite of the snow.

Vicinity: Near Fort Collins

Maps: Big Narrows (*USGS*)
Cache La Poudre, Big Thompson (*Trails Illustrated, #101*)

Information: http://colorado.utahtrails.com/mountmcconnel.html
http://www.fs.fed.us/arnf/ *(Roosevelt National Forest)*
phone: (970) 498-2770 *(Canyon Lakes Ranger District)*

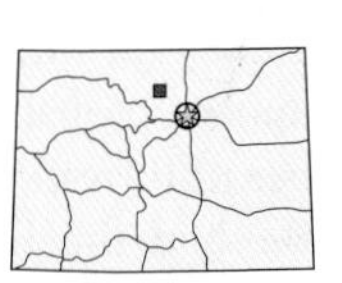

Drive north from Fort Collins on Highway 287 for 10 miles until you reach Highway 14, then turn west and follow Highway 14 for another 23 miles to the Mountain Park Recreation Area. When you reach Mountain Park turn left and cross the bridge on the south side of the highway. The trailhead is on the left side of the road into Mountain Park about 250 yards beyond the bridge.

By Colorado standards Mount McConnel is scarcely a mountain at all but rather an 8,000-foot hill of the northeast side of the Front Range. Nevertheless its location, just west of Fort Collins and high above the beautiful Poudre River Valley, has made it a popular hike. Like many of the trails in Colorado, the trail to the top of Mount McConnel was built in the mid-1930s by the Civilian Conservation Corps. More recently the lower part of the trail has been made into a nature walk with interpretive plaques at key points along the way that provide information about the history and ecology of the area.

The nature walk portion of the Mount

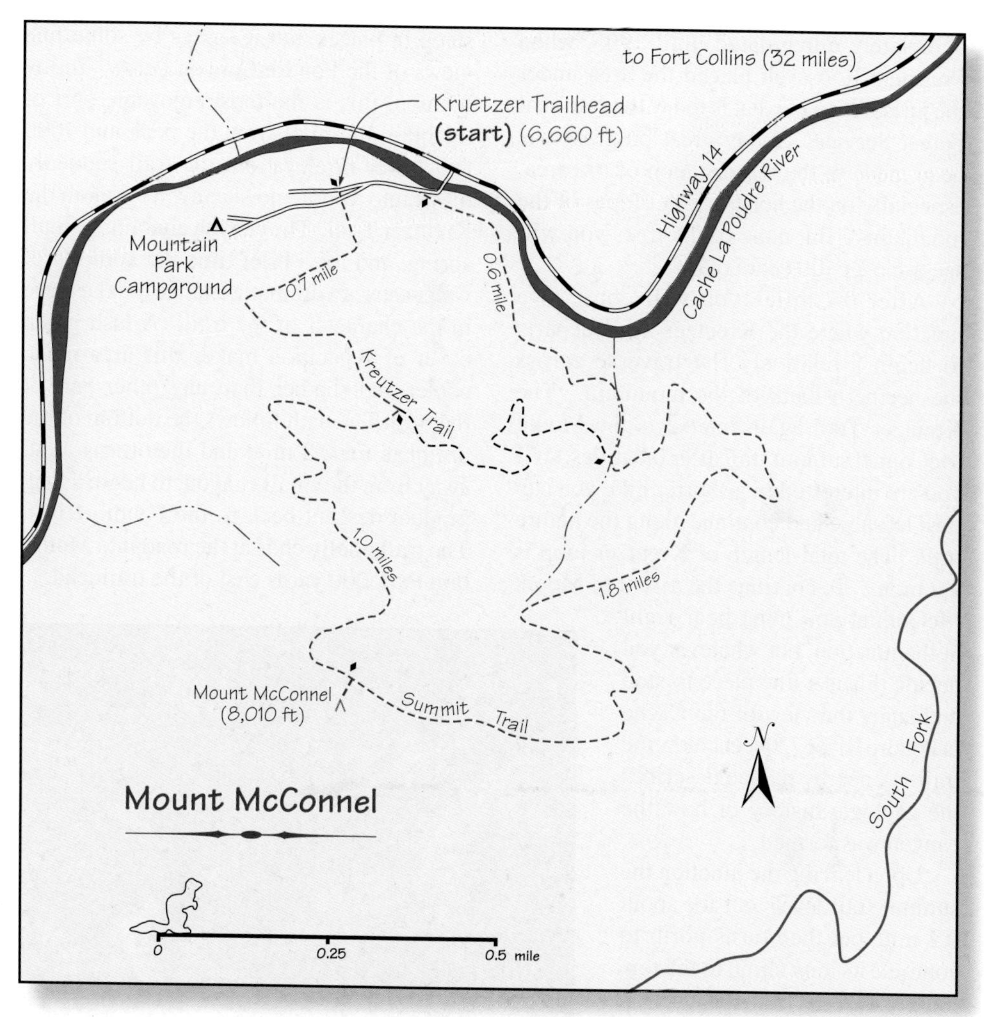

McConnel Trail is called the Kreutzer Trail in recognition of William R. Kreutzer, a Colorado resident who in 1898 became the first official forest ranger in the United States. Kreutzer worked for the Forest Service for 41 years, finally serving as the Supervisor of Roosevelt National Forest before his retirement in 1939. Mount McConnel itself was named after another early forest ranger, R. C. McConnel, who served in the Poudre District of Roosevelt National Forest in the early 1900s. The mountain became part of the Cache La Poudre Wilderness Area in 1980.

From the lower parking area the trail first climbs a short distance to cross the upper Mountain Park Road, and then continues a long gradual assent through an open forest of ponderosa pine and Douglas fir. One thing you may notice is that there are no very old trees. The reason is that from 1868 until the turn of the century the hills in this area were essentially stripped of all their timber. The trees were initially cut to provide ties for the Union Pacific and Denver Pacific Railroads, and later to satisfy the demand for lumber in Fort Collins and other nearby settlements. The Logging activities were completely unregulated until 1905, when President Roosevelt placed the area under the jurisdiction of what is today the National Forest Service. Today great progress has been made in the reforestation of the area, especially on the north-facing slopes of the mountains. But none of the trees you will see are over 100 years old.

After 0.7 miles you will come to a junction where the Kreutzer Trail departs to begin a relatively flat traverse across the northern flank of the mountain. The Kreutzer Trail again intersects the Mount McConnel summit trail after 0.8 miles, so if you are interested in a shorter hike you can turn left here and continue along the nature trail. The total length of Kreutzer loop is 2.2 miles. To continue the assent of Mount McConnel you must bear right at the junction, but whatever you decide this is a fine place to stop and enjoy the view of the Cache la Poudre River 720 feet below the trail. A nearby plaque describes the geologic history of how the canyon was formed.

Upon leaving the junction the summit trail levels out for about 0.2 mile but then turns north to continue its long climb to the top. Finally, 1.0 mile from the junction the route crosses the rocky summit of the mountain. The peak is rather nondescript. At 8,010 feet, it is well below timberline and the view is not particularly notable. There is, however, a nice view of the Mummy Range along the northern boundary of Rocky Mountain National Park.

As you begin your descent down the east side of the mountain you will soon notice that the trail has become more primitive. The route down is very rocky and steep in places, but it passes by some fine views of the Poudre Canyon below. In my opinion, this is the most enjoyable part of the hike. 1.8 miles from the peak and 1000 feet lower in elevation, the trail suddenly drops into a cool, moist canyon to rejoin the Kreutzer Trail. The canyon contains a small spring, and for a brief time the addition of water causes a dramatic change to take place in the character of the trail. A lush green cover of vegetation makes this area much cooler and shadier than any other part of the trail. The path follows the bottom of the drainage for 0.2 mile and then turns west, away from the small canyon, to begin a long gradual descent back to the Poudre River. The trail finally ends at the road into Mountain Park 200 yards east of the trailhead.

Cash La Poudre River, from the Kreutzer Trail

Greyrock Mountain

★ **day hike**

Distance:	7.5 miles (loop)
Walking time:	5 1/2 hours
Elevations:	2,255 ft. gain/loss Greyrock Trailhead (start): 5,558 ft. lower trail junction: 5,800 ft. upper trail junction: 6,990 ft. Greyrock summit: 7,613 ft.
Trail:	Mostly easy and well maintained. The last 0.9 mile to the summit is a slickrock trail marked by cairns. A small amount of scrambling may be necessary.
Season:	The trail is open year round, but expect some snow during the winter.
Vicinity:	West of Fort Collins
Maps:	Poudre Park (*USGS*) Cache la Poudre (*Trails Illustrated, #101*)
Information:	http://colorado.utahtrails.com/greyrock.html http://www.fs.fed.us/arnf/ *(Roosevelt National Forest)* phone: (970) 498-2770 *(Canyon Lakes Ranger District)*

Drive west of Fort Collins on Highway 14. When you pass the junction with highway 287 (Teds Place) check your odometer and continue west for another 8 miles. Look for a sign marking the Greyrock Trail parking area on your left.

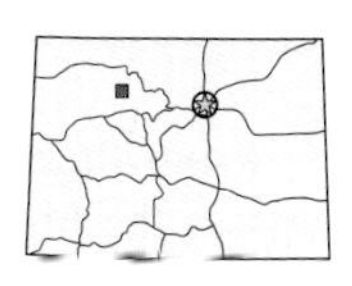

Greyrock Mountain, as the name suggests, is a large outcropping of gray granite located above the Poudre Canyon west of Fort Collins. But this is no ordinary granite outcropping. It is a huge, tent-shaped pyramid of stone that rises over 600 feet above the grassy meadow at its base. Local residents have always admired the landmark, both for its scenic setting and its unusual size and shape. But among hikers seeing Greyrock for the first time one emotional response seems to dominate: almost everyone experiences an overpowering urge to climb to the top.

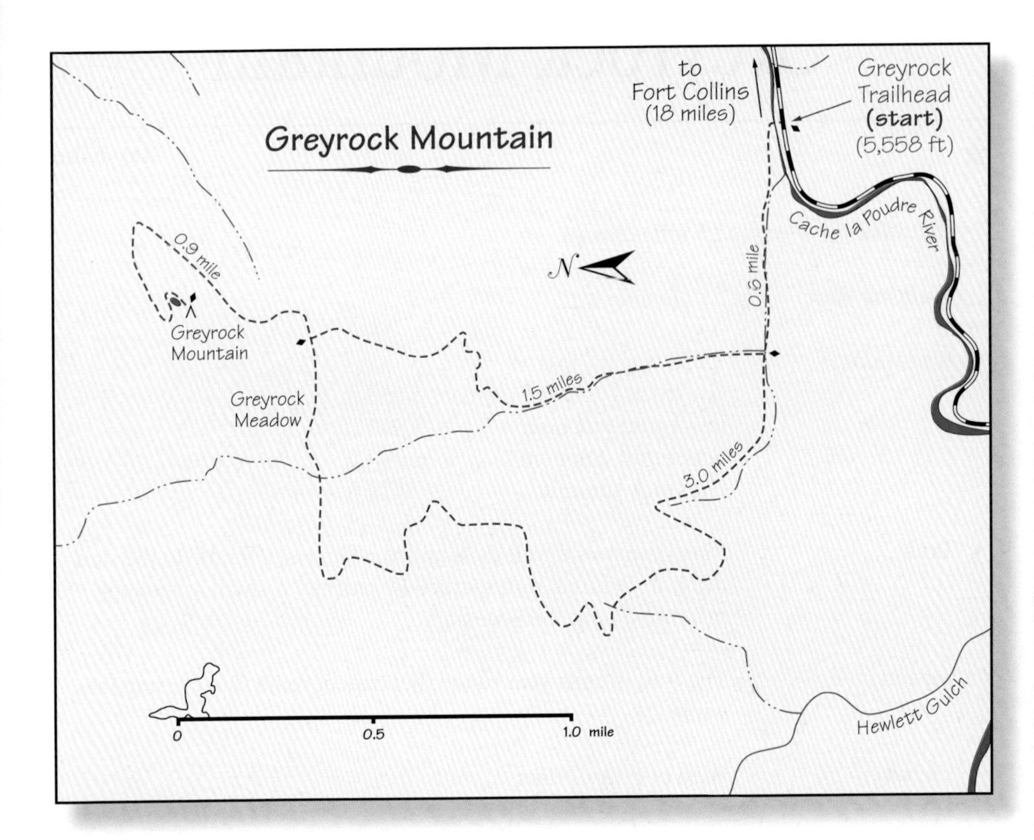

Fortunately there is a relatively easy route to the top. The Greyrock Summit Trail was built in the 1930s by the Civilian Conservation Crops, and in 1978 a second connecting trail called the Greyrock Meadows Trail was completed. Together, these two routes make it possible to do the loop hike described here.

From the parking area the trail first crosses the highway and then drops down to enter a small footbridge across the Cache la Poudre River. Once on the north side of the river the path makes an abrupt left turn and begins working its way westward up a shallow drainage. Then, about fifteen minutes after leaving the river, the trail comes to a junction where the newer Greyrock Meadows Trail begins. I suggest you bear left at this point onto the Meadows Trail and use the steeper Summit Trail as your return route.

The Meadows Trail continues following the drainage in a westerly direction for another 1.0 mile, and then begins a long, gradual climb up the north side of Poudre Canyon. The south-facing slope has very few trees, and the views back down into the canyon are magnificent. As you climb higher you will also be able to look down into Hewlett Gulch to the west.

After an elevation gain of 1200 feet the Meadows Trail levels out briefly and then looses 200 feet as it drops back down into the Greyrock Meadows. Now, for the first time, you will be able to see Greyrock Mountain. There are other outcroppings of granite here and there on the edge of the meadow, but Greyrock is the one that stands out. The trail proceeds along the flat bottom of the meadow in an easterly direction for 0.3 mile, then rises slightly before finally rejoining the Summit Trail just a few hundred yards south of the mountain.

Beyond the second junction the Summit Trail first turns east and then begins a long 180-degree counter clockwise spiral that winds up the side of the mountain and ultimately approaches the summit from the north. This is the only really strenuous part of the entire hike; the elevation gain is 620 feet over 0.9 mile.

As formidable as Greyrock Mountain looks from below, the trail up is not bad. The route takes advantage of many cracks and faults in the granite block and even passes through one flat grassy area near the top. Most surprising of all is the existence of a shallow pond of water just 30 feet below the summit. Amazingly, this 30-foot diameter depression usually contains water for most of the summer, although the water is not clean enough to drink untreated.

The summit is just a short scramble up from the pond. From there you can easily see the trail junction 500 yards to the south, and the trail through Greyrock Meadows is also clearly in view. The town of Fort Collins spreads across the plains in the east, and in the distant southwest is the Mummy Range of Rocky Mountain National Park.

To complete the loop hike you must turn left at the trail junction south of Greyrock Mountain, and return to the trailhead on the Summit Trail. This trail is considerably steeper than the Meadows Trail, however it is 1.5 miles shorter and there is more water along the way. After the first 0.9 mile it drops into a deep ravine, then the trail follows the rocky bottom of the ravine down to the first junction. From there you can retrace your steps the last 0.6 mile to the trailhead.

Greyrock Mountain above Greyrock Meadow

Homestead Meadows

★★ **day hike**

Distance:	9.4 miles (round trip)
Walking time:	6 hours
Elevations:	1,480 ft. gain/loss Lion Gulch Trailhead (start): 7,320 ft. Irvin Homestead: 8,600 ft. Brown Homestead: 8,680 ft.
Trail:	Easy, well marked and well maintained trail
Season:	Midsummer through mid-fall. There is usually snow on the trail from mid-November through mid-June.
Vicinity:	Near Estes Park
Maps:	Panorama Peak (*USGS*) Cache la Poudre/Big Thompson (*Trails Illustrated, #101*)
Information:	http://colorado.utahtrails.com/homesteadmeadows.html http://www.fs.fed.us/r2/arnf/ *(Roosevelt National Forest)* phone: (970) 295-6700. *(Canyon Lakes Ranger District)*

Drive east out of Estes Park to the junction of Highway 36 and Highway 34, then turn south on Highway 36 toward the town of Lyons. 8.5 miles from the junction, or 100 feet beyond milepost 8, you will see the trailhead and parking area on the right side of the road.

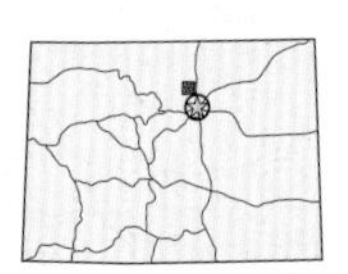

If you are interested in Colorado's early settlers and want to learn more about how and where they lived this hike will be of special interest to you. Homestead Meadows was added to the National Registry of Historic Places in 1990, and it is now a protected area managed by the Forest Service. The area contains no fewer than eight century-old homesteads. Many of the original buildings are still standing, and the trails leading to the homesteads are the old wagon roads that residents once used to access their homes. The sites provide a fascinating window into what life on the frontier was like at the turn of the last century.

To make the hike even more interesting the Forest Service has placed plaques at each of the eight homesteads to provide information about who lived there. One plaque describes a teenage girl who rode

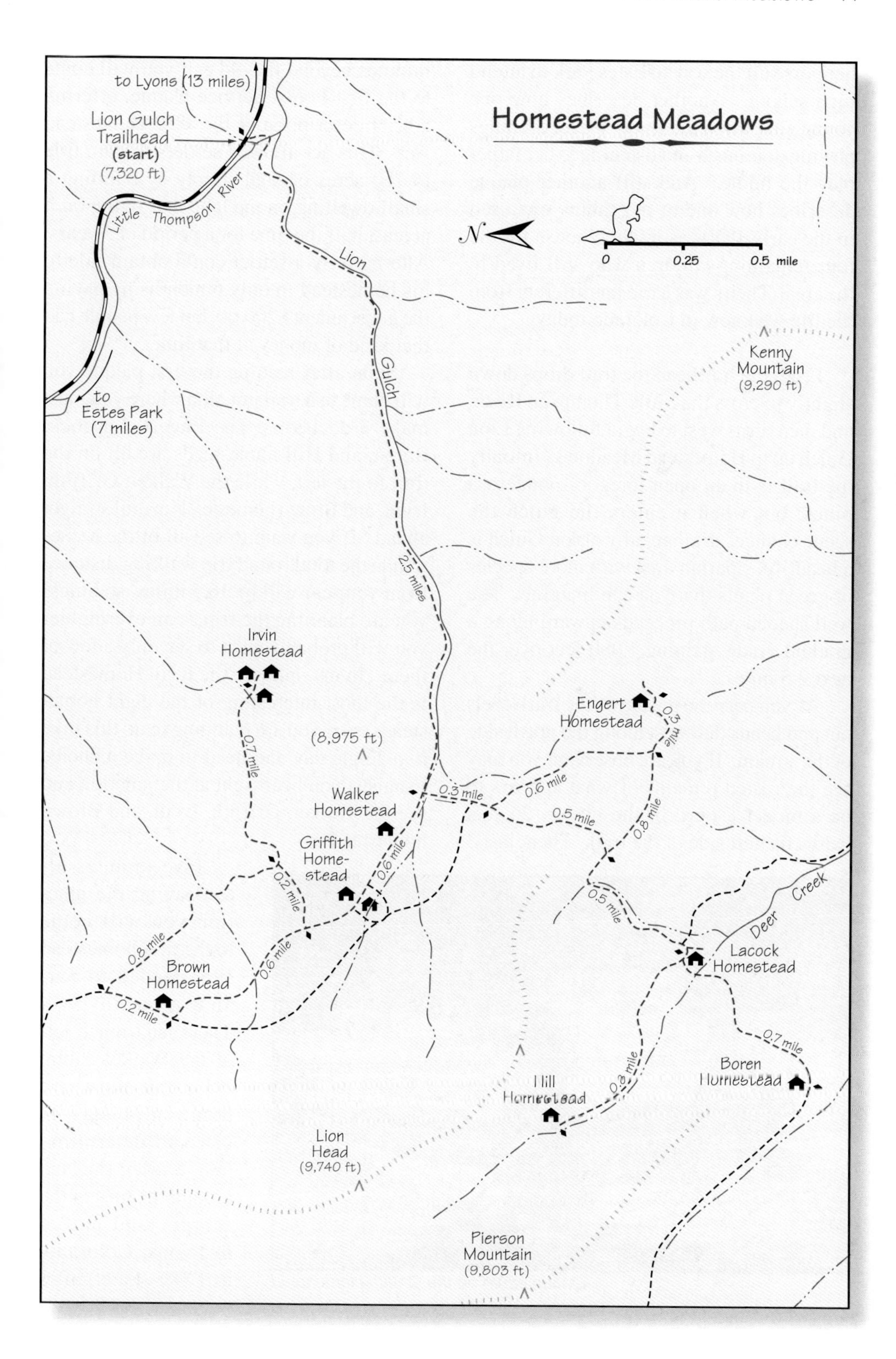
Homestead Meadows
to Lyons (13 miles)
Lion Gulch Trailhead (start) (7,320 ft)
Little Thompson River
to Estes Park (7 miles)
N
0
0.25
0.5 mile
Lion Gulch
2.5 miles
Kenny Mountain (9,290 ft)
Irvin Homestead
0.7 mile
(8,975 ft)
Engert Homestead
0.3 mile
0.6 mile
0.3 mile
Walker Homestead
0.5 mile
0.8 mile
Griffith Home-stead
0.6 mile
0.2 mile
0.5 mile
Deer Creek
0.8 mile
Brown Homestead
0.6 mile
0.2 mile
Lacock Homestead
0.7 mile
Boren Homestead
0.8 mile
Hill Homestead
Lion Head (9,740 ft)
Pierson Mountain (9,803 ft)

her horse all the way to Estes Park to attend high school. Another describes how one young girl passed the lonely winter evenings playing dominoes and listening to her father play the fiddle. And still another plaque describes how one of the cabins was used in the early 1950s as a schoolhouse for the four remaining children who still lived in the area. Theirs was a life far different from the life we know in Colorado today.

From the trailhead the trail drops down slightly to cross the Little Thompson River, and then turns west to begin following Lion Gulch up to Homestead Meadows. Initially the trail is in an open forest of ponderosa pines, but when it enters the gulch the scene changes dramatically. Lion Gulch is a beautiful riparian area with more species of green plants that you can imagine. The well shaded path proceeds upward along a gradual grade, gaining 1,080 feet over the next 2.5 miles.

As you near the meadows the trail levels out and heads due west along the north side of the stream. If you are observant you may see the rusted remains of what appears to be a model-T Ford in the bushes 25 feet below the left side of the trail. Then, just 3 minutes beyond the old car, you will come to the first Forest Service plaque, offering a brief description of the 1862 Homestead Act. This act allowed settlers to gain title to 160 acres of land simply by building a small dwelling on the land and living on it at least half the time for a period of 5 years. Alternatively a settler could obtain title to his homestead in only 6 months by paying the government $200.00, but few people had that kind of money at that time.

Soon after reading the first plaque you will come to a trail junction where you must make a decision. The Engert, Laycock, Boren, and Hill homesteads are all on the trail to the left, while the Walker, Griffith, Irvin, and Brown homesteads are all straight ahead. If you want to see all of the homesteads the total round trip walking distance from your car will be 16.5 miles, so unless you are planning the trip as an overnighter you will probably want to see only a few of them. In my opinion, the Irvin Homestead is the most interesting of the eight homesteads, so if you are planning to do this hike in a single day and need to make a choice I suggest you bear right at the junction and see the Walker, Griffith, Irvin, and Brown homesteads.

A fallen cabin on the Griffith Homestead

Five minutes after leaving the junction you will come to the first homestead site, deeded to Sarah Walker in 1914. There isn't much left of the Walker cabin, but Sarah must have been a lady filled with grit and determination. She left England around the turn of the century and moved to Lyons, Colorado, in 1908. Later, after loosing her husband and two children, she settled in Homestead Meadows and lived there until around 1925. She was the only single woman to homestead in the area.

Another 0.2 mile beyond the Walker homestead you will come to the remains of three old cabins on a plot of land that was purchased from the state of Colorado by William Griffith in 1923. Griffith lived there until his death in 1936.

From the Griffith homestead to the Irvin homestead is 1.1 miles along an old wagon road that once served a sawmill on the Irvin property. Along the way you will pass two other trails that branch off to the left towards the Brown homestead. You will probably want to visit the Brown property on the way back.

The Irvin homestead was first deeded to Frank Irvin in 1917 and later owned by R. J. Nettleton. Nettleton operated a sawmill there and also raised rabbit pelts for sale to the US Army during World War II. In the 1960s the homestead was developed as a hunting camp, and there are still at least 7 buildings on the property in various states of disrepair. Unfortunately there is not much left of the old sawmill except an old gear rack and a sledge that was probably used for dragging logs to the mill.

Retracing your footsteps 0.7 mile from the Irvin homestead will bring you back to the beginning of the Meadow Loop Trail that passes the Brown homestead. Turn right here and walk north on Road 120. After 15 minutes you will arrive at a junction where you must turn left onto Road 120A. The Brown homestead is a 5-minute walk from the junction.

The 320-acre Brown homestead was first deeded to brothers Harry and Cloyd Brown in 1917 and 1919, and Harry raised cattle and sold timber from the property until the 1930s. Today the property still has one cabin standing on it. The old cabin contains a number of interesting artifacts including an old-fashion stove.

Road 120A enters private property just

The Irvin Homestead

The Brown Homestead

south of Brown's Cabin, but 200 feet beyond the cabin the Meadow Loop Trail departs from the road and heads out through the trees for 0.6 mile back to the Irvin sawmill logging road. When you reach the road you must turn right to retrace your steps back past the Griffith and Walker homesteads and down Lion Gulch to the trailhead.

The Engert, Laycock, Boren, and Hill Homesteads

You can visit these homesteads by turning south at the trail junction below the Walker homestead. A visit to these four additional sites will add another 7.1 miles, round trip, to the length of the hike.

After you have walked 0.2 mile from the junction you will meet another old wagon road. Bear left on this road and continue for another 0.1 mile to another will marked road on the left that goes to the Engert Cabin. The distance from the second junction to the Engert property is 0.9 mile.

Charles Engert received his deed to this land in 1921. Unlike the other settlers in the area, however, he considered the cabin to be more of a vacation home than a residence. He had a job as the postmaster of Lyons, and he was able to fulfill the Homestead Act's 6 months/year residency requirement only by leaving his wife alone on the land for long periods of time during the summers. The cabin is falling down now, but you can still see some of the chairs inside where Mrs. Engert spent her lonely evenings reading or knitting.

From the Engert cabin it is a 1.6 mile walk on to the Laycock homestead. Walk back 0.3 miles west of Engert's property to a secondary road that branches off to the left. This road joins the main road after 0.8 mile, where you must turn left for the last 0.5 mile to the Laycock homestead. Just before you reach the Laycock property you will notice another road branching off to the right. Disregard this road and continue straight for another 100 yards down a narrow path to the Laycock cabin.

William Laycock was the first settler in Homestead Meadows, receiving his certificate of patent in 1889. But it was a later resident, William Turner House, that had the greatest impact on the meadows. House, a grandson of the Engerts, lived on the Laycock homestead from 1933 to 1952, longer than any of the other settlers. He was heavily involved in ranching and logging, and he eventually enlarged his holdings by buying five other homesteads. The House family grew hay for their cattle in the field south of the cabins, and you can still see a few pieces of broken farm equipment in the trees on the edges of the field.

The Boren Cabin, 0.7 mile beyond the Laycock homestead, was home to Robert Boren and his two young daughters, Mina and Joel. They were one of the few families who lived year round in the meadows. Mina, who was 13 when her father received the deed to the property in 1906, spoke disparagingly of the cold lonely winters spent feeding the cattle, chopping wood, and shoveling mountains of snow. But in spite of their isolation the Borens were a gregarious people who often invited travelers to stay with them in their mountain home.

A 20-minute walk north from the Laycock homestead on Trail 1007 will bring you to the last of the Homestead Meadows homesteads: the Hill homestead. This property was homesteaded by Clayton Hill in 1916. He received his certificate of patent in 1921 and promptly sold his holdings to a lady named Daisy Baber. Although Baber resold the land after just a few years, in 1952 she published a book about frontier life in Colorado titled *Injun Summer: an Old Cowhand Rides the Ghost Trails*. Perhaps some of her inspiration for the book came from the time she spent in Homestead Meadows.

The Engert Homestead

Finch and Pear Lakes

Rocky Mountain National Park
overnight hike

Distance:	11.4 miles (round trip)
Walking time:	day 1: 3 1/2 hours day 2: 4 1/2 hours
Elevations:	1,900 ft. gain/loss Allenspark Trailhead (start): 8,940 ft. Finch Lake: 9,912 ft. Pear Lake: 10,582 ft.
Trail:	Well marked, well maintained trail
Season:	Midsummer through mid-fall. There is usually snow on the trail from mid-November through June.
Vicinity:	Rocky Mountain National Park, near Estes Park
Maps:	Allenspark (*USGS*) Rocky Mountain National Park (*Trails Illustrated, #200*)
Information:	http://colorado.utahtrails.com/finchpearlake.html http://www.nps.gov/romo/ *(Rocky Mountain National Park)* phone: (970) 586-1242. *(Rocky Mountain National Park)*

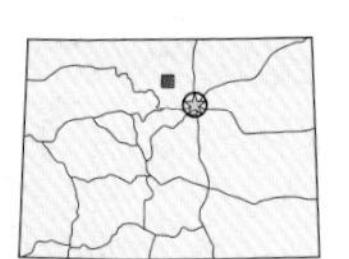

Drive south from Estes Park to the intersection of Highway 36 and Highway 7, then follow Highway 7 another 16 miles to the town of Allenspark. Turn off Highway 7 into Allenspark, and within 0.1 mile you will come to the Allenspark Post Office. Turn right at the Post Office, make a note of your odometer reading, and drive west on County Road 90. At 0.6 miles you will pass the Triple Creek Ranch. At 0.7 miles you will see a major road leaving on the right; keep going straight at this point. At 1.3 miles you will come to a major fork in the road where you must turn right. At 1.4 miles you will see a small sign on the right marking the Allenspark Trailhead and parking area.

Finch Lake is a popular destination among people looking for an easy overnight hike with a campsite in heavy timber next to a pretty alpine lake. The one-way distance to the lake is only 3.8 miles over a well maintained trail, and there are several fine campsites on the north side of the lake. If you want more privacy you can walk another 2.0 miles up the trail to Pear Lake where there are also several backcountry campsite.

In my opinion Finch Lake is a nicer place to spend the night than Pear Lake, but as scenery goes Pear Lake is the most dramatic. From Pear you can enjoy an exhilarating view of Elk Tooth Ridge 0.8 mile to the south and Mount Copeland 1.0 mile to the west. The rugged, cliff-strewn slopes of the mountain rise abruptly from the water's edge in an uninterrupted ascent to the 13,176-foot summit. Ogalalla Peak (13,138 ft.) is also visible further up the valley where Elk Tooth Ridge meets the Continental Divide.

Many people begin this hike at Finch Lake Trailhead near the Wild Basin Ranger Station, but starting there will add 1.5 miles to the round trip distance and 460 feet to the elevation gain. The 11.4-mile walk from Allenspark Trailhead described below can easily be completed in a single day, but Finch Lake is such a pleasant place to camp it would be a shame not to stay for a night. Campsites at both Finch and Pear Lakes can be reserved by calling the Backcountry Office of Rocky Mountain National Park at (970) 586-1242. Sometimes camping permits can also be obtained without reservations at the Wild Basin Ranger Station, but only if there are sites available. The cost of a camping permit is $15.00/night.

see map page 80

Day 1 (3.8 miles)

From the Allenspark Trailhead the route begins by climbing gradually through a forest of limber and lodgepole pines along a very well maintained path. After 0.7 mile you will come to the first trail junction where another well marked trail branches off to the right toward the Wild Basin Ranger Station. From there the path continues another 1.0 mile to the next junction where two more trails branch off to the right toward the Wild Basin Ranger Station. Again this junction

Wild Basin Ranger Station Trail Junction

is well marked with signs, but there are four trails leaving this intersection and if you aren't paying attention you can easily take the wrong one. If you start going downhill you have taken the wrong turn.

As you leave the second trail junction you will notice that you are skirting along the edge of an old burn area. The trees in this area were burned by a forest fire that started in the northern part of Wild Basin in 1978. For a while the fire threatened the town of Allenspark, but fortunately it was stopped before it got that far. The trail enters the burn area a short distance beyond the trail junction and stays there for about ten minutes.

It is encouraging to see how fast the forest is coming back after the 1978 Wild Basin fire. A dense stand of young lodgepole pines, 15-20 feet high, now covers the area, and healthy populations of squirrels, chipmunks, and birds have found homes among the burned trees. The fire also opened up some impressive panoramas of the northern mountains that cannot be seen inside the mature forest.

0.4 mile before arriving at Finch Lake

the trail crosses a small unnamed stream on a log bridge, then a short distance later it begins a 250-foot descent to the lake. You will first see the lake glinting through the trees on your left before the trail bends around its north side where the backcountry campsites are located.

Day 2 (7.6 miles)

Before returning to the trailhead be sure to take the side trip to Pear Lake and back. The round trip distance to Pear is only 3.9 miles, an easy walk if you leave your backpack at your campsite, and you will be well rewarded. The trail continues west from the camping area for 0.2 mile before coming to another log bridge across Cony Creek. It then begins a long gradual climb up the valley toward Pear Lake. In all you will gain about 650 feet over the next 1.7 miles.

0.3 mile before reaching the upper lake the trail comes to another log bridge where it crosses Pear Creek. You will also see a sign here directing you to the Pear Creek Campsite. Then just a few minutes beyond Pear Creek the trail ends on the east side of the lake.

Pear Lake, being closer to timberline, is much more open than Finch Lake, with unimpeded views on all sides. The landscape is dominated by Mount Copeland, and it is easy to see how glacial ice grinding its way down the slopes of the imposing mountain once gouged out the bowl that would later become Pear Lake. Many older maps refer to Pear Lake as a reservoir, and indeed it was once dammed to store water for farms on the east side of the Front Range. The old earthen dam has been breached for many years, however, and now the lake is almost as pristine as it ever was.

The walk from Pear Lake back to Finch Lake takes about an hour, and from there it is another 2½ hours back to the trailhead. The way back is all downhill except for a 250-foot elevation gain as you leave Finch Lake.

Finch Lake

Bluebird Lake

★★

Rocky Mountain National Park
overnight hike

Distance: 13.8 miles (round trip)

Walking time: day 1: 5¾ hours
day 2: 5 hours

Elevations: 2,930 ft. gain/loss
Wild Basin Trailhead (start): 8,500 ft.
Ouzel Lake: 10,020 ft.
Bluebird Lake: 10,978 ft.
Pipit Lake: 11,420 ft.

Trail: Good trail as far as Bluebird Lake, but some miner scrambling is required over the last 0.8 mile to Pipit Lake.

Season: Late summer. There is usually snow on the trail from mid-November until mid-July.

Vicinity: Rocky Mountain National Park, near Estes Park

Maps: Allens Park, Isolation Peak (*USGS*)
Rocky Mountain National Park (*Trails Illustrated, #200*)

Information: http://colorado.utahtrails.com/bluebirdlake.html
http://www.nps.gov/romo/ *(Rocky Mountain National Park)*
phone: (970) 586-1242. *(Rocky Mountain National Park)*

Drive south from Estes Park on Highway 7. Just before reaching Allens Park you will see a road on the right marked by a sign that says "Rocky Mountain National Park, Wild Basin Area". Turn right here and drive 2.7 miles to the end of the road, where you will find the parking area, ranger station, and trailhead.

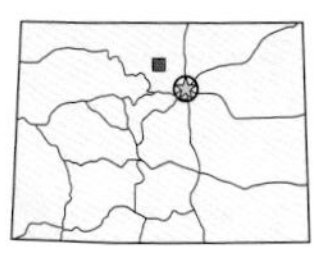

Isolated as it is in the southeastern corner of Rocky Mountain National Park, Wild Basin seems almost to be a private reserve for hikers. There are no paved roads here and no visitors centers–only pristine alpine lakes, rushing waterfalls, and about 30 miles of foot trails. In 1974 the Park Service proposed that Wild Basin be included as part of a new Enos Mills Wilderness Area. Congress still has not acted on their recommendations, but to their credit they are already managing the area as if it were

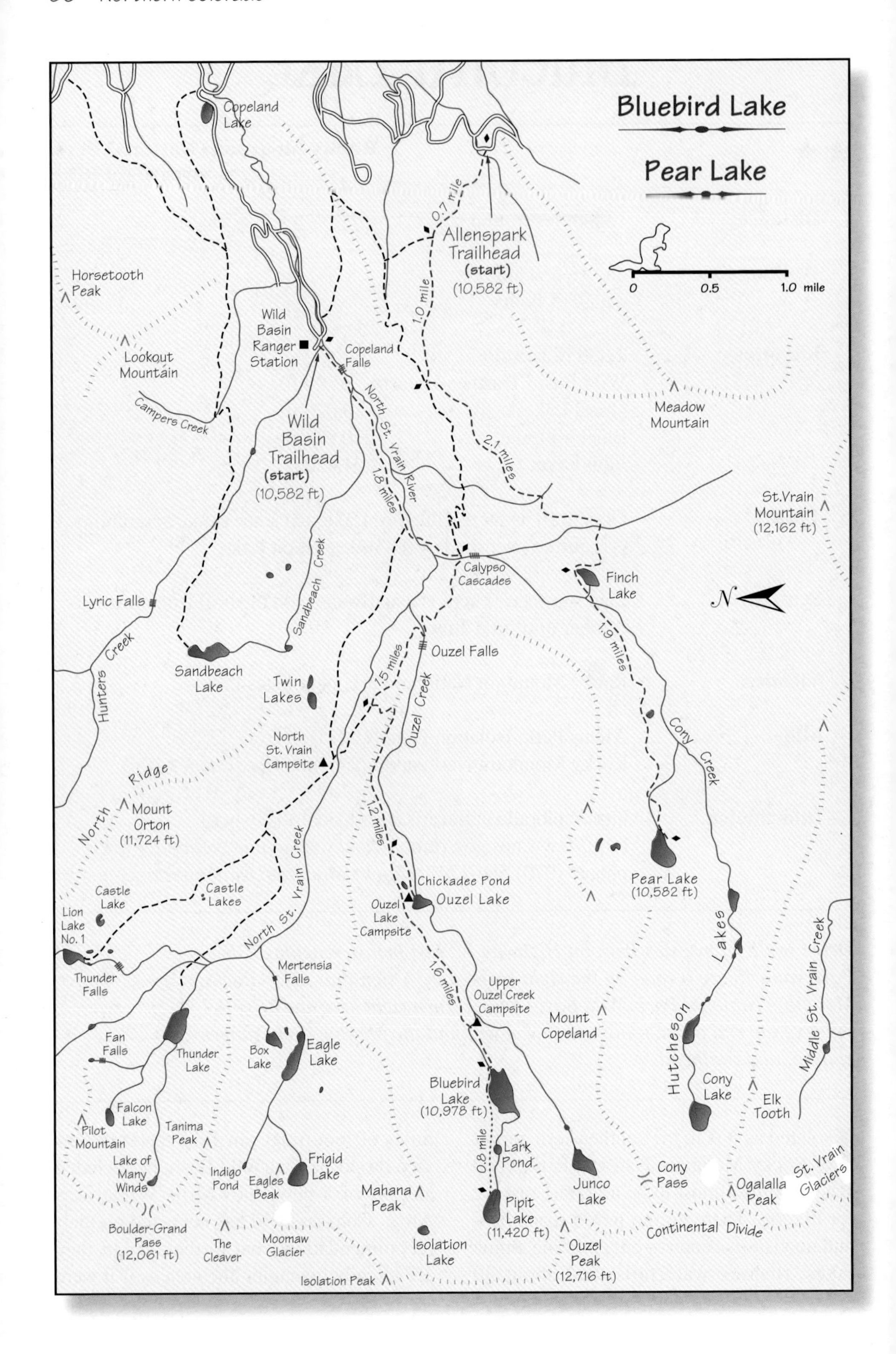
Bluebird Lake
Pear Lake
0
0.5
1.0 mile
N
Copeland Lake
Allenspark Trailhead
(start)
(10,582 ft)
0.7 mile
1.0 mile
Horsetooth Peak
Wild Basin Ranger Station
Copeland Falls
Lookout Mountain
Campers Creek
Wild Basin Trailhead
(start)
(10,582 ft)
North St. Vrain River
1.8 miles
2.1 miles
Meadow Mountain
St.Vrain Mountain
(12,162 ft)
Sandbeach Creek
Calypso Cascades
Finch Lake
Lyric Falls
Hunters Creek
Ouzel Falls
1.9 miles
Sandbeach Lake
Twin Lakes
1.5 miles
Ouzel Creek
Cony Creek
North St. Vrain Campsite
North Ridge
Mount Orton
(11,724 ft)
1.2 miles
Pear Lake
(10,582 ft)
Castle Lake
Castle Lakes
Chickadee Pond
Ouzel Lake
Ouzel Lake Campsite
North St. Vrain Creek
Lion Lake No. 1
Thunder Falls
Mertensia Falls
1.6 miles
Upper Ouzel Creek Campsite
Mount Copeland
Hutcheson Lakes
Middle St. Vrain Creek
Fan Falls
Thunder Lake
Box Lake
Eagle Lake
Bluebird Lake
(10,978 ft)
Cony Lake
Elk Tooth
Falcon Lake
Pilot Mountain
Tanima Peak
0.8 mile
Lark Pond
Lake of Many Winds
Indigo Pond
Eagles Beak
Frigid Lake
Mahana Peak
Pipit Lake
(11,420 ft)
Junco Lake
Cony Pass
Ogalalla Peak
St. Vrain Glaciers
Continental Divide
Boulder-Grand Pass
(12,061 ft)
The Cleaver
Moomaw Glacier
Isolation Lake
Ouzel Peak
(12,716 ft)
Isolation Peak

a designated wilderness.

The hike described here visits three of Wild Basin's lakes and three of its waterfalls. It can be done in one long day, but in my opinion a single day is not enough to really appreciate the beauty of the area. Unfortunately, the area is very popular among backpackers and the Park Service will only allow campers in certain places, so reservations are a necessity if you intend to spend the night on the trail. You can obtain a reservation by calling the Backcountry Office of Rocky Mountain National Park at (970) 586-1242 between March 1 and May 15 of the year you are planning your trip. Sometimes camping permits can also be obtained without reservations at the Wild Basin Ranger Station near the trailhead, but only if there are sites available. The cost of a camping permit is $15.00/night.

The best campsite to use for this hike is the Upper Ouzel Creek Site, located 0.4 mile below Bluebird Lake. This site is situated in a picture book location with plenty of wild flowers, a cascading stream and a tent site with an unforgettable view of the canyon below. The Ouzel Lake Site is nice too, especially if you want to do a little fishing. A distant third choice would be the North St. Vrain Site.

Day 1 (5.7 miles)

From the ranger station the trail starts out by following the North St. Vrain Creek, a rocky, fast flowing mountain stream that sometimes seems to be just one continuous cascade. The torrent at Copeland Falls, ten minutes from the trailhead, provides a good introduction to what lies ahead. But don't stop too long–it gets better.

A mile beyond Copeland Falls the path crosses the North St. Vrain Creek on a foot bridge, then climbs south along Cony Creek for a short distance to the second point of interest: Calypso Cascades. Here the turbulent water of Cony Creek makes its final, chaotic descent down a steep ravine to the confluence of the two streams. The cold liquid dances wildly over the granite boulders in a kind of animated mating ritual as it prepares to join the equally restless North St. Vrain. Best of all, the trail crosses Cony Creek on another foot bridge just below Calypso Cascades, so hikers have a perfect vantage point from which to view to spectacle.

0.8 mile after leaving Calypso Cascades

Bluebird Lake Trail

Upper Ouzel Creek Backcountry Campsite

the trail comes to another foot bridge across Ouzel Creek, where hikers can again witness an impressive display of natures artistry. A hundred feet west of the bridge the creek plunges over a 30-foot vertical drop in the streambed to form Ouzel Falls. The view from the bridge is fair, but it is worthwhile at this point to leave the established trail and proceed along a primitive hiker-made trail on the south side of the stream to the base of the waterfall. Your reward will be a face full of spray and a full frontal view of Ouzel Falls.

Before the trail reaches Ouzel Falls you will begin to notice signs of a forest fire that occurred in 1978 after a lightening strike near Ouzel Lake. Twenty minutes after leaving the Falls the trail comes to a junction where the Bluebird Lake Trail separates from the Thunder Lake Trail, and as you climb out of the North St. Vrain Drainage towards Bluebird Lake the fire damage becomes much more pronounced. The fire burned for two months and destroyed a total of 1050 acres before fire fighters could extinguish it.

It has been 30 years since the fire and nature is well on the way to repairing the damage. Notice the thousands of little lodgepole pines that are springing up throughout the burned areas. Lodgepole pines are always among the first trees to germinate after a fire in this region. In fact they do not reproduce well in the absence of fire because the tree's resin cements the cones together so tightly that the seeds cannot easily be released. But when a fire like 1978 Wild Basin Fire takes place it softens the resin in the lodgepole pinecones and scatters millions of new seeds across the blackened landscape.

Ouzel Lake lies on the left side of the trail 1.6 miles from the Thunder Lake Trail Junction. If you are planning to camp there you will be pleased to see that the fire never quite reached the shore of the lake, and it remains a beautiful place to spend the night. The campsite is at the end of the spur trail leading to the north side of the lake. The lake is quite shallow, but nevertheless a significant population of brook trout and greenback cutthroat trout manages to survive the winters, making Ouzel a popular lake for fly fishermen. The greenback cutthroats are unusually pretty fish, with spotted green backs and blood red gills. They are a threatened species, however, and the Park Service requires you to use barbless hooks and release any greenbacks you might catch.

The Upper Ouzel Creek Campsite is situated another mile past Ouzel Lake, beyond the western boundary of the 1978 fire. This site would be my first choice for this hike. The Upper Ouzel Creek Site is conveniently located near Bluebird Lake, and, in my opinion, it is also one of the prettiest and most comfortable campsites in Rocky Mountain National Park.

Day 2 (8.1 miles)

After leaving the Upper Ouzel Creek Campsite the trail becomes much steeper, climbing 400 feet before it reaches Bluebird Lake, 0.4 mile later. The trail is also much more primitive here, and if you are hiking before mid-July you will probably encounter snow on this part of the trail. This is all a preamble for the wild and beautiful Bluebird Lake which suddenly comes into view only a few feet before your arrival. The lake sits right on the edge of timberline, surrounded by gray granite and blue sky with Ouzel Peak rising above its western side.

Although no trace of the previous construction is now visible, it is interesting to note that until recently Bluebird Lake had a dam on its eastern side. The dam was built over a hundred years ago by irrigation farmers east of the Continental Divide. Then, in 1988, the National Park Service purchased the water rights to the lake from the city of Longmont with the intention of dismantling the dam. In order to minimize the environmental impact demolition crews broke up the concrete using only hand tools, and the debris was flown out by helicopter. Amazingly, not a trace of the old dam is now visible.

Pipit Lake is an easy 40-minute off-trail scramble from Bluebird Lake; if you like wild places you should include it in your itinerary. The easiest way to get there is to cross Ouzel Creek just before the outlet of Bluebird Lake and proceed across the north side of the lake in a westerly direction. Bear to the right of the granite outcropping on the lake's west side and climb to the plateau above the lake. From there it is an easy walk up the drainage past Lark Pond to Pipit Lake. The total distance is about 1.0 mile and the elevation gain is 440 feet. At 11,420 feet above sea level Pipit is well above timberline. It is only 1,000 feet below the Divide in an almost perfectly circular bowl with Mahana Peak directly north and Ouzel Peak directly south. And it definitely has the wild feel of a place not too many people visit.

From Pipit Lake it is an easy scramble back to Bluebird Lake, and from there you can retrace your steps back to the Wild Basin Trailhead.

Bluebird Lake

Longs Peak

Rocky Mountain National Park
overnight hike

Distance:	15.0 miles (round trip)
Walking time:	day 1: 6 1/2 hours day 2: 8 1/2 hours
Elevations:	4,950 ft. gain/loss Longs Peak Trailhead (start): 9,400 ft. Chasm Lake Junction: 11,540 ft. Boulderfield Camp: 12,740 ft. Longs Peak: 14,255 ft.
Trail:	Good trail as far as the Boulderfield Camp. There is no trail beyond Boulderfield, but the route is generally well marked. A great deal of scrambling is required for the last 1.5 miles between the Keyhole and the summit.
Season:	Late summer. There is usually snow and ice on the mountain until mid-July, and unless you are an experienced climber I would not recommend this hike before then. The best time to climb Longs Peak is from mid-July through August.
Vicinity:	Rocky Mountain National Park, near Estes Park
Maps:	Longs Peak (*USGS*) Rocky Mountain National Park (*Trails Illustrated, #200*)
Information:	http://colorado.utahtrails.com/longspeak.html http://www.nps.gov/romo/ *(Rocky Mountain National Park)* phone: (970) 586-1242 *(Rocky Mountain National Park)*

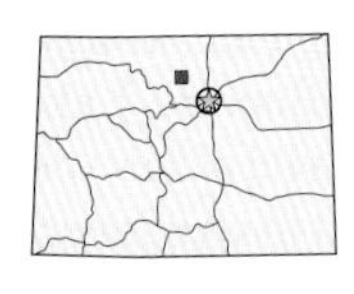

Drive 9.2 miles south from Estes Park on Highway 7 until you see a sign directing you to the Longs Peak Ranger Station in Rocky Mountain National Park. Turn right here and drive another 1.1 miles, following the signs to Longs Peak Ranger Station. The trailhead is located on the left side of the ranger station

Note: If you are doing this hike as an overnighter you will need to obtain a backcountry permit and reserve a campsite at the Boulderfield Camp. Unfortunately there are only 9 sites at Boulderfield and they are usually booked solid for months in advance, so plan ahead and make your reservations early. For more information call the Rocky Mountain National

Park Backcountry Office at (970) 586-1242 or visit their website at www.nps.gov/romo/visit/park/camp/guide.html

---

Longs Peak is undisputedly one of the outstanding mountain peaks of the American West. Entire books have been written about the majestic mountain, its rich history, its challenging assent routes and its rugged beauty. The first recorded sighting of the mountain was made by Stephen Long in 1820, but it was known to Indians and French trappers long before that. The mountain men referred to Longs Peak and nearby Mount Meeker as *Les Deux Orielles*, or The Two Ears. Interest in climbing the peak picked up in 1865 after the well-publicized conquest of the Matterhorn in Europe, and three years later a successful assent of Longs Peak was led by Major John Wesley Powell.

Powell's assent of Longs Peak added greatly to the mountain's fame, and by 1878 a tour operator named Elkanah Lamb was making a good living charging $5.00/party to guide sightseers from his lodge to the summit. Lambs business was later sold to a naturalist named Enos Mills, who with a total of 297 assents probably climbed Longs Peak more times than anyone before or since. Mills loved the area and campaigned hard to have it protected. More than any other man, it can be said that he was responsible for the creation of Rocky Mountain National Park in 1915. Today Longs Peak is easily the most popular mountain climbing destination in Colorado; around 4,000 climbers reach its summit every year.

Of the hundred or so published routes up Longs Peak the one described here is the easiest. Nevertheless, it is by far the most strenuous hike in this book. There is also an element of danger: according to Park Service statistics 55 people have been killed on the mountain since Powell's original assent. If you are in good physical condition and are properly prepared the risk is minimal, but don't take the mountain lightly. Make sure you know what to expect, and, above all, be prepared to turn back at the first sign of bad weather.

Bad weather has claimed many lives on Longs Peak. People have been killed by lightning, by hypothermia and, most commonly, by slipping on the wet or icy granite after a storm. Although the climb described here is not technically difficult, there is considerable exposure along some parts of the route. The last 250 feet, called the Homestretch, is particularly dangerous when wet. As climber Gerry Roach says, "Sudden summer storms can turn the Homestretch into a bobsled run."

If you have done much hiking in the

Northeast Face of Longs Peak

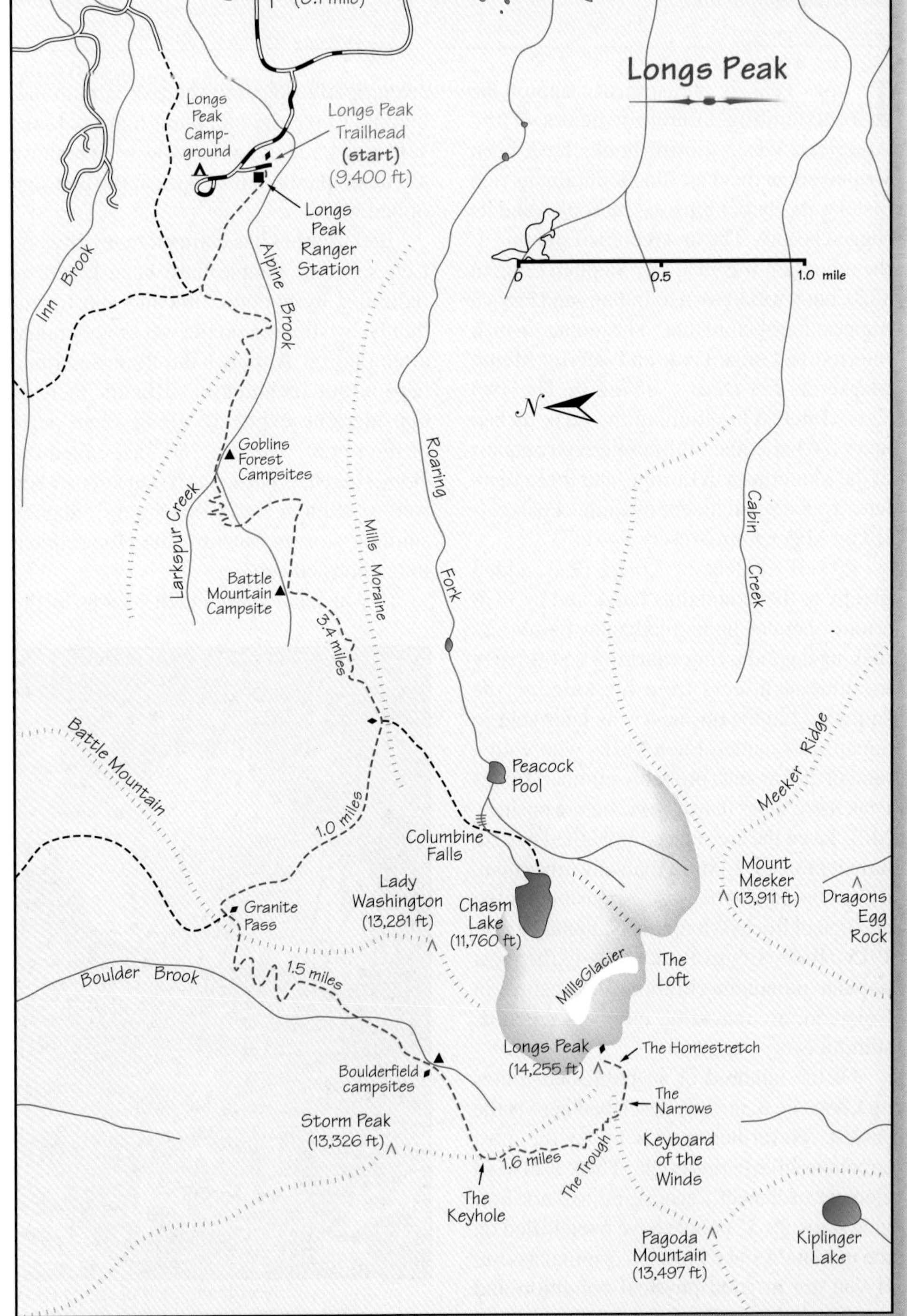

Longs Peak
to Highway 7
(0.1 mile)
Longs Peak Campground
Longs Peak Trailhead
(start)
(9,400 ft)
Longs Peak Ranger Station
Inn Brook
Alpine Brook
0
0.5
1.0 mile
N
Roaring Fork
Cabin Creek
Goblins Forest Campsites
Larkspur Creek
Mills Moraine
Battle Mountain Campsite
3.4 miles
Battle Mountain
1.0 miles
Peacock Pool
Meeker Ridge
Columbine Falls
Mount Meeker
(13,911 ft)
Dragons Egg Rock
Lady Washington
(13,281 ft)
Chasm Lake
(11,760 ft)
Granite Pass
Mills Glacier
The Loft
Boulder Brook
1.5 miles
Longs Peak
(14,255 ft)
The Homestretch
Boulderfield campsites
The Narrows
Storm Peak
(13,326 ft)
1.6 miles
The Trough
Keyboard of the Winds
The Keyhole
Pagoda Mountain
(13,497 ft)
Kiplinger Lake

Climbing from Boulderfield into the Keyhole

mountains of Colorado you probably already know that there are frequent thundershowers in the afternoons, and for that reason it is important to plan your hike so that you will be off the mountain by noon. To be safe you should leave the Boulderfield camping area by 7:00 a.m. This will put you at the summit of Longs Peak by 10:30 a.m. If the weather still looks good you can then enjoy a leisurely lunch on the peak before starting down, but if the clouds have already began to gather don't tarry at the top.

The hike described below assumes that you will be spending one night at the Boulderfield Camp. This is the most enjoyable way to climb Longs Peak, but unfortunately there are not many campsites at the Boulderfield and you must normally make reservations far in advance to get a site. Alternatively, many people spend a night at the Longs Peak Campground near the trailhead and do the entire hike the following day. This makes for a long, grueling day that will probably stretch your endurance to the limit, but a surprising number of people do it. If you plan to climb Longs Peak in only one day you should start out from the trailhead around 3:00 a.m. and plan to be on the mountain for 13 hours. During the summer you will meet dozens of like-minded hikers, their flashlights bobbing back and forth through the trees as they make their way up the trail to the Boulderfield.

Day 1 (5.9 miles)

From the trailhead to the Boulderfield Camp is a long, gentle but unrelenting climb of 3,350 feet. For the first 2.1 miles you will be walking through a well-shaded conifer forest, but shortly after the trail crosses Alpine Brook the forest begins to thin and soon gives way to the knurled, twisted krummholz growth that marks the transition into the Alpine Tundra Life Zone. Then, 3.4 miles from the trailhead, the trail reaches the junction with the Chasm Lake Trail. Longs Peak rises majestically 1.4 miles southeast of the junction, with Mount Lady Washington (13,281 ft.) on its right and Mount Meeker (13,911 ft.) on its left. Together these peaks form what has been called Colorado's greatest mountain cirque.

Like the last drop of champaign in the bottom of a wineglass, Chasm Lake lies at the bottom of the impressive cirque. If you still have time and energy after climbing Longs Peak you might want to take the 1.6-mile side trip down to the lake. Directly west of the picturesque lake you can see the famous east face of Longs Peak, a sheer 1,800-foot wall of granite that has long held a special fascination for rock climbers. Yosemite National Park's Half Dome is probably the only wall in the United States that can compare with it. Look up on the right side of the east face and you will see a particularly well known climbing challenge called the Diamond. The Diamond is considered by many to be the ultimate technical climb—it was first scaled only in 1960.

Traversing across The Narrows

From the Chasm Lake Junction the trail continues climbing for another 540 feet to the top of Granite Pass, then turns south at the Granite Pass Junction for the final 1.5 miles to the Boulderfield Camp. Pause to look across the tundra at the north face of Longs Peak as you approach the Boulderfield. From 1925 until the early 1970s the north face was the most popular route to the summit of the mountain. The Park Service maintained two sets of cables on the east side of the face to help climbers up the most difficult pitches, but the cables were removed in 1973 and now most people use the Keyhole assent route described here.

Ascending through The Trough

The Boulderfield Camp is located in a wide, flat tundra directly north of the peak. As the name suggests, the area is filled with boulders, and there is very little shelter. The tent sites generally consist of ten-foot-diameter clearings where the stones have been laboriously removed and stacked into walls around the perimeter. The low walls around the sites offer a modicum of protection from the high-altitude winds that frequently howl across the tundra, but you will still need to fasten your tent securely to the ground.

Day 2 (8.8 miles)

The round trip distance from Boulderfield Camp to the top of Longs Peak and back is only 3.2 miles, but in this case distances are deceiving. The route is well defined, but there is no trail and the climb is extremely strenuous. You should begin climbing by 7:00 a.m. and allow at least 5 hours for the round trip—more if, like me, you are past your prime.

First you must climb from the Boulderfield Camp to the Keyhole, an odd-shaped opening in the ridge that runs north from Longs Peak to Storm Peak. The elevation gain to the Keyhole is only 400 feet, but to get there you must negotiate a 0.4-mile obstacle course of loose granite boulders. The rocks come in all shapes and sizes, and they frequently move when you step on them, so be careful.

When you arrive at the Keyhole you will notice a small but very well built circular hut just to the left of the opening. This hut was built as a memorial to Agnes Vaille who froze to death on the mountain after a successful winter assent in 1925.

After passing through the Keyhole the route turns south along the west side of the Longs Peak-Storm Peak Ridge. There is very little net elevation change for the next 0.5 mile, and there are no more loose boulder fields to negotiate, but there is a great deal of scrambling along this part of the hike. The route first climbs slightly then descends and then climbs again as it works its way around the large, flat slabs of granite that cover this part of the ridge like scales on the neck of a dragon.

The views from the west side of the Longs Peak-Storm Peak Ridge are fantastic. The route is situated high above the beautiful Glacier Gorge (page 99), with Black Lake clearly visible 2,500 feet below. On the other side of Glacier Gorge the Continental Divide is profiled by a long line of thirteeners marching south along the skyline like a column of victorious soldiers. Although there is no trail the Park Service has blazed the route from the Keyhole all the way to the summit with a series of red and yellow circles painted on the rocks, so if you are observant you shouldn't have any trouble finding your way.

0.5 mile from the Keyhole the route intersects a long, steep couloir of loose rock, know locally as the Trough. The Trough runs all the way from the bottom of Glacier Gorge to a point within 400 feet of the summit, and the route uses it as a means of getting nearer to the goal. After turning left into the Trough the route heads straight up the slope, gaining a chest-pounding 550 feet of elevation in less than 0.3 mile. This is, by far, the most strenuous part of this hike, and the high altitude only adds to the difficulty.

Just below the summit of Longs Peak

Looking across the Loft from the summit of Longs Peak

There is also the danger of getting hit by a rock dislodge by someone above you, so be careful.

At the top of the Trough the route levels out and begins a traverse below the south side of the peak. Here the mountain drops off precipitously to a slabby area below that has been whimsically called the Keyboard of the Winds. Fortunately there is a conveniently situated ledge above the cliffs that makes the traverse possible. This ledge is known as the Narrows. There is considerable exposure below the Narrows, but if the weather is good and there is no ice it is not particularly dangerous. That is definitely not the case, however, if there is ice on the ledge. Icy conditions often persist until mid-July; consequently I would not recommend this hike before then.

After traversing the south side of the mountain for 300 yards the route turns abruptly north and proceeds up a steep slab of smooth granite called the Homestretch. The elevation gain on the Homestretch is about 250 feet, and with soft rubber soles the gradient is just below the maximum angle possible for friction walking. Most people will not be able to friction-walk up the granite, but fortunately the rock is fractured with several long, parallel cracks that extend up the left side of the pitch. The scramble up the cracks is not too difficult, and with the summit clearly in view spirits are usually high by this time.

The top of Longs Peak is a surprisingly flat, boulder-strewn field some 100 feet wide and 500 feet long. If you are hiking in late summer you will probably see at least a hundred other climbers resting on the summit and possibly many more. Relax and enjoy your accomplishment, but be sure to keep one eye on the weather. The moment clouds begin to gather you should start down. The weather can change amazingly quickly in Colorado's mountains, and it will take you at least two hours to get back down to the Boulderfield Camp and another three hours from there to the trailhead.

Flattop Mountain/Hallett Peak

★★★

Rocky Mountain National Park
day hike

Distance: 9.4 miles (round trip)

Walking time: 7 hours

Elevations: 3,275 ft. gain/loss
Bear Lake Trailhead (start): 9,480 ft.
Flattop Mountain: 12,324 ft.
Hallett Peak: 12,713 ft.

Trail: Good trail as far as Flattop Mountain, but there is no developed trail for the last 0.4 miles up Hallett Peak. Some miner scrambling is necessary.

Season: Midsummer through mid-fall. There is usually snow on the trail from mid-November through mid-July.

Vicinity: Rocky Mountain National Park, near Estes Park

Maps: McHenrys Peak (*USGS*)
Rocky Mountain National Park (*Trails Illustrated, #200*)

Information: http://colorado.utahtrails.com/flattophallett.html
http://www.nps.gov/romo/ *(Rocky Mountain National Park)*
phone: (970) 586-1206 *(Rocky Mountain National Park)*

From the Beaver Meadows Visitor Center on the east side of Rocky Mountain National Park you must drive west, following the signs to Bear Lake. The hike starts at the Bear Lake Trailhead.

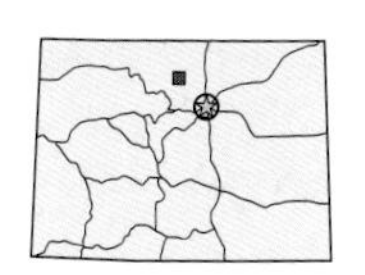

This hike will take you to the top of two well known peaks on the Continental Divide in the center of Rocky Mountain National Park. The two peaks rise majestically above Bear, Dream, and Emerald Lakes, and are constantly photographed by hikers walking through the Tyndall Gorge to those lakes. (See photograph page 104). Hallett Peak has a particularly distinctive shape, and few who have seen it from below do not relish the thought of climbing to its summit. The cliffs facing the Tyndall Gorge on its eastern side present a difficult technical challenge, but the trail described here approaches the summit of Hallett Peak from the relatively easy western side.

see map page 103

Begin by walking north from the Bear Lake Trailhead along the eastern shore of Bear Lake. As you walk, pause to look west at your destination: Hallett Peak on the left flanked by Flattop Mountain on its right. Within 200 yards you will come to a trail junction where a sign directs you to the right along the path to Flattop Mountain. From that junction the trail begins climbing north through a picturesque field of granite boulders towards the Bierstadt Lake Trail junction 0.3 mile later. There you must bear left. Finally, 0.8 mile after leaving the trailhead you will come to the third well-marked junction where the trail to Flattop Mountain departs on the left.

After leaving the third trail junction the path begins climbing up a moderate but unrelenting grade that persists for the next 3.3 miles, all the way to the summit of Flattop Mountain. The climb is long, but there are several diversions along the way. After 0.7 mile you will arrive at a gorgeous overlook point that lies directly above Dream Lake. The shimmering lake is 500 feet below the trail at this point, and five miles to the south you can see the distinctive shape of Longs Peak, the parks only fourteener, silhouette prominently on the skyline.

1.1 miles beyond the Dream Lake Overlook, at about the point where the trail crosses the tree line, you will come to a second overlook point above Emerald Lake. The lake lies directly below the overlook, 1,200 feet down in the bottom of the Tyndall Gorge. Distant views of the surrounding mountains also open up as you leave the forest behind. Bierstadt Lake is particularly obvious–a small, round, isolated lake 2.6 miles to the northeast on a bench above Glacier Basin.

0.3 mile before reaching the summit of Flattop Mountain the trail approaches the rim of the Tyndall Gorge, from where you can see the Tyndall Glacier below you and Hallett Peak on the opposite side of the canyon. From there it is an easy 10-minute walk the rest of the way up Flattop. The mountain is well named. It is so flat on top that you will scarcely be able to tell where the actual summit is. The land all along the west side of the Continental Divide is

Flattop Mountain Trail

Looking south along the Continental Divide from Hallett Peak

relatively flat in this area, rising gently from the west only to drop precipitously on the other side of the Divide. It is interesting to note that this pattern is repeated frequently throughout the West's north/south mountain ranges. It is also a feature of the Sierra Nevada Range in California.

In order to climb Hallett Peak you must walk south from Flattop, circumscribing the rim of Tyndall Gorge, and then turn east up the western slope of Hallett. There is no developed trail along this portion of the hike, but the route is easy. From the saddle between Flattop and Hallett you must gain 400 feet to reach the second summit. Many landmarks of Rocky Mountain National Park can be seen from the top of Hallett Peak. Grand, Granby, and Shadow Mountain Lakes are clearly visible on the west side of the Continental Divide, as are many of the lakes on the east side of the Divide.

Andrews Glacier

Most people return from Hallett Peak the same way they came, but for the adventurous there is another alternative: returning by way of Andrews Glacier. This choice will add 0.9 mile and about 45 minutes onto the total length of this hike. Andrews Glacier, located 1.2 miles south of Hallett Peak, offers a feasible route for descending from the crest of the Continental Divide down to Loch Vale where there is a good trail back to the Bear Lake Road. When conditions are right the descent down the face of the glacier is easy, but there is some danger and caution is advised.

The best time of year to do the Hallett Peak/Andrews Glacier hike is midsummer, when the snow on the trails has melted but there is still plenty of snow covering the glacier. By late August conditions on the glacier are no longer ideal. Water running under the snow can form hidden snow bridges, especially on the edges of the glacier, and serious injuries have been incurred by people falling through these bridges. Also, a period of warm weather followed by a freezing night will inevitably cause a layer of ice to form over the glacier making a safe descent all the more difficult. If you loose your footing and go into an uncontrollable slide down the glacier you run the risk of either slamming into an exposed boulder or sliding into the freezing water of Andrews Tarn at the bottom of the glacier.

Andrews Glacier

Getting from Hallett Peak to the top of Andrews Glacier will take you about 45 minutes. First you must descend 400 feet along the crest of the Divide to the top of Chaos Canyon. This canyon also has a glacier at its head, but the Chaos Glacier is much too steep and unstable for a safe descent. Neverthe-less it is worth pausing to enjoy the view down the Canyon. Lake Haiyaha is clearly visible in the bottom of the gorge from this viewpoint. From Chaos Canyon it is another 0.7 mile to the top of Andrews Glacier. There is no trail between Hallett Peak and Andrews Glacier, but, again, the route is not difficult.

When descending the glacier pick the path that is the least steep and do not go too close to the edges. The total elevation loss is about 550 feet over a horizontal distance of 0.3 mile. The average angle of descent is only about 20 degrees, so if the surface is not icy it is not difficult to arrest a slide. But if the surface of the glacier is icy the situation can be much different. In that case do not attempt a descent unless you have an ice axe and know how to use it!

As you approach the bottom of the glacier you should angle to the right, so you can get off the snow before coming too close to the lake below. Andrews Tarn is located directly below the snow, and if you slip near the lake you could easily slide right into the ice cold water. On the east side of the tarn you will find a rough trail that leads the last 0.9 mile down to the Loch Vale. Once you reach the Loch Vale Trail turn left, and 3.2 miles later you will arrive at Glacier Gorge Junction on the Bear Lake Road. From there you can ride a park service shuttle back to your car. (See page 102 for a complete description of the trail from Loch Vale to Glacier Gorge.)

Odessa and Fern Lakes

★★★★★

Rocky Mountain National Park
day hike

Distance: 9.1 miles (including 0.7-mile walk to shuttle bus stop)
(plus 10.5 miles by Park Service shuttle bus)

Walking time: 6 hours

Elevations: 1,140 ft. gain, 2,500 ft. loss

Bear Lake Trailhead (start):	9,480 ft.
highest point:	10,600 ft.
Odessa Lake:	10,020 ft.
Fern Lake:	9,540 ft.
Fern Lake Trailhead:	8,120 ft.

Trail: Well maintained, easy to follow

Season: Midsummer to mid-fall. The higher parts of the trail are usually covered with snow from mid-November through early July.

Vicinity: Rocky Mountain National Park, near Estes Park

Maps: McHenrys Peak (*USGS*)
Rocky Mountain National Park (*Trails Illustrated, #200*)

Information: http://colorado.utahtrails.com/odessalake.html
http://www.nps.gov/romo/ *(Rocky Mountain National Park)*
phone: (970) 586-1206 *(Rocky Mountain National Park)*

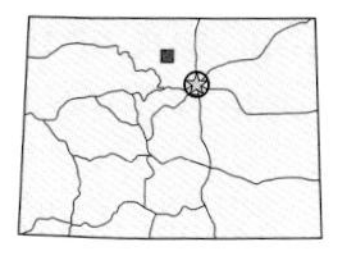

Drive west from the Beaver Meadows Visitor Center, following the signs to Bear Lake. The hike starts at the Bear Lake Trailhead.

The hike ends at the Fern Lake Trailhead near Moraine Park Campground, where you can board a park service shuttle bus for a free ride back to Bear Lake. The shuttle buses also stop at several other places along the way, including the Moraine Park Museum, Hollowell Park, and Glacier Basin Campground, so you can begin the hike at any of these places. During the summer the shuttles leave Moraine Park approximately every 30 minutes.

This extraordinary hike features a number of scenic attractions, including two of the prettiest lakes in Rocky Mountain National Park. Furthermore the Park Service has implemented a shuttle system that allows hikers to walk the trail one way and

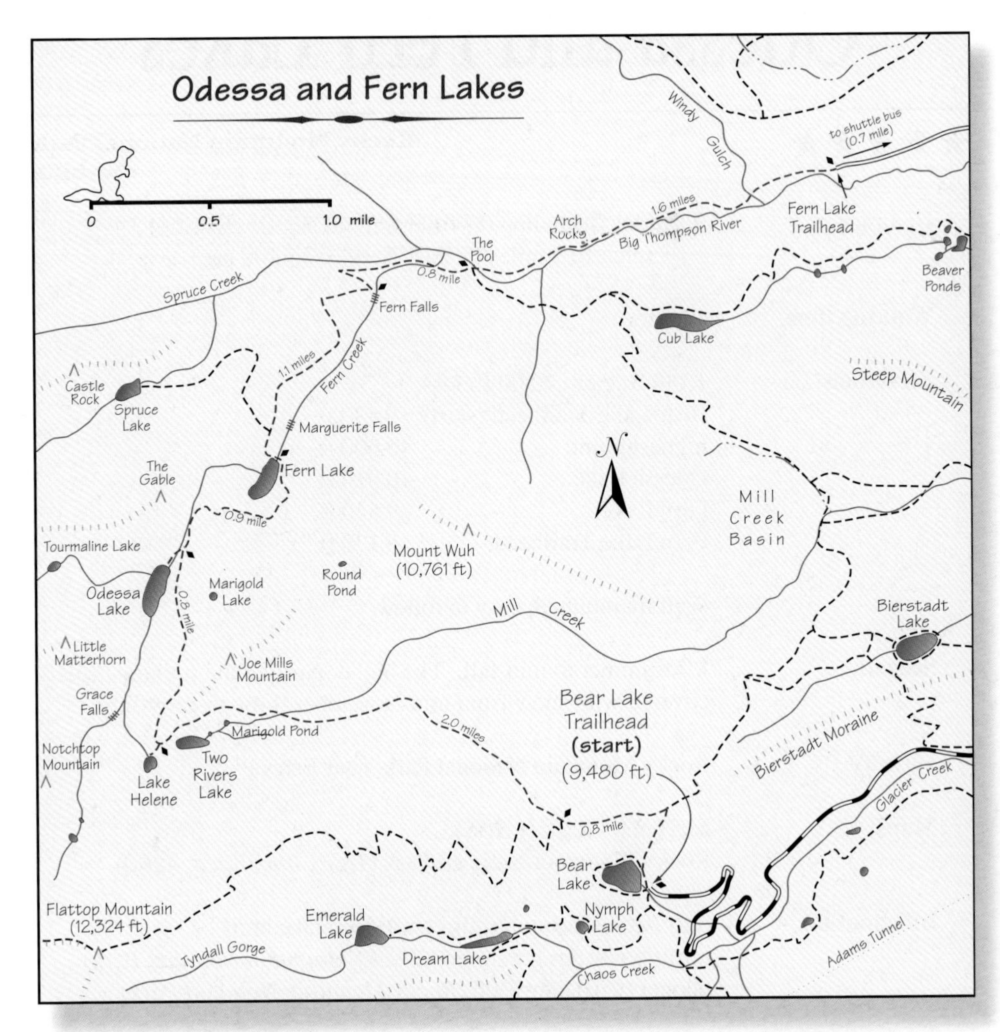

ride a shuttle back to the starting point. If you start at the Bear Lake Trailhead the route is almost all downhill!

From the trailhead you must turn north and circle along the eastern shore of Bear Lake for 0.1 mile until you see a sign directing you to Flattop Mountain and Odessa Lake. Bear right at the sign and continue north through a picturesque field of lichen-covered granite and schist boulders. Negotiating this jumble of huge boulders without a trail would be a nightmare, but on the trail it is a pleasant walk. The trail climbs northward away from the lake for 0.3 mile, then turns west at the Bierstadt Lake trail junction to continue a relatively gentle climb up the eastern slopes of Continental Divide.

0.8 mile from the trailhead you will come to another trail junction where the Flattop Mountain Trail branches off to the left. Bearing right at the junction the path continues climbing through the lodgepole pine forest for the next 2.0 miles, finally reaching the highest point of the hike on the southern side of Joe Mills Mountain. As the trail levels out you will see Two Rivers

Lake followed by Lake Helene just below and 100 yards to the left of the trail. Watch for a short hiker-made spur that drops down to Lake Helene, meeting it near its outlet on the northwest side.

Odessa Lake

The views in this area are sensational. The mountains slope up relatively gradually on the west side of the Continental Divide, but on the east side the topology plunges abruptly downward forming a succession of cliffs, escarpments, tarns, and waterfalls. Helene Lake lies just 0.6 mile east of the Divide, below a long line of 12,000-foot peaks.

From Helene Lake trail junction the main path makes a hairpin turn to the right and begins a 0.8-mile descent down the western side of Joe Mills Mountain into Fern Creek Canyon. Soon you will see Odessa Lake 500 feet below the left side of the trail. The land is too steep and rocky to support many trees in this area, so the panorama of rugged country across the canyon is almost unobstructed. Odessa Lake looks so close you could almost hit it with a stone.

As the trail passes above Odessa it starts to level out, and 200 yards beyond the lake you will come to another spur trail that doubles back along Fern Creek to the lake's northern outlet. When you reach the shore you will be treated to a gorgeous view of upper Fern Creek Canyon, framed by Little Matterhorn and Notchtop Mountain on the right and Flattop Mountain on the left.

Fern Lake is only 0.9 mile below Odessa Lake. Many people hike to Fern Lake from the Fern Lake Trailhead 3.5 miles further east, so there are usually many more people at Fern than Odessa. Both lakes are very pretty, but Odessa is still my personal favorite. There is also a Park Service Patrol Cabin at Fern Lake, but it is usually unoccupied.

The next major point of interest is Fern Falls, a roaring cascade of white water located 1.1 mile below Fern Lake. The trail switchbacks near the bottom of the fall, and the roar is deafening. Dozens of broken trees and logs at the bottom of the fall attest to the force of the water as it plunges down the streambed. Fern Falls is actually just one of several falls along Fern Creek below Fern Lake, although it is the most impressive one and the only one that is easily viewed from the trail. The creek looses just over 1,000 feet of elevation in its 1.2-mile descent from Fern Lake to the Big Thompson River.

0.7 mile below Fern Falls, just below the confluence of Fern Creek with the Big Thompson River, the trail crosses a bridge above the Big Thompson. The River flows through a deep pool above the bridge that is a popular stopping point for hikers coming up from the lower trailhead. There is also a trail junction at the Pool, where the Cub Lake Trail joins the Fern Lake Trail.

The last 1.7 miles before the Fern Lake Trailhead is along the relatively calm Big Thompson River. There are a number of tranquil river scenes along the way, but the most interesting feature on this segment of the hike is a collection of a dozen or so house-size granite boulders called the Arch Rocks. This odd accumulation of boulders lies on the otherwise flat riverbank, and the trail winds right through the middle of them. They almost appear to have been placed here by some giant that just got tired of carrying them around.

When you reach the Fern Lake Trailhead you will still have to do another 0.7 mile of road walking to get to the shuttle bus stop. The buses run every half-hour. If you are going to Bear Lake you will have to change busses at the Park & Ride facility near Sprague Lake.

Fern Creek

Glacier Gorge

Rocky Mountain National Park
day hike

Distance:	9.0 miles (round trip)
Walking time:	$5^3/_4$ hours
Elevations:	1,380 ft. gain/loss Glacier Gorge Junction Trailhead (start): 9,240 ft. Mills Lake: 9,940 ft. Black Lake: 10,620 ft.
Trail:	Well marked, well maintained
Season:	Midsummer through mid-fall. The higher parts of the trail are usually covered with snow from November through early July.
Vicinity:	Rocky Mountain National Park, near Estes Park
Maps:	McHenrys Peak (*USGS*) Rocky Mountain National Park (*Trails Illustrated, #200*)
Information:	http://colorado.utahtrails.com/glaciergorge.html http://www.nps.gov/romo/ *(Rocky Mountain National Park)* phone: (970) 586-1242 *(Rocky Mountain National Park)*

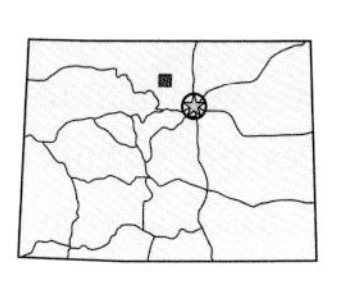

Drive into Rocky Mountain National Park from Estes Park on Highway 36. 1.5 miles beyond the visitor center you will come to the turnoff to Moraine Park and Bear Lake. Turn left here and proceed another 8.4 miles to the Glacier Gorge Junction parking area. The trailhead is just across the road from the parking lot.

Note: The parking lot at Glacier Gorge Junction is not very big, and during the busy summer months it is often difficult to find a parking space. Between June 14 and September 28, however, the Park Service operates a convenient shuttle service to Glacier Gorge Junction and Bear Lake from the Park & Ride facility near Glacier Basin Campground 3.5 miles away. The shuttle runs every 15 minutes, with the last shuttle leaving Glacier Gorge Junction at about 7:30 p.m.

The Rocky Mountains are a consequence of a little understood subterranean force that began pushing up the earth's crust in western North America some 65 million years ago—about the same time the age of the dinosaurs was coming to an end. The

Alberta Falls

land continued to rise for the next 60 million years before reaching its present height, but the initial uplift marked only the first phase in the formation of the Colorado Rockies. Nature's real artistry began about 3 million years ago with the onset of the Ice Age. Since that time the Rocky Mountains have been encased in ice at least a half dozen times, and a succession of glaciations have gouged out valleys, cleaved off peaks, and excavated alpine lakes throughout the range. This sculpting process came to an end when the glaciers subsided some 10,000 years ago, and today a fine example of nature's handiwork is preserved in the 409 square miles of Rocky Mountain National Park.

see map page 103

Glacier Gorge is an example of a U-shaped canyon that was carved by the Pleistocene glaciers. Again and again over the past 3 million years the gorge has been filled with rivers of ice that slowly flowed from Black Lake, to Glacier Gorge Junction and Moraine Park. At its deepest point the ice was probably in excess of 1,500 feet thick, entirely sufficient to carve the valley into its present form. Like giant, slow motion bulldozers the glaciers excavated rock from the canyon bottom and deposited it into tills and moraines further down the valley.

From Glacier Gorge Junction Trailhead the trail proceeds into the woods in a general southerly direction. Within a few feet of the trailhead you will see a junction where the trail to Bear Lake branches to the right. Keep to the left at this point, following the signs to Mills Lake and Black Lake. There is another junction 0.4 miles from the trailhead where the trail to Glacier Basin branches off to the left. Here you should bear right.

Thirty minutes after leaving the parking lot you should arrive at Alberta Falls, the first point of interest on this hike. Here Glacier Creek tumbles down a series of cascades, including a continuous drop of about 25 feet. It is not a particularly high waterfall, but it is very pretty. Also, the trail passes by a perfect vantage point for photographing the fall. You probably saw a lot of hikers on the trail up to this point, but most of them will turn around at Alberta Falls so you can expect less company from here on.

I might mention that about 150 yards before reaching Alberta Falls the trail passes directly over the Adams Tunnel, a 13-mile-long irrigation tunnel that was dug under the Continental Divide at the end of the Great

Glacier Gorge Trail

Depression to bring water to the eastern slopes of the Rockies. When the tunnel was completed in 1946 it was considered an engineering marvel. Adams tunnel is still in use, but don't bother to listen for the water. At this point the tunnel is 1,200 feet underground.

In the next 1.2 miles beyond Alberta Falls you will first see the North Longs Peak Trail branching off to the left (bear right here), and then you will come to a 4-way junction with trails leading to Sky Pond and Lake Haiyaha. Bear left at the second junction, following the signs to Mills Lake. The trail becomes slightly more primitive at this point, but it is still an easy walk. Within ten minutes the trail crosses Glacier Creek just below Glacier Falls. Don't expect too much from Glacier Falls, however. It is just a small cascade–not nearly as impressive as Alberta Falls.

0.6 mile after leaving the Lake Haiyaha/Sky Pond junction the trail opens up to a magnificent view of Mills Lake with Longs Peak, the highest summit in the park, almost directly behind it. The panorama is particularly fine in the morning when the water usually reflects a mirror smooth image of the famous peak. If you want to take a photograph, however, you had better have a wide angle lens for your camera.

The trail continues along the east side of Mills Lake and nearby Jewel Lake, finally ending 2.1 miles later in the large glacial cirque that contains Black Lake. The cirque, about a mile across, has been gouged from the eastern side of the Continental Divide with a large promontory of land called the Arrowhead defining its north side and another high ridge, the Spearhead, forming its southern boundary. If you are lucky enough to be there in early July, or after a rain, the dramatic scene will be accented with distant waterfalls crashing down the surrounding cliffs high above the lake. Another lake, appropriately called Frozen Lake, lies 960 feet higher than Black Lake near the base of the Spearhead, but it can't be seen from below. To reach it would require some rock climbing ability.

Upper Glacier Gorge

Loch Vale

Rocky Mountain National Park
day hike

Distance: 11.5 miles (loop)

Walking time: 7 1/2 hours

Elevations: 2,120 ft. gain/loss
Bear Lake Trailhead (start): 9,475 ft.
Emerald Lake: 10,080 ft.
Lake Haiyaha: 10,220 ft.
Sky Pond: 10,900 ft.

Trail: Mostly well marked and well maintained

Season: Midsummer through mid-fall. The trails to the upper lakes are usually covered with snow from November through early July.

Vicinity: Rocky Mountain National Park, near Estes Park

Maps: McHenrys Peak (*USGS*)
Rocky Mountain National Park (*Trails Illustrated, #200*)

Information: http://colorado.utahtrails.com/lochvale.html
http://www.nps.gov/romo/ *(Rocky Mountain National Park)*
phone: (970) 586-1242 *(Rocky Mountain National Park)*

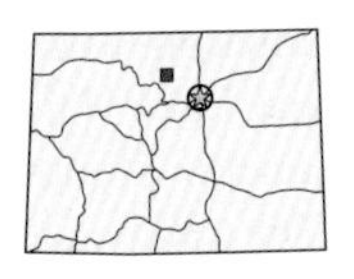

Drive into Rocky Mountain National Park from Estes Park on Highway 36. 1.5 miles beyond the Beaver Meadows Visitor Center you will come to the turnoff to Bear Lake, where you must turn left and proceed another 9.1 miles to the Bear Lake parking area. The trailhead is at the end of the parking area near the ranger station.

Note: After 10:00 a.m. during the summer it may be difficult to find a parking space at Bear Lake. The Park Service does, however, provide a convenient shuttle service to the lake between June 14 and September 28 from a larger parking area near Glacier Basin Campground 4.2 miles east of the lake. The shuttle runs every 15 minutes, with the last shuttle leaving Bear Lake at 7:30 p.m.

With over 350 miles of trails to choose from Rocky Mountain National Park is truly a hiker's paradise, but in my opinion the greatest concentration of beautiful alpine scenery lies in the vicinity of Bear Lake. Four trails leave Bear Lake in different di-

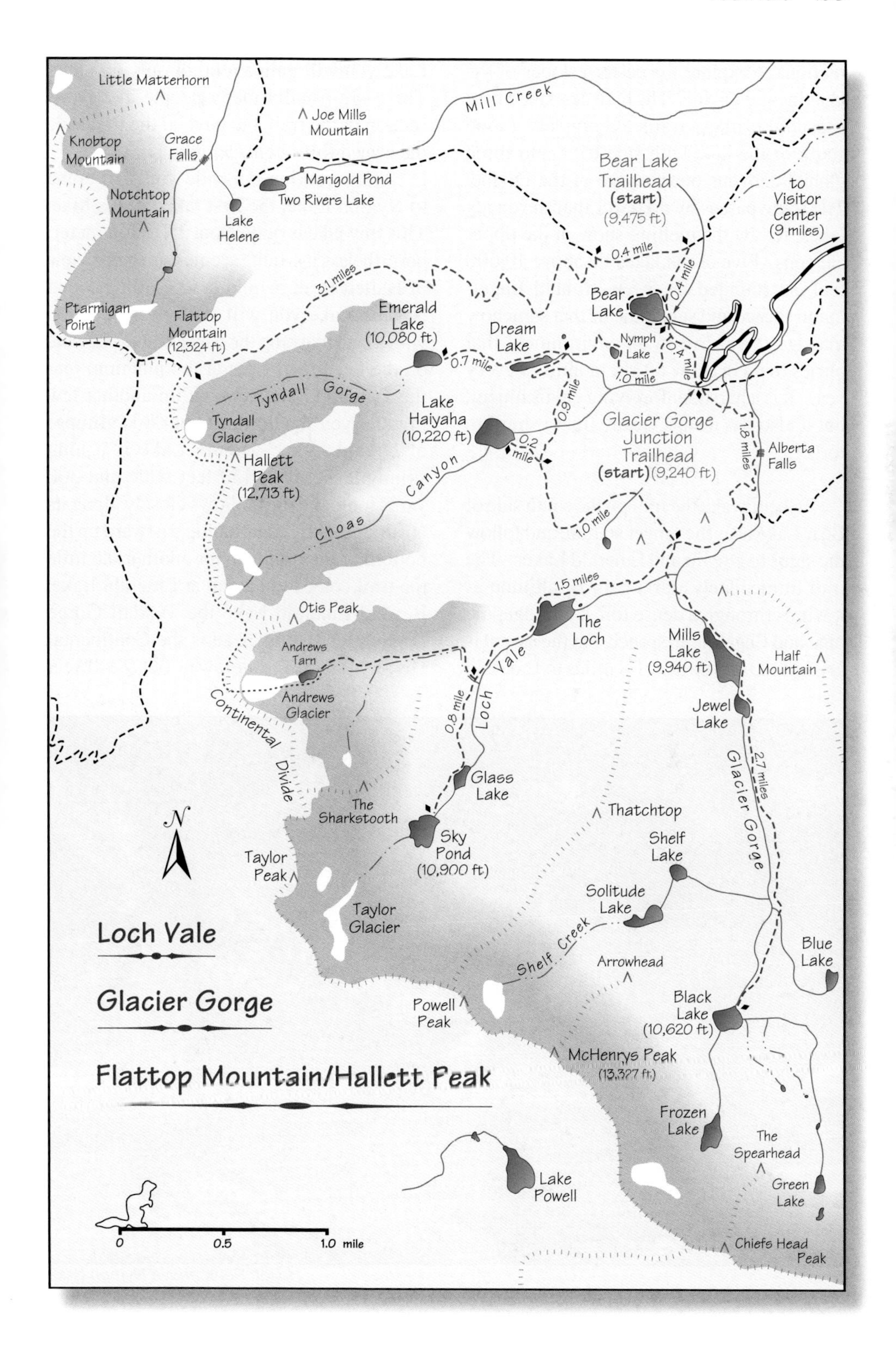
Little Matterhorn
Knobtop Mountain
Grace Falls
Joe Mills Mountain
Mill Creek
Marigold Pond
Two Rivers Lake
Notchtop Mountain
Lake Helene
Bear Lake Trailhead (start) (9,475 ft)
to Visitor Center (9 miles)
0.4 mile
0.4 mile
3.1 miles
Bear Lake
Ptarmigan Point
Flattop Mountain (12,324 ft)
Emerald Lake (10,080 ft)
Dream Lake
Nymph Lake
0.4 mile
0.7 mile
1.0 mile
Tyndall Gorge
Lake Haiyaha (10,220 ft)
0.9 mile
Glacier Gorge Junction Trailhead (start) (9,240 ft)
Tyndall Glacier
0.2 mile
1.8 miles
Alberta Falls
Hallett Peak (12,713 ft)
Canyon
Choas
1.0 mile
1.5 miles
Otis Peak
The Loch
Mills Lake (9,940 ft)
Half Mountain
Andrews Tarn
Loch Vale
Andrews Glacier
0.8 mile
Jewel Lake
Continental Divide
2.7 miles
Glass Lake
The Sharkstooth
Thatchtop
Glacier Gorge
Sky Pond (10,900 ft)
Shelf Lake
Taylor Peak
Solitude Lake
Taylor Glacier
Loch Vale
Shelf Creek
Blue Lake
Arrowhead
Glacier Gorge
Powell Peak
Black Lake (10,620 ft)
McHenrys Peak (13,327 ft)
Flattop Mountain/Hallett Peak
Frozen Lake
The Spearhead
Lake Powell
Green Lake
0
0.5
1.0 mile
Chiefs Head Peak

rections to explore the eastern slopes of the Continental Divide. The hike described here uses two of these trails to complete a loop south of the lake with side trips into three glacial canyons on the edge of the Divide. The route passes by no fewer than seven icy lakes, fed by the melting snow in the upper canyons. Five of the lakes lie above 10,000 feet, surrounded by a few stunted Engelmann spruce and subalpine fir that somehow manage to survive in an environment that buries them in snow for six months of every year. It is a harsh, unforgiving environment, but it also has a stark beauty that is hard to forget.

To begin take the trail on the south side of Bear Lake near the ranger station, and follow the signs to Dream and Emerald Lakes. The trail immediately starts gaining altitude as it winds through a dense forest of lodgepole pine and Engelmann spruce, but the assent is gradual. Over the next 1.8 miles to Emerald Lake you will gain a total of only 605 feet. There are usually many people along this section of the trail, but beyond the first mile the crowd thins considerably.

After walking 0.5 mile you will come to Nymph Lake, the first lake on this hike. This tiny lake is only about 250 in diameter; nevertheless it is quite scenic with a fine view of Hallett Peak behind it. 0.4 mile beyond Nymph Lake you will see a trail junction with a sign marking the way to Lake Haiyaha on the left. Bear right at the junction, into the Tyndall Gorge, and within another few minutes you should catch your first glimpse of Dream Lake. Dream Lake is a long skinny lake, about 150 feet wide and 300 yards long; the trail follows closely along its north side. After continuing eastward up the bottom of the drainage for another 0.6 mile the trail comes to an end at Emerald Lake. Beyond Emerald Lake the Tyndall Gorge is very steep; at its head is the Continental Divide, only 1.1 mile away but 2240 feet

Hallett Peak above Nymph Lake

higher in elevation. Looking up the gorge you can see Flattop Mountain (12,324 ft.) on the right, Hallett Peak (12,713 ft.) on the left, and the Tyndall Glacier reaching downward between the two. It is an impressive sight.

Lake Haiyaha

From Emerald Lake you must backtrack to the trail junction below Dream Lake and turn south. After walking 0.9 miles on this trail you will come to another junction where a short spur trail leads into Chaos Canyon for 0.2 miles to Lake Haiyaha. This junction, like all of the trail junctions in this area, is well marked with signs, so you shouldn't have any trouble finding your way. Lake Haiyaha is just slightly larger than Emerald Lake. Roughly circular in shape and about 250 yards in diameter, it is located at the foot of a huge pile of granite boulders, obviously deposited by the ancient glacier that once filled Chaos Canyon. Again there is a permanent snowfield at the top of the canyon, but the view is not quite as dramatic as Tyndall Gorge.

Back on the main trail below Lake Haiyaha, you must continue south for another 1.0 mile to the next trail junction at the mouth of Loch Vale. This is a major junction with four trails branching off from it, but again the trail signs will tell you which way to go. You should bear right at the junction and proceed in an easterly direction into Loch Vale. This is the longest and, in my opinion, the most interesting glacial valley you will explore on this hike. You must walk 2.3 miles from the junction to reach the end of the trail at Sky Pond, but the walk through the sub-alpine valley is well worth the time and energy spent.

After you have walked about 20 minutes from the junction you will come upon the Loch, a 450-yard-long lake that is the largest of the seven lakes encountered on this hike. From the Loch the trail meanders up the valley along the north side of a small stream called Icy Brook before reaching a minor obstacle: Timberline Falls. Timberline is not really a waterfall, but rather a cascade. It lies directly in the center of the canyon, and

Emerald Lake Trail

there is no easy way around it; consequently the trail goes straight up the streambed. You might get a little water splashed on you at this point, but unless there is a lot of snow this is not normally a problem.

Almost directly above the fall you will run into Glass Lake, where at first the trail seems to end. But don't give up. If you climb about 20 feet above the right side of the lake you should see a faint trail skirting around its western side. If you can't find the trail just continue working your way upstream through the stunted forest and after about 15 minutes you will reach Sky Pond. Sky Pond is the last of the seven lakes visited on this hike and, at 10,900 feet, it is also the highest. It lies just on the edge of timberline near the bottom of the Taylor Glacier. Taylor Peak (13,153 ft.), the highest point on the horizon west of the lake, marks the crest of the Continental Divide only a half mile behind the lake.

When you are finished savoring the view from Sky Pond make your way back to the 4-way trail junction below the Loch, and from there follow the eastern trail that leads to Glacier Gorge Junction. From the 4-way junction it is only 2.2 miles back to Bear Lake, but there is one more point of interest along the way: Alberta Falls. This much-photographed waterfall is located only 0.6 miles from the Glacier Gorge Junction parking lot, and it is a very popular short hike among park visitors. Expect a dramatic increase in the number of hikers you will encounter on this last section of the trail.

Once you reach Glacier Gorge Junction it is a short 15-minute walk back to Bear Lake where the hike began. Alternatively, you may want to end your hike at the Glacier Gorge Junction Trailhead. The Park Service shuttle to Bear Lake also stops at Glacier Gorge Junction, and during the summer the buses run about every 15 minutes.

Sky Pond

Lulu City

★

Rocky Mountain National Park
day hike

Distance:	7.4 miles (round trip)
Walking time:	4 hours
Elevations:	320 ft. gain/loss Colorado River Trailhead (start): 9,040 ft. Lulu City: 9,360 ft.
Trail:	Well marked, well maintained
Season:	Summer through mid-Fall. The trail is usually covered with snow from mid-November through early June.
Vicinity:	Rocky Mountain National Park, near Grand Lake
Maps:	Fall River Pass (*USGS*) Rocky Mountain National Park (*Trails Illustrated, #200*)
Information:	http://colorado.utahtrails.com/lulucity.html http://www.nps.gov/romo/ *(Rocky Mountain National Park)* phone: (970) 586-1242 *(Rocky Mountain National Park)*

Drive 10.2 miles north from the Kawuneeche Visitor Center on the west side of Rocky Mountain National Park where you will see a sign marking the turnout to the Colorado River Trailhead on the left side of the road. The trailhead is at the end of the turnout on the north side of the parking lot.

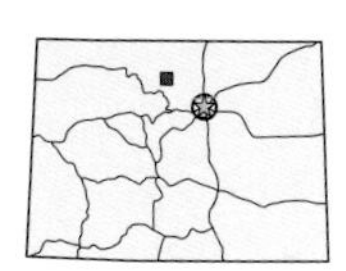

The mid-1800s was a time of great expectations in Colorado. Gold was discovered near Denver in 1858 and soon the territory's population began to swell with an influx of prospectors and dreamers. One of the hopefuls was Joe Shipler, a prospector who spent close to a decade searching for precious metals west of the Never Summer Mountains before moving into what is now Rocky Mountain National Park. In 1879, soon after entering the Kawuneeche Valley on the west side of the park, Shipler made two promising silver claims, and within months scores of other miners began to arrive in hopes of sharing his good fortune. Hopes ran high as the get-rich-quick enthusiasts flocked in, and by 1881 the small valley was home to an estimated 500 people. The center of population was Lulu City, a mining camp near the headwaters of the Colorado River.

At its peak Lulu possessed at least ten commercial buildings, including a clothing

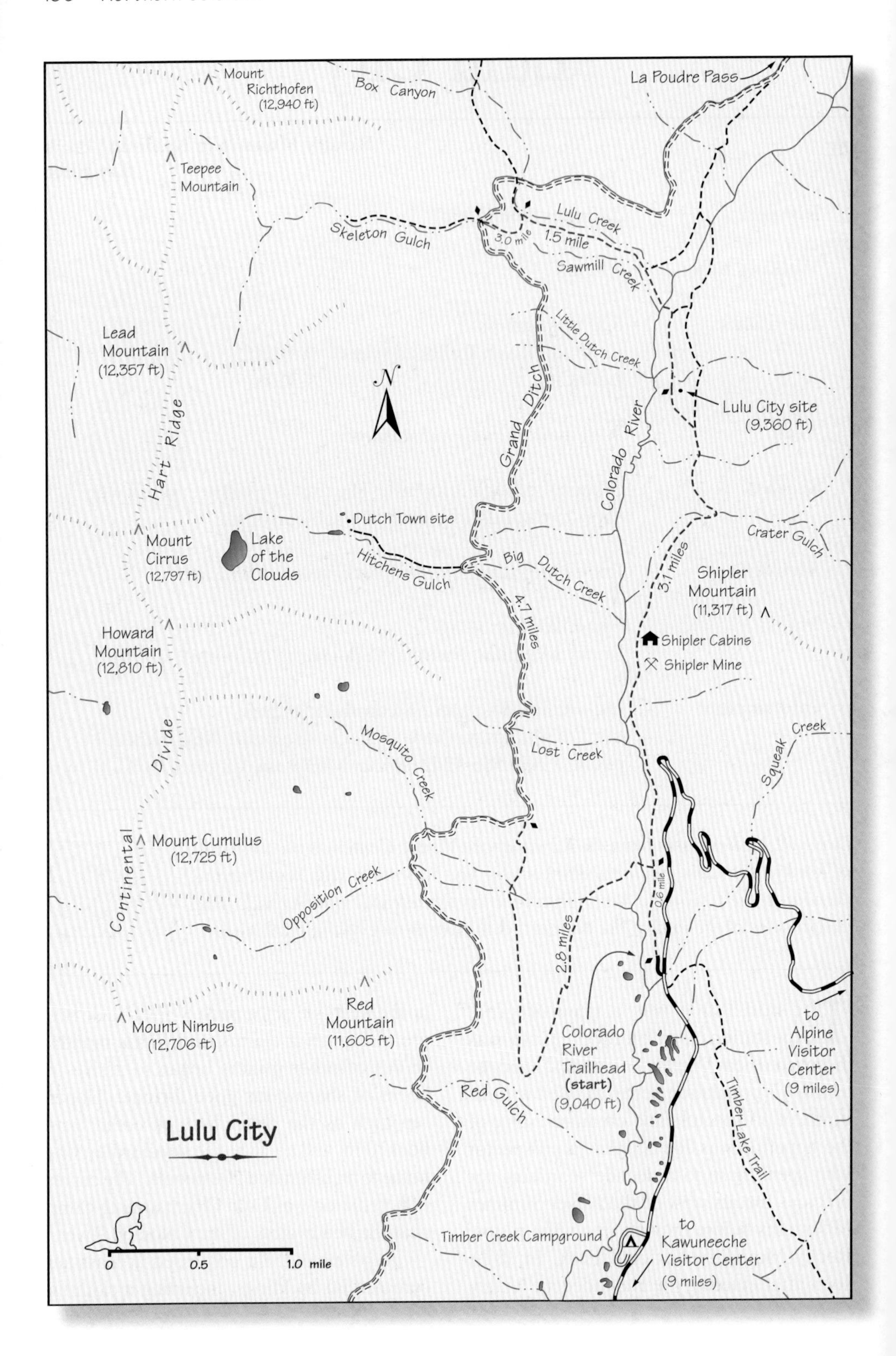

Mount Richthofen (12,940 ft)
Box Canyon
La Poudre Pass
Teepee Mountain
Lulu Creek
Skeleton Gulch
3.0 mile
1.5 mile
Sawmill Creek
Little Dutch Creek
Lead Mountain (12,357 ft)
N
Grand Ditch
Colorado River
Lulu City site (9,360 ft)
Hart Ridge
Dutch Town site
Mount Cirrus (12,797 ft)
Lake of the Clouds
Hitchens Gulch
Big Dutch Creek
3.1 miles
Crater Gulch
Shipler Mountain (11,317 ft)
4.7 miles
Howard Mountain (12,810 ft)
Shipler Cabins
Shipler Mine
Mosquito Creek
Lost Creek
Squeak Creek
Divide
Continental
Mount Cumulus (12,725 ft)
0.6 mile
Opposition Creek
2.8 miles
Red Mountain (11,605 ft)
Mount Nimbus (12,706 ft)
Colorado River Trailhead (start) (9,040 ft)
to Alpine Visitor Center (9 miles)
Red Gulch
Timber Lake Trail
Lulu City
Timber Creek Campground
to Kawuneeche Visitor Center (9 miles)
0
0.5
1.0 mile

Lulu City Trail

store, an assay office, a hotel and, of course, a brothel. The stagecoach arrived three times a week from Fort Collins and Grand Lake, and two sawmills were kept busy churning out lumber for new buildings. But the heyday was short lived. The mines proved disappointing, and soon the initial euphoria began to ebb. By the fall of 1883 most of the miners had left and the town was largely deserted.

Interestingly, Joe Shipler never left with the other miners, but continued to live on his claim near the Colorado River for the next 30 years. What prompted him to choose this lonely lifestyle? Was it his lingering hope of striking it rich in his silver mine? More likely it was a deep attachment for his beautiful mountain home that kept him from leaving. The remains of his cabins can still be seen today, not far from his abandoned mine.

From the parking area the trail meanders northward at a gentle grade along the east shore of the Colorado River. The Colorado is barely a creek at this point, giving little indication that it will eventually become the largest river in the western United States. The walk is a pleasant one, through a forest of lodgepole pine and Engelmann spruce, with occasional glimpses through the trees of the riparian area along the river. Watch the meadows, as it is not unusual to see deer, elk, and even moose in this area.

After you have walked just 0.6 mile you will see a signed trail junction where a trail to the left leads to the Grand Ditch. This trail offers an interesting loop hike which I will elaborate on later, but first let's discuss the shorter hike to Lulu City. Bearing right, the trail continues along the eastern shore of the Colorado River for another 1.4 miles to the first major point of interest: Shipler's cabins.

Shipler's cabins are situated on the edge of a lovely meadow at the base of Shipler's Mountain. From his home Joe Shipler could look across the river at Hart Ridge, 3 miles away, where a series of high peaks rise three thousand feet above the valley. Game was plentiful, and in one of his letters Shipler described catching 583 trout in a single day! Seeing this place makes it easier to understand why he didn't want to leave.

Shipler's cabins became part of the national park shortly after he abandoned them in 1914. But, sadly, no effort was ever made

Shipler's Cabins

Headwaters of the Colorado River

to preserve this bit of history and today they are in an advanced state of decay. Shipler's silver mine is also nearby. The trail passes below it just before arriving at the cabins. (Look for the mound of yellowish tailings above the right side of the path.) Also, with a little searching you can find the remains of an old mining trolley in the trees, just below the tailings on the left side of the trail.

Lulu City is located north of the Shipler cabins 1.7 miles further up the trail. Most hikers are disappointed by what they see when they get there; there are one or two obvious remains of cabins, but nothing to accurately portray the thriving community that once existed at Lulu. Many of the original logs and other remnants were scavenged by later settlers elsewhere in the valley. And most of what wasn't carried away has since been covered over by nature. However, if one is willing to spend some time exploring off the trail there is more to see than first meets the eye.

Grand Ditch

Although the round-trip hike to Lulu City is the most interesting and picturesque short hike along the Colorado River trail, there are several other worthwhile trails in the area. For someone interested in a longer hike I suggest combining the trail to Lulu City with the Grand Ditch trail to form a 13.6 mile loop.

Begin by walking along the Colorado River trail toward Lulu City for 0.6 mile, then turn left at the junction with the Grand Ditch Trail. As the sign at the junction indicates, it is 2.8 miles from there to the ditch. The trail gains 1,200 feet in elevation before reaching the Grand Ditch, but the gain is gradual and the climb is not a tiring one. Moreover, once you reach the ditch you will be at the highest point of the hike.

The Grand Ditch was originally conceived in the late 1800s as a way to bring water across the Continental Divide for the purpose of irrigating dry farm land near Fort Collins. It was a huge undertaking at that time. Most of the excavation work had to be done by hand, and it took 30 years just to complete the first 8 miles. The final 6 miles were dug as a public works project in the 1930s when better equipment became available.

Today the canal winds northward high on the western side of the Kawuneeche Valley for about 14 miles before crossing the divide at La Poudre Pass. There it empties its water into the Cache la Poudre watershed on the Atlantic side of the divide. Each year the Grand Ditch diverts some 40,000 acre-feet of water that would otherwise flow into the Colorado River, and channels it to the eastern side of the Rocky Mountains.

When the trail reaches the Grand Ditch turn right and walk along the jeep road that parallels the eastern side of the canal for the next 4.7 miles. On the way you will pass five streams that flow down from Hart Ridge to add their water to the Ditch. Big Dutch Creek, the second of these streams, flows out of Hitchens Gulch, a shallow canyon that contains the remains of another old mining camp. This camp was named Dutch Town, and like Lulu City it dates back to the 1880s. If you are interested, there is a trail to Dutch Town that begins just north of where Big Dutch Creek empties into the Ditch. The trail to Dutch Town is only 0.7 mile each way, but don't expect too see too much of the town when you get there. Like Lulu city, there isn't a great deal left of the old abandoned camp.

2.7 miles beyond Hitchens Gulch you will come to another foot bridge where the Skeleton Gulch trail crosses the Grand Ditch. Turn right here; this is the path you must take to return back to the Colorado River Trail and Lulu City. You should see a Park Service sign marking the trail as you leave the Grand Ditch. From there it is 1.8 miles to Lulu City.

Just five minutes after leaving the Grand Ditch you will come to Ditch Camp, where workers on the Grand Ditch once maintained a camp, and soon afterward you will see another trail junction where you must turn right. Again, the Park Service has placed a sign at this junction pointing the way to Lulu City. Just after leaving Ditch Camp the trail immediately starts loosing elevation at a fairly steep grade. This trail is the old stagecoach road that once connected Lulu City to Fort Collins. As you go down you will probably wonder how in the world the horses could pull a stagecoach up this trail—especially with a full load of passengers!

Soon you will come to the first of three trails that branch off to La Poudre Pass; in all cases you should bear right. Then, 1.1 miles after leaving the Ditch Camp, the trail reaches the Colorado River. The river here is only two miles from its point of origin, and it is hardly a shadow of the mighty river it will eventually become. Cross the creek on the log bridge and soon you will see another trail branching off on the left for La Poudre Pass. Bear right again, and in 0.4 miles you will arrive at Lulu City. From there it is 3.7 miles along the trail described earlier to the trailhead.

Note: There are several nice campsites along the Grand Ditch. If you wish to make this an overnight hike I suggest you camp at Dutch Town, Skeleton Gulch, or on the Old Stage Road, but be sure to get a backcountry permit first at the Kawuneeche Visitor Center.

The Grand Ditch

East Inlet

★★★★★

Rocky Mountain National Park
overnight hike

Distance:	15.6 miles (round trip)
Walking time:	day 1: 5 1/2 hours day 2: 5 1/2 hours
Elevations:	2,100 ft. gain/loss East Inlet Trailhead (start): 8,380 ft. Lake Verna: 10,180 ft. Spirit Lake: 10,300 ft.
Trail:	Excellent, well maintained trail most of the way.
Season:	Midsummer through mid-Fall. There is usually snow on the upper parts of the trail from mid-November through June.
Vicinity:	Rocky Mountain National Park, near Grand Lake
Maps:	Shadow Mountain, Isolation Peak (*USGS*) Rocky Mountain National Park (*Trails Illustrated, #200*)
Information:	http://colorado.utahtrails.com/eastinlet.html http://www.nps.gov/romo/ *(Rocky Mountain National Park)* phone: (970) 586-1206 *(Rocky Mountain National Park)*

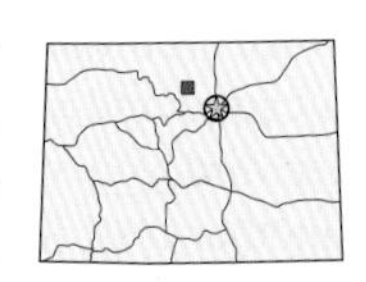

Drive south from the Kawuneeche Visitor Center on Highway 34 for 1.4 miles, then turn right toward the town of Grand Lake. Follow the signs to the public boat launching area on the far side of Grand Lake for the next 2.3 miles. As you approach the boat launching area you will see a sign directing you to the Rocky Mountain National Park access parking area on the left. The trailhead is on the east side of the parking lot.

Note: Overnight backpackers in Rocky Mountain National Park must obtain a backcountry permit before beginning their trip. Only a small number of permits are issued each day, so it is best to plan ahead. You can obtain day-of-trip permits in person at the Kawuneeche Visitor Center after 8:00 a.m., or you can make reservations for a future date by calling (970) 586-1242. Telephone reservations are not accepted during the busy season from May 16 until October 1.

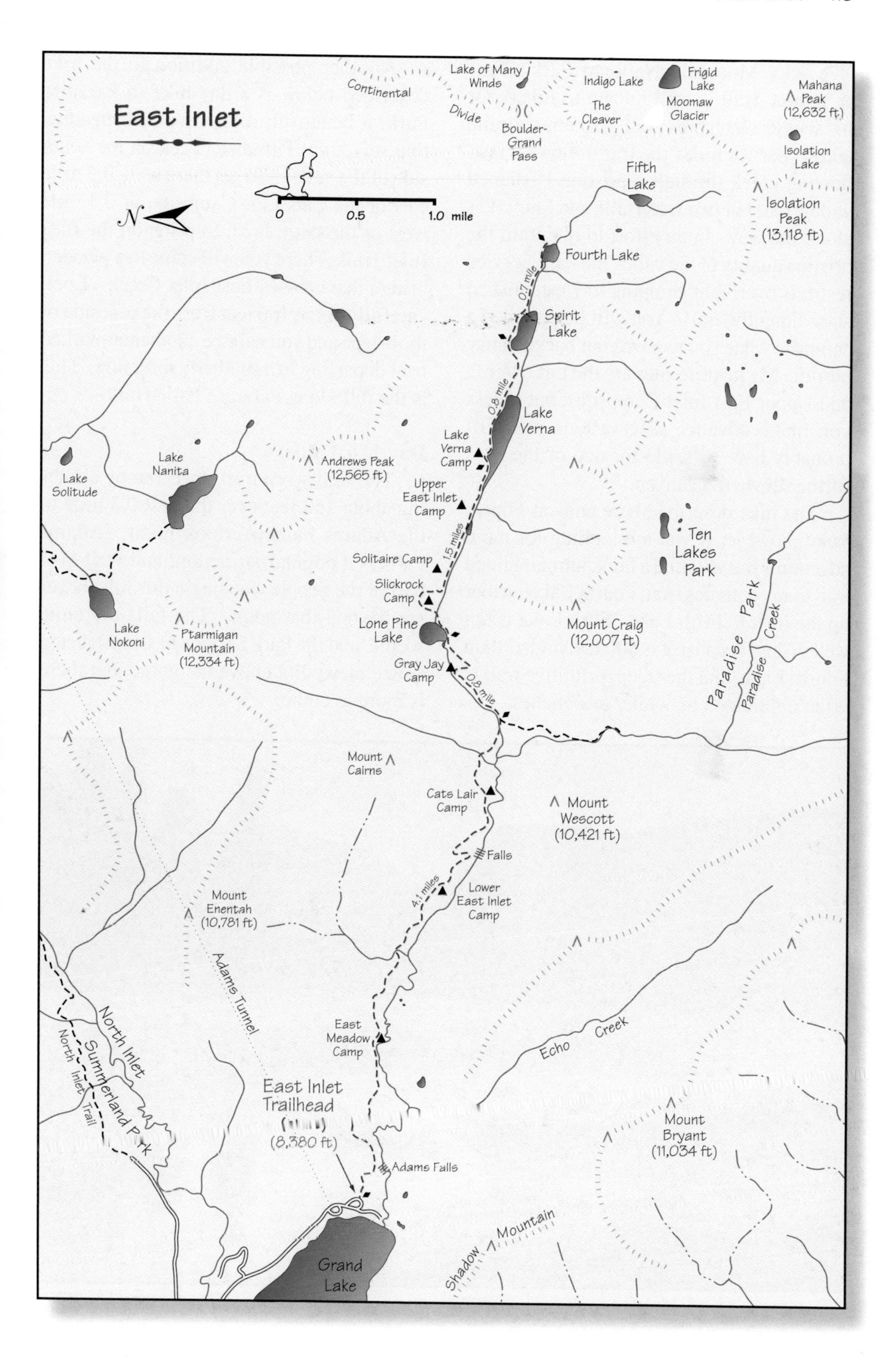

East Inlet
0
0.5
1.0 mile
N
Continental
Divide
Lake of Many Winds
Boulder-Grand Pass
Indigo Lake
The Cleaver
Frigid Lake
Moomaw Glacier
Mahana Peak (12,632 ft)
Isolation Lake
Fifth Lake
Isolation Peak (13,118 ft)
Fourth Lake
0.7 mile
Spirit Lake
0.8 mile
Lake Verna
Lake Verna Camp
Andrews Peak (12,565 ft)
Upper East Inlet Camp
1.5 miles
Lake Solitude
Lake Nanita
Ten Lakes Park
Solitaire Camp
Slickrock Camp
Lone Pine Lake
Mount Craig (12,007 ft)
Lake Nokoni
Ptarmigan Mountain (12,334 ft)
Gray Jay Camp
0.8 mile
Paradise Park
Paradise Creek
Paradise
Mount Cairns
Cats Lair Camp
Mount Wescott (10,421 ft)
Falls
4.1 miles
Lower East Inlet Camp
Mount Enentah (10,781 ft)
Adams Tunnel
North Inlet
Summerland Park
North Inlet Trail
East Meadow Camp
Echo Creek
East Inlet Trailhead (8,380 ft)
Mount Bryant (11,034 ft)
Adams Falls
Shadow Mountain
Grand Lake

Rocky Mountain National Park's East Inlet Trail is well known to hikers for its scenic waterfalls and gorgeous alpine lakes. For 7.8 miles the trail follows a fast-flowing creek through a pristine U-shaped valley, passing two waterfalls and four lakes along the way. In an effort to maintain the pristine quality of the valley the Park Service restricts overnight camping to 7 established sites along the trail. You will be assigned a campsite when you receive your backcountry permit. My favorite sites are the Lake Verna and Upper East Inlet Campsites, but unless you make advance reservations you will probably have to settle for one of the sites further down the canyon.

The hike described here ends at Fourth Lake; however if you are looking for more adventure you will find a faint, unmaintained trail than continues from Fourth Lake further up the inlet to Fifth Lake. Fifth Lake is not well visited because it is 500 feet higher than Fourth Lake, and the steep, primitive trail is often obliterated by winter avalanches.

Another possible addition to the hike described below is a day hike to Paradise Park, a beautiful, seldom-visited meadow that surrounds Paradise Creek on the south side of the valley. To get there walk 0.5 mile east of the Cats Lair Campsite, or 0.4 mile west of the Gray Jay Campsite, on the East Inlet Trail. There you will come to a wooden bridge that crosses East Inlet Creek. Look carefully about 100 feet from the east side of the bridge and you will see another unmarked trail departing in a southerly direction. This is the mile-long Paradise Park Trail.

Day 1 (6.4 miles)

The well-worn trail starts out by climbing about 150 feet over the first 0.3 mile to the Adams Falls overlook point. Adams Falls is a popular attraction, and well over half of the people who begin this hike never get beyond that point. The falls are quite scenic, and the Park Service has constructed a nice viewpoint above the gorge, but there is more to come.

East Meadow

East Inlet Trail above the Lower East Inlet Campsite

From Adams Falls the trail continues westward with practically no elevation change. 1.1 miles beyond the falls you will pass a spur trail leading to the East Meadow Campsite, and soon afterward the forest of lodgepole pine gives way to a magnificent meadow. For the next mile the trail meanders along the north side of the park, offering many fine views of the tranquil, grass-lined river bordered by distant mountains.

As you near the east end of the meadow the trail passes back into the trees and crosses a bridge where a small tributary flows in from the north. Another ten minutes will bring you to the Lower East Inlet Campsite, and beyond that the trail begins climbing in order to reach the higher plateaus in the back of the valley where the lakes are located.

The next 0.5 mile is much more strenuous than the first 2.5 miles of this hike. The trail climbs 400 feet and then levels off again as it passes by another dramatic waterfall. You will come to a place where the trail descends briefly across a large horizontal slab of granite before turning to double back into the woods. The roar of the rushing water will tell you there is something to see nearby, and when you walk 30 feet from the right side of the tail it will be become clear where the noise is coming from. Here the river is pinched into a slot only a few feet across, below which it crashes down through a tortuous channel to the valley below. Walk to the water's edge and feel the power of the rushing torrent, but be very careful. If you slip into the deluge you will be hopelessly swept away.

The Cat's Lair Campsite is located 0.6 mile further east from the water fall, and 0.6 mile beyond that the trail again begins to climb up to the next plateau. Again, the elevation gain is about 400 feet over 0.5 mile.

East Inlet Creek below the Cat's Lair Campsite

As you near the end of your climb you will see the Gray Jay Campsite on your left, and just a short distance beyond that you will arrive at Lone Pine Lake, the first of four lakes passed on this hike. Like many of Colorado's alpine lakes, these lakes are all tarns that were gouged out of the East Inlet during the last ice age when the valley was covered by a glacier. Today they lie like a string of pearls along the gently sloping plateau near the top of the inlet.

Beyond Lone Pine Lake the trail passes the Slickrock Campsite and proceeds for another mile up a gentle grade to Lake Verna, the prettiest of all the East Inlet lakes. The Lake Verna Campsite is a fine place to set up camp for the night, but two good alternatives are Solitaire and Upper East Inlet. Hopefully you were able to reserve one of these three when you obtained your backcountry permit.

Day 2 (9.3 miles)

Continuing eastward from the Lake Verna Campsite you will come to a sign indicating that the trail is no longer maintained; nevertheless you really should visit the last two lakes on the plateau before returning to the trailhead. In general the trail is still easy to follow, but you will probably have to climb over a few more fallen trees that would have otherwise been cleared by the Park Service. The path follows closely along the north shore of Lake Verna until it reaches its eastern end, then continues on through the forest for another 0.3 mile to Spirit Lake.

Spirit Lake is also a beauty. It is only half the size of Lake Verna, but it is in more of a meadow-like setting with the rugged profile of the Continental Divide directly behind it. Furthermore, few hikers get as far as Spirit Lake, so you will probably have it all to yourself.

Staying on the north side of the drainage, the trail leaves Spirit Lake and continues another 0.3 mile to Fourth Lake. The terrain between Spirit and Fourth Lakes is flat and grassy with lots of water. Sometimes the trail is overgrown with grass and hard to follow, but don't stray to close to the creek or you will find yourself in a bog.

As stated earlier, if the hike to Fourth Lake is not enough for you you may want to climb on up to Fifth Lake, the last lake in East Inlet. This will involve a strenuous 480-foot climb, however, over a trail that may or may not be there. Fifth Lake is located on a third glacial plateau above the other lakes, and the route up the drainage is often subject to avalanches and rock slides. Consequently, there is no permanent trail beyond Fourth Lake. However the hike to Fifth Lake can make for an interesting outing. The lake sits just below the Continental Divide at an elevation of 10,860 feet.

Lone Pine Lake

Mount Audubon

Indian Peaks Wilderness Area
day hike

Distance:	7.4 miles (round trip)
Walking time:	$5^1/_2$ hours
Elevations:	2,720 ft. gain/loss Mount Audubon Trailhead (start): 10,510 ft. Mount Audubon: 13,223 ft.
Trail:	Good trail except for the last 0.5-mile scramble to the summit.
Season:	Midsummer through mid-fall. The trail is generally covered with snow from mid-November until mid-July.
Vicinity:	Near Boulder
Maps:	Ward (*USGS*) Indian Peaks (*Trails Illustrated, #102*)
Information:	http://colorado.utahtrails.com/mountaudubon.html http://www.fs.fed.us/arnf/ *(Roosevelt National Forest)* phone: (303) 541-2500 *(Boulder Ranger District)*

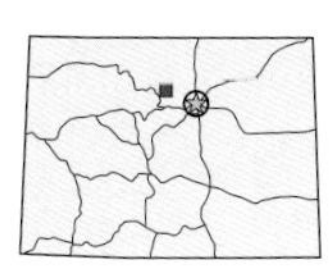

Drive east of Boulder on Highway 119 for 17 miles to the town of Nederland, then turn north on Highway 72 and drive another 11.6 miles to the town of Ward. As you pass through Ward you will see a paved road on the left next to a large sign that says "Brainard Lake Recreation Area". Turn left here and drive west for 4.8 miles to Brainard Lake. (Before you continue be sure to stop and take in the fantastic panorama of Mount Audubon from the viewpoint beside the lake.) From Brainard Lake follow the signs for another 1.0 mile to the Mitchell Lake Trailhead. You will find the Beaver Creek/Mount Audubon Trailhead on the north side of the parking lot.

On the way to Brainard Lake you will pass through a toll gate where you must pay $5.00 to enter the area; however if you intend to camp near the lake at the Pawnee Campground let the attendant know so you can get a $5.00 refund when you leave. (You can make advance reservations for the Pawnee Campground by calling (877) 444-6777)

Mount Audubon, though one of the highest summits in the Indian Peaks Wilderness Area, is also one of the easiest peaks to climb. The high, rounded mountain

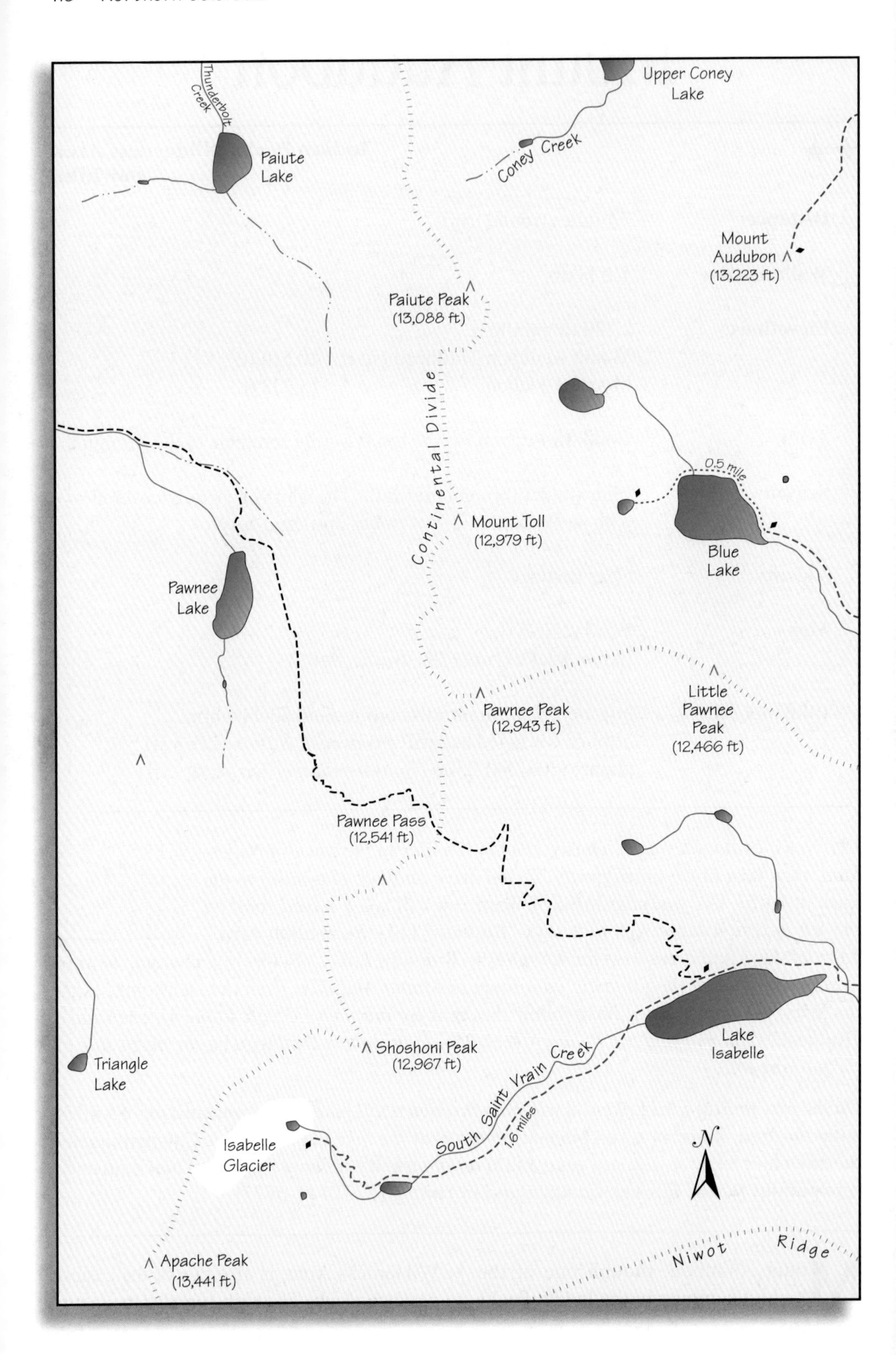

Thunderbolt Creek
Paiute Lake
Coney Creek
Upper Coney Lake
Mount Audubon (13,223 ft)
Paiute Peak (13,088 ft)
Continental Divide
0.5 mile
Mount Toll (12,979 ft)
Blue Lake
Pawnee Lake
Pawnee Peak (12,943 ft)
Little Pawnee Peak (12,466 ft)
Pawnee Pass (12,541 ft)
Shoshoni Peak (12,967 ft)
Lake Isabelle
Triangle Lake
South Saint Vrain Creek
1.6 miles
Isabelle Glacier
N
Apache Peak (13,441 ft)
Niwot Ridge

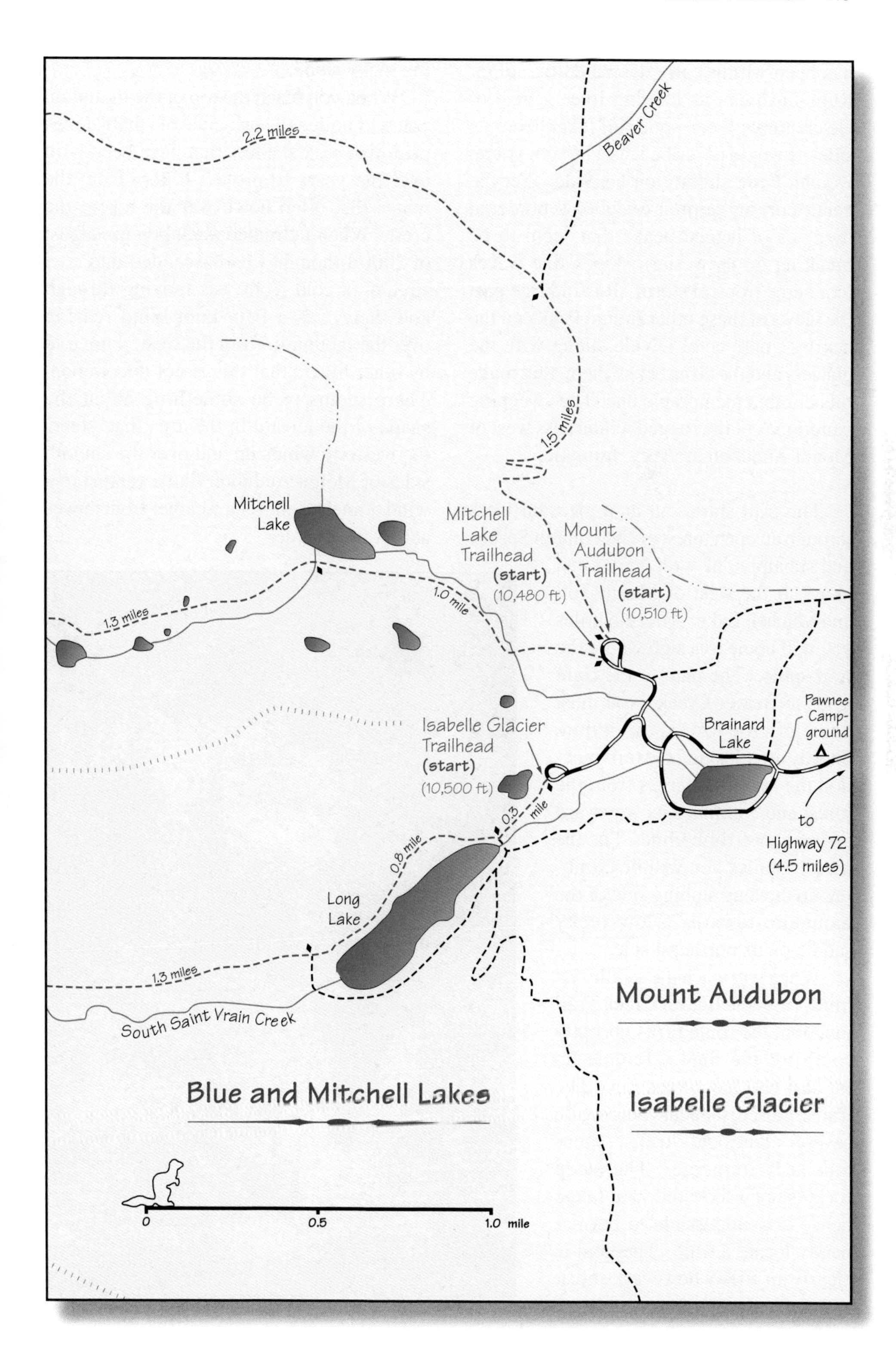

2.2 miles
Beaver Creek
1.5 miles
Mitchell Lake
Mitchell Lake Trailhead (start) (10,480 ft)
Mount Audubon Trailhead (start) (10,510 ft)
1.0 mile
1.3 miles
Isabelle Glacier Trailhead (start) (10,500 ft)
Brainard Lake
Pawnee Campground
to Highway 72 (4.5 miles)
0.3 mile
0.8 mile
Long Lake
1.3 miles
South Saint Vrain Creek
Mount Audubon
Blue and Mitchell Lakes
Isabelle Glacier
0
0.5
1.0 mile

has been whimsically described by author Ruth Cushman as looking like "a dish of ice cream with one spoonful taken from its side". I would describe it as a buxom young woman lying slightly on her side. Yet the gentle curving summit Audubon is bordered by a sea of jagged peaks that seem to be breaking on its western slopes like waves in a fierce tropical storm. It is in large part the views of these other Indian Peaks on the nearby Continental Divide, along with the glaciers and the tarns below them, that make this climb a memorable one. The sweeping panoramas of the rugged wilderness west of Mount Audubon are very dramatic.

The trail starts out as a pleasant walk through an open forest of Engelmann Spruce and subalpine fir with occasional views to the west of Mount Toll and Mitchell Lake. After 1.5 miles you will come to a sign where the trail splits. The path to the right leads to Beaver Creek; you must bear left for Mount Audubon. Shortly after leaving the trail junction the route immerges from the forest and continues its westward assent above timberline. For the next 1.5 miles you will be climbing up the long sloping side of the mountain towards a low rocky saddle on its northeast side.

When you reach the saddle, 1.7 miles from the Beaver Creek Trail junction, the route turns abruptly south for the final scramble up the last 630 feet to the top. The trail almost disappears here while several additional "trails" spontaneously immerge. The steep rocky slope is covered with talus; hence it is impossible to permanently locate a trail. The goal is clearly in view, however, and it isn't difficult to pick your way up the rocky slope.

When you reach the top of the mountain you will notice the presence of a half-dozen primitive rock shelters that have been built over the years to protect hikers from the winds that often howl over the top of the crest. When I climbed Audubon in August of 2000 I thought I had ascended into a jet stream—a cold front was moving through and there was a fifty-knot wind roaring over the mountain from the west. I am told by other hikers that this is not uncommon. There seems to be something about the shape of the terrain in the area that steers the westerly winds up and over the smooth sides of Mount Audubon like a venturi in a wind tunnel whenever a weather front moves across the Divide.

Mount Audubon Trail

Blue and Mitchell Lakes

★★

Indian Peaks Wilderness Area
day hike

Distance:	5.6 miles (round trip)
Walking time:	3 1/2 hours
Elevations:	950 ft. gain/loss Mitchell Lake Trailhead (start): 10,480 ft. Blue Lake: 11,310 ft.
Trail:	Popular, well maintained trail as far as Blue Lake
Season:	Midsummer through mid-fall. The trail is generally covered with snow from mid-November until mid-July.
Vicinity:	Near Boulder
Maps:	Ward (*USGS*) Indian Peaks (*Trails Illustrated, #102*)
Information:	http://colorado.utahtrails.com/bluelake.html http://www.fs.fed.us/arnf/ *(Roosevelt National Forest)* phone: (303) 541-2500 *(Boulder Ranger District)*

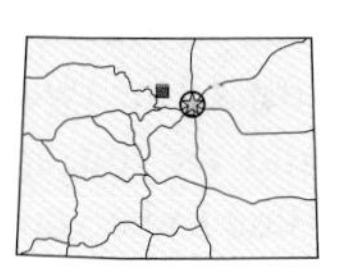

Drive east of Boulder on Highway 119 for 17 miles to the town of Nederland, then turn north on Highway 72 and drive another 11.6 miles to the town of Ward. As you pass through Ward you will see a paved road on the left next to a large sign that says "Brainard Lake Recreation Area". Turn left here and drive west for 4.8 miles to Brainard Lake. From Brainard Lake follow the signs for another 1.0 mile to the Mitchell Lake Trailhead. You will find the Mitchell and Blue Lakes Trail on the north side of the parking lot.

On the way to Brainard Lake you will pass through a toll gate where you must pay $5.00 to enter the area; however if you intend to camp near the lake at the Pawnee Campground let the attendant know so you can get a $5.00 refund when you leave. (You can make advance reservations for the Pawnee Campground by calling (877) 444-6777)

This is one of those hikes that offers a big reward for relatively little work. Blue Lake is only 2.4 miles from the Mitchell Lake Trailhead with an elevation gain of just 830 feet, yet it is one of the prettiest lakes you will see in the Front Range. It is just above timberline with the picturesque Mount Toll rising above the Continental Divide on its western side, and it is deep enough to have a cold steely blue color. As an added bonus, a 20-foot waterfall pours into the lake from the foot of Mount Toll, fed by the year-round snowfields that adorn its steep slopes.

see map page 119

The trail begins as a pleasant half-hour walk through a lush green forest of conifers and pines to the southern shore of Mitchell Lake 0.9 mile away. Mitchell is a tree-lined lake, some 400 yards long and 150 yards wide, with a fine view of Mount Audubon from its eastern side. it is a favorite among fly fishermen, although the fishing regulations here are quite strict.

Beyond Mitchell Lake the grade increases slightly as the trail climbs another 600 feet over the next 1.5 miles to Blue Lake. The route never strays far from the north side of the creek that joins the two lakes, and as you approach Blue Lake you will be treated to a number of splashing cascades below its outlet. Finally the trail reaches the lake's rocky eastern shore for a marvelous view across the calm water of Mount Toll on its western side.

Most people stop here, but it is worthwhile to walk another half-mile on the hiker-made trail that continues around the lake's north side and climbs to the source of the waterfall above its western shore. The primitive trail finally ends beside a small tarn, 200 feet across, where the melt from the snowfields above collects before draining into the lake. Try to be there in the morning, when the eastern sun is shining directly on Mount Toll and its snowfields, and the water is calm enough to reflect images of the picturesque peak.

Mount Toll above Blue Lake

Isabelle Glacier

★★★★★

Indian Peaks Wilderness Area
day hike

Distance:	8.0 miles (round trip)
Walking time:	5¼ hours
Elevations:	1,500 ft. gain/loss Long Lake Trailhead (start): 10,500 ft. Lake Isabelle: 10,868 ft. Isabelle Glacier: 12,000 ft.
Trail:	Easy and well marked as far as Isabelle Lake, but very steep and rocky for the last 0.5 mile.
Season:	Midsummer through mid-fall. The trail is generally covered with snow from mid-November until mid-July.
Vicinity:	Near Boulder
Maps:	Ward, Monarch Lake (*USGS*) Indian Peaks (*Trails Illustrated, #102*)
Information:	http://colorado.utahtrails.com/isabelleglacier.html http://www.fs.fed.us/arnf/ *(Roosevelt National Forest)* phone: (303) 541-2500 *(Boulder Ranger District)*

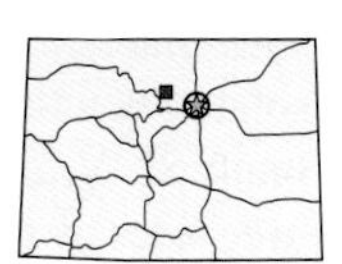

Drive east of Boulder on Highway 119 for 17 miles to the town of Nederland, then turn north on Highway 72 and drive another 11.6 miles to the town of Ward. As you pass through Ward you will see a paved road on the left next to a large sign that says "Brainard Lake Recreation Area". Turn left here and drive west for 4.8 miles to Brainard Lake. (Isabelle Glacier can be clearly seen from Brainard Lake.) From Brainard Lake follow the signs for another 1.0 mile to the Long Lake Trailhead and parking area.

On the way to Brainard Lake you will pass through a toll gate where you must pay $5.00 to enter the area; however if you intend to camp near the lake at the Pawnee Campground let the attendant know so you can get a $5.00 refund when you leave. (You can make advance reservations for the Pawnee Campground by calling (877) 444-6777).

I must admit I have a certain passion for glaciers, even small ones, but if I had to choose the one glacier in Colorado that stirs my soul the most, it would have to be Isa-

Lake Isabelle

belle Glacier. Isabelle lies hidden in a high, isolated bowl-shaped basin at the top of the South St. Vrain drainage. Surrounded on three sides by the rugged Shoshoni, Apache, and Navajo Peaks, and pinched off on the fourth side by the Niwot Ridge, Isabelle Glacier could not be in a more spectacular setting. The glacier is also intriguing from a geological point of view. It is fed by two opposing snowfields on the slopes of Shoshoni and Apache Peaks, and in the bottom of the bowl where the ice flows meet there are several large cracks that appear to be stress lines. Under the cracks lies a frozen lake that partially melts during the summer months and flows out under the moraine on the southeast side of the bowl. The pale, milky "glacier blue" color of the partially melted ice provides a striking contrast to the deep blue Colorado sky in late summer, and the trail ends at a perfect vantage point on the glacier's southern side. The view is stunning.

see map page 119

From the parking area the trail goes only 0.3 mile before immerging from the forest on the eastern shore of Long Lake. Long Lake, as the name suggests, is a slender elongated body of water that measures about 0.6 mile from end to end. The lake is quite pretty, but unfortunately the trail rarely comes closer than 200 feet from its shore and the water stays partially hidden behind a veil of trees.

The real scenery starts after leaving the west end of Long Lake. As the trail starts to climb up out of the forest the Indian Peaks along the Continental Divide begin to come into view, and by the time you reach Isabelle Lake, which is just below timber line, Pawnee, Shoshoni, Apache, and Navajo peaks are all prominently displayed on the skyline. Navajo Peak is the most scenic of the summits, and camera lenses along the trail seem to turn to it as surely as a compass needle points north. Navajo Peak is a classic cone-shaped mountain, 13,409 feet high, with a sharply pointed summit and a permanent snowfield called Navajo Glacier flowing down its northwest side.

The trail continues along the north side of Isabelle Lake to the junction with the Pawnee Pass Trail, and then bears left along the upper reaches of South St. Vrain Creek. More climbing is in order here; you still have another 1,100 feet of elevation gain to realize before arriving at the foot of Isabelle Glacier. Most other hikers will be left behind as you leave Isabelle Lake; only a small percentage of them make it all the way to the glacier.

A mile after you leave the lake you will come to a small picturesque tarn in the valley below the glaciers. You cannot see Isabelle Glacier yet, but Navajo Glacier is starkly apparent across the treeless tundra a half-mile southwest of the tarn. Navajo Peak looks to be little more than a stone's throw away, but actually it is 0.7 mile distant and 2,000 feet above the trail. The most common mountaineering route to the top of Navajo departs from the trail at this point, climbs to the top of Niwot Ridge, and approaches the peak from the side opposite Navajo Glacier.

Isabelle Glacier lies in a smaller basin 580 feet above the northwest side of the tarn. The trail, where it exists, is extremely rocky and steep, and you won't even see the glacier until you are right on top of it. But don't loose heart—it is there waiting for you. After about a half-hour of climbing you will see a 30-foot high moraine of broken granite that Isabelle has, over the centuries, pushed out of the basin, and on the other side of that moraine is the foot of the glacier.

One final note. It is tempting to walk out onto the bottom of Isabelle Glacier, but it is not wise to go too far—especially in late summer after considerable melt has occurred. As stated earlier, there is an ice lake under the snow, and as the water drains from this lake snow bridges are formed above it. If someone were to fall through the top into the icy water below it would be very difficult to get him out quickly.

Isabelle Glacier

Arapaho Glacier

Indian Peaks Wilderness Area
shuttle car required
day hike

Distance: 9.1 miles
(plus 21.1 miles by car)

Walking time: 6 1/2 hours

Elevations: 2,580 ft. gain, 2780 ft. loss

Fourth of July Trailhead (start):	10,160 ft.
glacier viewpoint:	12,700 ft.
Rainbow Lakes Trailhead:	9,960 ft.

Trail: Well marked and maintained

Season: Midsummer through mid-fall. The trail is generally covered with snow from mid-November through mid-July.

Vicinity: Near Boulder

Maps: East Portal, Monarch Lake (*USGS*)
Indian Peaks (*Trails Illustrated, #102*)

Information: http://colorado.utahtrails.com/arapahoglacier.html
http://www.fs.fed.us/arnf/ *(Roosevelt National Forest)*
phone: (303) 541-2500 *(Boulder Ranger District)*

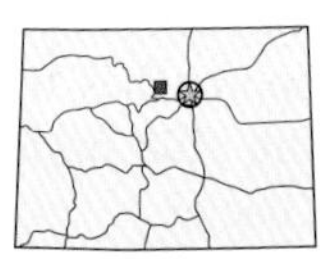

Drive east of Boulder on Highway 119 for 17 miles to the town of Nederland. When you reach the center of Nederland turn south on Highway 72 and drive for another 0.5 mile until you see a paved road on the right leading to the town of Eldora. Turn right here and drive through Eldora, following the signs to Buckingham Campground and the Fourth of July Trailhead at the end of the road. The trailhead is located 8.8 miles from the highway; the last 4.7 miles are unpaved but usually passable for most cars.

To reach the Rainbow Lakes Trailhead where the hike ends you must drive north of Nederland on Highway 72 for 6.9 miles where you will see a road on the left next to a sign that says "University of Colorado Mountain Research Station". Turn left here and follow the signs for 4.8 miles to the Rainbow Lakes Campground. Shortly after entering the campground you will see a small parking area on the right next to a sign that says "Glacier Rim Trail". This is where the hike will end and where you must leave a shuttle car.

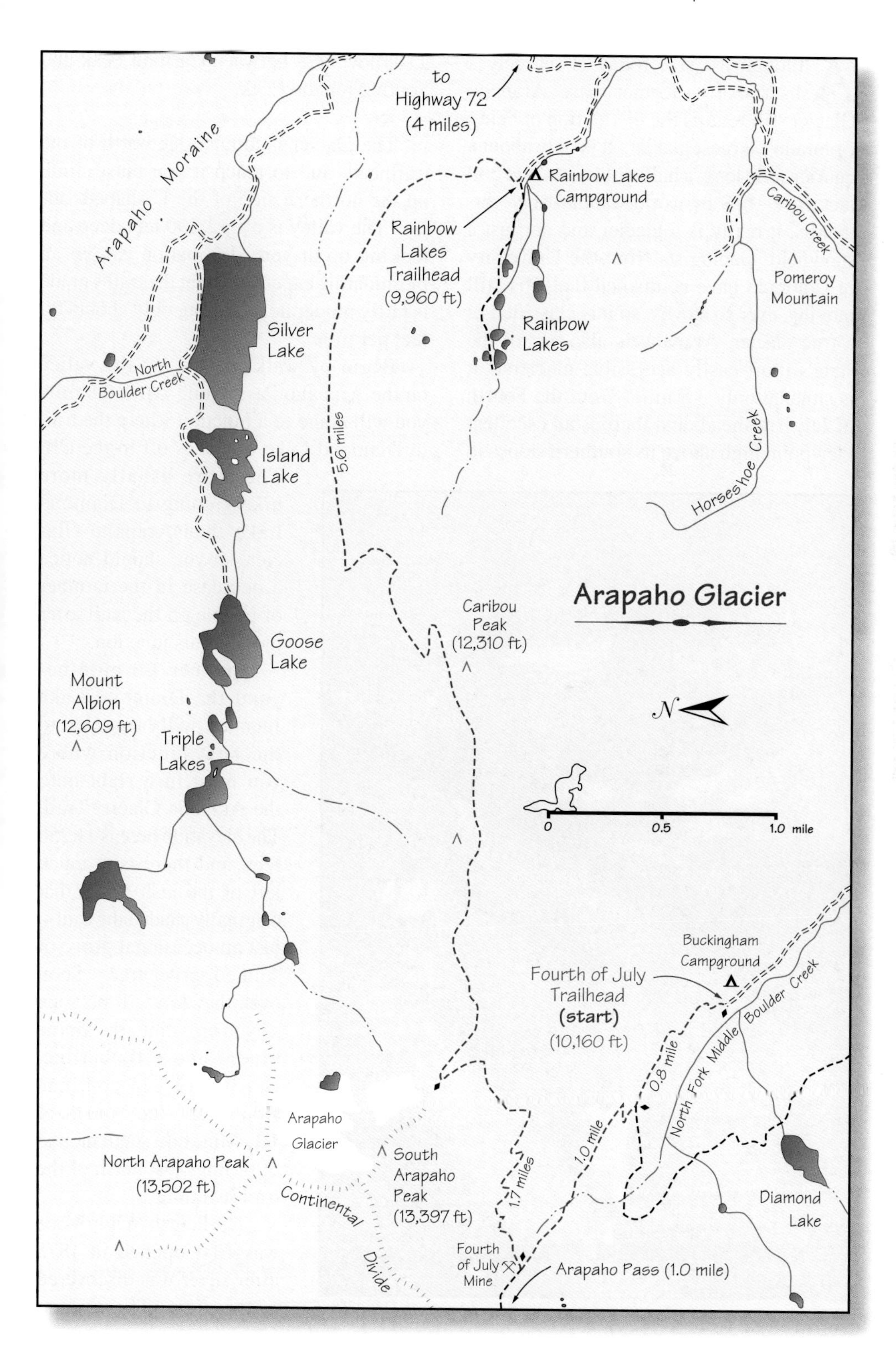
to
Highway 72
(4 miles)
Arapaho Moraine
Rainbow Lakes
Campground
Rainbow
Lakes
Trailhead
(9,960 ft)
Caribou Creek
Pomeroy
Mountain
Silver
Lake
Rainbow
Lakes
North
Boulder Creek
Island
Lake
5.6 miles
Horseshoe Creek
Arapaho Glacier
Caribou
Peak
(12,310 ft)
Goose
Lake
Mount
Albion
(12,609 ft)
N
Triple
Lakes
0
0.5
1.0 mile
Buckingham
Campground
Fourth of July
Trailhead
(start)
(10,160 ft)
Boulder Creek
North Fork Middle
0.8 mile
1.0 mile
Arapaho
Glacier
North Arapaho Peak
(13,502 ft)
South
Arapaho
Peak
(13,397 ft)
1.7 miles
Continental
Divide
Diamond
Lake
Fourth
of July
Mine
Arapaho Pass (1.0 mile)

Although it's size today is scarcely a shadow of its former mass, Arapaho Glacier still retains the distinction of being Colorado's largest glacier. It is only about a quarter-mile long, a half-mile wide, and 200 feet thick–tiny by world standards. Nevertheless, it really is a glacier and not just a snowfield. Geologists from the University of Colorado have confirmed that it is still moving, ever so slowly, so it is classified as a true glacier. Arapaho is also one of the state's most easily accessible glaciers. It is situated only 3.5 miles from the Fourth of July Trailhead, and there is an excellent viewpoint high above its southern slopes in a shallow pass between Caribou Peak and South Arapaho Peak.

The glacier is almost due north of the trailhead, and to reach it you must climb up the northern side of the U-shaped valley. The valley is over 2,500 feet deep and looking up at your destination can be an intimidating experience, but the trail's grade is fairly moderate, climbing only about 700 feet per mile.

Begin by walking west up the valley on the Arapaho Pass Trail. After 0.8 mile you will come to a junction where the trail to Diamond Lake branches off to the left. There are usually more hikers going to Diamond Lake than Arapaho Glacier, so you should notice a decrease in the number of people on the trail after passing this junction.

Arapaho Pass Trail

Another 1.0 mile beyond the Diamond Lake Junction will bring you to the next junction where you must turn right onto the Arapaho Glacier Trail. The elevation here is 11,250 feet, and there isn't much left of the lush forest that originally shaded the trail–just an occasional grove of stunted spruce trees. Soon even they too will be gone as you cross into the alpine tundra above timberline. But before you continue stop to see the Fourth of July Mine on a small mound of tailings just north of the trail junction.

The Fourth of July Mine was first opened in 1875 after silver was discovered in the area. The amount

Arapaho Glacier

of silver extracted from the claim proved disappointing, but that didn't prevent its unscrupulous owners from thinking up other unsavory ways to make their investment pay off. When the silver had played out they managed to convince others that a huge deposit of copper lay under the mine, and millions of dollars were made selling worthless stock to the victims of their scheme. Today it has been over a hundred years since the claim was worked but there are still a few pieces of rusting equipment scattered about, including a large boiler and parts of a wench.

From the Fourth of July Mine the trail continues climbing to the east for another 1.7 miles before it reaches the Arapaho Glacier Overlook. This part of the trail is all above timberline, and the views looking down into the North Fork of Middle Boulder Creek are gorgeous. Diamond Lake lies below in a basin above the south side of the valley, and you can clearly see the trail below winding up to Arapaho Pass west of the Fourth of July Mine. At the turn of the century there was a wagon road up the east side of Arapaho Pass, but no trace of it remains now.

Finally, about an hour after leaving the Fourth of July Mine, the trail arrives at the glacier viewpoint in a saddle on the ridge east of South Arapaho Peak. The viewpoint offers a superb overview of the ice field; it is about 500 feet above the bottom of the glacier and 700 feet below the top of South Arapaho Peak. The ice flow has pushed up a small moraine in front of the glacier and a small frozen lake, or tarn, fed by the melting snow, lies behind the natural dam. When I saw the glacier in 2000 there was a large vertical cleavage a few hundred feet behind the tarn where a section of the snow pack had broken away and slid downward. This fault afforded an opportunity to look at a cross section of the glacier and estimate the thickness of the milky blue ice: the vertical height of the cleavage appeared to be about 150 feet.

Seeing the glacier from the overlook

Ptarmigans on the Arapaho Glacier Trail

point gives one a compelling urge scramble down for a closer look, but unfortunately that is now illegal. In 1927 the city of Boulder acquired the Arapaho Glacier as part of a 3,685 acre land purchase from the federal government for the purpose of protecting the city's water supply. Boulder now has the distinction of being the only city in the United States that owns a glacier. It also owns several pristine lakes further down the valley that are strictly off limits to the public.

Many hikers climb to the summit of South Arapaho Peak after reaching the glacier overlook. The peak rises 700 feet above the trail to an elevation of 13, 397 feet. Although the climb is a very tiring scramble up an incline of about 30 degrees, it is not particularly difficult, and most climbers reach the top in about 45 minutes. It is also possible to traverse along the ridge from South Arapaho Peak to North Arapaho Peak, which at 13,502 feet is the highest mountain in the Indian Peaks Wilderness Area. The traverse to North Arapaho Peak is a more difficult scramble, however, than the climb up South Arapaho and takes at least another hour each way.

Soon after leaving the glacier overlook the trail passes the highest point on this hike and then slowly proceeds downhill along the ridge separating the North Boulder Creek drainage from the North Fork of Middle Boulder Creek. The views north of the ridge are very scenic; the valley below is decorated by a string of a half-dozen lakes that are fed by the Arapaho Glacier. Unfortunately these lakes are also owned by the city of Boulder, and hikers are not allowed to enter the valley. About 3.3 miles after leaving Arapaho Glacier, just before the trail again reaches timberline, you will begin to see a series of signs warning you not to venture north of the trail.

Finally, two miles before you reach the trailhead the trail again drops into a forest of spruce, subalpine fir and lodgepole pine as it descends to the Rainbow Lakes area, and soon it begins to follow a wire fence that Boulder claims to be the boundary line of its property. You should arrive at the Rainbow Lakes Campground about three hours after leaving the glacier overlook.

South Arapaho Peak

South Willow Falls

★

Eagles Nest Wilderness Area
day hike

Distance: 8.9 miles (round trip)

Walking time: 5½ hours

Elevations: 1,160 ft. gain/loss
Mesa Cortina Trailhead (start): 9,210 ft.
South Willow Falls: 10,120 ft.

Trail: Well marked, well maintained

Season: Summer through mid-fall. The higher parts of the trail are generally covered with snow from late November through late June.

Vicinity: Near Silverthorne

Maps: Frisco, Willow Lakes (*USGS*)
Vail, Frisco, Dillon (*Trails Illustrated #108*)

Information: http://colorado.utahtrails.com/southwillowfalls.html
http://www.fs.fed.us/r2/whiteriver/ (*White River National Forest)*
phone: 970-468-5400 . *(Dillon Ranger District)*

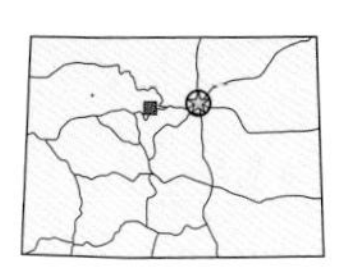

Take exit 205 from I-70 and drive north into Silverthorne. Just 0.3 mile after leaving the highway you will come to a stoplight where you must turn left onto Wildernest Road. After driving 0.2 mile south on Wildernest you will come to a bridge, beyond which the road forks. Bear right at the fork and within another 100 feet you will see Buffalo Drive where you must turn left. Continue west on Buffalo Drive, passing two car dealerships, and after 0.7 mile you will see Lake View Drive on the right. Continue 0.5 mile on Lake View to Aspen Drive; turn left and within 0.2 mile you will come to a parking lot on the right side of the road. The Trailhead is located near a Forest Service sign on the west side of the parking area.

This easy hike follows the Mesa Cortina Trail from the outskirts of Silverthorne into the Eagles Nest Wilderness Area where it meets South Willow Creek and the Gore Range Trail. It then follows the Gore Range Trail up the north side of the fast-flowing stream, finally to arrive at South Willow Falls. Those wanting a longer hike can continue from the falls to Red Buffalo Pass, Gore Lake and beyond. But the walk as far as South Willow Falls makes a nice day hike, and that is what I will describe here.

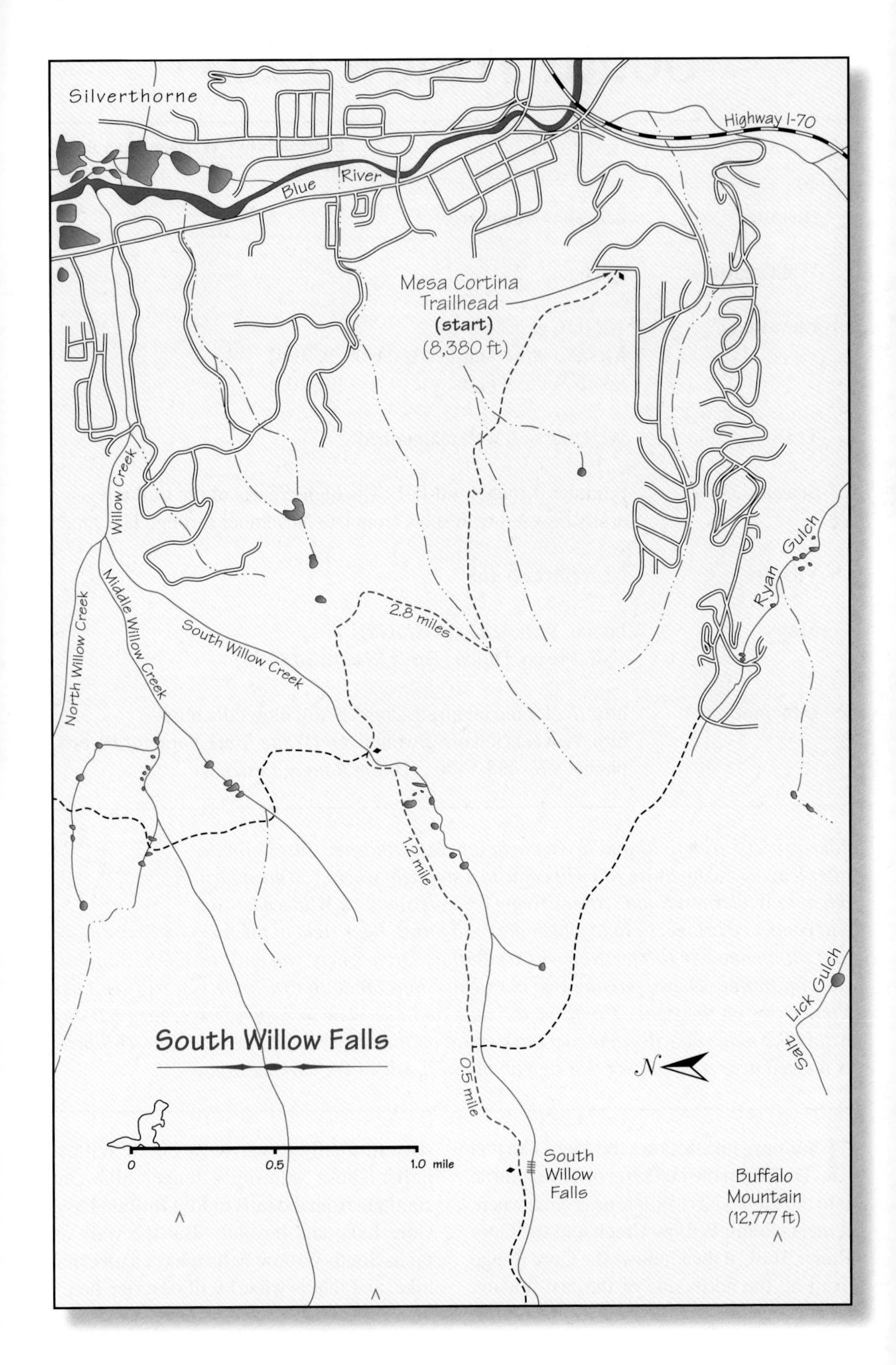

Silverthorne
Highway I-70
Blue River
Mesa Cortina Trailhead (start) (8,380 ft)
Willow Creek
North Willow Creek
Middle Willow Creek
South Willow Creek
2.8 miles
1.2 mile
0.5 mile
Ryan Gulch
Salt Lick Gulch
South Willow Falls
N
0
0.5
1.0 mile
South Willow Falls
Buffalo Mountain (12,777 ft)

South Willow Creek Trail

The trail is flat or even slightly downhill for the first 15 minutes, as it winds through several small meadows. The grassy, flower-filled parks, bordered by quaking aspen, make for a very pleasant beginning to the hike. The only distraction is the noise from traffic on nearby I-70. It will be nearly an hour before the highway noise completely disappears.

After about 20 minutes the trail crosses into the Eagles Nest Wilderness Area, and at about this point it shifts into a long, gentle uphill climb. Soon you will enter an area littered with fallen trees, probably felled by a windstorm many years ago. Most of the new trees in this area are lodgepole pine, but none of them appear to be more than about 50 years old. Fortunately the windfall area does not last long, and soon you are back in a shady forest of standing timber.

2.7 miles from the trailhead the trail crosses South Willow Creek and soon afterward arrives at sign marking the Gore Range Trail. This is a lovely area with several good campsites near the delightful fast-flowing stream. To reach the South Willow Falls you must turn left at the trail junction and follow the Gore Range Trail along the north side of the creek for another 1.7 miles. Notice the presence of many more Engelmann spruce and subalpine fir as you climb out of the montane forest into a subalpine life zone.

Not far from the trail junction the path passes several ponds where a colony of beaver have dammed the creek. Notice the dead trees that line the ponds–killed by the rising water level of the beaver ponds. Then, just over a mile from the Mesa Cortina Trail, you will come to another signed trail junction where the Buffalo Mountain Trail departs on the left.

You will know you are getting close to South Willow Falls when the trail passes

South Willow Falls

South Willow Creek Trail

under a dead tree that is leaning against a huge, 20-foot-high granite boulder on the left side of the trail. Beyond that point the path becomes much rockier, and soon you will see a large outcropping of granite ahead. Just before climbing over the wall of granite the trail makes a sharp right turn, but if you are observant you will notice another hiker-made trail leaving the main trail on the left side of the bend. Turn left here onto the hiker-made trail and within 100 yards you will come to the bottom of South Willow Falls.

Just before you reach the lower falls you will see the remains of an old cabin, probably built in the 1880s. According to author Mary Ellen Gilliland there was a flurry of mining activity in the area in the early 1880s, and many cabins were built along the creek at that time. Whoever lived in the cabin near the lower falls must have had a hearing impairment—the roar from the crashing water is deafening.

The best way to access the top of the falls is to return to the main trail and walk about 150 yards up a series of steep switchbacks. At the top of the switchbacks the trail levels out onto a polished slab of granite, worn smooth long ago by ice age glaciers. Leave the trail at this point and walk a short distance towards the river, where you can see and hear the water cascading down the streambed over a series of precipices and chutes towards the cabin at the bottom.

South Willow Creek

Pitkin Lake

★

Eagles Nest Wilderness Area
day hike

Distance: 9.4 miles (round trip)

Walking time: $6^3/_4$ hours

Elevations: 2,980 ft. gain/loss
Pitkin Creek Trailhead (start): 8,440 ft.
Pitkin Lake: 11,420 ft.

Trail: The trail is will maintained and easy to follow, but it is very steep in places—especially for the first 0.5 mile.

Season: Midsummer through mid-fall. The upper part of the trail is covered with snow most years from early July through mid November.

Vicinity: Near Vail

Maps: Vail East (*USGS*)
Vail, Frisco, Dillon (*Trails Illustrated, #108*)

Information: http://colorado.utahtrails.com/pitkinlake.html
http://www.fs.fed.us/r2/whiteriver/ (*White River National Forest)*
phone: (970) 827-5715 *(Holy Cross Ranger District)*

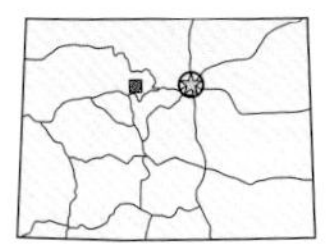

Take exit 180 off Highway I-70 6.3 miles east of Vail. Proceed to the stop sign on the north side of I-70 and turn right onto the frontage road. After another 0.2 mile you will see a small parking area on the right next to a Forest Service sign marking the trailhead. There is private property on both sides of the trailhead, so be sure your car is parked in the public parking area—not on the private property.

Located on the southern flank of the Gore Mountains, this trail is typical of hiking trails in the area. The route takes you up into a steep, heavily glaciated valley, through a series of hanging valleys with stunning scenery, and finally ends at a small lake nestled against the steep ridge in the center of the range. Although not all of the valleys have lakes in them, this same basic pattern is repeated again and again by trails in the Gore Range. With a few exceptions, the trails all dead-end high in the long glaciated valleys because there is no practical way out.

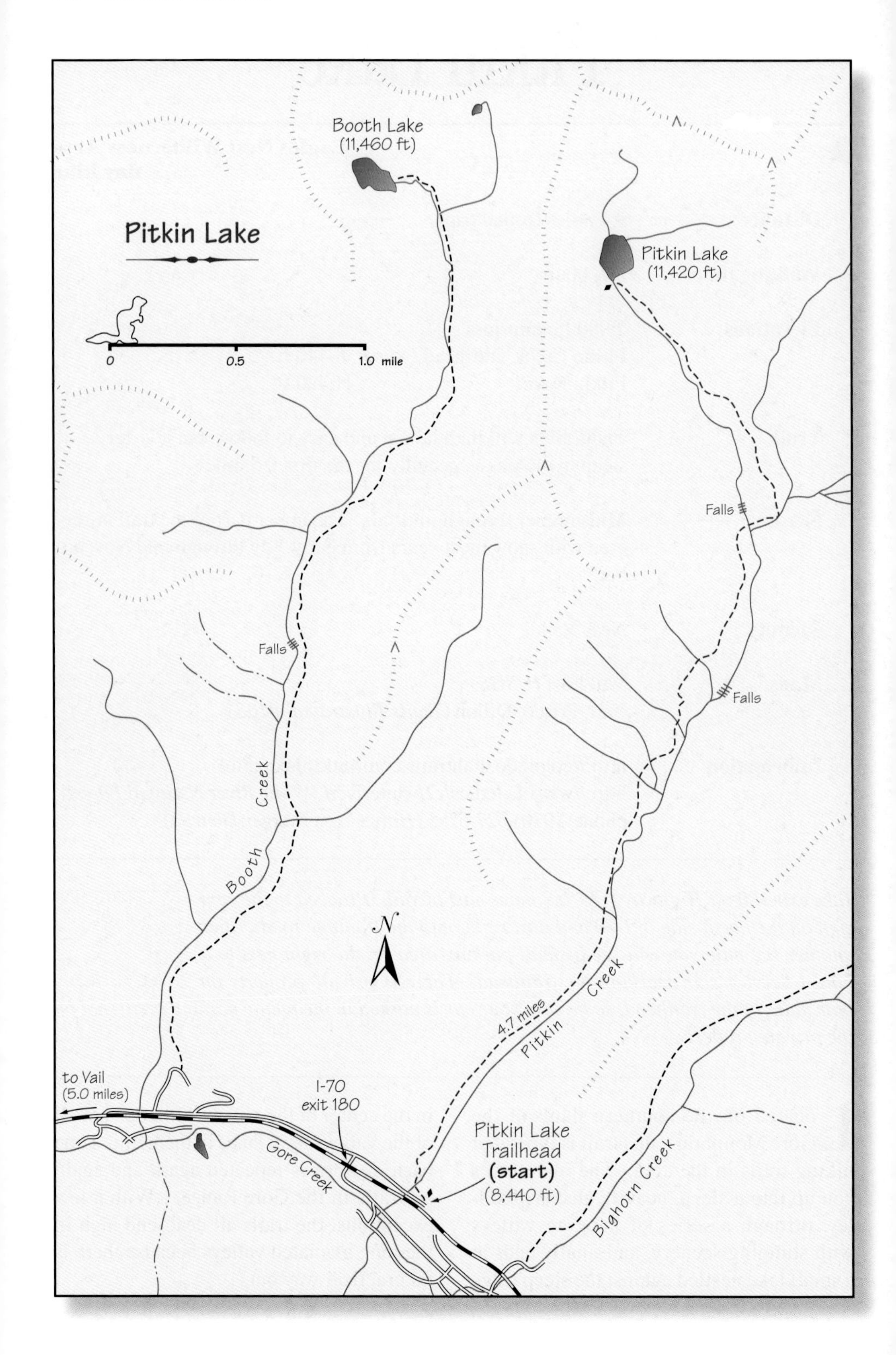
Pitkin Lake
0
0.5
1.0 mile
Booth Lake
(11,460 ft)
Pitkin Lake
(11,420 ft)
Falls
Falls
Falls
Booth Creek
N
4.7 miles
Pitkin Creek
Bighorn Creek
to Vail
(5.0 miles)
I-70
exit 180
Gore Creek
Pitkin Lake
Trailhead
(start)
(8,440 ft)

Pitkin Lake Trail

The Gore Range is one of the most rugged mountain ranges in Colorado. Surprisingly it does not contain any fourteen-thousand-foot peaks, but it does offer some prominent thirteeners. Pitkin Lake Basin, at the end of the trail, is nicely framed by two thirteen-thousand-foot peaks: West Partner (13,041 ft.) on the left and East Partner (13,057 ft.) on the right. East Partner is frequently climbed by walking up its south ridge, which begins on the east side of the lake.

The path starts by following the east side of Pitkin Creek, then after just 100 feet it crosses a small footbridge and continues up the west side of the streambed. There are several condominiums nearby, and for the first hundred feet you will almost feel as though you are walking through someone's backyard. Also I-70 is only a stone's throw from the trailhead and the road noise is overwhelming. But be patient; these signs of civilization will be gone soon enough.

For the first 0.5 mile the trail is very steep, but in about 15 minutes the trail reaches a plateau and levels out in a verdant meadow of grass and wildflowers. I-70 also disappears from sight and sound at this point, and you can begin enjoying the sounds of nature again. By the time the trail reaches the plateau it has already crossed into the Eagles Nest Wilderness Area, so take heart in the knowledge that this part of the forest will never be developed.

For the first 45 minutes of the hike the trail stays well above the west side of Pitkin Creek, then 1.5 miles from the trailhead the trail comes back to the stream, only to veer away again. Soon you will see a waterfall off to your right in the streambed of Pitkin Creek. The trail offers a fine view of the fall, although it never approaches closer than about 250 yards. When you see the fall you are a little more than half way to the lake.

Beyond the waterfall the grade increases again as the trail resumes its climb up the valley. It gains another 400 feet of elevation before reaching the next a bench, where you must cross a boulder field at the bottom of an old avalanche chute. Avalanches must be common in this canyon in the winter; notice the long vertical open areas on the opposite side of the valley where previous slides have knocked down the trees.

At 3.3 miles from the trailhead the path turns right and passes within 200 feet of the bottom of the second waterfall. This is also a flat area with some good campsites nearby, but for me the noise of the fall is a bit too intense to consider stopping. The trail crosses Pitkin Creek just below the waterfall, then stays on the east side of the drainage for the remainder of the climb.

The last 1.3 miles of the hike are frustrating because of the false summits. From the second waterfall you will climb a succession of three more benches, and each time you will probably swear that the lake must be just above you. But the third time you will be correct.

Pitkin Lake is a small lake, about 600 feet in diameter and almost perfectly round. It is surrounded on three sides by ridges, with thirteen-thousand-foot peaks on both the right and left. The lake is well above timberline so don't look for trees, but if you are there in August you won't be disappointed by the alpine wildflowers. The area is very pristine. Also, look for the native trout that spawn in the shallow water on the south side of the lake at the outlet in late summer.

Pitkin Lake

Gore Trail-Upper Cataract Lake

Eagles Nest Wilderness Area
3-day hike

Distance: 19.3 miles (loop)

Walking time: day 1: 5 1/2 hours
day 2: 4 hours
day 3: 3 1/2 hours

Elevations: 2,140 ft. gain/loss
Surprise Trailhead (start): 8,620 ft.
Upper Cataract Lake: 10,756 ft.
Mirror Lake: 10,570 ft.

Trail: Well marked, but poorly maintained in some sections.

Season: Midsummer through mid-fall. The trail is covered with snow from mid-November through June.

Vicinity: Eagles Nest Wilderness Area, near Silverthorne

Maps: Mount Powell (*USGS*)
Green Mountain Reservoir (*Trails Illustrated, #107*)

Information: http://colorado.utahtrails.com/goretrail.html
http://www.fs.fed.us/r2/whiteriver/ *(White River National Forest)*
phone: (970) 468-5400 *(Dillon Ranger District)*

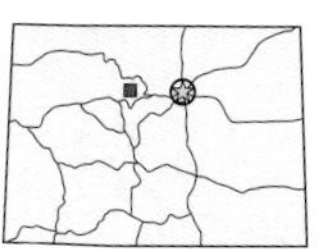

Exit I-70 at Silverthorne and drive north on Highway 9 towards Kremmling. After driving 16 miles you will see a sign marking the road to Green Mountain Reservoir on the left. Turn here, and 5.5 miles after leaving Highway 9 you will come to Cataract Creek Road on your left. Turn left again and drive for another 2.0 miles to Cataract Lake Campground. The Surprise Trailhead is located just 0.3 miles beyond the turnout to the campground.

Note: The Forest Service requires that you pay a users fee of $5.00 per day while your car is parked at the trailhead. You can purchase a permit at the toll booth near the entrance to the campground.

This hike offers a relatively easy three-day tour of six lakes in the Eagles Nest Wilderness Area. Two of the lakes, Upper Cataract and Mirror, lie just below the north side of Eagles Nest Peak, the rugged 13,397-foot peak for which the wilderness

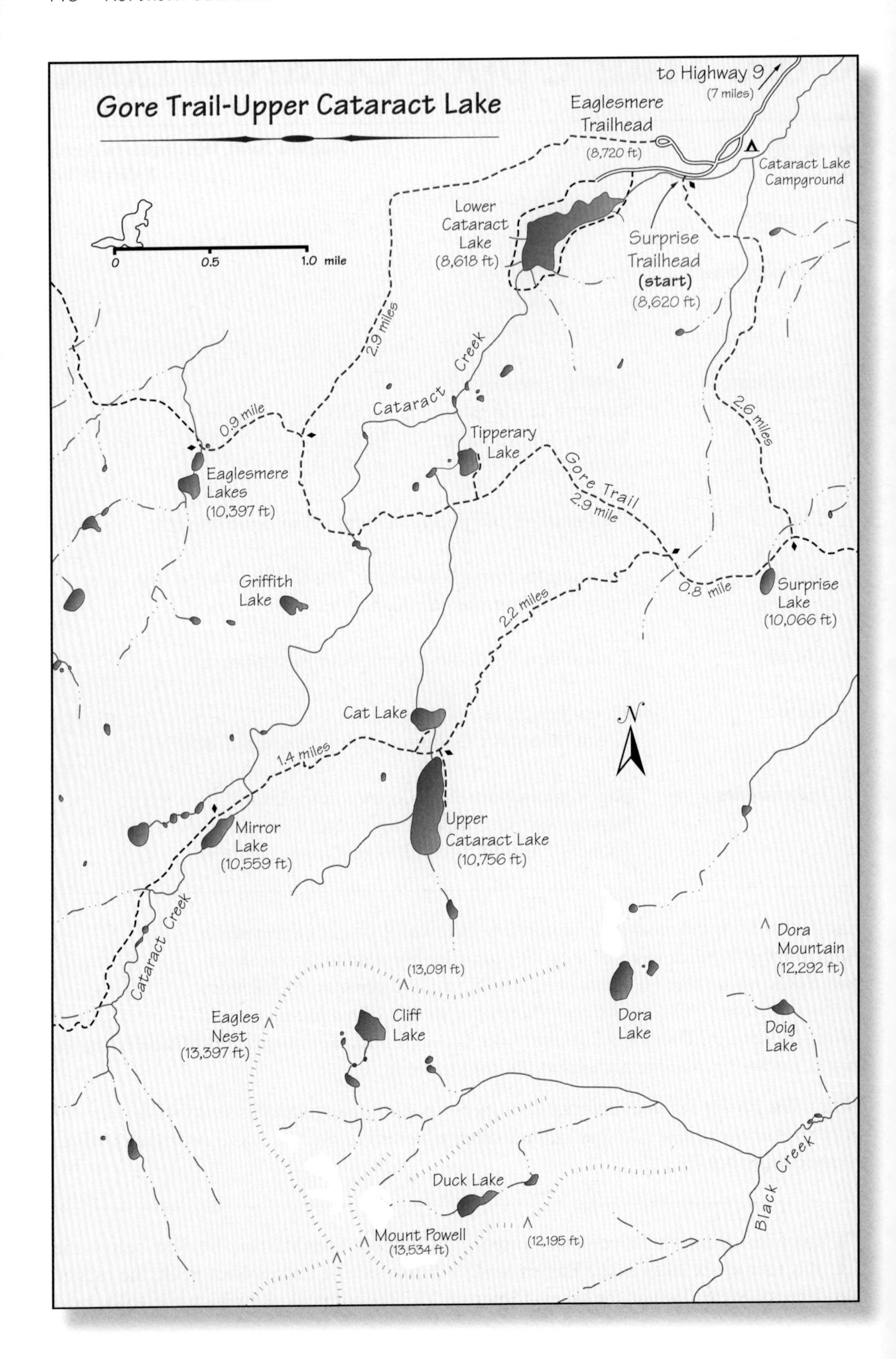

Gore Trail-Upper Cataract Lake
to Highway 9
(7 miles)
Eaglesmere Trailhead
(8,720 ft)
Cataract Lake Campground
Lower Cataract Lake
(8,618 ft)
Surprise Trailhead
(start)
(8,620 ft)
0
0.5
1.0 mile
2.9 miles
Cataract Creek
0.9 mile
Tipperary Lake
Eaglesmere Lakes
(10,397 ft)
Gore Trail
2.9 mile
2.6 miles
0.8 mile
Surprise Lake
(10,066 ft)
Griffith Lake
2.2 miles
Cat Lake
N
1.4 miles
Mirror Lake
(10,559 ft)
Upper Cataract Lake
(10,756 ft)
Cataract Creek
Dora Mountain
(12,292 ft)
(13,091 ft)
Eagles Nest
(13,397 ft)
Cliff Lake
Dora Lake
Doig Lake
Black Creek
Duck Lake
Mount Powell
(13,534 ft)
(12,195 ft)

was named. The Eagles Nest is but one of six local summits that extend along the jagged summit ridge for almost a mile, giving the crest the appearance of a serrated knife blade. Further south along the ridge, 1.2 miles from the Eagles Nest, is Mount Powell, the highest peak in the Gore Range. Mount Powell was named after Major John Wesley Powell, who in 1868 became the first known man to reach its summit.

The Gore Range is remarkably free of the mining activity that has despoiled many of Colorado's other mountain ranges over the past 150 years. Nevertheless its timber and water resources have long been coveted by special interests, and local conservation groups faced a daunting political battle in the mid-1970s when they fought to have the Gore Range protected from development. In the end the Forest Service's plan to sell logging concessions was thwarted, the Denver Water Department was forced to cancel its plans to divert water from the range east to Denver, and the U.S. Department of Transportation had to redesign and reroute I-70 south around the southern tip of the Gore Range. The citizens prevailed, and the Eagles Nest Wilderness Area was created in 1976.

Day 1 (5.8 miles)

From Surprise Trailhead the trail winds steadily upward through an elevation gain of 1,300 feet before arriving, 2.6 miles later, at the junction with the Gore Trail. The forest is surprisingly open near the bottom of the trail, with large open meadows and scattered groves of aspen. But after walking a mile or so you will begin to see fewer aspen and more spruce. There are an unusual number of fallen trees in the upper conifer forest, but the Forest Service has done a good job of cutting them away from the trail itself.

When you reach the Gore Trail turn right, and within 0.2 miles you will see Surprise Lake. Surprise Lake is small—only about

Cat Lake

Cataract Creek

a few minutes you will be on the north shore of the lake.

There are a number of nice campsites around Cataract Lake, the fishing is reasonably good, and the views of Eagles Nest Peak are marvelous. All things considered it is a great place to spend a night. Upper Cataract is very popular, however, and during the summer it is often crowded. If you crave more solitude there are also some nice campsites at Cat Lake, just north of the main trail.

Day 2 (7.7 miles)

Before leaving Upper Cataract Lake I suggest you stash your packs and walk to Mirror Lake, 1.4 miles further along the main trail. Mirror is also a very pretty lake with a nice view of the Eagles Nest from its western shore. The trail to the lake is a pleasant walk through open forest with about 300 feet of elevation gain. There are also some nice places to camp on the northwest side of the lake if you want to extend your trip.

After you have seen Mirror Lake you will have to retrieve your packs at Cataract and retrace your steps for 2.2 miles back to the Gore Trail. When you reach the junction turn left and proceed in a westerly direction. The trail descends gradually for 1.4 miles before reaching the signed spur trail to Tipperary Lake. Tipperary is 200 feet below the main trail, and the descent is quite steep. There are a few campsites at the lake but, unfortunately, Tipperary is a favorite among horseback riders, and there is a great deal of horse manure around the campsites. I sug-

200 yards across—but because it is so close to the trailhead it is a popular destination for day hikers. You may even see a few tents there. 0.6 mile beyond Surprise Lake there is another signed junction, where you must leave the Gore Trail and bear left towards Upper Cataract Lake.

The trail continues upward through dense forest for 1.7 miles after leaving the Gore Trail before coming to an open area with welcome views of the mountain peaks above. You will also be able to see Cat Lake from here, 250 feet below the trail. 0.2 mile later you should see a sign marking the spur trail to Cataract Lake. Turn left and within

gest you continue on for another 0.7 mile to Cataract Creek. Cataract Creek is a very scenic spot along the Gore Trail to stop for the night, and there is a great camping spot just before the trail crosses the creek.

Day 3 (5.8 miles)

0.8 mile after leaving Cataract Creek you will come to another trail junction, where the trail to Lower Cataract Lake leaves the Gore Trail. You will have to bear right here when you return to Lower Cataract, but first take off your packs and continue along the Gore Trail for another 0.9 mile to the Eaglesmere Lakes. These lakes are very popular with day hikers. They aren't as pretty as Mirror or Upper Cataract, but as long as you are so close you should take the time to see them. About 20 minutes from the junction you will come to a swampy area where a small sign points the way up a shallow drainage that leads to the lakes. You will come to the first lake about 200 feet from the main trail, and the second lake will appear soon afterward. The second is the nicer of the two.

After you recover your pack at the junction it is another 2.9 miles down to the Eaglesmere Trailhead on the north side of Lower Cataract Lake. You will notice that this section of trail is in much better condition than the Gore Trail. As you descend you will begin to see more lodgepole pine and aspen, and finally large open areas with fine views over Lower Cataract Lake. Notice the waterfall above the south end of the lake. This is Cataract Falls, after which the creek and the lake were named. Also, one cannot help but notice the unusual abundance of mariposa lilies along this part of the trail. These are the stunning cup-shaped flowers on tall slender stems with three white petals surrounding a yellow interior.

When you reach the Eaglesmere Trailhead it is an easy 0.3 mile walk down the road to the lower Surprise Trailhead where the hike began.

Upper Cataract Lake

Lost Lakes - Devils Causeway

Flat Tops Wilderness Area
3-day hike

Distance: 22.3 miles (loop)

Walking time:
day 1: $4\frac{1}{4}$ hours
day 2: $3\frac{1}{4}$ hours
day 3: $8\frac{1}{4}$ hours

Elevations:
3,330 ft. gain/loss

Stillwater Trailhead (start):	10,280 ft.
Causeway Lake:	10,420 ft.
West Lost Lake:	10,296 ft.
Devils Causeway:	11,800 ft.

Trail: The trail is good in the forested areas. There is no trail on the top of the Flat Tops, but the route is easy to follow.

Season: Midsummer through mid-Fall. The trail is covered with snow from mid-November through June.

Vicinity: Near Steamboat Springs and Yampa

Maps:
Devils Causeway, Trappers Lake (*USGS*)
Flat Tops NE (*Trails Illustrated, #122*)

Information:
http://colorado.utahtrails.com/lostlakes.html
www.fs.fed.us/r2/mbr/ *(Routt National Forest)*
phone: (970) 638-4516 *(Yampa Ranger District)*

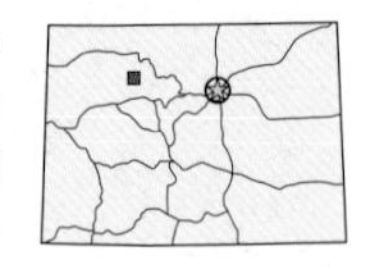

Take the Wolcott exit from I-70 (exit no. 157) and drive north on Highway 131 for 42 miles to the town of Yampa. (If you are starting at Steamboat Springs, drive south for 31 miles to Yampa.) Drive through Yampa and bear left on the west side of the town, following the signs to Stillwater Reservoir. The pavement ends after 7 miles, becoming a graded gravel road that ends 10 miles later at the Stillwater Reservoir. The Stillwater Trailhead is located near the earthen dam at the end of the road.

Hikers are often surprised when they first see the Flat Top Mountains of northern Colorado. Most of the state's other prominent mountain ranges are crowned with rugged peaks of Precambrian granite, gneiss and schist. In contrast, the crest of the

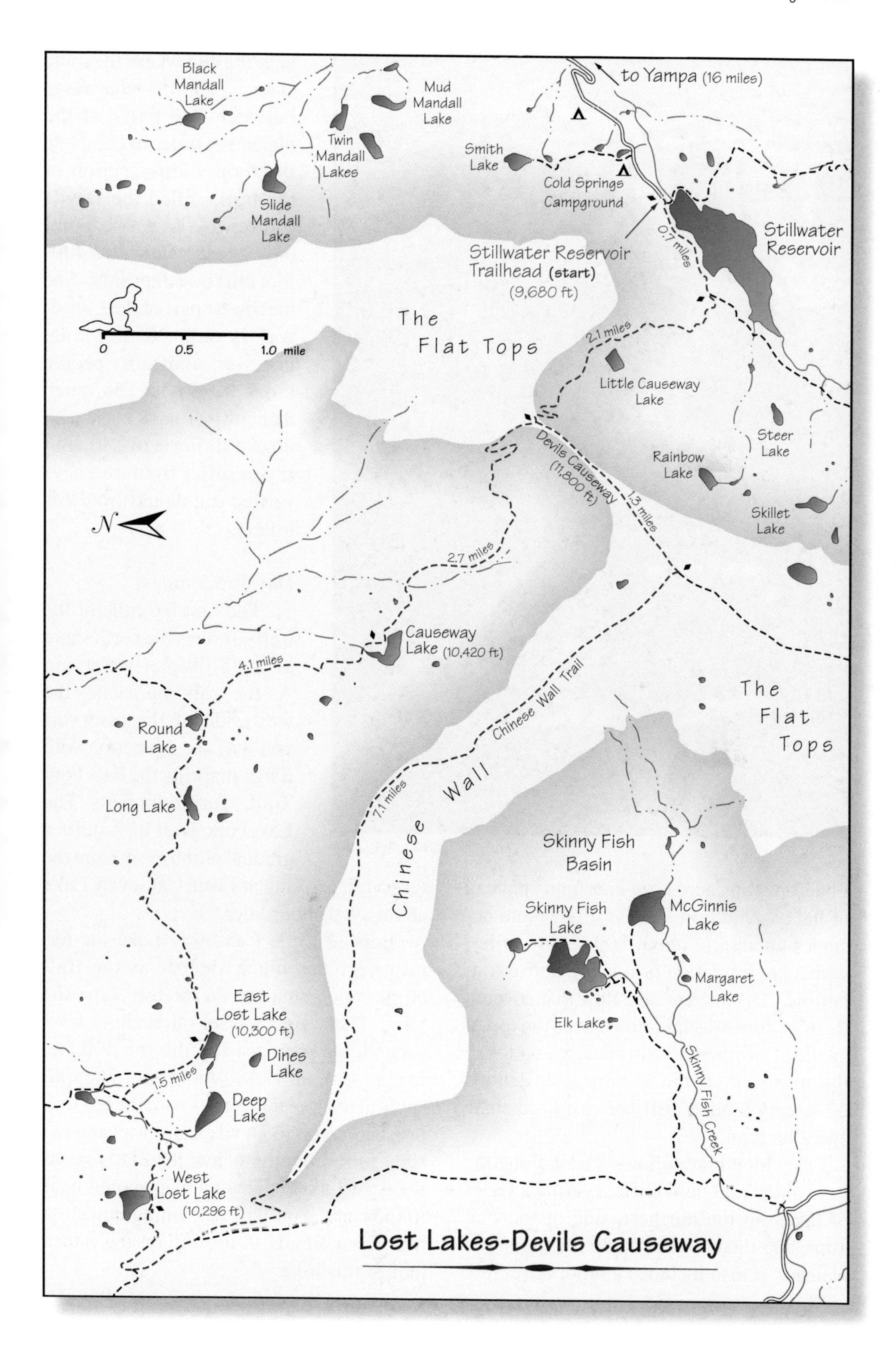

Black Mandall Lake
Mud Mandall Lake
Twin Mandall Lakes
Slide Mandall Lake
Smith Lake
to Yampa (16 miles)
Cold Springs Campground
Stillwater Reservoir
Stillwater Reservoir Trailhead (start)
(9,680 ft)
0.7 miles
0
0.5
1.0 mile
The Flat Tops
2.1 miles
Little Causeway Lake
Devils Causeway (11,800 ft)
1.3 miles
Steer Lake
Rainbow Lake
Skillet Lake
N
2.7 miles
Causeway Lake (10,420 ft)
4.1 miles
Round Lake
Chinese Wall Trail
The Flat Tops
Long Lake
7.1 miles
Chinese Wall
Skinny Fish Basin
Skinny Fish Lake
McGinnis Lake
Margaret Lake
Elk Lake
East Lost Lake
(10,300 ft)
Dines Lake
1.5 miles
Deep Lake
Skinny Fish Creek
West Lost Lake
(10,296 ft)
Lost Lakes-Devils Causeway

East Lost Lake

Flat Tops runs across an enormous plateau of flat basaltic lava. The vast tableland occupies an area of about 500 square miles, with a large fraction of it being above timberline. The ancient lava flow that covered the Flat Tops was laid down over the top of an older sedimentary formation, and today the boundaries of the lava are often defined by steeply eroded cliffs of rusty red shale and alluvium.

This loop hike follows a trail along the base of the alluvium cliffs, visiting a series of lakes on the northern side of the Flat Tops, and then returns along the top of the plateau. It also includes a bit of adventure near the end where the route crosses a knife-edge ridge between two parts of the plateau in order to complete the loop. This section of the trail, called the Devils Causeway, is at one point only 4 feet wide with a 400-foot cliff on either side. The narrowest part of the Causeway is only 20 feet long, however, and most people cross it without too much difficulty (I have even seen dogs walking across it). But if you suffer from excessive vertigo you should avoid this hike.

Day 1 (5.5 miles)

The first 0.6 mile of the trail parallels the north shore of the Stillwater Reservoir. As the trail approaches the west side of the reservoir you will see a junction with a sign marking the East Fork Trail. Turn right here. The East Fork Trail then starts a gradual climb away from the reservoir, arriving at Little Causeway Lake about a half-hour later.

Beyond Little Causeway Lake the terrain becomes much steeper as the trail climbs into a small basin 250 feet above the lake. Then, after a brief interlude of level ground, the path goes up the last 400 feet to the top of an 11,580-foot pass. The trail splits at the top of this pass with the left fork proceeding up to Devils Causeway and the right fork dropping below the Flat Tops to the Lost Lakes. For now you should bear to the right. You will be coming down the trail from Devils Causeway on the return half of this hike.

North side of the Chinese Wall

Before leaving your vantage point at the summit of the pass you should stop to examine the route ahead. For the next eight miles you will be walking below a long succession of reddish-brown cliffs that define the northern side of the Chinese Wall. When you reach the western end of the Wall the trail will turn south and climb to the top of the Flat Tops before doubling back to the southern end of thc Devils Causeway.

An hour and a half after leaving the pass below Devils Causeway the trail passes the east side of Causeway Lake, and unless you got a very early start I suggest you spend the night here. Causeway is quite a pretty lake, the fishing is good, and there are plenty of excellent campsites. If you are interested in fishing, pay particular attention to the outlet on the north end of the lake. This is a spawning area for the lake's cutthroat trout, and you can often see 15-inch fish lazing along the bottom of the shallow, fast-flowing stream. Unfortunately they don't often take bait while they are spawning.

Day 2 (5.6 miles)

From Causeway Lake the trail winds lazily through the dense conifer forest past five more lakes before reaching West Lost Lake, the next recommended campsite. Round Lake, the next lake you will encounter, is located about 45 minutes from Causeway Lake. You will also see a trail junction here where you must bear left. Soon after leaving Round Lake you will see Long Lake, then, after another 2.0 miles, East Lost Lake. East Lost Lake is, in my opinion, the prettiest lake you will see on this hike. It is especially scenic early in the morning when the mirror-smooth water reflects the sun-drenched cliffs behind it. There is also a fine campsite near its western end. I have done this loop in the past as an overnighter, camping at East Lost Lake instead of Causeway and West Lost Lakes. This is a tiring trip, however, with 12.7 miles on the second day and little time to enjoy the scenic beauty of the area.

Trail south of West Lost Lake

Looking west from the top of the Flat Tops

In the next 0.6 mile after East Lost Lake you will pass two more trail junctions, where two other trails lead north past a nearby unnamed lake. Bear left in both cases. Then, after another ten minutes you will pass a third trail taking off to the south. This is the 0.3-mile-long spur that leads to Deep Lake. Deep Lake is also quite a pretty lake, and if you have the time you should definitely see it. There are no signs to mark the trail, but the junction is easy to spot. You will see the spur heading abruptly upward from the main trail near the bottom of a small drainage about 25 minutes after leaving East Lost Lake.

West Lost Lake, the recommended campsite for the second night, is just 15 minutes beyond the spur to Deep Lake. If it is still early in the day you may want to continue on, but it is better to resist this temptation because there are no other good campsites beyond West Long Lake. Better to spend the night here and get a good rest for the 11.2-mile walk back to the trailhead tomorrow. You will find some good campsites on the southwest side of the lake.

Day 3 (11.2 miles)

The third day of this hike is the most tiring; you still have an 11.2-mile walk across the Flat Tops ahead of you to complete the loop. Unfortunately, unless you spend a night above timberline, there is really no way to break up the trip. But although this portion of the hike is a bit long it is certainly not without its compensations. During the summer large sections of the Flat Tops are decorated with a stunning array of wildflowers, and the views from the edge of the mesa into the valleys below are superb.

For the next 2.5 miles after leaving West Lost Lake the trail climbs to the top of the Flat Tops, finally reaching relatively level ground on the north end of the mountain at an altitude of 11,600 feet. The top of the mesa is just high enough to be devoid of trees yet low enough to be covered with a carpet of grasses and wildflowers, and an exhilarating feeling of freshness and openness seems to pervade the air. It is a marvelous diversion from the dense conifer forest below the mountain.

Soon after reaching the top of the Flat Tops the trail begins to grow faint, and the presence of many sheep trails on the tundra also adds confusion. Unfortunately, sheep are allowed to graze in the wilderness area in the summer and parts of the fragile tundra have been seriously degraded by their presence. Just remember to stay on the north, or highest side of the plateau, and don't be tempted to follow any trail that goes south more than a few hundred yards from the crest of the mesa. Most of the sheep trails lead to the lower southern side where there is more water. As you proceed, pause occasionally to look down from the top of the cliffs and enjoy the fine views of the Chinese Wall and the Lost Lakes below.

After you have walked about 3.0 miles along the top of the mesa you will begin to notice a series of widely spaced poles and monuments that have been erected by the Forest Service to mark the trail. The Forest Service route, however, veers away from the crest of the Flat Tops, and it is more interesting to continue walking nearer the rim. Either way, you will eventually run into the well-used trail leading to Devils Causeway. When you reach this trail turn left, and after about 20 minutes you will see the unique formation.

The Devils Causeway is actually a thin strip of land that forms a bridge between two of the Flat Tops mesas. At its narrowest point the bridge is only four feet wide. There is an almost sheer drop of 400 feet on either side, and for some people walking across the Causeway can be an unnerving experience. The total length of the span is about 200 feet, and no technical skill is required to make the traverse. Were it not for the exposure it would be an easy walk—just watch your footing and don't stop to look over the edge. If you are absolutely terrified of heights you can always get down on all fours and crawl across. The really narrow part is only 20 feet long.

On the north side of Devils Causeway the trail drops down 200 feet to the top of the pass between Causeway and Little Causeway Lakes, and from there you must retrace your footsteps for 2.8 miles back to Stillwater Reservoir and the trailhead.

Crossing the Devils Causeway

Hooper and Keener Lakes

Flat Tops Wilderness Area
day hike

Distance:	7.7 miles (round trip)
Walking time:	5 hours
Elevations:	1,400 ft. gain/loss Stillwater Trailhead (start): 10,270 ft. Hooper Lake: 10,864 ft. Keener Lake: 10,780 ft.
Trail:	Generally well marked and well maintained
Season:	Midsummer through mid-fall. The higher parts of the trail are often covered with snow from late November through June.
Vicinity:	Near Steamboat Springs and Yampa
Maps:	Orno Peak, Dome Peak (*USGS*) Flat Tops NE, Trappers Lake (*Trails Illustrated, #122*)
Information:	http://colorado.utahtrails.com/hooperlake.html www.fs.fed.us/r2/mbr/ *(Routt National Forest)* phone: (970) 638-4516 *(Yampa Ranger District)*

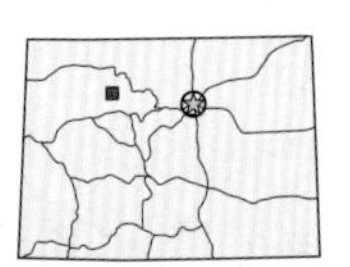

Take the Wolcott exit from I-70 (exit no. 157) and drive north on Highway 131 for 42 miles to the town of Yampa. (If you are starting at Steamboat Springs, drive south for 31 miles to Yampa.) Drive through Yampa and bear left on the west side of the town, following the signs to Stillwater Reservoir. The pavement ends after 7 miles, becoming a graded gravel road that ends 10 miles later at the Stillwater Reservoir. The Stillwater Trailhead is located near the earthen dam at the end of the road.

The unpredictable nature of Colorado weather dictates that you should always begin your hikes as early in the morning as possible, but on this particular trail there are several additional reasons why you should get an early start. First, the Stillwater Trailhead is also where the popular hike to the Devils Causeway begins (page 144), and by 9:00 a.m. the limited parking space at the trailhead is often completely filled. Second, both Hooper and Keener lakes are situated directly east of a long stretch of spectacular cliffs below Flat Top Mountain, and the early morning views from across the lakes are

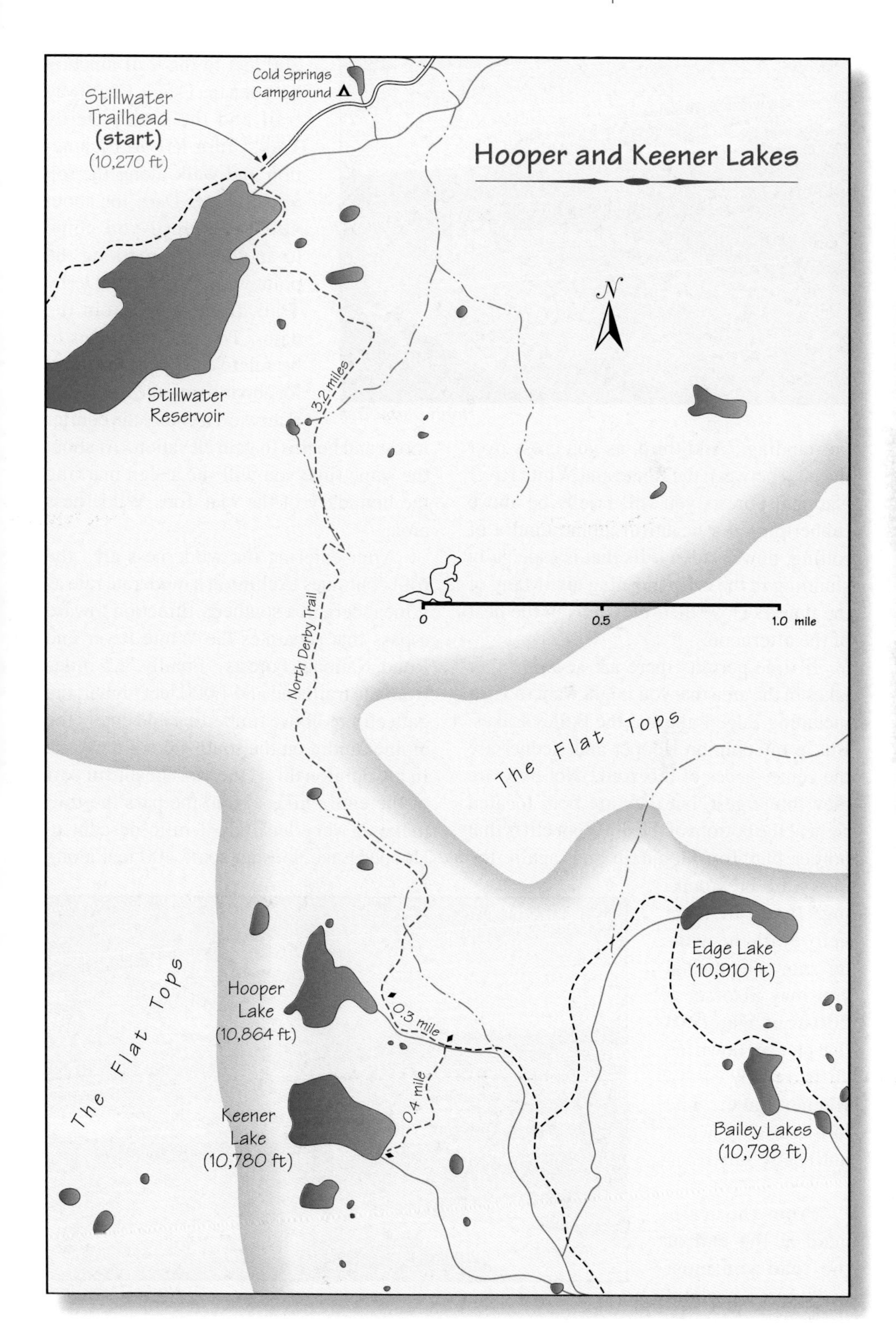

Hooper and Keener Lakes
Cold Springs Campground
Stillwater Trailhead (start) (10,270 ft)
Stillwater Reservoir
3.2 miles
N
North Derby Trail
0
0.5
1.0 mile
The Flat Tops
The Flat Tops
Edge Lake (10,910 ft)
Hooper Lake (10,864 ft)
0.3 mile
0.4 mile
Keener Lake (10,780 ft)
Bailey Lakes (10,798 ft)

North Derby Trail

outstanding. And third, as you cross over the pass between the Route and White River National Forests you will briefly be above timberline on a beautiful alpine tundra of rolling, flower-laden hills that is especially stunning in the crisp morning air. Many of the flowers close their blossoms in the heat of the afternoon.

If time permits there are several other lakes in the area that you might want to visit, including Edge Lake and the Bailey Lakes. But in my opinion Hooper and Keener are the centerpieces of this trail. Not only are they the largest, but they are both located right at the bottom of the 600-foot cliffs that border Flat Top Mountain and, again, the views are breathtaking. If you are there before all the winter snow has melted you may also see a 200-foot waterfall that plunges down the cliffs directly east of Keener Lake. The fall is usually active until early July.

From the trailhead at the end of the road you must walk east for about 200 feet to the trail junction between the Devils Causeway trail and the North Derby Trail. Turn left at the junction and walk along the top of Stillwater Dam for about 400 yards until you come to another sign marking the point where the North Derby Trail drops down from the dam. The trail continues to be relatively open and level for about 10 minutes, but soon afterward it enters the conifer forest and begins to gain elevation. At about the same time you will see a sign marking the boundary of the Flat Tops Wilderness area.

After entering the wilderness area the trail continues to climb at a moderate rate as it meanders in a southerly direction toward a pass that separates the White River and Routt National Forests. Finally, 2.2 miles from the trailhead and 1,000 feet higher, the path climbs above timberline and enters the alpine tundra on the south side of the pass. In my opinion this is the most beautiful part of the entire hike. From the pass the trail makes a very leisurely 1-mile descent to Hooper Lake, loosing some 400 feet along

North Derby Trail

Hooper Lake

the way and reentering an open forest just before it reaches the lake. There are flat top mountains on both sides of the trail here, however the mountain on the east side where Edge Lake is located is not as impressive as the one on the west side of the trail. The path is rather vague in a few places in this grassy alpine meadow and you may loose it. When in doubt keep to the west. If you loose the trail and stray too far to the east you can easily miss the lakes.

As the trail approaches Hooper Lake it turns to the west, but then just before arriving at the lake it swings again to the east, away from the lake, and never actually gets closer than about 150 feet from the water. It is conceivable that if one were not paying attention he could miss the lake, although it's eastern arm is visible from the trail. Of the two lakes visited on this hike, Hooper is the best one for camping. There are plenty of nice camp sites along the east side of the lake.

From Hooper Lake the trail follows the drainage eastward for just 0.2 mile before passing the spur that leads to Keener Lake. There are no signs at the junction and the trail is not terribly distinct, but if you are observant you will easily spot it. Look for a small stone monument, and also a collection of bleached white bones—the remains of a deer that must have died there many years ago. From the junction it is another 0.4-mile walk through the well-shaded forest to the lake. Just before reaching the lake the trail breaks out of the trees into a small clearing on the east side of the water with an exquisite view of Flat Top Mountain above the far shore. There is no need to go farther–this is the best place you will find to stop for a lunch break before heading back to the trailhead.

Keener Lake

Skinny Fish and McGinnis Lakes

★★

Flat Tops Wilderness Area
day hike

Distance: 6.2 miles (round trip)

Walking time: 4 hours

Elevations: 1,100 ft. gain/loss
Skinny Fish Trailhead (start): 9,235 ft.
Skinny Fish Lake: 10,192 ft.
McGinnis Lake: 10,158 ft.

Trail: Well marked, well maintained

Season: Midsummer through mid-fall. The higher parts of the trail are generally covered with snow from late November through mid-June.

Vicinity: Near Meeker and Yampa

Maps: Devils Causeway (*USGS*)
Flat Tops NE, Trappers Lake (*Trails Illustrated, #122*)

Information: http://colorado.utahtrails.com/skinnyfishlake.html
http://www.fs.fed.us/r2/whiteriver/ (*White River National Forest*)
phone: (970) 878-4039 (*Blanco Ranger District*)

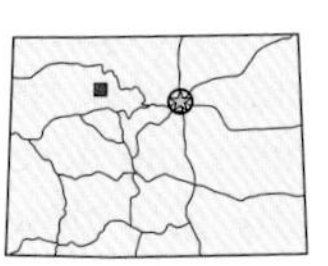

Drive east out of Meeker on Highway 13 for 1.5 miles until you see a sign on the right directing you to Trappers Lake. Turn here and continue for another 39 miles on County Road 8 until you come to the junction with Forest Road 205. Turn right again, following the signs to Trappers Lake, and 6.5 miles after leaving the junction you will see the Skinny Fish Lake Trailhead on your left. You can also get to Road 205 and the Skinny Fish Lake Trailhead by driving west from Yampa on County Road 17. See page 157 for further instructions.

This relatively easy hike will take you to two gorgeous lakes in the Flat Tops Wilderness Area. The lakes are beautifully situated below the Flat Tops on the west side of the picturesque Chinese Wall, and their shores are shaded by a prolific forest of Engelmann spruce and subalpine fir. The fishing is relatively good in both lakes, and if you wish to spend more than one day in the area there are plenty of good camp sites nearby. It is unfortunate that the area around Trappers Lake suffered a devastating

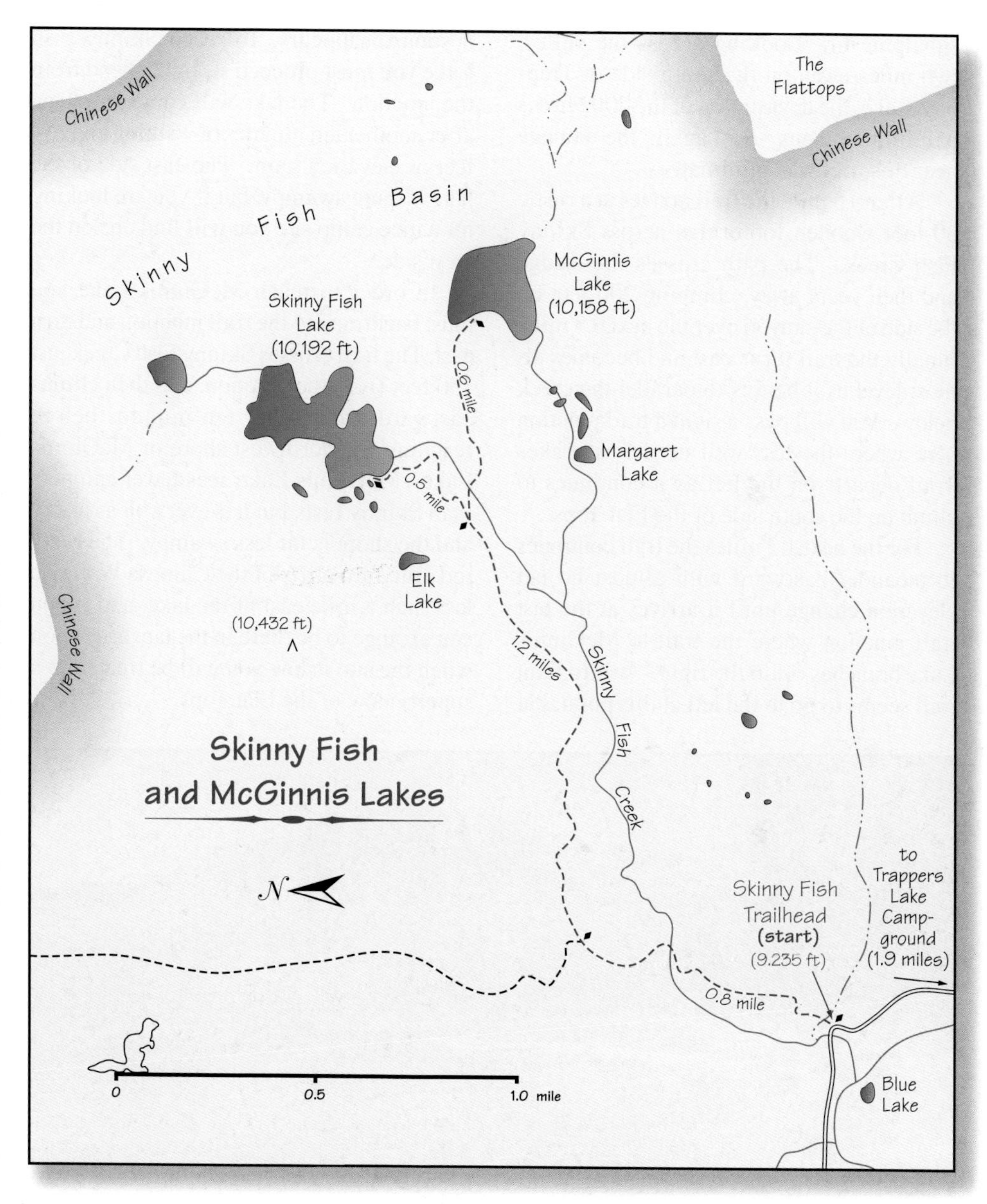

fire during the summer of 2002, and some brief sections of this trail do pass through the burned area. However most of the burn occurred south and west of the lakes, and the damage in the Skinny Fish drainage was not extensive. Both lakes are still delightful places to spend an afternoon, and the trails are almost as scenic as ever.

Immediately after leaving the parking area the trail crosses a small stream, and then begins to climb upward through a lush meadow of yellow wildflowers and scattered groves of quaking aspen. The parking area below continues to be visible for the next 10 minutes before the trail finally enters the primary forest of Engelmann spruce and subalpine fir. Looking across the valley, two miles away on the south side of Trappers Lake, the devastation of the 2002 fire is painfully obvious. But, again, the damage near this trail was minimal.

After 0.5 mile the trail arrives at a rustic 30-foot wooden footbridge across Skinny Fish Creek. The path crosses the bridge and then veers away, climbing 200 feet up the side of the canyon over the next 0.3 mile. Finally the trail turns east and becomes almost level as it begins to parallel the creek below. You will pass a signed trail junction here where the less well used Lost Lakes Trail departs on the left as it continues to climb up the south side of the Flat Tops.

For the next 1.2 miles the trail continues to meander eastward with almost no net elevation change until it arrives at the last trail junction where the trail to McGinnis Lake branches off to the right. A third faint trail seems to go to the left at this point, but it soon disappears. To reach Skinny Fish Lake you must proceed straight ahead from the junction. The lake will come into view after another ten minutes of walking and 150 feet of elevation gain. The east side of the lake is quite swampy, but if you are looking for a nice camp site you will find one on the west side.

In order to reach McGinnis Lake you must backtrack to the trail junction and turn east. The trail crosses Skinny Fish Creek just 150 feet from the junction, and then climbs eastward for another ten minutes before reaching the northwest shore of McGinnis Lake. McGinnis Lake sees fewer campers than Skinny Fish, but it is every bit as pretty and the shore is far less swampy. The rusty red alluvium cliffs of the Chinese Wall rise less than a mile east of the lake, and if you can arrange to be there in the late afternoon when the sun is low you will be treated to a superb view of the Flat Tops.

Skinny Fish Lake

Flat Tops

Flat Tops Wilderness Area
shuttle car required
day hike

Distance:	9.5 miles (plus 67 miles by shuttle car)
Walking time:	6 hours
Elevations:	1,730 ft. gain, 1,130 ft. loss Scotts Lake Trailhead (start): 9,680 ft. Flat Top Mountain: 11,410 ft. Stillwater Trailhead: 10,280 ft.
Trail:	Well marked, easy to follow
Season:	Midsummer through mid-fall. The trail is covered with snow from mid-November through June.
Vicinity:	Near Steamboat Springs, Meeker, and Yampa
Maps:	Devils Causeway, Trappers Lake (*USGS*) Flat Tops NE (*Trails Illustrated, #122*)
Information:	http://colorado.utahtrails.com/flattops.html www.fs.fed.us/r2/mbr/ *(Routt National Forest)* http://www.fs.fed.us/r2/whiteriver/ *(White River National Forest)* phone: (970) 638-4516 *(Yampa Ranger District)*

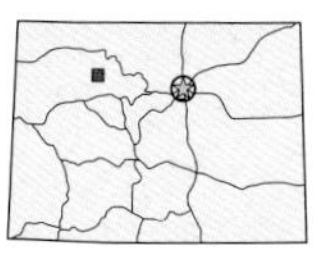

Take the Wolcott exit from I-70 (exit no. 157) and drive north on Highway 131 for 42 miles to the town of Yampa. (If you are starting at Steamboat Springs, drive south for 31 miles to Yampa.) Drive through Yampa and bear left on the west side of the town, following the signs to Yamcolo Reservoir and Stillwater Reservoir. The pavement ends after 7 miles, becoming a graded gravel road that ends 10 miles later at the Stillwater Reservoir. The Stillwater Trailhead is located near the earthen dam at the end of the road. This is where the hike will end and where you should leave a shuttle car.

To get to Trappers Lake, where the hike begins, return to Yampa and drive north on Main Street for 0.5 mile until you see a sign marking County Road 17. Turn left onto this road and follow the signs to Dunkley Pass. You will be driving first on Road 17 and finally on Road 8. All but the first 5.4 miles will be on a graded gravel road. 7 miles beyond Dunkley Pass you will come to a junction in the road where you must bear left, or south. 10 miles further you will cross Ripple Creek Pass, and 6 miles beyond Ripple Creek Pass you will come to Forest

Road 205 where you must turn left toward Trappers Lake. From that point on the road is clearly marked with signs directing you to Trappers Lake. Just before you get to Trappers Lake you will see a road on the right leading to the campground. Take this road across a small wooden bridge, and 1.0 mile further you will see a parking lot on the left side of the road where the Scotts Lake Trailhead is located.

The unusual flat-topped mountains of the Flat Tops Wilderness Area provide a unique opportunity to hike in an alpine-tundra ecological environment without a great deal of tiring elevation gain. Most high-altitude hikes in Colorado are in very rugged terrain with little level ground. But in the Flat Tops once you have climbed above timberline there is very little up and down on the trails. A hike on the top of the Flat Tops is more of a pleasant stroll through fields of high alpine wildflowers, with panoramas of a vast treeless tundra, more like what one would expect to find in northern Canada.

The reason that the mountains are so flat can be traced to a period of prolonged volcanic activity that occurred in Colorado about 35 million years ago. During that time the underlying sedimentary rock was covered with a thick layer of hard basaltic lava. Later, when the land began to rise and erode the basalt acted like a capstone, protecting the softer rock beneath. Today we see flat topped mountains in the places that were covered by the ancient lava flows, while the surrounding valleys and canyons are sculpted from the softer underlying sedimentary layers.

Near the junction with the Chinese Wall Trail

The best time to hike on the Flat Tops is in early July, while there are still patches of snow above timberline. While the snow is melting there are hundreds of tiny streams and rivulets on the mountains, feeding diminutive alpine lakes and nourishing a panoply of alpine wildflowers. The growing season is very short at these elevations, so the tiny flowers must complete their life cycle and bear seeds very quickly. Most species burst into bloom almost immediately after the snow cover is gone, causing the tundra to explode in a profusion of July color. Be warned, however, that mosquitoes are a problem at this time of year, so if you are hiking in July be sure to take along some insect repellent.

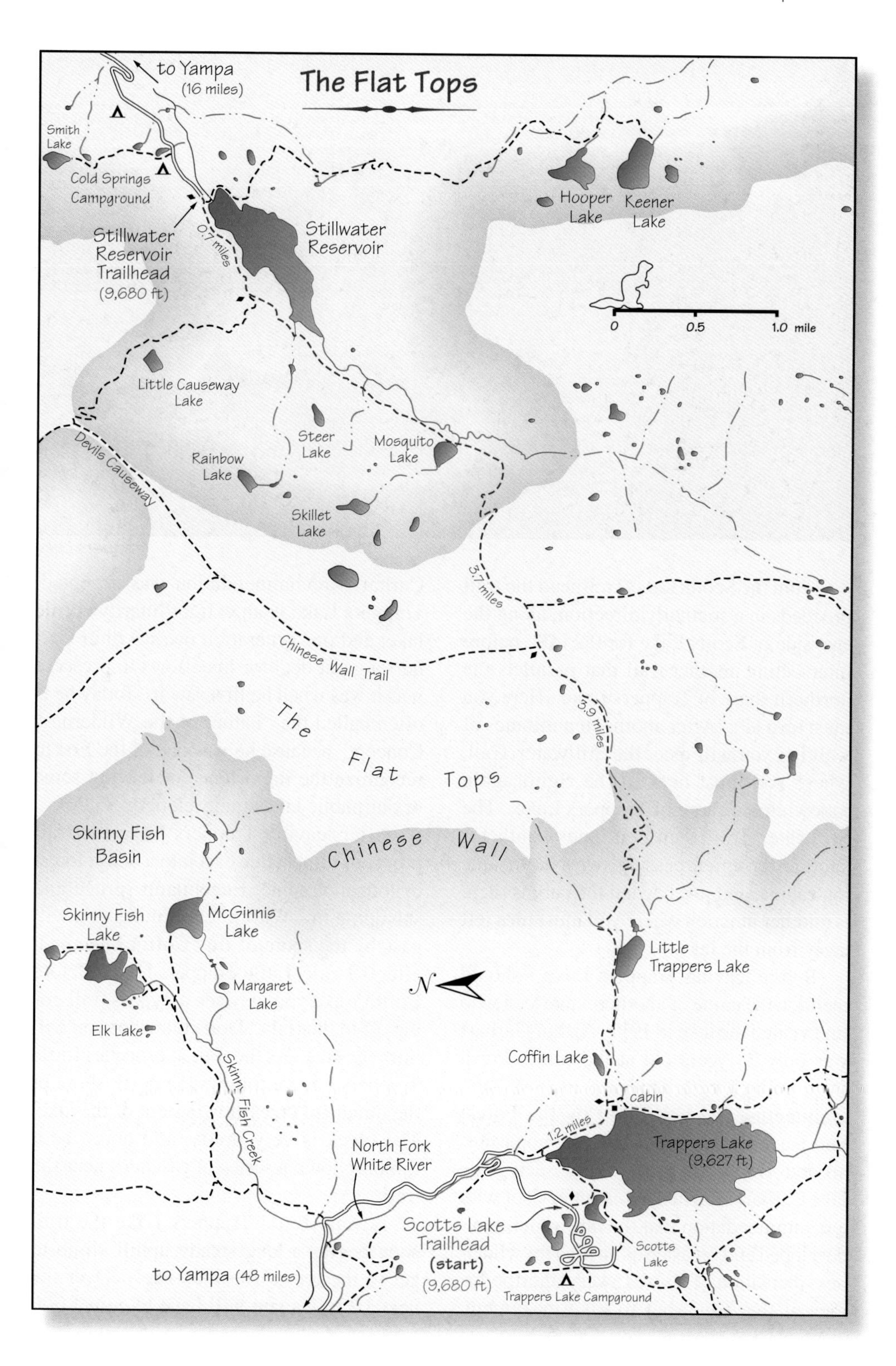
The Flat Tops
to Yampa (16 miles)
Smith Lake
Cold Springs Campground
Stillwater Reservoir Trailhead (9,680 ft)
0.7 miles
Stillwater Reservoir
Hooper Lake
Keener Lake
0
0.5
1.0 mile
Little Causeway Lake
Devils Causeway
Steer Lake
Mosquito Lake
Rainbow Lake
Skillet Lake
3.7 miles
Chinese Wall Trail
3.9 miles
The Flat Tops
Skinny Fish Basin
Chinese Wall
Skinny Fish Lake
McGinnis Lake
Little Trappers Lake
N
Margaret Lake
Elk Lake
Skinny Fish Creek
Coffin Lake
cabin
1.2 miles
Trappers Lake (9,627 ft)
North Fork White River
Scotts Lake Trailhead (start) (9,680 ft)
Scotts Lake
to Yampa (48 miles)
Trappers Lake Campground

Trappers Lake

From the Scotts Lake Trailhead the trail proceeds in a southerly direction, along the east side of Scotts Lake for 0.2 mile before intersecting another trail that parallels the northern shore of Trappers Lake. Here you must turn left. After another ten minutes of walking you will meet the Stillwater Trail, where you must bear to the right, again following the shore of Trappers Lake. The Stillwater Trail then continues south for another 0.5 mile, passing two picturesque log cabins, and just beyond the cabins there is another junction where you must turn left away from the lake.

Before leaving Trappers Lake I should mention the name of another American who first visited the lake in 1919. Arthur Carhart was only 27 years old at the time. Fresh from college with a degree in landscape architecture, he was hired by the Forest Service to survey a road and plot homesites around Trappers Lake. After seeing the lake Carhart returned to his supervisor with a recommendation that the lake remain undeveloped and set aside as an area for wilderness recreation. This was a very unorthodox idea at that time, but to his amazement, Carhart's recommendation was accepted. Trappers Lake is an extraordinarily scenic lake, and our generation owes Arthur Carhart a great deal for his efforts to preserve it as it was when he first saw it. Today he is often called the "Father of the Wilderness Concept" because he was one of the first to recognize the importance of leaving some of our public lands undeveloped.

After leaving Trappers Lake the trail proceeds almost due east into a dense forest of lodgepole pine, Engelmann spruce and subalpine fir. Within ten minutes you will pass by the shore of tiny Coffin Lake and, after 0.9 mile, Little Trappers Lake. Before Coffin Lake you may see a bypass trail going off to the right. Don't take it or you will miss the lake. As the trail approaches Little Trappers Lake it follows the north shore of the unnamed creek flowing out of the lake. The creek is very pretty, and noisy, as it tumbles down a series of cascades near the trail.

Beyond Little Trappers Lake the trail soon begins a long steady uphill climb to get to the top of the Flat Tops. Over the next 1.7 miles you will have to gain 1,000 feet of elevation before the trail levels out again. But the climb is an interesting one. Watch the size of the trees diminish as you gain altitude. The Engelmann spruce go from over 100 feet to five feet high before they disappear completely at about 11,000 feet.

Once you reach the top of the Flat Tops the trees are replaced by a tundra of flowers and grasses. Thousands on individual dots of color litter the ground. Individually, each flower is a masterpiece of design. Some are shaped like little yellow teacups, some look like miniature purple elephant heads, complete with ears and trunks, and some look so much like bells you can almost hear them chiming in the wind. Together the alpine flowers produce delightful blends of blue, purple, white, green, and especially yellow across the rolling highland. Elsewhere, much of the Flat Tops tundra has been destroyed by grazing sheep, but for some reason the land along this trail has been exempted from the grazing. It remains pristine.

3.9 miles after leaving Trappers Lake the trail arrives at a junction where an old weathered sign marks the beginning of the Chinese Wall Trail. Continue straight ahead at this point, staying on the Stillwater Trail. Then, 0.3 mile later, you will see yet another sign marking the beginning of the West Mountain Trail on your right. Again, continue straight.

The West Mountain Trail marks the highest point on this hike (11,412 feet), and a short way beyond that point the Stillwater Trail begins its descent to Stillwater Reservoir. The trail makes the descent in four distinct stages. First it drops about 200 feet into a small basin on the eastern side of the mountain. Then after a brief respite it drops another 200 feet into a slightly larger and flatter basin. Next it looses another 400 feet of elevation before leveling out once again on the shore of Mosquito Lake. Finally, 0.2 mile beyond Mosquito Lake, the trail begins its final 300 feet of gradual descent to the Stillwater Trailhead. The last four miles of the trail follow the western side of Stillwater Creek and Stillwater Reservoir.

Stillwater Reservoir

Dark Canyon

Raggeds Wilderness Area
day hike

Distance:	13.6 miles (round trip) (plus 14.3 miles by shuttle car)
Walking time:	8 1/2 hours
Elevations:	1,260 ft. gain, 3,360 ft. loss Horse Ranch Park Trailhead (start): 8,920 ft. top of Devils Stairway: 8,200 ft. Erickson Springs Trailhead: 6,820 ft.
Trail:	Generally well marked and easy to follow.
Season:	Midsummer through mid-fall. The upper parts of the trail are usually covered with snow from mid-November through early July.
Vicinity:	near Crested Butte
Maps:	Marcellina Mountain, Paonia Reservoir *(USGS)* Kebler Pass *(Trails Illustrated, #133)*
Information:	http://colorado.utahtrails.com/darkcanyon.html http://www.fs.fed.us/r2/gmug/ *(Gunnison National Forest)* phone: (970) 527-4131 *(Paonia Ranger District)*

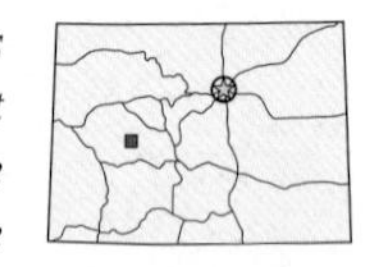

Drive west through Crested Butte on Whiterock Avenue. This road runs into the Kebler Pass Road on the edge of town, and from there you must continue driving west to the pass. After 6.9 miles you will arrive at the top of Kebler Pass, and from there another 4.5 miles will bring you to the signed road on the right leading to Horse Ranch Park. Turn right into Horse Ranch Park and drive the last 0.4 mile, bearing right at the last two junctions, to the trailhead. This is where the hike begins. (Note: if you don't have a 4WD vehicle you may have to park in the lower 2WD parking area and walk the last 0.2 mile.)

To reach the Erickson Springs Trailhead where the hike ends you must continue west on the Kebler Pass Road for another 13.4 miles from the Horse Ranch Park turnoff to the Erickson Springs Recreation Area. Turn right into the recreation area and drive 0.5 mile to the trailhead and parking area at the end of the road.

Dark Canyon is often explored as a short day hike from the Erickson Springs Trailhead. From there the trail follows along the north side of Anthracite Creek, entering almost immediately into one of the most scenic parts of Dark Canyon. Anthracite Creek is a fast-flowing stream that is very popular with fly fishermen, and Erickson Springs Campground is conveniently located just a few hundred feet from the trailhead. The walk up Anthracite Creek makes a fine alternative to the hike described below if a shuttle to the Horse Ranch Park Trailhead cannot be arranged. If a shuttle can be arranged, however, I recommend beginning your hike at Horse Ranch Park. The total distance between the two trailheads is 13.6 miles, which may be too long for some, but the trail is an easy, mostly downhill path. Furthermore you probably won't see anyone else until you reach Anthracite Creek.

Another alternative is to begin the hike at the Ruby Anthracite Trailhead instead of at Horse Ranch Park. The 5-mile-long Ruby Anthracite Trail meets the Horse Ranch Park Trail at a well marked junction 8.5 miles north of Horse Ranch Park, so if you choose this route the hike will be 3.5 miles shorter. The disadvantage is that the trail crosses Ruby Anthracite Creek, necessitating a 760-foot climb out of the canyon to meet the Horse Ranch Park Trail. Furthermore this trail is not as well used and may be harder to follow. The Ruby Anthracite Trailhead, however, is easy to find. It is located on the Kebler Pass Road 7.3 miles from the Erickson Springs turnoff going toward Crested Butte. The trailhead is clearly marked by a highway sign on the left side of the road.

From Horse Ranch Park the trail immediately enters a dense forest of aspen trees as it meanders up a gentle grade in a northerly direction. There are several ponds of water along the left side of the path, and after a half-hour the trail passes through a swampy meadow that contains at least three large beaver dams. Beavers are very shy animals

Marcellina Mountain

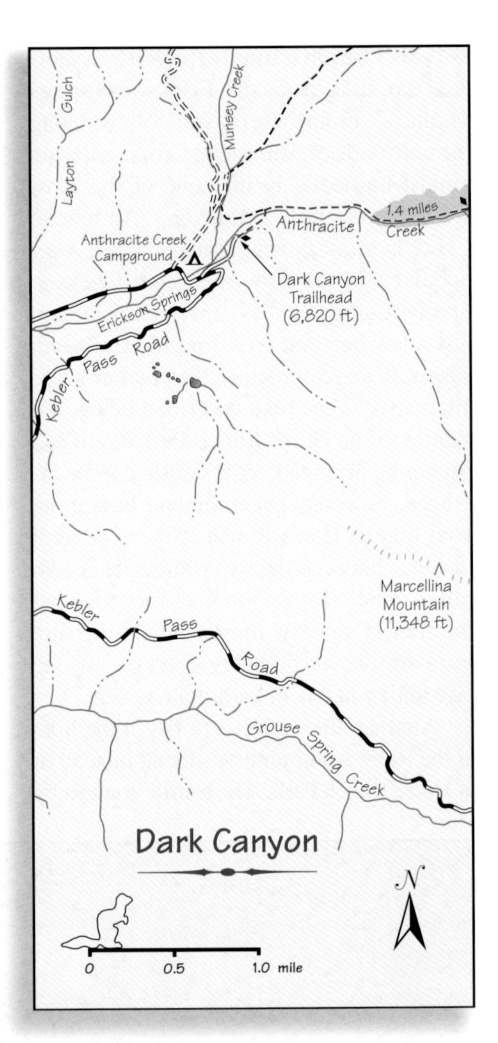

and it rare to see them, but the fresh mud and newly cut aspen sticks on their dams prove their presence.

For the first hour the trail seldom breaks out of the trees, so your views of the surrounding countryside will be limited. But after 1.7 miles the trail crosses a low ridge with a fine view of Marcellina Mountain and Ruby Anthracite Canyon to the west. At 9,400 feet this ridge represents the highest point on the Dark Canyon Trail.

Ten minutes after leaving the ridge you will come to a trail junction where an old, weathered sign marks the trail to O-Be-Joyful Pass on the right. Bear left at the junction and in another 0.2 mile you will come to Dyke Creek. Dyke Creek usually contains little more than a small trickle of water–you will have no trouble getting across it with dry feet–but it does mark the boundary of the Raggeds Wilderness Area. The remainder of the hike will be within the confines of the wilderness area.

Anthracite Creek

Over the next 5.6 miles the trail crosses three more named drainages, Gold Creek, Sardine Creek, and Silver Creek, as well as several unnamed ones. All flow westward, down the slopes into Ruby Anthracite Creek, but most of them carry very little water. Silver Creek stands out as the exception. Not only does Silver Creek have a respectable flow rate, but it is also quite pretty. The stream is shaded by a large grove of blue spruce trees, and there are several nice campsites in the area. If you plan to make this hike an overnight excursion and want

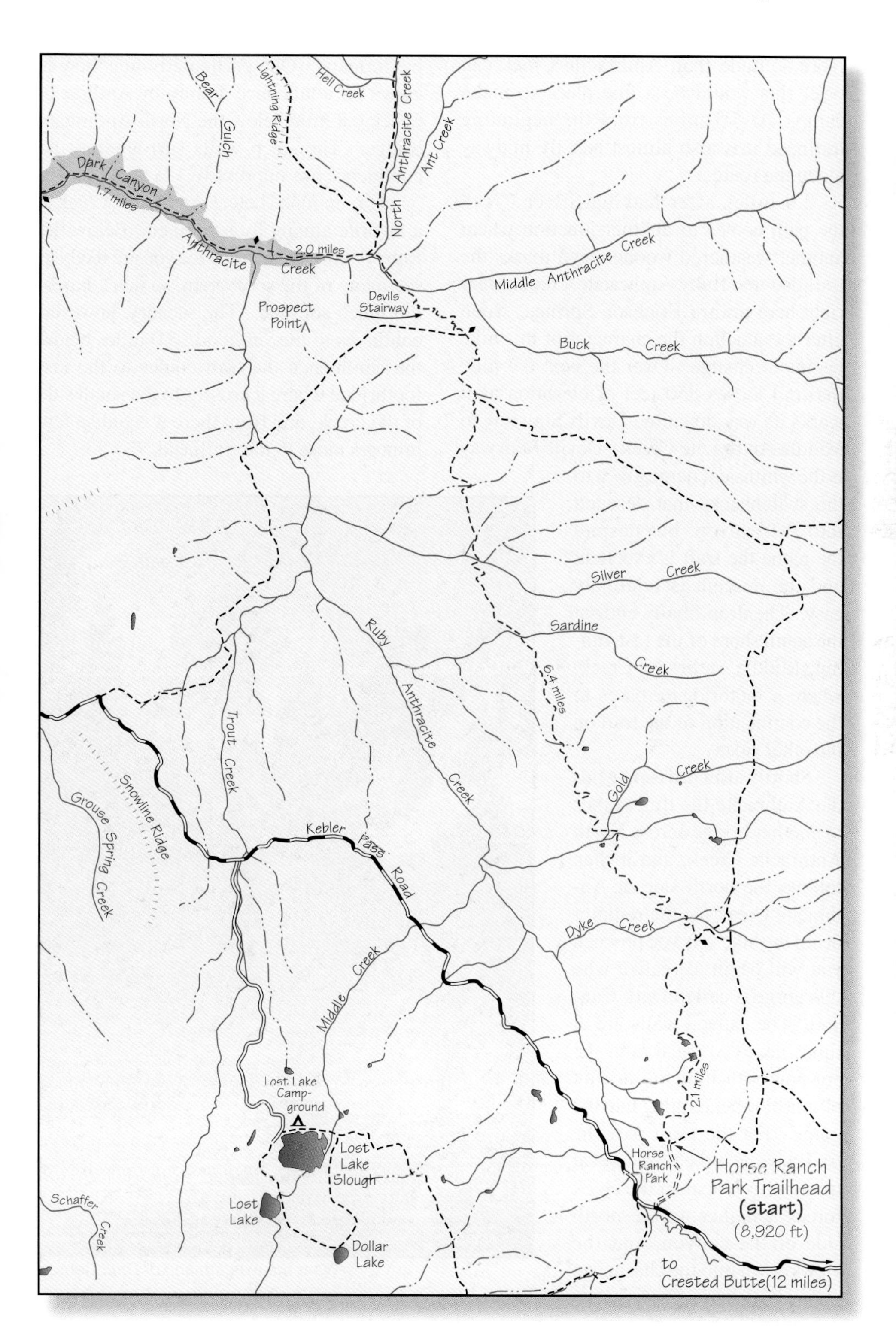
Bear Gulch
Lightning Ridge
Hell Creek
North Anthracite Creek
Ant Creek
Dark Canyon
1.7 miles
Anthracite Creek
2.0 miles
Middle Anthracite Creek
Prospect Point
Devils Stairway
Buck Creek
Silver Creek
Sardine Creek
Ruby Anthracite Creek
6.4 miles
Gold Creek
Trout Creek
Snowline Ridge
Grouse Spring Creek
Kebler Pass Road
Dyke Creek
Middle Creek
Lost Lake Campground
Lost Lake Slough
Lost Lake
Dollar Lake
Schaffer Creek
2.1 miles
Horse Ranch Park
Horse Ranch Park Trailhead
(start)
(8,920 ft)
to Crested Butte(12 miles)

more solitude than Anthracite Creek can offer this would be a fine place to make camp. At 6.5 miles from the beginning trailhead it is also almost exactly midway along the route.

2.0 miles after leaving Silver Creek the path comes to another junction where another weathered wooden sign marks the trail down to Ruby Anthracite Creek. Bear right here toward Erickson Springs. Soon after the junction the character of this hike begins to change. Over the next 0.9 mile the trail looses 850 feet of elevation as it works its way down the Devils Stairway to Middle Anthracite Creek. Devils Stairway is the whimsical name given to the switchbacks that descend into the canyon, but despite the name the trail is excellent and the descent is relatively easy. The drop finally ends at the south shore of the fast-running Middle Anthracite Creek, where a footbridge crosses to the continuation of the trail on the other side.

Shortly after crossing Middle Anthracite the trail comes to another bridge across North Anthracite Creek, and it then follows the north side of Anthracite Creek for the remainder of the hike. As you proceed you will begin to realize why this gorge is called Dark Canyon. The canyon walls are at times nearly vertical, and the volcanic cliffs limit the amount of sunshine penetrating into the gorge. For the most part the trail stays near the water, but at times the rubble near the creek forces it higher up the north side of the canyon, and the views down into the chasm can be dramatic. One particularly fine view is above the confluence with Ruby Anthracite Creek 0.8 mile below the North Anthracite bridge. The steep walls surrounding the confluence are impressive.

As mentioned before Anthracite Creek is a favorite among fly fishermen. Below the Ruby Anthracite confluence you are likely to see many of the sportsmen, so don't expect too much solitude. The scenery, however, continues to the very end. 3.0 miles below the confluence the trail comes to the last footbridge where it crosses to the south side of the creek, and from there it is only a few minutes more to the trailhead.

Near the western end of Dark Canyon

Lamphier Lake/Gunsight Pass

Fossil Ridge Wilderness Area
day hike

Distance: 7.4 miles (round trip to all points of interest)

Walking time: 5 1/4 hours

Elevations: 2,150 ft. gain/loss
Lamphier Lake Trailhead (start): 10,040 ft.
Lamphier Lake: 11,700 ft.
Gunsight Pass: 12,167 ft.

Trail: well maintained as far as Lamphier Lake.

Season: Midsummer through mid-fall. The higher parts of the trail are usually covered with snow from November through mid-July.

Vicinity: Near Gunnison

Maps: Fairview Peak *(USGS)*
Gunnison/Pitkin *(Trails Illustrated, #132)*

Information: http://colorado.utahtrails.com/lamphierlake.html
http://www.fs.fed.us/r2/gmug/ *(Gunnison National Forest)*
phone: (970) 641-0471 *(Gunnison Ranger District)*

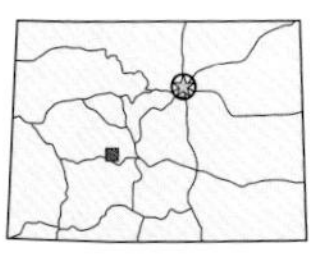

Drive east of Gunnison on Highway 50 for 11.5 miles to the town of Parlin. Shortly after entering Parlin you will see a sign marking a paved road on the left that goes to Ohio and Pitkin. Turn left here and continue another 8.5 miles to the town of Ohio. In the center of Ohio you will see another sign marking the graded gravel road to Gold Creek. Turn left again and drive north for 6.8 miles to the Gold Creek Campground. The Lamphier Lake Trailhead is located on the left side of the road just 250 yards beyond the entrance to the campground. Don't be confused by the Fossil Ridge Trailhead. It is also on the left side of the road, but only 70 yards beyond the entrance to the Gold Creek Campground.

Like most of the alpine lakes in Colorado, Lamphier Lake is a glacial tarn that was scooped out of the surrounding rock during the last ice age. The well-protected lake lies just below timberline, and is surrounded on three sides by Broncho Mountain, Square Top Mountain, and Fossil Mountain. Lamphier is particularly scenic early in the morning when Square Top Mountain is reflected from its shaded, mirror-smooth surface; if

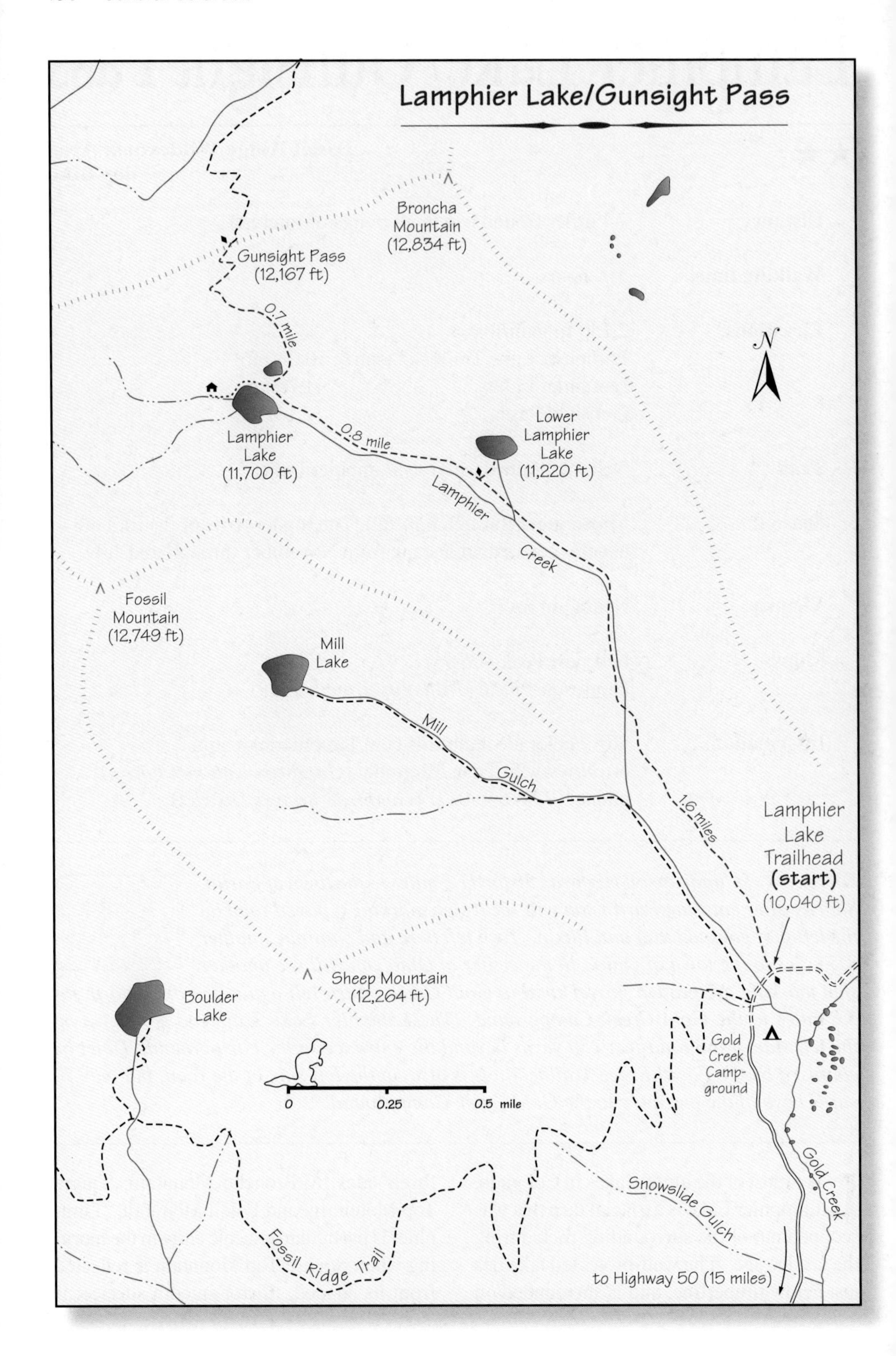

Lamphier Lake/Gunsight Pass
Broncha Mountain (12,834 ft)
Gunsight Pass (12,167 ft)
0.7 mile
Lamphier Lake (11,700 ft)
0.8 mile
Lower Lamphier Lake (11,220 ft)
Lamphier Creek
N
Fossil Mountain (12,749 ft)
Mill Lake
Mill Gulch
1.6 miles
Lamphier Lake Trailhead
(start)
(10,040 ft)
Boulder Lake
Sheep Mountain (12,264 ft)
Gold Creek Campground
0
0.25
0.5 mile
Gold Creek
Snowslide Gulch
Fossil Ridge Trail
to Highway 50 (15 miles)

you are interested in seeing this morning spectacle you will find several fine camping sites in the trees along its eastern shore.

Although Lamphier lies in a bowl of granite and schist, the ridge above the west side of the lake is capped with an unusual layer of limestone. Looking up at the ridge you can easily distinguish the difference in color and texture between the granite and its sedimentary overburden. Most of Colorado was once covered with sedimentary rock, but in the 45 million years since the Rocky Mountains were uplifted most of the overlying sedimentary deposits have eroded away. The ridge above Lamphier Lake is called Fossil Ridge because, like most limestone formations, it is rich in fossils.

The trail to Lamphier Lake is initially very rocky as it climbs up what must be a deposit of rubble left behind by the ancient glacier. Fortunately the grade not steep, and after the first mile the trail is not so rocky. After a half-hour the route crosses to the west side of Lamphier Creek and then, five minutes later, crosses back to the east. The trail stays on the east side of Lamphier Creek for the remainder of the hike.

25 minutes after the second crossing of Lamphier you will cross another small creek that drains Lower Lamphier Lake. According to most maps there is a spur trail that follows this drainage up to the lower lake, but that is wrong. There is no trail up the drainage below Lower Lamphier Lake. The trail to Lower Lamphier Lake actually begins another 0.2 mile up the main trail from the drainage, but the spur is unmarked and because of the error on the maps few people visit Lower Lamphier Lake. That is a pity because the lake is certainly worth visiting. It is nearly as big as the upper lake, and it is only a 4-minute walk from the main trail.

Make a note of the time as you cross the small creek that drains Lower Lamphier Lake, and when you have walked another 5-6 minutes start looking for an unmarked trail on the right. It is easy to miss the trail

Fossil Ridge above Lamphier Lake

Lower Lamphier Lake

if you aren't looking for it, but if you are observant you should be able to see it. There are also two old blaze marks on nearby trees at the point where the unmarked trail branches off.

The trail to Lower Lamphier Lake is easy to follow once you have found it. It runs in a northeasterly direction with very little change in elevation for 0.2 mile before ending on the southern shore of the lake. Lower Lamphier appears to be somewhat shallower than its sister lake but it is still very pretty, and the fact that you will probably have the lake all to yourself only adds to the serenity.

0.8 mile after passing the spur to Lower Lamphier Lake the trail passes the east side of the larger upper lake. The scenery in this area is magnificent, with Fossil Ridge looming high above the west side of the calm water. There is also a small cabin nearby that you will probably want to check out. The cabin is not visible from the lake but it is only a short distance away. Walk to the west side of the lake and follow a shallow drainage upward to a small grassy meadow 100 yards from the water. When you reach the middle of the meadow turn to your right and look up into the trees. There, 200 feet from the bottom of the drainage you will see the log structure. The cabin appears to have been built sometime in the early 1900s, but it is still in remarkably good condition.

After passing Lamphier Lake the trail seems to dead end on the west side of a nearby pond. To reach Gunsight Pass you should leave the trail and walk around the east side of the pond to a drainage on its north side. There, 150 feet north of the pond on the left side of the drainage, you will see a 6-foot vertical pole. This pole marks the beginning of the trail up to Gunsight Pass. The trail is marked by a series of poles and cairns that climb up the rocky slope to the pass 467 feet above the lake.

From the name one might expect Gunsight Pass to be a well-defined notch in the saddle between Square Top Mountain and Broncho Mountain. However, in my opinion, the pass looks nothing like a gunsight. Rather it is simply the lowest point in the gently sloping saddle, only 667 feet lower than nearby Broncho Mountain. Nevertheless there are splendid views from the top of the pass into Lamphier Creek Basin to the south and Brush Creek Basin to the north. Although this hike ends here you can see the trail below continuing down to Brush Creek and on to South Lottis Trailhead on the northern edge of the Fossil Ridge Wilderness Area.

Cabin near Lamphier Lake

Maroon - Snowmass Trail

Maroon Bells - Snowmass Wilderness
shuttle car required
2-day hike

Distance: 16.3 miles
(plus 21 miles by car)

Walking time: day 1: 8 hours
day 2: 4 1/4 hours

Elevations: 3,120 ft. gain, 4,282 ft. loss
Maroon Lake Trailhead (start): 9,580 ft.
Buckskin Pass: 12,462 ft.
Snowmass Lake: 10,980 ft.
Maroon-Snowmass Trailhead: 8,420 ft.

Trail: Popular, well maintained trail

Season: Midsummer through mid-fall. The higher parts of the trail are usually covered with snow from mid-November through late July.

Vicinity: near Aspen

Maps: Maroon bells, Snowmass Mountain, Capitol Peak *(USGS)*
Maroon Bells *(Trails Illustrated, #128)*

Information: http://colorado.utahtrails.com/maroonsnowmass.html
http://www.fs.fed.us/r2/whiteriver/ *(White River National Forest)*
phone: 970-925-3445 *(Aspen Ranger District)*

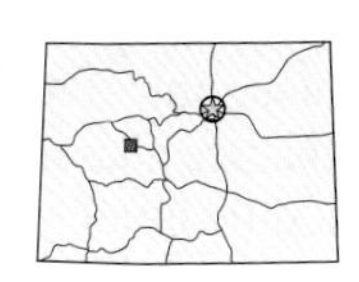

Drive 0.5 mile west of Aspen on Highway 82 until you reach Maroon Creek Road, then turn left and continue south for another 9.5 miles. The Maroon Creek Road ends at Maroon Lake where the trailhead is located, and overnight parking is permitted in the large lot a few hundred yards east of the lake. When planning this hike you should be aware that the road to Maroon Lake is closed to most traffic during the summer months between the hours of 8:30 a.m. and 5:00 p.m. Alternatively, the Roaring Fork Transit Agency provides daily bus service between the Ruby Park bus terminal in Aspen and Maroon Lake during the summer. The buses run about every 20 minutes from 9:00 a.m. to 5:00 p.m., and the fare is only $5.00 for a round trip.

The hike ends at the Maroon-Snowmass trailhead, near Snowmass Village. To get there drive 4.2 miles west of Aspen on Highway 82 to Brush Creek Road. Turn left on Brush

Creek Road and drive another 4.8 mile to Divide Road. Turn right on Divide Road and after another 1.3 miles you will arrive at the Krabloonic Restaurant and dog kennels. From there you must continue straight on a narrow dirt road that descends from the paved road. The dirt road ends after 1.8 miles at the entrance to the Snowmass Falls Ranch. You will see the trailhead and parking area just outside the entrance gate to the ranch.

There is also public bus service between Aspen and Divide Road most of the year. The buses leave Ruby Park every 30 minutes and stop at Divide Road on their way to Snowmass Village. When you get off the bus at Divide Road you will still have a 3.1-mile walk to the trailhead, but their are so many other hikers traveling this route in the summer that your chances of hitching a ride to the trailhead are good. The first bus leaves Aspen for Snowmass Village at 6:15 a.m., and the last bus leaves Snowmass at 1:15 p.m.

If you don't have two cars you can use the public buses to get to and from Aspen and the trailheads for this hike, but since the last bus leaves Snowmass Village at 1:15 in the afternoon it is only practical to use the buses if you do the hike in reverse. That is, you should start at the Maroon-Snowmass Trailhead and finish at Maroon Lake. The disadvantages: (1) this will add another 1,160 feet of elevation gain to the hike, and (2) you will miss the early morning view of the Maroon Bells peaks over Maroon Lake and Crater Lake – two of the most beautiful sights in all of Colorado.

The Maroon Bells-Snowmass Wilderness Area is one of Colorado's oldest wilderness areas, and in the 45 years since its creation it has also become one of the state's most popular outdoor recreational destinations. Tens of thousands of visitors flock to Maroon Lake every summer to see the famous Maroon Bells Peaks, and thousands more feel compelled to walk the tails into the heart of the Elk Mountains. If you are looking for solitude this isn't where you should be, but if you seek inspiration this is definitely your hike. There are a few scenes along this trail, especially on the first day, that are guaranteed to make your blood run a little faster.

Day 1 (8.5 miles)

As you begin this hike your eyes will invariably be drawn to two purplish, bell-shaped peaks that rise about three miles southwest of the lake. These are the famous Maroon Bells: Maroon Peak (14,156 ft.) on the left and North Maroon Peak (14,014 ft.) slightly in front of it on the right. If you are fortunate enough to be starting out in the early morning calm of a clear day you will also see a reflection of the Bells in the smooth, shaded water of Maroon Lake. This composition has stirred the hearts of many

Below Buckskin Pass (Maroon Peak on left)

Len Shoemaker Ridge above Crater Lake

an artist over the years, and as a result the Maroon Bells are now among the most photographed mountains in Colorado.

As the trail proceeds along the north shore of Maroon Lake you will soon see a large pile of wood protruding from the water about 20 feet from the shore. This is an old beaver lodge. There are beaver in the lake, although they are not often seen. After 0.4 mile the trail leaves the western end of Maroon Lake and begins climbing up the valley towards Crater Lake. For the next half hour the Maroon Bells will continue to be directly in front of you and rarely out of sight.

1.8 miles from the trailhead you will come to a trail junction where you must turn right to stay on the Maroon-Snowmass Trail, but before turning you should first continue straight for 0.1 mile to Crater Lake and another exquisite view of the Maroon Bells. North Maroon Peak is only 1.0 mile from the west end of Crater lake, and again the setting is unforgettable—especially early in the morning. Another well known fourteener is also visible above the opposite shore of the lake: Pyramid Peak (14,018 ft.) lies just 1.2 miles to the southeast.

From the Crater Lake trail junction the path climbs unrelentingly for the next 2.8 miles before reaching the top of the pass. With an elevation gain of 2,340 feet, this is the most grueling part of the entire hike. But you can take heart in knowing that once you reach Buckskin Pass the remainder of the hike will be almost entirely downhill. The route gets slightly steeper as you near the pass, but the trail is good and there are plenty of switchbacks to ease the climb. At 1.8 miles you will see another sign marking the trail on the right to Willow Lake. Bear left at that point for the last 0.8 mile to the top of Buckskin. Just before you reach the top of the pass you should see a secondary trail branching off

Snowmass Creek

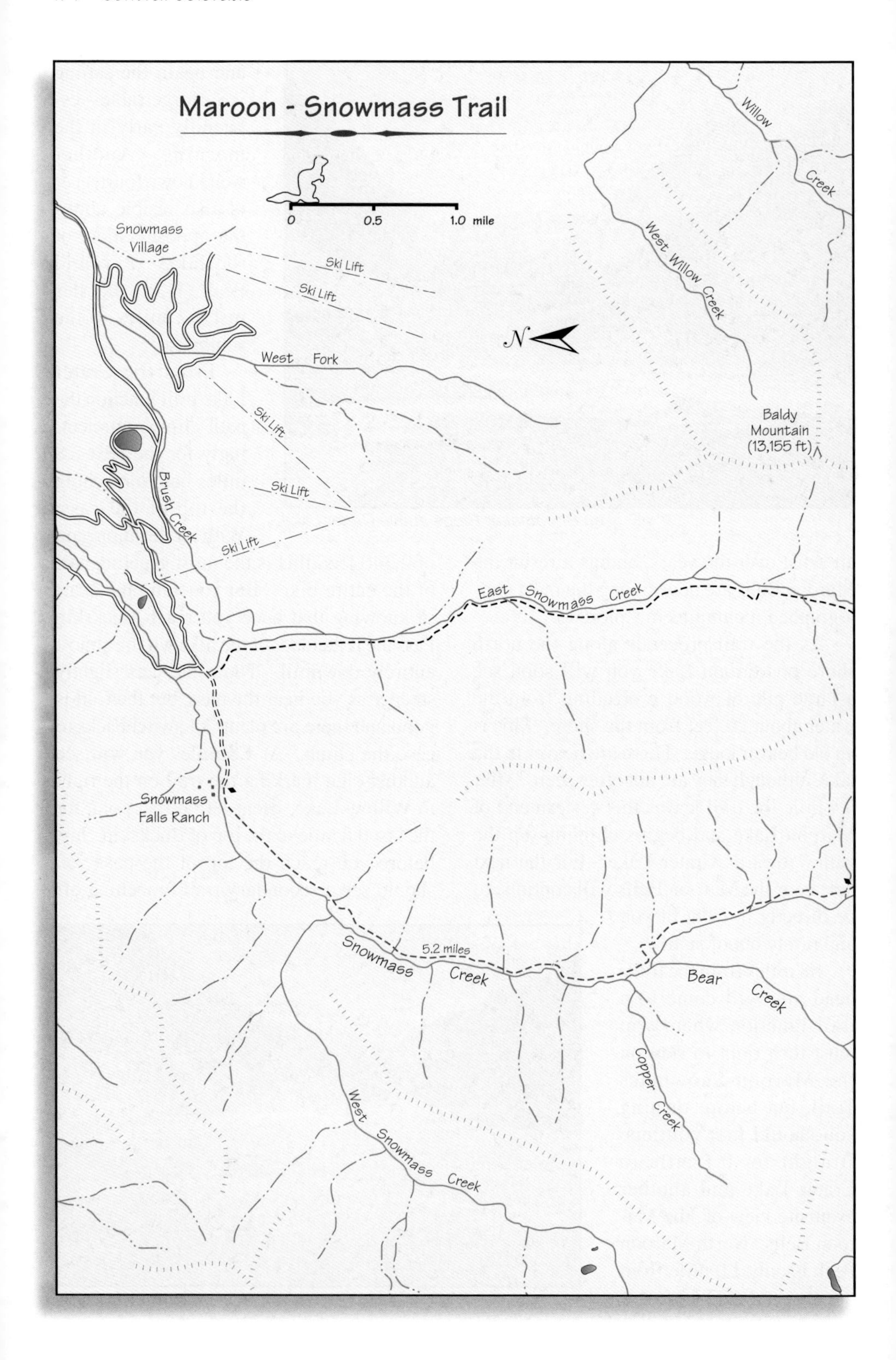

Maroon - Snowmass Trail
0
0.5
1.0 mile
N
Snowmass Village
Ski Lift
Ski Lift
West Fork
Ski Lift
Ski Lift
Ski Lift
Brush Creek
Willow Creek
West Willow Creek
Baldy Mountain (13,155 ft)
East Snowmass Creek
Snowmass Falls Ranch
5.2 miles
Snowmass Creek
Bear Creek
Copper Creek
West Snowmass Creek

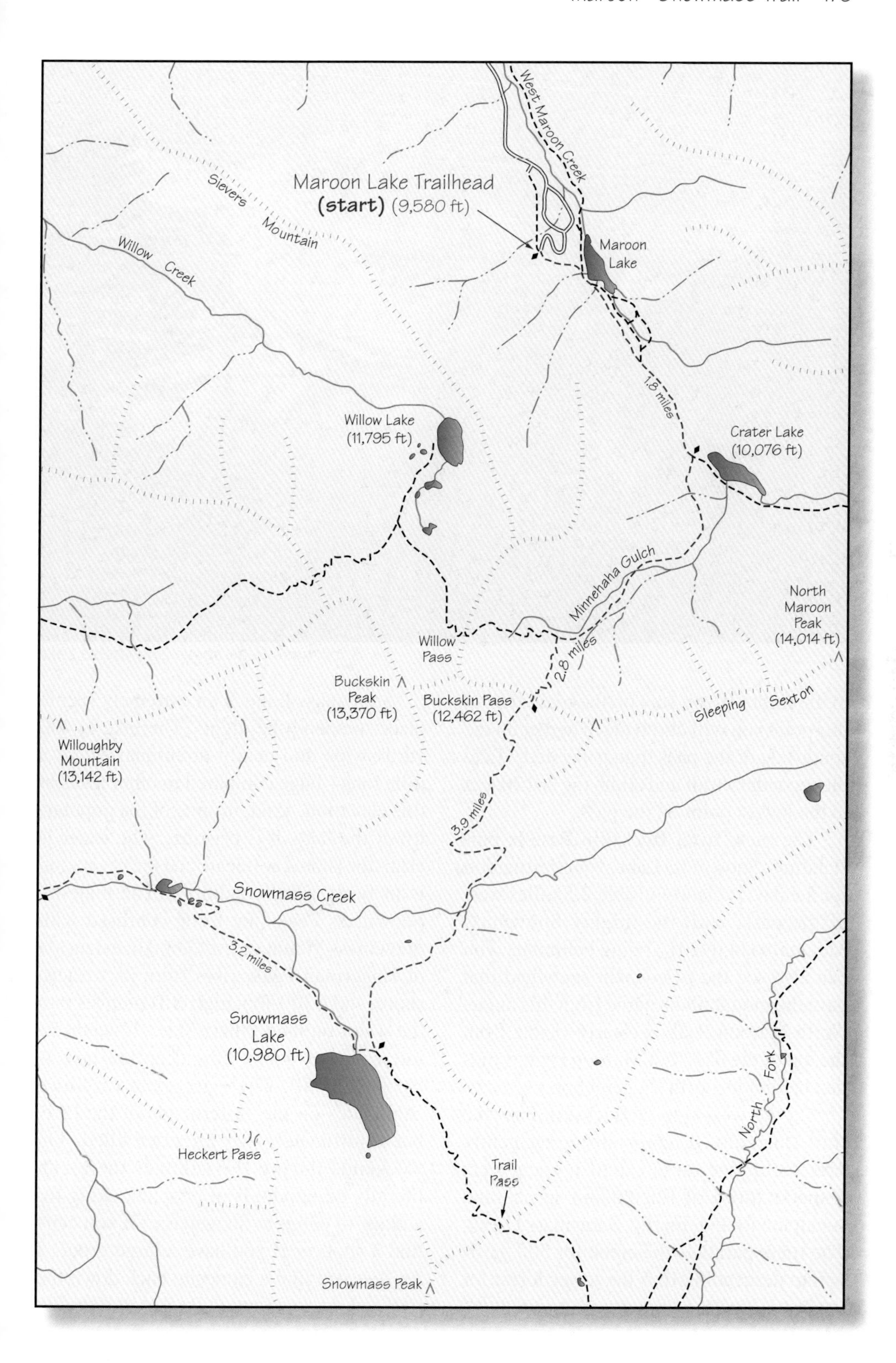
West Maroon Creek
Maroon Lake Trailhead
(start) (9,580 ft)
Sievers
Mountain
Willow
Creek
Maroon
Lake
1.8 miles
Willow Lake
(11,795 ft)
Crater Lake
(10,076 ft)
Minnehaha Gulch
North
Maroon
Peak
(14,014 ft)
Willow
Pass
2.8 miles
Buckskin
Peak
(13,370 ft)
Buckskin Pass
(12,462 ft)
Sleeping
Sexton
Willoughby
Mountain
(13,142 ft)
3.9 miles
Snowmass Creek
3.2 miles
Snowmass
Lake
(10,980 ft)
North
Fork
North
Heckert Pass
Trail
Pass
Snowmass Peak

Snowmass Peak above Snowmass Lake

to the right. If you stay on the main trail at this point you will climb much higher up the south side of the pass than is needed. Take the secondary trail and climb the last 20 feet to the lowest point on the pass.

The view from Buckskin Pass is outstanding. Snowmass Lake, your destination for the day, is clearly visible 2.5 miles west of the pass, with the mighty Snowmass Mountain (14,092 ft.) rising behind it. You can also see the permanent snowfield that gave the mountain its name from this angle. North Maroon Peak is clearly visible from the top of the pass, but Maroon Peak is hidden behind its northern neighbor.

On the west side of Buckskin Pass the trail starts down again, dropping gently over the alpine tundra until it encounters a sparse forest of Engelmann spruce and subalpine fir and, finally, Snowmass Creek. The route parallels the creek for 300 yards before descending into the lower forest for the last 1.3 miles to Snowmass Lake.

Snowmass Lake is an extremely scenic place to spend the night. The lake is 400 yards wide and nearly three-quarters of a mile long—huge compared to other lakes at this elevation. And, in spite of the popularity of the lake, it is pristine. The water is clear, the shores are clean, and the vegetation is in fairly good condition. The majestic Snowmass Peak (not to be confused with Snowmass Mountain), a 13,600 ft. extension of Hagerman Peak, rises from its western shore, and a 300-foot high cliff plunges into the water on its northern side. It would be interesting to know how deep the lake is below the cliff. There are some very nice camp sites on the eastern side of the lake, but unfortunately they are often filled. On weekends during the summer there can literally be hundreds of people looking for a place to camp at Snowmass. If you can't find a spot, or if you have a large group, I suggest you find a campsite back down the trail a short way toward Buckskin Pass.

Day 2 (8.4 miles)

The second day of this hike, while not as scenic as the first day, is nevertheless a very pleasant walk along a fast-flowing creek with little or no elevation gain. After leaving Snowmass Lake the trail proceeds downhill for 1.6 miles before leveling out in a flat marshy area beside Snowmass Creek. The trail continues down the west side of the drainage until it comes to a large log jam that has dammed up the stream to form a wide, shallow pond. This log jam is locally known as the Beaver Dam, although to me it doesn't look like the work of beavers. In any case you must cross the stream at this point, walking across the lose logs to the eastern side.

For the next 5.8 miles the trail winds uneventfully along the western side of Snowmass Creek. Most of the time the trail is immersed in a dense forest of spruce, subalpine fir, and aspen, but on occasion the forest opens up to provide views of the valley or the mountains beyond. A particularly notable clearing occurs about 1.7 miles below the Beaver Dam where there is a fine panorama of Copper Creek Valley and Capital Peak (14,130 ft.), 3.7 miles away.

The maps indicate that there are three large lakes, the Pierre Lakes, in the upper reaches of the nearby Bear Creek drainage. These lakes are only 4.0 miles up Bear Creek from the confluence with Snowmass Creek, but unfortunately there is no trail. Getting to the lakes would involve 3100 feet of elevation gain and a lot of difficult uphill bushwacking. I have never talked to anyone who has seen the lakes, but they certainly look intriguing on the maps. The largest one is almost the size of Snowmass Lake. It lies in a large, flat bowl at an elevation of 12,180 feet, about a mile east of Capital Peak. It must be beautiful in its isolation.

The trail finally ends at the entrance to the Snowmass Falls Ranch. The last mile or so of the route crosses a portion of the ranch, and you will pass through two unlocked gates at the ranch boundaries. Be sure to close the gates as you cross into the private land. The Snowmass Falls Ranch also provides horseback tours to Snowmass Lake, and you will probably see a few horses along this part of the trail.

Copper Creek Valley (Capitol Peak right of center)

Conundrum Creek - Gothic

Maroon Bells - Snowmass Wilderness
shuttle car required
2-day hike

Distance: 17.6 miles
(plus 118 miles by car)

Walking time: day 1: 7 1/2 hours
day 2: 7 1/4 hours

Elevations: 4,260 ft. gain, 3060 ft. loss

Conundrum Creek Trailhead (start):	8,760 ft.
Conundrum Hot Springs:	11,200 ft.
Triangle Pass:	12,900 ft.
Copper Lake:	11,321 ft.
Copper Creek Trailhead:	9,960 ft.

Trail: Well maintained and easy to follow.

Season: Midsummer through mid-fall. The higher parts of the trail are usually covered with snow from November through mid-July.

Vicinity: Between Aspen and Crested Butte

Maps: Hayden Peak, Maroon Bells, Gothic *(USGS)*
Aspen, Maroon Bells, Crested Butte *(Trails Illustrated, #127, #128 and #131)*

Information: http://colorado.utahtrails.com/conundrumcreek.html
http://www.fs.fed.us/r2/whiteriver/ *(White River National Forest)*
phone: 970-925-3445 *(Aspen Ranger District)*

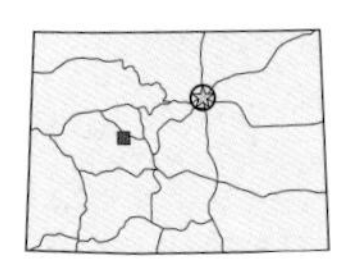

Drive west from Aspen on Highway 82 for 0.5 miles to the large round-about. Take the Castle Creek Road exit from the round-about and drive south for 5.0 miles until you see a small sign marking the Conundrum Creek Road. Turn right here and continue southwest on the gravel road for another 1.1 miles to the Conundrum Creek Trailhead and parking area. This is where the hike begins.

To get to the Copper Creek Trailhead where the hike ends you must drive from Aspen to Crested Butte on Highways 82 and 133 and the Kebler Pass Road. When you arrive at Crested Butte proceed to the west side of town and turn left on Highway 135. Drive north on this road for 7.8 miles to the town of Gothic, then continue north for another 0.6 miles to a signed road on the right. This road ends after 0.5 miles at the Copper Creek Trailhead.

Aspen, probably the best known town in the Colorado Rockies, is famous largely because of its location on the northern edge of the spectacular Elk Mountains. Six of the state's fabled 14,000-foot peaks are located in this range, including the Maroon Bells, the most recognizable of all of Colorado's fourteeners. The area has long been noted for its scenic beauty, and in 1964 Congress established the Maroon Bells-Snowmass Wilderness Area south of Aspen. This was one of Colorado's five original wilderness areas, and today it receives more visitors each year than any other Forest Service managed land in the state.

The crest of the Elk Mountains runs roughly in a northwest-southeast direction some 14 miles south of Aspen, and hikers often backpack across the mountains to the town of Crested Butte on the other side of the ridge. People interested in doing this trip generally have three trails to choose from.

The shortest route across the Elk Mountains is the 10-mile-long West Maroon Creek Trail, which begins ten miles out of Aspen on Maroon Creek Road. This trail follows West Maroon Creek to its source, then crosses West Maroon Pass and descends along the East Fork of the Crystal River to a trailhead near Schofield Pass. From there it is 14 miles by road to Crested Butte.

Also departing from the Maroon Creek Road is the East Maroon Creek Trail. This trail follows East Maroon Creek to its source, then climbs over the East Maroon Pass and descends along Copper Creek to the Copper Creek Trailhead nine miles north of Crested Butte.

The third route across the Elk Mountains is the Conundrum Creek trail that I will describe below. At 17.1 miles, this is the longest route from Aspen to Crested Butte, but in my opinion it is also the most interesting. The thing that makes the trail so special is that it offers an opportunity to spend a night camping near Conundrum Hot Springs.

At 11,200 feet above sea level the Conundrum Springs are the highest hot springs in Colorado and probably in the United States. They are situated near the headwaters of Conundrum Creek at the top of a valley that could not be more beautiful. An afternoon spent bathing in one of the springs' pools, relaxing tired muscles while enjoying the fabulous view down Conundrum Valley, can be a truly memorable occasion.

Day 1 (8.3 miles)

From the trailhead the path proceeds southward up the wide, forested valley

Conundrum Creek

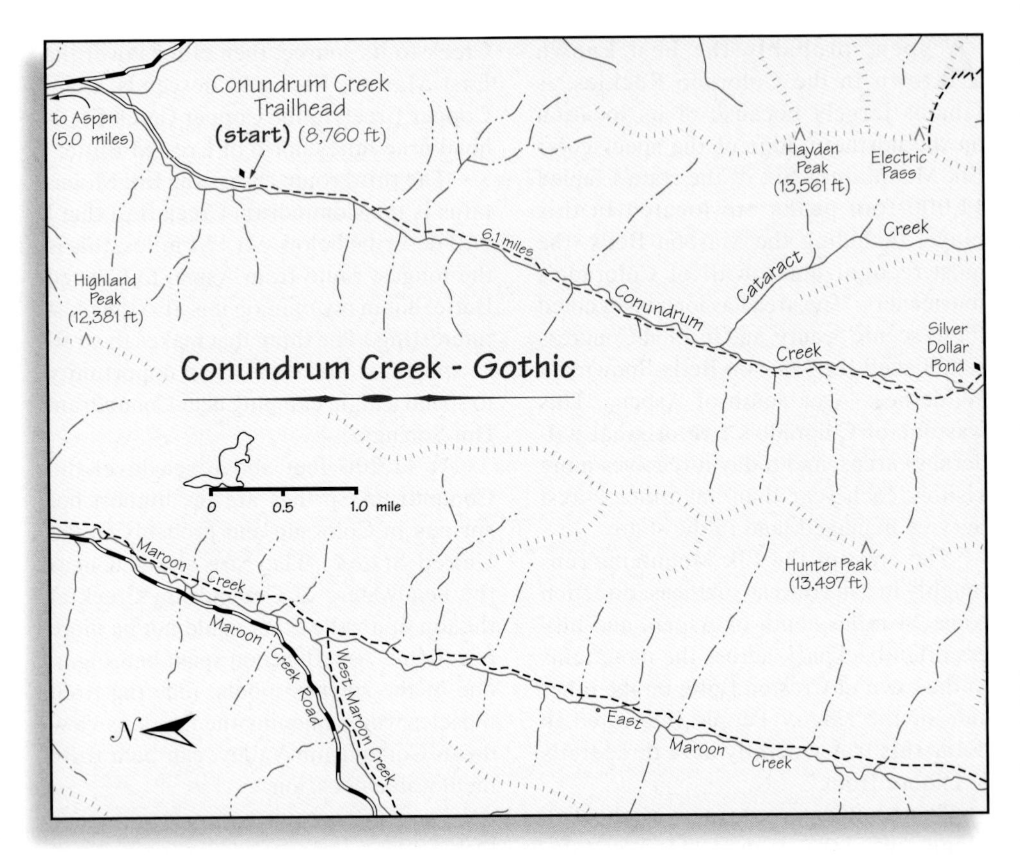

that surrounds Conundrum Creek. The classical U-shaped glacial valley is initially forested by large groves of aspen surrounding frequent open meadows, but as you go higher the forest becomes a patchwork of aspen and conifer. After 1.6 miles the trail passes the remains of two old log cabins in the center of a large meadow, then it ducks back into the trees again on the east side of the creek.

A mile beyond the cabins the trail crosses a log bridge to the west side of the creek. There are several large beaver dams just beyond the bridge. You probably won't be lucky enough to see a beaver, but there must be many of them in this area.

One hour above the first bridge the trail comes to a second bridge where it crosses again to the east side of the creek. Pause here to study the skyline for a moment. Electric Pass, the highest named pass in Colorado, is the dip on the horizon due east of the second bridge. This 13,300-foot pass is easily reached by trail from its eastern side (see page 186), and a continuation of that trail descends the rocky slopes below the pass to meet the Conundrum Creek Trail 0.4 mile north of the bridge. The trail down from the pass is very primitive and steep, with a 900-foot talus slope of extremely unstable rock near the top. Occasionally an adventurous hiker will follow it down to the creek, but I have never heard of anyone climbing up to the pass on this trail.

The trail stays on the east side of the creek for another 20 minutes before crossing back again for the last 2.0 miles to the hot springs. As you approach the

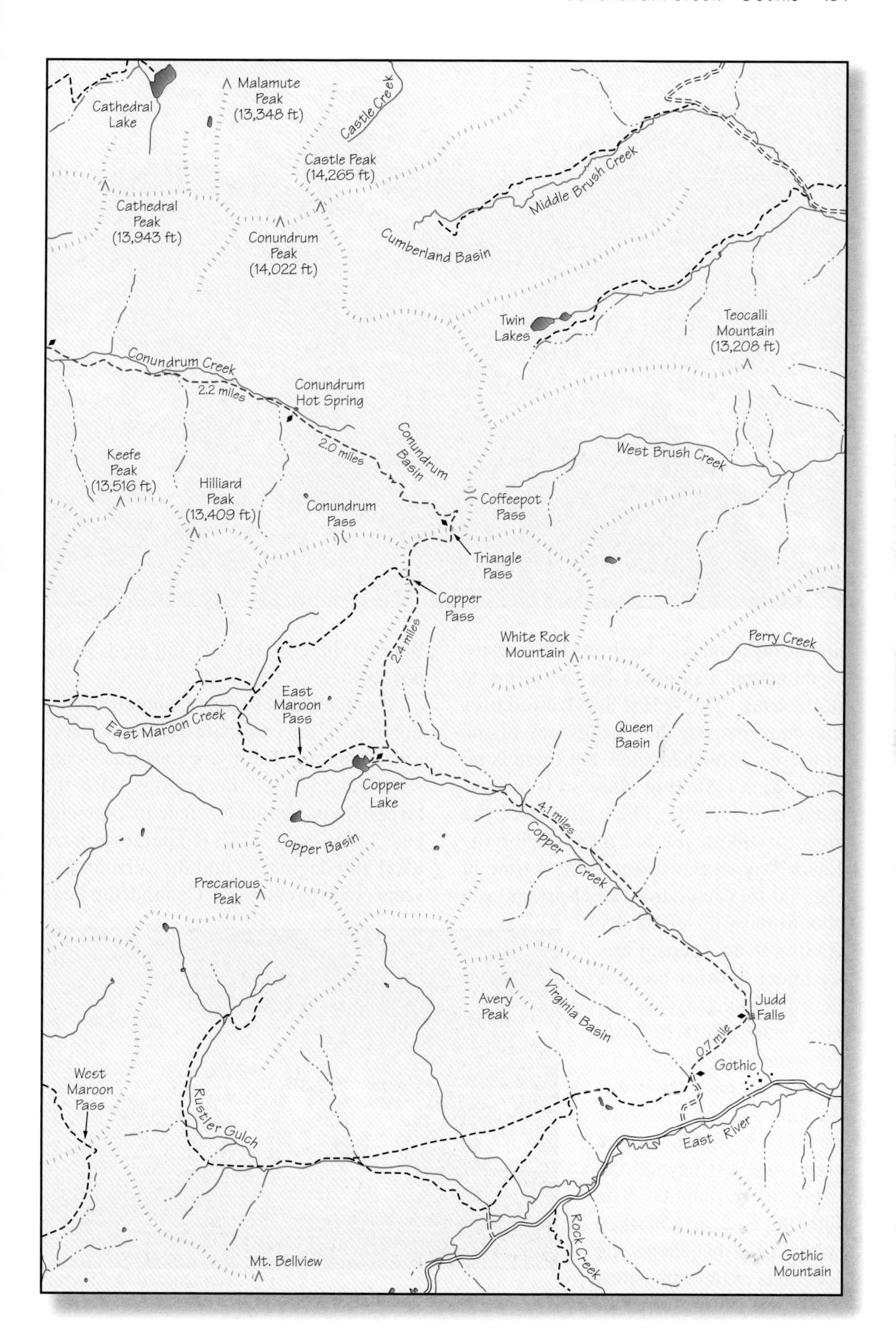

Malamute Peak (13,348 ft)
Cathedral Lake
Castle Creek
Castle Peak (14,265 ft)
Middle Brush Creek
Cathedral Peak (13,943 ft)
Conundrum Peak (14,022 ft)
Cumberland Basin
Twin Lakes
Teocalli Mountain (13,208 ft)
Conundrum Creek
2.2 miles
Conundrum Hot Spring
2.0 miles
Conundrum Basin
West Brush Creek
Keefe Peak (13,516 ft)
Hilliard Peak (13,409 ft)
Conundrum Pass
Coffeepot Pass
Triangle Pass
Copper Pass
2.4 miles
White Rock Mountain
Perry Creek
East Maroon Pass
East Maroon Creek
Queen Basin
Copper Lake
4.1 miles
Copper Creek
Copper Basin
Precarious Peak
Avery Peak
Virginia Basin
Judd Falls
0.7 mile
Gothic
West Maroon Pass
Rustler Gulch
East River
Rock Creek
Mt. Bellview
Gothic Mountain

Conundrum Hot Springs

hot springs you will begin to see a series of numbered campsites on the left side of the trail. The Forest Service requires that campers near the springs stay in one of these established sites, but there is no reservation system in place so it is first-come-first-served. There are 18 of the sites, so unless you are there during the Labor Day weekend (the busiest time of the year for Conundrum Hot Springs) you should have no difficulty finding an unoccupied site. Camping in other areas is permitted only if your site is at least a quarter-mile from the hot springs.

As you pass campsites 4a and 4b you will see an old log cabin on the right, and just beyond the cabin the trail splits. The junction is clearly marked with a sign that shows the locations of the campsites. Bear left here for the last 150 yards to the hot springs.

As mentioned before, Conundrum Hot Springs is an exquisite place to spend an afternoon. There are four hiker-constructed pools at the springs with the largest being about 15 feet in diameter and 3 feet deep. The temperature is an ideal 100 degrees F, and the surrounding scenery is spectacular. Conundrum Peak

Conundrum Hot Springs

(14,022 ft.) and Castle Peak (14,265 ft.) soar high above the east side of the creek, and to the north Conundrum Valley seems to stretch on forever. You are unlikely to find solitude at the springs, but for me that is not a distraction. An evening spent relaxing in the hot water talking to fellow hikers about the wonders of Colorado's mountains can be very pleasant indeed.

Day 2 (9.3 miles)

On the west side of Conundrum Creek, 150 yards from the hot springs, you will see the trail junction with a sign indicating the way to Triangle Pass. Turn south at the junction to begin the climb up to the pass. Very soon the trail passes the last few Engelmann spruce and subalpine fir trees as it crosses above timberline and climbs up the west side of Conundrum Basin.

Ahead lies a confused jumble of alpine peaks and saddles; four major ridges come together above Conundrum Basin, and it is unclear at first which saddle the trail will use as it crosses over the crest of the Elk Mountains. Initially the path appears to be headed for Coffeepot Pass, the lowest pass to the other side. But a glance at a map will confirm that this route would lead to the West Brush Creek drainage. Just before reaching Coffeepot Pass the trail veers to the right and climbs another 160 feet to the top of Triangle Pass.

From the summit of Triangle Pass the path ahead is clearly visible for at least two miles. Although some sections have been severely damaged by rock slides the trail is well defined and it is obvious that a great deal of effort has been expended in building it. Just below the pass the trail turns west and begins a long traverse below the ridge as it descends gradually into the Copper Creek drainage. 0.6 mile from the top of the pass there is a trail junction where another trail ascends to the right over Copper Pass and eventually joins the East Maroon Creek Trail. The distinctive peak rising in the distance directly behind Copper Pass is Maroon Peak (14,156 ft.).

2.1 miles after leaving Triangle Pass the trail finally reaches timberline and

Conundrum Creek

Trail up the north side of Triangle Pass

enters a grove of trees. Within another 50 yards you will come to a signed trail junction where a spur trail to Copper Lake branches off to the right. If you are in a terrible hurry you can bypass the lake, but doing so would only save 0.4 mile, so it would be a shame not to see it. Turn right here and within 0.2 mile you will come to the East Maroon Pass Trail. Copper Lake is easily visible through the trees below this second junction.

By now you have probably become so spoiled by the incredible scenery on this hike that Copper Lake may be something of a disappointment to you. It is not the prettiest lake in the area, but it is still worth a look. It is also a fairly popular overnight stop for backpackers walking between Aspen and Crested Butte through East Maroon Pass, so you may see other people there. There are several established campsites just south of the lake.

Walk south from Copper Lake on the East Maroon Pass Trail and within 0.4 miles it will rejoin the Copper Creek Trail. From there it is a somewhat uneventful 3.8 miles down the Copper Creek drainage to Judd Falls, where another 0.7-mile spur trail will take you to the Copper Creek Trailhead.

The last four miles of this hike are, in my opinion, a huge disappointment. For one thing almost the entire distance is along an old mining road. This area is now part of the Maroon Bells-Snowmass Wilderness Area and vehicles are no longer allowed on the road; nevertheless the scars from previous vehicles are so well established that it will take many more decades for them to disappear. Furthermore, the road generally stays far from the creek, seemingly following the least scenic part of the valley. But my greatest misgiving along this part of the hike is the presence of large numbers of cows. As you approach Judd Falls there are so many cows hanging around the trail that you may occasionally have to detour through the bushes to get around them. The cows uproot young trees, trample the

Copper Creek Canyon, viewed from the south side of Copper Pass

ground cover, muddy the riparian areas, and generally degrade the wilderness experience to the point where you might as well be on a farm.

Shortly after exiting the wilderness area you will see a viewpoint above Judd Falls on the left. Until recently there was a trail from Judd Falls down to the town of Gothic, but in the late 1990s the land on the east side of town was acquired by the Rocky Mountain Biological Laboratory and there is now a gate across this section of trail. A nearby sign directs hikers to a bypass trail that leads to the new trailhead northeast of Gothic. Follow this trail for ten minutes, past more cows, until you see a sign that says "Private Property: Access Courtesy of the Rocky Mountain Biological Laboratory". (From the looks of the area the primary interest of scientists working for the Rocky Mountain Biological Laboratory must be to study the detrimental affects of overgrazing.) From the sign it is another 8-minute walk along another jeep road to the Copper Creek Trailhead.

Judd Falls

Electric Pass

★

Maroon Bells - Snowmass Wilderness Area
day hike

Distance: 8.7 miles (round trip)

Walking time: 7 hours

Elevations: 3,755 ft. gain/loss
Cathedral Lake Trailhead (start): 9,880 ft.
Cathedral Lake: 11,866 ft.
Electric Pass: 13,500 ft.
Electric Pass Peak: 13,635 ft.

Trail: Generally well maintained and easy to follow.

Season: Midsummer through mid-fall. The higher parts of the trail are usually covered with snow from November through early July.

Vicinity: Near Aspen

Maps: Hayden Peak (USGS)
Aspen, Independence Pass *(Trails Illustrated, #127)*

Information: http://colorado.utahtrails.com/electricpass.html
http://www.fs.fed.us/r2/whiteriver/ *(White River National Forest)*
phone: 970-925-3445 *(Aspen Ranger District)*

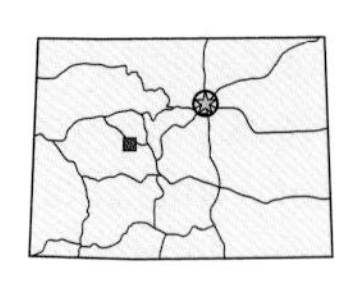

Drive west from Aspen on Highway 82 for 0.5 miles to the large round-about. Take the Castle Creek Road exit from the round-about and drive south for 12.0 miles until you see a small sign just 10 feet north of milepost 12 that says "Trailhead". Turn right here and drive 0.6 miles to the trail-head and parking area at the end of the road.

This hike is most notable for the panoramas that can be seen from the summit of Colorado's highest named mountain pass. No fewer than five of the state's 14,000-foot peaks can be seen from the 13,500-foot vantage point. The area is also home to a fair number of mountain goats, and when I did this hike in the summer of 2002 there were four of the shaggy white animals waiting for me at the top of the pass. They let me get within 100 feet of them, but that seemed to be their limit. They studied me until their curiosity was satisfied and then calmly ambled on up the ridge toward Cathedral Peak.

From the trailhead the path climbs slowly

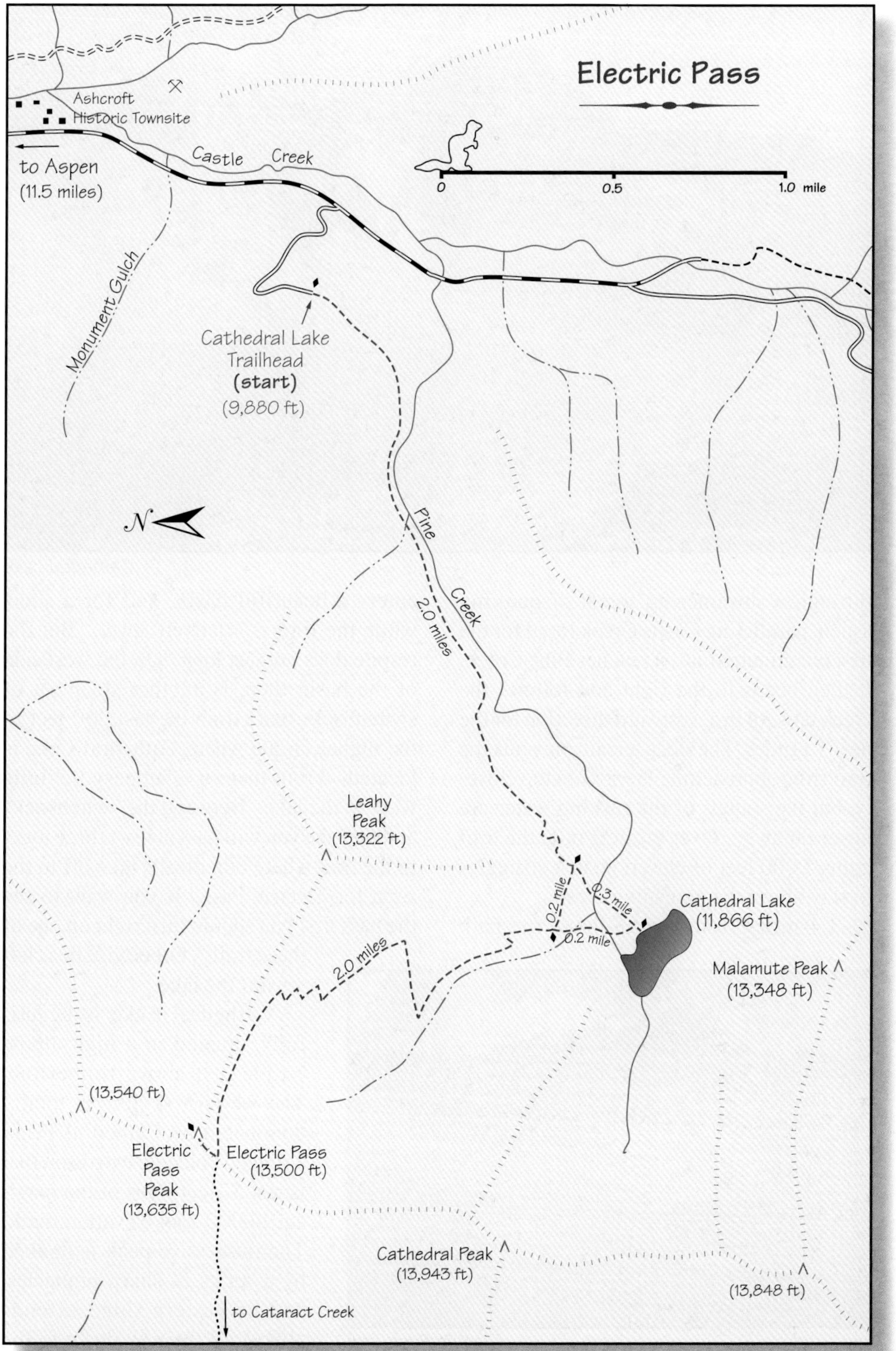

Electric Pass

0
0.5
1.0 mile

N

Ashcroft
Historic Townsite
to Aspen
(11.5 miles)
Castle Creek
Monument Gulch
Cathedral Lake
Trailhead
(start)
(9,880 ft)
Pine Creek
2.0 miles
Leahy
Peak
(13,322 ft)
0.2 mile
0.3 mile
0.2 mile
Cathedral Lake
(11,866 ft)
Malamute Peak
(13,348 ft)
2.0 miles
(13,540 ft)
Electric
Pass
Peak
(13,635 ft)
Electric Pass
(13,500 ft)
Cathedral Peak
(13,943 ft)
(13,848 ft)
to Cataract Creek

Cathedral Lake

through a shimmering forest of quaking aspen, paralleling Castle Creek Road for the first ten minutes until it reaches Pine Creek. It then bends to the right and follows the creek upward in a westward direction for the next 1.1 miles. The steep terrain prevents the trail from approaching the stream too closely, but the sounds of the rushing water are never far away. Over the next mile the trail gains 1,000 feet of elevation as it struggles to stay above the cascading creek.

1.4 miles from the trailhead the path enters a beautiful basin, and for a short while the trail is relatively level. But the respite does not last long. On the west side of the basin there is another steep set of switchbacks that climb the last 200 feet to the higher cirque where Cathedral Lake is located. From there it is an easy 0.3-mile walk to the lake. Between the switchbacks and the lake you will pass at least three forks in the trail where other trails take off to the right for Electric Pass. If you want to see the pass first you should turn right on one of these trails. Otherwise bear left toward the lake.

Electric Pass Trail

Cathedral Lake is beautifully situated in a high alpine cirque just above timberline. The western skyline is totally dominated by Cathedral Peak, a rugged volcanic extrusion that is just 57 feet short of the magical 14,000-foot elevation mark. The impressive peak is flanked by a series of sharp pinnacles, and its eastern ridge extends almost all the way down to the northwest side of the lake. Many people choose to spend a night on the eastern side of the lake and climb to Electric Pass the following day.

From Cathedral Lake an obvious trail goes north up the alpine tundra to the saddle below Leahy Peak and then turns west to Electric Pass. The first 1.7 miles of the trail to the Leahy Peak saddle are very well defined and easy to follow, but many people mistakenly think when they reach the saddle they are at Electric Pass. Although the views from the saddle are nice, the best is yet to come. When you reach the saddle below Leahy Peak turn left and follow a less well defined trail that continues westward. The trail soon begins to traverse across a talus slope and the footing can be a little tricky, but with care it is really not that difficult. From the Leahy Peak saddle to the pass is a 20-minute walk with 300 feet of additional elevation gain.

The trail does not stop at Electric Pass. Rather it makes a sharp right turn and continues another 300 yards to the top of a nearby peak that is unofficially called Electric Pass Peak. This peak is just 140 feet higher than the pass, and most people climb it before hiking back down. Nearby Cathedral Peak is also a tempting goal. Its summit is only 450 feet above the trail, but the obstacles along the ridge would make it a very difficult climb

Most dramatic are the views to the west of Electric Pass. Conundrum Creek Valley lies 3,300 feet below the ridge, and beyond that lies a vast expanse of 13,000- and 14,000-foot peaks that include Pyramid Peak and the Maroon Bells. There is an old trail that continues down the west side of Electric Pass to Conundrum Creek, but it is now seldom used. From the pass the steep, unmaintained trail immediately drops down 1,000 feet of loose scree before finally reaching solid ground near Cataract Creek. The last few miles of the trail between Cataract Creek and Conundrum Creek are clearly visible below, but I wouldn't recommend this route.

View into Upper Cataract Creek Basin from Electric Pass

Lost Man Loop

Hunter–Fryingpan Wilderness Area
shuttle car or bicycle required
day hike

Distance: 8.2 miles (loop)
(plus 4.0 miles by car or bicycle)

Walking time: 4 3/4 hours

Elevations: 2,350 ft. gain, 1,330 ft. loss
Lost Man Trailhead (start): 10,490 ft.
Lost Man Pass: 12,820 ft.
Roaring Fork Trailhead: 11,510 ft.

Trail: Excellent, well marked trail

Season: Midsummer through mid-fall. The higher parts of the trail are usually covered with snow from mid-November through early July.

Vicinity: Near Aspen

Maps: Mount Champion, Independence Pass *(USGS)*
Aspen, Independence Pass *(Trails Illustrated, #127)*

Information: http://colorado.utahtrails.com/lostmanlake.html
http://www.fs.fed.us/r2/whiteriver/ *(White River National Forest)*
phone: 970-925-3445 *(Aspen Ranger District)*

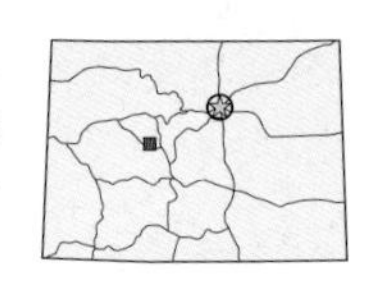

Drive 13.7 miles east of Aspen on Highway 82 to Lost Man Campground. On the north side of the highway, directly opposite the entrance to Lost Man Campground, you will see a short road leading to a parking area near the Lost Man Trailhead where the hike begins.

The Roaring Fork Trailhead is located 4.0 miles further up Highway 82 towards Independence Pass. You should leave a bicycle or a shuttle car at the Roaring Fork Trailhead to complete the loop when you finish the hike. (It is a very easy bicycle ride from Roaring Fork Trailhead back to Lost Man Trailhead – all downhill.)

Note: The ghost town of Independence is just 1.1 miles west of Roaring Fork Trailhead on the south side of Highway 82. If you have time after your hike you should stop and see this well preserved mining camp that was abandoned around the turn of the century. There is also at least one old miner's cabin just across the highway from the Roaring Fork Trailhead.

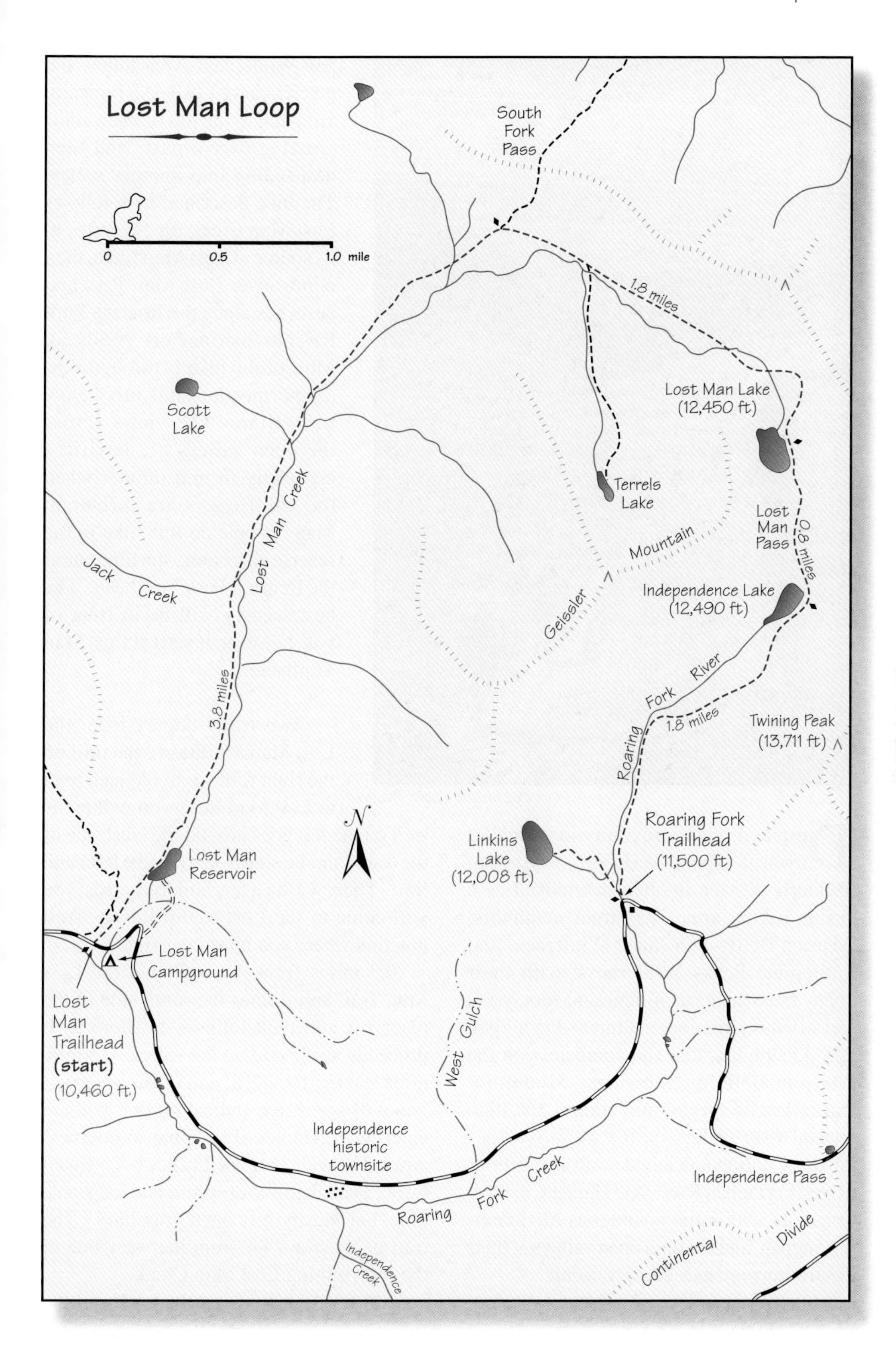

Lost Man Loop
0
0.5
1.0 mile
South
Fork
Pass
1.8 miles
Scott
Lake
Lost Man Creek
Lost Man Lake
(12,450 ft)
Terrels
Lake
Lost
Man
Pass
0.8 miles
Mountain
Geissler
Independence Lake
(12,490 ft)
Jack
Creek
3.8 miles
River
Fork
Roaring
1.8 miles
Twining Peak
(13,711 ft)
N
Linkins
Lake
(12,008 ft)
Roaring Fork
Trailhead
(11,500 ft)
Lost Man
Reservoir
Lost Man
Campground
Lost
Man
Trailhead
(start)
(10,460 ft)
West Gulch
Independence
historic
townsite
Roaring Fork Creek
Independence Pass
Independence
Creek
Continental Divide

Lost Man Loop Trail

Despite its close proximity to the resort town of Aspen, the Hunter–Fryingpan Wilderness Area is often overlooked as a prime hiking area. Its larger neighbors, Maroon Bells–Snowmass Wilderness and Collegiate Peaks Wilderness, with their many famous fourteen-thousand-foot peaks get all the attention. Hunter–Fryingpan has no summits that can compete with the Maroon Bells or Snowmass Mountain, but rather its special attraction is the high glacial river valleys on the western slopes of the Continental Divide. Roaring Fork River, Fryingpan River, and Hunter Creek all originate within the boundaries of Hunter-Fryingpan, and the high open valleys at their headwaters are exceedingly scenic.

Most of the trails in the Hunter–Fryingpan Wilderness Area follow the glacier-carved valleys, typically climbing to the top of one valley, crossing over a pass, and then descending into another valley. The hike described here follows Lost Man Creek for 5.5 miles to its source at Lost Man Lake, then climbs over Lost Man Pass and descends along the Roaring Fork River to Roaring Fork Trailhead. Most of the hike is through sub-alpine meadowland just below timberline. The views across the open valleys are terrific–especially in midsummer when the wildflowers are in bloom. Many people do this hike in the reverse direction, starting out at the Roaring Fork Trailhead. The best scenery will be in front of you, however, if start at Lost Man Trailhead.

Two trails depart from the Lost Man Trailhead: the trail on the right follows an old jeep road to Lost Man Reservoir, while the trail on the left goes around the west side of the reservoir. Be sure to start on the left hand trail. Then, within a few hundred yards, you will come to the Lost Man/Midway Trail junction where you must bear right.

0.3 miles from the trailhead the Lost Man Trail approaches the south side of the reservoir and then follows its shore as it proceeds northward up the valley. 0.8 mile after leaving the north end of the reservoir you will see a sign indicating that you are entering the Hunter–Fryingpan Wilderness Area. The wide U-shaped valley is vegetated by occasional groves of spruce and lodgepole pine, but mostly it is open grassland. The trail never strays far from the west side of the fast running Lost Man Creek.

About 3.0 miles from the trailhead the

trail begins making a long sweeping turn to the east as it follows the creek bed. Then, at mile 3.8 it meets the junction with South Fork Pass Trail. This trail makes an interesting side trip for people wishing to make this a two-day hike. Deadman Lake is only two miles from the junction along South Fork Pass Trail, and their are plenty of fine campsites nearby. Unfortunately, there are no fish in Deadman Lake—probably because the winters are occasionally severe enough to kill all of the fish.

Unless you are making a side trip to Deadman Lake, bear right at the South Fork Pass junction and continue climbing eastward along the north shore of Lost Man Creek. The scenery in the upper reaches of the Lost Man Creek Valley is especially dramatic. The valley climbs eastward for 1.6 miles to a point just below the ridge of the Continental Divide then turns abruptly south into a small bowl wherein lies Lost Man Lake. By the time you reach the lake you will be well above timberline, and the rocky shore that surrounds the small lake is typical alpine tundra. Beyond the lake the trail climbs steeply to the ridge south of the lake, gaining 400 feet in 0.3 mile. When you reach the top of the ridge you will be in Lost Man Pass (12,820 ft.), the highest point on the hike.

The last 2.3 miles of trail are all downhill. From the top of Lost Man Pass the route winds down to the west side of Independence Lake, then continues on down the Roaring Fork drainage to the trailhead. Like Lost Man Lake, Independence Lake is located in a small bowl west of the Continental Divide. It is also about the same size and elevation and deep enough that it does not freeze solid in the winter. The fishing is fair to good in both lakes. Independence Lake is an easy 2.0 mile walk from the Roaring Fork Trailhead; consequently you are likely to see many more hikers on this last section of the trail. But most of these hikers will miss the best part of the loop. Although the scenery along Roaring Fork is nice, it can't really compare to the grandeur of the upper Lost Man Creek Drainage.

Finally, 0.2 mile before you reach the highway, you will see another short spur trail departing on the right for Linkins Lake. If you still have energy left you might want to make the 0.8 mile round-trip side trip to Linkins, but be advised that the trail involves another steep and tiring climb. You must gain another 400 feet of elevation in 0.4 mile. Linkins Lake is situated right on the edge of timberline at an elevation of 12,008 feet. It lies on a small bench at the base of a north-south ridge called Greissler Mountain. From the Linkins Lake trail junction it is a five-minute downhill walk to the point where Roaring Fork crosses the highway at the trailhead.

Lost Man Lake

Kroenke Lake

★★★★★

Collegiate Peaks Wilderness Area
shuttle car required
overnight hike

Distance:	12.9 miles (plus 17.4 miles by shuttle car)
Walking time:	day 1: 8 hours day 2: 2 hours
Elevations:	3,000 ft. gain, 3040 ft. loss Denny Creek Trailhead (start): 9,900 ft. Hartenstein Lake: 11,451 ft. Browns Pass: 12,020 ft. Kroenke Lake: 11,500 ft. North Cottonwood Trailhead: 9,860 ft.
Trail:	well marked, easy to follow
Season:	Midsummer through mid-fall. The higher parts of the trail are usually covered with snow from late November through mid-July.
Vicinity:	Near Buena Vista
Maps:	Mount Yale *(USGS)* Buena Vista–Collegiate Peaks *(Trails Illustrated, #129)*
Information:	http://colorado.utahtrails.com/kroenkelake.html http://www.fs.fed.us/r2/psicc/ *(San Isabel National Forest)* phone: (719) 486-0749 *(Leadville Ranger District)*

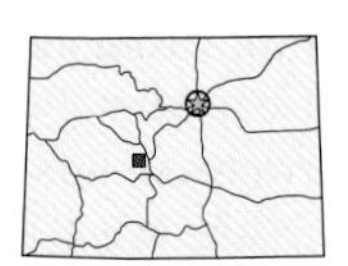

Drive south from Leadville on Highway 24 for 34 miles to the town of Buena Vista. When you come to the stoplight in downtown Buena Vista turn right and continue on County Road 306 toward Cottonwood Pass. After driving 2.6 miles you will see a sign on the right marking the road to North Cottonwood Creek (County Road 361). Turn right again and follow County Road 361 for the next 2.4 miles to the junction with County Road 365 where you must turn left. Road 365 ends after 5.3 miles at the North Cottonwood Trailhead and parking area. The road is initially a good graded gravel road, but after about 2.0 miles it begins to deteriorate. Ordinary cars can usually make it all the way to the trailhead, but drive with care! This trailhead is where the hike ends and where you must leave a shuttle car.

To get to the Denny Creek Trailhead where the hike begins you must return to the junction of Road 361 and Road 306 and continue driving west on County Road 306 toward Cottonwood Pass. 9.7 miles from the junction you will see a sign on the right marking the Denny Creek Trailhead and parking area.

This hike has it all: two gorgeous lakes, a short walk along the Continental Divide, and memorable views of several 14,000-foot Collegiate Peaks. At 12.9 miles it is a relatively easy backpack trip with a choice of two lakes as campsites. If you get an early start you will probably want to spend the night at Kroenke Lake, 8.2 miles from the Denny Creek Trailhead. If you get a late start, however, you can also camp at Hartenstein Lake which is only 3.0 miles from the trailhead. Either lake is a beautiful place to spend the night. The hike described here begins at the Denny Creek Trailhead, but you can just as easily do the trip in the opposite direction.

Day 1 (8.9 miles):

The trail follows the west side of Denny Creek for the first 1.0 mile, then crosses the creek on a primitive log bridge as it continues to climb toward the Continental Divide. 0.3 mile beyond Denny Creek you will come to a well-marked trail junction where the trail to Mount Yale departs on the right. Up to that point the trail is so wide it sometimes looks more like a jeep road than a foot path, but beyond the junction the trail soon narrows down. Also, as you gain elevation the forest seems to thin a bit, yielding occasional views of the mountains north and west of the trail.

0.7 miles from the Mount Yale trail junction you will come to another well-marked junction where the Hartenstein Lake trail leaves on the left. You could complete this

Hartenstein Lake (with Mount Yale in background)

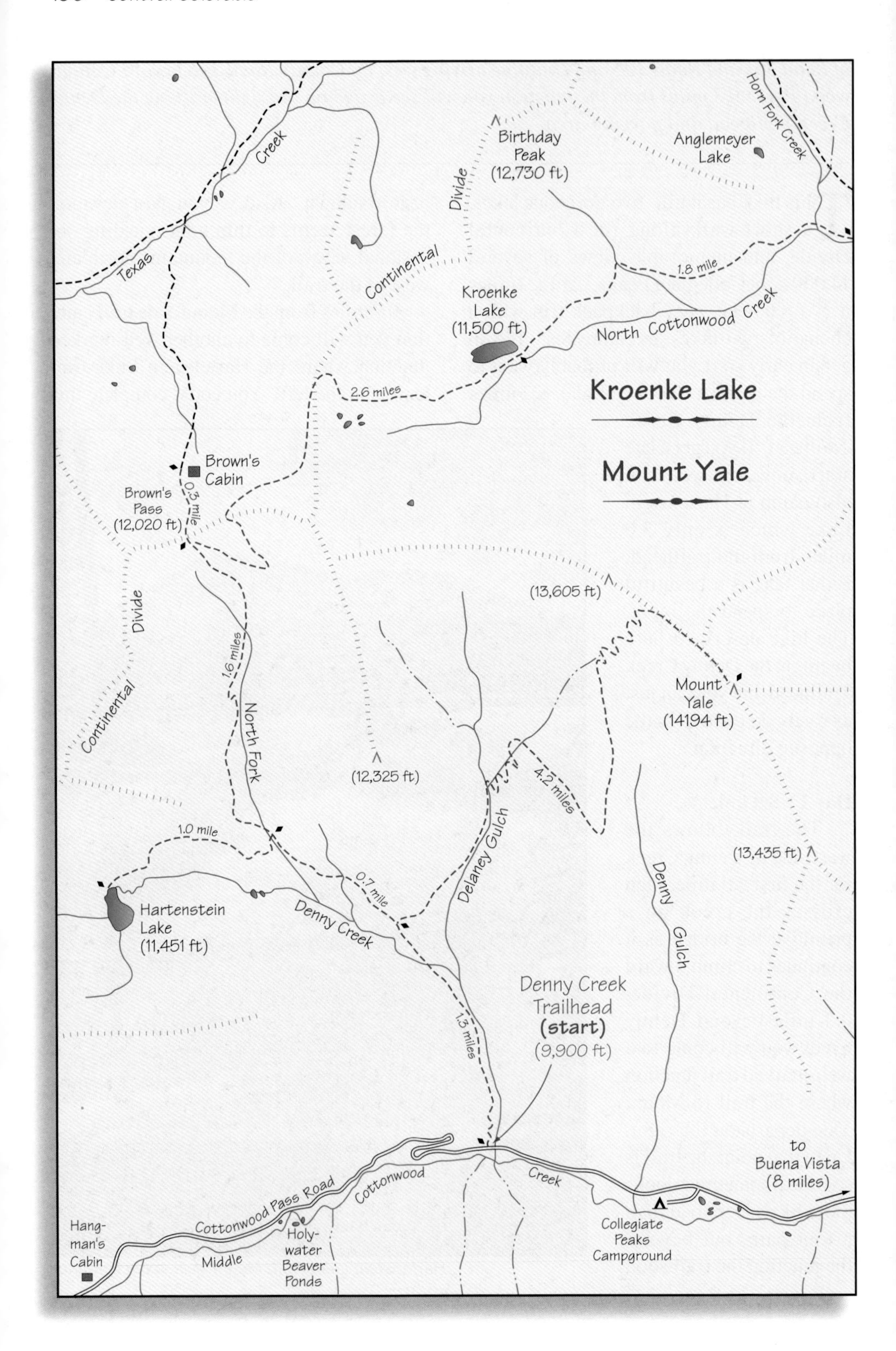

Kroenke Lake
Mount Yale
Birthday Peak (12,730 ft)
Anglemeyer Lake
Horn Fork Creek
Texas Creek
Continental Divide
Kroenke Lake (11,500 ft)
1.8 mile
North Cottonwood Creek
2.6 miles
Brown's Cabin
Brown's Pass (12,020 ft)
0.3 mile
(13,605 ft)
1.6 miles
North Fork
Mount Yale (14194 ft)
(12,325 ft)
4.2 miles
Delaney Gulch
1.0 mile
(13,435 ft)
0.7 mile
Hartenstein Lake (11,451 ft)
Denny Creek
Denny Gulch
Denny Creek Trailhead (start) (9,900 ft)
1.3 miles
to Buena Vista (8 miles)
Cottonwood Pass Road
Cottonwood
Creek
Middle
Hang-man's Cabin
Holy-water Beaver Ponds
Collegiate Peaks Campground

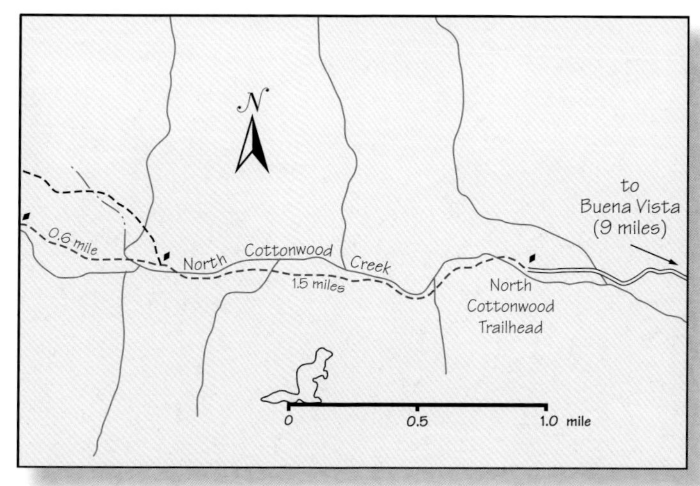

view of Mount Yale further to the east. Finally, when you reach Browns Pass the full glory of the Collegiate Peaks Wilderness Area opens up before you. Texas Creek runs through the deep canyon directly below the pass, and above the north side of the canyon a long like of dramatic mountain peaks marches east to west across the skyline. First in line is Mt. Columbia, followed by Mt. Harvard. Then there is Emerald Peak, a near fourteener, with Missouri Mountain, Mt. Belford and Mt. Oxford behind it. And finally, further to the west, the distinctive Three Apostles.

hike without taking the detour to Hartenstein, but it is such a pretty lake it would be a shame to miss it. It is just a half-hour's walk from the main trail over an easy path with an elevation gain of only 330 feet. As you approach Hartenstein you will notice a treeless slope above the north side of the lake that is swept clean almost every winter by avalanches. The slope descends 1,200 feet from the ridge above at an almost constant 30-degree angle—a perfect avalanche chute. Not a place you would want to be in late winter or early spring! There are some excellent campsites where the trail ends at Hartenstein Lake, and if it is late in the day you may want to consider spending the night there instead of pushing on to Kroenke Lake.

The Kroenke Lake Trail crosses the North Fork of Denny Creek just a few yards beyond its junction with the Hartenstein Lake Trail, and from there it climbs another 900 feet over a distance of 1.6 miles to the summit of Browns Pass. This part of the hike is very pleasant. The trail is situated in an alpine bowl just east of the Continental Divide, and as you pass above timberline you will have an unimpeded

Campsite at Hartenstein Lake

The Three Apostles, as seen from Brown's Pass

300 feet below the north side of Browns Pass you can see the remains of an old broken-down cabin, Browns Cabin, that was once well known to hikers in the area. Before the 1990s the hundred-year-old cabin was still intact and backpackers frequently used it as an overnight stop. The cabin had a large attic and an iron stove, and there was plenty of room to roll out sleeping bags on the floor. Unfortunately, sometime in the late-1990s the winter snow-load proved to be too much for the old shelter and the roof collapsed. Now Browns Cabin is little more than a gigantic pile of logs, but it is still fun to visit and poke around in the debris. A detour to the cabin and back will add 0.7 mile to the length of this hike.

From Browns Pass the trail climbs up the ridge that defines the Continental Divide, then zigzags along the north side of the Divide for 1.4 miles to a saddle at the head of North Cottonwood Creek. This is all alpine tundra country, well above timberline, and walking across it on a carpet of grass and wildflowers with the spectacular Collegiate Peaks rising dramatically above Texas Creek on your left and Mount Yale on your right is an exhilarating experience. The trail between Browns Pass and Kroenke

Brown's Cabin

Lake is easily my favorite part of this hike.

Upon reaching the basin above North Cottonwood Creek the trail makes a long descending turn around the north side of the bowl (in order to avoid a snowfield), and then heads east down the drainage towards Kroenke Lake. Finally, 0.8 mile after leaving the Divide, the path arrives at a terrific overlook point above the lake and then makes its way down the last 300 feet to the water's edge. You will find several excellent campsites along the south side of the lake.

Day 2 (4.0 miles)

The trail leaves on the east side of Kroenke Lake, first crossing the bog below the lake, and then pursuing a route above the north side of North Cottonwood Creek. Soon you will enter a dense, pristine forest of Engelmann spruce and subalpine fir as you make your way down the stream along the well traveled path. Over the next 2.5 miles the trail crosses several minor tributaries of North Cottonwood Creek before finally coming to Horn Fork. The trail crosses Horn Fork on a rickety log bridge, and 30 minutes later arrives at the well-marked Horn Fork Trail Junction. The Horn Fork Trail is the route most often used by hikers climbing Mt. Harvard and Mt. Columbia. These two fourteeners are popular hiking destinations, so you can expect to see many more hikers on the trail between this junction and the North Cottonwood Trailhead.

The last 1.5 miles of this hike are particularly pleasant. North Cottonwood Creek picks up a substantial amount of water from Horn Fork, and after leaving the trail junction the path never strays far from the dancing, tumbling waters of the fast-flowing mountain stream. The route follows the south shore of the creek for 1.1 miles to the wilderness boundary, then after another 0.3 mile it crosses the stream, soon to end at the North Cottonwood Creek Trailhead and parking area.

Kroenke Lake

Mount Yale

Collegiate Peaks Wilderness Area
day hike

Distance: 10.9 miles (round trip)

Walking time: 8 ½ hours

Elevations: 4,300 ft. gain/loss
Denny Creek Trailhead (start): 9,900 ft.
Mount Yale: 14,196 ft.

Trail: Generally well marked and easy to follow. The last 0.6 mile, however, is a scramble up a rocky, boulder-strewn ridge with no trail.

Season: Midsummer through mid-fall. There is usually snow on the trail from early November through mid July.

Vicinity: Near Buena Vista

Maps: Mount Yale *(USGS)*
Buena Vista–Collegiate Peaks *(Trails Illustrated, #129)*

Information: http://colorado.utahtrails.com/mountyale.html
http://www.fs.fed.us/r2/psicc/ *(San Isabel National Forest)*
phone: (719) 486-0749 *(Leadville Ranger District)*

Drive south from Leadville on Highway 24 for 34 miles to the town of Buena Vista. When you come to the stoplight in downtown Buena Vista turn right and continue on County Road 306 toward Cottonwood Pass. After driving 12.9 miles you will see a sign on the right marking the Denny Creek Trailhead and parking area.

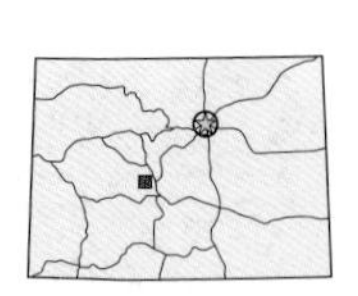

Mount Yale is one of fifteen 14,000-foot peaks in Colorado's Sawatch Mountain Range. The range is a favorite hiking area, and writers frequently refer to it with whimsical phrases such as "the pinnacle of the North American continent", or "the roof of the Continental Divide". The truth is that this 80-mile-long stretch of mountains contains more fourteeners than any other range in Colorado, and all of them, including the three highest peaks in the state, are relatively easy class-2 climbs. This abundance of climbing opportunities combined with good trails and plenty of scenic beauty combine to make the Sawatch Range

see map page 196

a favorite among hikers.

Yale is typical of the Sawatch fourteeners. It is a high, rounded hump with broad sloping shoulders and a rocky, talus-covered summit. It is one of the well-known Collegiate Peaks that were surveyed in 1869 by Harvard University Professor J. D. Whitney and subsequently named after famous universities. Whitney named the highest peak in his survey Mount Harvard, and he named the one thought to be the second highest Mount Yale, after his alma mater. Unfortunately for graduates of Yale it was later discovered that the nearby Mount Princeton is one foot higher than Mount Yale!

Trail to the summit of Mount Yale

The trail begins by climbing upward toward Browns Pass through an open forest of lodgepole pine and spruce. The grade is moderate, but unrelenting. The route follows the west side of Denny Creek, and although the water is not often visible you can hear the cascading stream behind the screen of trees to the right of the trail.

After 10 minutes of walking the trail crosses the boundary into the Collegiate Peaks Wilderness Area, and 20 minutes later it crosses a log bridge to the east side Denny Creek. 0.3 miles beyond the bridge you will come to a fork where the trail to Mount Yale branches off the Browns Pass Trail. As indicated by the Forest Service sign, you must turn right at the junction.

From the junction the Mount Yale Trail turns abruptly to the northeast and begins climbing away from Denny Creek. After 15 minutes the path begins following the left side of a small ravine called Delaney Gulch. Eventually the trail crosses to the east side of Delaney Creek in the bottom of the gulch and then begins a long series of switchbacks as it works its way up through the trees toward timberline.

After gaining about 800 feet of elevation from the Browns Pass trail junction the path enters a grassy area where most of the trees were long ago chopped down, and if you watch carefully you will see the remains of an old broken-down cabin. The structure is just 20 feet from the right side of the trail, but it is now so deteriorated it is hardly recognizable as a cabin. If the rotting logs could talk they would probably tell a story of another lonely prospector whose backbreaking work was never adequately rewarded.

The trail turns south as it crosses the tree line and then loops back around to the north for an imposing view of your goal, Mount Yale. The view from this angle is intimidating, to say the least. The bare, rocky dome of Yale stands like a giant sleeping monster 2,000 feet above the trail with long summit ridges spreading out west and southeast of the mountain. The entire remainder of the route is visible from this prospective. The trail climbs 1,300 feet in a northerly direction to intersect the western ridge, and then follows the knife-edge up the last 700 feet to the summit. The climb is not technically difficult, but it is obvious that a great deal of lung-busting work remains to be done before you can call the peak your own.

The trail remains reasonably good and the grade relatively moderate until it nears the base of the summit ridge. Then as it switchbacks up the side of the ridge it gets progressively steeper and rockier. When it reaches the top of the ridge the trail disappears altogether, and for the last 0.6 mile you are left to pick your own way across the boulders. In some places the easiest route is directly on top of the ridge, in others it is easier to walk on the right or south side. There is one false summit that is easiest to avoid by bearing to the right. The ridge levels out near the end, and the last 100 yards of the climb is an easy walk.

Once you have reached the top of Mount Yale your efforts will be well rewarded. Some people claim that they can see over half of Colorado's fourteeners from the summit of Yale. I have my doubts about that claim, but you can certainly see a lot of them. The view to the north is particularly dramatic, with Columbia, Harvard, Missouri, Oxford, Belford, and Huron Peaks all clearly visible. The lake just below the north side of Yale is Kroenke Lake and farther to the west, nestled in a grove of trees, you can see Hartenstein Lake.

photo by Joe Pacal

Mount Harvard, as seen from the summit ridge of Mount Yale

Lake Ann

★

Collegiate Peaks Wilderness Area
4WD vehicle useful
day hike

Distance:	7.0 miles (round trip)
Walking time:	4 3/4 hours
Elevations:	1,260 ft. gain/loss South Clear Creek Trailhead (start): 10,565 ft. Lake Ann: 11,805 ft.
Trail:	well marked, easy to follow
Season:	Midsummer through mid-fall. The higher parts of the trail are usually covered with snow from November through early July.
Vicinity:	Near Leadville
Maps:	Winfield *(USGS)* Buena Vista, Collegiate Peaks *(Trails Illustrated, #129)*
Information:	http://colorado.utahtrails.com/lakeann.html http://www.fs.fed.us/r2/psicc/ *(San Isabel National Forest)* phone: (719) 486-0749 *(Leadville Ranger District)*

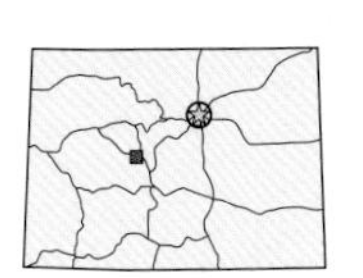

From the stoplight in the center of Leadville you must drive south on Highway 24 for a distance of 18.9 miles. Turn right when you see a sign directing you to Vicksburg and Winfield, and continue west on County Road 390 for another 11.6 miles, past historic Vicksburg to the abandoned mining town of Winfield. When you reach Winfield you must turn left along a smaller dirt road for the last 2.1 miles to the trailhead. The road gets very rough near the end, so if you are driving an ordinary passenger car you will have to stop just south of Winfield and walk the last 1.7 miles. 4WD vehicles should be able to make it all the way to the trailhead. 0.7 mile beyond Winfield the road comes to a junction where you must bear right; then 1.3 miles later the road ends at a parking area near the trailhead.

Lake Ann is an alpine gem that lies just south of the Continental Divide and west of three picturesque summits known as the Three Apostles. The lake is also on the Continental Divide Trail; consequently it is a popular camping area for summer backpackers. From Lake Ann the trail climbs another 800 feet to the top of the Divide and then drops down its south side towards Illinois Creek. For those that seek more solitude

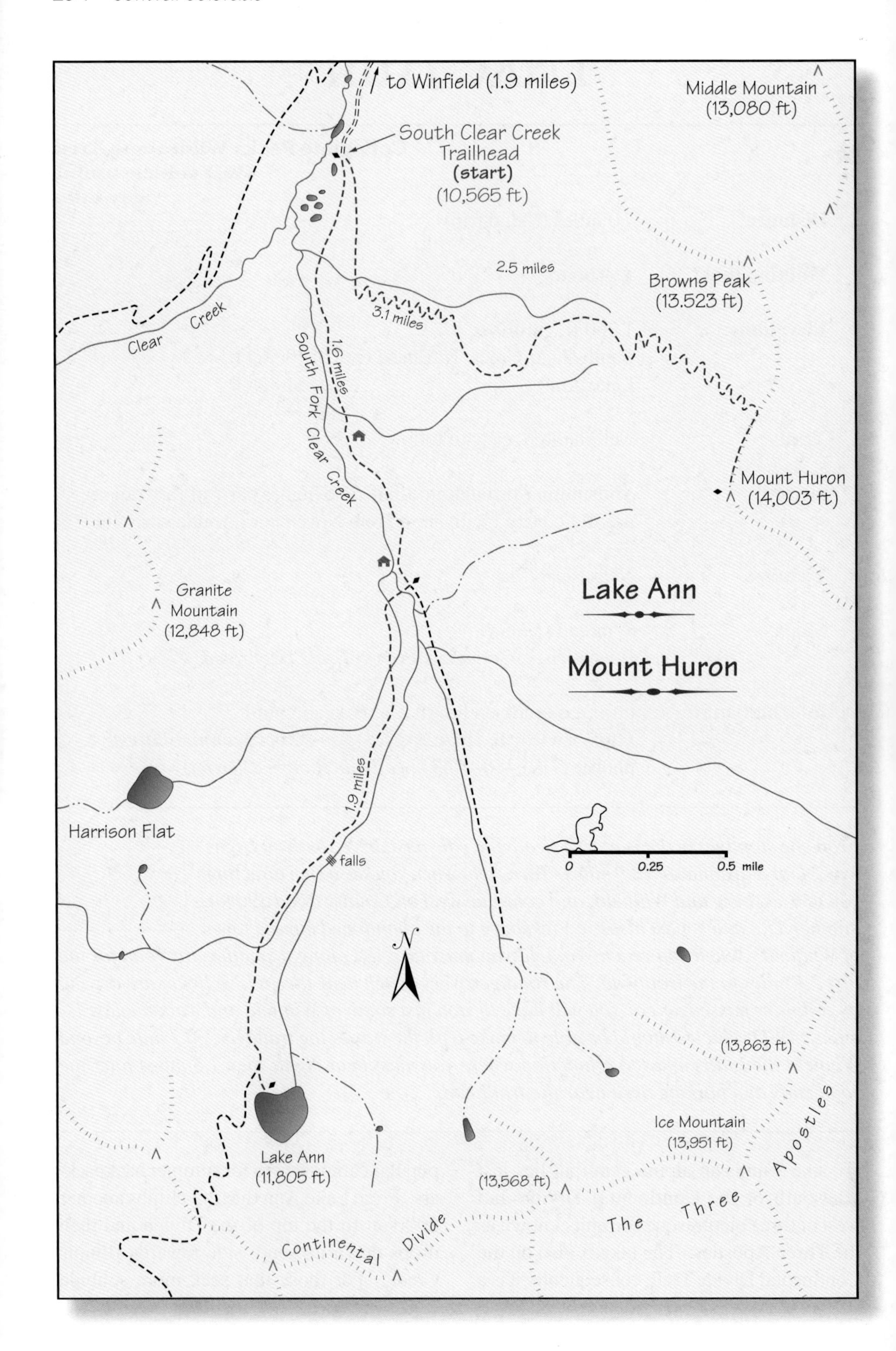

to Winfield (1.9 miles)
Middle Mountain
(13,080 ft)
South Clear Creek
Trailhead
(start)
(10,565 ft)
2.5 miles
Browns Peak
(13.523 ft)
3.1 miles
Clear Creek
South Fork Clear Creek
1.6 miles
Mount Huron
(14,003 ft)
Granite
Mountain
(12,848 ft)
Lake Ann
Mount Huron
1.9 miles
Harrison Flat
falls
0
0.25
0.5 mile
N
(13,863 ft)
Ice Mountain
(13,951 ft)
Lake Ann
(11,805 ft)
(13,568 ft)
The Three Apostles
Continental Divide

The Three Apostles

than the Lake Ann Trail can provide there are two other short spur trails along the way, one leading to the Three Apostles Basin east of Ann Lake and the other leading to Harrison Flats on the west side of the lake. Harrison Flats also contains two additional unnamed lakes.

For the first 1.5 miles the trail follows the South Fork of Clear Creek through a very pretty valley with Huron Peak above the east side and Granite Mountain to the west. Huron Peak, with an elevation of 14,003 feet, is one of Colorado's two lowest fourteen-thousand-foot peaks. The trail to the top of Huron leaves from the same trailhead as Lake Ann (see page 207), and if you see other cars in the parking area the chances are they belong to peak baggers looking for an easy fourteener to climb.

After walking for 20 minutes you will pass by an old miner's cabin 60 feet from the left side of the trail. The cabin is located about 200 yards north of the Forest Service sign that marks the Collegiate Peaks Wilderness boundary. Unfortunately, all that is left of the cabin now are the first three rows of

Huron Peak, from the Lake Ann Trail

logs at the bottom of the four walls. There is at least one other cabin further up the Lake Ann Trail. The second one is located on the opposite side of the creek 0.7 mile beyond the first. Although the second cabin is 100 yards from the right side of the trail it is easy to spot if you are paying attention.

Just 3 minutes beyond the second cabin the trail arrives at a junction with the Lake Ann trail departing on the right. The trail on the left continues to follow the South Fork of Clear Creek for another 1.0 mile to a steep basin on the north side of the Three Apostles. The basin is very pretty, but the best views of the Apostles lie closer to the trail junction. The problem is that the Three Apostles Basin trail ends so close to the ridge that it is impossible to see all three of the summits at one time.

Continuing on the trail to Lake Ann the path crosses the South Fork of Clear Creek just 50 feet from the junction, and from there it follows the Lake Ann drainage the last 1.8 miles to the lake. Unlike the first half of the hike, the trail above the junction is immersed in a forest of spruce and subalpine fir, so the views are limited. There are, however, a couple of nice cascades along the way. One particularly nice waterfall is located 0.8 mile from the junction. Look for a hiker-made trail on the left that leads to a viewpoint below the fall just 30 feet from the main trail.

Finally, 300 yards before reaching the lake the trail crosses timberline and climbs the last 80 feet through a treeless alpine meadow of grass and wildflowers. Two short spur trails leave the main trail at this point: the left spur drops down the last 150 yards to Lake Ann, and the right spur heads west toward Harrison Flats.

Lake Ann lies directly below a rugged 13,000-foot ridge that in this area defines the Continental Divide. The Continental Divide Trail continues up toward a pass on the right, and if you are in the mood for another 800 feet of climbing there is a great view of Mount Huron and Lake Ann from the pass. One of the Three Apostles is visible from the lake, but unfortunately the other two summits are too far to the east to be seen.

Lake Ann

Mount Huron

★

Collegiate Peaks Wilderness Area
4WD vehicle useful
day hike

Distance: 6.2 miles (round trip)

Walking time: 5 1/4 hours

Elevations: 3,440 ft. gain/loss
Mount Huron Trailhead (start): 10,565 ft.
Mount Huron: 14,003 ft.

Trail: Generally well maintained and easy to follow.

Season: Midsummer through mid-fall. The higher parts of the trail are usually covered with snow from mid-November through early July.

Vicinity: Near Leadville

Maps: Winfield *(USGS)*
Buena Vista, Collegiate Peaks *(Trails Illustrated, #129)*

Information: http://colorado.utahtrails.com/mounthuron.html
http://www.fs.fed.us/r2/psicc/ *(San Isabel National Forest)*
phone: (719) 486-0749 *(Leadville Ranger District)*

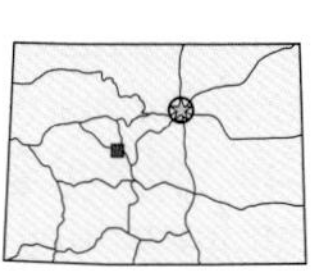

From the stoplight in the center of Leadville you must drive south on Highway 24 for a distance of 18.9 miles. Turn right when you see a sign directing you to Vicksburg and Winfield, and continue west on County Road 390 for another 11.6 miles, past historic Vicksburg to the abandoned mining town of Winfield. When you reach Winfield you must turn left along a smaller dirt road for the last 2.1 miles to the trailhead. The road gets very rough near the end, so if you are driving an ordinary passenger car you will have to stop just south of Winfield and walk the last 1.7 miles. 4WD vehicles should be able to make it all the way to the trailhead. 0.7 mile beyond Winfield the road comes to a junction where you must bear right; then 1.3 mile later the road ends at a parking area near the trailhead. Walk 150 feet south of the parking area to the Ann Lake Trailhead, then look to your left and you will see another lesser-used trail departing up the slope near a sign that says "Mount Huron Trail".

Mount Huron lies 0.6 mile north of the Continental Divide, at the top of a long ridge that includes Brown's Peak (13,523 ft.). It is best known for its terrific views

Mount Huron Trail

of the Three Apostles, three well known thirteeners that lie directly south of Huron on the Continental Divide. Ice Mountain, the middle Apostle, is just 52 feet lower than Mount Huron, and has the reputation among peak baggers of being one of the most treacherous of the high thirteeners. Mount Huron also provides an interesting perspective of Ann Lake (page 203), a high hanging lake that lies just below the northwest side of the Three Apostles.

see map page 204

There are also several notable points of historic interest along the road to the trailhead. History buffs will certainly want to stop and spend some time at the old Vicksburg and Winfield mining settlements. These towns were alive with activity in the 1880s when there was an explosion of mining activity in Clear Creek Valley north and west of Huron Peak. There were at least a half-dozen towns in the area, but Winfield and Vicksburg are the best preserved. Neither town prospered for more than a few years, but in their heyday they both had hotels, schools, post offices, and, of course, saloons. Winfield was the largest, with a peak population of about 1,500 people. 1.7 miles beyond Winfield, or 0.4 miles before the trailhead the road passes the remains of the old Baker Mine. Baker Mine was one of the area's major mines in the 1880s, and there are still a lot of fallen buildings and mining artifacts scattered nearby.

A good plan is to spend some time checking out these remnants of Colorado's colorful past, and then camp at the trailhead the night before you climb Mount Huron. You will find a beautiful place to camp beside Clear Creek, just next to the parking area at the end of the road.

Upon leaving the trailhead the Mount

Huron Trail begins a gradual climb up the eastern side of Clear Creek Valley. After 0.4 mile the grade increases somewhat, then begins a long series of short switchbacks as it climbs up the slope in an easterly direction. The trail is in excellent condition, not rocky and not particularly steep, and it is shaded by a thick forest of spruce and subalpine fir.

Finally, after an elevation gain of 1,300 ft. the trail suddenly breaks out of the trees for a marvelous view of the Three Apostles. As you approach timberline the grade becomes gentler and the trail turns to the northeast, entering an amazingly flat bench of alpine tundra below the ridge that separates Browns Peak from Mount Huron. If you are there in early August you will find this bench covered by a panoply of wildflowers. The luxury of a level path through the alpine garden lasts only briefly, however. Within 0.3 mile the trail comes to the eastern side of the basin and begins climbing again through long a series of switchbacks toward the summit ridge.

Another 1,200 feet of elevation gain will bring you to the top of the long ridge connecting Browns Peak to Mount Huron. Browns Peak lies 1.8 miles north of Mount Huron along the crest of the ridge only 130 feet higher than the ridge's lowest point. Many hikers choose to climb Browns Peak on the way down from Huron.

The trail intersects the ridge 500 feet below the top of Mount Huron and turns south for the final knee-busting assent to the summit. Like most fourteeners, the summit of Huron is covered by jagged boulders and loose scree that make the last few hundred yards of the assent the most difficult. In this case, however, these obstacles are not really daunting. The trail continues to be quite recognizable nearly all the way to the top. Once on the summit of Huron you can enjoy a great panoramic view, not only of the Three Apostles and the Continental Divide, but also of Colorado's rugged Sawatch Mountains. This range contains 15 of Colorado's 55 celebrated fourteeners, and at least 6 of them are visible from Huron.

The Three Apostles, as seen from the summit of Mount Huron

Missouri Gulch–Mount Belford

★★★★

Collegiate Peaks Wilderness Area
day hike

Distance:	9.7 miles (round trip)
Walking time:	8 hours
Elevations:	4,660 ft. gain/loss Missouri Gulch Trailhead (start): 9,540 ft. Elkhead Pass: 13,220 ft. Mount Belford: 14,197 ft.
Trail:	Most of the trail is well maintained and easy to follow. The return route down the northwest ridge of Mount Belford, however, is very steep.
Season:	Midsummer through mid-fall. The trail is covered with snow from mid-November through June.
Vicinity:	Near Leadville
Maps:	Mount Harvard, Winfield *(USGS)* Buena Vista–Collegiate Peaks *(Trails Illustrated, #129)*
Information:	http://colorado.utahtrails.com/mountbelford.html http://www.fs.fed.us/r2/psicc/ *(San Isabel National Forest)* phone: (719) 486-0749 *(Leadville Ranger District)*

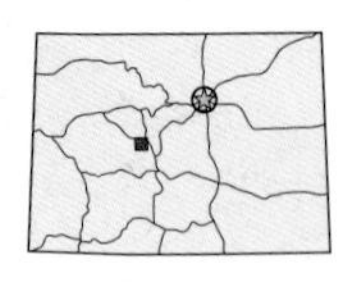

Drive south of Leadville on Highway 24 for 19 miles until you see a sign directing you to Vicksburg and Winfield on the right. Turn here onto a gravel road and drive for another 7.7 to another sign marking the Missouri Gulch parking area on the left. The trailhead is on the south side of the large parking area.

Note: before leaving this area you should be sure to check out the Vicksburg Museum, just a few hundred feet beyond the turnoff to the trailhead. Vicksburg was a well known silver mining camp in the 1870s and 1880s. It has been partially restored by the Clear Creek Canyon Historical Society, and a small museum is open to visitors during the summer. There is also a museum at the Winfield mining camp, four miles further up the road.

This hike, with its 4,660 feet of elevation gain, is a relatively strenuous choice, but the rewards are ample. After climbing for the first two miles the trail finally levels

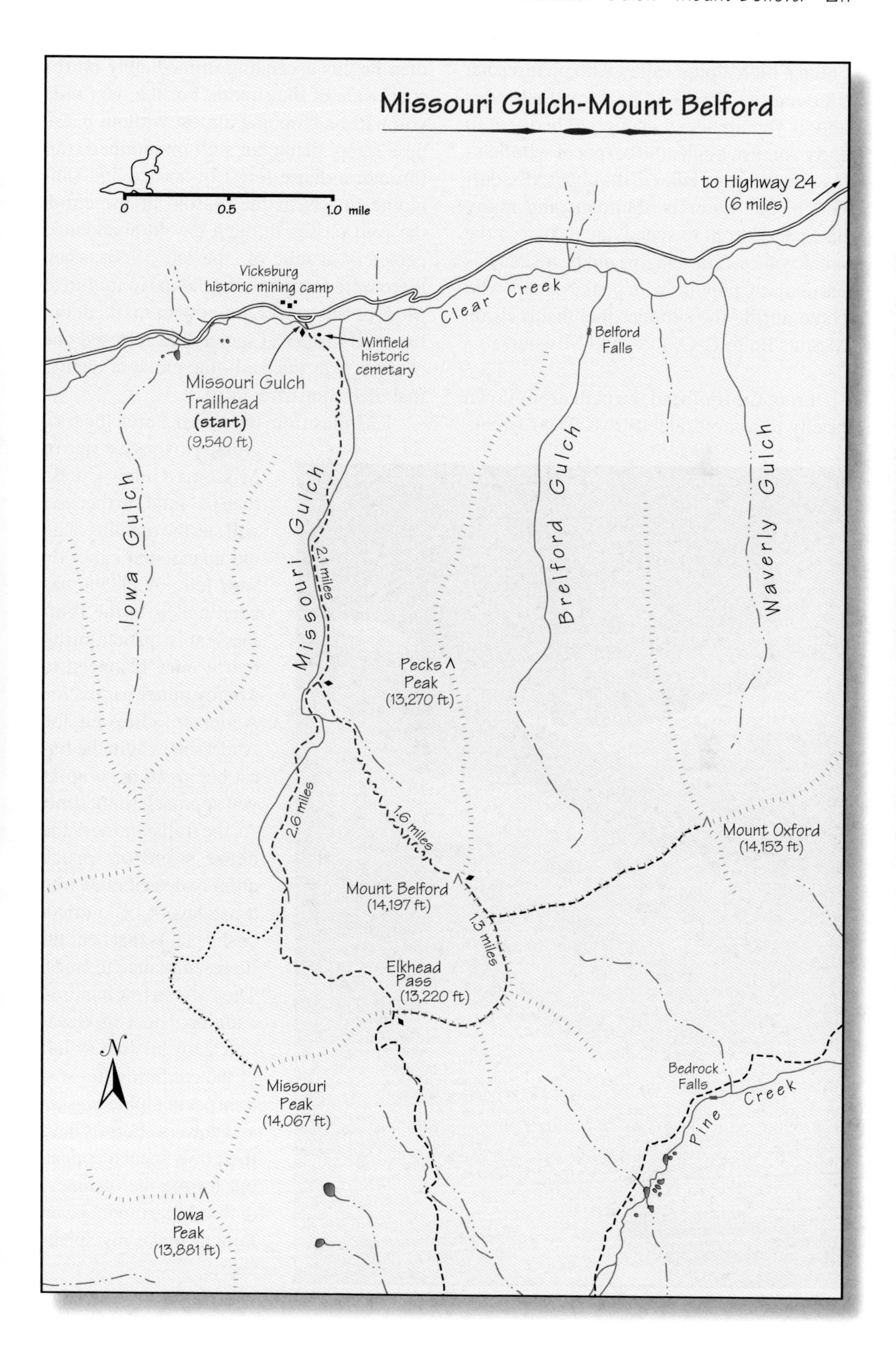
Missouri Gulch-Mount Belford
0
0.5
1.0 mile
to Highway 24
(6 miles)
Vicksburg
historic mining camp
Clear Creek
Winfield
historic
cemetery
Belford
Falls
Missouri Gulch
Trailhead
(start)
(9,540 ft)
Iowa Gulch
Missouri Gulch
2.1 miles
Brelford Gulch
Waverly Gulch
Pecks
Peak
(13,270 ft)
2.6 miles
1.6 miles
Mount Oxford
(14,153 ft)
Mount Belford
(14,197 ft)
1.3 miles
Elkhead
Pass
(13,220 ft)
N
Missouri
Peak
(14,067 ft)
Bedrock
Falls
Pine Creek
Iowa
Peak
(13,881 ft)

out in a high alpine valley with picturesque fourteen-thousand-foot peaks on both sides and, if you are lucky enough to be there in early August, a splendid carpet of wildflowers. There are no lakes in the upper Missouri Gulch, but water is abundant and many backpackers opt to spend day or two in the scenic valley. The hanging alpine meadow is particularly popular with peak baggers who come during the summer months to climb Mounts Belford, Oxford, and Missouri.

From the trailhead the path drops down briefly to a footbridge across Clear Creek, then begins ascending immediately on the south side of the stream. For the next mile you will be climbing almost without pause up a steep, tiring but well maintained trail through a dense forest of spruce and subalpine fir. Near the bottom of the climb the trail passes through an old abandoned cemetery, a relic of the late 1800s when there were many mining camps in this area. Most of the graves are now unmarked, but the local historical society has restored one of them near the trail—the grave of a child that died soon after birth.

1.3 miles from the parking area the trail crosses to the east side of Missouri Gulch Creek, then 0.3 mile further you will see the remains of an old abandoned cabin on your left. A plaque has been nailed to the roofless cabin proclaiming that it once belonged to a hardy miner named Joe Anderson. Beyond Joe Anderson's cabin the forest begins to open up as you approach timberline. As the trail continues the dense stand of spruce quickly deteriorates into a patchwork of knurled, bushy plants that bear little resemblance to trees. Then after a few hundred additional feet of elevation gain all that is left of the confining forest is a carpet of alpine grasses and flowers. Forests have their own special appeal, but for me the openness of the alpine tundra never fails to make my spirits soar.

Upper Missouri Gulch

As you emerge from

Looking north from Mount Belford

the forest you can see the summit Belford Peak clearly on your left. It is a gentle peak, as fourteeners go, more like a high rolling hill that a mountain. The ridge on the west side of Missouri Gulch, by contrast, is a very rugged formation, bordered by cliffs and talus slopes. The highest point on this ridge, near the southern end, is Missouri Peak (14,067 ft.).

After you have walked 0.5 mile from Joe Anderson's cabin you should see a trail junction with a sign marking the trail to Mount Belford, on the left, and Elkhead Pass, on the right. Either route will take you to the top of Mount Belford, but the more direct trail on the left is 2.3 miles shorter. Nevertheless, the elevation gain is the same and the trail on the right is much less steep. I suggest you continue to Elkhead Pass before climbing Belford, enjoying the beauty of upper Missouri Gulch, and use the steeper trail on the left for your return journey.

The Elkhead Pass trail continues climbing gradually for another 2.6 miles, gaining another 1,580 feet before it reaches the pass. Sandwiched in between two fourteeners at an elevation of 13,220 feet, Elkhead is almost the highest mountain pass in Colorado. The only one higher is the 13,300-foot Electric Pass, near Aspen. To the north you can look down into the Missouri Gulch, through which you have come, and to the south, in front of the Continental Divide, is the remote Missouri Basin. Seeing Missouri Peak above the west side of the pass is a great incentive to push on to Belford, the higher of the two peaks.

The trail to Belford begins by heading due east from Elkhead Pass, then it makes a long sweeping turn to the left as it follows the southern ridge to the summit. The grade continues to be gradual, and were it not for the altitude it would be an easy walk to the top. The trail gains only 980 feet in 1.3 miles. After a mile you will see a spur trail branching off to the right toward Mount Oxford, then less than 10 minutes later you will encounter the small outcropping of rock that marks the summit of Mount Belford. From there you can look down on both Missouri

Mount Belford summit

Peak and Mount Oxford, the two closest fourteeners. The large, prominent peak that juts up three miles to the southeast, on the other side of Missouri Basin, is Mount Harvard (14,420 ft.), the third highest peak in Colorado.

The return route goes down Belford's northwest ridge for 1.6 miles to intersect the Missouri Gulch Trail. The route is very steep—it looses 2,560 in only 1.6 miles—so you will be glad you are going down this way and not up. The route is exciting because for the entire distance you are looking directly down into the lush green tundra of the Missouri Gulch. The trail is not difficult but it is slippery in places, so watch your footing. Once you reach the Missouri Gulch Trail you can retrace your steps for the last 2.1 miles to the trailhead.

Mount Oxford and Missouri Peak

Some hikers climb both Mount Belford and Mount Oxford together, although doing this in one day makes for a very long, tiring walk. Including Mount Oxford in the hike described here will add another 2.4 miles onto the walking distance and 1,230 feet onto the elevation gain, making a total of 12.1 miles and 5,890 feet gain. The total walking distance can be trimmed somewhat if you turn right at the trail junction in Missouri Gulch and bypass Elkhead Pass. This route will take you straight up the northwest ridge to the top of Mouth Belford, shaving 2.3 miles of the total hiking distance. But this plan will also bring the total elevation gain up to 6,000 feet.

Joe Anderson's cabin

The most enjoyable way to climb Mount Oxford is to spend a night in upper Missouri Gulch and climb both Belford and Oxford the following day. If you camp near the trail junction in Missouri Gulch you can visit Elkhead Pass, Mount Belford, and Mount Oxford all with only 7.9 miles of walking and 3,790 feet of elevation gain.

Setting up a camp in Missouri Gulch will also give you the option of climbing Missouri Peak, the area's third fourteener. Unlike Belford and Oxford there is no easy trail up Missouri, but it is nevertheless a popular climb. The safest way to approach the summit of Missouri Peak is as follows:

Continue south from the trail junction in Missouri Gulch toward Elkhead Pass. The trail proceeds in a southerly direction for about 1.8 miles before it swings to the east to begin the final climb up to the pass. At the point where the trail turns east, about 0.8 miles from the top of the pass, you should leave the trail and walk due west. Ahead you will see a break in the cliffs below Missouri Peak's northwest ridge, with grassy slopes extending most of the way up to a 13,700-foot saddle. This will be your route to the crest of the summit ridge.

Once you have climbed the 1,100 feet from Missouri Gulch to Missouri Peak's northwest ridge there is a relatively easy route to the summit. The highest point lies at the southern end of the ridge, 0.7 miles from the saddle. You will encounter two notable obstacles on your walk along the crest of the ridge: First, you will have to climb over a false summit that rises 230 feet above the south side of the saddle. Then, just before you reach the peak you will encounter some rocky outcrops that can be bypassed on the west side of the ridge.

If you are camped near the trail junction in Missouri Gulch the hike to the top of Missouri Peak will involve about 6.2 miles of walking, round trip, and 2,480 feet of elevation gain. This is a fairly easy day hike, except for the strenuous off-trail climb from Missouri Basin to the summit ridge.

Lamas tethered near the top of Mount Belford

La Plata Peak

★★★

Collegiate Peaks Wilderness Area
day hike

Distance:	9.2 miles (round trip)
Walking time:	7 1/2 hours
Elevations:	4,250 feet gain/loss La Plata Trailhead (start): 10,160 ft. La Plata Peak: 14,361 ft.
Trail:	Good trail except for some minor scrambling over boulder fields near the summit.
Season:	Midsummer through mid-fall. The upper parts of the trail are generally covered with snow from November through early July.
Vicinity:	Near Leadville
Maps:	Independence Pass, Mount Elbert *(USGS)* Aspen, Independence Pass *(Trails Illustrated, #127)*
Information:	http://colorado.utahtrails.com/laplatapeak http://www.fs.fed.us/r2/psicc/ *(San Isabel National Forest)* phone: (719) 486-0749 *(Leadville Ranger District)*

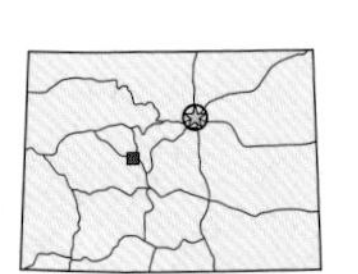

Drive south from Leadville on Highway 24 for 15 miles until you come to the junction with Highway 82. Turn right here towards Aspen and Twin Lakes and drive for another 14.8 miles where you will see a sign marking the La Plata Trailhead. The trailhead parking area is on the right side of Highway 82 near the junction with the South Fork Lake Creek Road.

La Plata Peak lies in the Sawatch Range near the center of Colorado's Rocky Mountains. This 80-mile-long range of mountains contains more 14,000-foot peaks than any other range in the lower 48 United States. La Plata is the fourth highest peak in the range and the fifth highest in Colorado. Like most Sawatch peaks, La Plata is a relatively easy class-2 climb, but the feature that really gives it a personality of its own is the spectacular Ellingwood Ridge. This rugged 2-mile-long ridge up the northeast side of the mountain has intrigued mountaineers since La Plata was first climbed in 1873. The imposing ridge was named after Albert Ellingwood who first scaled La Plata via this route in 1921.

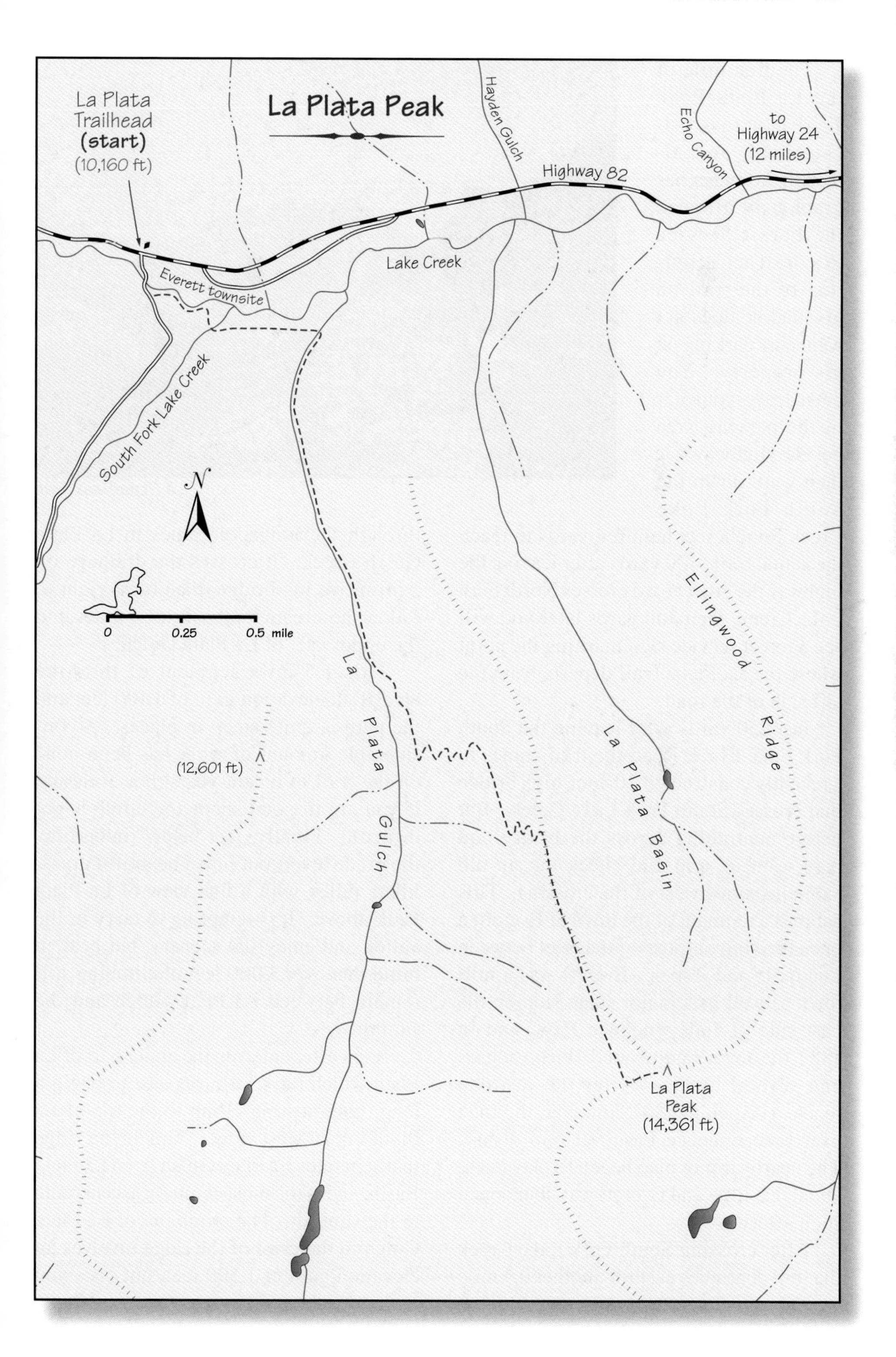
La Plata Peak
La Plata Trailhead
(start)
(10,160 ft)
Hayden Gulch
Echo Canyon
to Highway 24
(12 miles)
Highway 82
Lake Creek
Everett townsite
South Fork Lake Creek
N
0
0.25
0.5 mile
La Plata Gulch
Ellingwood Ridge
La Plata Basin
(12,601 ft)
La Plata Peak
(14,361 ft)

La Plata Peak Trail

The first mile of the La Plata Peak Trail is across private land, and although the owner has graciously allowed the Forest Service to construct a portion of the trail on his land he does not want cars parking on his property. You must leave your car in the parking area beside Highway 82, then walk down the South Fork Lake Creek Road a few hundred yards to reach the actual trail. 100 yards after leaving the highway the gravel road crosses North Fork Lake Creek, then 300 yards later you will see a forest service sign marking the point where the La Plata Trail departs from the left side of the road.

Just 250 yards after leaving the South Fork Lake Creek Road the trail comes to a recently constructed 20-foot-high bridge that crosses South Fork Lake Creek. But before continuing across the bridge you may want to stop and check out an old cabin just northwest of the crossing. This cabin is a remnant of the town of Everett, a once thriving outpost on the road between Leadville and Aspen. Everett was a mill town as well as a major stage stop on the east side of Independence Pass, and in 1882 the town had around thirty houses and several hotels. After the railroad reached Aspen in 1887, however, the road over Independence Pass fell into disuse. The nearby mines also began to play out at about that time and Everett was abandoned soon afterward.

After crossing South Fork Lake Creek the trail continues east for another 0.4 mile through the lodgepole pines to La Plata Gulch Creek. It crosses the drainage on a primitive log bridge, then turns right to follow the stream for the next 1.5 miles into the upper part of La Plata Gulch.

This 1.5-mile segment of the hike entails an elevation gain of 1,100 feet and the path is quite steep in places. A considerable amount of work has been done on the trail in recent years, however, and if you are in good shape the climb is not difficult. Finally, just below timberline, the grade levels out into a beautiful grass-filled valley with a fine view of La Plata Peak above. It is tempting to tarry in the valley and enjoy the scenery, but bear in mind that over 3,000 feet of climbing still remain between La Plata Gulch and the summit.

Soon after entering the upper part of La Plata Gulch the trail turns east to begin a long, lung-busting climb to the top of La Plata's northwest ridge. This is the ridge that separates La Plata Gulch from La Plata Basin, and is the most common ascent route to the summit. The climb out of La Plata Gulch to the crest of the ridge involves an elevation gain of 1,500 feet, but once you reach the top you will be treated to a gorgeous view of La Plata Basin and the rugged Ellingwood Ridge.

Ellingwood Ridge rises up the northeast side of La Plata Peak, and climbers occasionally make the ascent to the summit along that ridge. As you can see from your vantage point on the northwest ridge, the ascent up the Ellingwood Ridge is much more difficult that the trail described here.

Once you reach the top of the northwest ridge the trail simply follows the crest of the ridge for the last 1.0 mile to the summit of La Plata. The first 0.5 mile along the ridge is quite straightforward, but about halfway along you will enter a boulder field where the trail becomes harder to follow. There is also a semi-permanent snowfield near the left side of the ridge at this point, and the ascent is marginally easier if you stay near the edge of the snowfield as you climb. The boulder field ends about halfway up the snowfield, and there you will again see a clear trail veering off to the west side of the ridge.

When you are about 300 feet below the summit the trail turns slightly to the right and climbs into a saddle between La Plata's summit and a small rocky knob on its west side. The trail then climbs the last 150 feet up another boulder field on the west side of the peak.

There are good views all around from the summit of La Plata, but the most interesting landmarks are to the north. Mount Elbert, the highest point in Colorado, rises above the surrounding summits only 6.3 miles away in the direction of magnetic north. Mount Massive, the state's second highest peak is about 20 degrees west of Mount Elbert and 4.9 miles more distant. Directly below the summit you can admire the rugged Ellingwood Ridge rising up the north side of the mountain between the La Plata Basin and Crystal Lake Creek and be thankful that there is an easier way down.

Ellingwood Ridge

Mount Massive

Mount Massive Wilderness Area
day hike

Distance: 13.4 miles (round trip)

Walking time: 10 hours

Elevations: 4,380 ft. gain/loss
Mount Massive Trailhead (start): 10,060 ft.
Mount Massive: 14,421 ft.

Trail: The trail is well maintained for the first 6.1 miles, but just below the summit it becomes very rocky and somewhat confusing.

Season: Midsummer through mid-fall. The higher parts of the trail are usually covered with snow from November through early July.

Vicinity: Near Leadville

Maps: Mount Massive *(USGS)*
Aspen, Independence Pass *(Trails Illustrated, #127)*

Information: http://colorado.utahtrails.com/mountmassive.html
http://www.fs.fed.us/r2/psicc/ *(San Isabel National Forest)*
phone: (719) 486-0749 *(Leadville Ranger District)*

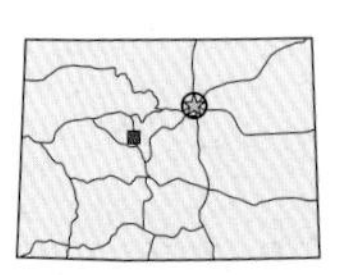

Drive south from downtown Leadville on Highway 24 for 3.9 miles to the junction with Road 300. Turn right here and drive west, following the signs to Halfmoon Campground. 0.8 mile after leaving Highway 24 you will see a sign directing you to turn south onto Road 11. Stay on Road 11 for 1.3 miles, and just before the pavement ends you will see another unpaved road on the right marked by another sign pointing the way to Halfmoon Campground. This is the continuation of Road 11. Turn right here and drive the last 3.9 miles to Halfmoon Campground. Continuing on past Halfmoon Campground for another 1.5 miles will bring you to the well-marked Mount Massive Trailhead and parking area.

As you may already know, Mount Massive is the second highest peak in the Colorado Rockies. At one time it was thought to be the highest peak, but a later survey determined that the nearby Mount Elbert was slightly higher. Mount Massive, however, will always reign supreme in one respect. As its name suggests, the sheer volume of the mountain is far larger than any other fourteener in Colorado. The

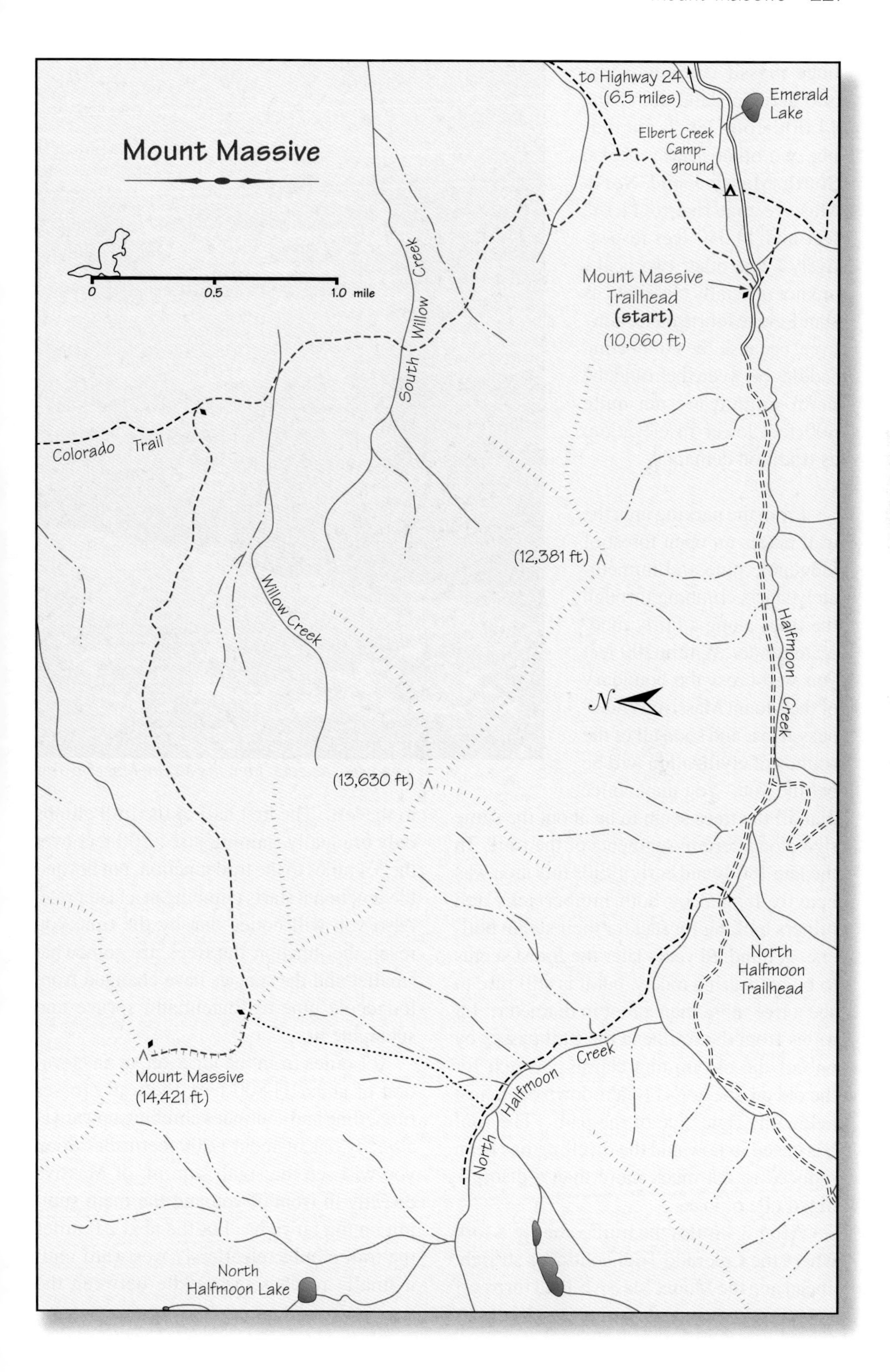
Mount Massive
0
0.5
1.0 mile
to Highway 24
(6.5 miles)
Emerald
Lake
Elbert Creek
Camp-
ground
Mount Massive
Trailhead
(start)
(10,060 ft)
South Willow Creek
Colorado Trail
Willow Creek
(12,381 ft)
Halfmoon Creek
N
(13,630 ft)
North
Halfmoon
Trailhead
Mount Massive
(14,421 ft)
North Halfmoon Creek
North
Halfmoon Lake

huge massif contains some 300 acres of land above the 14,000-foot level, including two other nearby peaks, South Massive and North Massive that rise to 14,132 feet and 14,340 feet respectively. The other two peaks are not officially classified as stand-alone fourteeners, however, because the connecting saddles between them and the main summit are not quite 300 feet lower in elevation, as tradition demands.

Leadville, as seen from the Mount Massive Trail

From the parking area the trail enters an open forest of lodgepole pine and immediately starts climbing through the trees along a fairly moderate grade. Within 200 feet you will cross the boundary of the Mount Massive Wilderness Area, and soon all of the sounds of civilization will be behind you. You may notice that all the trees seem to be about the same size along certain segments of the trail. In the late 1800s and early 1900s this area was heavily logged by both lumberjacks and miners looking for fuel for their steam boilers. A hundred years later the forest seems to be recovering nicely, but it is still rare to see a tree more than a foot in diameter. 1.8 miles from the trailhead the trail passes by one of the old mining claims. Watch for the old prospector's broken-down cabin just below the right side of the path. The roof has caved in now and the dwelling has been reduced to not much more than a disorganized pile of logs,

After 3.4 miles the trail comes to a fork where the Colorado Trail continues straight ahead and the Mount Massive Trail turns off to the left. The first half of the trail climbs only gradually, gaining just 1,200 feet over the 3.4 miles to the trail junction, but beyond the junction it starts climbing at a faster rate. Also you will notice that by the time you reach the junction the trees are somewhat smaller and the species have changed from lodgepole pine to Engelmann spruce and subalpine fir.

0.7 miles from the junction, at an elevation of about 11,800 feet, the trail crosses timberline and continues climbing upward at a steady rate of about 1,200 feet/mile. Soon you will see the south summit of Massive directly in front of you and the main summit on the far right. For the next 2.0 miles the trail climbs relentlessly westward until it finally reaches the saddle between the two peaks.

Once you reach the saddle you must turn north along a much more primitive trail for the last 0.6 mile. This part of the trail can be confusing. The ridge is extremely rocky, and the trail is vague with many false spurs diverging from the main route. The easiest way stays high near the crest of the ridge. You will cross a false summit just 200 yards before reaching the top of Mount Massive, then the trail looses 50 feet of elevation and climbs back to the main summit.

Several landmarks stand out as you survey mountains below, including Mount Elbert, Colorado's highest peak. The higher summit is just 5 miles away on the south side of Halfmoon Creek. From this perspective Massive appears to be the higher of the two, but Elbert wins by a scant 12 feet. On most days Leadville and Turquoise Lake are clearly visible to the east, and to the west you can look directly down onto the North Halfmoon Lakes at the head of North Halfmoon Creek.

North Halfmoon Trail

If you have a shuttle car or don't mind 2.5 miles of road walking you might want to consider returning to the Mount Massive Trailhead via a different route. Look carefully when you return to the saddle that connects Mount Massive to its south summit and you will see a primitive trail that turns right for an abrupt descent down the southwest side of the saddle. This hiker-made trail is extremely steep—it looses 2,700 feet in only 1.1 miles—and it is not well defined. The trail ultimately intersects the North Halfmoon Trail on the east side of North Halfmoon Creek, then follows the creek for another 3.1 miles to North Halfmoon Trailhead.

The North Halfmoon Trailhead is located on Forest Road 11 just 2.5 miles beyond the Mount Massive Trailhead. This segment of road is very rough, however, and you will need a 4WD vehicle if you intend to drive on it. Just before the road crosses North Halfmoon Creek you will see a sign on the right marking the trailhead and parking area where you should leave your shuttle car.

The distance from the summit of Mount Massive to the North Halfmoon Trailhead is only 3.1 miles, compared to 6.7 miles to the Mount Massive Trailhead. Even if you have to road walk the last 2.5 miles between the two trailheads it is still 1.1 miles shorter to return via the North Halfmoon Trail.

For several years an organization called the Colorado Fourteeners Initiative has been involved in building a proper trail from North Halfmoon Creek to the top of Mount Massive, and when they finish their work this alternative route will probably be the most popular way to climb the mountain. As this book goes to press, however, the trail is still far from complete.

Mount Massive summit

Mount Elbert

★★ **day hike**

Distance:	8.8 miles (round trip)
Walking time:	7 1/2 hours
Elevations:	4,400 ft. gain/loss Mount Elbert Trailhead (start): 10,040 ft. Mount Elbert: 14,440 ft.
Trail:	Well marked, easy to follow
Season:	Midsummer through mid-fall. The higher parts of the trail are usually covered with snow from November through early July.
Vicinity:	Near Leadville
Maps:	Mount Massive, Mount Elbert *(USGS)* Aspen, Independence Pass *(Trails Illustrated, #127)*
Information:	http://colorado.utahtrails.com/mountelbert.html http://www.fs.fed.us/r2/psicc/ *(San Isabel National Forest)* phone: (719) 486-0749 *(Leadville Ranger District)*

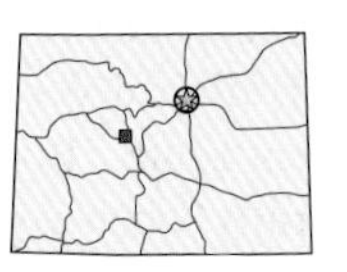

Drive south from downtown Leadville on Highway 24 for 3.9 miles to the junction with Road 300. Turn right here and drive west, following the signs to Halfmoon Campground. 0.8 mile after leaving Highway 24 you will see a sign directing you to turn south onto Road 11. Stay on Road 11 for 1.3 miles, and just before the pavement ends you will see another unpaved road on the right marked by another sign pointing the way to Halfmoon Campground. This is the continuation of Road 11. Turn right here and drive the last 3.9 miles to Halfmoon Campground. Continuing on past Halfmoon Campground for another 1.0 miles will bring you to the well-marked Mount Elbert Trailhead and parking area.

Mount Elbert is not the most scenic fourteener in Colorado, but it can certainly hold its own—and it does happen to be the highest mountain in the state! The peak was named in 1871 after Samuel Elbert, the territorial governor of Colorado, and it was first climbed 3 years later by members of the Hayden Survey Expedition. At that time no one realized that Mount Elbert was the highest peak in Colorado. That honor was mistakenly bestowed upon Pikes Peak and later upon Mount Massive. We now know,

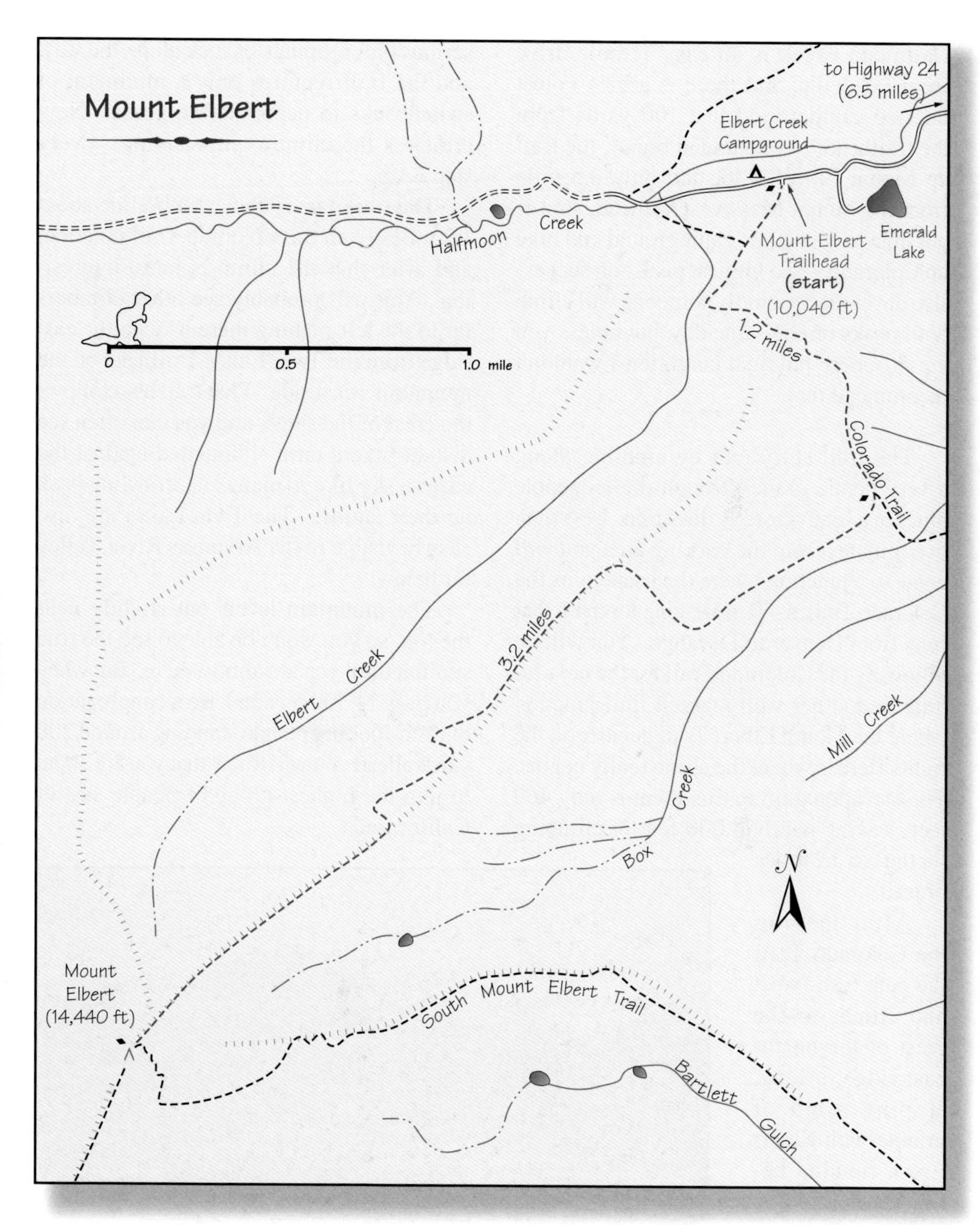

however, that the stately Mount Elbert is not only the highest peak in Colorado, but it is the second loftiest summit outside Alaska in the entire United States. Only Mount Whitney in California is higher.

There are three separate trails leading to the top of Mount Elbert, from the north, south, and east, and on a clear summer day you can usually see people ascending the peak from all three directions. Each of the routes has its own merits, but the most popular trail begins at Halfmoon Creek and climbs the mountain's northeast ridge. That is the route I will describe here.

Halfmoon Creek is an easy 11-mile drive from Leadville, and there is a nice Forest Service campground just 100 yards from the trailhead. As an added bonus, the trail up Mount Elbert is located only 0.5 mile from the Mount Massive Trailhead, so it is possible to stay at the campground and hike up Colorado's two highest peaks on successive days. Occasionally someone will climb both peaks on the same day, but unless you are in superb physical condition I wouldn't recommend that.

The trail starts out by ambling along a very gentle grade through the lodgepole pines in a southwesterly direction. Less than five minutes from the parking area you will come to a junction where the route joins the Colorado Trail, a 471-mile-long footpath that runs from Denver to Durango. You will be following the Colorado Trail for the next 1.0 mile to another well-marked trail junction where the Mount Elbert Trail departs on the right. Here is where the climb really begins. The elevation gain to this point is only 460 feet, leaving nearly 4,000 feet of climbing for the last 3.2 miles of trail.

After leaving the Colorado Trail the path turns west and climbs to the crest of the northeast ridge, a long, sloping ramp of granite with Elbert Creek running below its north side and Box Creek to the south. The top of the ridge is almost obstacle-free and provides a perfect platform for a trail. There are no serious outcroppings of rock along the way, and the trail requires only a minimum of switchbacks to negotiate the grade. Nevertheless the climb is unrelenting. Every step is up.

The trail passes above timberline about 1.3 miles from the Colorado Trail junction, and after that the climb is more interesting. You will probably see other climbers far to the left inching there way up the east ridge from the Twin Lakes Trailhead on the mountain's east side. That trail also follows the crest of the ridge, and you can often see distant hikers on it silhouetted against the eastern sky like so many ants crawling back up their anthill. The Twin Lakes are also clearly visible in the Arkansas River Valley far below.

The mountain levels out slightly near the top, so you won't be able to see the true summit until you are almost there. But when you pass 14,300 feet and see a congregation of tired-looking people standing around 200 yards ahead you will know that you are about to join the highest group of people east of California.

Ascending the northeast ridge of Mount Elbert

Missouri Lakes/Holy Cross City

★★★★★

Holy Cross Wilderness Area
overnight hike

Distance:	10.6 miles (loop)
Walking time:	day 1: 6 hours day 2: 2 1/2 hours
Elevations:	2,770 ft. gain/loss Missouri Lakes Trailhead (start): 10,000 ft. Fancy Pass: 12,380 ft. Fancy Lake: 11,540 ft. Holy Cross City: 11,340 ft.
Trail:	Excellent trail, but very steep in places. A portion of the trail to Holy Cross City is actually a 4WD jeep road.
Season:	Midsummer through mid-fall. The higher parts of the trail are generally covered with snow from late November through mid-July.
Vicinity:	Near Leadville
Maps:	Mount of the Holy Cross, Mount Jackson *(USGS)* Holy Cross, Ruedi Reservoir (*Trails Illustrated, #126*)
Information:	http://colorado.utahtrails.com/missourilakes.html http://www.fs.fed.us/r2/whiteriver/ (*White River National Forest)* phone: (970) 827-5715 *(Holy Cross Ranger District)*

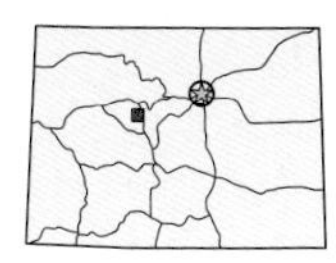

Drive east of Vail on I-70 and take the Minturn exit 171. Continue south, through Minturn, on Highway 24 for 14 miles until you see a sign marking the Homestake Road on your right. Turn here and drive south on the Homestake Road for 7.7 miles to the junction with the Missouri Creek Road. Turn right again and follow the Missouri Creek Road for 2.2 miles to a point where the road makes a sudden hairpin turn to the right. Stop at the turn and look to your left. 150 feet from the road you will see a large sign marking the Missouri Lakes Trailhead where the hike begins.

The Fancy Creek Trailhead, where the hike ends, is located on the left side of Missouri Creek Road just a hundred yards north of the Missouri Lakes Trailhead.

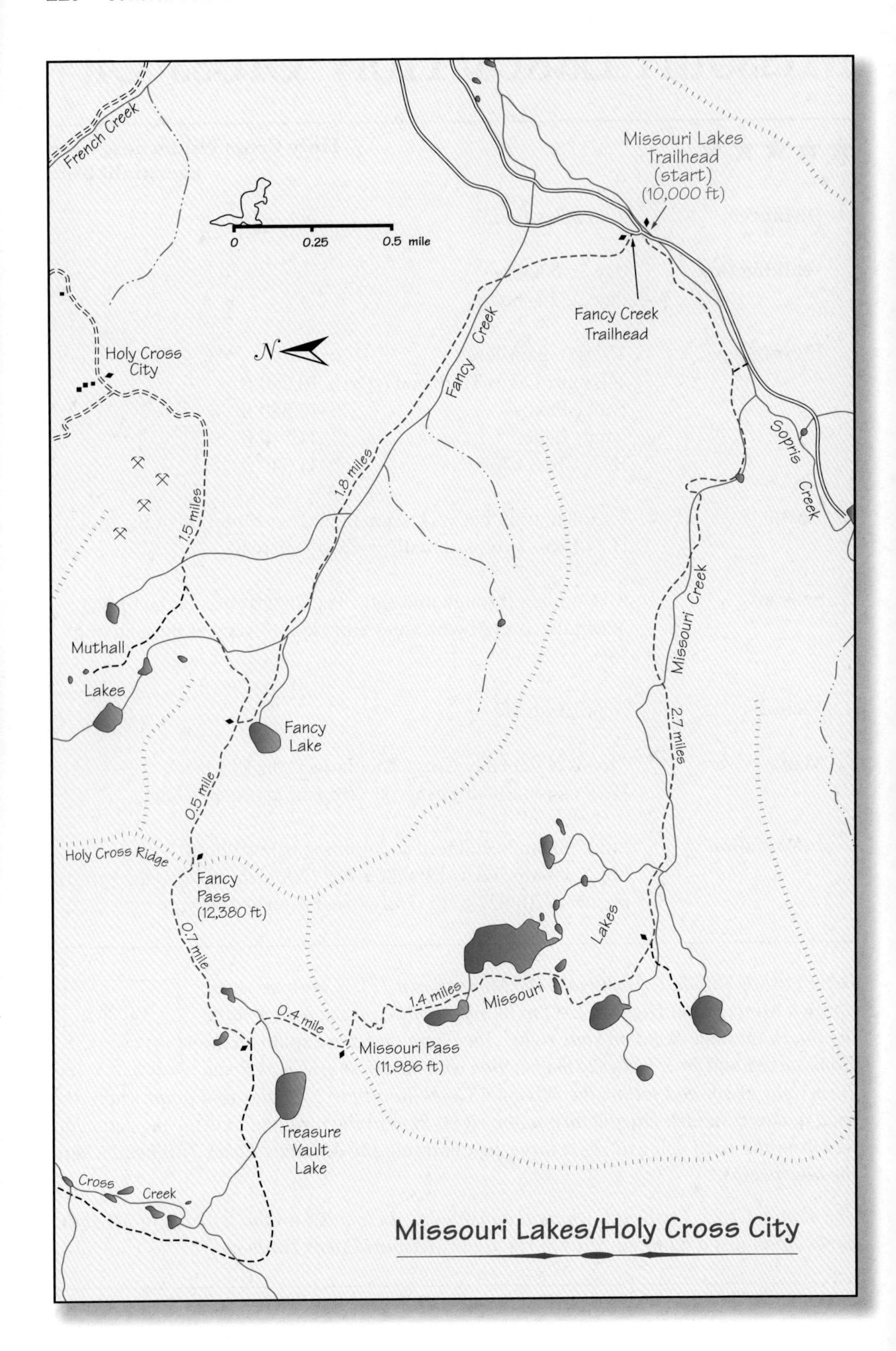

French Creek
Missouri Lakes Trailhead (start) (10,000 ft)
0
0.25
0.5 mile
Fancy Creek Trailhead
N
Holy Cross City
Fancy Creek
Sopris Creek
1.8 miles
1.5 miles
Missouri Creek
Muthall Lakes
Fancy Lake
2.7 miles
0.5 mile
Holy Cross Ridge
Fancy Pass (12,380 ft)
0.7 mile
Lakes
1.4 miles
Missouri
0.4 mile
Missouri Pass (11,986 ft)
Treasure Vault Lake
Cross Creek
Missouri Lakes/Holy Cross City

This loop hike offers three scenic rewards, any one of which would be enough to make the trip worthwhile. The first treat is the beautiful Missouri Lakes Basin, with four large lakes and a half-dozen smaller ones surrounded on three sides by peaks nearly 13,000 feet high. The second point of interest is the view into the spectacular Cross Creek glacial valley from the summits of Missouri Pass and Fancy Pass. And the third reward is the opportunity to walk through Holy Cross City, a late 1800s mining town that lies just outside the wilderness boundary.

The hike can be completed without too much difficulty in one 8 hour day; however a more leisurely walk of two days will allow you to better enjoy the exceptional scenery and the historical mining town of Holy Cross. If you are getting off to a late start you will find a number of fine campsites in the Missouri Lakes Basin only three miles from the trailhead. Otherwise, Fancy Lake is a fine place to pitch camp for the night. In addition to the itinerary suggested here there are several opportunities for more off-trail exploration, especially in the area west of Holy Cross City.

As you begin this hike you will notice the presence of a large aqueduct that goes underground near the trailhead. This structure provides a poignant reminder of the uphill battle faced by western conservationists in their never-ending struggle to protect the region's wilderness. There is almost always something in these wild places that somebody wants; in the case of the Holy Cross Wilderness it is water.

In 1962 the cities of Aurora and Colorado Springs obtained the water rights to much of the land that is now included in the Holy Cross Wilderness Area. Work began almost immediately on the Homestake Water Diversion Project, and by the time the wilderness was designated in 1980 the first phase of the water collection plan had been completed. The boundaries of the new wilderness area had to be adjusted to exclude the roads, pipes, and reservoirs created by the project, but local environmentalists were able to prevent phase two of the Homestake Project from proceeding. Today most of the land within the Holy Cross boundaries is still pristine; however sections are still at risk. For the past 20 years concerned citizens have been waging a series of legal battles to prevent Aurora and Colorado Springs from dewatering the high alpine valleys of Cross Creek and Fall Creek. The fight continues today, with no guarantee that the courts won't ultimately rule against them.

Missouri Lakes Basin

Looking west into Cross Creek Basin from Fancy Pass

Day 1 (5.8 miles)

For the first mile the trail to Missouri Lakes seems to be following an old abandoned roadbed. Actually a huge pipe is buried under this section of trail; it intercepts Missouri Creek just outside of the wilderness area to carry water from the drainage to Homestake Reservoir (all part of the Homestake Water Diversion Project). 0.6 mile from the trailhead the path meets one of the service roads for the aqueduct, where there is an alternative trailhead. Beyond that the trail veers west and north, and after another 0.4 miles it enters Holy Cross Wilderness Area.

I almost always experience a feeling of excitement, anticipation and relief when I see one of the familiar wooden signs that mark wilderness area boundaries. But nowhere is that feeling more intense than along the Missouri Lakes trail. It is impossible not to notice the difference before and beyond that sign. On one side, the forest as God created it; on the other, the forest as Man has modified it. It is a lesson that is bound to stick in the mind of anyone who walks this trail.

For the next 1.7 miles the route never strays far from the delightfully picturesque Missouri Creek. Log footbridges cross the stream on several occasions, once just below a particularly pretty cascade where the creek cuts through a layer of black schist. Finally the trail breaks out of the trees into the Missouri Lakes Basin, a relatively flat, open pocket of alpine tundra that lies just below timberline. 1,500 feet above the basin the deep blue sky touches a rugged surrounding skyline of granite and schist peaks. And scattered amidst the wildflowers on the bottom of the tundra are a half dozen cold blue lakes, the largest of which is a quarter-mile long.

For the next mile the trail meanders through the basin, passing by three of the largest lakes. If you want to see the fourth lake you must turn left on a 0.3 mile spur trail that leaves the main trail shortly after you enter the basin. As you near the northern side of the basin the trail begins to climb, and soon you will start switchbacking up the stony terrain towards Missouri Pass, the low point on the surrounding ridge. The trail is fairly steep in a few places, but it doesn't last long. After a 400-foot climb you will reach the top, where you should pause to look back for another fine view of the Missouri Lakes Basin before you cross the pass.

Looking north from Missouri Pass you can see almost the entire length of Cross Creek Valley, with its headwaters below you at Treasure Vault Lake. On the east side of Cross Creek is Holy Cross Ridge, which culminates on the north end of the valley at the Mount of the Holy Cross. Below the pass you can see most of the trail that will take you past Treasure Vault Lake and on up to the top of Fancy Pass.

Treasure Vault Lake

From the top of Missouri Pass the trail descends for 0.4 mile to a junction on the northeast side of Treasure Vault Lake. From there it turns east and begins climbing again for another 0.7 mile until it reaches the top of Fancy Pass. The view from the top of Fancy Pass is even grander than the view from Missouri Pass. From Fancy your eyes will be drawn westward, across Cross Creek Valley, to the long line of 12,000- and 13,000-foot peaks that extend for miles across the heart of the Holy Cross Wilderness to Eagle Peak (13,049 ft.) on the western side of the protected area.

If you are a student of geology, you may also notice that the rock on the northwest side of Missouri Pass and Fancy Pass is almost entirely granite, whereas on the opposite side of these passes there is a great deal of schist. Apparently the ancient magma intrusion that created the granite in this area must have stopped near the ridge between these two passes.

Trail from Fancy Pass to Fancy Lake

From Fancy Pass the trail drops abruptly downward, making an extremely steep descent to Fancy Lake. The trail looses 800 feet in 0.5 mile without the luxury of a switchback. Along the way you will see pieces of old mining equipment that were hauled over the pass in the late 1800s to mines on the east side of the ridge. Moving heavy iron machinery over this kind of terrain with only horses and men must have been a back-breaking task.

You will be able to see Fancy Lake as you descend from the pass. When you reach the same elevation as the lake, 0.5 mile from the summit, you should see a vague trail branching off to the right. Follow this trail the last 0.1 mile to the lake. Fancy Lake is a good place to spend the night. At this point you are only 1.8 miles from the trailhead, but spending the night here will allow you to enjoy the mountain air, as well as make a 3.0 mile side trip to Holy Cross City the next morning.

Day 2 (4.8 miles)

Before descending to the Fancy Creek Trailhead you should take a side trip to Holy Cross City, a historic mining town that was flourishing 125 years ago. The remnants of this once booming town are an easy 1-hour walk from Fancy Lake and there is a lot to see in the area. In order to get there you must walk back 200 yards to the point where the Fancy Lake Trail leaves the main trail coming down from Fancy Pass. Turn right at the junction and follow the old jeep road in an easterly direction. The old abandoned road meanders along the side of the mountain with very little change in elevation for 1.5 miles before arriving at a small meadow where the main part of the town was once located. At least 7 cabins are easily visible from the road in this area, although only two of them are still standing. You will also see a massive array of old mining equipment scattered across the landscape.

During its heyday from 1880 to 1884 there were four mining companies operating in Holy Cross City. The town also supported two stamp mills, two general stores, a post office, a hotel and several boarding houses. For a brief time the 300 or so people who lived there even enjoyed a daily mail service and stagecoach connection, but the glory days were short lived. After 1884 the mines began to play out, and by the late 1890s the town was completely deserted.

In order to complete the hike you must backtrack to Fancy Lake and continue down the Fancy Creek Trail to the bottom of the valley. The trail is very steep in places, loosing 1,460 feet of elevation in just 1.8 miles. It closely follows the north side of Fancy Creek with no switchbacks to impede its rate of descent. The path finally ends just outside the Holy Cross Wilderness Area near a huge water intake pipe where the whole of Fancy Creek is swallowed up and channeled into the Homestake Reservoir for later use by the cities of Aurora and Colorado Springs.

Holy Cross City

Fall Creek Pass/Tuhare Lakes

★★★★★

Holy Cross Wilderness Area
overnight hike

Distance:	14.3 miles (round trip)
Walking time:	day 1: 6 hours day 2: 6 1/4 hours
Elevations:	4,400 ft. gain/loss Holy Cross Jeep Road parking area (start): 10,280 ft. Hunky Dory Trailhead: 11,160 ft. Fall Creek Pass: 12,590 ft. Lake Constantine: 11,371 ft. Upper Tuhare Lake: 12,365 ft.
Trail:	Mostly well marked and well maintained; however the trail up to the Tuhare Lakes requires some miner scrambling.
Season:	Late summer through early fall. The higher parts of the trail are generally covered with snow from mid July until late November.
Vicinity:	Near Leadville
Maps:	Mount of the Holy Cross *(USGS)* Holy Cross, Ruedi Reservoir (*Trails Illustrated, #126*)
Information:	http://colorado.utahtrails.com/fallcreekpass.html http://www.fs.fed.us/r2/whiteriver/ *(White River National Forest)* phone: (970) 827-5715 *(Holy Cross Ranger District)*

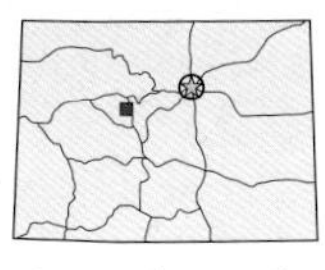

Drive east of Vail on I-70 and take exit 171 to Minturn. Continue south, through Minturn, on Highway 24 for 14 miles until you see a sign marking Homestake Road on your right. Turn here and drive south on Homestake Road for 7.7 miles to the junction with the Missouri Creek Road. Turn right again and follow the Missouri Creek Road for the next 2.2 miles to a junction where the Homestake Collection System Road (Forest Road 727) departs on the right. Turn right here and drive north, past the Fancy Lake Trailhead, for the last 1.8 miles. The road becomes increasingly primitive after leaving the Fancy Lake Trailhead, but with care most cars with reasonably high clearance should be able to make it. You will pass two other primitive spur roads along the way where you must bear right. Finally you will come to a large parking area where you can leave your car. On the north side of the parking area there is a spur that leads 100 feet further into the woods to intersect the Holy Cross Jeep Road.

There are two ways to hike to the Tuhare Lakes: you can walk south from the Half Moon/Fall Creek Trailhead (nearer Minturn) for a distance of 5.4 miles, or you can walk north from the Hunky Dory Trailhead for a distance of 5.2 miles. It is much easier to drive to the Half Moon/Fall Creek Trailhead, so most people begin the hike from there, but in my opinion the trail from Hunky Dory is much more interesting than the northern route. For that reason I will describe the southern trail. The hike from the Hunky Dory Trailhead takes you past the Seven Sisters Lakes and over Fall Creek Pass before dropping down to the Tuhare Lakes Trail. Furthermore, Holy Cross City is just a 15-minute walk from the Hunky Dory Trailhead. You might want to take a side trip to see that historic ghost town before beginning this hike. (See page 227.)

In order to reach Holy Cross City just continue walking past the Hunky Dory Trailhead along the Holy Cross Jeep Road for another 0.8 mile. The town has been deserted for 120 years and, to my knowledge, no effort has ever been made to preserve any of the buildings or other artifacts, so don't expect to find any pristine structures. But during its heyday in the early 1880s Holy Cross City was a bustling place, and a great deal of ore from the surrounding mines was processed there. The short-lived town possessed two general stores, a hotel, a post office, and even a stagecoach connection with Leadville, 30 miles away. From the road you can still see the remains of a half-dozen cabins, two of which are still standing, and, of course, tons and tons of discarded iron mining machinery scattered across the ground. The mines themselves are mostly located in the hills above the north side of the townsite.

Day 1 (6.3 miles)

Years ago it was possible to reach the Hunky Dory Trailhead by driving a stock 4wd vehicle 1.5 miles up the Holy Cross Jeep Road. The road, however, has not been

Lake number four of the Seven Sisters Lakes

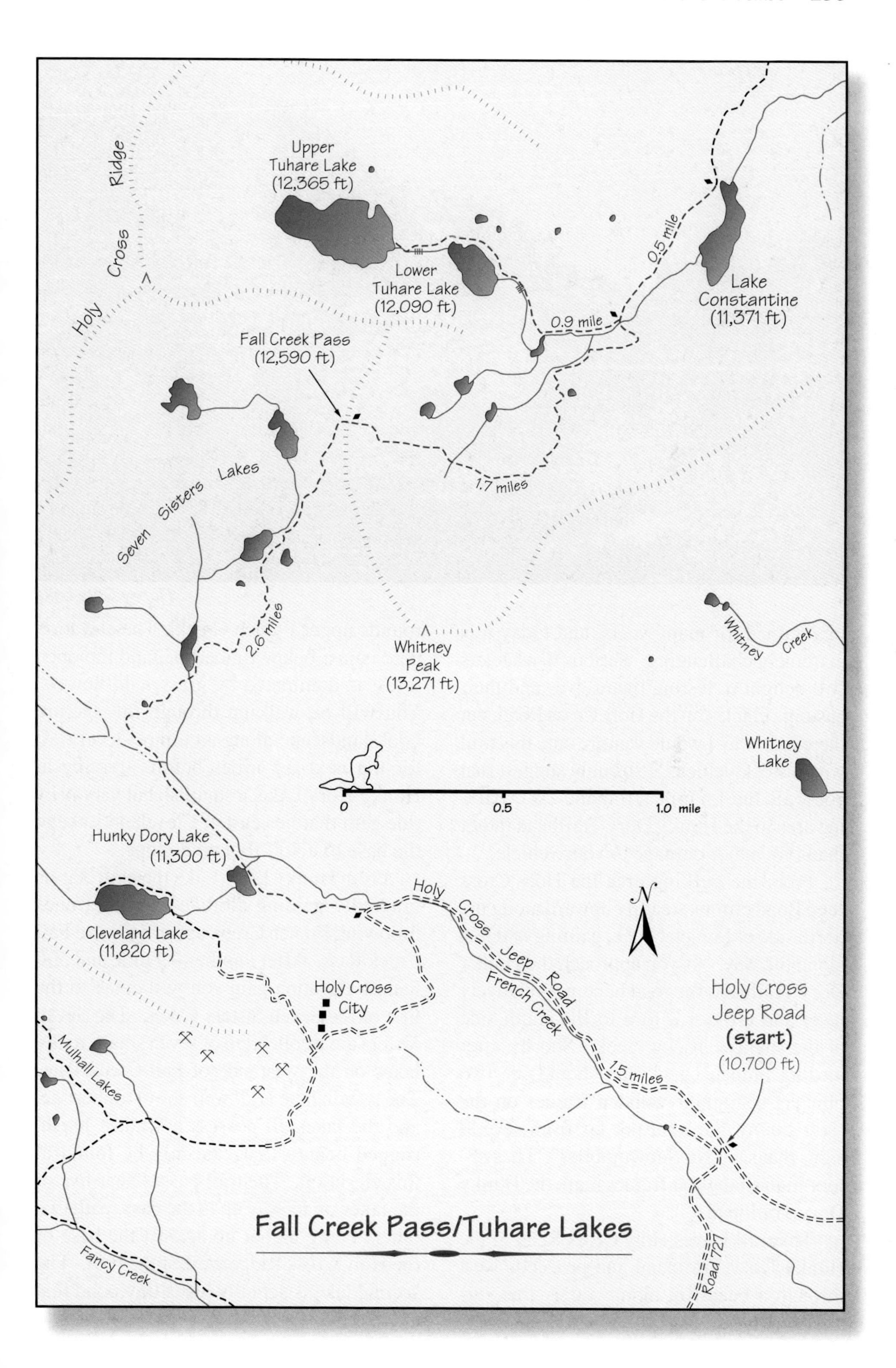

Upper
Tuhare Lake
(12,365 ft)
Holy Cross Ridge
Lower
Tuhare Lake
(12,090 ft)
Lake
Constantine
(11,371 ft)
0.5 mile
0.9 mile
Fall Creek Pass
(12,590 ft)
Seven Sisters Lakes
1.7 miles
2.6 miles
Whitney
Peak
(13,271 ft)
Whitney Creek
Whitney
Lake
0
0.5
1.0 mile
Hunky Dory Lake
(11,300 ft)
Cleveland Lake
(11,820 ft)
Holy Cross Jeep Road
French Creek
Holy Cross
City
Mulhall Lakes
1.5 miles
Holy Cross
Jeep Road
(start)
(10,700 ft)
Road 727
Fancy Creek
N
Fall Creek Pass/Tuhare Lakes

Hunky Dory Lake

maintained for many years, and today it is extremely challenging. Serious 4-wheelers still delight in testing themselves and their custom vehicles on the Holy Cross Road, but there is no way I would venture onto this trail with a stock vehicle. I strongly suggest that you walk the 1.5 miles from the 2WD parking area to the Hunky Dory Trailhead rather than risk major damage to your vehicle.

From the parking area the Holy Cross Jeep Road climbs steadily upward along the north side of French Creek, gaining 880 feet along the way. As you approach the Hunky Dory Trailhead the road becomes relatively level and crosses a ford to the south side of the shallow, rocky creek. Shortly after fording French Creek you should see two obvious triangular wooden frames on the right side of the road not far from several signs that say "No Snowmobiles". These 8-foot-high triangular frames mark the Hunky Dory Trailhead.

The trail leaves Holy Cross Road at the Hunky Dory Trailhead and proceeds west through a beautiful alpine valley that surrounds upper French Creek. The elevation here is just below timberline, and the open forest is dominated by grass wild flowers. You will be walking through this picture book landscape along an almost level trail for the next 0.5 miles before arriving at Hunky Dory Lake, a smallish but very pristine gem that lies east of Cleveland Lake at the base of a 400-foot talus slope.

From Hunky Dory Lake the path begins gradually gaining altitude as it continues following French Creek upward toward Fall Creek Pass. After another 0.9 mile and 500 feet of elevation gain you will come to the first of the Seven Sisters Lakes. The Seven Sisters are a collection of seven small, rocky lakes on the west side of Fall Creek Pass. The terrain here is all well above timberline, and the lakes all possess a kind of harsh, rugged beauty that can only be found at this elevation. The trail passes near five of the lakes on its way up to the pass, with two others being higher up against the base of the Holy Cross Ridge west of the trail. The second lake is actually just a tiny pond that you will see on your left 15 minutes after leaving the first lake. It hardly qualifies as a lake by my definition, but I guess "Seven Sisters" sounds more interesting than the "Six Sisters Lakes".

Shortly after passing the baby sister lake the trail goes between two more lakes as it climbs steadily toward the highest point of this hike. Another 15 minutes will bring you to the last lake, and just beyond that you will be on the summit of Fall Creek Pass. As you cross to the east side of the pass you will notice the presence of much more vegetation than could be found on the rocky west side. The trail descends through a broad, flat alpine meadow that seems to be filled with fat, lazy marmots. For the first 0.7 mile after crossing Fall Creek Pass the trail makes a leisurely descent through thick blankets of wildflowers (late July to mid August) before turning north to begin a much more serious descent into Fall Creek Valley.

As you cross timberline the trail passes another small but delightfully pretty alpine lake as the views to the north open before you. Lake Constantine is soon visible directly ahead, and in the back of a distant alpine basin on your left your eyes will be drawn to a long graceful waterfall that cascades down from an unseen source. Actually, the source of this magnificent waterfall is the lower Tuhare Lake, your next day's destination. The trail you must follow to reach the lake climbs just to the right of the waterfall.

Finally, after loosing 1,100 feet from the summit of Fall Creek Pass, the trail arrives at Fall Creek. Upon crossing the stream on a primitive log bridge you will see a sign

North side of Fall Creek Pass

Lake Constantine

marking the Tuhare Lakes Trail junction. The elevation where the trail crosses the creek is still 11,500 feet, which would be above the tree line in many parts of Colorado, but here the forest is well timbered. There are a number of fine campsites in this area, and you probably will not want to climb to the Tuhare Lakes until the next day. The lakes and the waterfalls are prettiest in the morning when the sun is in the east.

If you are looking for privacy you might want to consider another campsite a short distance up the Tuhare Lakes Trail. This site is located 0.3 mile from the trail junction in a very pleasant area near a pond on the left side of the trail. The disadvantage is that this site is about 300 feet higher than the trail junction, and some scrambling is required to get there. In general, you will find that the Tuhare Lakes Trail is much more primitive than the Fall Creek Trail, with some hand over hand scrambling required in a few places. This can be a problem if you are carrying a heavy backpack.

If it is still early in the day my choice would be to continue down the Fall Creek Trail for another 0.5 mile to Lake Constantine where there are many attractive lake side campsites, especially on the south and west sides of the lake. Constantine is a good-sized lake, over 0.3 mile long and 100 yards wide. It is well timbered with Engelmann spruce, and if you are packing a fishing pole you will find that the fishing is not bad.

Day 2 (8.0 miles)

In order to see the Tuhare Lakes you must backtrack 0.5 mile from Lake Constantine to the trail junction and turn right. As noted before, this is a primitive trail with a

Waterfall below the Tuhare Lakes

good deal of elevation gain, so it is best to leave your backpack at the Tuhare Lakes trail junction before beginning the climb. Within just a few minutes of leaving Fall Creek the trail comes to a granite outcropping where some scrambling is necessary. Following that it reaches a plateau where you can enjoy a few minutes of level ground before again continuing the climb. The waterfall on the north side of the canyon will be in full view as you continue upward, and the scenery just keeps getting better.

The trail climbs steadily up the right side of the stream, passing the northeast side of the waterfall, before finally reaching level ground again on the east side of Lower Tuhare Lake. Again, you are well above timberline at this point, so don't expect any shade. The trail to the upper lake continues around the northern side of the lower lake and follows the north side of the drainage upward for another 275 feet of elevation gain. Once again, there is a waterfall below the outlet of the upper lake, and the trail climbs up the north side of the fall. Finally, just below the upper lake the trail drops into the creek itself where you must depend on a series of stepping stones to avoid getting you feet wet. The lake will greet you as you step out of the drainage.

Nestled snugly against the east side of Holy Cross Ridge at an altitude of 12,365 feet, Upper Tuhare Lake is very cold, very remote, very pristine, and very big—more than twice the size of the lower lake. It is unusual to find such a large lake so high in the mountains of Colorado. The Holy Cross Ridge which provides the backdrop for upper Tuhare Lake is punctuated by two unnamed high thirteeners, the one on the northeast side of the lake being just 169 feet shy of 14,000 feet. The fabled Mount of the Holy Cross (14,005 ft.) is unfortunately not visible from the lake shore, although it lies at the top of the ridge only a mile north of the upper lake.

Upper Tuhare Lake

Buffalo Meadows Loop

★

Buffalo Peaks Wilderness Area
day hike

Distance:	11.4 miles (loop)
Walking time:	7 1/2 hours
Elevations:	1.900 ft. gain/loss Rich Creek Trailhead (start): 9,950 ft. highest point: 11,560 ft.
Trail:	Well marked, easy to follow
Season:	Midsummer through mid-fall. The higher parts of the trail are usually covered with snow from November through early July.
Vicinity:	near Breckenridge and Fairplay
Maps:	Jones Hill, South Peak *(USGS)* Leadville, Fairplay *(Trails Illustrated, #110)*
Information:	http://colorado.utahtrails.com/buffalomeadows.html http://www.fs.fed.us/r2/psicc/ *(Pike National Forest)* phone: (719) 836-2031 *(South Park Ranger District)*

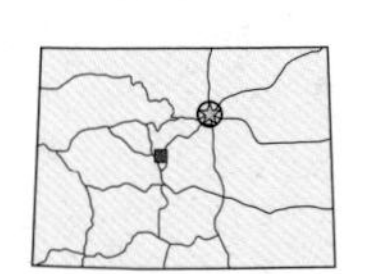

Take exit 203 from I-70 and drive south on Highway 9 to the town of Fairplay. Turn right at the highway junction on the east side of Fairplay and continue south on Highway 285 for another 4.8 miles. There you must turn right onto County Road 5 and drive west toward Weston Pass. 7.0 miles after leaving the highway you will come to another junction with County Road 22. Bear right at this junction, again following the signs to Weston Pass, and after another 3.0 miles you will see the Rich Creek Trailhead and parking area on the left.

The Buffalo Meadows Loop is a somewhat long but very pleasant day hike that will take you through an interesting variety of mountain ecosystems. The route starts at the South Fork of the South Platte River and follows Rich Creek, a smaller tributary, to its headwaters. It then crosses a gentle alpine pass and drops down into the wide grassy valley known as Buffalo Meadows. From there the trail follows the Rough and Tumbling Creek down into a gorgeous riparian area that includes numerous beaver dams and lodges. Finally, the trail climbs up over the ridge that separates Rough and Tumbling Creek from the South Fork South Platte and returns to the trailhead.

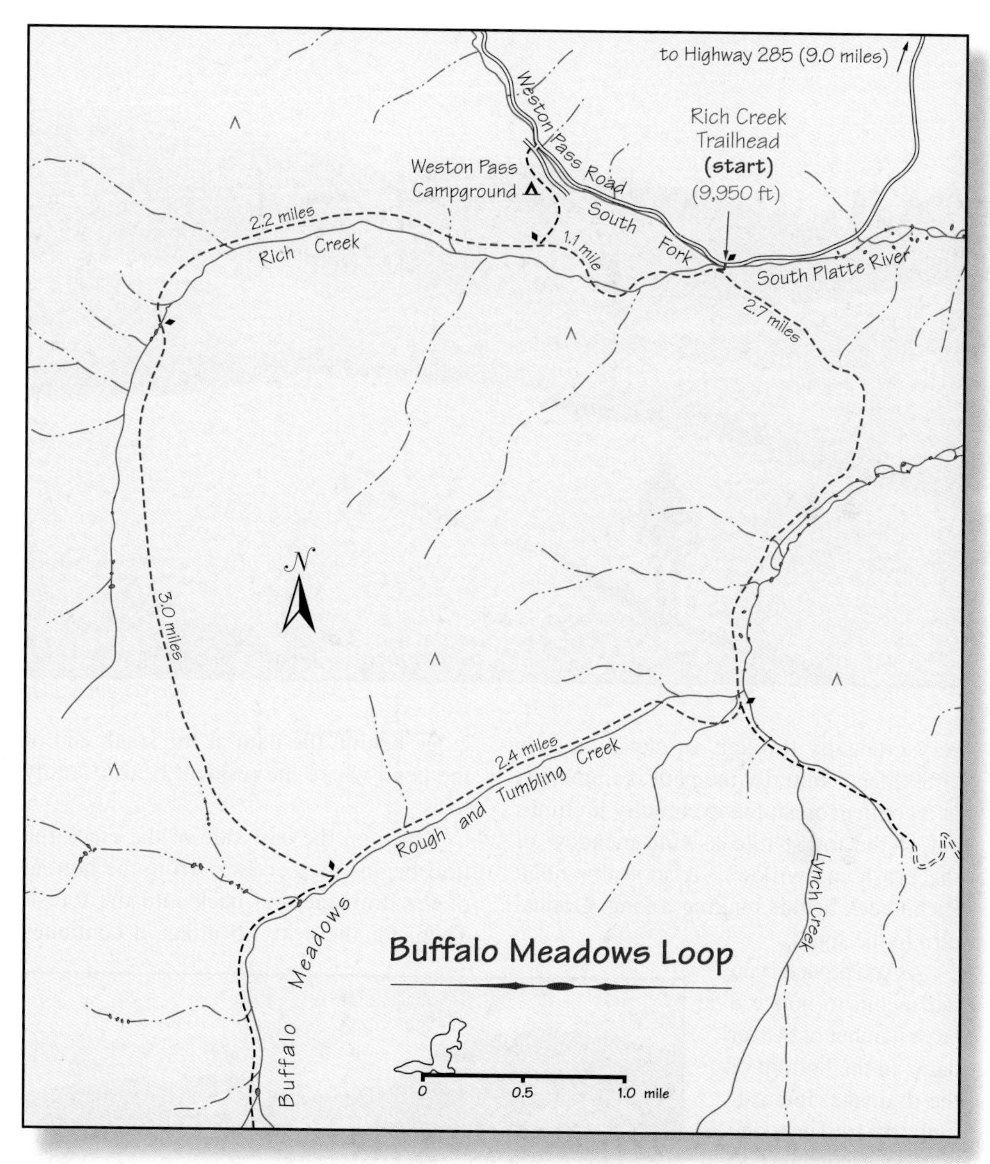

Immediately after leaving the parking area the trail crosses a well-constructed bridge that spans the South Fork of the South Platte River. Once on the south side of the river the trail turns right, and within 200 feet you will see a sign marking the beginning of the Buffalo Meadows loop. This loop can be walked in either direction, but the hike I describe below assumes you will bear right at the sign and begin by following Rich Creek.

Over the next 30 minutes the trail crosses Rich Creek three times, finally coming to a junction above the north side of the creek where a spur trail branches off toward the Weston Pass Campground. Continue straight ahead at this junction, following the north side of Rich Creek in a westerly direction. The trail stays on the right side of the creek for the next 2.1 miles, climbing

Rich Creek Valley

very gradually through an elevation gain of 800 feet. Initially the path is immersed in a conifer forest, but eventually it climbs out of the forest into a wide meadow of sagebrush and willows. Also at this point Rich Creek begins making a long, gradual turn to the south.

As you proceed you will begin to notice a large number of beaver dams in the bottom of the drainage. Interestingly, the trail uses one of the larger dams to cross to the east side of the creek. You may get your feet wet at this point, but most people find it great fun to walk across the narrow, spongy 80-foot dam made of willows and mud. Notice the lodge behind the dam at the south end of the pond where the resident beaver family lives.

Once on the east side of the creek the trail begins to veer away from the bottom of the drainage and back into the forest. Then, for the next 1.6 miles, it continues

Looking east from the Tumble Creek Trail

its gradual climb to the top of the low pass that separates Rich Creek from Rough and Tumbling Creek. After crossing the pass the path descends 1.4 miles to Rough and Tumbling Creek and Buffalo Meadows.

When the trail reaches the valley floor you will come to another junction where the Rich Creek Trail joins the Tumble Creek Trail. In order to complete the loop you must turn left here, but before doing so you may want to follow the Tumble Creek Trail further south into the heart of Buffalo Meadows. The trail extends for another 5.5 miles, finally ending at Fourmile Creek on the southern boundary of the Buffalo Peaks Wilderness Area.

The trail eastward along the Rough and Tumbling Creek is almost level for the next 1.0 mile. Then as the meadow gives way to forest the trail begins to loose elevation. The stream also begins to flow faster now as in descends through a steep V-shaped canyon. For the next 1.4 miles the water cascades noisily downward through a streambed full of boulders and fallen logs, making it clear how Rough and Tumbling Creek got its name.

0.5 mile before the end of the steep canyon the trail veers away to the south and then returns to Rough and Tumbling Creek at its confluence with Lynch Creek. The Tumble Creek Trail also intersects the Lynch Creek Trail at the confluence, but the trails are well posted with signs directing you northward along the Tumble Creek Trail.

For the next 1.3 miles the trail climbs slowly northward along the slopes on the west side of the Rough and Tumbling Creek. The personality of the creek is much different in this area. It has become a slow moving, meandering stream in the bottom of a lush, flat-bottomed valley filled with quaking aspen. This stretch of the Rough and Tumbling is a beaver's paradise, and, predictably enough, dozens of beaver dams can be seen below the trail.

After about 30 minutes the Rough and Tumbling Creek turns east, and the trail begins climbing northward up the ridge that separates it from the trailhead. Most of the climb is through thick groves of aspen, but as you cross over to the north side of the ridge you will again find yourself in a familiar forest of Engelmann spruce, subalpine fir and, surprisingly, a fair amount of bristlecone pine. The ridge tops out 400 feet above Rough and Tumbling Creek, and from there the trail descends 350 feet back to the South Fork South Platte River and the trailhead.

Tumble Creek Trail

Mounts Democrat, Lincoln, Bross

★★ **day hike**

Distance:	8.2 miles (loop)
Walking time:	$6^1/_2$ hours
Elevations:	3,470 ft. gain/loss Kite Lake Trailhead (start): 12,020 ft. Mount Democrat: 14,148 ft. Mount Lincoln: 14,286 ft. Mount Bross: 14,172 ft.
Trail:	The route down from Mount Bross involves a 0.7 mile descent over a very steep trail with loose rock. It is not particularly dangerous if you are careful, but be sure you have good boots and long pants. The last 0.9 mile of the ascent up Mount Democrat is also very rocky.
Season:	Midsummer through mid-fall. The trail is covered with snow from mid-November through June.
Vicinity:	near Breckenridge and Fairplay
Maps:	Climax, Alma *(USGS)* Breckenridge–Tennessee Pass *(Trails Illustrated, #109)*
Information:	http://colorado.utahtrails.com/mountdemocrat.html http://www.fs.fed.us/r2/psicc/ *(Pike National Forest)* phone: (719) 836-2031 *(South Park Ranger District)*

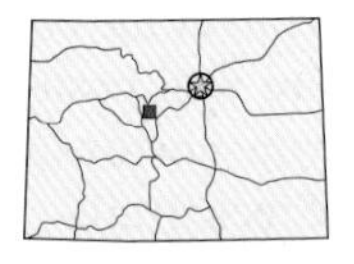

Drive south from Breckenridge on Highway 9 towards Fairplay. 16 miles from Breckenridge (or 6 miles north of Fairplay) you will come to the town of Alma where you must turn right. As you drive into the center of Alma look for a small sign marking the road up Buckskin Creek to Kite Lake (County Road #8). Take this road and proceed in a westerly direction for 5.5 miles until the road ends at the Kite Lake Campground. The last mile of the road is quite rough, but with care almost any car should be able to make it. It is necessary to ford Buckskin Creek about 0.4 mile from the end of the road, and some drivers may opt to park here and walk the last few hundred yards to the lake. The creek bed is quite firm, however, and most cars should be able to drive across. Most hikers camp at Kite Lake and do the hike the next day. The campground is conveniently located at the beginning of the trail, and it is seldom full.

In Colorado you can't really call yourself a serious outdoorsman until you have climbed at least a few of the state's 55 fourteen-thousand-foot peaks. This trail is a peak-baggers delight, because it will allow you to ascend to the tops of no fewer than three fourteeners within the space of a single day. The trailhead is located in the bottom of a high alpine basin that lies just south of Mount Democrat, Mount Cameron, Mount Lincoln, and Mount Bross. The elevation of the basin is only 2,270 feet below the highest peak, and the summits are all connected by a high rocky ridge that circles the north side of the basin.

One thing that stands out along this trail is the abundance of mining activity. These mountains are full of precious mineral deposits, and prospectors have been combing them in search of wealth for the past 150 years. Miners have never been known for their tidiness, and on this hike you will seldom be out of site of their refuse. There are old mine shafts and fallen-down shacks everywhere–even near the peaks themselves. The peaks were named by miners shortly after the Civil War. Mount Lincoln, or course, for Abraham Lincoln, and Mount Bross for a miner named William Bross. No one really knows who named Mount Democrat, but it is easy to assume it was a southerner who didn't like Lincoln and his Republican Party.

Begin by following the trail north from the Kite Lake Campground, along the bottom of the basin. Directly ahead you can see a low spot on the ridge between Mount Democrat, on the left, and Mount Cameron, on the right. This saddle is your first goal. Below the pass you can also see an old abandoned wooden building standing beside the trail, a remnant of the mining fever that once swept the valley. The trail climbs at a steady rate of 1,200 feet per mile until it reaches the saddle.

When you reach the saddle turn left for the climb up the eastern side of Mount Democrat. You only have 770 feet of climbing left, but you will soon discover that the going is harder in the thin air. Also, the good trail is now behind you. Still, there is a primitive trail all the way to the top, and you will find the climb less strenuous if you try to stay on it. Democrat is the lowest of the four peaks featured on this hike, but it is probably the most interesting of the four. There are no jeep roads on the mountain and, consequently it seems more pristine. On a clear day at least ten of the area's other fourteeners are visible from the top. To the north you can also look down on the world's largest molybdenum mine at Climax, just 1.8 miles away on the north side of the Continental Divide.

Mount Lincoln, from Cameron Peak

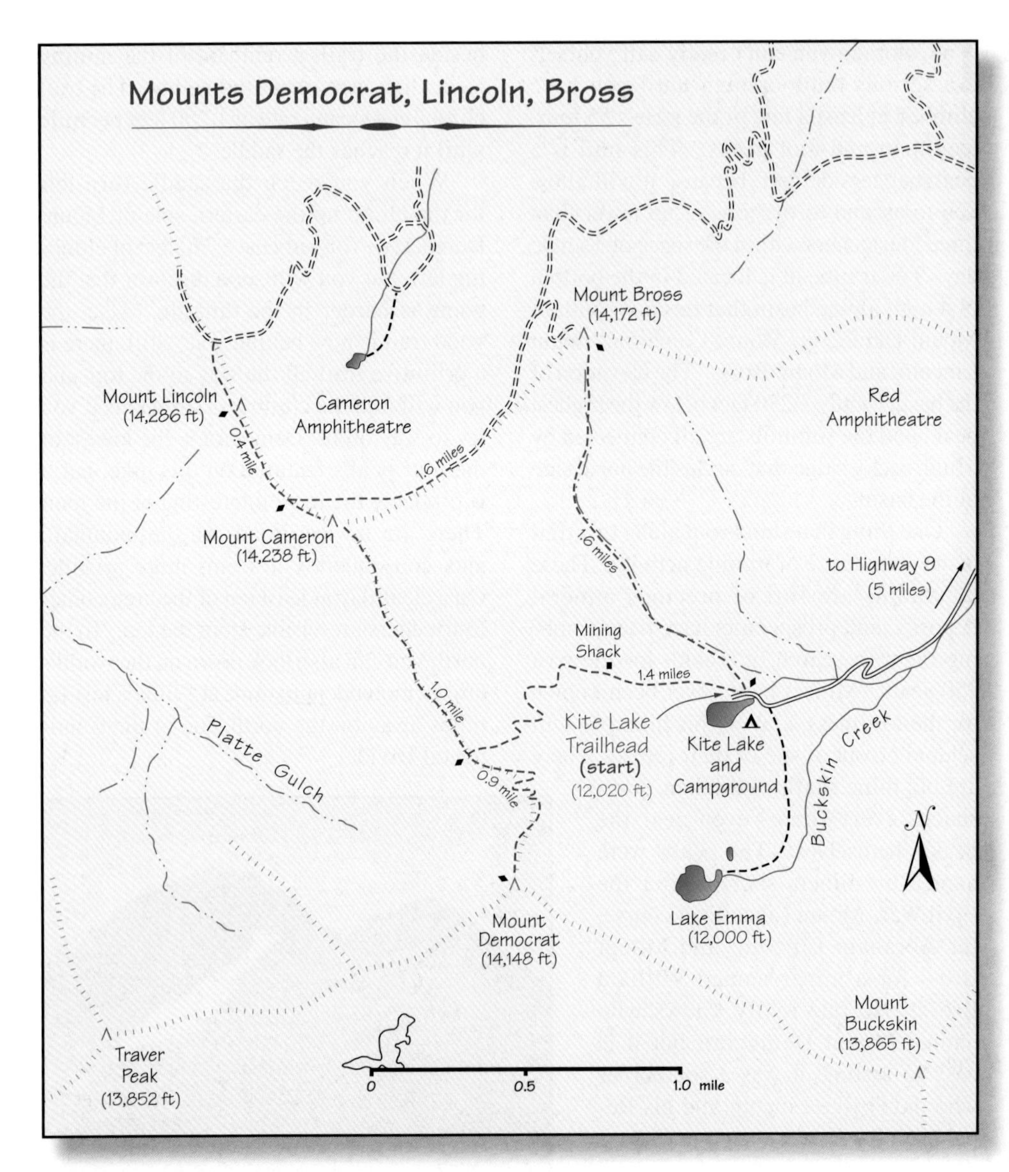

From the top of Mount Democrat you will have to retrace your steps back to the saddle in order to begin the 860-foot climb up Mount Cameron. This time the climb is somewhat easier because the trail is better and not as steep. The peak does not have a steep, well defined summit like Mount Democrat, but is more of a rounded knob on the top of the ridge. It's summit is only 140 feet higher than the saddle between Cameron and Lincoln. For this reason Mount Cameron is not officially included in the list of Colorado's 14,000-foot peaks, but few people climb Democrat and Lincoln without including Mount Cameron in their itinerary.

As you can see from this prospective, once you reach the top of Mount Cameron it is an easy 20-minute walk to get to the summit of Mount Lincoln. The terrain is

View from the summit of Mount Democrat

much less rocky here and the elevation gain is modest. Unfortunately there are dozens of old mines around the summit of Lincoln, including one that is less that 200 yards from its peak. There is also a jeep road that passes only 0.3 mile east of the summit. All of the human activity definitely detracts from the experience, but Mount Lincoln is still an interesting peak. Unlike the other peaks on this hike it has a very distinctive outcropping of rock at the summit that rises a short distance above the talus slopes.

To reach Mount Bross, the last peak on this hike, you must walk back to the eastern side of Mount Cameron then turn south and walk across the wide, flat ridge that connects it with Bross. About half way along the ridge you will come upon a jeep road that continues all the way to the summit. I would like to think this road is not used very often, but I have seen at least one 4WD vehicle on this road, probably owned by someone who has a claim on this mountain.

The top of Bross is so flat it is hard to determine where the actual summit is. There are several monuments on the top, but the true summit is on the northwest side in the vicinity of a rock shelter that someone has built.

Stand at the highest point on Mount Bross and look southwest. About a hundred yards away you will see a steep, talus-filled gully that drops off the west side of the mountain into the Kite Lake Basin below. There is a vague trail in the bottom of the gully, and this is the route you must follow to complete the loop back to the trailhead. The trail is very steep, but if you are going down and not up it isn't too bad. Just proceed with care and be prepared to slip here and there on the loose rocks. Hopefully you are wearing boots and long pants for this part of the hike, so you will have some protection against twisted ankles and scratched legs. After 0.7 mile and 1,500 feet of elevation loss the gully reaches the side of the basin, and from there a more inviting trail crosses the alpine tundra for the last 0.7 mile back to the trailhead.

Quandary Peak

day hike

Distance:	6.2 miles (round trip)
Walking time:	$5^1/_4$ hours
Elevations:	3,450 ft. gain/loss Quandary Peak Trailhead (start): 10,850 ft. Quandary Peak: 14,265 ft.
Trail:	Generally well marked and easy to follow.
Season:	Midsummer through mid-fall. The higher parts of the trail are usually covered with snow from November through mid-July.
Vicinity:	near Breckenridge
Maps:	Breckenridge *(USGS)* Breckenridge–Tennessee Pass *(Trails Illustrated, #109)*
Information:	http://colorado.utahtrails.com/quandarypeak.html http://www.fs.fed.us/r2/whiteriver/ *(White River National Forest)* phone: (970) 468-5400 *(Dillon Ranger District)*

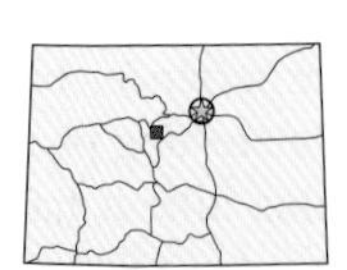

Take exit 201 from I-70 and drive south on Highway 9 to the town of Breckenridge. When you reach the center of town you will pass through a stoplight at the intersection of Highway 9 and Ski Hill Street. Check your odometer at this point and continue south for another 7.9 miles until you see a graded gravel road on the right near a sign that says "Blue Lakes Road". Turn here and in just 200 yards you will come to a smaller road near a sign that says "Quandary Peak Trailhead 0.1 mile". Turn right again and drive for the last 250 yards to a small parking area on the right. The trailhead is 150 feet beyond the parking area on the opposite side of the road.

As Colorado's fourteeners go, Quandary Peak is a relatively easy hike. Like all fourteeners, getting to the top requires a significant expenditure of energy, but the climb is only 3.1 miles long and there is now an excellent trail most of the way. Before 2001 the trail was much more primitive, but it has since been significantly improved by an organization called the Colorado Fourteeners Initiative. The trail has been rerouted up the south side of the mountain's east ridge, and long sections of stone stair steps have been

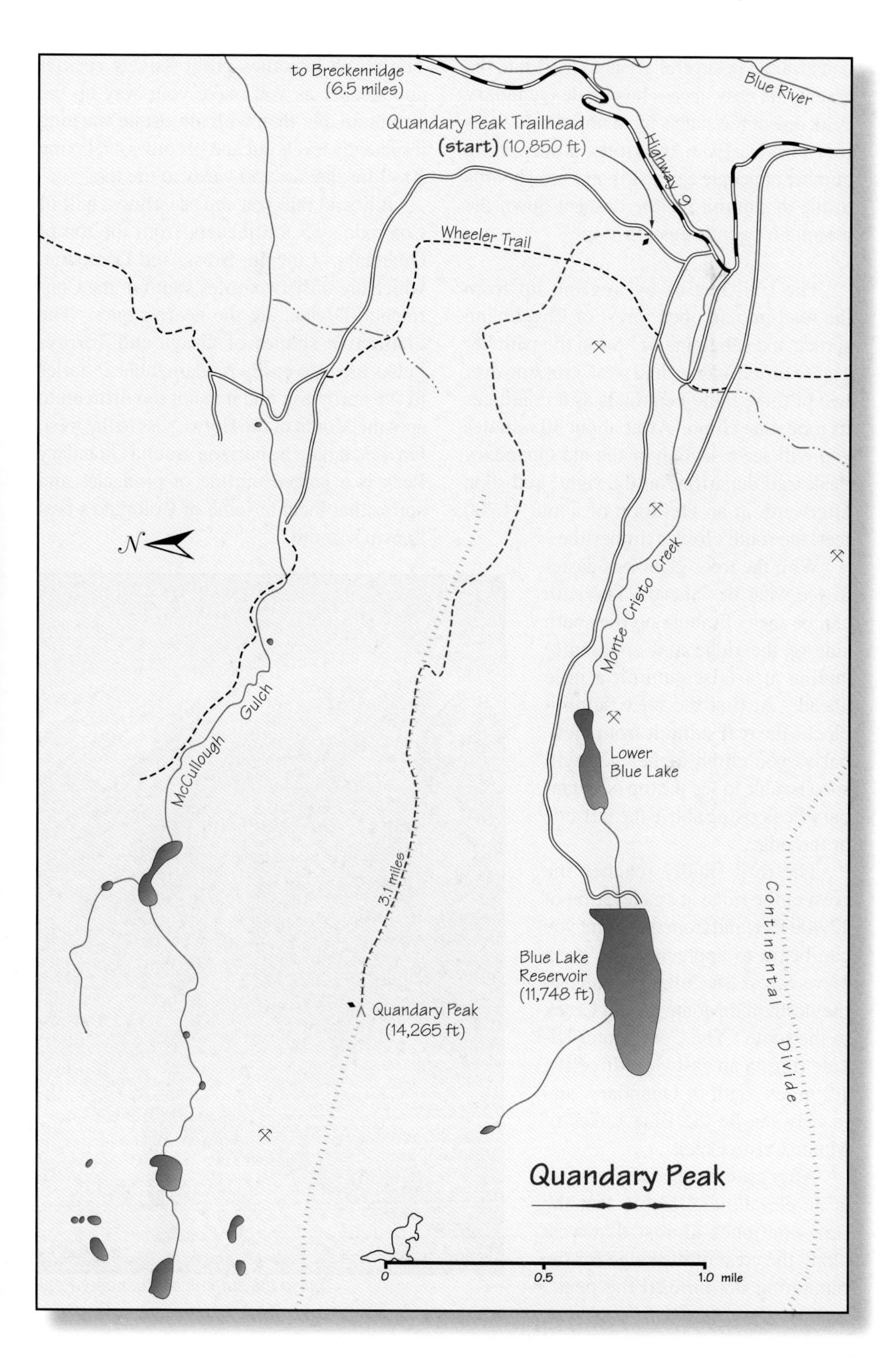
to Breckenridge
(6.5 miles)
Blue River
Quandary Peak Trailhead
(start) (10,850 ft)
Highway 9
Wheeler Trail
Monte Cristo Creek
McCullough Gulch
3.1 miles
Lower
Blue Lake
Blue Lake
Reservoir
(11,748 ft)
Quandary Peak
(14,265 ft)
Continental Divide
Quandary Peak
0
0.5
1.0 mile

constructed in several areas to facilitate the assent. Its easy access has made Quandary Peak one of the state's most popular 14,000-foot climbs. Even in winter a surprising number of people carry skis and snowboards to the to summit for the descent down the mountain's gentle eastern slopes.

The trail begins by angling up from the road into an open forest of Engelmann spruce and subalpine fir. Soon the path begins to turn from north to west, crossing over two or three faint jeep roads as it continues its moderate climb. After about 30 minutes you will see a section of the old Quandary Peak trail departing on the right, and soon afterward, at an elevation of about 11,700 feet, the route crosses timberline.

With the trees gone it is easier to see what lies ahead. The path can be seen climbing up the south side of the ridge and apparently ending at a false summit a mile ahead. At first the false summit blocks the real summit from view, but as you climb higher you will soon be able to see the top of Quandary Peak rising above the left side of the ridge.

The trail finally reaches the crest of the ridge at an elevation of 12,900 feet, and from that point you can begin to appreciate the great views across McCullough Gulch to the north and Monte Cristo Creek to the south. The Continental Divide runs in an east-west direction 1.2 miles south of Quandary, and in between lie the Blue Lakes of Monte Cristo Creek.

After crossing the false summit at an elevation of 13,146 feet the trail continues almost due west along the crest of the ridge for the remaining 0.9 mile to the peak. The climb becomes progressively rockier and steeper as you make your way up the mountain, but then with almost no warning it suddenly levels out and becomes a relaxing stroll for the last 150 yards to the top.

It is said that you can see almost half of Colorado's 55 fourteeners from the top of Quandary. Lincoln, Bross, and Democrat, which are only two miles south of the Continental Divide, are the nearest ones. The distinctive shapes of Grays and Torreys Peaks are also easily recognizable 25 miles to the northeast, and it is not too difficult to spot the Mount of the Holy Cross to the west. On a clear day the horizon around Quandary Peak is a jagged outline of pinnacles and spires that include some of Colorado's best known summits.

Trail to the summit of Quandary Peak

Mohawk Lakes

★★★ **day hike**

Distance:	6.6 miles (round trip)
Walking time:	$4^{3}/_{4}$ hours
Elevations:	1,700 ft. gain/loss Spruce Creek Trailhead (start): 10,380 ft. Lower Mohawk Lake: 11,820 ft. Upper Mohawk Lake: 12,080 ft.
Trail:	Popular, well marked trail
Season:	Midsummer through mid-Fall. The trail is covered with snow from mid-November through mid-July.
Vicinity:	near Breckenridge
Maps:	Breckenridge *(USGS)* Breckenridge–Tennessee Pass *(Trails Illustrated, #109)*
Information:	http://colorado.utahtrails.com/mohawklakes.html http://www.fs.fed.us/r2/whiteriver/ *(White River National Forest)* phone: (970) 468-5400 *(Dillon Ranger District)*

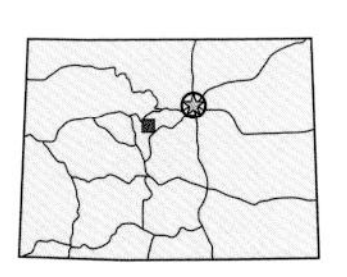

Drive south from Breckenridge on Highway 9 for 2.5 miles until you see a small sign marking Spruce Creek Road. Turn right here and continue southwest on Spruce Creek Road for another 1.2 miles to the Spruce Creek Trailhead, where the hike starts.

As you can see from the map the Spruce Creek Trail meets Spruce Creek Road once again 2.1 miles later near the end of the road. Consequently, it is possible to begin the hike at the end of Spruce Creek Road and bypass the first 2.1 miles of this hike. The last 0.5 mile of the road, however, is extremely rough, even for 4WD vehicles.

One would be hard pressed to find a prettier hike than the Mohawk Lakes Trail. The two Mohawk Lakes are very scenic and, as an added bonus, there is a nice waterfall in the creek below the lakes. There are also a number of interesting relics in the area from Colorado's late 1800s mining boom. Mining camps were built in the vicinity of Mayflower Lake and Lower Mohawk Lake in the 1880s, and today some of the log cabins in these two camps can still be seen. Of course, most of the cabins

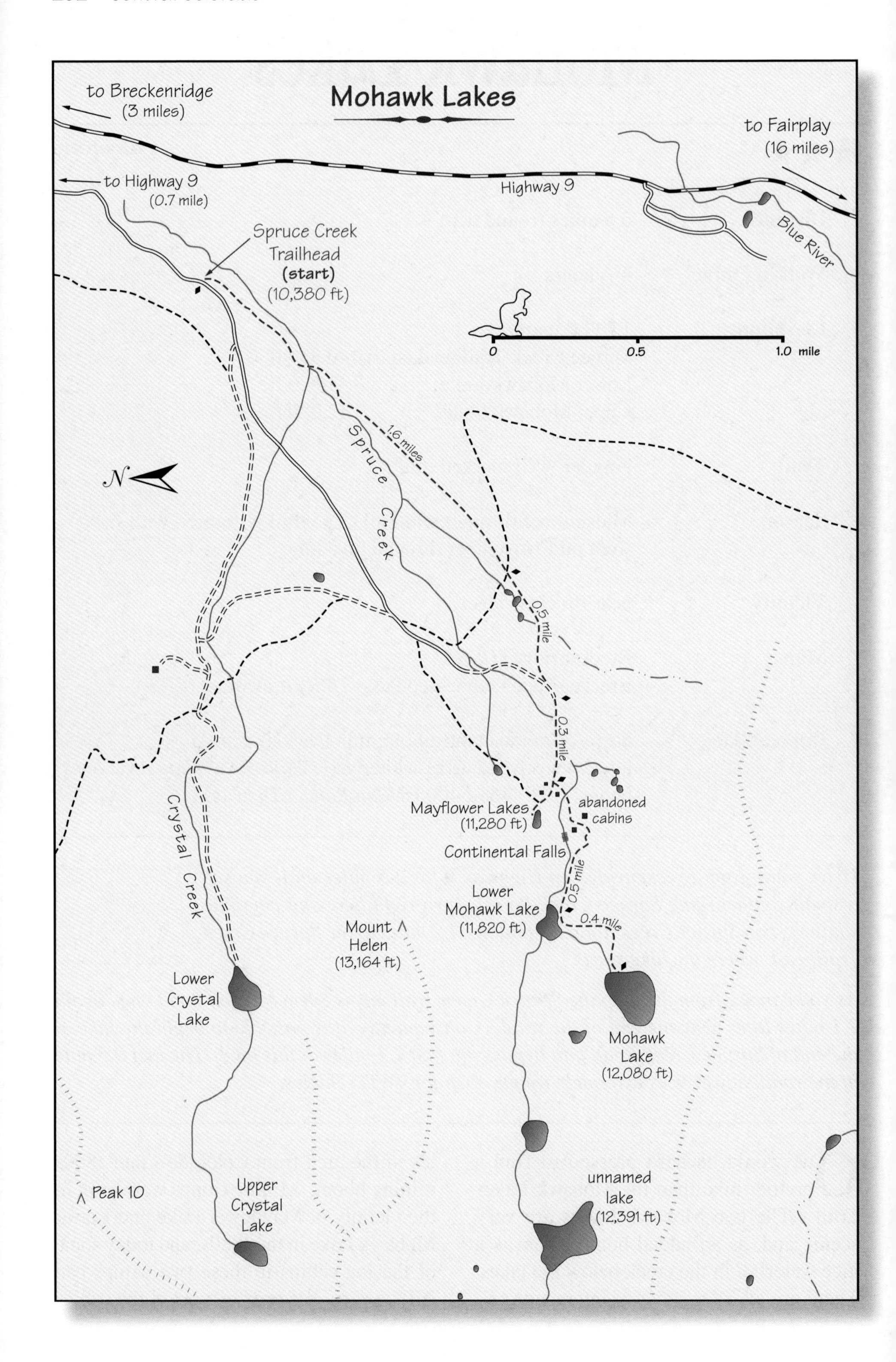
Mohawk Lakes
to Breckenridge
(3 miles)
to Fairplay
(16 miles)
to Highway 9
(0.7 mile)
Highway 9
Blue River
Spruce Creek
Trailhead
(start)
(10,380 ft)
0
0.5
1.0 mile
N
1.6 miles
Spruce Creek
0.5 mile
0.3 mile
Mayflower Lakes
(11,280 ft)
abandoned
cabins
Continental Falls
0.5 mile
Lower
Mohawk Lake
(11,820 ft)
0.4 mile
Crystal Creek
Mount
Helen
(13,164 ft)
Lower
Crystal
Lake
Mohawk
Lake
(12,080 ft)
Peak 10
Upper
Crystal
Lake
unnamed
lake
(12,391 ft)

have long since collapsed, but one has recently been restored and it is occasionally used as a bivouac by overnight campers. It contains a primitive sleeping loft and even a wood-burning stove to warm cross-country skiers and other winter visitors.

Trail to Upper Mohawk Lake

From Spruce Creek Trailhead the trail immediately enters a dense forest of Engelmann spruce and lodgepole pine and starts following the north side of Spruce Creek. After 0.5 mile it crosses the creek and begins to climb gradually above the south side of the drainage. About 25 minutes after leaving the creek you will come to a signed junction where the Wheeler Trail crosses Spruce Creek Tail, and soon afterword the forest opens up to a large meadow with picturesque views of Mount Helen (13,164 ft.) on the right.

Ten minutes after the Wheeler Trail junction the trail intersects the upper end of Spruce Creek Road. The creek is used as a source of water for communities in the Blue River Valley below, and you will probably notice the presence of a large underground water tank on the north side of the road. Walk up the road for a few hundred feet until it ends at the outlet of a small reservoir, and look for the continuation of the trail on your right. The path is marked by a small sign pointing the way to Mayflower Lake and the Mohawk Lakes.

Shortly after leaving the road you will come to another sign where a short spur trail to Mayflower Lake leaves the main trail. You should turn right here for the side trip to Mayflower Lake. The lake itself is rather small and uninteresting, but nearby you can see the intriguing remains of an old, abandoned mining camp—a town where men once struggled against a highly contagious affliction known as "gold fever".

Gold was discovered at the nearby Mayflower Mine in 1887, and for a brief time the mine sporadically yielded ore as rich as 30 ounces of gold per ton. But the euphoria was short-lived; the mines soon played out and the camps were vacated. In the end there was but one resident left. A hermit named Tom Davidson continued to live with his cat in one of the cabins near Mayflower Lake until his death around 1920.

As you continue on toward Mohawk Lakes you will soon come to the remains of an old stamping mill. Nearby is a cabin that has recently been restored and is occasion-

Continental Cabin

ally used by hikers and cross-country skiers. It is the only one of the dozen or so cabins in the area that still has a roof on it. Inside is a crude plaque inscribed with the words:

Welcome to Continental Cabin, 11,402 feet, circa 1883, the last bastion of freedom in this here Summit County. May the peace of these surroundings be felt by you and yours while you stay. The cabin was saved from filth and decrepitness on October 21, 1989 for the purpose of nothing more than sheer enjoyment.

The bottom of Continental Falls is only a few hundred feet north of Continental Cabin; you should check it out before continuing on to Mohawk Lakes. A primitive trail to the Falls begins a hundred feet east of the cabin, behind the roofless remains of another cabin.

From the hikers' cabin the trail switchbacks up the south side of Spruce Creek for 0.4 mile, climbing 400 feet to the lower Mohawk Lake. Just before you reach the lake you will see the remains of an old wooden tower that was once part of a tramway for lowering ore to the mill below. There are also a few broken-down cabins on the west end of the lake along with the tailings from several abandoned mines. However these artifacts of human occupation no longer distract from the beauty of the lake. It has been over a century since the mines were worked, and the old weathered, roofless cabins now seem to fit perfectly with the wild scenery. They are now simply a small reminder of Colorado's colorful past.

The trail continues along the south side of the lower lake for a hundred yards, then veers away to begin the climb to the upper lake. The upper lake is only 300 feet higher than Lower Mohawk Lake, but that small elevation gain is enough to make a big difference in vegetation. Lower Mohawk Lake is just below timberline, but Upper Mohawk is above that magic elevation and no trees grow here. The lake is also much deeper and wider than the lower lake, and there are no obvious mines in the area to mar its pristine beauty.

Upper Mohawk Lake

Grays and Torreys Peaks

Mount Evans Wilderness Area
day hike

Distance:	9.0 miles (round trip to both peaks)
Walking time:	7 hours
Elevations:	3,640 ft. gain/loss Grays Peak Trailhead (start): 11,240 ft. Grays–Torreys saddle: 13,707 ft. Grays Peak: 14,270 ft. Torreys Peak: 14,267 ft.
Trail:	Generally well marked and easy to follow.
Season:	Midsummer through mid-fall. The higher parts of the trail are usually covered with snow from November through mid-July.
Vicinity:	near Georgetown
Maps:	Grays Peak *(USGS)* Idaho Springs, Georgetown *(Trails Illustrated, #104)*
Information:	http://colorado.utahtrails.com/grayspeak.html http://www.fs.fed.us/r2/arnf/ *(Arapaho National Forest)* phone: (303) 567-3000 *(Clear Creek Ranger District)*

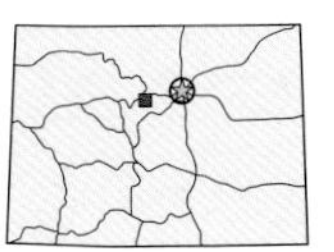

Drive west from Georgetown on I-70 for 6.3 miles to the Bakersville exit 221. There you must leave the highway and proceed south on Forest Road 189 for 3.1 miles to the Grays Peak Trailhead. There are two road junctions along the way, but in each case signs have been posted pointing the way to the trailhead. Ordinary cars can sometimes reach the trailhead, but be warned that Road 189 is not well maintained and high clearance vehicles are recommended.

Grays and Torreys Peaks are the two highest points on the Continental Divide. Torreys was named after John Torrey, an early nineteenth-century botanist who is best remembered for his work in classifying North American flora. Grays Peak was named in recognition of Asa Gray, also a well known botanist in the mid 1800s, whose research on variations in plant species provided important evidence in support of Charles Darwin's Theory of Evolution.

The Grays Peak Trail has recently been designated as a National Recreational Trail, and it is one of the best maintained of any of

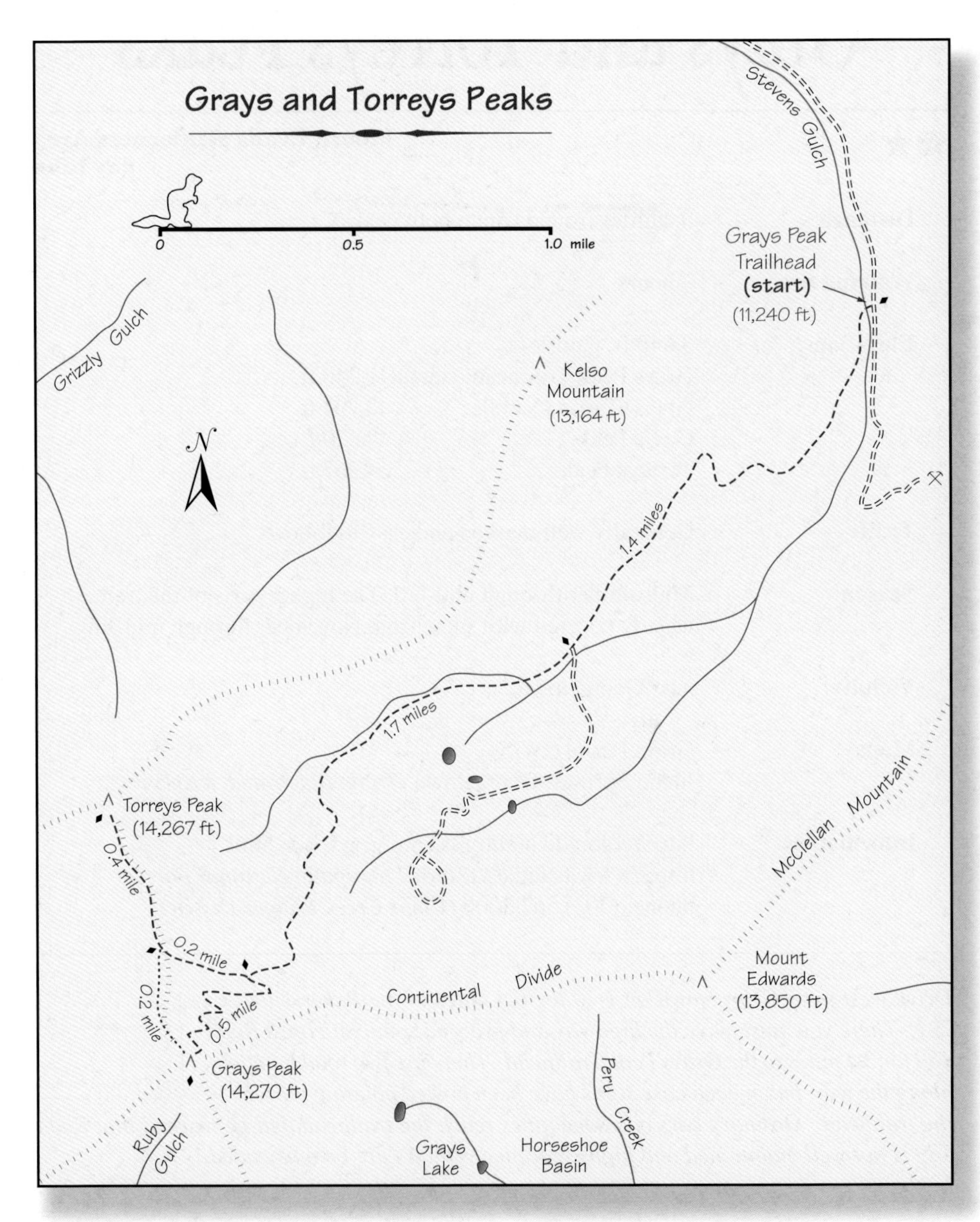

the fourteener trails. The trail approaches the peak through a gorgeous glacial valley with Kelso Mountain (13,164 ft.) on one side and Mount Edwards (13,850 ft.) on the other. The valley ends at the foot of the Continental Divide below the saddle connecting Grays Peak with Torreys.

Asa Gray and John Torrey were close friends and associates; hence it is fitting that Grays and Torreys Peaks are only 0.7 mile apart with an easy connecting ridge between them. The round trip distance up Grays, the higher peak, is 8.0 miles, but adding Torreys to the itinerary lengthens the hike by only

Mount Edwards (left) and Grays Peak (right)

one extra mile and 600 feet of additional elevation gain. Consequently, they are often climbed in combination.

The trail begins by crossing the creek at the bottom of Stevens Gulch on a steel bridge. It then parallels the creek as it makes a long, gradual climb along the west side of the valley. Finally, after a distance of 1.4 miles and an elevation gain of 800 feet the trail enters the high alpine plateau that forms the headwaters of Stevens Gulch. This beautiful alpine meadow is devoid of trees but filled with low-lying thickets of Scouler willows; it also offers a magnificent view of Grays and Torreys Peaks.

You will probably want to pause for a few minutes at this point to study the route up the two peaks. The trail ahead can be clearly seen switchbacking up the northeast flank of Grays Peak. You should also be able to see another obvious trail, marked by a series of 7 large stone monuments, that leaves one of the switchbacks below Grays and goes to the saddle below Torreys. Your route will take you up the switchbacks to the top of Grays, then down the ridge to the saddle and up the other side to Torreys. When you make your descent from Torreys you will be returning back to the saddle again, then taking the connecting trail that goes from the saddle down to the Grays Peak Trail.

The presence of the switchbacks on Grays Peak make this climb a relatively easy one. The grade is not too steep and the trail is well defined all the way to the top. About half way up you will see a sign marking the junction with the Torreys Peak Trail. If you plan to climb only Torreys you must turn right here, but if you are climbing both Grays and Torreys it is slightly easier to go up Grays first. After another 700 feet of elevation gain up the remaining switchbacks the trail tops out on the crest of the Continental

Torreys Peak from the summit of Grays Peak

Divide. Turn right here and continue west for another 200 yards to the summit.

Before you can climb Torreys Peak you will have to descend 563 feet to the saddle between the two peaks. The easiest way to do this is to continue northwest from Grays, following the crest of the Continental Divide all the way down to the saddle. This route is steep near the top, but there is a crude hiker-made trail all the way down. Once you reach the saddle you can continue following the Divide up the ridge to the summit of Torreys. Again, many people have done this in the past, and a crude, hiker-made trail is visible most of the way. The trail generally keeps to the west side of the ridge to avoid cliffs on the east side.

When you are ready to leave Torreys Peak simply retrace your steps back to the saddle and use the connecting trail to return to the switchbacks below Grays Peak. Once you reach the Torreys/Grays Junction it is 3.5 miles back to the trailhead. Note: the connecting trail does not begin precisely at the bottom of the saddle. Rather, it starts near a large rock monument 50 feet up the ridge on the Grays Peak Side. It starts higher in order to avoid a large patch of snow on the east side of the saddle that never seems to melt.

There are several great views from the top of Grays and Torreys, including Quandary Peak, the peaks of the Gore Range, and the Breckenridge ski slopes. Silverthorne and Dillon are only 15 miles west of the Grays and Torreys, and you can see a long section of I-70 from the summits. But for me the most impressive sight is of Mounts Evans and Bierstadt and the Sawtooth Ridge between them. There is an outstanding view of these two fourteeners southeast from Torreys with Grays Peak, Mount Edwards, and the Continental Divide in the foreground.

Torreys Peak from the saddle connecting Grays and Torreys Peaks

Chicago Lakes

★

Mount Evans Wilderness Area
day hike

Distance:	9.2 miles (round trip)
Walking time:	6 1/2 hours
Elevations:	1,750 ft. gain/loss Chicago Lakes Trailhead (start): 10,650 ft. lowest point: 10,320 ft. Lower Chicago Lake: 11,420 ft. Upper Chicago Lake: 11,740 ft.
Trail:	Generally well marked and easy to follow. Includes a mile of road walking and 0.1 mile of scrambling over boulders.
Season:	Midsummer through mid-fall. The higher parts of the trail are usually covered with snow from November through mid-July.
Vicinity:	Near Idaho Springs
Maps:	Idaho Springs, Mt. Evans (*USGS*) Idaho Springs, Georgetown (*Trails Illustrated, #104*)
Information:	http://colorado.utahtrails.com/chicagolakes.html http://www.fs.fed.us/r2/arnf/ (*Arapaho National Forest*) phone: (303) 567-3000 (*Clear Creek Ranger District*)

Exit I-70 at Idaho Springs and drive south on Highway 103 for 12.9 miles to the Echo Lake Lodge. The trailhead is located in the Echo Lake Lodge parking lot, just off Highway 103.

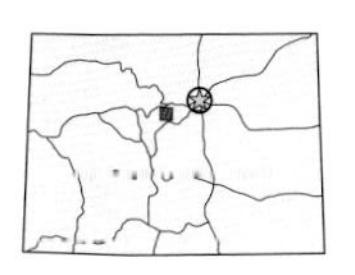

The downside of the Chicago Lakes hike is that in includes a mile of monotonous road walking followed by another mile through the scorched remains of an old forest fire. Fortunately, the fire stopped short of the lakes themselves, and it is the last mile of the trail that really makes the hike worthwhile. The Chicago Lakes are extraordinarily scenic. The first lake is tucked away in the back of a steep glacial valley with thousand-foot granite cliffs plunging down to its eastern shore. The second lake rests 400 yards further south above a 300-foot wall of broken cliffs and steep grassy slopes.

In my opinion this hike is not worth-

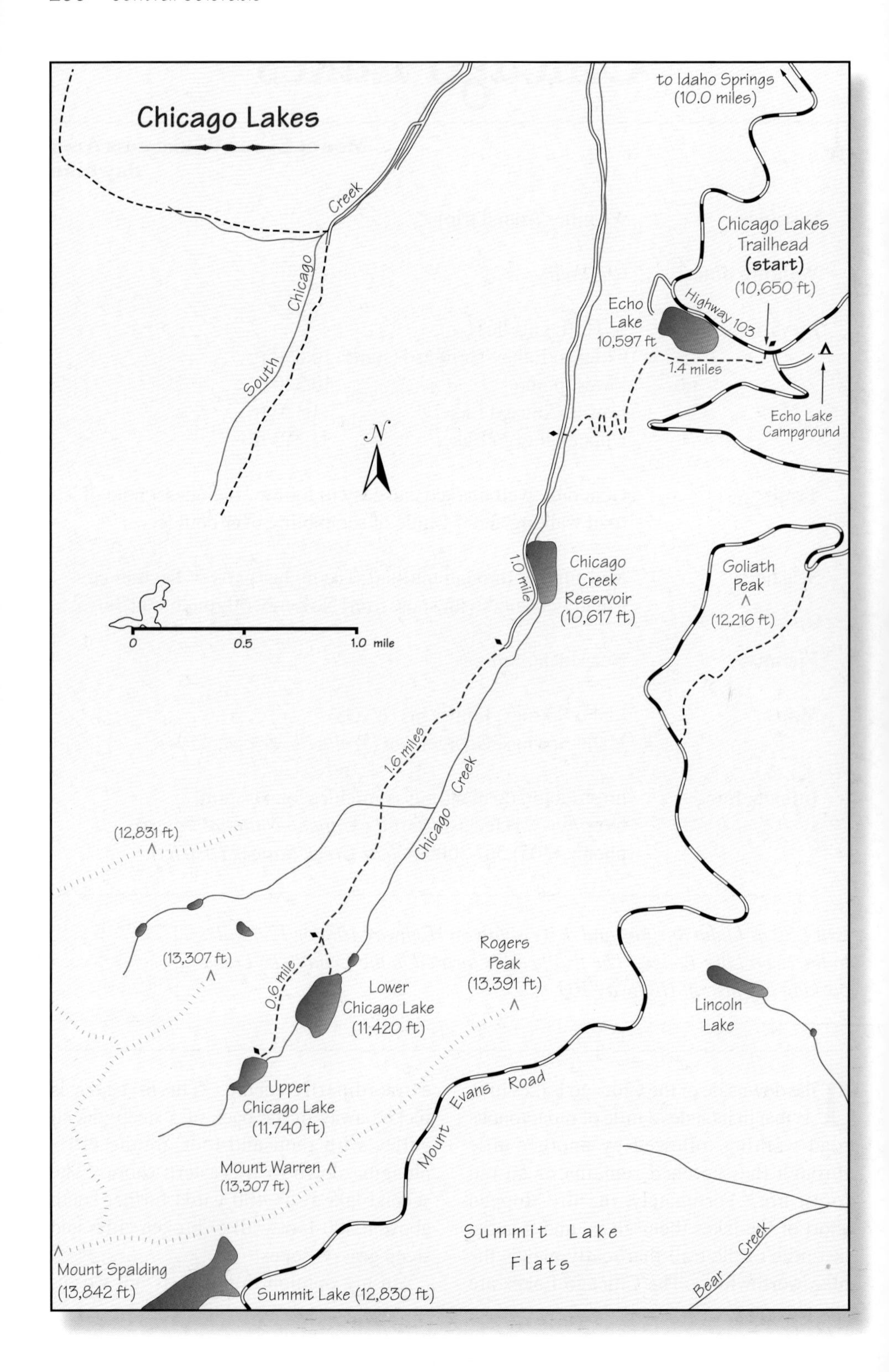
Chicago Lakes
to Idaho Springs
(10.0 miles)
Creek
Chicago
South
Chicago Lakes
Trailhead
(start)
(10,650 ft)
Echo
Lake
10,597 ft
Highway 103
1.4 miles
Echo Lake
Campground
N
Chicago
Creek
Reservoir
(10,617 ft)
1.0 mile
Goliath
Peak
(12,216 ft)
0
0.5
1.0 mile
1.6 miles
Chicago
Creek
(12,831 ft)
(13,307 ft)
0.6 mile
Lower
Chicago Lake
(11,420 ft)
Rogers
Peak
(13,391 ft)
Lincoln
Lake
Upper
Chicago Lake
(11,740 ft)
Mount Evans Road
Mount Warren
(13,307 ft)
Summit Lake
Flats
Mount Spalding
(13,842 ft)
Summit Lake (12,830 ft)
Bear Creek

while unless you plan to go all the way to the upper lake. The lower lake is very attractive, but its scenic rewards are just not sufficient to justify two hours of walking on a road and through a burned area. The rugged beauty of the upper lake and the awesome view looking down onto the lower lake from above are the real prizes of the hike. The lakes are especially pretty in late morning, before the wind picks up but after the sun is high enough to clear the surrounding cliffs.

From the parking lot a well groomed trail heads west along the southern shore of Echo Lake. When the path reaches the west side of the lake it seems to split into several smaller divergent trails, but the correct one is clearly marked by a wooden sign. The trail climbs up over a low ridge and then turns south along the eastern side of the Chicago Creek Valley. At first the path descends slowly toward the bottom of the valley, then it enters a series of switchbacks that take it down more quickly. Finally, 0.8 mile after leaving Echo Lake the trail levels out on valley floor, and shortly afterward it runs into the Chicago Creek Road.

The Chicago Creek Road was built by the Forest Service and the city of Idaho Springs in order to provide access to Chicago Creek Reservoir. This reservoir has long been a major source of water for Idaho Springs, and when the Mount Evans Wilderness Area was created in 1980 its boundaries were deliberately drawn to exclude the reservoir. The route follows Chicago Creek Road up the canyon for the next 1.0 mile, past the Chicago Creek Reservoir and on to the wilderness boundary. Ideally this hike would begin at the wilderness boundary where the Chicago Creek Road ends, but unfortunately the road is closed to private vehicles so there is really no way to avoid the road walk.

You will probably feel a sense of relief

Echo Lake

when you leave the road and begin walking into the Mount Evans Wilderness Area, but prepare yourself for further disappointment. The trail enters the burned area almost immediately after crossing the wilderness boundary, and for the next 1.3 miles it meanders through the skeletal remains of a wasted forest.

Finally, at an elevation of about 11,300 feet, the trail climbs out of the burned area, and 15 minutes later you will see the first lake in a large bowl below the left side of the path. The land around the lake is very marshy, and for that reason the trail stays 150 feet above the water as it passes its west side. There is a spur trail that cuts down through the willows to the lake shore below, but the mud and the underbrush deter many people from using it.

The second lake is 320 higher than the first one, and once the trail reaches the southern side of the lower lake it begins climbing up the steep moraine that separates them. For the most part the trail is easy to follow, but at one point it seems to disappear into a pile of house-size boulders. Just continue straight up through the rocky maze and after a short while the trail will reappear.

Finally the path reaches the top of the moraine and dips back down over the grassy tundra to the shore of the upper lake. This lake is almost entirely surrounded by thousand-foot granite cliffs, and the scene looking south across the lake into the back of the basin is very dramatic. Also, before you leave the area be sure to walk back to the edge of the cliffs east of the trail for a look down at Chicago Creek and the lower lake. It is a panorama you will not soon forget.

Lower Chicago Lake as seen from Upper Chicago Lake

Mount Bierstadt

★★★

Mount Evans Wilderness Area
day hike

Distance:	6.3 miles (round trip)
Walking time:	$4^3/_4$ hours
Elevations:	2,550 ft. gain/loss Guanella Pass Trailhead (start): 11,669 ft. Bierstadt Willows: 11,510 ft. Mount Bierstadt: 14,060 ft.
Trail:	Generally good except for some minor scrambling near the top.
Season:	Midsummer through mid-fall. The higher parts of the trail are usually covered with snow from November through early July.
Vicinity:	Near Georgetown
Maps:	Mt. Evans (*USGS*) Idaho Springs, Georgetown (*Trails Illustrated, #104*)
Information:	http://colorado.utahtrails.com/mountbierstadt.html http://www.fs.fed.us/r2/arnf/ *(Arapaho National Forest)* phone: (303) 567-3000 *(Clear Creek Ranger District)*

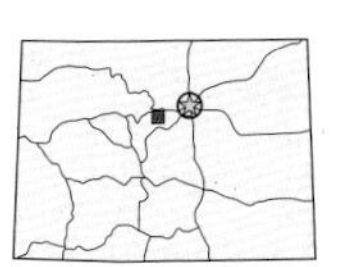

Take exit #228 from I-70 and drive into the downtown area of historic Georgetown. As you enter the town you will see a series of signs directing you to the Guanella Pass Road. Follow these signs and you will arrive at Guanella Pass 10.6 miles after leaving Georgetown. The trailhead is located on the left side of the road at the top of the pass. There are actually two parking lots at the pass, each with a separate trail departing for Mount Bierstadt. But don't be confused–the trails merge within 200 feet.

Mount Bierstadt was named after Albert Bierstadt, a nineteenth-century landscape artist who first visited the American West as a member of a Rocky Mountains Survey Team in 1859. Bierstadt's resulting works soon catapulted him to fame, and he spent most of the rest of his life painting a series of dramatic landscapes of the West. Today he is recognized as one of the greatest American artists of all time. It is fitting that one of Colorado's fourteeners should be named after him.

Serious mountaineers often climb Bierstadt in combination with Mount Evans.

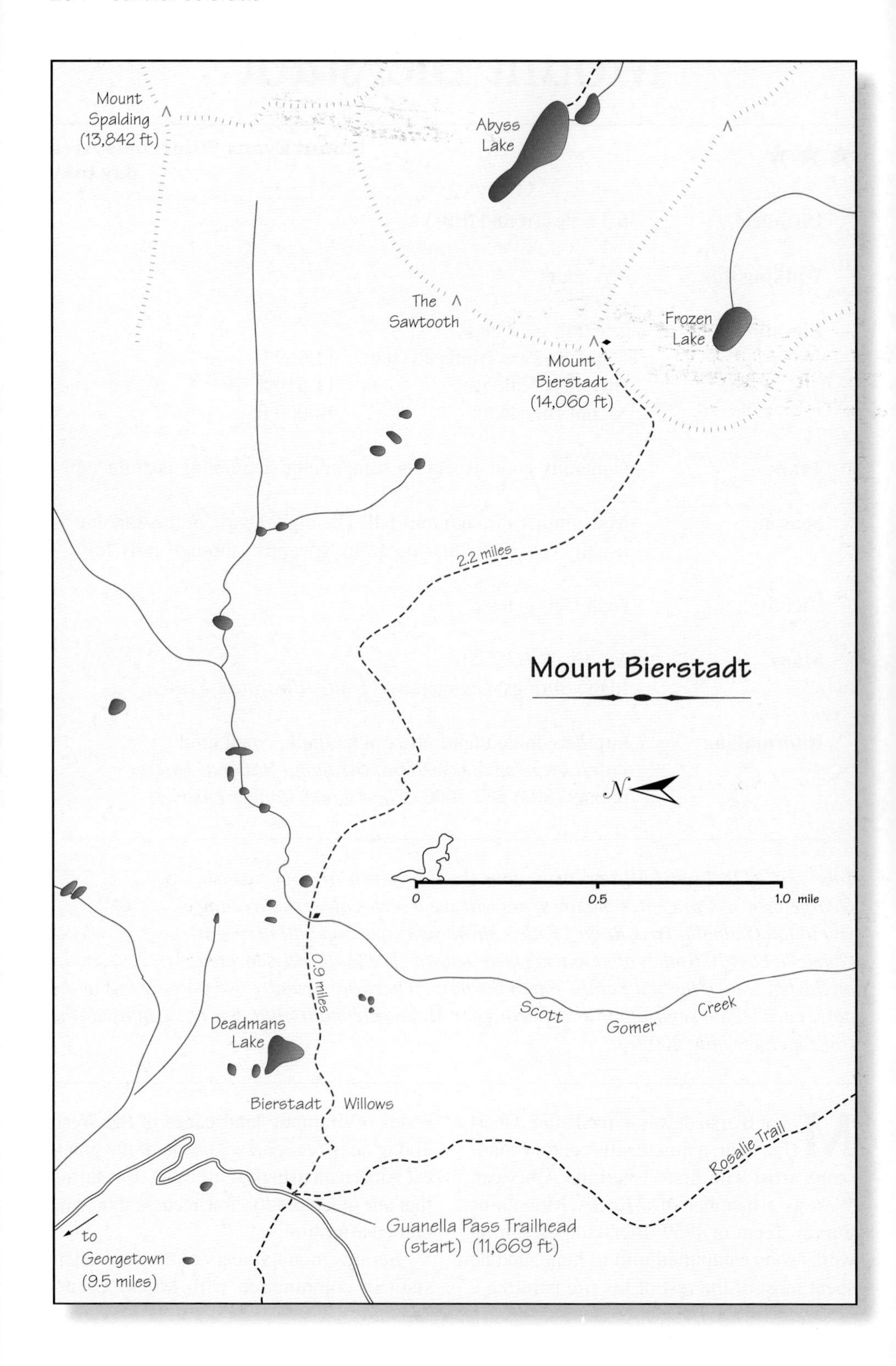
Mount Spalding (13,842 ft)
Abyss Lake
The Sawtooth
Frozen Lake
Mount Bierstadt (14,060 ft)
2.2 miles
Mount Bierstadt
N
0
0.5
1.0 mile
0.9 miles
Scott Gomer Creek
Deadmans Lake
Bierstadt Willows
Rosalie Trail
Guanella Pass Trailhead (start) (11,669 ft)
to Georgetown (9.5 miles)

The double ascent requires a traverse from Bierstadt to Evans across a formidable looking ridge that includes a step called the Sawtooth. There is a great view of Bierstadt and the Sawtooth from the Guanella Pass Trailhead, but unfortunately Mount Evans is hidden behind the ridge and can't be seen from that perspective. The traverse between the two peaks doesn't look any easier when viewed from the top of Bierstadt, but it is actually not as technically difficult as it appears. It is usually rated as a class-3 climb.

The trail looses 160 feet of elevation in the first 0.8 mile as it descends toward Scott Gomer Creek. This area is a marshland filled with dense thickets of Scouler willows that once presented a serious obstacle to hikers. Many older maps and guidebooks warn that the trail is impassable in spring, and suggest that Mount Bierstadt is best climbed in the winter when the bog is frozen. Fortunately, considerable work has been done on this trail in the last eight years, and there are now boardwalks across the worst parts of the marsh. The Bierstadt Willows are no longer as intimidating as they once were.

After crossing Scott Gomer Creek the trail continues east for another 1.1 miles, heading for the top of a ridge on the northwest side of the summit. When you reach the crest of this ridge you will be treated to a fine view of the Sawtooth and the rugged basin below it.

Once the trail reaches the crest of the northwest ridge it turns south and continues to gain altitude as it makes a long sweeping turn to the east. Finally the trail levels out and seems to end at the base of a rocky outcropping 250 feet below the summit. A large stone monument has been erected at this point to make it easier for hikers to pick up the trail again on the return trip.

There are a few cairns marking the way beyond the stone monument, but you are basically on your own from that point on. The route is not particularly difficult but it does involve some minor scrambling over large boulders. What you see from below is actually a false summit. Bear slightly to the left of the hill as you climb and work your way around its north side, then climb up the last 50 feet to the top of the true summit.

Mount Evans lies west of Mount Bierstadt above Lake Fork and Abyss Lake. Evans is easily identified because of the observatory that has been built on its summit. It is also interesting to look at the east side of the Sawtooth from Bierstadt. The usual route for the traverse follows the east side of the ridge until it reaches a point just below the Sawtooth. Then it climbs to the opposite side of the ridge and ties into a narrow, exposed ledge near the bottom of the Sawtooth's west face.

Ascending the southwest side of Mount Bierstadt

Goose Creek

★★★★

Lost Creek Wilderness Area
day hike

Distance: 9.0 miles (round trip to all points of interest)

Walking time: 5 1/2 hours

Elevations: 1,030 ft. loss/gain
Goose Creek Trailhead (start): 8,200 ft.
Shafthouse: 8,680 ft.

Trail: Excellent, well marked trail

Season: Summer through mid-fall. The road to the trailhead is generally closed until early June.

Vicinity: South of Denver

Maps: McCurdy Mountain (*USGS*)
Tarryall Mountains, Kenosha Pass (*Trails Illustrated, #105*)

Information: http://colorado.utahtrails.com/goosecreek.html
http://www.fs.fed.us/r2/psicc/ (*Pike National Forest)*
phone: (303) 275-5610 *(South Platte Ranger District)*

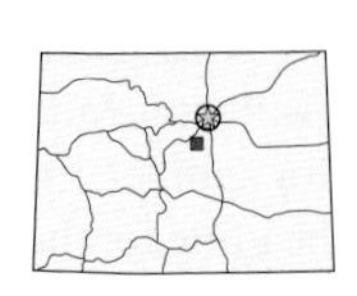

Drive southwest from Denver on Highway 285 through Conifer to Pine Junction. When you reach Pine Junction you will come to a stop light where you must turn left onto Pine Valley Road (County Road #126) toward Dekkers. Continue south on Pine Valley Road for 22 miles until you come to the Cheeseman Lake Road (Forest Road #211) on the right. It is easy to miss Cheeseman Lake Road; it is a gravel road marked only by a small sign on the left side of Pine Valley Road. Turn onto the Cheeseman Lake Road and continue south, following the signs to Goose Creek and the JVL Lost Valley Ranch. After 3.1 miles you will come to a major fork in the road where you must bear left. Another 5.3 miles will bring you to a poorly marked junction where you must turn right onto Forest Road #211. Follow this road for 4.8 miles, over a wooden bridge and past a burned-out campground, until you see a sign directing you to the Lost Creek Wilderness and Goose Creek Trail on the right. Turn here onto Forest Road #558 and drive the last 1.5 miles to the Goose Creek Trailhead and parking area.

Driving to the Goose Creek Trailhead is a depressing experience. On June 8, 2002 it was reported that a fire was burning in Tappan Gulch, 9 miles south of Goose

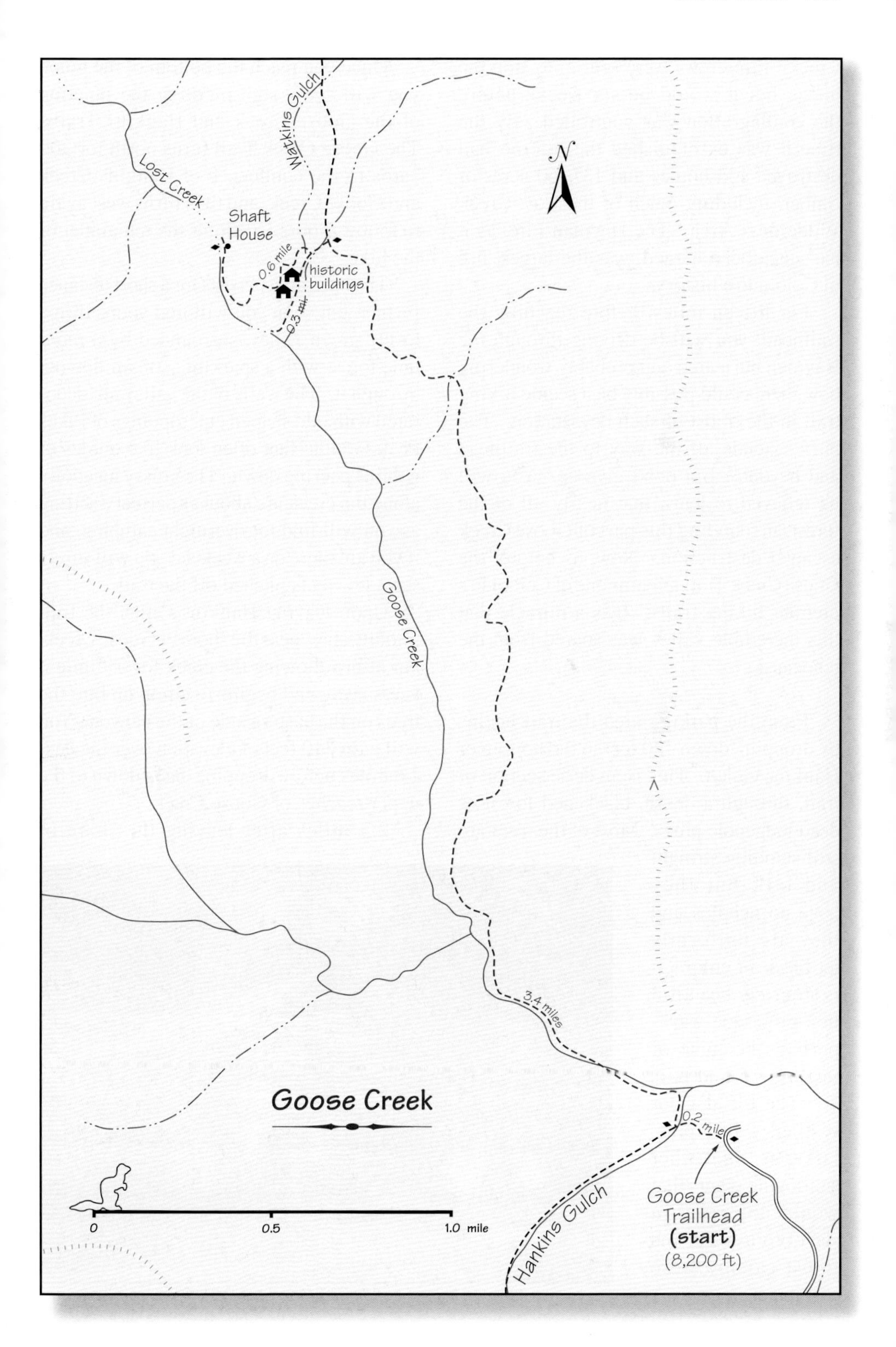

Watkins Gulch
Lost Creek
Shaft House
0.6 mile
historic buildings
0.3 mi.
N
Goose Creek
3.4 miles
Goose Creek
0.2 mile
Hankins Gulch
Goose Creek Trailhead
(start)
(8,200 ft)
0
0.5
1.0 mile

Creek. Fire crews were sent in to stop the blaze, but it would be six weeks before the conflagration was controlled. By the time it was extinguished the inferno had destroyed 133 homes and 137,760 acres of timber, including much of the Lost Creek Wilderness Area. The Hayman Fire, as it has since been named, was the largest fire in Colorado's history.

For fifteen miles, before reaching the trailhead, you will be driving through the Hayman burn area and probably wondering how there could possibly be a scenic hiking trail in the midst of such devastation. The burn extends all the way to the trailhead and beyond. But don't give up. You will be relieved to learn that nearly all of the forest surrounding this part of Goose Creek escaped destruction. Now, as before, the Goose Creek Trail remains one of Colorado's premier hiking trails. It is a miracle that this incredible valley was spared from the holocaust.

From the parking area the trail begins by dropping down 120 feet to the bottom of Hankins Gulch. This is an eerie section of trail, through a dense, blackened forest of dead lodgepole pines. Most of the trees are still standing straight and tall, but they have no needles and they are uniformly jet black in color. It is strangely beautiful in a grotesque way—perhaps because of the lush ground cover. The forest floor is filled with lupine, larkspur, and other sun-loving plants that would not grow in such profusion if the forest canopy were still intact.

Once you reach the bottom of the gulch you will see a sign marking the junction of the Goose Creek and Hankins Trails. The Goose Creek Trail turns north for 200 yards to the confluence of Hankins Creek and Goose Creek, and then turns west again to follow Goose Creek for the remainder of the hike.

The burn area persists for a short distance further, but soon you will find yourself in a lovely green valley, surrounded by a montane forest with a sparkling stream flowing through it. The walls of the valley are decorated with odd shaped outcroppings of Pikes Peak Granite that often look like hordes of goblins peering down. The grassy meadows along the creek are about as perfect a setting as you will find for overnight camping, and if you are there on a weekend you will surely see a few tents pitched off the trail.

Upon leaving Hankins Gulch the trail initially stays near the shore of Goose Creek, but after following the creek for 0.9 mile it veers away and begins to climb up into the trees on the eastern side of the canyon. You will gain 540 feet of elevation over the next 1.6 miles before dropping back down to the upper reaches of Goose Creek.

2.3 miles after leaving the shore of

Historic buildings of the Lost Park Reservoir Company

Goose Creek the trail comes to another junction marked by a sign directing you to the "Historic Buildings" on the left. The historic buildings consist of two intact cabins and one that has already collapsed; they are located in a clearing about 100 yards down the slope from the main trail. These cabins were built between 1891 and 1913 to accommodate employees of the Antero and Lost Park Reservoir Company, a company that was trying create a reservoir by damming up Lost Creek.

Lost Creek originates 15 miles north of Goose Creek in the Kenosha Mountains. As it flows south, however, it disappears underground and emerges again further south. In fact it does this no fewer than 11 times, finally emerging for the last time as Goose Creek. The ground in this area consists of a jumble of granite boulders with many voids between; hence the river's strange behavior. If you will walk down the slope for 200 yards below the historic buildings, then walk upstream for another 200 feet, you can see where Lost Creek bubbles up out of the ground to become Goose Creek.

The Lost Park Reservoir Company thought that by drilling a shaft into the granite bedrock above Goose Creek and pumping concrete into the voids they could effectively dam up Lost Creek and form the Lost Park Reservoir. It was a bold idea, and with our modern technology it would probably work. But turn of the century drilling technology was not adequate for the job, and the project ultimately failed.

The last thing you must see before walking back to your car is the shafthouse site where the Lost Park Reservoir Company engineers attempted to drill into the jumble of granite boulders. The trail to the shafthouse begins just 100 feet north of the first historic cabin. Follow this trail for 0.4 mile and you will come upon the old steam engine that was used to drill the shaft. The actual shafthouse is not there anymore, but the steam engine is a fascinating artifact in itself. It must have taken a great deal of effort to get it to this site.

The trail to the shafthouse presents a fascinating display of strange and unusual rock formations, and just beyond the shafthouse the trail enters an area that is wonderfully unique. In the words of author Michael Green:

> *Massive rocks of all shapes and sizes rise up everywhere creating images of creatures and objects for your imagination to find. ...It is a maze of narrow passageways, box canyons, and catacombs. A mysterious, secret place where trees seem to grow out of solid rock as they cling to tiny cracks, their roots straining to find soil.*

Goose Creek Trail

Castlewood Canyon

★★

Castlewood Canyon State Park
day hike

Distance:	5.9 miles (loop)
Walking time:	3 1/2 hours
Elevations:	690 ft. loss/gain Lake Gulch Trailhead (start): 6,610 ft. Castlewood Canyon Dam: 6,350 ft.
Trail:	Well marked, well maintained
Season:	Year round. There may occasionally be some snow on the trail during the winter months.
Vicinity:	South of Denver
Maps:	Castle Rock South, Russellville Gulch (*USGS*) Castlewood Canyon State Park brochure
Information:	http://colorado.utahtrails.com/castlewood.html http://www.coloradoparks.org/castlewood/ *(Castlewood Canyon State Park)* phone: (303) 688-5242 *(Castlewood Canyon State Park)*

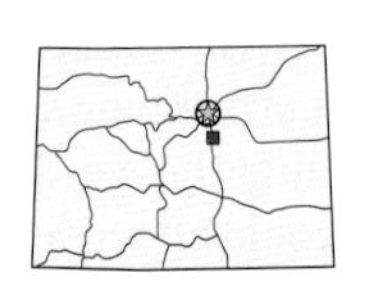

Drive south of Denver on Highway 25 for 25 miles to the town of Castle Rock and take exit 182 east on Highway 86. 7.3 miles after leaving Highway 25 you will come to a stoplight on the west side of Franktown; turn right here and drive south on Highway 83. After another 4.9 miles you will see a sign marking the entrance to Castlewood Canyon State Park on the right. Turn here and drive 0.6 miles to the visitor center, where you must pay an entrance fee of $4.00/car. Canyon Point Picnic Area, where the hike begins, is 0.4 miles beyond the visitor center. Look for the Lake Gulch Trailhead on the north side of the parking lot near the restrooms.

Thundering like a mountain on the move, the wall of water surged through Parker, tumbled down Cherry Creek toward suburban Denver. Logs, tree-trunks, tons of debris were swept along as the billion-gallon deluge widened out to more than a mile. Cherry Creek was a battering-ram of water, boiling over its embankments. At 7 o'clock it burst into Denver, ripped out six bridges in swift succession. Just ahead of it were police cars and fire engines, sirens a-scream, racing the residents to safety.

A stampede of 5,000, many clad in night cloths, fled from the lowlands.

Time Magazine, *August 14, 1933*

This riveting article describes the wall of water that surged into Denver after the failure of the Castlewood Dam seventy-five years ago. Built in 1890, Castlewood Dam had been in service for 43 years when it ruptured. Two people were killed, but it would likely have been thousands had it not been for the actions of an alert telephone operator named Nettie Driscoll who was on duty that night 20 miles downstream. She was informed of the failure at about 2:00 a.m. by the dam caretaker, and managed to

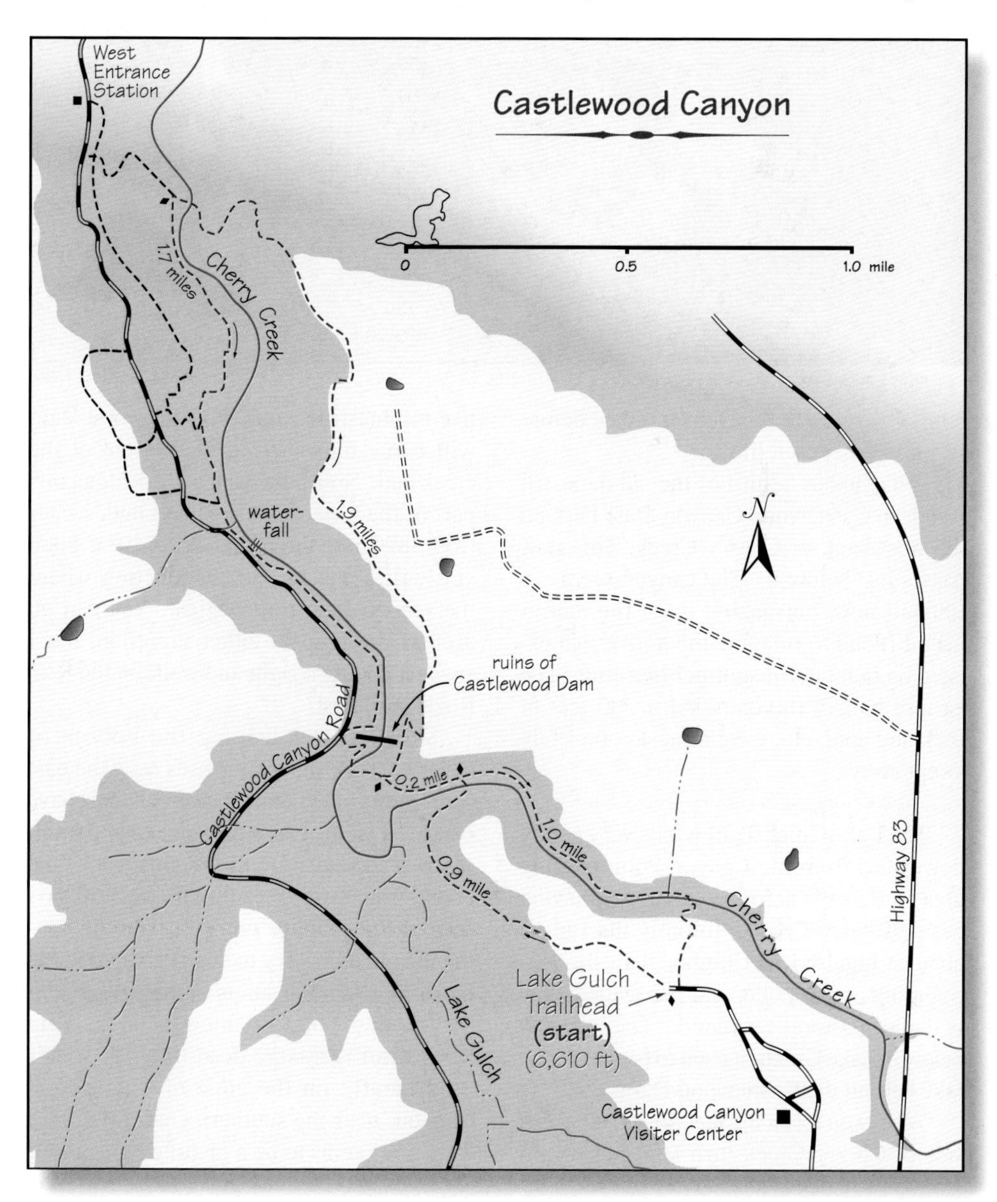

Castlewood Dam

relay a warning to the Denver police before fleeing for her own life.

Today about a third of the old dam still stands in Castlewood Canyon State Park on the west bank of Cherry Creek. This trail passes just below it. The canyon seems so tranquil now, but gazing up at the dam it isn't difficult to imagine the horror that existed on that fateful summer morning. The eastern half of the dam, some 300 feet of rock and concrete, were almost completely swept away.

The Lake Gulch Trail winds very gently downward from the Canyon Point parking area for 0.9 mile before coming to a junction beside Cherry Creek. Initially the trail is about a hundred feet higher than the surrounding countryside, and the scene below is one of pastoral farmland. The meadow below is Lake Gulch; it used to be part of the lake behind the Castlewood Dam.

When you reach the junction on the north side of Cherry Creek turn left, and within five minutes the ruins of Castlewood Dam will come into view in the bottom of the creek bed. Notice the lack of trees along this part of the hike. This area was underwater from 1890 until the dam broke in 1933. Soon you will come to another junction where the second loop trail begins. You can go around the loop in either direction, but I suggest you turn right and walk on the Rim Rock Trail first.

Shortly after leaving the bottom of Cherry Creek the trail passes near the east shore ruins of the dam. The break must have occurred on the east side, since only a small piece of the dam remains on this side of the creek. When you reach the rim you will pass several fine vantage points for photographing the old dam. Try to be in this area in the morning when the sun is in the east.

Another point of interest on the Rim Rock Trail is a large dead tree that stands prominently on the edge of Castlewood Canyon, near the southern end of the trail. This tree seems to be a favorite hangout for

Turkey Vulture above Castlewood Trail

a flock of turkey vultures that live in the area, and two or three of the ungainly birds can almost always be seen perched over the rim on its branches. There are also a large number of hawks in the area that love to soar over the eastern side the canyon.

The Rim Rock Trail follows the rim of the Castlewood Canyon for 1.5 miles before dropping back inside the canyon. Then, just after crossing Cherry Creek, it arrives at the northern junction with the Creek Bottom Trail. Turn left at the junction and continue along the creek back to the dam ruins. As you may have noticed, the forest on the top of the rim consists almost exclusively of juniper and Ponderosa pine, but in the shaded canyon there is also a lot Douglas fir. None of the trees in the canyon are very old though; the flood of 1933 must have destroyed all of the vegetation immediately below the dam.

1.1 miles after passing a picturesque waterfall the trail once again arrives at the dam ruins. Looking up at the remains of the structure one can't help but be impressed by the work of the nineteenth century engineers. But there were some disastrous shortcomings in their design. Unlike modern dams, the Castlewood Dam was not arched, but rather built straight across the canyon; no excavation was done in the bottom of the streambed under the dam's foundation; and the dam did not have an interior water barrier to prevent it from leaking.

After leaving the dam the trail crosses back to the east side of Cherry Creek and soon passes the southern end of the Rim Rock Trail. 0.2 mile later it arrives at the Inner Canyon Trail where you should turn left for the final 1.2 miles back to the parking lot. The Inner Canyon Trail continues along a particularly scenic section of Cherry Creek before climbing out of Castlewood Canyon just south of the trailhead.

Cherry Creek

The Crags

★ **day hike**

Distance:	4.0 miles (round trip)
Walking time:	2 1/2 hours
Elevations:	720 ft. gain/loss The Crags Trailhead (start): 10,080 ft. The Crags viewpoint: 10,800 ft.
Trail:	Generally well marked and easy to follow
Season:	Summer through mid-fall. The higher parts of the trail are generally covered with snow from late November through late June.
Vicinity:	Near Colorado Springs
Maps:	Pikes Peak, Woodland Park (*USGS*) Pikes Peak (*Trails Illustrated, #137*)
Information:	http://colorado.utahtrails.com/thecrags.html http://www.fs.fed.us/r2/psicc/ (*Pike National Forest*) phone: (719) 636-1602 *(Pikes Peak Ranger District)*

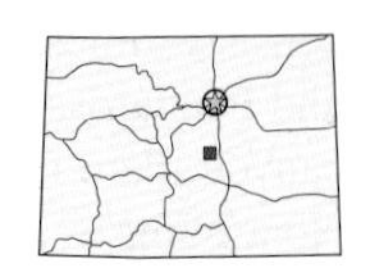

Drive West of Colorado Springs for 24 miles on Highway 24. When you reach the tiny town of Divide turn left at the street light and drive south on Highway 67 for another 4.2 miles. There you will see a gravel road on the left marked by a sign that says "Crags Campground 3½ miles". Turn here and follow the signs for the next 3.1 miles to the Crags Campground. The trailhead and parking area are on the east side of the campground 0.3 mile from the entrance.

Many mysteries still surround the formation of the Rocky Mountains, but one of the most intriguing puzzles concerns the formation of Pikes Peak on the southern tip of the Front Range. Pikes Peak was created some 60 million years ago when a large deposit Pikes Peak Granite was pushed up from deep within the earth. The puzzling thing is that after the rock reached the earth's surface it seemed to expand and flow outward, eventually covering many square miles of much younger sedimentary rock. This wouldn't seem unreasonable if the rock had been in liquid or plastic form, but in this case the material was far from liquid. It was solid Precambrian granite that had cooled and crystallized a billion years before it was pushed to the surface. It is difficult to imagine

The Crags

N

to Highway 67 (2 miles)

The Crags

The Crags Trailhead **(start)** (10,080 ft)

The Crags Campground

Fourmile Creek

0 0.25 0.5 mile

solid granite being squeezed out of the earth like toothpaste from a tube and then flowing horizontally like cold molasses across the earth's surface. But that appears to be exactly what happened.

Granite is an igneous rock that can only form under extreme temperatures and pressures, so it was definitely not in a liquid or plastic state when the extrusion took place. The Pikes Peak Granite, however, is so badly fractured and jointed that it must have been subjected to enormous forces while it was being pushed to the surface. The beautiful, pinkish boulders that surround the peak often look like they have been pushed through a meat chopper.

Bristlecone Pines near the end of the Crags Trail

Granite is normally a hard, smooth material that stands up well to the forces of erosion, but on Pikes Peak the stubby interlocking crystals of quartz, feldspar, hornblende and mica are filled with hairline cracks. Because of the fractured texture of the stone it is highly vulnerable to the forces of erosion, and over the years the rocky outcroppings that surround the peak have eroded into a weird gallery of unlikely shapes. To a large extent it is the spires and pinnacles of Pikes Peak Granite surrounding the trail that make this short walk so delightful.

From the Crags Campground the trail proceeds eastward through a narrow valley that is alternately filled with Engelmann spruce, quaking aspen, and open meadows. The valley is surprising pretty, especially in the grassy areas where there are nice views of the granite pinnacles on the south side of the small canyon.

After 10 minutes the trail comes to a junction where a smaller spur branches off to cross Fourmile Creek on the right. Bear left at this point, walking straight up the valley. The trail continues for the next mile at an almost level grade, then begins climbing up into the trees near the head of the creek. At this point the trail is much less distinct but still relatively easy to follow. Finally, after an elevation gain of 500 feet from the trailhead, the trail seems almost to disappear altogether.

Don't stop at the apparent end of the trail, but continue climbing straight ahead for another 300 yards. After an additional 200 feet of elevation gain you will come to the end of a high promontory where there are great views of the Pikes Peak Granite formations as well as the Catamount Reservoirs 2.5 miles to the north. As an added bonus, there is also a small grove of bristlecone pine trees at the top of the promontory. There is no way to know how old these particular trees are, but bristlecone pines have been known to live over 4,000 years—longer than any other higher organism on earth They always seem to grow on windswept ridges where little else can survive.

The Crags

Brush Creek Lakes

Sangre De Cristo Wilderness Area
day hike

Distance: 8.0 miles (round trip)

Walking time: 6 hours

Elevations: 2,100 ft. gain/loss
Peerless Mine Trailhead (start): 9,600 ft.
Lower Brush Lake: 11,404 ft.
Upper Brush Lake: 11,540 ft.

Trail: Very rocky in places. Also, the trail between the lower and upper lakes is not well defined.

Season: Midsummer through mid-fall. The road to the trailhead is usually not passable before early July.

Vicinity: Near Westcliffe

Maps: Electric Peak *(USGS)*
Sangre de Cristo Mountains *(Trails Illustrated, #138)*

Information: http://colorado.utahtrails.com/brushcreeklakes.html
http://www.fs.fed.us/r2/psicc/ *(San Isabel National Forest)*
phone: (719) 269-8500 *(San Carlos Ranger District)*

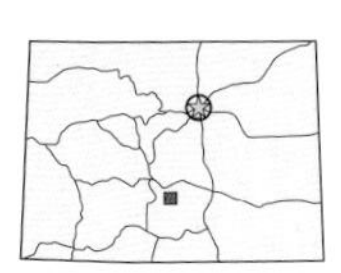

Drive 12.8 miles north of Westcliffe on Highway 69 to the farming community of Hillside. Just 0.2 mile before arriving at the Hillside Post Office you will see a sign marking the road to Lake Creek Campground on the left. Turn here onto County Road 198 and drive west for 2.9 miles to the Lake Creek Campground. Shortly after passing the road into the campground you will come to a junction where you must turn left onto Road 337. From there you should follow the signs for another 1.1 miles to the Duckett Creek Trailhead.

Continue driving south from the Duckett Creek Trailhead on Forest Road 337 for another 0.9 mile until you come to another junction where you must turn right onto Road 331. Forest Road 331 ends at the Peerless Mine Trailhead 1.5 miles later. Don't be confused when you pass two more junctions where Roads 333 and 331A depart on the right. Just stay on road 331. The road becomes significantly rougher as it approaches the trailhead. With care most cars can make it to the end, but a high clearance vehicle is advisable.

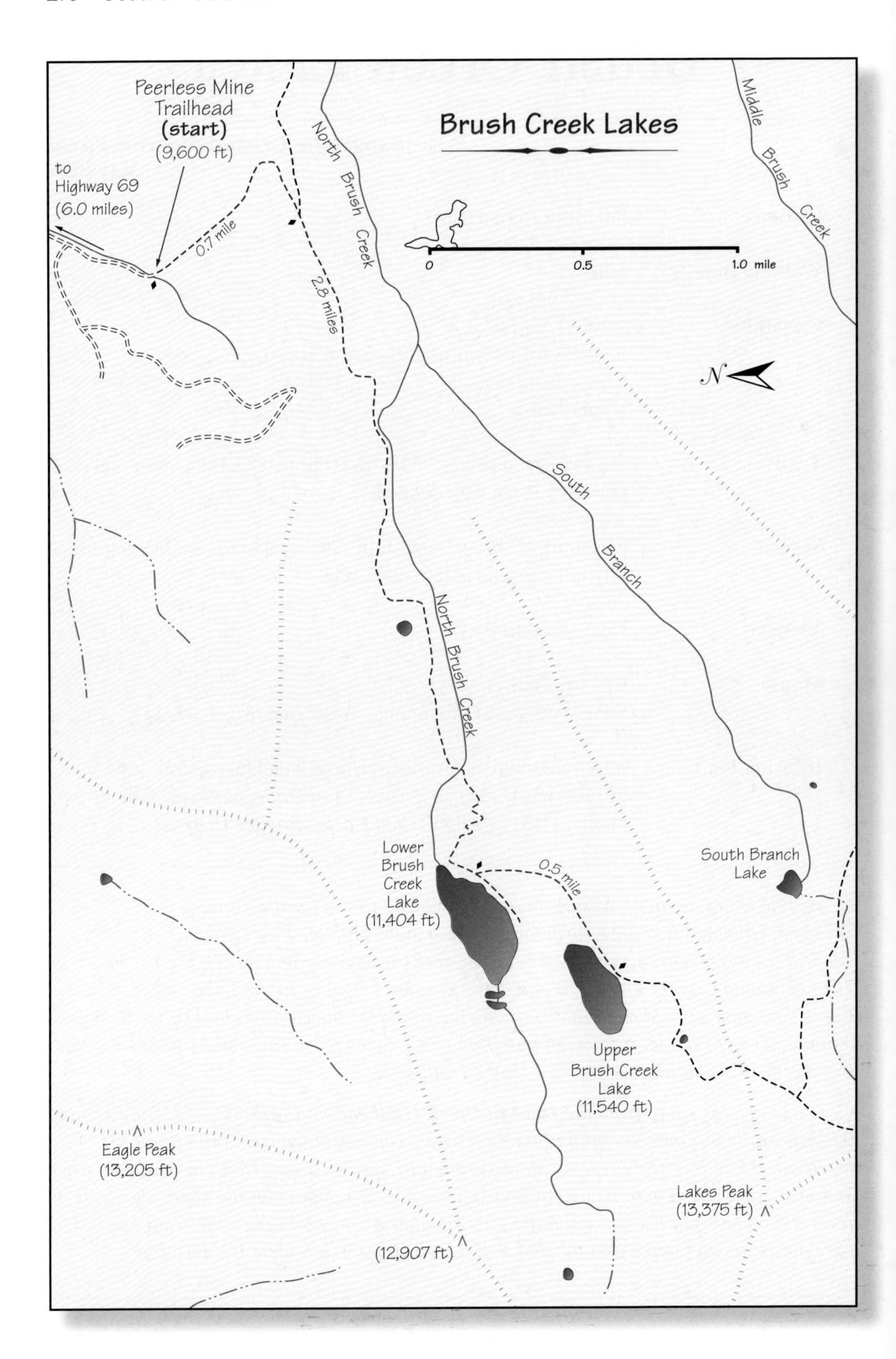
Brush Creek Lakes
Peerless Mine
Trailhead
(start)
(9,600 ft)
to
Highway 69
(6.0 miles)
0.7 mile
2.8 miles
North Brush Creek
Middle Brush Creek
0
0.5
1.0 mile
N
South Branch
North Brush Creek
Lower
Brush
Creek
Lake
(11,404 ft)
0.5 mile
South Branch
Lake
Upper
Brush Creek
Lake
(11,540 ft)
Eagle Peak
(13,205 ft)
Lakes Peak
(13,375 ft)
(12,907 ft)

It is common for hikers to begin this trek at the North Brush Creek Trailhead near the end of Forest Road 337; however in my opinion it makes better sense to start at the Peerless Mine Trailhead described here. The round trip distance to the lakes from Peerless Mine is nearly five miles shorter; hence it is relatively easy to walk from there to the lakes as a day hike.

The Brush Creek Lakes are two of the largest lakes in the Sangre de Cristo Range, and the fishing can be good. Also, they are not as frequently visited as many other lakes in the vicinity, so you can usually expect more solitude there. The lakes are situated right on the edge of timberline in a picturesque alpine cirque just east of Thirsty Peak (13,213 ft.) and Lakes Peak (13,375 ft.). Unfortunately the talus slopes below the surrounding peaks extend all the way to the water's edge, and the jagged boulders make it impossible to enjoy a pleasant stroll around the lakes. Furthermore, good campsites near the lakes are limited.

The trail starts behind the old mining shack on the east side of the parking area. The trail register is located in the trees 30 feet from the shack, and from there you will see a rock-strewn path that proceeds straight up the slope under a heavy canopy of aspen and lodgepole pine. Perhaps the reason this trail is not often used is because many of the people who visit the Brush Creek Lakes do so by horseback, and it would be difficult for a horse to negotiate this rocky path. After 15 minutes, however, the trail becomes a better walking path, less rocky and less steep, and soon afterward to breaks out of the trees onto the rim of North Brush Canyon. Here you will be treated to a fine view into the deep glacier-carved gorge with Wet Mountain Valley at its mouth and Lakes Peak above its western side.

The vista is brief; within 200 feet the trail heads back down into the trees as it descends westward into the canyon. After loosing about 200 feet over the next 10 minutes you will come to a trail junction where the Peerless Mine Trail meets the North Brush Creek Trail. Here you must turn right as you proceed to the headwaters of North Brush Creek.

North Brush Creek

For the next hour the trail remains immersed in a dense forest of lodgepole pine, gradually changing to Engelmann spruce, as it follows the north side of the canyon. The grade is generally level and the walking is easy. Then, 2.2 miles from the trail junction ,the path crosses to the south side of the creek and begins climbing up the slope toward the lower lake. From there you must climb another 440 feet over the next half-mile to reach the lower lake.

My first impression upon gazing across Lower Brush Lake was one of disappointment. The shore of the lake is so rocky it is not easily accessed from the trail, and although Thirsty Peak makes a fine backdrop above the western shore I didn't find the lake to be particularly inspirational. There are a few reasonable campsites in a grove of trees on the lake's southern shore, but elsewhere there is too little soil for trees.

Although most maps show the trail continuing on from the lower lake to the upper lake, the trail essentially disappears once it enters the trees on the south side of the lower lake. The easiest way to get to the upper lake is to head upward in a southwesterly direction from a point near the outlet of the lower lake. After gaining 120 feet of elevation you will find a good trail that follows the grassy area at the base of the talus slopes south of the lakes. Following this trail for another 400 yards will bring you to the most accessible southern shore of the upper lake.

Again, the rocks and the willows that surround Upper Brush Lake preclude the possibility of a leisurely walk around its shore. However I found this lake to be very attractive in a wild and rugged sort of way. It sits right on the edge of timberline, and the only trees you will see are stunted survivors of the harsh winter snows. The skyline is dominated by Thirsty and Lakes Peaks, the air is crisp and clear, and one cannot help but feel the spiritual presence of nature in such a place. It is a world far different from the man-made world in which most of us live our daily lives.

Upper Brush Creek Lake

Lakes of the Clouds

Sangre de Cristo Wilderness Area
day hike

Distance:	9.1 miles (round trip)
Walking time:	6 1/2 hours
Elevations:	2,230 ft. gain/loss Gibson Creek Trailhead (start): 9,400 ft. Lower Lake: 11,470 ft. Upper Lake: 11,630 ft.
Trail:	Well marked, but extremely rocky in places.
Season:	Midsummer through mid fall. The trail is generally covered with snow from late November through early July.
Vicinity:	Near Westcliffe
Maps:	Beckwith Mountain, Electric Peak *(USGS)* Sangre de Cristo Mountains *(Trails Illustrated, #138)*
Information:	http://colorado.utahtrails.com/lakesofclouds.html http://www.fs.fed.us/r2/psicc/ *(San Isabel National Forest)* phone: (719) 269-8500 *(San Carlos Ranger District)*

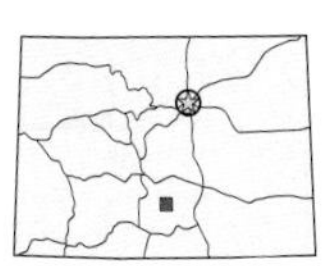

Drive south out of Westcliffe on Highway 69 and on the outskirts of town, just 0.2 mile from the city center, you will see a sign marking Hermit Lane. Turn right here and drive toward the mountains. Hermit Lane continues due west for 6.1 miles before coming to a signed junction where you must bear right to reach the Gibson Creek Trailhead. From that point the road bends to the north, finally ending 1.6 miles later at a T-junction with North Taylor Road. Turn left at the T and drive another 0.7 mile to the trailhead and parking area.

Three very pleasant high-altitude lakes on the east side of the Sangre de Cristo Mountains are the goal of this hike. The lakes are situated on the edge of timberline in a high alpine valley that is almost completely surrounded by 13,000-foot peaks. One of the peaks, Spread Eagle Peak (13,423 ft.) is only 0.6 mile southeast of the lower lake, and is a popular climb for those looking for an additional challenge. All three lakes also support a thriving population of cutthroat trout, and if you want to spend more time in the area you will find some nice camping spots beneath the trees on the

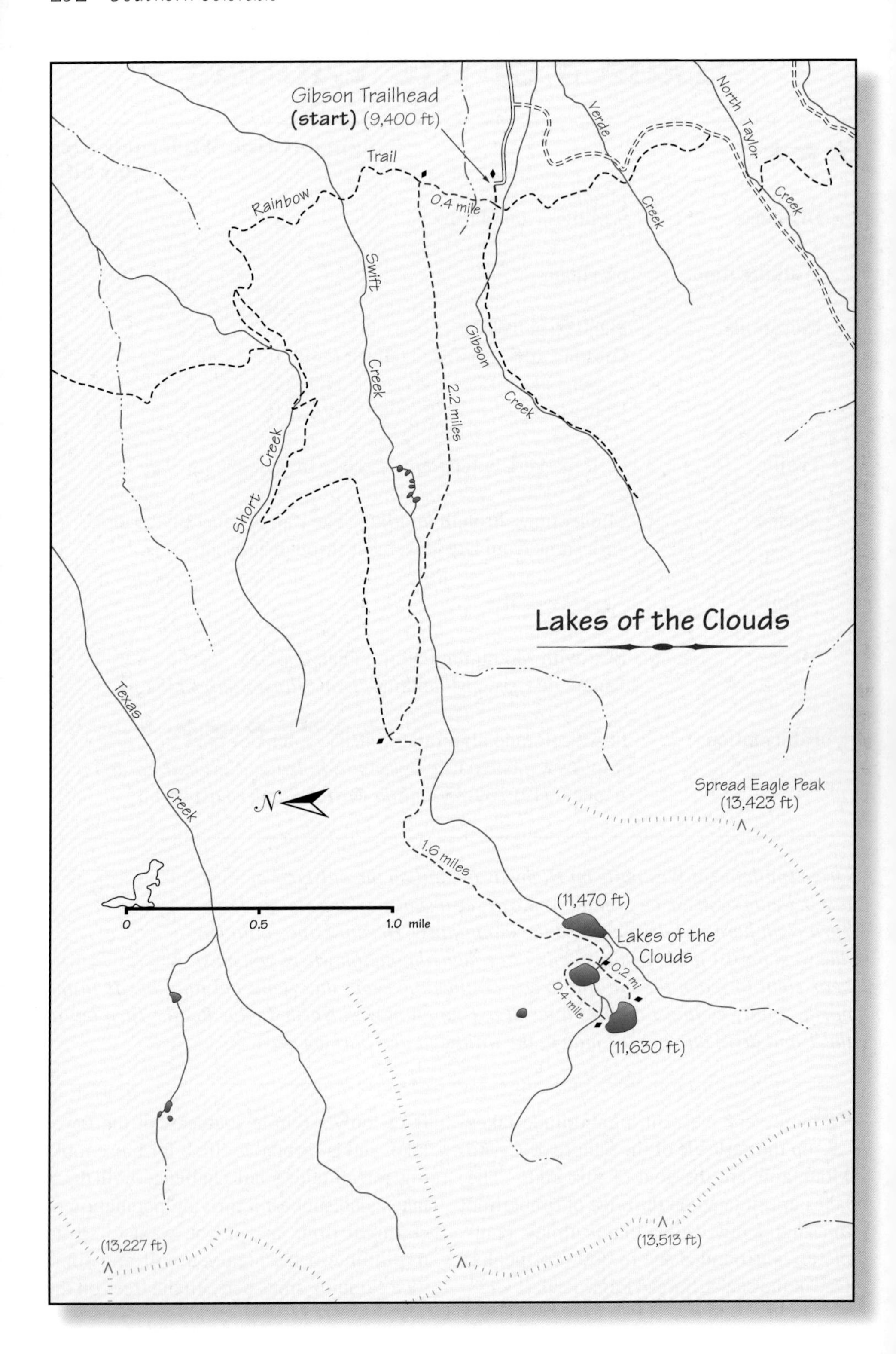
Gibson Trailhead
(start) (9,400 ft)
Trail
Rainbow
0.4 mile
Verde
Creek
North
Taylor
Creek
Swift
Creek
Gibson
Creek
2.2 miles
Short
Creek
Lakes of the Clouds
Texas
Creek
N
Spread Eagle Peak
(13,423 ft)
1.6 miles
(11,470 ft)
Lakes of the
Clouds
0.2 mi
0.4 mile
(11,630 ft)
0
0.5
1.0 mile
(13,227 ft)
(13,513 ft)

Lower Lake of the Clouds

north side of the lower lake.

From the trailhead a short spur trail proceeds west through a grove of aspen trees for about 100 yards before joining the Rainbow Trail. The Rainbow Trail is a popular 100-mile-long ATV route that runs just outside the wilderness boundary along the eastern side of the Sangre de Cristos. Many of the footpaths that enter these mountains begin on the Rainbow Trail, so it is frequently used by backpackers and ATV riders alike.

Turn right when you reach the Rainbow Trail and walk north for another 0.5 mile until you see a sign marking the beginning of the Swift Creek Trail. There you must turn west again to begin the long trek upward to the headwaters of Swift Creek where the Lakes of the Clouds are located. The grade is only moderately steep, but the rocky terrain makes walking difficult for the first mile. Erosion seems to have removed every last bit of the soil from the path, leaving only rocks.

For 1.6 miles the trail follows the south side of the Swift Creek glacial valley, then it dips down to cross the creek. When you first arrive at the water's edge it appears that there is no way to cross without getting your feet wet. But if you walk upstream for 30 feet you will come to a place where a few well-placed logs make the crossing much easier.

The gradient of the streambed increases dramatically above the creek crossing, causing the trail to get steeper as it climbs up the north side of the canyon. As you climb you can hear the roar of the water crashing downward over a series of long cas-

Swift Creek and the Lower Lake of the Clouds

Trail between the second and third lakes

cades below the trees on your left. After 5 minutes the path again levels out, and if you are observant you will see a vague spur trail branching off toward a viewpoint above one to the waterfalls. Unfortunately, however, the view is seriously obstructed by the trees, and to get closer would require some major bushwhacking.

0.7 mile after crossing the stream the trail arrives at the junction where the Swift Creek Trail meets the Lakes of the Clouds Trail. Soon it approaches the water again, passing through an area of near-perfect creek-side campsites, and then heads upward along the base of a steep scree field. Finally, as you approach timberline, the path levels out to become a more pleasant walk. You should arrive at the lower Lake of the Clouds about 45 minutes after leaving the trail junction.

The most notable thing you will see as you approach the lower lake is the distinctive Spread Eagle Peak, a cone-shaped thirteener that rises from the south shore of the lake just over a half-mile away. The mountain is most impressive when viewed around sunset during the summer months when the sun is in the northwest. It towers above the lake like a gigantic Egyptian pyramid.

The trail proceeds along the western side of the lower lake for 200 yards before veering away toward the outlet of the middle lake. Just before reaching the outlet the trail splits, with the right fork circling around the middle lake and the left fork going directly to the south shore of the upper lake. The trail to the right eventually ends on the edge of a

Spread Eagle Peak and the Middle Lake of the Clouds

large bog that occupies the northern shore of the upper lake.

Spread Eagle Peak

As mentioned before, Spread Eagle Peak is a common destination for people who want to spend more time in the area and are looking for an additional challenge. The standard route to the top of this 13,423-foot peak begins on the south shore of the upper lake. Head southeast through the woods above the lake for 200 yards until you run into a north-flowing drainage. Follow this drainage up the slope for about 0.4 mile, then veer to the left of the drainage towards the saddle on the ridge above. When you reach the saddle simply turn east and make your way along the top of the ridge for the last 0.7 mile to the summit. The total distance of this climb from the upper lake is 3.4 miles round trip with an elevation gain of 1,800 feet.

Lakes of the Clouds Trail

As is indicated on the map, there are two trails leading to the Lakes of the Clouds. The trail described above is the Swift Creek Trail, but it is also possible to use the Lakes of the Clouds Trail that starts further north on the Rainbow Trail. The Lakes of the Clouds Trail is actually a better trail than the one described here–less rocky and not as steep. But it is also 0.4 miles longer and requires another 1.3 miles of walking along the Rainbow Trail to reach the trailhead. There are some nice views into Swift Water Canyon from the Lakes of the Clouds Trailhead, but other than that the scenery along both trails is substantially the same.

If you do this hike along the Lakes of the Clouds Trail the round trip distance will be 3.4 miles longer than the hike already described. Just for the sake of diversity you might want to consider using the Lakes of the Clouds Trail for your return trip from the lakes. In that case add 1.7 miles onto the length of the hike. The elevation gain along either trail is about the same.

Frozen waterfall above the Upper Lake of the Clouds

Venable and Comanche Trails

Sangre De Cristo Wilderness Area
day hike

Distance:	12.2 miles (loop)
Walking time:	9 hours
Elevations:	3,900 ft. gain/loss Comanche/Venable Trailhead (start): 9,000 ft. Venable Lakes: 12,000 ft. Venable Pass: 12,800 ft. Comanche Lake: 11,660 ft.
Trail:	Well marked, easy to follow
Season:	Midsummer through mid-fall. The higher parts of the trail are generally covered with snow from mid-November through early July.
Vicinity:	Near Westcliffe
Maps:	Rito Alto Peak, Horn Peak *(USGS)* Sangre de Cristo Mountains *(Trails Illustrated, #138)*
Information:	http://colorado.utahtrails.com/venabletrail.html http://www.fs.fed.us/r2/psicc/ *(San Isabel National Forest)* phone: (719) 269-8500 *(San Carlos Ranger District)*

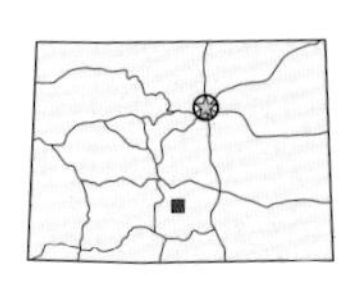

Drive south from the town of Westcliffe on Highway 69 for a distance of 3.4 miles, then turn right onto Schoolfield Road. Drive west for another 6.6 miles, following the signs to Alvarado Campground and the Comanche/Venable Trailhead. 0.2 miles before you reach the campground you will see sign directing you to the right for the last 0.5 mile to the trailhead.

The Venable Trail begins on the right side of the parking area, and the Comanche Trail begins on the left. This loop can be walked in either direction, but since the Venable Trail is not quite as steep most people begin there and return on the Comanche Trail.

The Venable and Comanche trails together form a popular loop hike into the Sangre de Cristo Wilderness Area. The route follows Venable Creek up to the crest of the Sangre de Cristo Range, then traverses the west side of Spring Mountain. From there it crosses Comanche Pass and follows the Comanche Trail back to the trailhead.

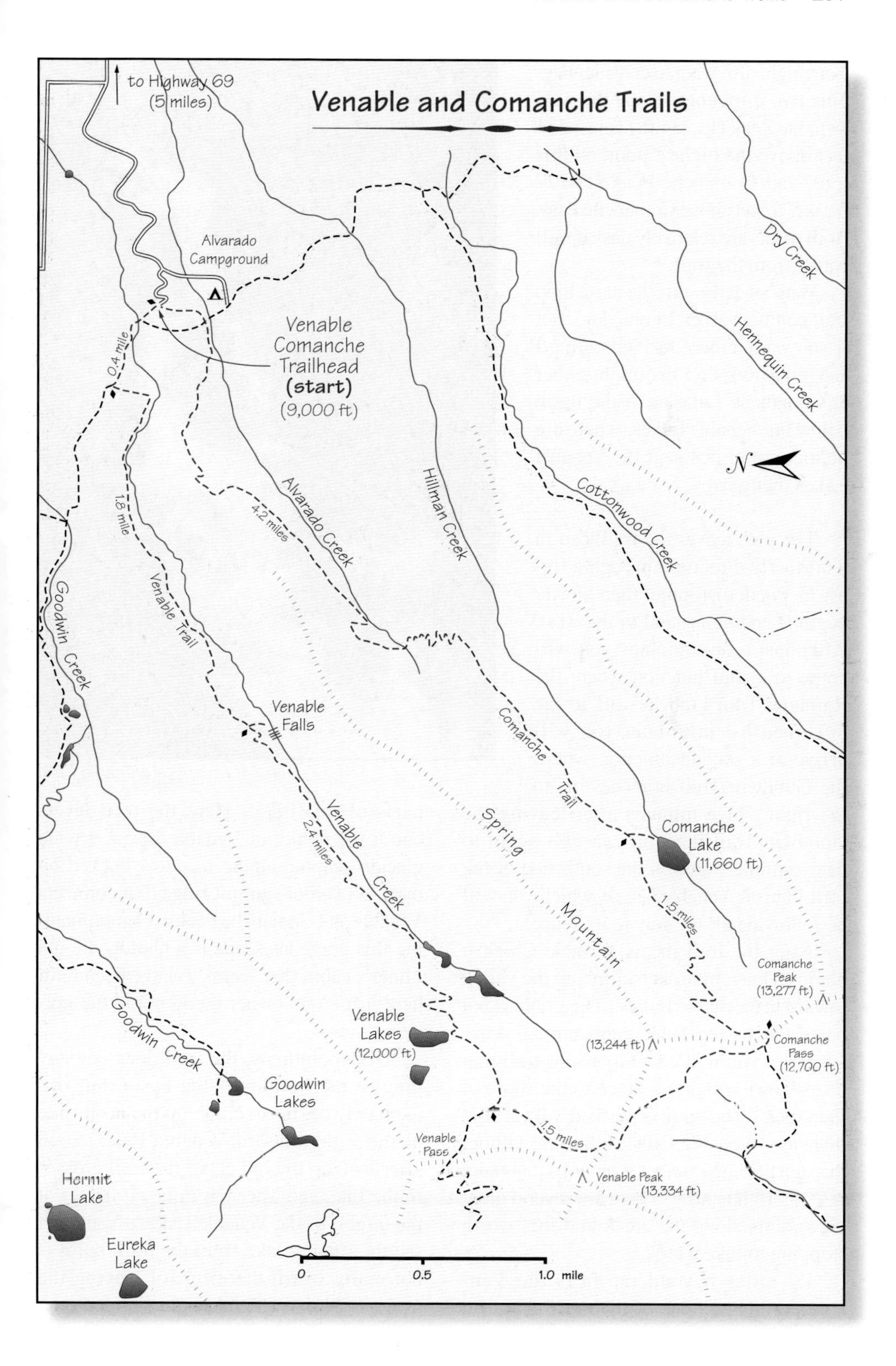

Venable and Comanche Trails
to Highway 69
(5 miles)
Alvarado Campground
Venable Comanche Trailhead
(start)
(9,000 ft)
0.4 mile
1.8 mile
4.2 miles
Alvarado Creek
Hillman Creek
Cottonwood Creek
Dry Creek
Hennequin Creek
N
Goodwin Creek
Venable Trail
Venable Falls
Venable Creek
2.4 miles
Comanche Trail
Spring Mountain
Comanche Lake
(11,660 ft)
1.5 miles
Comanche Peak
(13,277 ft)
Comanche Pass
(12,700 ft)
(13,244 ft)
Venable Lakes
(12,000 ft)
Goodwin Creek
Goodwin Lakes
1.5 miles
Venable Pass
Venable Peak
(13,334 ft)
Hermit Lake
Eureka Lake
0
0.5
1.0 mile

You might also want to consider bagging two thirteeners along the way. Venable Peak (13,334 ft.) is just 554 feet above the highest point on this trail, and Comanche Peak (13,277 ft.) is 577 feet above Comanche Pass. Both peaks are relatively easy uphill walks from the trail.

With an early start the basic loop trail can be walked in one day. But if you want a more relaxed outing I suggest you spend one night either at Comanche Lake or in the basin below the Venable Lakes. There are no nice campsites near the Venable Lakes themselves.

Venable Falls

The path leaves the trailhead in a northerly direction through a forest of Ponderosa pine, then slowly begins bending around to the west. After just a few minutes you will come to a trail junction where the Rainbow Trail branches off to the left, then 0.3 mile later you will arrive at a second junction where the Goodwin Trail branches off to the right. Five minutes after leaving the Goodwin Trail junction you will begin to hear running water on the south side of the trail. This is Venable Creek, which you will be following all the way to its source.

After the trail meets Venable Creek it begins a long, unbroken climb up the valley toward the Venable Lakes. The grade is not particularly steep, but it is unrelenting. After 1.8 miles you will come to a spur trail that drops down a short distance to the shore of the creek. The spur is marked with a sign that says "Venable Falls", but even without the sign the noise makes it obvious that there is a waterfall nearby. There are several great viewpoints along the creek and it is worth stopping to take a look.

1.3 miles beyond the falls the Venable Trail enters one of the most beautiful parts of this hike. Here the trail levels out at the mouth of Venable Basin, a wide glacier-sculpted alpine meadow backed by the 13,000-foot summit ridge that connects Venable and Comanche Peaks. Complimenting this gorgeous scene is a photogenic old miner's cabin that seems to have been built here just so its owner could enjoy the gorgeous view.

Disappointingly, the trail does not stay long in the bottom of the basin, but immediately begins to climb up the north side of the valley toward Venable Pass. Soon after leaving the old cabin the trail crosses timberline, and after 0.6 miles it arrives at the largest of the Venable Lakes. You can't see the smaller lake from the trail, but it is not really worth the effort of leaving the trail to visit it. The lakes are situated on a high, rocky bench, quite removed from the picturesque valley below, and they are not particularly scenic.

0.4 mile after leaving Venable Lakes the trail comes to another junction. If you turn right here you will be heading toward Venable Pass, but in order to complete the loop you must bear left toward Comanche Pass. The next 0.6 mile of trail is an exciting segment. The path gains another 340 feet before reaching 12,780 feet, the highest point on this hike, and crossing to the west side of the ridge. The last few hundred yards are along a very narrow constructed trail with significant exposure on the left side. I wouldn't want to attempt this trail in icy conditions. In warm, dry weather the danger is minimal, but it is definitely exciting.

As the trail crosses the ridge Venable Peak seems almost close enough to hit with a rock. If you have the time and inclination to bag a thirteener it is an easy 20-minute scramble to the top. The summit is 0.3 mile from and 554 feet above the trail.

After crossing the ridge the trail heads south with very little change in elevation toward Comanche Pass. It reaches the pass after 1.0 mile, crosses to the east side of the ridge, and starts down into Comanche Lake basin. Again, it is tempting to bag another named thirteener before starting down. Comanche Peak is just 0.3 mile further up the summit ridge—an easy 20-minute walk away. The peak is 577 feet above Comanche Pass, but the terrain is not particularly difficult.

From Comanche Pass the trail heads down the north side of the basin, loosing 1,040 feet of elevation and passing Comanche Lake after 1.5 miles. Comanche Lake is much prettier than the Venable Lakes and there are a few nice camping areas nearby, but the basin itself is not a pretty as Venable Basin. From the lake it is another 4.2 miles of uneventful downhill walking to the trailhead.

Comanche Lake

Humboldt Peak

★★★★

Sangre De Cristo Wilderness Area
4WD vehicle useful
day hike

Distance:	7.4 miles (round trip)
Walking time:	5 3/4 hours
Elevations:	2,870 ft. gain/loss South Colony Lakes Trailhead (start): 11,200 ft. Upper South Colony Lake: 12,030 ft. Humboldt Peak: 14,064 ft.
Trail:	Generally good except for some minor scrambling near the top.
Season:	Midsummer through mid-fall. The road to the trailhead is usually impassable from mid-November until early July.
Vicinity:	Near Westcliffe
Maps:	Crestone Peak *(USGS)* Sangre de Cristo Mountains *(Trails Illustrated, #138)*
Information:	http://colorado.utahtrails.com/humboldtpeak.html http://www.fs.fed.us/r2/psicc/ *(San Isabel National Forest)* phone: (719) 269-8500 *(San Carlos Ranger District)*

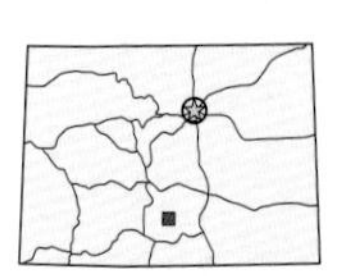

Drive south of Westcliffe on Highway 69 for 4.5 miles until you see a sign directing you to Music Pass. Turn right here onto Colfax Road and continue south for another 5.5 miles. Colfax Road ends at a T junction where you must turn right onto Road 120, following the signs to South Colony Trailhead. 1.4 miles from the T junction you will come to a 2WD parking area, beyond which the road crosses 1.5 miles of private land. From there the road becomes quite rocky, although, with care, most passenger cars can still proceed for a few more miles. The road crosses the Rainbow Trail 2.2 miles after leaving the 2WD parking area, and although at this point you are still 3.2 miles from South Colony Trailhead you will soon find the road impossibly rough for a 2WD vehicle. There are, however, plenty of places to pull out along the way when you decide to park and continue on foot. If you are driving a 4WD vehicle you will find the road moderately difficult, but manageable. The road finally ends at a large parking area 5.3 miles from the lower 2WD parking area. The trailhead is marked by a locked gate at the end of the road and a sigh that says "South Colony Lakes 1.5 miles".

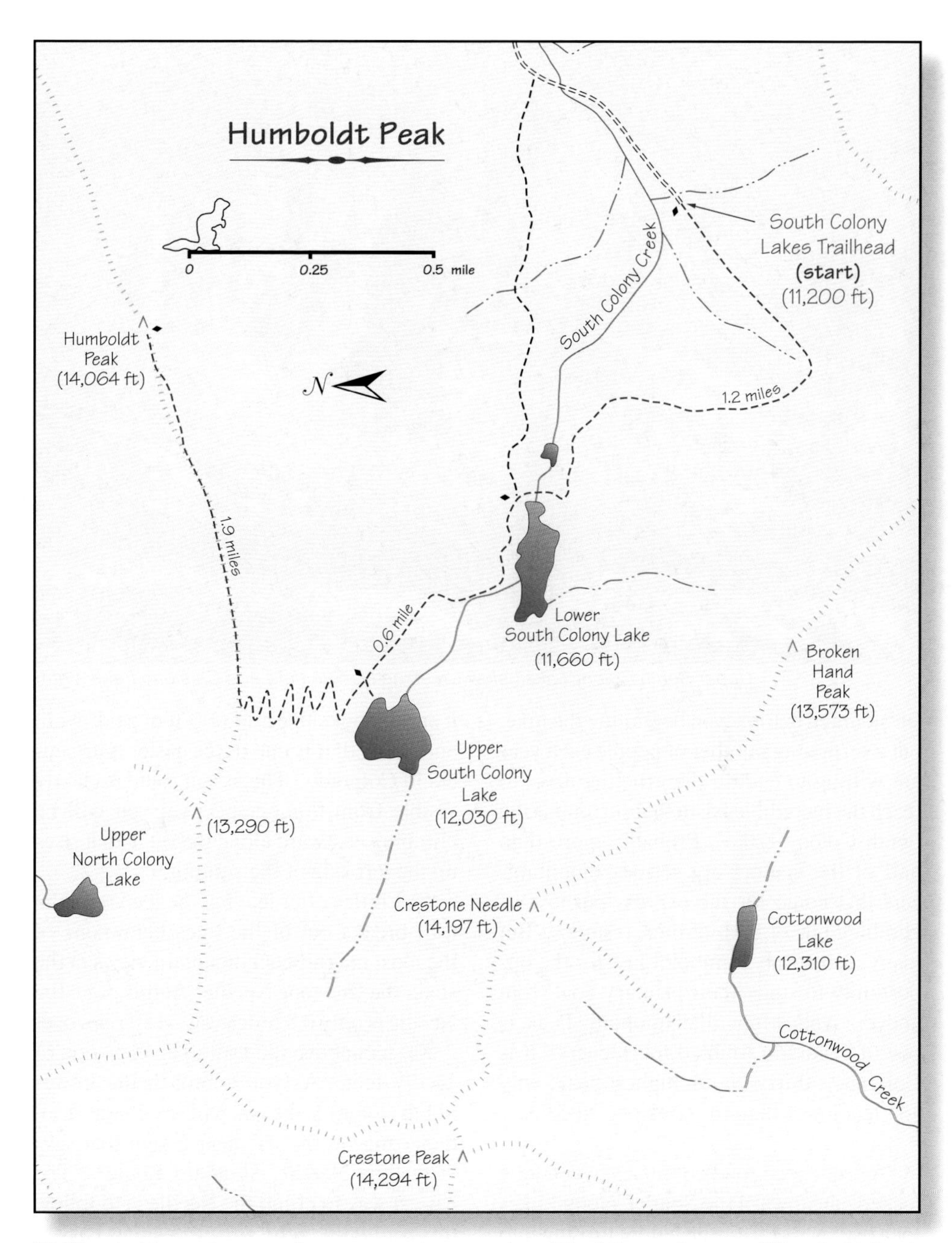

Humboldt, on its own, is not a particu larly notable peak. It is a relatively easy climb with no challenging obstacles and only one well traveled route. It is, however, located in a spectacular part of the Sangre de Cristo Mountains, and therein lies its attraction. The hike to the top of Humboldt Peak passes some of the most notable mountain scenery in Colorado, including the South Colony Lakes, Crestone Peak, and the Crestone Needle. The 5-mile jeep road to the trailhead is a daunting obstacle that must be

Upper South Colony Lake below Crestone Needle (left) and Crestone Peak (right)

surmounted before even beginning the hike, but a surprising number of people each year are willing to endure the grueling drive to reach the incredible basin that surrounds the South Colony Lakes. Probably more than half of the visitors are serious mountaineers that come for the express purpose of climbing one or both of the Crestones. But many also climb Humboldt just for the opportunity to study their primary goal from above. And, after all, Humboldt Peak is one of Colorado's fabled fourteeners. It is Colorado's thirty-eighth highest peak, only 133 feet lower than the Crestone Needle.

A crude jeep road continues beyond the locked gate toward the South Colony Lakes for a distance of 0.4 mile before turning into a foot path. From there the trail turns north as it meanders along the slope with very little elevation gain toward the lower lake. Humboldt Peak rises directly in front of you along this section of trail. It seems so close it hardly looks like a 14,000-foot peak at all, and, indeed, it is one of the easier fourteeners in Colorado. The assent route is clearly visible from this perspective; you will be climbing eastward along the ridge that rises up the left side of the summit.

0.7 miles after leaving the jeep road the trail breaks out of the trees below one of the most magnificent mountain views in the state: the Crestone Needle. At this point the Needle is only 0.8 mile away, yet it rises over 2,500 feet above the trail to an elevation of 14,197 feet. As you approach the Lower South Colony Lake you will see a vague trail departing on the left near a sign that says "Crestone Needle, Standard Route". The easiest way to climb the Needle is to follow this trail west, across Broken Hand Pass to the southwest side of the mountain. There climbers can find a non-technical class-3 route to the summit of the Needle.

Just beyond the Crestone Needle Trail the path crosses South Colony Creek and emerges on the eastern shore of the Lower South Colony Lake. As you leave the lower lake you will pass an unsigned junction where another trail departs to the east. That trail eventually ends back at the South Colony Jeep Road about 0.4 mile below the trailhead. If you left a vehicle at the end of the road you should take care not to get sidetracked onto that trail on the return portion of the hike.

The trail to the upper lake continues its gradual climb away from the lower lake, soon crossing timberline and entering the alpine tundra that fills the upper basin. All heads will be turned to the west as you proceed, toward the breathtaking view of Crestone Peak and the Crestone Needle from the upper lake. A climbing route that is considered to be one of the finest technical climbs in Colorado begins at Upper South Colony Lake and proceeds directly up the northeast ridge, or arête, of the Crestone Needle. This route, rated 5.7 in difficulty, was first accomplished in 1925 by Albert Ellingwood, and it is now called the Ellingwood Arête Route. The entire route can clearly be seen from Upper South Colony Lake, and one cannot help but admire those who have climbed the mountain along this highly exposed ridge.

After leaving the upper lake the trail begins switchbacking northward to the top of Humboldt Peak's west ridge, finally topping out after an elevation gain of 830 feet. Once on the crest of the ridge the path turns east to follow it for the last 0.8 mile to the summit. The first half of the ridge trail is easy, gaining about 900 feet over 0.5 mile. But as you approach the peak you will be challenged by a field of sharp-edged thousand-pound boulders that you must pick your way through. Take care not to break a leg while boulder-hopping up this part of the climb. There is no easy way up the boulder field, but the terrain is slightly gentler on the south side of the ridge, so try to keep on that side as you climb. Unfortunately, this section of the trail is not well defined, and there are many misplaced cairns that try to lure you to the north side of the ridge. Follow only the larger monuments of stone, ignoring some of the smaller cairns, and, arduous though it is, you will be following the least difficult course.

Finally, after an elevation gain of 2,034 feet from Upper South Colony Lake the route breaks out onto the west side of the summit, and from there it is a simple walk over the last 200 yards to the mountain's highest point. From there you will be treated to glorious views in nearly every direction. The North Colony Lakes are below you to the north, shadowed by Colony Baldy, a high thirteener on the north side of North Colony Creek. Kit Carson Peak (14,165 ft.) lies 2.7 miles west, just to the right of Crestone Peak. And, of course, the South Colony Lakes are in full view to the south.

Humboldt Peak

Music Pass/Sand Creek Lakes

Sangre De Cristo Wilderness Area
4WD vehicle useful
day hike

Distance:	8.8 miles (round trip)
Walking time:	6 hours
Elevations:	1,910 ft. gain/loss Music Pass Trailhead (start): 10,700 ft. Grape Creek Trailhead: 9,200 ft. Music Pass: 11,395 ft. Upper Sand Creek Lake: 11,745 ft. Lower Sand Creek Lake: 11,471 ft.
Trail:	Well marked, easy to follow
Season:	Midsummer through mid-fall. The higher parts of the trail are generally covered with snow from mid-November through mid-July.
Vicinity:	Near Westcliffe
Maps:	Beck Mountain, Crestone Peak *(USGS)* Sangre de Cristo Mountains *(Trails Illustrated, #138)*
Information:	http://colorado.utahtrails.com/musicpass.html http://www.nps.gov/grsa *(Great Sand Dunes National Park)* phone: (719) 378-6399 *(Visitor Center)*

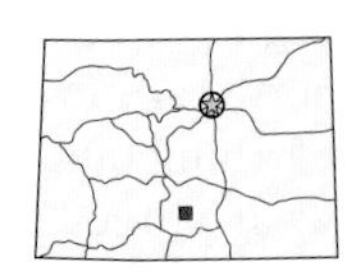

Drive south from the center of Westcliffe on Highway 69 for 4.8 miles until you see a sign marking the road to Music Pass Trailhead. Turn right here and continue south on Colfax Lane until the road ends at a T-junction 5.6 miles from the highway. You will see a sign at the junction indicating that you must turn left to proceed to the Music Pass Trailhead. Another 5.2 miles will bring you to the Grape Creek Trailhead where you must park if you are not driving a 4WD vehicle. From there an extremely rocky 4WD road continues upward for another 2.9 miles to the Music Pass Trailhead.

Who wouldn't want to walk to a place with a name like Music Pass? The pass was given this poetic name because some claim they can hear musical sounds when the wind blows over the surrounding mountains. I have not personally

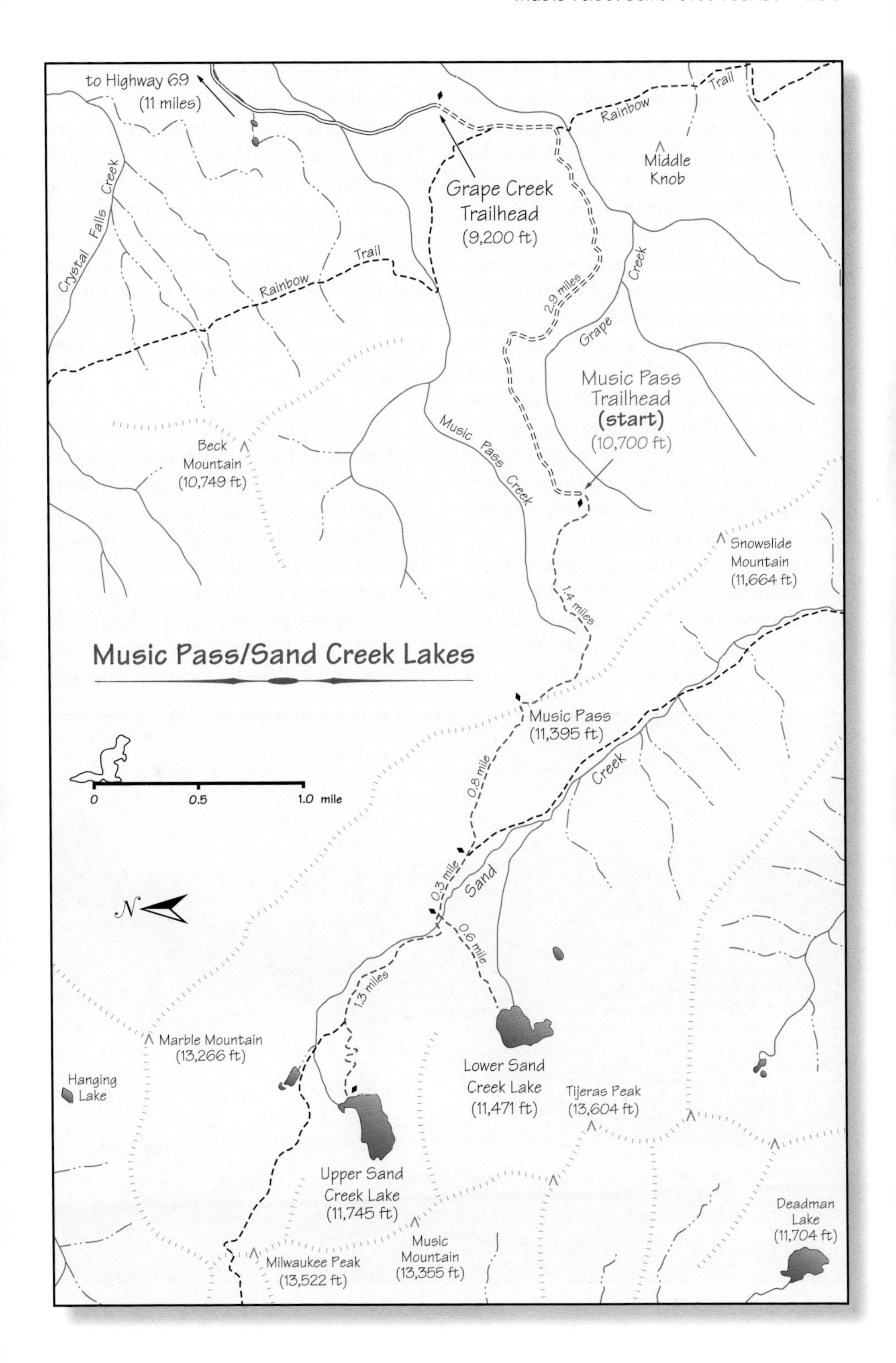

Music Pass/Sand Creek Lakes
to Highway 69 (11 miles)
Grape Creek Trailhead (9,200 ft)
Rainbow Trail
Middle Knob
Crystal Falls Creek
Grape Creek
2.9 miles
Music Pass Trailhead (start) (10,700 ft)
Music Pass Creek
Beck Mountain (10,749 ft)
Snowslide Mountain (11,664 ft)
1.4 miles
Music Pass (11,395 ft)
0.8 mile
Sand Creek
0.3 mile
0.6 mile
1.3 miles
0
0.5
1.0 mile
N
Marble Mountain (13,266 ft)
Hanging Lake
Lower Sand Creek Lake (11,471 ft)
Tijeras Peak (13,604 ft)
Upper Sand Creek Lake (11,745 ft)
Music Mountain (13,355 ft)
Milwaukee Peak (13,522 ft)
Deadman Lake (11,704 ft)

experienced that sensation, but I can attest to the magnificent mountain scenery that surrounds Music Pass and the Sand Creek Lakes. Even if you miss the legendary music, the hike across Music Pass to the lakes below can be a memorable endeavor.

Many years ago it was possible to drive a 4WD vehicle all the way from the Grape Creek Trailhead to the summit of Music Pass, but that is no longer possible. Motor vehicles are still allowed on the first 2.9 miles of the road, as far as the Music Pass Trailhead, but the final 1.4 miles of the old Music Pass Road have long since been blocked off and converted to a foot path. From the looks of the trail it has been many years since it was used by vehicles. There is now little evidence that the trail was once a road.

The following discussion assumes that you are beginning your hike at the Music Pass Trailhead, but I must warn you that the last 2.5 miles of the road to this trailhead are extremely steep and rocky and you won't make it if you don't have a 4WD vehicle. If you don't have a 4WD vehicle you will have to leave your car at the Grape Creek Trailhead and walk the last 2.9 miles to the trailhead. You may be lucky enough to get a ride up in the back of another hiker's pickup; otherwise you must add another 5.8 miles onto the round trip walking distance and 1,500 feet to the elevation gain for this hike. In that case it is probably better to plan the hike as an overnighter rather than a day hike.

From the parking area at the end of Music Pass Road the trail immediately enters a dense conifer forest as it begins climbing toward the pass. Initially you won't see much but trees, but after about 45 minutes the forest starts to become more open, giving you some great views of the Wet Mountain Valley on the east side of the Sangre de Cristo Range. Finally, just before reaching the pass you will pass a sign indicating that

The west side of Music Pass

you are entering the Great Sand Dunes National Preserve, an extension of the Great Sand Dunes National Park on the western side of the range. This point also marks the eastern boundary of the Sangre de Cristo Wilderness Area.

More great views await you at the top of the pass where the trail begins its descent into Sand Creek Valley. Unfortunately you won't be able to see the lakes from this vantage point, but the vista to the west where the backbone of the mountain is punctuated by Tijeras Peak (13,604 ft.), Music Mountain (13,356 ft.), and Milwaukee Peak (13,522 ft.) is sure to give you pause. These three majestic thirteeners lie directly above the west side of the Sand Creek drainage, and as you press on toward the lakes they seem to grow ever more imposing.

Sand Creek

400 feet below the west side of Music Pass you will come to a junction where a lesser-used trail branches off to the left and proceeds downstream along the east side of Sand Creek. Bearing right at the junction the trail becomes almost level as it follows the 11,000-foot contour upstream toward the lakes. Then, 0.3 mile beyond the junction with the lower Sand Creek Trail you will come to another junction where the trail splits on its way to the Upper and Lower Sand Creek Lakes.

I suggest you turn left at this junction and visit Lower Sand Creek Lake first, so you can enjoy it before the sun is too high. Shortly after leaving the junction the path crosses to the west side of the creek and begins gaining elevation as it makes its way toward the lower lake. The forest is so dense in this area you can't see much of the terrain ahead, but after 30 minutes of relatively easy walking you will suddenly break out of the trees on the northeast shore of Lower Sand Creek Lake. Here the sight of Tijeras Peak rising above the opposite side of the lake will almost knock you off your feet! The towering summit lies less than a half-mile from the lake shore, and seeing it from this perspective is a view you will not soon forget. The best time to be there is in the morning while the sun is in the east, but, impressive as the scene is, it is difficult to get a good photograph of the mountain and the lake together. Tijeras Peak is so high and so close you will need a very wide angle lens just to get the entire mountain in one frame.

In order to reach the Upper Sand Creek Lake you must backtrack to the junction beside Sand Creek and turn left. The trail follows the east side of the creek for a short distance, then turns west to cross the stream and again begins climbing through the trees in a northwesterly direction. After 0.7 mile you will pass another vague trail on the right that climbs over Milwaukee Pass and drops into the Cottonwood Creek drainage on the west side of the mountains. Bearing left at that junction for another 0.5 mile will bring you to Upper Sand Creek Lake.

The upper lake is just 275 feet higher than the lower lake but it is very close to timberline; hence there are very few trees to impede the view of the mountains. Music Mountain looms large across the lake. It is easier to photograph, but it is not as imposing as the view of Tijeras Peak from the lower lake. A fair number of bighorn sheep live in the mountains around the Sand Creek Lakes, and they often hang out on the rocky slopes above the upper lake. Being the same color as the rocks they are hard to spot, but they are often heard. Listen for the occasional sounds of small rocks rolling down the talus slopes on the west side of the lake. Chances are they were dislodged by a clumsy bighorn sheep. The fishing is exceptional in both of the Sand Creek Lakes, but if you are planning to spend the night at one of them you will find a better choice of campsites at the lower lake.

(Thanks to Pete Ross, whose GPS coordinates proved invaluable in determining the locations of the trails for this hike.)

Upper Sand Creek Lake

Willow Lake

Sangre De Cristo Wilderness Area
day hike

Distance:	7.7 miles (round trip)
Walking time:	$5\frac{3}{4}$ hours
Elevations:	2,700 ft. gain/loss Willow Creek Trailhead (start): 8,880 ft. Willow Lake: 11,564 ft. Upper Willow Lake: 12,325 ft.
Trail:	Well used, well maintained trail.
Season:	Midsummer through mid-fall. There is generally snow at Willow Lake from mid-November through early July.
Vicinity:	Near Crestone
Maps:	Crestone, Crestone Peak *(USGS)* Sangre de Cristo Mountains *(Trails Illustrated, #138)*
Information:	http://colorado.utahtrails.com/willowlake.html http://www.fs.fed.us/r2/riogrande/ *(Rio Grande National Forest)* phone: (719) 655-2547 *(Saguache Ranger District)*

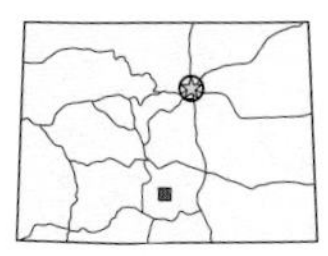

Drive north from Alamosa or south from Poncha Springs on Highway 17 to the farming community of Moffat. On the south side of Moffat you will see a highway sign marking the road to Crestone. Turn here and drive east for 12.6 miles until you come to a 4-way-stop intersection in the center of Crestone. Turn right at the stop sign and continue the last 2.3 miles to the end of the road where the trailhead and parking area are located.

Note: The last 1.2 miles of the road from Crestone are posted "4WD only". Ordinary cars can often make it all the way, but if your car has low clearance you may have to park at the beginning of the 4WD road and walk the rest of the way.

This is one of the most popular hikes on the western side of the Sangre de Cristo Wilderness Area. For me, the thing that makes it so special is a magnificently situated waterfall that plunges 150 feet into the eastern side of Willow Lake. The best time to photograph this picture-perfect scene is in the late afternoon when the sun is low in the west. If you are fortunate enough to be there at that magical late afternoon mo-

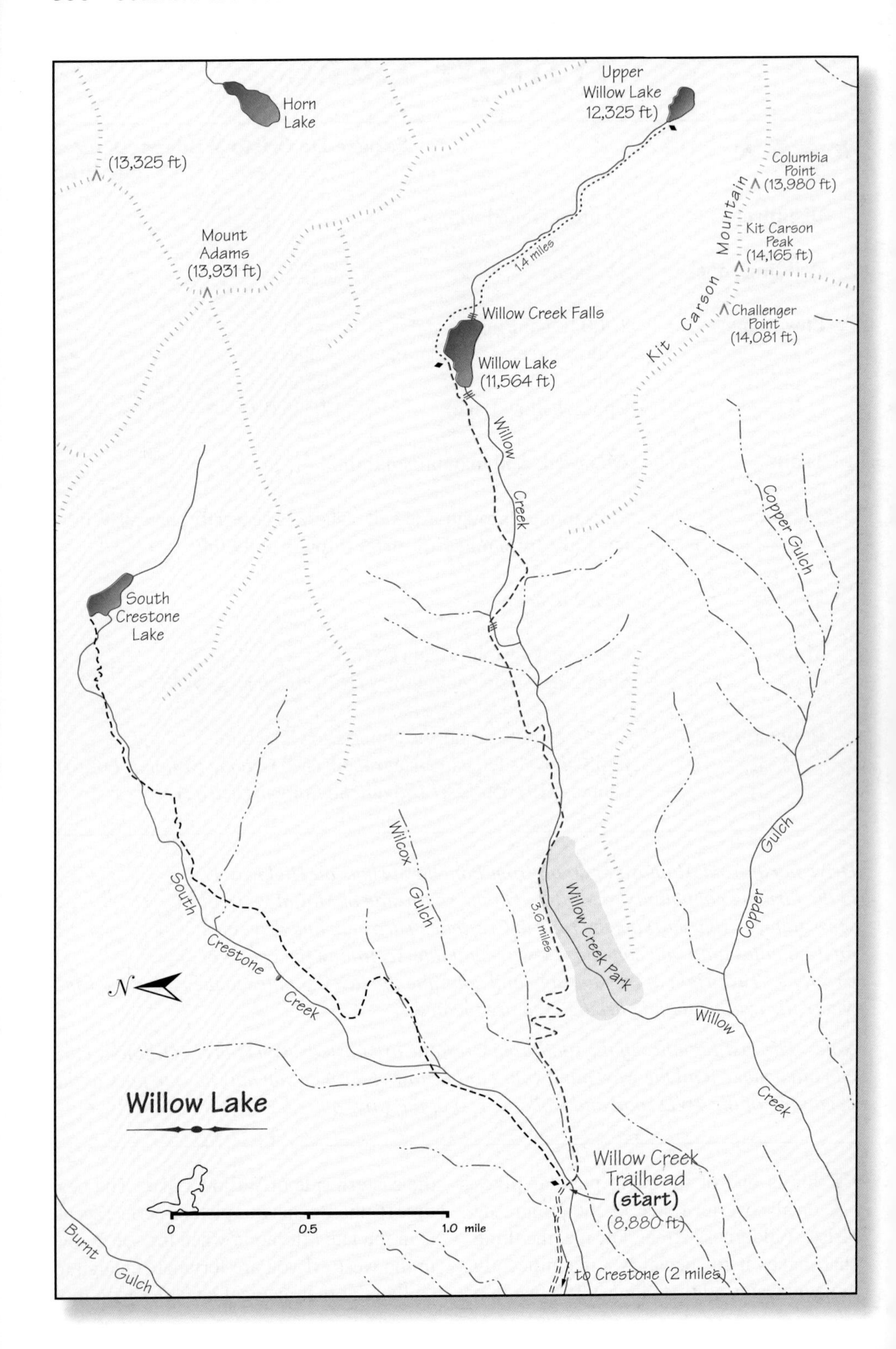
Horn Lake
Upper Willow Lake 12,325 ft)
(13,325 ft)
Columbia Point (13,980 ft)
Mount Adams (13,931 ft)
1.4 miles
Kit Carson Mountain
Kit Carson Peak (14,165 ft)
Challenger Point (14,081 ft)
Willow Creek Falls
Willow Lake (11,564 ft)
Willow Creek
Copper Gulch
South Crestone Lake
Wilcox Gulch
South Crestone Creek
3.6 miles
Willow Creek Park
Copper Gulch
Willow Creek
N
Willow Lake
Willow Creek Trailhead
(start)
(8,880 ft)
0
0.5
1.0 mile
Burnt Gulch
to Crestone (2 miles)

ment when the lake is in shade but the fall is still in full sunlight, and when the water is calm, you will be treated to a prize-winning view of the fall's reflection off the lake. It is rare, however, for the water to be calm at that time of day.

Another reason people are drawn to Willow Lake is that it is a popular staging area for the assent of Kit Carson Peak (14,165 ft.) and Challenger Point (14,081 ft.). Both of these fourteeners, along with Columbia Point (13,980 ft.) are located on the ridge directly above the south side of the Willow Creek drainage. The 3,600-foot assent to the summits of Kit Carson Peak and Challenger Point begins just above the east side of Willow Lake.

From the parking area the trail goes east for 100 yards before coming to a well-marked junction between the Willow Creek Trail and the South Crestone Trail. Turn right here onto the Willow Creek Trail. Immediately upon leaving the junction the path dips down into a shallow depression, crosses Crestone Creek and the Wilcox Gulch drainage in quick succession, then climbs out to a meadow on the south side of the drainages. Upon reaching the higher ground of the meadow the trail proceeds eastward along the south side of Wilcox Gulch.

The route follows Wilcox Gulch for 0.3 mile, then turns to begin a series of long, gentle switchbacks upward to the top of the ridge that separates the Wilcox Gulch drainage from Willow Creek. After 40 minutes of climbing through an open forest of Douglas fir and white fir the trail reaches the top of the ridge, then it drops slightly down the south side of the ridge toward Willow Creek.

Willow Creek, at this point, flows through a large treeless meadow called Willow Creek Park. The 500-yard-long meadow is very picturesque, but it seems oddly out of place in this rugged terrain. Though it is completely surrounded by dense timber it is completely treeless and almost perfectly flat. It appears to be the remnant of an ancient lakebed that eventually filled with silt and was transformed into a grassy park. The trail stays well above the north side of the meadow, but along the way you will pass several spur trails that drop down to its northern side. During the summer you can usually see the tents of at least one or two backpacking parties camping on the perimeter of the park.

As you walk above Willow Creek Park notice the cleavage in the mountains on the east side of the meadow. This is the gorge through which Willow Creek flows and it is the route you will follow to the lake. The

Willow Creek Park

Waterfall below Willow Lake

trail continues to descend until it reaches the eastern end of the park, loosing about 100 feet in all, then starts uphill again. Shortly after leaving the meadow you will pass a Forest Service sign marking the Sangre de Cristo Wilderness Area boundary. Beyond the sign the trail becomes significantly rockier as it enters the Willow Creek Gorge, but the grade continues to be relatively gentle.

As you ascend through the canyon that surrounds Willow Creek the terrain becomes more and more rugged and the trail does a great deal of meandering as it searches for the easiest way forward. Initially it stays high above the north side of the creek, but about 1.0 mile after crossing the wilderness boundary the trail comes back to Willow Creek once again. As it nears the creek the path passes an impressive waterfall, then just above the fall it crosses to the south side of the creek.

After winding up a series of short, rocky switchbacks through a steep boulderfield the trail finally crosses again to the gentler north side of the creek and remains there for the last 0.6 mile to the lake. This part of the hike is extremely scenic. Just before reaching the lake you will pass one more waterfall, then after a few more minutes you will be at the lake.

Willow Lake could not be prettier. It is located just below timber line, and although it is surrounded by 13,500-foot peaks its shores are adorned with towering conifers that grow right to the water's edge. But the major attraction of Willow Lake is its magnificent waterfall. The eastern side of the lake is bordered by a 150-foot cliff that lies directly across the Willow Creek drainage, and the resulting waterfall gives Willow Lake a unique element of beauty.

Upper Willow Lake

Upper Willow Lake is an easy 1.0 mile walk beyond the lower lake with 760 feet of additional elevation gain. Don't expect the upper lake to be as visually attractive as the lower lake. Nevertheless the walk through the alpine tundra of upper Willow Creek Basin, with Kit Carson Mountain on the right and the Sangre de Cristo summit ridge on the left, makes for an interesting extension to this hike.

There is a primitive trail around the north end of Willow Lake to the bench above the waterfall. The trail follows the lakeshore for 300 yards, then ascends through a heavy undergrowth of willows to the more open terrain above the fall. From there the faint trail continues east along the south side of the creek for a short distance before it disappears. You may see a few cairns above the fall marking another route that ascends the northern flank of Kit Carson Mountain. As mentioned before, this is a popular route for peak baggers wishing to climb Challenger Point and Kit Carson Peak. The route from Willow Lake to Challenger Point is a relatively easy 1.4 mile climb with 2,520 feet of elevation gain, and from Challenger climbers can make a slightly more difficult traverse along the summit ridge to Kit Carson Peak.

The easiest route to Upper Willow Lake follows along the south side of the creek. You will see bits and pieces of a trail along the way, but nothing that lasts very long. There are several large groves of willows in the bottom of the basin, but you can usually find an easy way through them. Most of the route is across a grassy tundra and the walk is not difficult.

The upper lake lies at the bottom of a deep pocket with steep scree fields on three sides and towering mountains above. Past rockslides have deposited huge boulders in and around the lake. Look up at the sides of the valley northeast of the lake and you can see abundant scratch marks, polished surfaces and other evidence of the glaciers that once filled the basin. Fifty thousand years ago the ice above the upper lake must have been at least a thousand feet thick. The glaciers are gone now, but looking at the stark landscape of Upper Willow Basin it is not difficult to imagine the forces that once carved the Willow Lakes.

Willow Lake

South Zapata Lake

Sangre De Cristo Wilderness Area
day hike

Distance:	9.2 miles (round trip)
Walking time:	6 1/2 hours
Elevations:	2,800 ft. gain/loss Zapata Falls Trailhead (start): 9,080 ft. Zapata Falls: 9,400 ft. South Zapata Lake: 11,900 ft.
Trail:	Well used, well maintained trail
Season:	Midsummer through mid-Fall. The higher parts of the trail are generally covered with snow from late June through mid-November.
Vicinity:	Near the Great Sand Dunes National Park
Maps:	Twin Peaks *(USGS)* Sangre de Cristo Mountains *(Trails Illustrated, #138)*
Information:	http://colorado.utahtrails.com/zapatalake.html http://www.fs.fed.us/r2/riogrande/ *(Rio Grande National Forest)* phone: (719) 274-8971 *(Conejos Peak Ranger District)*

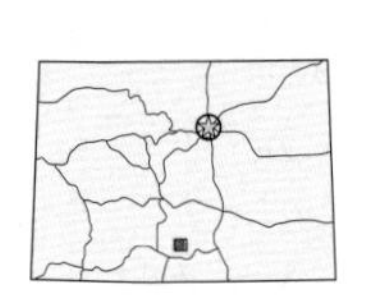

Drive south from Great Sand Dunes National Park on Highway 150. 5.4 miles from the park entrance, or 2.7 miles beyond the paved connecting road to Highway 17, you will see a sign marking a gravel road that leads to Zapata Falls. Turn left here and continue the last 3.6 miles to the Zapata Falls Trailhead and parking area.

Note: 0.4 mile before arriving at the Zapata Falls Trailhead you will see another sign marking the South Zapata Lake Trailhead. It is possible to begin your hike on this little-used connecting trail, but if you do you will miss seeing Zapata Falls. I suggest that you drive on to the Zapata Falls Trailhead and begin your hike there. If you are planning to park overnight, however, you should leave your car at the first trailhead.

A hidden waterfall, several old miner's cabins, and a high alpine lake are the rewards of this hike. The Zapata Falls are only 0.5 mile from the trailhead, and that is as far as most people get. The cabins are less than a mile beyond Zapata Falls, and they are

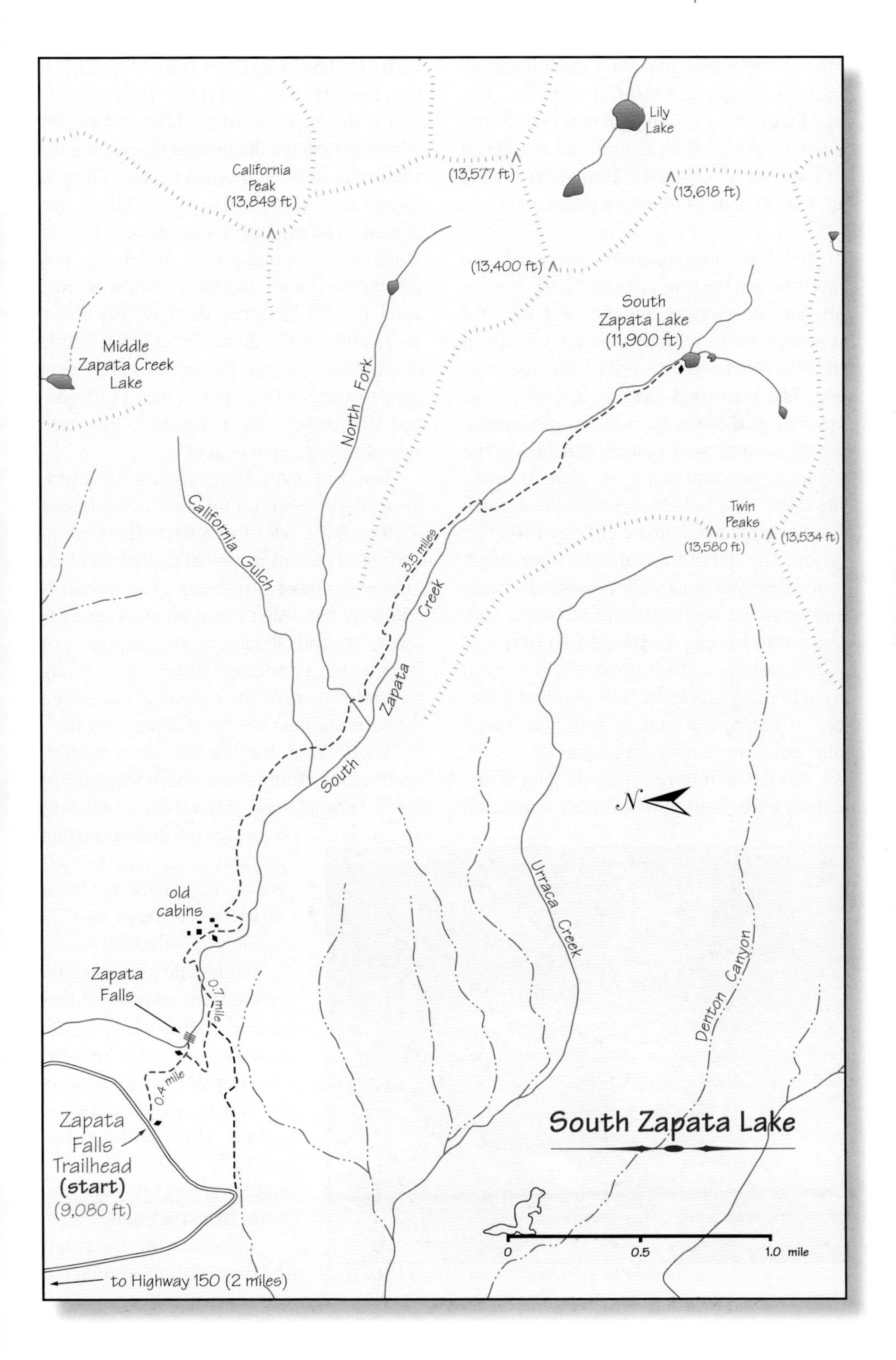
Lily Lake
California Peak (13,849 ft)
(13,577 ft)
(13,618 ft)
(13,400 ft)
South Zapata Lake (11,900 ft)
Middle Zapata Creek Lake
North Fork
California Gulch
3.5 miles
South Zapata Creek
Twin Peaks
(13,580 ft)
(13,534 ft)
N
old cabins
Zapata Falls
0.7 mile
0.4 mile
Urraca Creek
Denton Canyon
Zapata Falls Trailhead
(start)
(9,080 ft)
South Zapata Lake
0
0.5
1.0 mile
to Highway 150 (2 miles)

also a worthwhile goal for a short day hike into the Sangre de Cristo Mountains. The real highlight of this hike, however, is South Zapata Lake, a small alpine lake at the end of the trail in a majestic basin surrounded by 13,000- and 14,000-foot peaks.

It will become apparent when you begin this hike that the trail to Zapata Falls is actually an old jeep road, and although the road is now closed to vehicles the first 0.5 mile of the hike is not as pretty as it might otherwise be. The jeep road ends in a shady, tree-covered glen at the base of the mountains, where several well-placed benches invite hikers to stop and enjoy the scenery below the falls. The falls themselves are located inside a large notch in the cliff face 100 feet beyond the end of the trail, and if you want to see them you must wade through the water and enter the notch. Inside the dark, sunless grotto you can see the 30-foot ribbon of water crashing down from above. But if you want to photograph the falls you had better have a waterproof camera with high-speed film and a super-wide-angle lens.

100 feet before reaching the end of the Zapata Falls Trail you will pass a junction with a sign pointing the way to the South Zapata Lake Trail on your right. Turn here and follow the trail toward the lake as it begins climbing through the juniper trees along the south side of South Zapata Creek. There is a great view to the north along this section of trail. The expansive sand dunes of Great Sand Dunes National Park are clearly visible 9 miles away, and the Crestone Needle and Crestone Peak rise dramatically above the skyline in the distance. After 0.3 mile of climbing the trail passes the connecting path to the South Zapata Lake Trailhead, and 10 minutes later it crosses to the north side of South Zapata Creek.

Just 5 minutes after crossing the creek the trail passes the remnants of at least three old log cabins, one of which is still in reasonably good condition. What a pleasant place to live this must have been. The terrain is relatively flat, water is not far away, and the cabins are well shaded by an open forest of Douglas fir. The occupants were most likely miners who spent their summers scouring the surrounding hills for precious metals.

Shortly after leaving the cabins the trail resumes its climb above the north side of South Zapata Creek. After 0.6 mile you will see a sign informing you that you have crossed the boundary of the Sangre de Cristo Wilderness Area, and 20 minutes later the trail passes by another old miner's cabin on the right. About all that is left of this cabin is the first four courses of logs and the fireplace. The cabin is located near the bottom of a large scree field and has probably sustained considerable damage through the years from rock slides.

Old miner's cabin near South Zapata Lake Trail

Upon leaving the cabin the trail continues along the

South Zapata Creek

bottom of the scree field for the next 1.0 mile before again crossing South Zapata Creek. Once on the south side of the creek the trail climbs 400 feet through the spruce and subalpine fir to the edge of timberline, and then breaks out into a lovely alpine meadow for the last 0.6 mile to the lake. If it is early in the summer you may have trouble following the trail through the tall grass that fills the meadow, but the route is obvious. Finally, after gaining 140 feet over the last 0.5 mile you will cross a low ridge and step onto the north shore of the lake.

South Zapata is a relatively small lake, scarcely 200 yards in diameter, but the ruggedly beautiful setting of the tiny alpine tarn compensates for its diminutive size. The lake is situated high above timberline in the back of the South Zapata Basin with the crest of the Sangre de Cristo Mountains for a backdrop. Ellingwood Peak (14,042 ft.) is less than a mile away, and the view of the fourteener from across the lake is an impressive sight. Blanka Peak, Colorado's forth-highest summit is only 1.4 miles away, but it is effectively hidden by Ellingwood Peak.

South Zapata Lake

Ruybalid Lake

South San Juan Wilderness Area
day hike

Distance:	9.4 miles (round trip)
Walking time:	6 1/2 hours
Elevations:	2,370 ft. gain/loss Ruybalid Lake Trailhead (start): 8,810 ft. Ruybalid Lake: 11,180 ft.
Trail:	Generally well marked and easy to follow.
Season:	Summer through mid-fall. The upper parts of the trail are usually covered with snow from mid-November through early June.
Vicinity:	South of Alamosa
Maps:	Spectacle Lake *(USGS)* South San Juan/Del Norte *(Trails Illustrated, #142)*
Information:	http://colorado.utahtrails.com/ruybalidlake.html http://www.fs.fed.us/r2/sanjuan/ *(San Juan National Forest)* phone: (970) 264-2268 *(Pagosa Ranger District)*

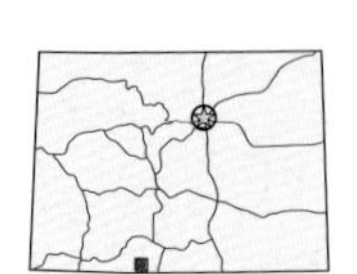

Drive west from Antonito for 22 miles or north from Chama, New Mexico for 28 miles on Highway 17 until you come to a well-marked gravel road leading north to Spectacle Lake Campground and Platoro. Turn here and drive north along the east side of the Conejos River. After 6.3 miles you will pass the Spectacle Lake Campground, and 1.4 miles later you will see Old Bridge Road, quickly followed by Record Bridge Road and the Rocky Mountain Lodge. Turn left on Record Bridge Road. After 0.2 mile the road crosses the Conejos River on Record Bridge and ends in a grassy field that serves as the parking area. The trailhead is marked by a small sign 150 feet south of the bridge.

Ruybalid Lake is one of several seldom-visited lakes that dot the top of a large mesa on the west side of the Conejos River. Although the mesa and its environs comprise the southwestern third of the rugged San Juan Mountains and the Continental Divide runs along the west side of the mesa, the terrain here is surprisingly gentle. This part of the San Juans also receives far fewer visitors than the more challenging mountains further north, and that, for many, is part of its attraction.

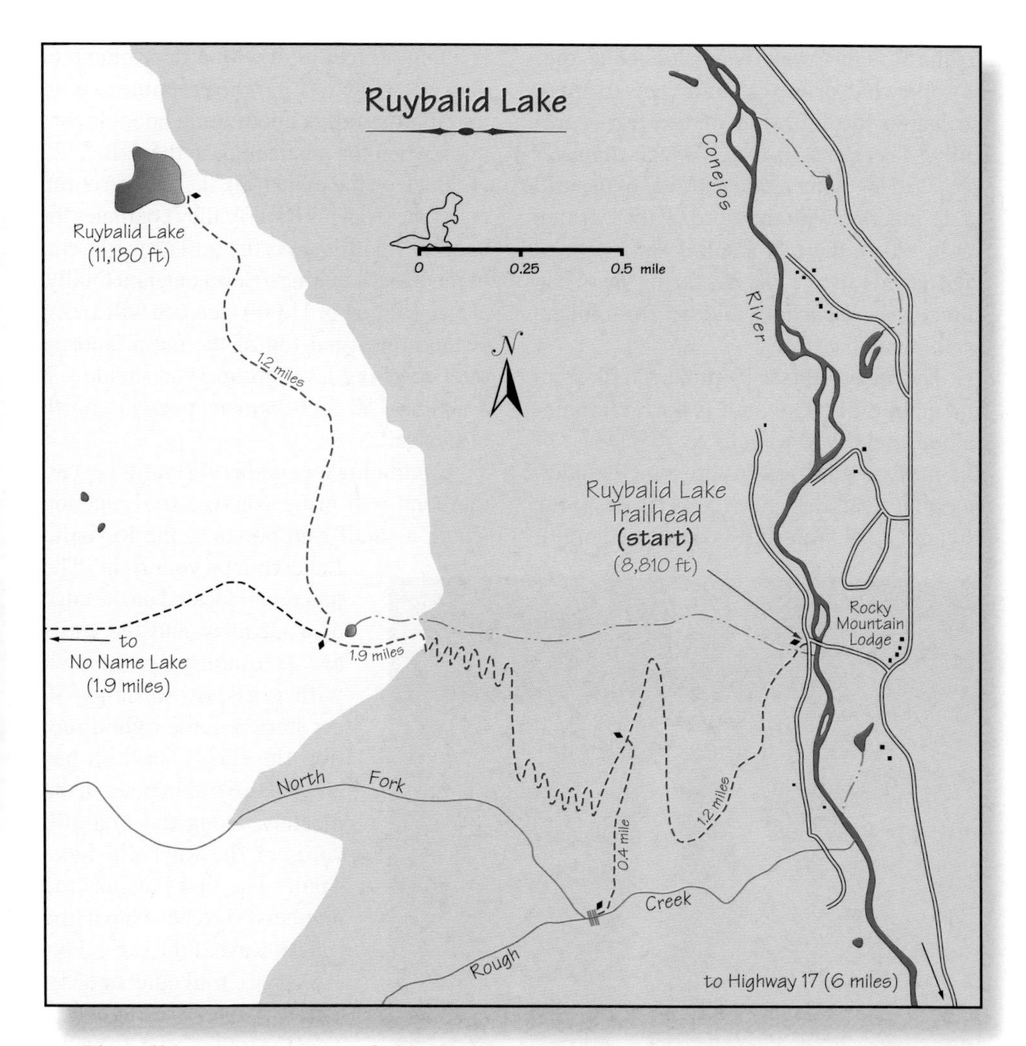

The wild, remote nature of the South San Juans was dramatically brought to the public's attention in the fall of 1979, when a grizzly bear was killed about 10 miles west of Ruybalid Lake. Until then it had been almost 30 years since a grizzly had been seen in Colorado. There have not been any other confirmed grizzly sightings since than, but there is a great deal of circumstantial evidence that there are still grizzlies living in the area.

After leaving the parking area the trail winds along the eastern edge of a horse pasture near the Conejos River for a few hundred yards, before entering a dense grove of aspen trees. Soon afterward it crosses the boundary of the South San Juan Wilderness Area and begins climbing up the west side of the Conejos River Valley. This is the most strenuous part of the hike. The trail gains 2,100 feet of elevation over the next 2.5 miles before finally leveling out on the top of the mesa. Fortunately the grade is not extremely steep, and there are several nice views of the Conejos Valley along the way.

After 30 minutes of walking you will come to a spur trail on the left that leads to the Rough Creek Waterfall. The spur is somewhat primitive and easy to miss, so watch the left side of the trail carefully. There is a 10-foot, 18-inch-diameter bleached log lying on the left side of the trail at the junction with the word "Falls" written on it. Also, there is a small hand-painted sign nailed to a tree, but it is facing the wrong direction and partially hidden from hikers walking up the trail.

The waterfall is a 10-minute walk from the main trail. The path is not well maintained, and if you want to get to the base of the fall you will need to do some boulder-hopping near the end. Nevertheless, the Rough Creek Waterfall is worth seeing. It is about 80 feet high with a fair volume of water flowing over it. The best time to photograph the fall is about three hours before noon when the sun is high in the east.

Back on the main trail, the upward climb out of the Conejos River Valley continues for another 1.5 miles. As the trail nears the rim of the mesa it begins to level out, and finally, at an elevation of 11,000 feet, you will arrive at the almost-flat top of the mesa. Shortly after reaching level ground you should see a shallow 150-foot-diameter pond just north of the trail.

Continuing for another 100 yards beyond the pond will bring you to a trail junction where a small sign points to the Ruybalid Lake Trail on your right. The junction is located on the edge of a meadow and the trails are frequently overgrown with grass, so to help you get started in the right direction the forest services has erected two 6-foot poles in the meadow along the first 100 yards of the Ruybalid Lake Trail. The first pole has the number 855 etched onto it (the trail to Ruybalid Lake is Forest Service trail number 855). The two poles are aligned in a northeast direction from the trail junction.

Turn right at the junction and when you get to the second pole you will see a faint trail heading into the woods in a northwesterly direction. After the trail leaves the meadow it is much easier to follow. The path winds through an open forest of Engelmann spruce and subalpine fir for about 1.2 mile before ending on the south shore of Ruybalid Lake.

Rough Creek Fall

Ruybalid Lake Trail

Ruybalid is a very pretty lake in a tranquil sort of way. There are no dramatic cliffs or rugged mountain peaks near the lake, but its shores are well vegetated with tall trees and abundant ground cover, and there are several fine campsites along its southern shore. Considering its location, the 250-yard-diameter lake is surprisingly large. The surrounding terrain is relatively flat and there are no streams flowing into the lake. Furthermore it is situated right on the rim of the Conejos Valley, separated from the canyon below by an insignificant rise in the land of less than 20 feet. One has to wonder where all the water comes from.

Ruybalid Lake is just one of several lakes located on the mesa above the Conejos River; the next one, No Name Lake, lies about 1.2 miles to the west. You can reach No Name Lake by returning to the Ruybalid trail junction and continuing west on the better-marked trail for another 2.7 miles, but you will find that Ruybalid Lake is the prettier of the two. The terrain surrounding No Name is much flatter and less scenic than the environs of Ruybalid, and furthermore it does not offer the striking view of the Conejos River Valley that can be seen from Ruybalid. Most of the people who go on to No Name Lake are horseback riders. The gently rolling terrain west of Ruybalid Lake is perfect for horseback riding, but if you are walking the hike to No Name Lake is, in my opinion, not worth the extra effort.

Ruybalid Lake

Fourmile Creek

★★★★★

Weminuche Wilderness Area
day hike

Distance:	10.6 miles (round trip)
Walking time:	7 hours
Elevations:	1,980 ft. gain/loss Fourmile Trailhead (start): 9,200 ft. Fourmile Falls: 9,760 ft. Fourmile Lake: 11,185 ft.
Trail:	Easy to follow, but often extremely rocky.
Season:	Midsummer through mid-Fall. The upper parts of the trail are generally covered with snow from mid-November through late June.
Vicinity:	Near Pagosa Springs
Maps:	Pagosa Peak *(USGS)* Weminuche Wilderness *(Trails Illustrated, #140)*
Information:	http://colorado.utahtrails.com/fourmilecreek.html http://www.fs.fed.us/r2/sanjuan/ *(San Juan National Forest)* phone: (970) 264-2268 *(Pagosa Ranger District)*

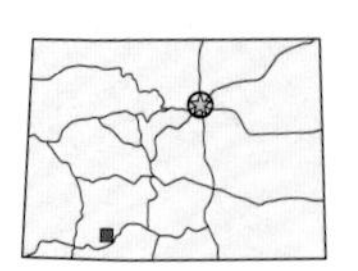

Drive to the center of Pagosa Springs on Highway 160 and turn north at the stop light on 5th street. Immediately after turning north you will see a fork in the road where you must bear to the left. This is the beginning of Fourmile Road which ends 13.2 miles later at the Fourmile Trailhead. There are two major forks along the way where you must bear right, but in each case the road is clearly marked with road signs.

The highlights of this hike are two gorgeous waterfalls that are located 3.0 miles from the trailhead. The falls are an easy walk from the road with an elevation gain of only 750 feet, and upon reaching them most people go no further. There are several more waterfalls along Fourmile Creek, however, and the additional 2.3-mile walk to the head of the fast-flowing mountain stream will yield additional rewards. The trail finally ends at Fourmile Lake, a 600-foot diameter tarn hidden in the back of a basin on the northeast side of Pagosa Peak.

If you want to experience Fourmile

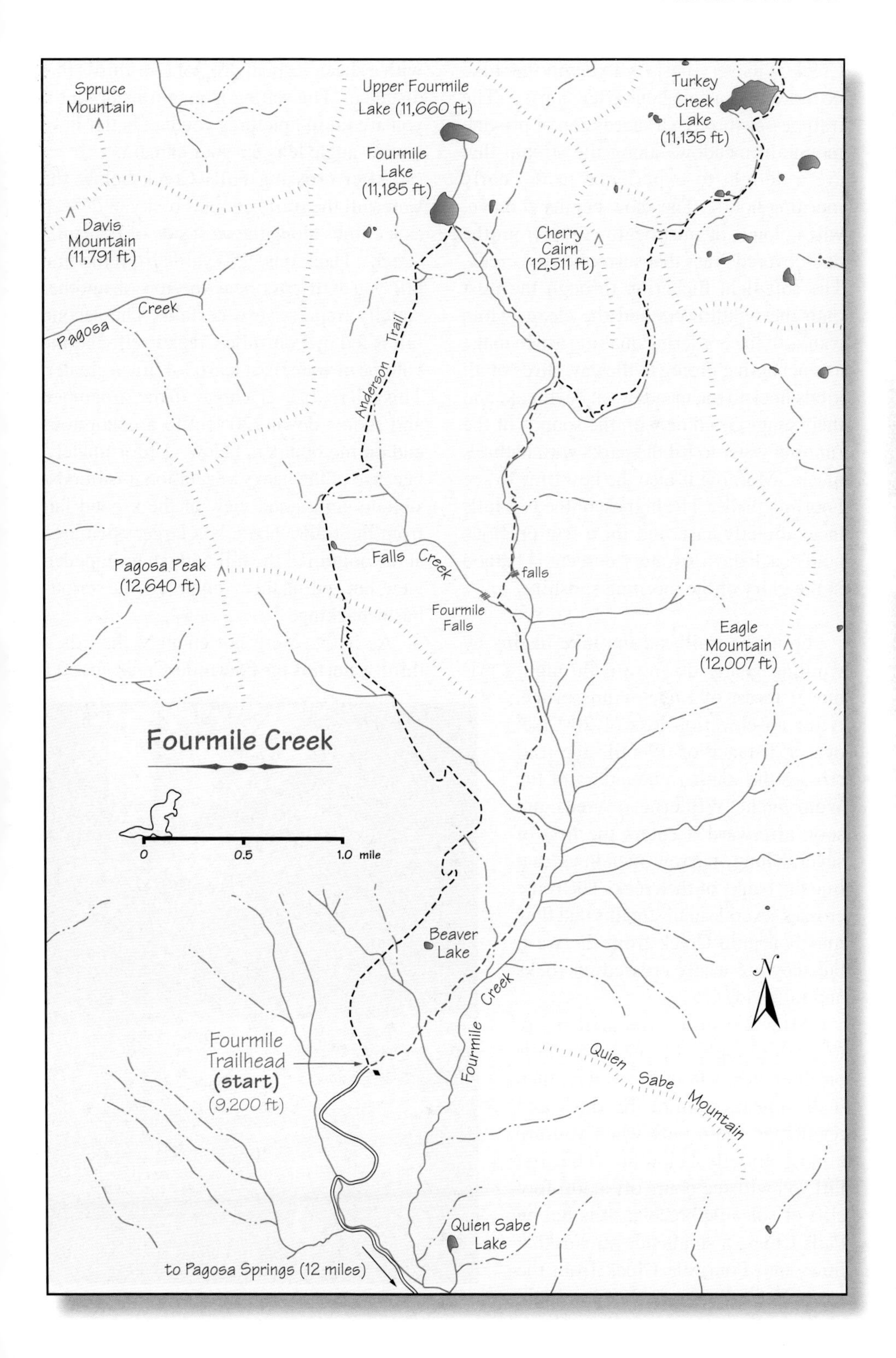
Spruce Mountain
Upper Fourmile Lake (11,660 ft)
Turkey Creek Lake (11,135 ft)
Fourmile Lake (11,185 ft)
Davis Mountain (11,791 ft)
Cherry Cairn (12,511 ft)
Pagosa Creek
Anderson Trail
Falls Creek
falls
Pagosa Peak (12,640 ft)
Fourmile Falls
Eagle Mountain (12,007 ft)
Fourmile Creek
0
0.5
1.0 mile
Beaver Lake
Fourmile Creek
N
Fourmile Trailhead
(start)
(9,200 ft)
Quien Sabe Mountain
Quien Sabe Lake
to Pagosa Springs (12 miles)

Creek at its very best try to begin this hike no more than a half-hour after sunrise. The trail passes through a succession of pristine mountain meadows along the stream that are a delight to experience in the early morning hours. The show begins at dawn, when clouds of mist begin rising from the due-covered grass that surrounds the creek. The soft light flickering through the mist onto the wildflowers and the clean, white trunks of the bordering quaking aspen make an enchanting prolog to the day. Birds of all kinds flock to the meadows at daybreak, and their songs combine with the sounds of the running water to fill the parks with nature's music. Morning is also the best time to see Fourmile Falls. The highest of the two falls faces directly east, and for a few precious hours each day its watery descent is bathed in the glory of the morning sunshine.

From the trailhead the hike begins by winding gently downward through a primeval forest of Engelmann spruce. After an elevation loss of 200 feet over a distance of 0.7 mile the trail crosses the southern boundary of the Weminuche Wilderness Area, and soon afterward it enters the first of several long, narrow meadows that line the banks of the creek. The route crosses several small streams that flow into Fourmile Creek from the west, but they are easily crossed on rocks and fallen logs.

After 2.6 miles you will begin to catch glimpses of one of the falls on the north side of the valley, then it disappears behind the trees and reemerges again only when you are almost directly below it. The first fall you will see pours off a 300-foot cliff of volcanic breccia. It is fed by Falls Creek, a small side stream that flows into Fourmile Creek from the west. The fall is some 250 feet high, with a sheer vertical drop of two-thirds that distance. The setting is magnificent, but if you are taking pictures you had better have a wide-angle lens for your camera.

After crossing Falls Creek below the waterfall the trail becomes rocky and steep as it climbs along the west side of Fourmile Creek. Then, only 250 yards from the first fall you will pass near the top of another equally impressive waterfall. The second fall is fed by Fourmile Creek itself, and the volume of water is at least 3-4 times greater. This fall roars over a break in the streambed and shoots down 120 feet to a calamitous end on the boulders below. Unfortunately, because of the heavy vegetation it is impossible to get a good view of the second fall from the trail. There is a large, open area at the bottom of the fall with an unimpeded view, but getting there requires some serious bushwhacking.

As if two were not enough, there is a third waterfall on Fourmile Creek just 0.1

Fourmile Creek Trail

mile above the second fall. The third one does not have a long vertical drop like the first two, but it is still worth pausing to look at. The gradient of the creek (and the trail!) is so steep after the first 3.0 miles that waterfalls are inevitable, and as you proceed upward you will be treated to one cascade after another. If you are doing this hike in early summer before the spring runoff has ended the rushing water is particularly dramatic.

Fourmile Falls

Five minutes beyond the third waterfall the trail crosses to the east side of the creek. Older maps indicate that there was once a steel bridge across the creek at this point, but now there is scarcely a trace of the old span. It has been gone for at least 20 years, but fortunately there is a fallen log nearby so it is possible to cross the water without getting your feet wet.

The trail stays on the east side of the water for only about 10 minutes before crossing back again. When you are back on the west side pause to look 200 yards upstream and you will see yet another dramatic cascade of whitewater roaring down another chute in the streambed. This is also a fine area for camping if you are carrying a tent. The forest is open and flat for some distance below the cascade, and one couldn't ask for a more inspirational place to spend a night.

Soon the trail crosses to the east side of the creek for the second time, where it will remain for the rest of the way to the lake. After 15 minutes you will see a sign at a trail junction where the trail to Turkey Creek Lake branches off to the right. Bear left here and soon you will enter the southern end of another long alpine meadow that lines the shores of Fourmile Creek. The trail stays in the meadow for 0.7 mile before climbing into the trees on its northern side. Finally it climbs the last 200 feet to end at the southern shore of Fourmile Lake.

Fourmile Lake is a very pretty alpine jewel, completely surrounded with trees and

Fourmile Creek Trail

bordered on three sides by 12,000-foot ridges. The nicest campsites are on the northern shore, and the fishing is reputed to be good. Upper Fourmile Lake lies 475 feet higher and 0.3 mile further north. There is no trail leading to the upper lake, but the route is not difficult. Just follow the drainage upward from the north end of the lower lake and after fifteen minutes of climbing you should arrive at Upper Fourmile Lake.

Anderson Trail

The Anderson Trail provides an alternate route from the end of Fourmile Road to Fourmile Lake, and many people do this hike as a loop. The Anderson Trail is not as steep and rocky as the second half of the Fourmile Creek Trail; however it is 2.0 miles longer and 400 feet higher. Unlike the Fourmile Creek Trail, the Anderson Trail generally stays high on the eastern slopes of Pagosa Peak rather than following a creek. It is a much better trail for horses, and I suspect that is the primary reason it was originally constructed.

The route up Fourmile Creek is such a scenic trail that I personally prefer to return the same way, but if you decide to do this hike as a loop I suggest you save the Anderson Trail for the return trip. That way you will see the waterfalls and meadows earlier in the day when the light is best, and you will be walking on the easier Anderson Trail at the end of the day when you have less energy to spare.

The Anderson Trail begins at the same trailhead as the Fourmile Creek Trail, and it ends at the source of Fourmile Creek on the south side of the lake. When you reach the end of the Fourmile Creek Trail you will see the stream that drains the lake on your left. Cross to the west side of the creek and within 20 feet you will see a small wooden sign nailed to a tree beside the lake that marks the beginning of the Anderson Trail.

Fourmile Lake

Rainbow Hot Springs

★★

Weminuche Wilderness Area
day hike

Distance:	9.4 miles (round trip)
Walking time:	5 1/2 hours
Elevations:	1,000 ft. gain/loss Rainbow Trailhead (start): 8,160 ft. Rainbow Hot Springs: 8,990 ft.
Trail:	Mostly well marked and easy to follow.
Season:	Summer through mid-Fall. The upper parts of the trail are generally covered with snow from Late November through mid-June.
Vicinity:	Near Pagosa Springs
Maps:	Saddle Mountain, South River Peak *(USGS)* Weminuche Wilderness *(Trails Illustrated, #140)*
Information:	http://colorado.utahtrails.com/rainbowsprings.html http://www.fs.fed.us/r2/sanjuan/ *(San Juan National Forest)* phone: (970) 264-2268 *(Pagosa Ranger District)*

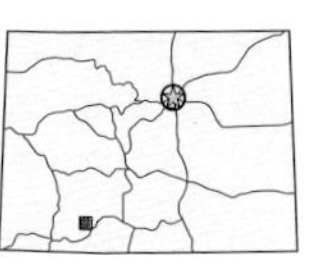

Drive northeast from Pagosa Springs on Highway 160 for 14.5 miles until you see a sign marking the West Fork Road on your left. Turn onto West Fork Road and continue north for another 3.1 miles, past Wolf Creek Campground and West Fork Campground, to the end of the road. (Just beyond Wolf Creek Campground you will come to a fork in the road where you must bear left towards West Fork Campground.) When you reach the end of the road you will see a sign marking the trailhead.

Your reward at the end of this hike will be a rare opportunity to lie back and immerse your tired body in a waste-deep pool of warm spring water on the shore of a scenic, fast-flowing mountain stream. The spring flows from a small fissure on the east side of the West Fork San Juan River and tumbles down the rock face into two small pools that have been constructed by previous hikers. The lower pool, about 20 feet long and 8 feet wide, is situated right on the shore of the river. Its temperature averages 95 degrees F, but if that is not hot enough you can climb up to the slightly smaller up-

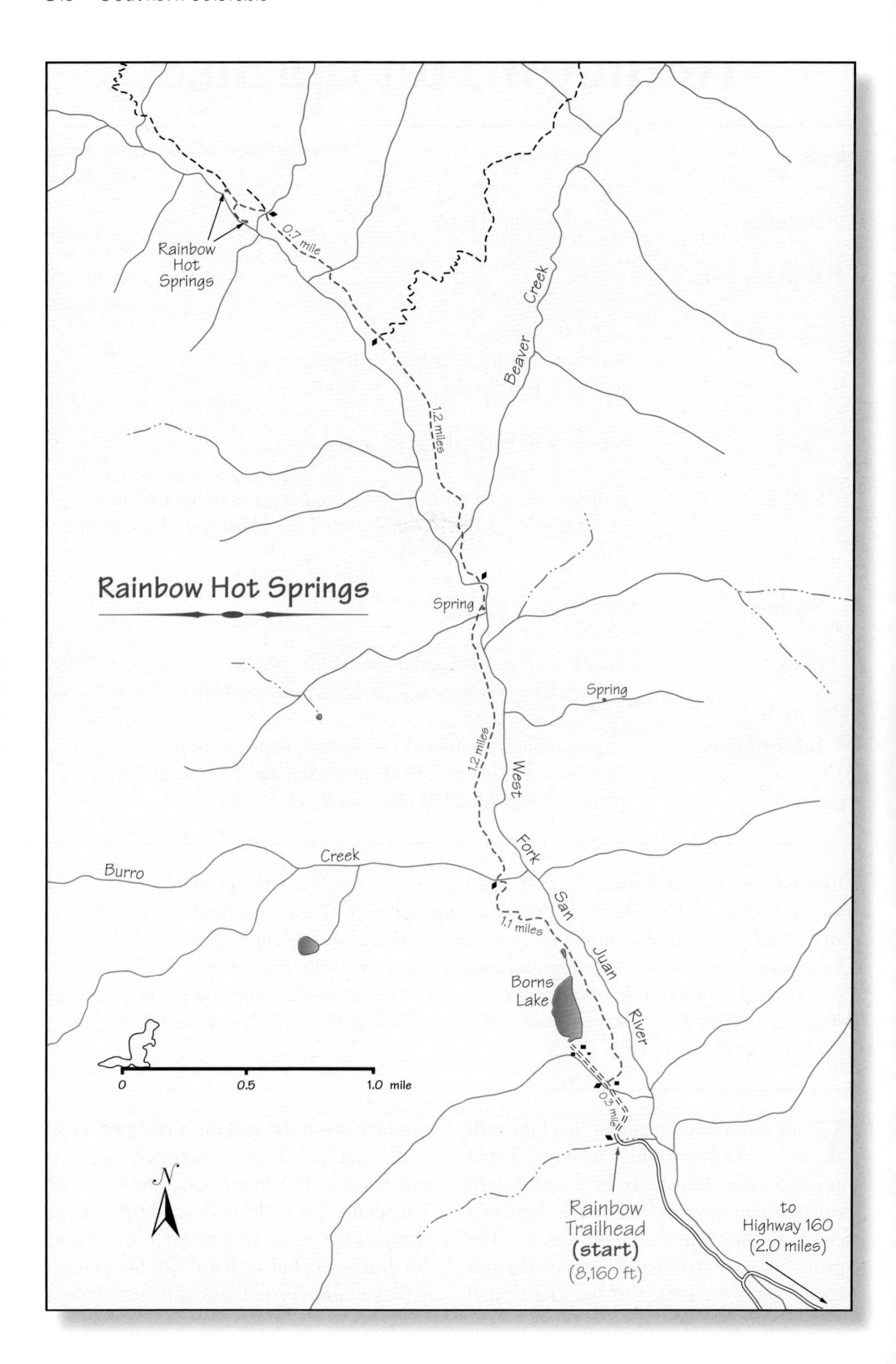

Rainbow Hot Springs
Rainbow Hot Springs
0.7 mile
Beaver Creek
1.2 miles
Spring
Spring
1.2 miles
West Fork San Juan River
Burro Creek
1.1 miles
Borns Lake
0.3 mile
0
0.5
1.0 mile
N
Rainbow Trailhead
(start)
(8,160 ft)
to Highway 160 (2.0 miles)

per pool. The smaller pool is 15 feet closer to the spring and 10 degrees hotter. Most people cannot stay in the upper pool for longer than about 15 minutes, but there is always the option of cooling off in the 50-degree water of the river.

Although Rainbow Hot Springs is not well known outside southwestern Colorado it is quite popular among local hikers and you are unlikely to have the springs all to yourself. Nevertheless it can be a very enjoyable hike. There are also a number of fine campsites in the open forest above the springs, and many people do this hike as an overnighter.

When you leave the parking area you will initially be walking on a jeep road that runs through an inholding of privately owned land within San Juan National Forest. Soon you will pass several summer homes, and after 10 minutes you will come to a well-signed junction where the Rainbow Trail departs from the right side of the road. The road actually ends 0.2 miles beyond the junction on the south side of a large privately-owned lake, but numerous signs make it abundantly clear that visitors are not welcome at the lake and hikers are expected to stay on the trail! The residents here could legally close the trail if they felt that their rights were being abused, so I suggest that we all comply with the signs and respect their privacy.

Soon after leaving the road the trail turns north and begins following the rim of West Fork Canyon. The canyon cannot generally be seen from the trail, but there are a few viewpoints along the way and it is very impressive. The steep V-shaped gorge has been cut from a relatively soft strata of volcanic tuff by the cascading river 300 feet below the rim.

0.8 mile after leaving the jeep road the trail finally leaves the private land and enters San Juan National Forest. Then, 0.2 mile later you will see a sign indicating that you have entered the Weminuche Wilderness Area. The forest of huge Douglas fir and Engelmann spruce is so pretty in this area it is reassuring to know that it will never be developed.

Within 250 feet after passing the wilderness area sign the trail comes to the first of three large bridges that have been constructed by the Forest Service. This one crosses Burro Creek, a tributary on the west side of the West Fork. From Burro Creek the trail continues high along the west side of the West Fork of the San Juan River for another 1.2 miles before crossing it on the second bridge. Then just 0.2 mile further it crosses Beaver Creek on the third bridge.

Before the mid 1980s there were no bridges across West Fork and Beaver Creek,

West Fork San Juan River

Rainbow How Springs

so it was necessary to ford these rivers in order to reach the hot springs. Both streams carry a substantial flow of water, especially in early summer, and wading through the icy, chest-deep water was often hazardous. Finally, after a backpacker was drowned trying to cross West Fork, the Forest Service decided to improve the trail and bridges were constructed across West Fork and Beaver Creek.

After crossing Beaver Creek the trail climbs about 200 feet up the east side of the canyon and continues north. 1.0 mile from Beaver Creek you will come to a trail junction where the Beaver Creek Trail heads east towards the Continental Divide. Bear left at this point.

In the next 0.7 mile after leaving the Beaver Creek Trail Junction the trail crosses two more small drainages. Immediately after the second drainage you will come to a fork in the trail where you must turn left, and within 200 feet the path passes through a well-used campsite about 90 feet above the east side of the river. The rim of the canyon is only 20 feet from the campsite, and from there you can look down at the two small bathing pools that comprise Rainbow Hot Springs directly below the camp.

There are several other campsites in the area, but there are no signs indicating the presence of the hot springs and there are no good trails leading to them. They are easy to miss if you aren't paying attention. In order to reach the hot springs you must continue northward along the rim of the canyon for another 100 yards to a point where there is an easier access to the river. Once you reach the river you can double back along its shore to the pools where your reward awaits you.

If you are in the mood for some exploration you will find another small pool 250 yards upstream from the first pools. The third pool lies 10 feet from the water in a flat grassy area that is much easier to access than the first two pools. In my opinion, however, it is not as interesting as the first pools.

Rainbow How Springs

Piedra River Trail

★

shuttle car required
day hike

Distance:	10.5 miles (plus 47.3 miles by car)
Walking time:	5 3/4 hours
Elevations:	200 ft. gain, 700 ft. loss Piedra River Trailhead (start): 7,620 ft. First Fork Trailhead: 7,100 ft.
Trail:	Well marked and easy to follow
Season:	Summer through mid-fall. There is usually snow on the trail from late November through early June.
Vicinity:	Near Pagosa Springs
Maps:	Oakbrush Ridge, Bear Mountain, Devil Mountain *(USGS)*
Information:	http://colorado.utahtrails.com/piedrariver.html http://www.fs.fed.us/r2/sanjuan/ *(San Juan National Forest)* phone: (970) 264-2268 *(Pagosa Ranger District)*

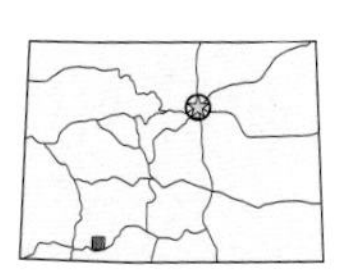

Drive west from Pagosa Springs on Highway 160 for 22 miles. 5.5 miles after passing the junction with Highway 151 you will come to the Piedra River Resort where there is a gravel road departing on the right. This is Forest Road 622 or County Road 166, and it is marked by a sign that says "National Forest Service Access, First Fork Road". Turn right here and drive 11.8 miles to the Piedra River Bridge. The First Fork Trailhead is located on the north side of the bridge. This is where the hike ends and where you must leave a shuttle car.

To reach the Piedra River Trailhead where the hike begins you must return to Highway 160 and drive back toward Pagosa Springs for a distance of 19.3 miles. 2.5 miles before reaching the center of Pagosa Springs you will come to a stop light where Piedra Road meets the highway. Turn left here and proceed north on Piedra Road for 15.9 miles until you come to the bridge across the Piedra River. (The road is paved for about 8 miles, and beyond that it is an excellent gravel road.) 0.2 mile beyond the Piedra River bridge you will see a small sign directing you to the Piedra River Trailhead and parking area just off the left side of the road. This is where the hike begins.

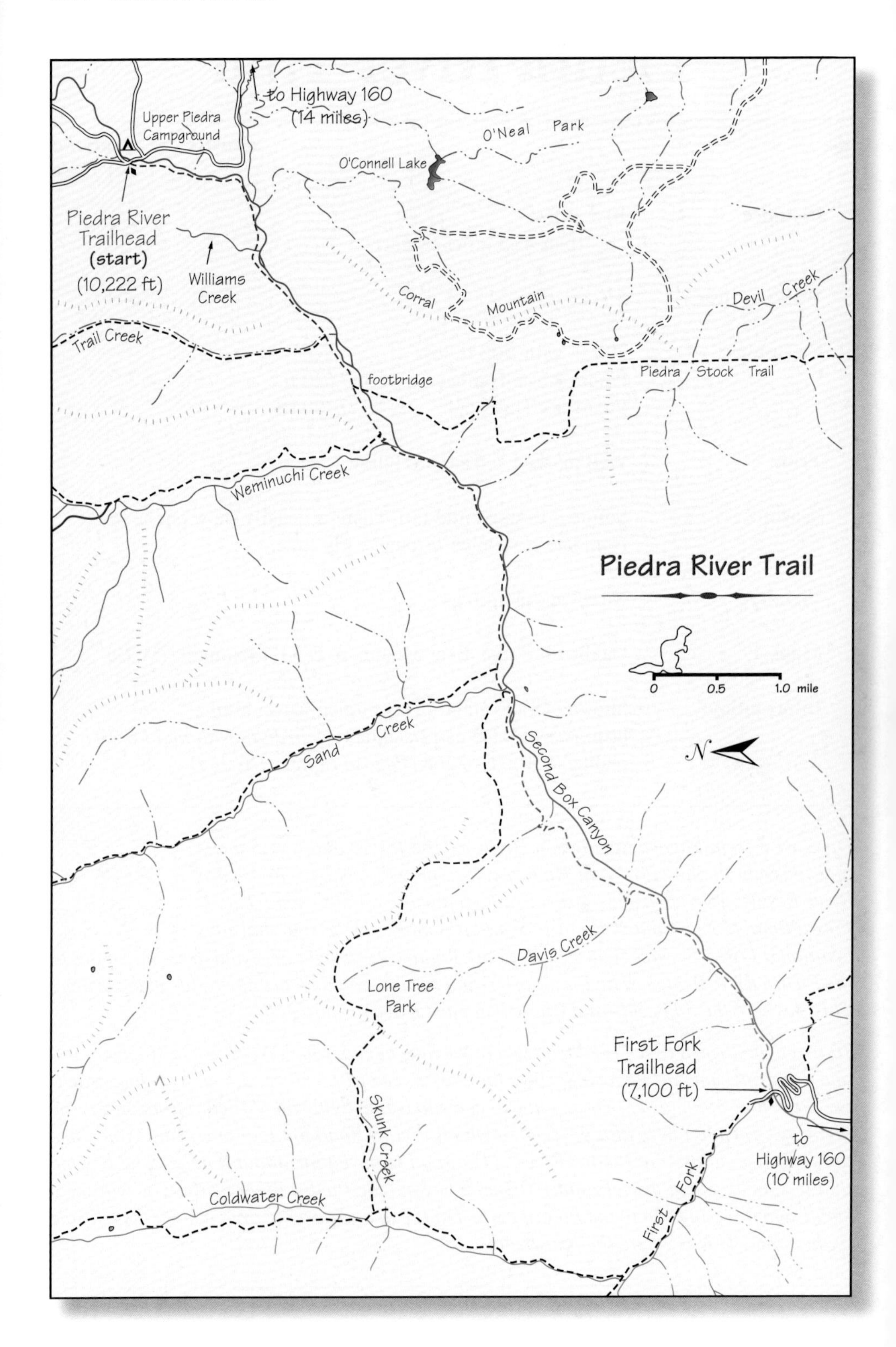

Piedra River Trail
to Highway 160 (14 miles)
Upper Piedra Campground
O'Neal Park
O'Connell Lake
Piedra River Trailhead (start) (10,222 ft)
Williams Creek
Corral Mountain
Devil Creek
Trail Creek
footbridge
Piedra Stock Trail
Weminuchi Creek
0 0.5 1.0 mile
N
Sand Creek
Second Box Canyon
Davis Creek
Lone Tree Park
First Fork Trailhead (7,100 ft)
to Highway 160 (10 miles)
Skunk Creek
Coldwater Creek
First Fork

Because of water rights issues in the Piedra River watershed this area missed being declared a Wilderness Area in the 1993 Colorado Wilderness Act. Fortunately, however, because of its vast expanse of old-growth forest it was decided to make it a "Special Management Area". Consequently, the virgin forest is now protected against future logging and road building activities, and its 62,550-acre size makes it the largest such forest preserve in the state.

Fishermen have a special appreciation for the Piedra River area. The river and its tributaries are teaming with fish, with rainbow trout and brown trout being particularly abundant. The Piedra River is also the site of an experimental project to reintroduce the endangered river otter back into its native habitat. But even if you aren't carrying a fishing pole or looking for river otters there is enough great scenery along the river to make this trail a worthwhile walk.

From the trailhead the well-used trail meanders southward for the first mile, passing through a particularly interesting area where the river is overhung by cliffs on the east side. After a mile the river makes an abrupt 90-degree turn and begins flowing westward through a long, narrow flat-bottomed valley. 0.6 mile after the turn it crosses a small bridge that spans Williams Creek, then it continues in a southwest direction along the north shore of the Piedra.

The trail crosses Trail Creek about a half hour beyond Williams Creek, and 10 minutes later you will notice another trail branching off to the left. This is the Piedra Stock Driveway Trail, a lesser used trail that dips down to cross the Piedra River on another picturesque bridge and then veers away to the south. You should bear right at the trail junction and stay on the plateau above the north side of the river.

0.7 mile beyond the Piedra Stock Driveway junction the Piedra River Trail comes to another footbridge spanning Weminuche Creek. It then returns to the shore of the river

Junction of the Piedra River Trail and the Piedra Stock Trail

and closely follows its twists and turns for the next 3.0 miles. If you are a fisherman with an intent to spend the night along the river this section of the trail would be your best choice.

An hour and twenty minutes after leaving Weminuche Creek the trail crosses the third major side drainage on this hike, and this time there is no footbridge to assist your crossing. This tributary is called Sand Creek, and it is the only place along the trail where you must get your feet wet to get across. The water is only a foot deep and 15 feet wide, but there seems to be no easy way to cross it.

Sand Creek represents the beginning of a narrow part of the Piedra River Canyon called the Second Box, and 0.6 mile beyond the confluence the trail begins climbing up the north side of the canyon to get around the steep cliffs below. This part of the trail is, for me, a disappointment. River runners attest that the scenery inside the Second Box is dramatic, with the river rushing through the confines of the inner canyon, roaring through class IV rapids and pounding against the cliffs that line the shore. But, alas, from 500 feet above the canyon floor where the trail is located the river is seldom visible, and there is scarcely a hint of the spectacle that exists within the gorge. I suppose it would be impractical to construct a trail closer to the water at this point, but what a hike it would be if the route could follow the river through the Second Box!

After 2.0 miles the Second Box ends, and the trail returns to the bottom of the canyon again. This easily accessible stretch of river is a prime fishing area and you are likely to see fishermen as you approach the end of the hike. The trail stays close to the water for the next 1.5 miles, then climbs 100 feet above the shore for the last 0.5 mile before arriving at the First Fork Trailhead.

Piedra River

Powderhorn Lakes

★★

Powderhorn Wilderness Area
day hike

Distance:	10.6 miles (round trip)
Walking time:	6 1/2 hours
Elevations:	1,100 ft. gain/loss Powderhorn Lakes Trailhead (start): 11,020 ft. Lower Powderhorn Lake: 11,650 ft. Upper Powderhorn Lake: 11,859 ft.
Trail:	Generally well maintained and easy to follow.
Season:	Midsummer through mid-fall. The higher parts of the trail are generally covered with snow from mid-November until mid-July.
Vicinity:	Near Gunnison and Lake City
Maps:	Powderhorn Lakes *(USGS)* La Garita/Cochetopa Hills *(Trails Illustrated, #139)*
Information:	http://colorado.utahtrails.com/powderhornlakes.html http://www.co.blm.gov/ubra/ *(BLM, Montrose)* phone: (970) 240-5300 *(Uncompahgre Field Office)*

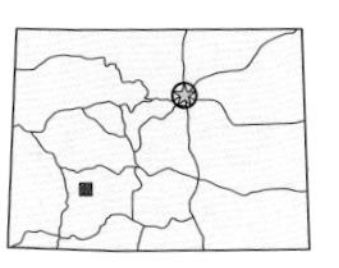

Drive north from the center of Lake City on Highway 149 for a distance of 25 miles until you see a graded gravel road departing on the right. This is County Road 58, the Indian Creek Road; it is located just 200 feet south of milepost 97. If you are driving south from Gunnison on Highway 149 you will come to the Indian Creek Road 20.4 miles after leaving the junction with Highway 50. Turn east onto Road 58 and continue for another 10.2 miles to the end of the road where you will see the trailhead and parking area.

The Powderhorn Lakes are the centerpiece of the Powderhorn Wilderness Area, a 60,100-acre preserve that in 1993 became Colorado's first BLM-managed wilderness. Like the rest of the San Juan Mountains, the geology of the Powderhorn Wilderness is volcanic, but here the topography is very different. Instead of the high, rugged peaks normally associated with the San Juans, the terrain in this area is comprised mostly of huge, flat mesas topped with treeless meadows that extend for miles across the alpine tundras. The mesas are the result of a vast amount of volcanic debris—up to 5,000 feet

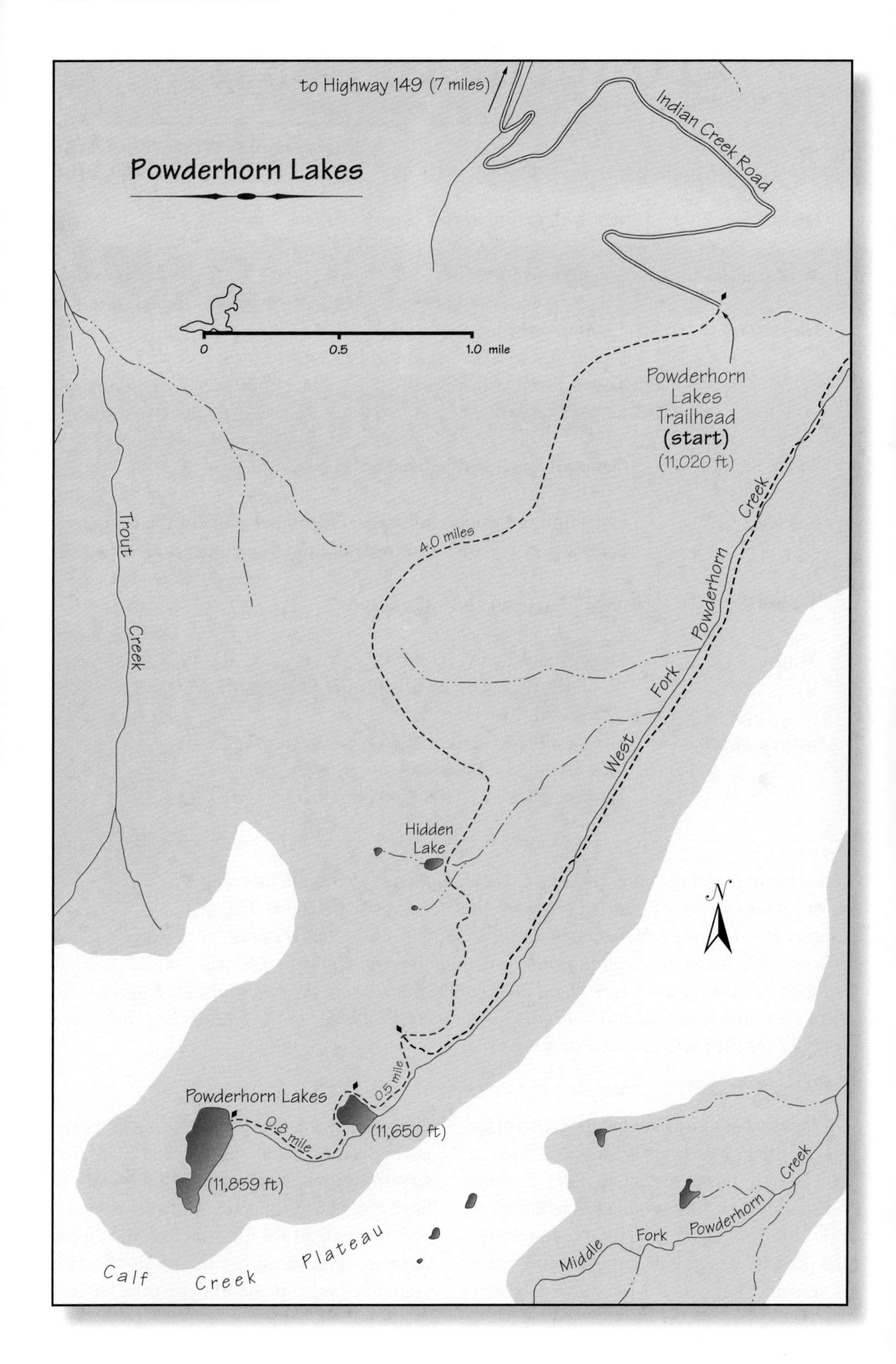

Powderhorn Lakes
to Highway 149 (7 miles)
Indian Creek Road
0
0.5
1.0 mile
Powderhorn Lakes Trailhead (start) (11,020 ft)
4.0 miles
Trout Creek
West Fork Powderhorn Creek
Hidden Lake
N
Powderhorn Lakes
0.5 mile
0.8 mile
(11,650 ft)
(11,859 ft)
Calf Creek Plateau
Middle Fork Powderhorn Creek

deep in some places—that was deposited in the area between 10 and 35 million years ago. The scenic Powderhorn Lakes are situated in a deep pocket 700 feet below the eastern side of one of the mesas.

The trail starts out by climbing at a moderate grade in a westerly direction through a well-shaded forest of Engelmann spruce. One thing you will immediately notice is the large number of dead trees lying scattered over the ground like sticks in some giant's game. It appears that the trees have been blown down by windstorms that must occasionally roar up the side of the mountain from the valleys below the trail. Fortunately the BLM and the Forest Service have done an excellent job of clearing the trail of fallen trees.

The trail climbs for 1.5 miles before approaching the top of a hill 850 feet above the trailhead and then drops slightly into a large alpine meadow. The lush meadow would appear to be an ideal habitat for elk. It is anywhere from 200 to 500 yards wide and descends gradually down the southern slopes of the hill toward the West Fork of Powderhorn Creek. The trail proceeds across the meadow and heads into the trees on its west side. It then turns south and skirts for a half-mile along the edge of the open grassy area.

Finally the path leaves the meadow entirely, and after another half-mile it passes by a 200-foot-diameter pond called Hidden Lake. This unimpressive lake is not even named on most maps, but it does provide a recognizable landmark to let you know you are getting close to your destination. Beyond Hidden Lake the terrain becomes much less uniform. The trail twists and turns in order to minimize changes in elevation and then, without any warning, it arrives at the bottom of the green, well-watered valley that surrounds the West Fork of Powderhorn Creek.

As you approach the creek you will see a sign on the trail directing you straight ahead

photo by Joe Pacal

Lower Powderhorn Lake

to the Powderhorn Lakes. Although it is not immediately obvious, this sign actually marks the junction between the Powderhorn Lakes Trail and the East Fork/Middle Fork Trail. The East Fork/Middle Fork Trail is not well used and you probably won't even be able to see it. But if you look directly south from the sign you will see a 5-foot juniper pole planted in the ground about 200 feet away. This pole marks the beginning of the East Fork/Middle Fork Trail.

The trail continues up the north side of the creek, avoiding the swampy center of the valley, for another 0.4 mile before arriving at Lower Powderhorn Lake. Lower Powderhorn, 200 yards across, is about a third the size of Upper Powderhorn. Like its larger sister lake, it lies against the base of the cliffs on the south side of the valley. There are a few nice campsites on the lake's northern shore, but if you are interested in spending a night I suggest you camp at the upper lake.

The trail to the upper lake continues to follow closely along the north side of the creek. Just above the lower lake there are several large beaver dams, so walk quietly in this area and you may see a beaver. As you approach the upper lake the trail becomes much less well defined, and eventually disappears altogether. But this shouldn't be a problem; upper Powderhorn Lake fills the entire western end of the valley, and it is impossible to miss.

The West Fork of Powderhorn Creek flows out of a glacial valley that was carved during the last ice age from the eastern side of Calf Creek Plateau. As often happened, the ice flow gouged out a deep depression at the head of the valley, and the depression later filled with water to form Upper Powderhorn Lake. Upper Powderhorn is surprising large for a glacial tarn. It is 0.4 mile long and 250 yards wide. The lake is very near timberline, but there are some nice campsites in a grove of trees on its east side if you are interested in doing this hike as an overnighter.

photo by Joe Pacal

Upper Powderhorn Lake

Uncompahgre Peak

Uncompahgre Wilderness Area
day hike

Distance:	7.2 miles (round trip)
Walking time:	5 1/2 hours
Elevations:	2,850 ft. gain/loss Nellie Creek Trailhead (start): 11,460 ft. Uncompahgre Peak: 14,309 ft.
Trail:	Generally well maintained and easy to follow.
Season:	Midsummer through mid-Fall. The upper parts of the trail are generally covered with snow from early November through mid-July.
Vicinity:	Near Lake City
Maps:	Uncompahgre Peak *(USGS)* Silverton, Ouray, Telluride, Lake City *(Trails Illustrated, #141)*
Information:	http://colorado.utahtrails.com/uncompahgrepeak.html http://www.fs.fed.us/r2/gmug/ *(Uncompahgre National Forest)* phone: (970) 641-0471 *(Gunnison Ranger District at Lake City)*

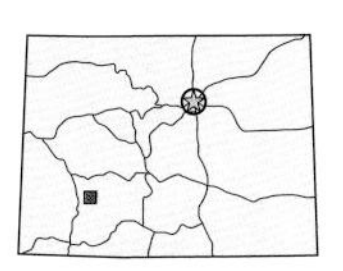

Drive west through Lake City on 2nd Avenue to Bluff Street, then turn left following the signs to Engineer Pass on the Alpine Loop Road. The pavement ends after only 0.2 mile, but a good gravel road continues west along Henson Creek. Continue west for another 4.9 miles beyond the pavement until you see a large sign on the right marking the beginning of the 4WD jeep road to the Nellie Creek Trailhead. Turn right here and drive the last 4.1 miles to the trailhead. Note: ordinary cars can make it as far as the Nellie Creek turnoff, but the last 4.1 miles to the trailhead is for 4WD vehicles only.

A "giant's top hat, slightly cocked to one side" is the way some climbers describe Uncompahgre Peak. As fourteeners go, it is a relatively easy climb, but there is really only one way to ascend the mountain. The peak is surrounded on three sides by vertical cliffs of crumbly volcanic rock, but fortunately the south side consists of a sloping ridge that is easily climbed with a minimum of scrambling.

Uncompahgre Peak was first climbed by members of the Hayden Survey in 1874.

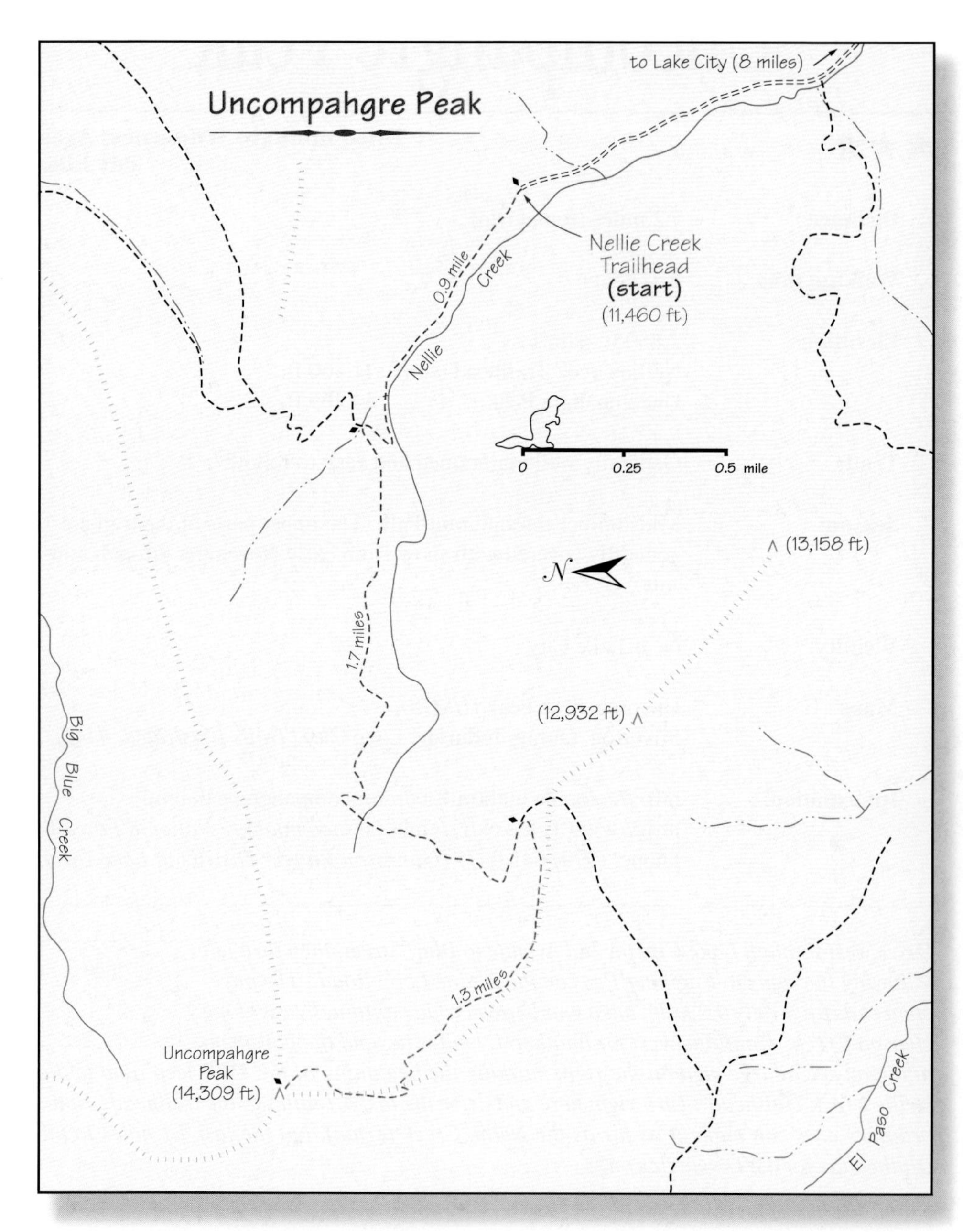

The mountain has long been recognized for its scenic beauty, and in the 1930s the area was included as one of the Forest Service's original Primitive Areas. In 1980 the peak became the centerpiece of the Big Blue Wilderness Area, later to be enlarged and renamed the Uncompahgre Wilderness Area.

For the first 0.9 mile the trail follows the upper reaches of Nellie Creek as it climbs out of the forest to the alpine tundra above. The streambed is littered with volcanic boulders that have rolled down from an ancient lava flow above the south side of the creek. Some of the more interesting rocks are so full of holes they look like giant blocks of Swiss Cheese. These strange boulders are the result of sputtering around the volcanic vents, where gobs of relatively cool putty-like lava piled up and hardened into loosely packed mounds of basalt.

After gaining 450 feet of elevation the trail comes to a junction where the Big Blue Trail leaves to the right. There shouldn't be any doubt that you must bear left at this point because Uncompahgre Peak dominates the skyline directly in front of the trail. It is also obvious from this perspective exactly where the trail will go. The shear cliffs on the north side of the mountain make an easy assent impossible from that direction, whereas the route from the south looks quite feasible.

For the next half-hour you will be walking westward across a gorgeous alpine tundra below the east side of the mountain. The elevation gain along this part of the hike is minimal, but after 1.0 mile the trail bends to the left and begins working its way up to the ridge on the south side of the peak.

When you reach the ridge a whole new panorama of scenery will open up on the west side of the mountain. The Matterhorn (13,590 ft.) lies just two miles away, and just behind that is the Wetterhorn (14,015 ft.). There is often a strong wind blowing up the ridge from the west, and you are also likely to see hawks and other soaring birds riding the air currents.

Half way up the ridge you will encounter a steep section of the trail where some scrambling is briefly necessary. Loose rocks can be a problem in this area, particularly if there are people directly above or below you. The steep part does not last long, however, and soon you will be back on the gently sloping top of the mountain. The last 250 yards of the climb is an easy walk with scarcely 120 feet of elevation gain.

Uncompahgre Peak Trail

Red Cloud and Sunshine Peaks

★★★ **day hike**

Distance:	11.0 miles (round trip)
Walking time:	8 1/2 hours
Elevations:	4,240 ft. gain/loss Silver Creek Trailhead (start): 10,420 ft. Red Cloud Peak: 14,034 ft. Sunshine Peak: 14,001 ft.
Trail:	Well marked, but very steep and slippery near the top.
Season:	Midsummer through mid-Fall. The upper parts of the trail are generally covered with snow from early November through mid-July.
Vicinity:	Near Lake City
Maps:	Red Cloud Peak *(USGS)* Silverton, Ouray, Telluride, Lake City *(Trails Illustrated, #141)*
Information:	http://colorado.utahtrails.com/redcloudpeak.html http://www.fs.fed.us/r2/gmug/ *(Uncompahgre National Forest)* phone: (970) 641-0471 *(Gunnison Ranger District at Lake City)*

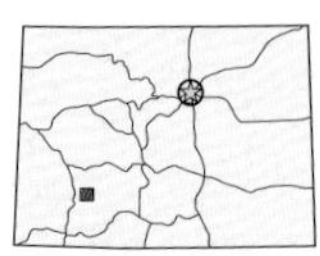

Drive south from Lake City on Highway 149 for 2.4 miles until you see a sign directing you to the San Cristobal Recreation Area. Turn right here onto County Road 30 and follow the signs toward Cinnamon Pass. After 4.1 miles you will come to the end of the pavement, and 12.0 miles later you will see a sign marking the Silver Creek Trailhead on the right side of the graded gravel road.

The main attraction of this hike is that it allows you to bag two of Colorado's coveted fourteen-thousand-foot peaks in a single day. True, at 14,001 feet Sunshine is just barely high enough to be classified as a fourteener, but it is still Colorado's 55th highest peak, and like Red Cloud it offers an exquisite panorama of the ruggedly beautiful San Juan Mountains. The trail up Handies Peak is just across the road from the Silver Creek Trailhead, and occasionally hikers climb all three of the fourteeners in a single day. But if this is your plan you had better get an early start and be prepared for a very

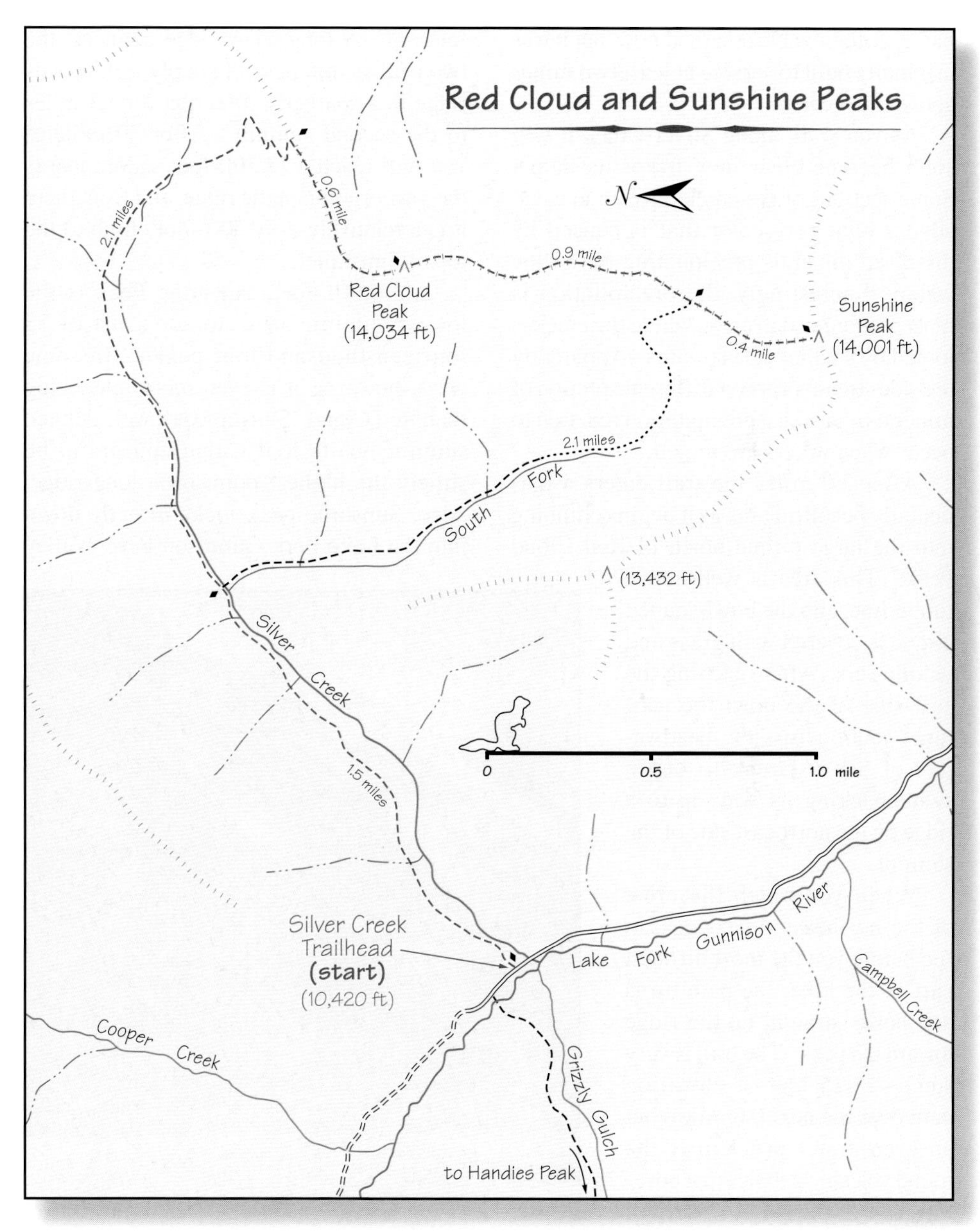

long, tiring day. (See page 336 for more information about the Handies Peak hike.)

For the first 3.0 miles the trail follows the north side of Silver Creek, occasionally straying as much as 300 yards from the water but more often staying within a few feet of the shore. Only after climbing into a large cirque north of Red Cloud Peak where Silver Creek originates does the trail finally leave the streambed to begin the climb to the summit ridge. You will probably notice that the first mile or so of the trail is actually an old, overgrown jeep or wagon road. It is barely recognizable as a road now, but it was originally built to service at least two mines above the creek.

As you walk along Silver Creek it will soon become clear how it got its name. Some sections of the creek have an unusual silvery blue-gray color that is caused by dissolved minerals precipitating out of the water. Interestingly, the precipitation is most pronounced in areas where the creek is joined by smaller side streams. Apparently the side streams carry a different solution of minerals, causing a precipitation reaction to occur when waters are mixed.

After 2.0 miles the trail enters a particularly beautiful area as it begins climbing into the large cirque north of Red Cloud Peak. This area is well above timberline, and the bowl-shaped cirque is covered with grass and wildflowers. After reaching the east side of the bowl the trail turns south across the headwaters of Silver Creek to begin switchbacking its way up to a ridge on the northeast side of the summit.

When you reach the crest of the northeast ridge you can see before you the most difficult part of the hike: the path turns and heads straight up the ridge toward the peak. The trail is very steep—1,025 feet of elevation gain over the next 0.6 mile—but an even grater problem is the round volcanic pebbles that cover the crest of the ridge. You will probably be slipping and sliding all the way up. After 0.4 mile the steep, slippery trail reaches a false summit, then it turns south for the last relatively easy 0.2 mile to the top.

The route from Red Cloud to Sunshine Peak is very straightforward. A long, easy ridge connects the two peaks, and the trail simply follows this ridge in a southerly direction for 1.3 miles to the second summit. After 20 minutes you will reach a 13,500-foot saddle that is the lowest point on the ridge, and from there it is a relatively easy 500-foot climb to the top of Sunshine.

At 14,001 feet, Sunshine Peak is the lowest summit on Colorado's list of 55 fourteen-thousand-foot peaks. In some ways, however, it is even more interesting than Red Cloud. Sunshine is a well-defined summit, while Red Cloud appears to be simply the highest point on a long ridge. Also, Sunshine peak looks directly down into the Lake Fork Gunnison River Valley

Upper Silver Creek Basin

where the trail starts. Both peaks offer fine views of many other fourteeners in the area, most notably Uncompahgre to the north and Handies to the west.

For the return portion of this hike many people choose to take a shortcut route down one of the gullies on the west side of the summit ridge. I don't recommend this. The steep western slopes of the two peaks are covered with loose talus, and it is almost impossible to make the descent without rolling rocks down on people below. Furthermore, the shortcut is not really that much shorter–it will get you back to the trailhead only about a half-hour sooner. The BLM has posted a sign on the summit ridge to discourage hikers from leaving the trail, and I highly recommend that you heed their advice. Nevertheless, so many people choose the shortcut route that I feel I should offer some information about it.

0.4 mile north of Sunshine Peak, where the trail passes the lowest point between Red Cloud and Sunshine, the Bureau of Land Management has posted a sign that says "Dangerous Area, This Is Not a Trail. Please Return Via Red Cloud". This saddle is the most common starting point for the shortcut down the talus slopes. There is a crude trail down the slope for about 100 feet, but soon the trail disappears leaving you to choose your own route. As you walk/slide down the steep slope you should angle somewhat to the north, because there are cliffs directly below the saddle.

After you have lost about 800 feet the slope begins to level out somewhat, and soon you will begin to see a trail descending along the east side of South Fork Silver Creek. At first it is marked only by cairns and stone monuments, but by the time you have descended to about 12,400 feet the trail is quite obvious. Just before reaching timberline the trail passes within 250 yards of an old mine on the left side of the gully, and five minutes later you will see the remains of an old cabin in a grove of Engelmann spruce beside the trail. The cabin undoubtedly belonged to the person working the mine. Fifteen minutes beyond the cabin the trail crosses Silver Creek and joins the main trail. From there you can retrace your steps the last 1.5 miles to the trailhead.

Sunshine Peak, as seen from Red Cloud Peak

Handies Peak

★★★★★

shuttle car required
day hike

Distance:	6.0 miles (plus 4.5 miles by car)
Walking time:	4 3/4 hours
Elevations:	2,450 ft. gain, 3,630 ft. loss American Basin Trailhead (start): 11,600 ft. Handies Peak: 14,048 ft. Grizzly Gulch Trailhead: 10,420 ft.
Trail:	Well maintained and easy to follow
Season:	Midsummer through mid-Fall. The upper parts of the trail are generally covered with snow from early November through mid-July.
Vicinity:	Near Lake City
Maps:	Handies Peak, Red Cloud Peak *(USGS)* Silverton, Ouray, Telluride, Lake City *(Trails Illustrated, # 141)*
Information:	http://colorado.utahtrails.com/handiespeak.html http://www.fs.fed.us/r2/gmug/ *(Uncompahgre National Forest)* phone: (970) 641-0471 *(Gunnison Ranger District at Lake City)*

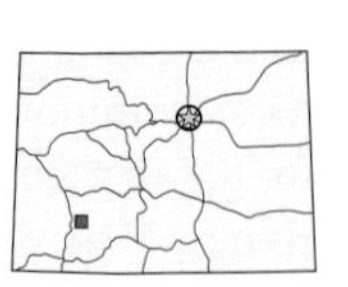

Drive south from Lake City on Highway 149 for 2.4 miles until you see a sign directing you to the San Cristobal Recreation Area. Turn right here onto County Road 30 and follow the signs toward Cinnamon Pass. After 4.1 miles you will come to the end of the pavement, and 12.0 miles later you will see a sign marking the Grizzly Gulch Trailhead on the left side of the graded gravel road. This is where the hike ends.

To get to American Basin where the hike begins you must continue west on County Road 30 towards Cinnamon Pass for another 3.6 miles. Turn left at the sign that says "American Basin" and drive another 0.9 miles. The trailhead and parking area are at the end of the road. The road is not well maintained beyond the Grizzly Gulch Trailhead, but most cars can still usually get as far as the American Basin turnoff. The last 0.9 miles, however, are for 4WD vehicles only.

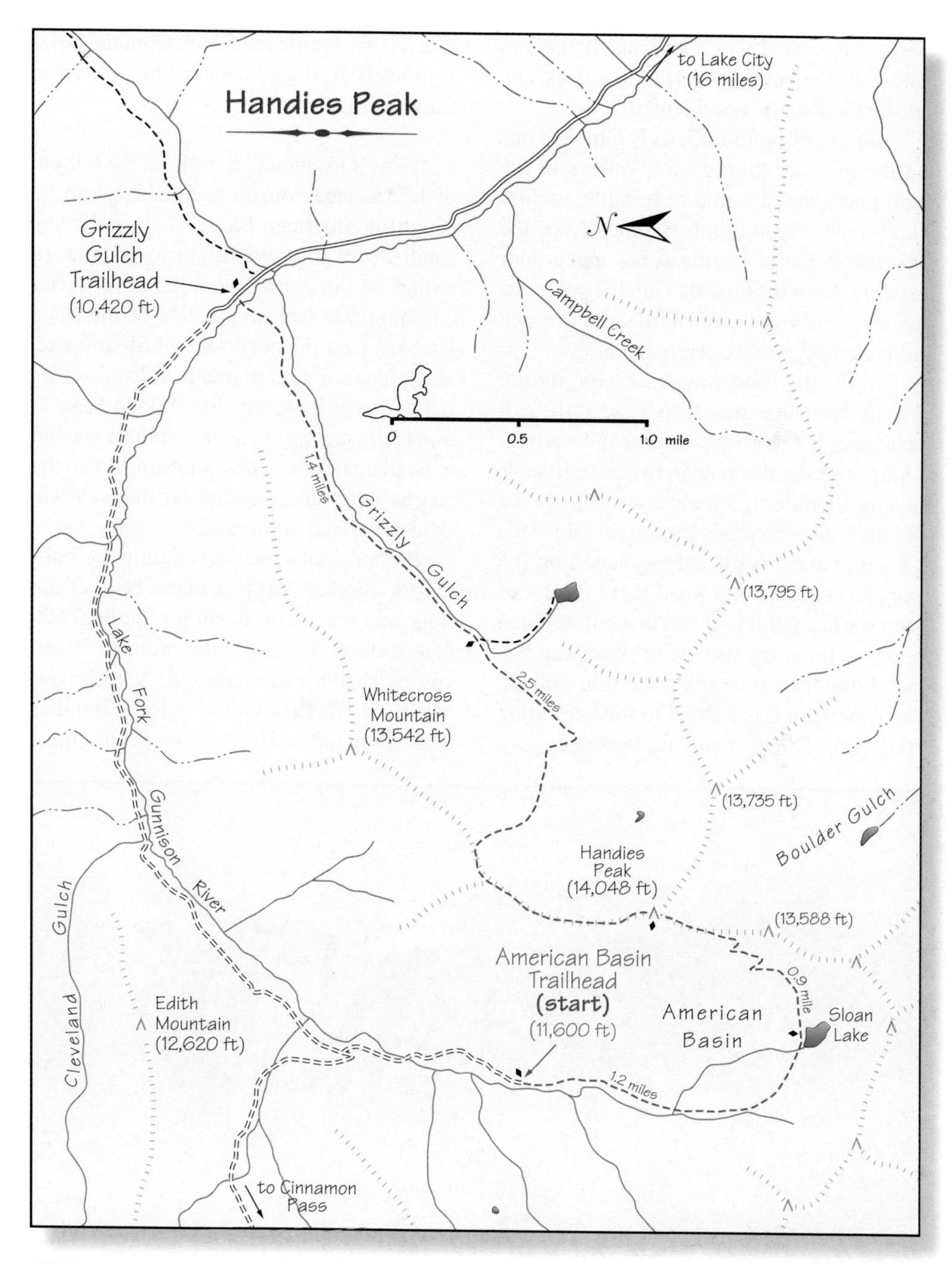

There are two commonly used trails to the summit of Handies Peak: one goes up through American Basin on the west side of the mountain, and the other approaches the peak from the east through Grizzly Gulch. Of these two alternatives the trail through American Basin is the most popular, simply because it is shorter. It is only 2.1 miles from the American Basin Trailhead to the summit, and the elevation gain is only 2,450 feet. The round trip hike from American Basin to the summit of Handies Peak can easily be done in 4 or 5 hours.

But in my opinion Grizzly Gulch is one of the most striking glacial valleys in the San Juans, and it would be a shame to miss it. I suggest you climb Handies from the American Basin Trailhead but make your descent down the Grizzly Gulch Trail to experience the joy of a downhill stroll through an incredibly beautiful alpine valley.

To do this one-way hike you should ideally have an extra car to leave at the exit trailhead, but there are several alternatives: One: since the distance between trailheads is only 4.5 miles it is quite feasible to do the shuttle with a mountain bike. Two: Since the Grizzly Gulch Trailhead is located on the popular Alpine Loop Road there is a lot of jeep traffic, and it isn't too difficult to hitch a ride as far as the turnoff to American Basin. From there it is only a 0.9 mile walk up the American Basin Road to the beginning trailhead. Three: If you are unable to get a ride it is a 4.5-mile road walk from the Grizzly Gulch Trailhead back to the American Basin Trailhead.

A well trodden path follows the bottom of the drainage from the trailhead up into the beautiful American Basin. The trail bears south for 0.8 mile and then turns east toward a ridge on the south side of the peak. After climbing 500 feet up the side of the ridge you will pass the north side of Sloan Lake, an alpine tarn with dramatic volcanic cliffs rising above its south side. Sloan Lake is especially pretty if you are fortunate enough to be there on a windless morning when the nearby cliffs are reflected off the smooth, shaded surface of the water.

From the lake the trail continues climbing for another 500 feet to the crest of the ridge and then turns north for the final 650 feet of elevation gain to the summit. When you reach the ridge you will see the real beauty of Handies unfold below. Handies Peak is surrounded by three gorgeous alpine

Sloan Lake, seen from the south ridge of Handies Peak

Looking north from the summit of Handies Peak

basins: American Basin, Grizzly Gulch, and Boulder Gulch. When you reach the crest of the ridge you will be able to look southeast into Boulder Gulch, and as you near the summit you will see Grizzly Gulch below the northeast side of the peak. Unlike American Basin, there has been no obvious mining activity in either of the two eastern basins, and both still retain their primal, untouched attraction. Boulder Gulch doesn't even have a trail going into it.

Upon reaching the summit of Handies Peak the trail continues north along the ridge between American Basin and Grizzly Gulch loosing altitude at an alarming rate. It reaches the 13,000-foot-level about 0.9 mile later and then turns southeast for the descent down into Grizzly Gulch. At this point, if you are like me, you will probably feel some excitement as the pristine valley below beckons you to enter and explore.

The glaciers that formed Grizzly Gulch carved the bottom of the valley into two distinct tiers. From the ridge the trail drops steeply to the first plateau and then levels out for the next quarter-mile. It then heads down again and, after loosing another 200 feet of elevation, levels out onto the second plateau. The trail stays on this tier for the next 1.3 miles, descending gradually down the tundra towards the trees below.

Look up to the right as you walk and you will see a hanging lake on the east side of the valley. This lake, located on a shelf 300 feet above the floor of Grizzly Gulch, is the headwaters of Grizzly Gulch Creek. A spur trail to the lake leaves the main trail near the point where the trail meets the creek.

At the edge of timberline, about 11,700 feet, the trail becomes much steeper as it passes from the alpine tundra into a forest of Engelmann spruce and subalpine fir. From there it is a pleasant walk down the north side of Grizzly Gulch Creek to the trailhead.

Grizzly Gulch`

Highland Mary Lakes

Weminuche Wilderness Area
4WD vehicle useful
day hike

Distance: 7.8 miles (loop)

Walking time: 5 3/4 hours

Elevations: 1,800 ft. gain/loss
Highland Mary Trailhead (start): 10,800 ft.
Highland Mary Lake (largest): 12,090 ft.
Verde Lakes: 12,186 ft.
Continental Divide: 12,600 ft.

Trail: Generally well marked and easy to follow.

Season: Midsummer through mid-fall. The higher parts of this trail are usually covered with snow from early November through mid-July.

Vicinity: Near Silverton

Maps: Howardsville *(USGS)*
Weminuche Wilderness *(Trails Illustrated, #140)*

Information: http://colorado.utahtrails.com/highlandmary.html
http://www.fs.fed.us/r2/sanjuan/ *(San Juan National Forest)*
phone: (970) 884-2512 *(Columbine Ranger District)*

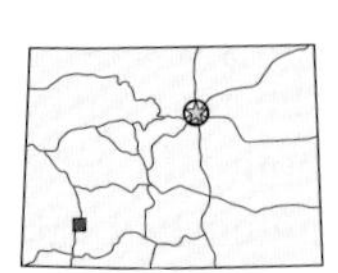

Drive north on Silverton's Main Street until you see a sign marking Highway 110 on the edge of town. Turn right at this sign and continue on Highway 110 for another 4.1 miles to the mining settlement of Howardsville. Just before entering Howardsville you will see a graded gravel road on the right with a sign that says "Stony Pass, 5 miles". Turn south here. This road follows Cunningham Creek for the next 3.6 miles. There are several forks in the road, one of which departs on the left for Stony Pass. In every case, however, you must bear to the right and continue driving along Cunningham Creek. The graded road finally ends at the Highland Mary Mill, an old mill for processing silver ore that was built beside Cunningham Creek in the late 1800s. From the mill there is a primitive jeep road that continues on to the trailhead, but if you are driving a passenger car you will have to park at the end of the graded road and continue on foot. The trailhead is 1.1 miles from the mill along the jeep road, or 0.6 mile along a shortcut trail that follows the west side of Cunningham Creek.

Just before the graded gravel road ends you will see the jeep road descending on the right to ford Cunningham Creek. Turn onto this road, drive across the creek, and bear right at a fork 100 yards above the west side of the water. The road proceeds in a northerly direction for a short distance, then turns south again to follow the west side of the stream. 0.9 mile after leaving the graded road you will see another spur that departs from the left side of the jeep road and again fords Cunningham Creek. Take this road across to the east side of the stream, then turn south and follow the water for another 150 yards to the trailhead.

The Highland Mary Lakes are a group of seven above-timberline lakes on the northwestern side of the Weminuche Wilderness Area. This trail passes by the two largest Highland Mary Lakes as well as the nearby Verde Lakes. But, in my opinion, the most interesting part of the hike is the second half of the trail. From the Verde Lakes the trail turns east and climbs to the top of the Continental Divide. It then follows the Continental Divide Trail for 1.0 mile before turning west again for the descent back to the trailhead. All but the first and last mile of the hike are above timberline.

I should mention an interesting bit of history regarding the Highland Mary Mine near the beginning of this hike. This mine was originally established by the Ennis brothers who emigrated from New York to Colorado in the early 1870s to try their luck at prospecting. Before leaving home they hired a spiritualist to tell them where to dig for gold. Given a map of the United States she confidently pointed to Cunningham Gulch and told them that this was the place where they would find a "Lake of Gold". The brothers struggled for over ten years, carefully following the mystic's instructions, until they had dug a mile-long tunnel into the mountain and discovered a number of high grade silver deposits, but they never struck gold. Finally, after spending a million dollars on the mine and $50,000 on the spiritualist, they went bankrupt. The Highland Mary Mine was taken over by new owners in 1895 and, ironically, by 1907 it had become the second largest silver producing mine in the Silverton area.

From the trailhead the trail begins climbing upward almost immediately along the left side of the creek. For the next 40 minutes you will rarely be out of sight or sound of Cunningham Creek as it tumbles and splashes down the steep grade through a series of delightful cascades. After 0.2 mile there is a fork in the trail with a misleading sign that says hikers should bear right and horses bear left. Be sure to bear right at this sign, or you will soon find yourself climbing out of Cunningham Gulch toward the Continental Divide.

The trail continues up the left side of the main drainage for another 0.9 mile, crossing two minor tributaries along the way. Then,

Second largest of the Highland Mary Lakes

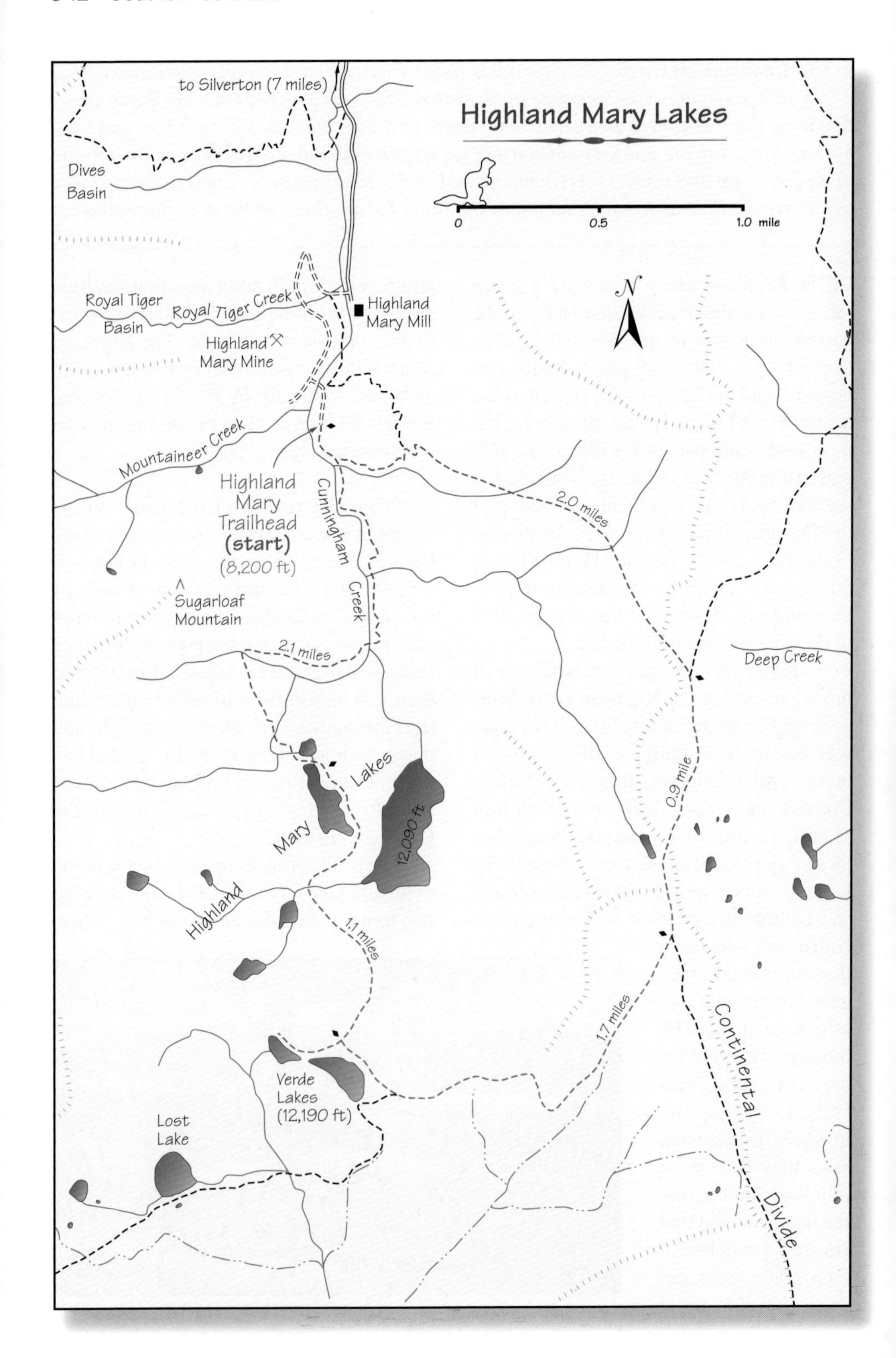

Highland Mary Lakes
0
0.5
1.0 mile
N
to Silverton (7 miles)
Dives Basin
Royal Tiger Basin
Royal Tiger Creek
Highland Mary Mill
Highland Mary Mine
Mountaineer Creek
Highland Mary Trailhead (start) (8,200 ft)
Cunningham Creek
Sugarloaf Mountain
2.0 miles
2.1 miles
Deep Creek
Highland Mary Lakes
12,090 ft
0.9 mile
1.1 miles
1.7 miles
Verde Lakes (12,190 ft)
Lost Lake
Continental Divide

Cunningham Creek

just above a picturesque waterfall and shortly after crossing the northern boundary of the Weminuche Wilderness Area, the path crosses over a conveniently placed log to the west side of Cunningham Creek. At this point the trail veers further west into another unnamed drainage and follows it out of the forest to the first of the Highland Mary Lakes. By the time you reach the first tiny lake you will be above timberline. Soon the second lake will come into view, quickly followed by the third. All of the lakes are well above timberline, with not a tree in sight. They are situated in the midst of a plain of gently rolling hills with the crest of the continental divide 1.0 mile to the east.

The third lake is the largest of the Highland Mary Lakes, 0.4 mile long and 300 yards wide. The trail continues south along its western shore and then bends westward to get around its swampy southwestern side. The path disappears into the tall grass at this point, but if you look further south you can see where it emerges again on the side of the hill a few hundred yards ahead. Continue following it in a southerly direction, and within 20 minutes you will arrive at the northern side of the two Verde Lakes.

Having reached the Verde Lakes, many hikers simply return to the Highland Mary Trailhead and same way they came, but a much more interesting route is to return by way of a loop trail that crosses over the Continental Divide. Colorado's higher altitude trails are often difficult to follow, and you may not immediately see the trail leading from Verde Lakes up to the top of the Divide. But fortunately the Forest Service has marked the route with a series of 7-foot poles placed along the route at intervals of a few hundred yards. If you just follow these poles up the slope on the east side of the lake you will soon run into the trail.

Largest of the Verde Lakes

As you climb up the slope your eyes will probably be drawn to a range of very rugged peaks four miles south of Verde Lake. This is the spectacular Grenadier Range, considered to be one of the highest concentrations of technical mountain climbing challenges in the state. While the Grenadiers do not contain any fourteen-thousand-foot peaks, they do contain over a dozen notable thirteeners. One sharply pointed, pyramid-shaped peak is particularly eye-catching. That is Arrow Peak (13,803 feet), considered to be one of the most difficult summits in Colorado.

After a climb of 1.1 miles and an elevation gain of only 600 feet above Verde Lake the trail arrives at the Continental Divide. Another trail comes in from the south at this point, but it is poorly marked and you probably won't even see it. This is the Continental Divide Trail. Continuing north along the Divide the path passes by a small lake that drains to the west, and then dips down on the eastern side of the Divide. (The Continental Divide is not well defined in this area, so don't be disappointed if you can't tell exactly where the magic line is.)

After another 1.2 miles you will come to another fork where you must leave the Continental Divide Trail and drop back down to the west to return to the Highland Mary Trailhead. Again, the better trail is the one you want; if you are not paying attention you may not even see the fork where the Continental Divide Trail departs. The trail drops steeply back down into the trees and continues into Cunningham Gulch, loosing 1,200 feet before it reaches the creek. 0.5 mile before you reach the creek you will come to an unmarked fork in the trail. If you go right you will meet the creek 0.2 mile below the trailhead; if you go left you will meet the creek 0.2 mile above the trailhead. Both routes are about the same distance to the trailhead, but if you parked you car on the main road near the Highland Mary Mine the trail on the right will get you to your vehicle a little faster.

Continental Divide Trail

Ice Lake Basin

★★★ **day hike**

Distance:	9.3 miles (round trip)
Walking time:	6 3/4 hours
Elevations:	2,870 ft. gain/loss Ice Lake Basin Trailhead (start): 9,840 ft. Ice Lake: 12,257 ft. Fuller Lake: 12,585 ft. Island Lake: 12,380 ft.
Trail:	Mostly well marked and easy to follow.
Season:	Midsummer through mid-fall. The upper parts of the trail are generally covered with snow from early November through mid-July.
Vicinity:	Near Silverton
Maps:	Ophir *(USGS)* Silverton, Ouray, Telluride *(Trails Illustrated, #141)*
Information:	http://colorado.utahtrails.com/icelake.html http://www.fs.fed.us/r2/sanjuan/ *(San Juan National Forest)* phone: (970) 884-2512 *(Columbine Ranger District)*

Drive 2.5 miles northwest of Silverton on Highway 550 until you see a graded road on the left near a sign that says "South Mineral Campground Road". Turn left here and continue for another 4.6 miles to the campground. The Ice Lake Basin Trailhead is on the right side of the road opposite the entrance to South Mineral Campground.

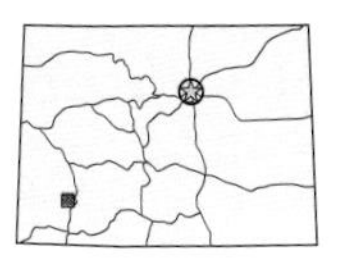

As the name suggests, Ice Lake Basin lies high above timberline in a corner of the San Juan Mountains known for its long winters and short summers. Ice Lake and its neighboring lakes are frozen for at least eight months of the year, and the valley they occupy is bordered by several snowfields that never completely melt. There are four named lakes within the basin and five or six unnamed ones, all remnants of the glaciers that long ago created the bowl-shaped valley. The basin is a textbook example of an alpine depression that was gouged out of the mountains by a long succession of glaciers

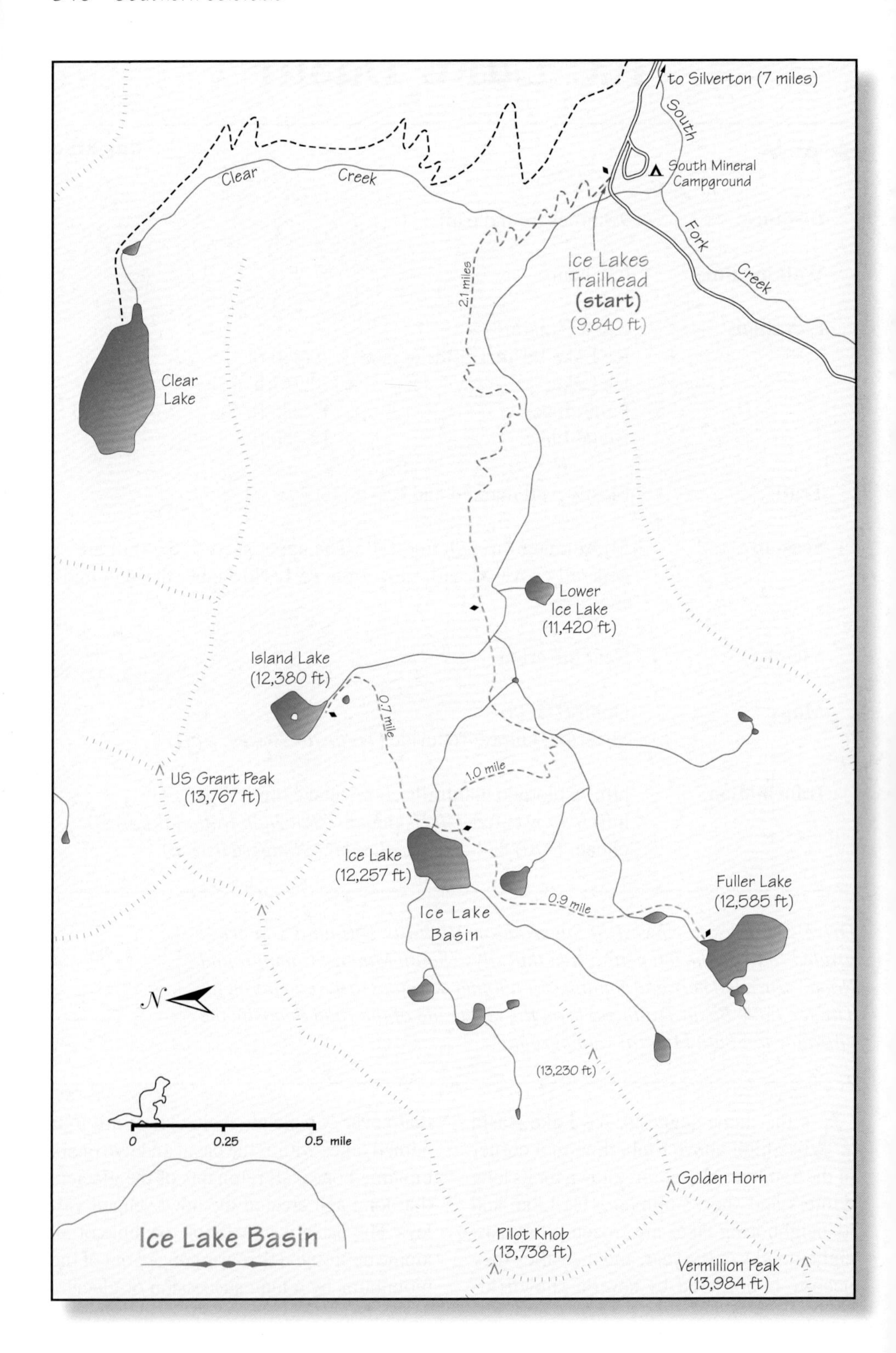
to Silverton (7 miles)
South
South Mineral Campground
Fork
Creek
Clear
Creek
Ice Lakes Trailhead
(start)
(9,840 ft)
2.1 miles
Clear Lake
Lower Ice Lake
(11,420 ft)
Island Lake
(12,380 ft)
0.7 mile
US Grant Peak
(13,767 ft)
1.0 mile
Ice Lake
(12,257 ft)
Ice Lake Basin
0.9 mile
Fuller Lake
(12,585 ft)
(13,230 ft)
0
0.25
0.5 mile
Golden Horn
Ice Lake Basin
Pilot Knob
(13,738 ft)
Vermillion Peak
(13,984 ft)

Ice Lake Basin Trail

that have periodically resided here over the past 900,000 years.

To the west the basin is bordered by a long crescent-shaped ridge of thirteen-thousand-foot peaks that were probably never completely covered with ice, but below them accumulations of ice and snow occasionally collected to produce intermittent glaciers that were, at times, over a thousand feet thick. Propelled by their own weight, the glaciers slowly moved eastward down the slopes of the mountain, and as they moved they left a bed of unseen destruction in their wake. Pushing and shoving, gouging and scraping like enormous earth-moving machines, the huge masses of ice changed the landscape completely. Today the glaciers are gone, but their legacy remains. All of the cirques and tarns of Ice Lake Basin, as well as the beautiful U-shaped South Mineral Valley below were sculpted by the glaciers of previous ice ages.

From the head of South Mineral Valley, the trail starts climbing almost immediately up the right side of the Ice Creek drainage. After 0.4 mile the path crosses Clear Creek, a tributary that cascades down a lovely waterfall just above the crossing. The trail then switchbacks up the slope and enters the forest again near the top of the waterfall. You will probably want to stop here for a few minutes to feel the spray and enjoy the view of the valley below.

Soon after leaving Clear Creek the route passes the remains of an old mining structure. The structure is now little more than a pile of broken timbers, but it looks like it might have once housed machinery for processing ore. From there you must continue the uphill climb for another 0.9 mile to the first plateau, where Lower Ice Lake is located.

One would expect the floor of a glacier-covered basin to slope steadily downward in the direction of the glacier's movement, but that is frequently not the case. High glaciated canyons are often shaped more like

Ice Lake Basin Trail

stair steps, with steep sections followed by plateaus. This irregularity may have resulted from the different hardnesses of the rock layers. Or it might be the result of the fact that the glaciation was not a single event, but rather occurred in many episodes. The last Ice Age lasted some 100,000 years, and before that there were many earlier ones.

The Lower Ice Lake basin or plateau offers a welcome stretch of level ground after the 1,600 foot climb from the trailhead. The flat area is about a half-mile long and a quarter-mile wide, with the Lower Ice Lake lying on its southern side. This lower basin serves as a confluence for three small streams that pour in from the lakes above: Island Lake, Ice Lake, and Fuller Lake. The terrain is very steep where these streams flow in, and if there has been a recent rain you will be treated to a spectacle of cascading waterfalls in the back of the small valley.

Fuller Lake

After you have crossed the Lower Ice Lake Basin the work begins again. The trail swings to the south, then goes through a series of grueling switchbacks before bending again to the north. Finally, after a climb of 800 feet, the trail levels out again just south of Ice Lake. The view from Ice Lake is beautiful in a harsh and desolate sort of way. The basin is enclosed by a ridge of thirteen-thousand-foot peaks with barren talus slopes extending all the way to the water. By this time you are well above timberline and the view is unimpeded by any vegetation more than 10 inches high. The crest of the ridge is serrated by heavily eroded spires of

Ice Lake

volcanic rock, but the peaks don't really look that high from this vantage point; they are only a thousand feet above the bottom of the basin. The terrain is high enough to foster permanent snowfields, and the lakes are clear and blue.

From Ice Lake the trail turns south and climbs another 330 feet to Fuller Lake, the highest and southernmost lake in the basin. The view looking back on Ice Lake with U.S. Grant Peak (13,767 ft.) in the background is gorgeous, but Fuller Lake itself is not as pretty as Ice Lake. The serenity is marred by the presence of a broken-down miner's cabin of recent vintage on the shore of the lake. Bits of aluminum siding are scattered about (in the lake as well as on the ground), and an old helicopter rotor blade forms a bench in front of the cabin.

In my opinion the prettiest and most interesting lake in Ice Lake Basin is Island Lake. To get there you must return to Ice Lake and look up the slope above the northeast corner of the lake. You should see a faint trail angling up the slope near the bottom of an old mine tailing. If you walk down the drainage for a few hundred feet below Ice Lake you will find the beginning of this trail near an easy spot to cross the creek. The trail continues up past the mine tailing for a short way, and then doubles back into a higher, hidden basin containing Island Lake.

Island Lake lies in the bottom of a steep sided bowl that looks for all the world like an extinct volcanic crater. Geologists assure us that the bowl was formed by glaciation, but a part of me remains unconvinced. Even the small island in the center suggests otherwise.

Many a swimmer has undoubtedly felt challenged by the small, rocky island that gives Island Lake its name. The island is situated only a hundred feet from the southern shore, but the water, even in late summer, is very cold. In the words of local writer, Sven Brunso, the lake "can provide a refreshing swim if you happen to have packed in your defibrillator to restart your heart after plunging into the 35-degree slurpee."

Island Lake

Bear Creek Trail

★★★★ **day hike**

Distance:	7.6 miles (round trip)
Walking time:	5 3/4 hours
Elevations:	2,640 ft. gain/loss Bear Creek Trailhead (start): 8,460 ft. Grizzly Bear Mining Camp: 9,900 ft. Yellow Jacket Mining Camp: 11,100 ft.
Trail:	Well maintained and easy to follow. This trail has been designated as a National Recreation Trail.
Season:	Midsummer through mid-fall. The trail is generally covered with snow from mid-November through June.
Vicinity:	Near Ouray
Maps:	Ouray, Ironton, Handies Peak *(USGS)* Silverton, Ouray, Telluride *(Trails Illustrated, #141)*
Information:	http://colorado.utahtrails.com/bearcreek.html http://www.fs.fed.us/r2/gmug/ *(Uncompahgre National Forest)* phone: (970) 240-5400 *(Ouray Ranger District)*

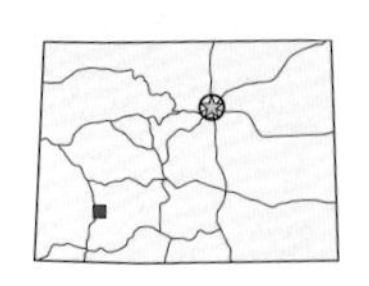

Drive south of Ouray on Highway 550 for 2.3 miles to where the road passes through a short tunnel. The Bear Creek Trailhead is located on the south side of the tunnel and the west side of the road. There is a large parking area opposite the trailhead on the east side of the road.

As described at the end of this chapter, this hike can also be done as a one-way hike starting at the top of Engineer Pass and ending at the Bear Creek Trailhead. A 4WD vehicle is required, however, to get to Engineer Pass. To reach the pass drive south of Ouray for 3.6 miles where you will see a sign on the left marking the beginning of the Alpine Loop Road. Engineer Pass is 9.8 miles up this 4WD road. You will encounter a number of forks along the way where, with one exception, you must always bear left. The only exception is a short spur road to Oh! Point, which departs on the left just 0.4 mile before the road reaches the pass.

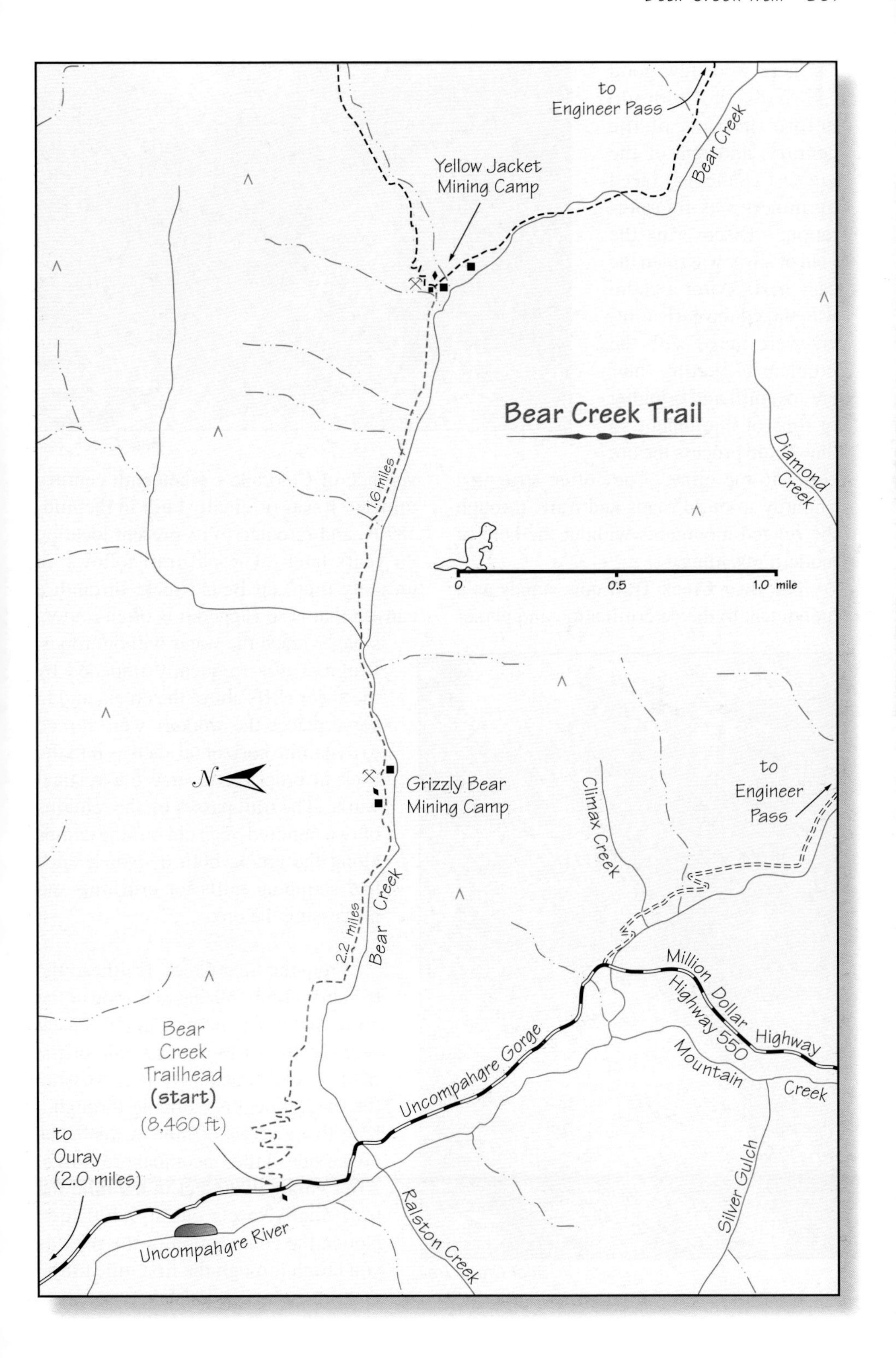

to
Engineer Pass
Bear Creek
Yellow Jacket
Mining Camp
Bear Creek Trail
Diamond
Creek
1.6 miles
0
0.5
1.0 mile
N
Grizzly Bear
Mining Camp
to
Engineer
Pass
Climax Creek
Bear Creek
2.2 miles
Million Dollar Highway
Highway 550
Mountain
Creek
Bear
Creek
Trailhead
(start)
(8,460 ft)
Uncompahgre Gorge
to
Ouray
(2.0 miles)
Uncompahgre River
Ralston Creek
Silver Gulch

Bear Creek Trail

There were few good roads in Colorado before the turn of the century, and one of the greatest challenges faced by miners was transportation. Discovering the gold or silver was often the easy part. After a claim was staked the early miners were faced with the problem of getting their ore to a mill and bringing in tons of equipment so they could process the ore closer to the mine. They often struggled mightily to build roads and trails through the rugged mountains without the help of modern machinery.

The Bear Creek Trail now stands as a monument to the determination and perseverance of Colorado's nineteenth century miners. It was originally built in the mid-1870s, and rerouted to its present location 20 years later. The old trail follows an unlikely route up Bear Creek, through a canyon that is so rugged it is often impossible to reach the water without ropes. Progress was frequently impeded by the sheer cliffs above the creek, and in some places the workers were forced to dynamite horizontal shelves into the rock in order to traverse the vertical walls. The trail passes by the remains of two hundred-year-old mining camps along the creek, both of which once had stamping mills for crushing and processing the ore.

Bear Creek Trail

From the Bear Creek Trailhead the trail first climbs 50 feet to the top of the highway tunnel and then doubles back over the tunnel to the east side of the road. Then, immediately after crossing the road, it begins climbing through a long tiring series of nine switchbacks up the side of the Uncompahgre Gorge. After gaining 900 feet in 0.9 mile the trail finally levels out at 9,400 feet. Notice the composition of the rock as you climb through the first mile of the

Unnamed waterfall on Bear Creek

trail. This is the Precambrian Uncompahgre Formation, which is comprised primarily of slate and quartzite. The shiny black slate is particularly interesting. It fractures into thin, brittle sheets that crackle like glass when you walk over them. Notice the ripple marks in some of the slate beds. The rock is composed of metamorphosed mudstone, and although it is at least 600 million years old it still bears the marks of the river bottom or mudflat where it was long ago deposited.

The trail levels out at the top of the Uncompahgre Formation and begins to turn south toward Bear Creek. Also at this point it begins to skirt along the base of the volcanic cliffs of the San Juan geologic formation. This thick, gray colored layer of tuff is only about 30 million years old, much younger than the underlying slate and quartzite. It is also very crumbly and easily eroded; the affects of erosion are everywhere apparent.

When the trail reaches Bear Creek it enters the most spectacular part of the route. The cliffs are too high to scale, and the creek bottom is too rugged for a trail; hence the miners were forced to blast a narrow path into the side of the vertical wall a hundred feet above the canyon bottom. There are no published statistics about people or animals falling into the canyon here, but the trail has been in use for over a hundred years and I would be surprised if there has never been an accident.

2.2 miles after leaving the trailhead you will pass by the wreckage of the Grizzly Bear Mining Camp, which according to the 1900 government census had a population of 24 people. At that time there was a bridge across the canyon giving access to the Grizzly Bear Mine on the other side. No trace of the wooden bridge remains now, but the ruins of several old cabins and some mining equipment are still evident along the trail. According to historic records the Grizzly Bear Mine reached its peak production in the mid 1890s under the ownership of

Yellow Jacket Mining Camp

George and Ed Wright and Milton Moore. In all, some $600,000 worth of silver and gold were extracted from the mine before it was closed.

From Grizzly Bear Mining Camp the trail meanders along Bear Creek for another 1.6 miles to the Yellow Jacket Mining Camp. The Yellow Jacket Camp was never as big as Grizzly Bear, but it is better preserved today and it is also in a very scenic area. The camp is situated in an open meadow above the creek, just below timberline at an elevation of 11,100 feet. A picturesque cabin still stands near the remains of a large stamp mill with a great deal of antique machinery scattered about. The mine itself is located above the mill on the north side of the creek. The Yellow Jacket Mine reached its peak production in 1915, a decade after the Grizzly Bear Mine had closed.

Engineer Pass Trailhead

If a 4WD shuttle can be arranged the easiest way to do this hike is to begin above Ouray at Engineer Pass and walk downhill all the way to Highway 550. The total distance of this one-way hike is 6.4 miles and the elevation loss is 4,340 feet. In addition to avoiding the uphill climb near the Bear Creek Trailhead, this option also offers a pleasant walk through the alpine tundra in the top of the Bear Creek Basin above Yellow Jacket Mine.

Looking northwest from the top of Engineer Pass you can see almost the entire route to the Yellow Jacket Mining Camp. The camp itself is hidden just below timberline in the first grove of trees below the pass, but if you look carefully you can see the yellowish tailings from the mine above the trees on the right side of the canyon. The trail starts out as a jeep road that drops west into the basin from the summit of the pass. After 0.4 mile the road turns into a footpath and makes a sweeping bend to the north. Soon afterward it crosses the creek and continues down the bottom of the drainage to the Yellow Jacket Mining Camp. From Yellow Jacket it is another 3.8 miles to the Bear Creek Trailhead.

Yellow Jacket Mining Camp

Blue Lakes

Mount Sneffels Wilderness Area
day hike

Distance:	8.6 miles (round trip to upper lake)
Walking time:	6 hours
Elevations:	2,370 ft. gain/loss Blue Lakes Trailhead (start): 9,350 ft. Lower Blue Lake: 10,980 ft. Upper Blue Lake: 11,720 ft.
Trail:	Well maintained and easy to follow.
Season:	Midsummer through mid-fall. The trail is generally covered with snow from mid-November through June.
Vicinity:	Near Ouray
Maps:	Mount Sneffels, Telluride *(USGS)* Silverton, Ouray, Telluride *(Trails Illustrated, #141)*
Information:	http://colorado.utahtrails.com/bluelakes.html http://www.fs.fed.us/r2/gmug/ *(Uncompahgre National Forest)* phone: (970) 240-5400 *(Ouray Ranger District)*

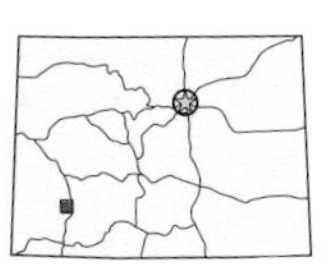

Drive west from Ridgway on Highway 62 for 4.4 miles until you see a sign marking the Dallas Creek Road. Turn left onto this graded gravel road and continue south for another 8.9 miles, following the signs to the Uncompahgre National Forest and Blue Lakes Trailhead. You will cross the National Forest boundary 7.2 miles after leaving the highway, and 1.7 miles further the road ends at the trailhead. There are many good places to camp near the end of the road if you want to spend the night there before beginning the hike.

Traveling west of Ridgway on Highway 62 one cannot help but be impressed by the long, rugged line of mountain peaks that lie directly south of the road. Nearly all of the summits rise above the 13,000-foot level, but there is one peak in particular that dominates the scene: Mount Sneffels. At 14,150 feet above sea level, Sneffels stands over 300 feet higher than its nearest neighbor; it is the only fourteener in the area.

In 1980 the land between Mount Sneffels and North Pole Peak, 7.5 miles to the west, was designated as the Mount Sneffels Wilderness Area, and today few outdoorsmen

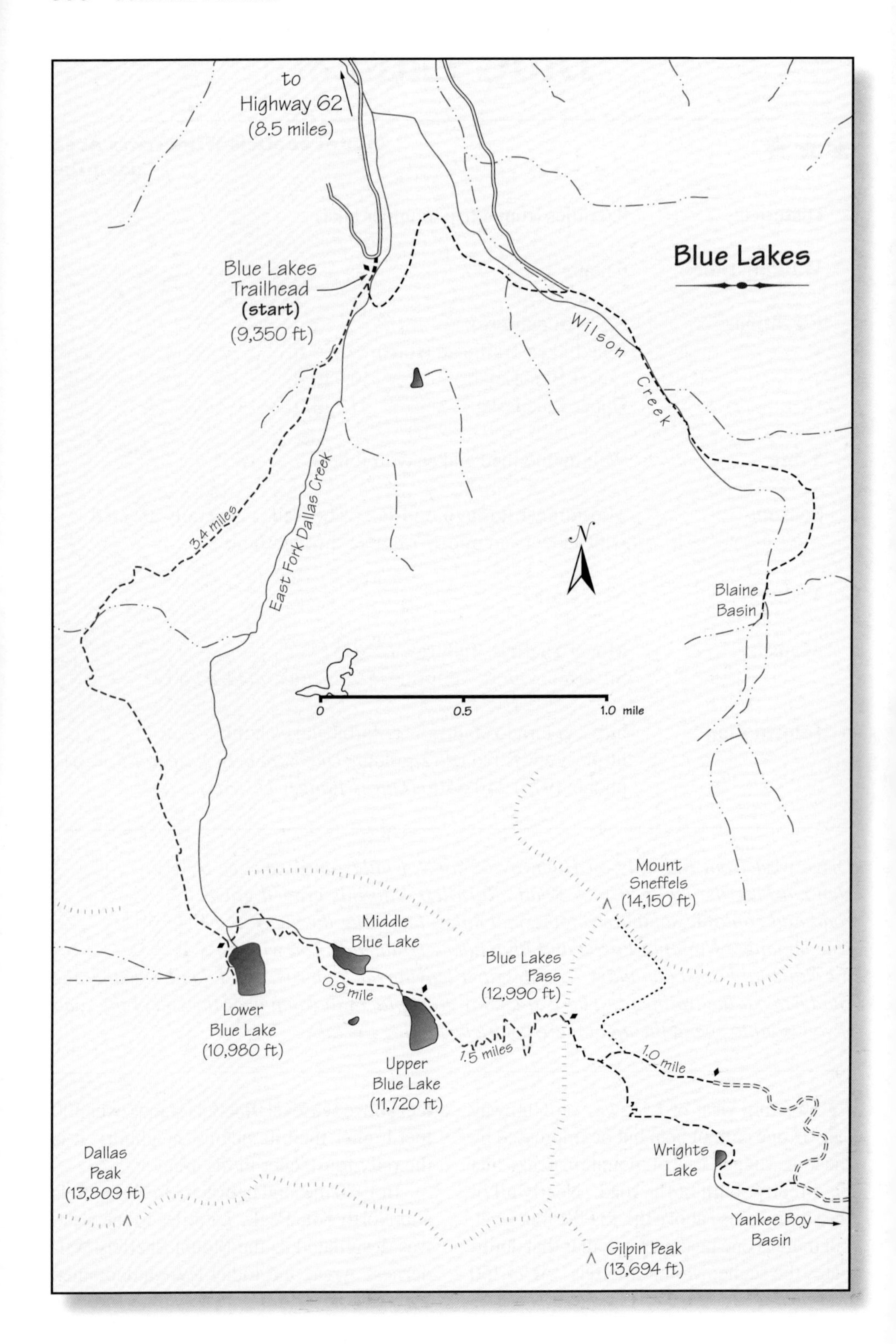

Blue Lakes
to
Highway 62
(8.5 miles)
Blue Lakes
Trailhead
(start)
(9,350 ft)
Wilson
Creek
East Fork Dallas Creek
3.4 miles
N
Blaine
Basin
0
0.5
1.0 mile
Mount
Sneffels
(14,150 ft)
Middle
Blue Lake
Blue Lakes
Pass
(12,990 ft)
0.9 mile
Lower
Blue Lake
(10,980 ft)
Upper
Blue Lake
(11,720 ft)
1.5 miles
1.0 mile
Wrights
Lake
Dallas
Peak
(13,809 ft)
Yankee Boy
Basin
Gilpin Peak
(13,694 ft)

can gaze at the dramatic mountain scenery without feeling the urge to explore. There are only a few trails leading into the wilderness area, but in my opinion the Blue Lakes Trail ranks among the best. The three Blue Lakes are the only large bodies of water in the 16,505-acre wilderness, and they are spectacularly situated in the East Dallas Drainage just west of Mount Sneffels. All of the lakes can easily be visited in one day, but if you are interested in an overnighter there are several excellent camp sites on the north side of the lower Blue Lake. Mount Sneffels can be clearly seen from all three lakes. It lies only 0.8 miles east of the upper lake, and in fact is often climbed as a day hike from the Blue Lakes

Middle Blue Lake

From the trailhead the path goes south for two hundred feet before arriving at the Blaine Basin Trail Junction. The Blue Lakes Trail bears right here and continues along the side of East Fork Dallas Creek for a short distance before turning up the west side of the steep valley. There are few level areas along the lower part of the trail; most of the time you will be angling upward along the steep sides of the drainage through a thick forest of Engelmann spruce. After 1.6 miles the trail enters a small, steep valley on the eastern side of Wolcott Mountain, then crosses the stream at the bottom of the drainage and resumes its uphill climb. Notice the absence of large trees in this small valley—a clear sign of avalanche activity. For 150 yards on the south side of the stream you won't see any trees taller than about 15 feet, and looking up you can easily imagine the torrent of snow that occasionally rages down the precipitous slopes of the mountain. Not a good place to be in the wintertime. After leaving the avalanche chute the trail bends to the left and continues climbing at a somewhat more gradual rate, finally returning to the East Fork of Dallas Creek some 1.4 miles later. Lower Blue Lake is just above the point where the trail reaches the creek.

Although this hike is described as a day hike, many people choose to spend the night at the lower Blue Lake. There are several fine campsites amidst a grove of tall trees along the western shore. When I camped there in the summer of 2000 I had a close encounter with a large red fox that seemed to be making a routine inspection of the campground about an hour before sunset. He was very daring, and although he was keeping a close eye on me he was at one point only 15 feet away. It was the only time I have ever seen this reclusive species so close, and the experience was thrilling. The fox stood about 2 feet high, larger than I would have expected, and he had the most beautiful coat I have ever seen on an animal. Shades of reddish brown, with an exquisite bushy tail fully three feet long tipped on the end with a large tuft of snowy white fur.

Campers can also enjoy a magnificent view of Mount Sneffels above the east side of Lower Blue Lake. The peak looks very foreboding from this angle, with a series of heavily eroded serrations on its slopes and jagged, rocky pinnacles on its ridges. The assent to the summit via the south slope is not as difficult as it looks from this angle, although it is certainly a challenging climb.

To reach the other two Blue Lakes you must backtrack to a trail junction just below Lower Blue Lake and turn right across a primitive log bridge that spans East Fork Dallas Creek. This trail climbs past the other lakes on its way to Blue Lakes Pass. The cirque in which the middle and upper lakes are located is 600 feet higher that lower Blue Lake, and as you climb up the east side of the lower basin you will be treated to a number of fine views of the lake below. Lower Blue is located in an almost perfectly circular bowl with extremely steep sides. Dallas Peak (13,809 ft.) rises from the jagged ridge south of the lake, and the scree from its heavily eroded slopes appears to be slowly filling the lake with rocks.

Lower Blue Lake

East Fork Dallas Creek

By the time you reach the upper basin you will be well above timberline, and as the trail levels off you will enter a world of gently rolling hills richly carpeted with the grasses and wild flowers of the alpine tundra. The trail first skirts around the west side of middle Blue Lake, the smallest of the three, and then climbs another 200 feet to the slightly larger upper lake. On a clear day the peaceful landscape of the upper basin seems to foster a mood of great tranquility. However, lest you forget where you are, the peaceful meadow is surrounded on three sides by a 13,000-foot ridge punctuated by Dallas Peak, Gilpin Peak, and Mount Sneffels. It is altogether a wondrous place to spend a few hours thinking about what it means to be alive on God's earth.

Yankee Boy Basin

The Blue Lakes can also be reached from Yankee Boy Basin near Ouray. Drive south from Ouray towards Silverton on Highway 550. Just 0.3 miles from town you will see a graded gravel road near a sign that says Camp Bird and Yankee Boy Basin. Turn right here and follow the signs for the next 9.6 miles to the end of the road at the top of Yankee Boy Basin. After 5.0 miles, just above the Camp Bird Mine, the road starts to get very rough, and you may not be able to get beyond that point with a 2WD car. Another 2.7 miles will bring you to a small parking area where the Forest Service has erected an outhouse. You definitely will not be able to get beyond that point without a 4WD vehicle.

1.0 mile beyond the Forest Service outhouse the road passes Wright's Lake Trailhead, where you can begin your hike to the Blue Lakes. Alternatively, if you are still driving (and your car is still in one piece!) you can continue another 0.9 mile to the Blue Lakes Trailhead at the end of the road and begin your hike from there. From the Wright's Lake Trailhead the distance to the top of Blue Lakes Pass is 1.6 miles with an elevation gain of 1,230 feet. If you begin at the end of the road the distance to the top of the pass will be 1.0 mile with an elevation gain of 600 feet. When you reach the summit of Blue Lakes Pass you will be treated to a gorgeous view of Upper Blue Lake 1,270 feet below. The trail down to the lake is 1.5 miles long.

Mount Sneffels

As mentioned earlier, Mount Sneffels is often climbed as a day trip from the Blue

Yellow-bellied Marmot

Lakes. If you are considering this, however, you should be aware that this climb is considerably more challenging than the other fourteener assents described in this book, and I would not recommend it unless you have had previous mountaineering experience. The south slope of Sneffels is usually classified as a class 2+ climb: harder than Colorado's class 1 and class 2 walkups, but not as hard as the class 3 routes up the Maroon Bells and the Crestones. In his book, *Colorado's Fourteeners*, Gerry Roach describes it as a good climb for "someone who has climbed all the easy fourteeners and wants a taste of what the harder ones are like".[6]

The easiest route up Sneffels begins on the Blue Lakes Trail just 0.5 mile below the east side of Blue Lakes Pass in Yankee Boy Basin. There you will see a large cairn marking the point where the Sneffels Trail departs from the Blue Lakes Trail. The faint trail first zigzags up a wide, rocky couloir to a 13,500-foot-high saddle between Sneffels and the nearby Kismet Peak. There is no trail above the saddle, but the established route continues westward up another small, steep couloir that extends to within 150 feet of the summit. Just before reaching the end of the smaller couloir you must exit via a 30-foot V-shaped crack on the left, and then scramble up the last 200 feet to the top.

If you intend to climb Sneffels I suggest you read Gerry Roach's description of the assent route before starting out. Another excellent description of this climb can be found in Kelvin Kent's *Ouray Hiking Guide*.[7]

---

[6] Gerry Roach, *Colorado's Fourteeners: from Hikes to Climbs*, Fulcrum Publishing, Golden, Colorado, 1999.
[7] Kelvin Kent, *Ouray Hiking Guide*, Wayfinder Press, Ridgway, Colorado, 1999.

Upper Blue Lake

Sneffels Highline Trail

★★★★

Mount Sneffels Wilderness Area
day hike

Distance:	13.4 miles (loop)
Walking time:	9 1/2 hours
Elevations:	3,500 ft. gain/loss Cornet Creek Trailhead (start): 8,900 ft. Pack Basin Pass: 12,250 ft. Mill Creek Basin: 11,100 ft. Epees Park: 9,640 ft.
Trail:	Well marked, well maintained
Season:	Midsummer through mid-fall. The trail is generally covered with snow from mid-November through June.
Vicinity:	Near Telluride
Maps:	Telluride *(USGS)* Silverton, Ouray, Telluride *(Trails Illustrated, #141)*
Information:	http://colorado.utahtrails.com/highlinetrail.html http://www.fs.fed.us/r2/gmug/ *(Uncompahgre National Forest)* phone: (970) 327-4261 *(Norwood Ranger District)*

This hike begins just 300 yards from downtown Telluride. Go to Aspen Street on the west side of the business district and walk north for 4 blocks until the street dead ends. There you will see a large signboard marking the trailhead.

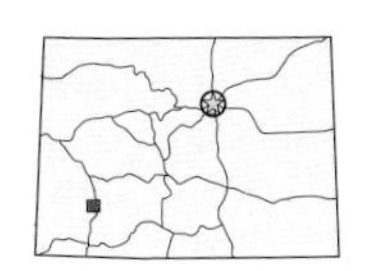

Where else but in Telluride could one ever expect to find a scenic 13-mile alpine loop trail that begins practically in the center of town! The Sneffels Highline Trail is a Colorado classic, and it is a fitting addition to one of the most interesting and picturesque towns in the state.

Telluride is almost completely surrounded by mountains, and hiking is a popular summer sport among its residents. Many of the nearby trails and bike paths follow old mining roads that were built during the first half of the last century. Some sections of the Sneffels Highline Trail also follow these older trails, but in 1990 the Forest Service undertook a project to create a loop by connecting several of the older trails north of the city. The result of the effort was the Snef-

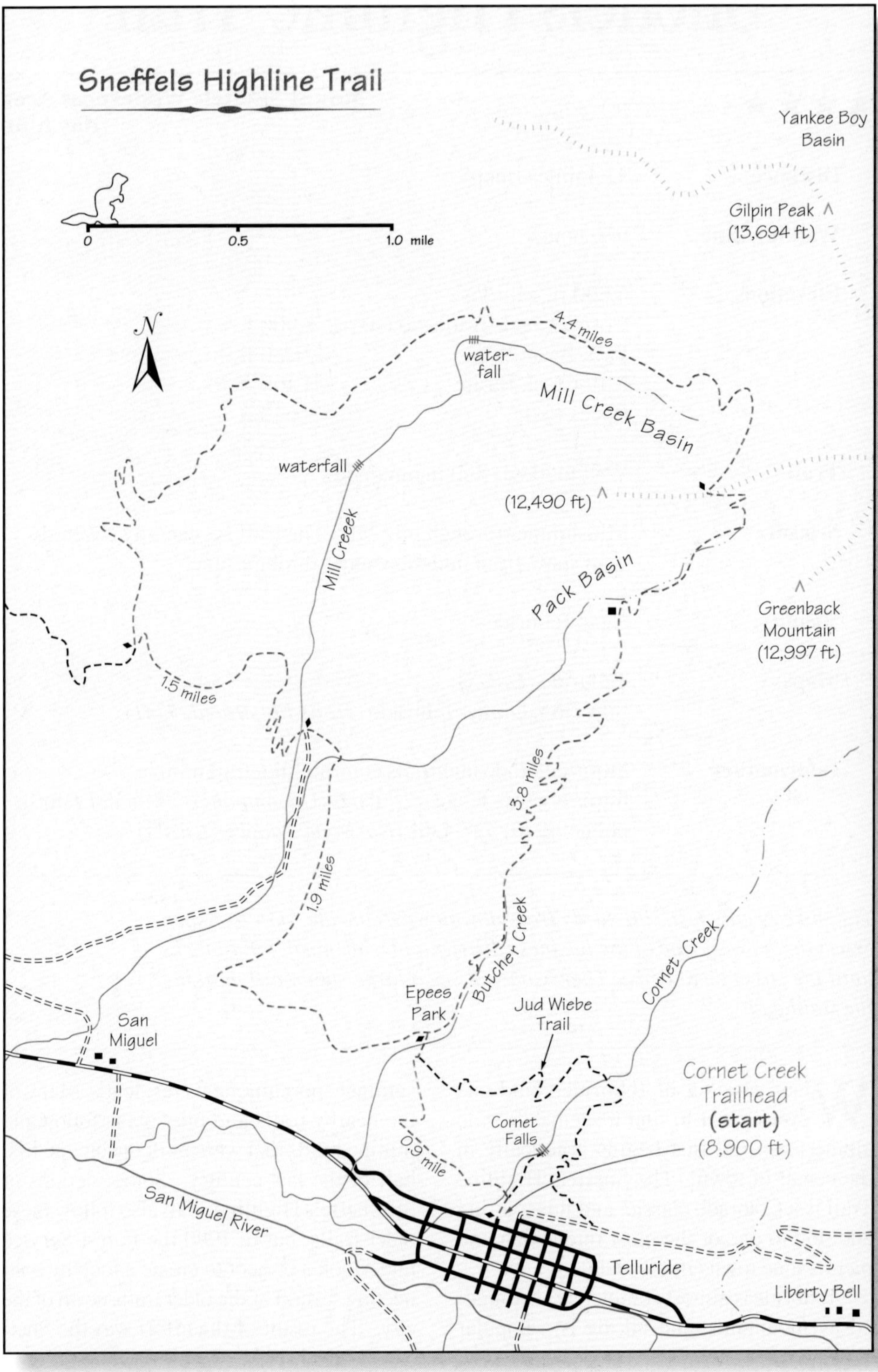

Sneffels Highline Trail
0
0.5
1.0 mile
N
Yankee Boy Basin
Gilpin Peak (13,694 ft)
4.4 miles
water-fall
Mill Creek Basin
waterfall
(12,490 ft)
Mill Creeek
Pack Basin
Greenback Mountain (12,997 ft)
1.5 miles
3.8 miles
1.9 miles
Butcher Creek
Cornet Creek
Epees Park
Jud Wiebe Trail
San Miguel
Cornet Creek Trailhead (start) (8,900 ft)
Cornet Falls
0.9 mile
San Miguel River
Telluride
Liberty Bell

fels Highline Trail. The trail was so named because two miles of the loop lie within the Mount Sneffels Wilderness Area, and it is hoped that someday this part of the trail will be extended further into the preserve.

The trail starts out along the east side of Cornet Creek, but after just 100 feet you will come to a small footbridge that you must cross to the west side of the stream. (The trail up the east side of the creek ends at Cornet Falls 0.2 miles away.) After crossing the bridge you will be on the Jud Wiebe Trail, named after a locally famous forest ranger who died of cancer in 1986.

As the path climbs along the slopes northwest of Telluride it passes some great views of the town and the valley below. Telluride is located in the bottom of a deep glacial valley with an extraordinarily flat bottom and high mountains on three sides. Many of the peaks on the north, east, and south sides of the town are over 12,000 feet high and a few exceed 13,000 feet. The town is an ideal location for a ski resort, and many sky runs are clearly evident on the slopes across of the valley. You can also see the gondolas on the Mountain Village tramway creeping slowly up the side of the mountain, and as you gain altitude the Mountain Village itself will begin to come into view.

Initially you will be walking through a forest of Douglas fir, but as the trail climbs higher it enters an aspen forest. After 0.9 mile you will come to a small sign marking the junction where the Mill Creek Trail departs from the Jud Wiebe Trail. The Mill Creek Trail is one of the trails that comprise the Sneffels Highline Loop, and you must bear left at this point. Within two minutes after leaving the Jud Wiebe Trail the path crosses Butcher Creek and comes to another junction. This is the start of the Sneffels

Ski trails above Telluride

Old miners cabin below Pack Basin

Highline Loop, and I suggest that you turn right at this point. Some hikers prefer to bear left at the junction because the uphill portion of the trail is not quite as steep if the hike is walked in a clockwise direction. However in my opinion the scenery is slightly better if the loop is followed in a counterclockwise direction, and that is the route I will describe here.

Between 1901 and about 1916 there was a large building in Epees Park, the flat area where the Jud Wiebe and Sneffels Highline Trail junctions are located. The building was called the "county pest house", and its purpose was a quarantine facility for victims of pestilence (diphtheria, scarlet fever, and other contagious diseases). Unfortunately there is no trace of the building now, but you can still see remnants of an historic waterline that once carried water through Eppes Park to the town below.

After leaving Epees Park the Sneffels Highline Trail follows Butcher Creek to its source, 0.6 miles away, and then continues climbing northward up the steep canyon. After you have climbed about 1,500 feet from the junction the trail passes a notch in the ridge between Butcher Creek Canyon and Lower Mill Creek Basin where you can enjoy a fine view of the rugged country that surrounds Mill Creek. The return part of the loop crosses the western side of Lower Mill Creek Basin, but the trail is well hidden below the dense forest and can't be seen from the notch.

Another 500 feet of elevation gain will bring you to the bottom of Pack Basin, an incredibly scenic alpine bowl that lies just below the western side of Mount Emma (13,581 ft.). The trail passes the remains of an old miner's cabin as it approaches the basin, and a short while later the forest suddenly ends at the edge of the tundra. The canopy of spruce and subalpine fir gives way to an open meadow of grasses and wildflowers, protected on two sides by a ring of 12,000- and 13,000-foot peaks. Ahead the trail can be seen switchbacking up the north side of

photo by Joe Pacal

Upper Mill Creek Basin

the bowl to the top of Pack Basin Pass.

The summit of Pack Basin Pass is one of those special places in Colorado where the magic of the mountains seems to penetrate deep into one's soul. The view to the south is across Pack Basin to the ski runs above Telluride and beyond to the Lizard Head Wilderness Area. The distant skyline is dominated by Lizard Head Rock and Mount Wilson (14,246 ft.), the highest point in the San Juan Range. To the north are Mill Creek Basin, Gilpin Peak (13,694 ft.) and Dallas Peak (13,804 ft.). Mount Sneffels, one of Colorado's best-known fourteeners, is just two miles away, but unfortunately it is hidden behind Gilpin Peak.

From the top of the pass the trail descends down the western slopes of Mount Emma into Mill Creek Basin. This part of the trail is north facing and the ground is usually covered with snow well into July. The snow can make for an exciting 500-foot glissade into Mill Creek Basin, and for that reason many Telluride residents prefer to do this hike in June. Once the trail reaches the bottom of the basin it continues along the north side of Mill Creek for the next mile, past an impressive waterfall, and then veers off to the right. Keep an eye out for elk along

Mill Creek Waterfall

the sides of the basin. This area is a favorite summer grazing area for the large animals and they are seen on a fairly regular basis. Soon after the waterfall the creek turns south and drops into Lower Mill Creek Basin while the trail continues eastward into the Mount Sneffels Wilderness Area.

The trail stays in the wilderness area for 2.0 miles, then turns south along the ridge separating Mill Creek from Eider Creek. After following the ridge for ten minutes you will come to a signed junction where the trail intersects the Deep Creek Trail. The route turns left at this point and begins descending down the east side of the ridge.

After following the Deep Creek Trail for 1.5 miles you will come to a junction near Mill Creek where another trail branches off to the south and follows the creek down to Last Dollar Road. You are only 0.5 miles from the road at this point, and if you choose to turn right you will arrive at the Telluride water treatment plant after a 15-minute walk. Most people, however, prefer to bear left at the junction in order to complete the loop back to the Cornet Creek Trailhead where the hike began. This choice requires an additional 2.3 miles of walking, but it also avoids the hassle of arranging a car shuttle from the water treatment plant.

Shortly after passing the spur trail to the water treatment plant the Deep Creek Trail crosses Mill Creek and turns south along the east side of the stream. This section of trail is known locally as the Waterline Trail because it follows the route of the old waterline that once brought water from Mill Creek to Telluride. Along the way you will see bits and pieces of the waterline and its associated equipment littering the forest. The Waterline Trail follows the contour of the land south and then east for 1.9 miles to Epees Park where the Sneffels Highline Loop began. From there you can retrace your steps the last 0.9 mile down the Jud Wiebe Trail to the Cornet Creek Trailhead.

Ridge separating Mill Creek Basin from Eider Creek Basin

Lizard Head Trail

★★★★★

Lizard Head Wilderness Area
shuttle car required
overnight hike

Distance: 11.2 miles
(plus 16 miles by shuttle car)

Walking time: day 1: 7 1/4 hours
day 2: 2 hours

Elevations: 2,580 ft. gain, 3,040 ft. loss
Lizard Head Pass Trailhead (start): 10,222 ft.
highest point: 12,070 ft.
Sunshine Mesa Trailhead: 9,760 ft.

Trail: Well marked, well maintained

Season: Midsummer through mid-fall. The higher parts of the trail are usually covered with snow from November through early July.

Vicinity: near Telluride

Maps: Paradox *(USGS)*

Information: http://colorado.utahtrails.com/lizardhead.html
http://www.fs.fed.us/r2/sanjuan/ *(San Juan National Forest)*
phone: (970) 882-7296 *(Dolores Ranger District)*

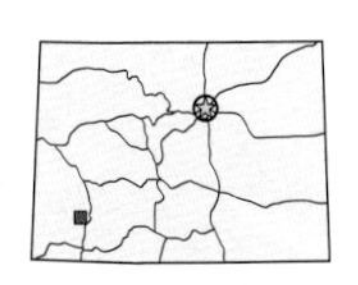

Drive west from Telluride for 3.4 miles to the 3-way junction on Highway 145. Bear right at the junction and continue west for another 2.6 miles until you come to County Road 63L, an initially paved road on your left that goes to the Ilium Church Camp. Turn south here and proceed the next 2.2 miles to Ilium. On the south side of the Ilium Camp there is a bridge that crosses the South Fork of the San Miguel River. Drive across the bridge and continue south along the west side of the river on County Road 63J. After 3.1 miles the road veers to the right and begins climbing steeply up the west side of the valley. There are several spur roads in this area that lead to private homes; just stay on the main road. 5.1 miles from Ilium the road passes several abandoned log buildings that were once part of an old dairy farm, and 300 yards later it ends at a locked gate. A nearby sign identifies this gate as the Wilson Mesa Trailhead (also called Sunshine Mesa Trailhead). This is where the hike ends and where you must leave your shuttle car.

To get to Lizard Head Pass where the hike begins you must return to Ilium and drive south on County Road 63L for 5.9 miles until it ends at Highway 145. Turn right onto the highway and continue the last 4.6 miles to the top of the pass. When you reach Lizard Head Pass you will see a sign directing you to a parking area above the north side of the pass where the Lizard Head Trailhead is located.

The Lizard Head is considered by many climbers to be the most difficult summit in Colorado. The crumbly neck of reddish-gray volcanic tuff rises 400 feet from its base to reach an elevation of 13,113 feet. The first known people to reach the top of the pinnacle were Albert Ellingwood and Barton Hoag who pioneered a route up the west face in 1920. Currently an estimated 20 to 30 people scale the peak each year, but the treacherous climb is definitely not for everyone. Impressive as it looks, the spire is little more than a heap of loose and unstable volcanic debris.

Many people hike the Lizard Head Trail only as far as the top of Bilk Basin and then return to Highway 145 by way of the Cross Mountain Trail. The total walking distance of this loop is 8.7 miles with a shuttle between the two trailheads of 2.2 miles on Highway 145. This shorter hike affords the same fine views of the Lizard Head as the hike described below, but it misses the dramatic scenery in Bilk Basin. Bilk Basin is well known for its waterfalls, one of which is 300 feet high.

Day 1 (8.0 miles)

From the top of Lizard Head Pass the trail heads northeast along the side of the hill with little change in elevation. It parallels the highway for a distance of 1.6 miles, but for most of that distance the highway cannot actually be seen from the trail. Finally, at a point above the west end of Trout Lake, the trail crosses into the Lizard Head Wilderness Area and begins climbing to the west. Over the next 0.9 mile the path gains 1,600 feet, climbing through a long series of switchbacks to the top of the Black Face Ridge.

The Lizard Head

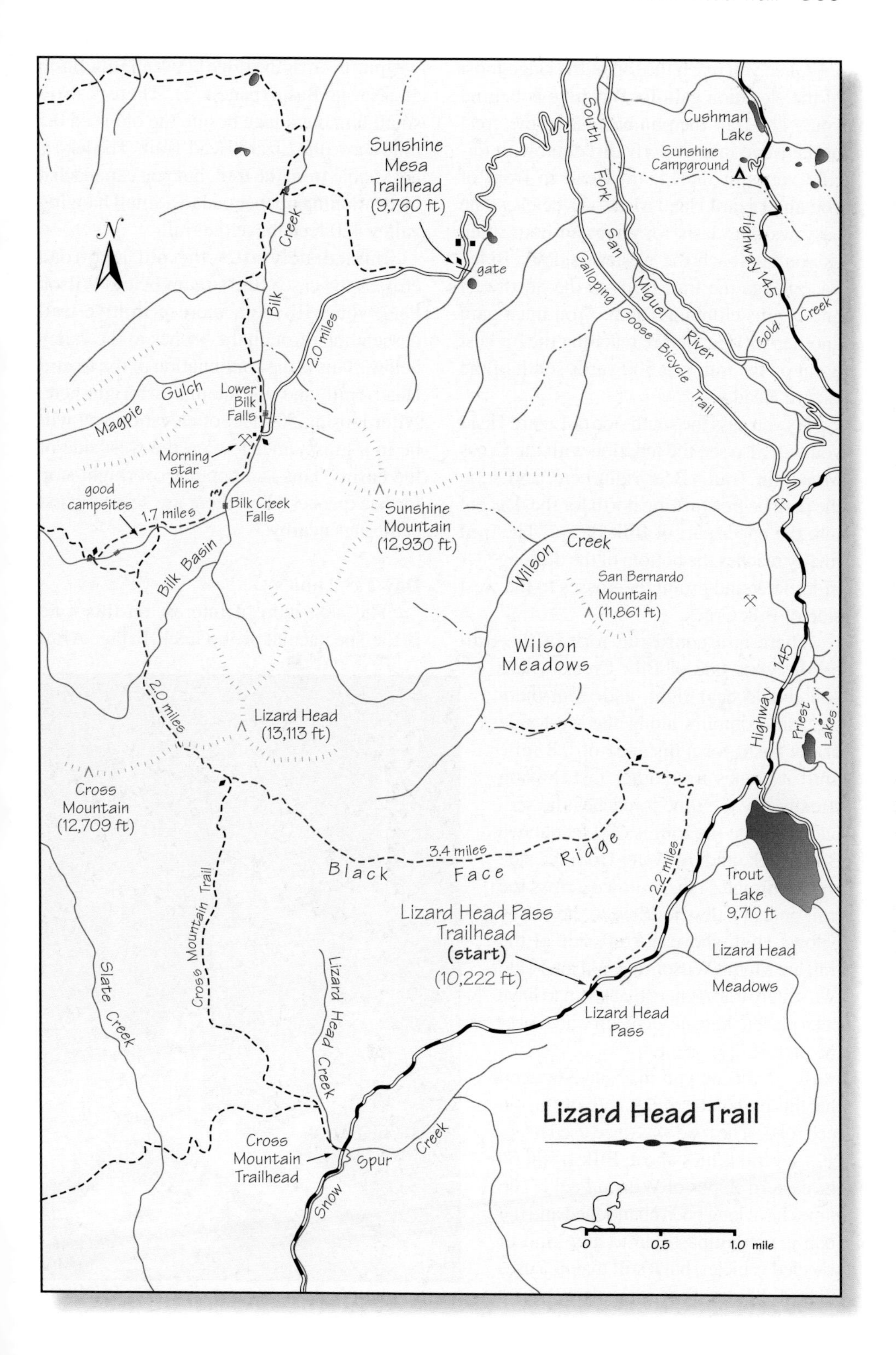
Sunshine
Mesa
Trailhead
(9,760 ft)
gate
South Fork San Miguel River
Galloping Goose Bicycle Trail
Cushman
Lake
Sunshine
Campground
Highway 145
Gold Creek
Bilk Creek
2.0 miles
Magpie Gulch
Lower
Bilk
Falls
Morning
star
Mine
good
campsites
1.7 miles
Bilk Creek
Falls
Bilk Basin
Sunshine
Mountain
(12,930 ft)
Wilson Creek
San Bernardo
Mountain
(11,861 ft)
Wilson
Meadows
Highway 145
Priest
Lakes
2.0 miles
Lizard Head
(13,113 ft)
Cross
Mountain
(12,709 ft)
3.4 miles
Black Face Ridge
2.2 miles
Trout
Lake
9,710 ft
Lizard Head Pass
Trailhead
(start)
(10,222 ft)
Lizard Head
Pass
Lizard Head
Meadows
Cross Mountain Trail
Slate Creek
Lizard Head Creek
Lizard Head Trail
Cross
Mountain
Trailhead
Snow Spur Creek
0
0.5
1.0 mile

Once you reach the top of the ridge most of the elevation gain for this hike is behind you. The trail then ambles along the crest of the ridge in a westerly direction with terrific views of the Lizard Head in front of you and Lizard Head Meadows below. The easy walking lasts for about an hour, then as you approach the western side of Black Face Ridge the trail turns to the northwest and begins climbing again. You must gain another 500 feet before reaching the highest point on the trail just 500 yards south of the Lizard Head.

As you pass the south side of Lizard Head you will also see the junction with the Cross Mountain Trail. Bear right here, and soon the path begins turning north for the descent into the upper part of Bilk Basin. The trail finally reaches the bottom of the drainage 1.1 miles later and promptly crosses to the west side of Bilk Creek.

There is a confusing fork in the trail on the west side of Bilk Creek where you should bear right, and from there the trail contours along the west side of the basin for a distance of 0.8 mile until it comes to another fast-flowing stream. By the time it reaches the second drainage the trail is 600 feet above Bilk Creek, and the water from the side stream tumbles noisily down across the trail on its restless journey to the valley below. High above the left side of the trail are Mount Wilson and Wilson Peak, two stately fourteeners that seem to have been placed there just to keep watch over the picturesque scene.

By this time you may have noticed that this part of the trail is actually an old jeep road. The road was once used to access several mines above Bilk Basin on the eastern slopes of Wilson Peak. The mines have long been abandoned and the road is now impassable to any kind of wheeled vehicles, but it still makes a useful trail. It is used occasionally by hikers wishing to cross the ridge between Bilk Basin and Navajo Basin (page 372). There is also a small unnamed lake beside the old road 0.5 mile above the Lizard Head Trail. The lake is not visible from the trail, but you can reach it by continuing up the road to a small hanging valley 420 feet above the trail.

Immediately after the old jeep road crosses the cascading stream below Wilson Peak you will see a more primitive trail descending through the bushes to the valley below. This is the continuation of the Lizard Head Trail, and you should turn right here. After loosing 500 feet of elevation you will be in a grassy meadow on the west side of the basin. This is a popular overnight stop for backpackers, and there are several good campsites nearby.

Day 2 (3.2 miles)

The next item of interest on this hike is the spectacular Bilk Creek Falls. After

Bilk Creek

leaving the meadow the trail continues to follow the stream coming down from Wilson Peak for another 0.4 mile before veering off to the north. Then after another 0.2 mile, near the confluence of Bilk Creek and its smaller tributary, the path turns east again and begins switchbacking back down to the valley floor. This is the point where Bilk Creek Falls first comes into view. The creek first plunges down a 150-foot cliff and then enters a 50-foot cascade that is followed by a sheer 100-foot drop. Of the five or six waterfalls in Bilk Basin this one is the most impressive.

When you first see Bilk Creek Falls the trail is several hundred yards away and the thick forest makes a good view impossible. However as you descend into the valley each switchback will bring you a little closer. The last switchback turns at a point that is only a few hundred feet from the base of the falls, and from there there is a very primitive and very steep hiker-made trail that drops the rest of the way down to the water. The view from the bottom of the falls is magnificent, but if you are taking photographs you had better have a wide-angle lens. I used a 24-mm lens for this photograph of Bilk Creek Falls.

0.5 mile after leaving the falls the trail leaves the Lizard Head Wilderness Area, and just beyond the boundary you will pass through the ruins of the old Morning Star Mine. The amount of junked equipment scattered about indicates that Morning Star must have been a thriving operation at one time. One of the most intriguing items is the hulk of an old 1950s vintage semi-truck trailer. It must have taken considerable effort to transport this trailer over the primitive road to the mine.

At the north end of the mining camp there is a sign marking another trail junction where you must leave the Lizard Head Trail and bear right to reach the ending trailhead. But before leaving the area you might want to take a short side trip down the Lizard Head Trail to see one last waterfall. If you bear left at the trail junction and continue down the Lizard Head Trail for just 250 yards you will pass the Lower Bilk Creek Falls.

After bearing right at the Morning Star Mine trail junction the trail crosses to the east side of Bilk Creek and begins following the old jeep road that once provided access to the mine. This last section of the trail is a pleasant walk of 2.0 miles through a shaded forest with a gradual elevation loss of 320 feet. After an hour you will come to the locked gate at Sunshine Mesa Trailhead where your shuttle is parked.

Bilk Creek Falls

Navajo Lake

Lizard Head Wilderness Area
day hike

Distance:	8.8 miles (round trip)
Walking time:	6 hours
Elevations:	2,060 ft. gain/loss Navajo Lake Trailhead (start): 9,340 ft. Navajo Lake: 11,154 ft.
Trail:	Well marked, well maintained
Season:	Midsummer through mid-fall. The higher parts of the trail are usually covered with snow from November through early July.
Vicinity:	Near Telluride
Maps:	Dolores Peak *(USGS)* Silverton, Ouray, Telluride, Lake City *(Trails Illustrated, #141)*
Information:	http://colorado.utahtrails.com/navajolake.html http://www.fs.fed.us/r2/sanjuan/ *(San Juan National Forest)* phone: (970) 882-7296 *(Dolores Ranger District)*

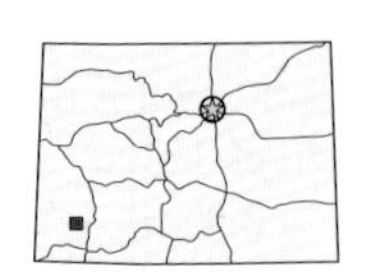

Drive west from Telluride for 3.4 miles to the junction with Highway 145, then turn left and drive south for 11.9 miles to the summit of Lizard Pass. Make a note of the mileage at the top of the pass and continue south for another 5.2 miles until you see a small sign marking Dunton Road (Forest Road 535) on the left. Turn towards Dunton, again making a note of your odometer reading. After 4.2 miles you will pass a junction with the Eagle Creek Road where you must continue straight. The turnoff to the Navajo Lake Trailhead is located 3.0 miles beyond the Eagle Creek Junction or 7.2 miles from Highway 145. When you reach the turnout turn right and drive the last 250 yards to the parking area and trailhead.

Navajo Lake is probably the most popular destination in the Lizard Head Wilderness Area. Not only is the lake itself an alpine gem, but it is located in a ruggedly beautiful basin that is surrounded on three sides by 13,000-foot ridges and three 14,000-foot peaks (Wilson Peak, Mount Wilson, and El Diente Peak). Peak baggers often use Navajo Basin as a base for climbing these three peaks.

The trail starts out in a northerly direc-

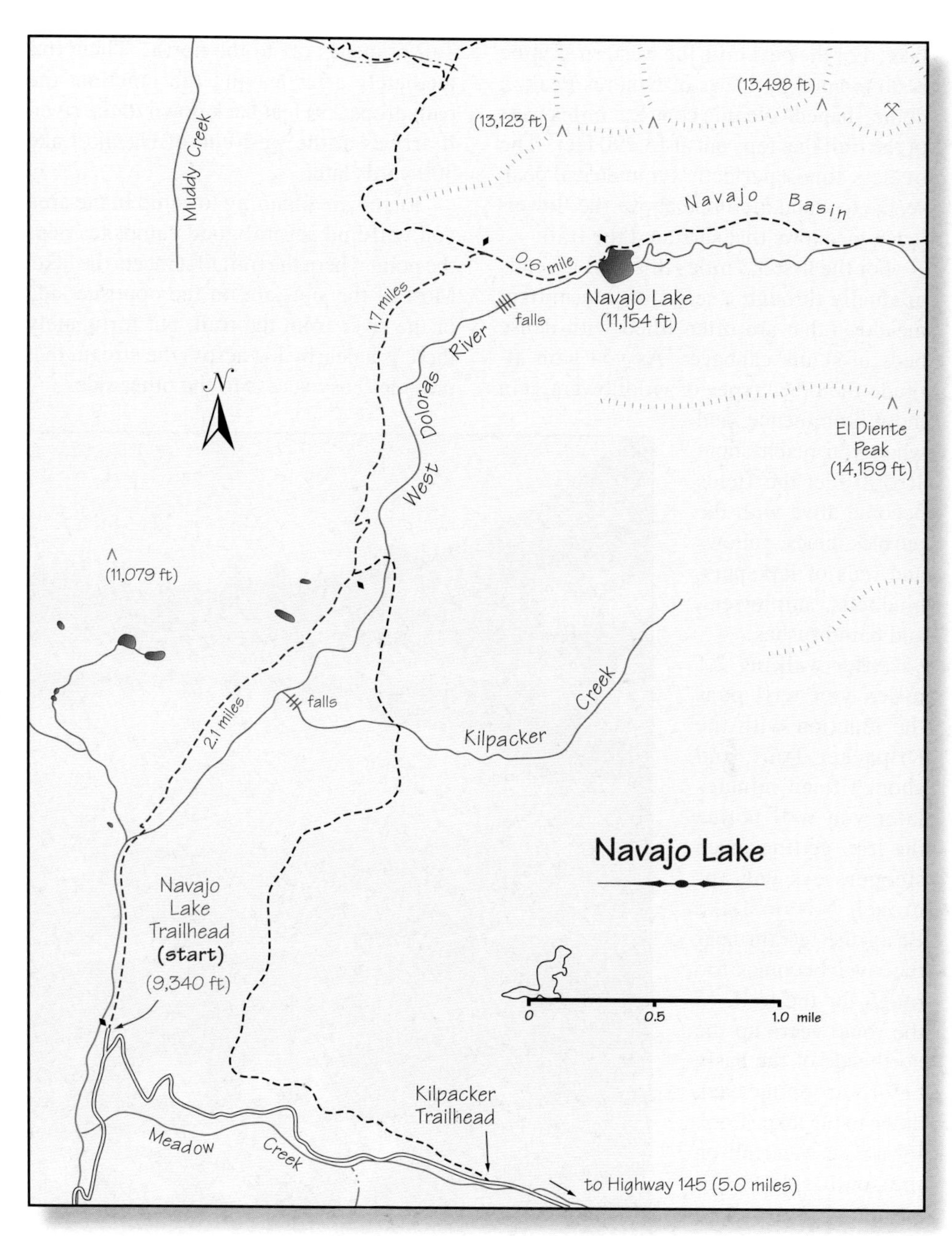

tion and proceeds through a series of grassy meadows along the east side of the West Dolores River. After five minutes you will see a wooden footbridge on the left where the Groundhog Trail crosses the river. Continue straight on the better-used Navajo Lake Trail at this point.

0.7 mile from the trailhead the path comes to a newly constructed footbridge across the West Dolores River, and then it continues to follow along the left side of the river for the rest of the way to the lake. For the next mile the western skyline is dominated by views of Dolores Peak, a dome-shaped volcanic cone 2.5 miles west of the trail that tops out at 13,290 feet. The treeless almost perfectly symmetrical peak seems to stand all alone above the flower-laden meadows that surround the trail.

For the first 3.3 miles this trail ascends gradually through a series of intermittent meadows that are often filled with dense beds of skunk cabbage. As you gain altitude the other types of wildflowers gain more prominence, and when you reach about 10,500 feet the fields become alive with the purples, blues, yellows and reds of larkspurs, bluebells, sunflowers, and paintbrushes.

After walking 2.1 miles you will pass the junction with the Kilpacker Trail, and about fifteen minutes later you will notice the trail getting much steeper. As you approach Navajo Lake Basin the terrain near the river becomes too rough for the trail, so the route veers up the north side of the basin before dropping back down to the lake. Look for a nice waterfall on the south side of the basin in this area.

After the trail has climbed 400 feet above the West Dolores River you will come to another trail junction where the Woods Lake Tail branches off to the north. Then, immediately after leaving the junction, the path drops 250 feet back down to the river. It arrives at the west end of Navajo Lake 300 yards later.

If you are planning to camp in the area you will find several good campsites near the point where the trail first meets the lake. Most of the sites are on the opposite side of the river from the trail, but fortunately there is a nearby log across the stream that provides easy access to the other side.

Navajo Lake

Black Canyon of the Gunnison

★

Black Canyon of the Gunnison National Park
day hike

Distance: 7.2 miles (round trip)

Walking time: 4 1/2 hours

Elevations: 870 ft. gain/loss
North Vista Trailhead (start): 7,700 ft.
Exclamation Point Overlook: 7,702 ft.
Green Mountain: 8,563 ft.

Trail: Well marked and easy to follow

Season: From late spring through late fall. The north rim of the park is usually closed by snow from mid-November through April.

Vicinity: Near Delta

Maps: Grizzly Ridge *(USGS)*
Black Canyon of the Gunnison *(Trails Illustrated, #245)*

Information: http://colorado.utahtrails.com/blackcanyon.html
http://www.nps.gov/blca/ *(Black Canyon of the Gunnison National Park)*
phone: (970) 641-2337 *(Park Headquarters)*

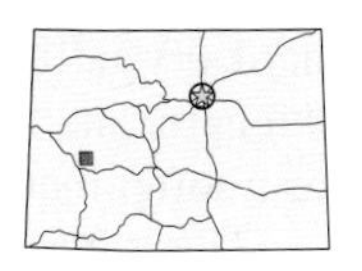

This hike begins at the ranger station on the north rim of Black Canyon of the Gunnison National Park. To get there drive east from Delta on Highway 92 for 32 miles to the farming community of Crawford. Continue past Crawford for another 3.2 miles until you come to the Black Canyon Road. Turn right here and follow the signs for another 12 miles to the ranger station where you will see a sign marking the trailhead.

The Black Canyon of the Gunnison River is surely one of the most awesome spectacles in Colorado. The canyon's average depth is 2,000 feet, and in many places it is much deeper. But the characteristic that makes the canyon so unusual is the sheerness of its walls. At the Painted Wall, for example, the gorge is 2,300 feet deep, yet the horizontal distance from the river to the edge of the north rim is scarcely 500 feet.

Adding to the visual effect of the seemingly bottomless chasm is the dark color of the metamorphic gneiss and schist that make up most of the inner canyon walls. This an-

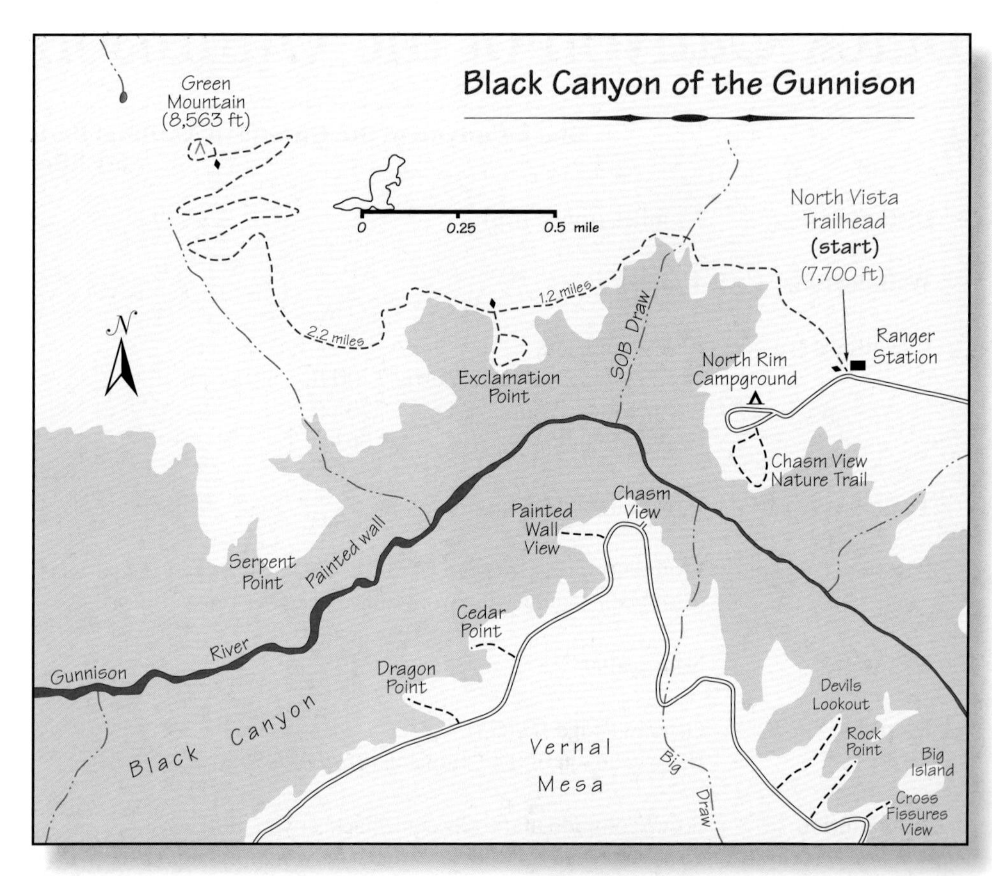

cient stone was formed during Precambrian time and is well over a billion years old. It is also extremely hard, and to a large extent that is why the walls are so sheer. The hard, crystalline rock has great compressive strength, and it does not erode away as fast as a softer material might.

There are scenic drives on both the north and south rims of the Black Canyon, and the Park Service has established overlook points on both rims from where you can gaze into the canyon. There are also several relatively safe, non-technical routes into the canyon if you are inclined to climb down to the water. These routes generally involve less than 2 miles, round trip, of scrambling, but the climb out is very strenuous. The rangers can tell you more about these routes.

The North Vista Trail described here

Black Canyon of the Gunnison

View from the top of Green Mountain

does not actually go inside the canyon, but it goes to the Exclamation Point Overlook which will give you a fine overview of the canyon. It also goes to the top of Green Mountain, which will give you as close to an aerial view of the canyon as you can get from the ground. Furthermore this trail is on the less-traveled north rim side of the park, where you might be able to enjoy a measure of solitude on your walk.

From the ranger station the trail proceeds west through the sagebrush and pinion/juniper forest for 0.3 mile to the edge of the Black Canyon Gorge. It then parallels the rim of the canyon above SOB draw for the next 0.9 mile, passing several unnamed overlook points along the way. Finally, 1.2 mile from the ranger station you will come to a signed spur trail that goes the last 0.2 mile to Exclamation Point.

Exclamation Point is situated high above a large bend in the canyon, giving you the opportunity to look down the gorge in two directions. The canyon is 1,900 feet deep at this point, and the Gunnison River is clearly visible below. Unlike the park's other viewpoints, there are no guardrails here, so be careful.

From Exclamation Point the trail veers away from the canyon through the pinion and juniper trees in a northwesterly direction. After 2.2 miles it breaks out of the trees at the top of a nearby hill called Green Mountain. Green Mountain is only 860 feet higher than the canyon rim, but it offers another interesting perspective on Black Canyon. You can also see several other nearby Colorado landmarks from the summit, including the San Juan Mountains, the West Elks, and Grand Mesa.

Looking into Black Canyon from Exclamation Point

Gunnison Gorge

★ **day hike**

Distance:	9.0 miles (round trip)
Walking time:	5 1/2 hours
Elevations:	1,230 ft. loss/gain Ute Park Trailhead (start): 6,520 ft. Gunnison River: 5,290 ft.
Trail:	Well maintained, well defined trail
Season:	Mid-spring through late fall. The primitive road to the trailhead is usually inaccessible from late November until April.
Vicinity:	near Delta
Maps:	Black Ridge *(USGS)* Black Canyon of the Gunnison *(Trails Illustrated, #245)*
Information:	http://colorado.utahtrails.com/gunnisongorge.html http://www.co.blm.gov/ubra/ *(BLM, Montrose)* phone: (970) 240-5300 *(Uncompahgre Field Office)*

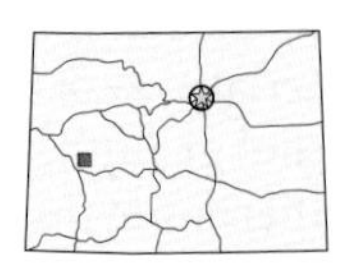

Drive south from Delta on Highway 50 for 8.8 miles until you see a paved road on the left and a sign that says "Carnation Road". Turn left here and drive for another 3.0 miles where Carnation Road ends at a gravel road called Road 6200. Turn left again and drive north on Road 6200. After driving about a mile on the gravel road you will begin to parallel an irrigation canal, and at 1.3 miles you will come to a fork where you must bear right across the canal. You are now on Road 2445. After crossing the canal you must drive another 2.5 miles on Road 2445 until it ends at Peach Valley Road. Turn left onto Peach Valley Road and drive north for 0.4 mile until you see another small sign next to an ungraded road on the right that says "Ute Trail 2.5 miles". The Ute Trailhead is at the end of this road. Ordinary cars can usually handle the first 1.4 miles of this ungraded road, but unless you have a pickup or other high clearance vehicle you will probably have to pull over and walk the last 1.1 miles to the trailhead.

The Gunnison Gorge Wilderness Study Area was established by the BLM in 1978 in order to preserve a 13-mile stretch of the Gunnison River below the Black Canyon of the Gunnison National Park while it is being considered as a possible

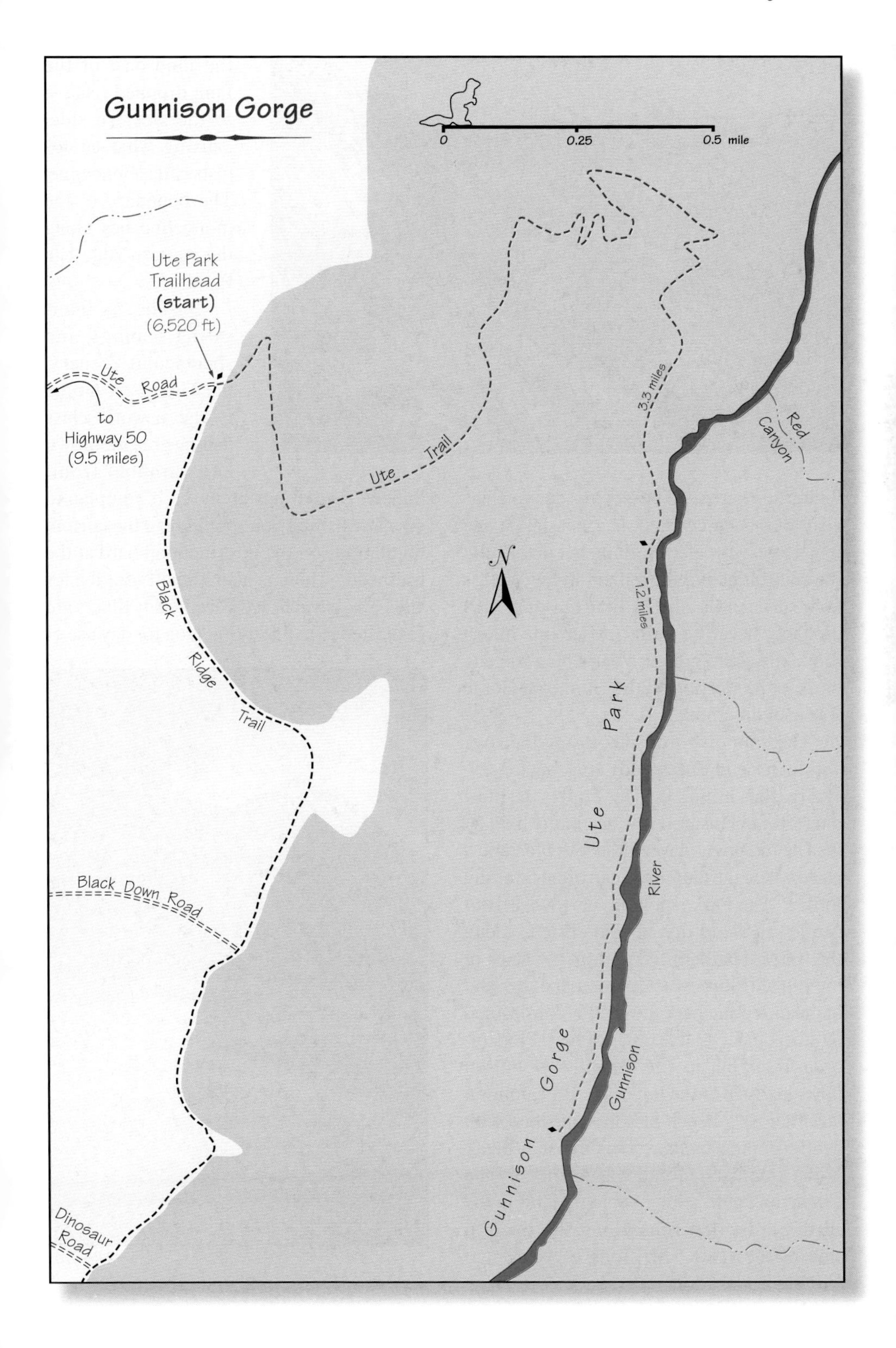
Gunnison Gorge
0
0.25
0.5 mile
Ute Park
Trailhead
(start)
(6,520 ft)
Ute Road
to
Highway 50
(9.5 miles)
Ute Trail
3.3 miles
Red Canyon
1.2 miles
Black Ridge Trail
Ute Park
River
Black Down Road
Gunnison Gorge
Gunnison
Dinosaur Road
N

Ute Trail

the land east of the fault dropped relative to the western side, causing what geologists call a monocline. The boundary of the monocline lies along the western edge Ute Park.

Besides its interesting geology and spectacular scenery, the Gunnison Gorge is also a world class fishing area for brown and rainbow trout. Special regulations apply, so if you plan to do some fishing you should read the current regulations on the information board at the trailhead. There is also a small user fee for Ute Park, payable at the trailhead; hikers are requested to pay $3.00/person for day use or

wilderness area. The scenic canyon has also long been coveted as a possible a site for a large hydroelectric dam, but thankfully the environmental movement in the West is now sufficiently strong that the dam will probably never be built. After this hike I think you will agree, it would be a tragedy of major proportions if the Gunnison Gorge was ever dammed.

There are five trails accessing the river within the wilderness study area, but for several reasons I think the Ute Trail is the most interesting. This trail was originally built by the Ute Indians as a way to access Ute Park, a place where the Gunnison can often be easily forded. Ute Park is a long, narrow shelf of gentle grassland that appears briefly along the western bank of the river in the heart of the rugged Gunnison Gorge. On either end of the mile-long park the river is constrained by steep, inaccessible cliffs of hard Precambrian rock, but in Ute Park the Gunnison flows lazily over the top of the Precambrian layer across a bench of soft sandstone with gently sloping banks. This unusual break in the Gunnison Gorge was formed by the Cimarron Fault, a long geologic fault in the earth's crust that runs along the western side of the river. Millions of years ago

Ute Trail

$5.00/person for overnight use.

From the rim of the canyon the trail winds down through a large amphitheater filled with pinion pine and juniper trees to the head of a small drainage 450 feet below the trailhead. It then follows the drainage to a bench of smooth, reddish Entrada Sandstone that lies some 700 feet above the river. Having reached this plateau the path turns northward for 0.7 mile before turning east again for another descent through a layer of black schist and gneiss. Surprisingly, when you finish the second descent you will be back at the top of the Entrada Sandstone again! This is because the trail makes its descent at the precise boundary of a monocline, and you must drop about 400 feet, just as the land has dropped, to stay on the top of the Entrada Formation.

Upon reaching the lower bench the trail turns south again and continues downward to Ute Park. But before you continue you should take a short spur trail a few hundred yards to the end of a long hourglass-shaped outcropping of slickrock sandstone that overlooks the river. At the end of the point you will be rewarded with a marvelous view of the gorge below.

About 0.8 mile further will bring you to the northern edge of Ute Park, and from there the trail continues south, along the river for another 1.0 mile to the southern edge of the park. As you walk notice the black cliffs of Precambrian rock on the west side of the park at the boundary of the monocline. Gradually the cliffs close in on the flat, sandy bench, making it impossible to continue.

This part of the Gunnison River is also popular among river rafters, and you will probably see some of them at the campsites in Ute Park. Most of the rafters put in at the end of the Chukar Trail about five miles further upstream and float to the North Fork River, a total of 13 miles. (All of their gear must be carried down the 1.1 mile Chukar Trail on pack animals.)

Gunnison River

Roubideau Trail/Pool Creek

★

shuttle car or bicycle required
day hike

Distance: 5.7 miles
(plus 2.8 miles by shuttle car or bicycle)

Walking time: 3 3/4 hours

Elevations: 1,010 ft. loss, 1,240 ft. gain

Roubideau Trailhead (start):	9,450 ft.
Pool Creek:	8,440 ft.
Pool Creek Trailhead:	9,680 ft.

Trail: Poorly marked. You should carry a compass on this hike in case you loose the trail.

Season: Midsummer through mid-fall. The road to the trailhead is usually closed from mid-November through early July.

Vicinity: Near Montrose

Maps: Antone Spring *(USGS)*

Information: http://colorado.utahtrails.com/roubideautrail.html
http://www.fs.fed.us/r2/gmug/ *(Uncompahgre National Forest)*
phone: (970) 327-4261 *(Norwood Ranger District)*

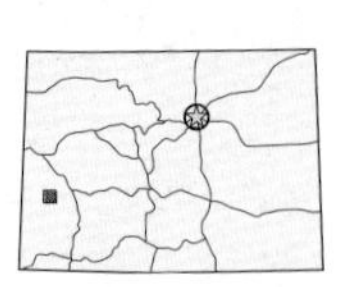

Look for the junction with Highways 50, 550, and 90 in downtown Montrose. Check your odometer here and turn west, staying on Highway 90 for the next 23.5 miles as it climbs out of the farmland into Uncompahgre National Forest. Finally you will come to a signed junction where Highway 90 turns to the left towards Nucla. Bear right at this junction and begin following the signs toward Columbine Pass. 5.4 miles after leaving Highway 90 you will come to a small road on the right that leads to the Pool Creek Trailhead, 0.2 miles off the main road. This is where the hike will end. (Don't confuse the Pool Creek Trailhead road with a logging road you will pass 1.9 miles earlier near a sign that says "Pool Creek".)

Exactly 1.6 miles past the turnout to Pool Creek Trailhead you will come to another road called the East Bull Road. Turn right here and drive north for 1.0 miles until you see a small cabin on the left side of the road near a large pasture. Just across the road from the cabin there is a small sign marking the Roubideau Trailhead where the hike begins.

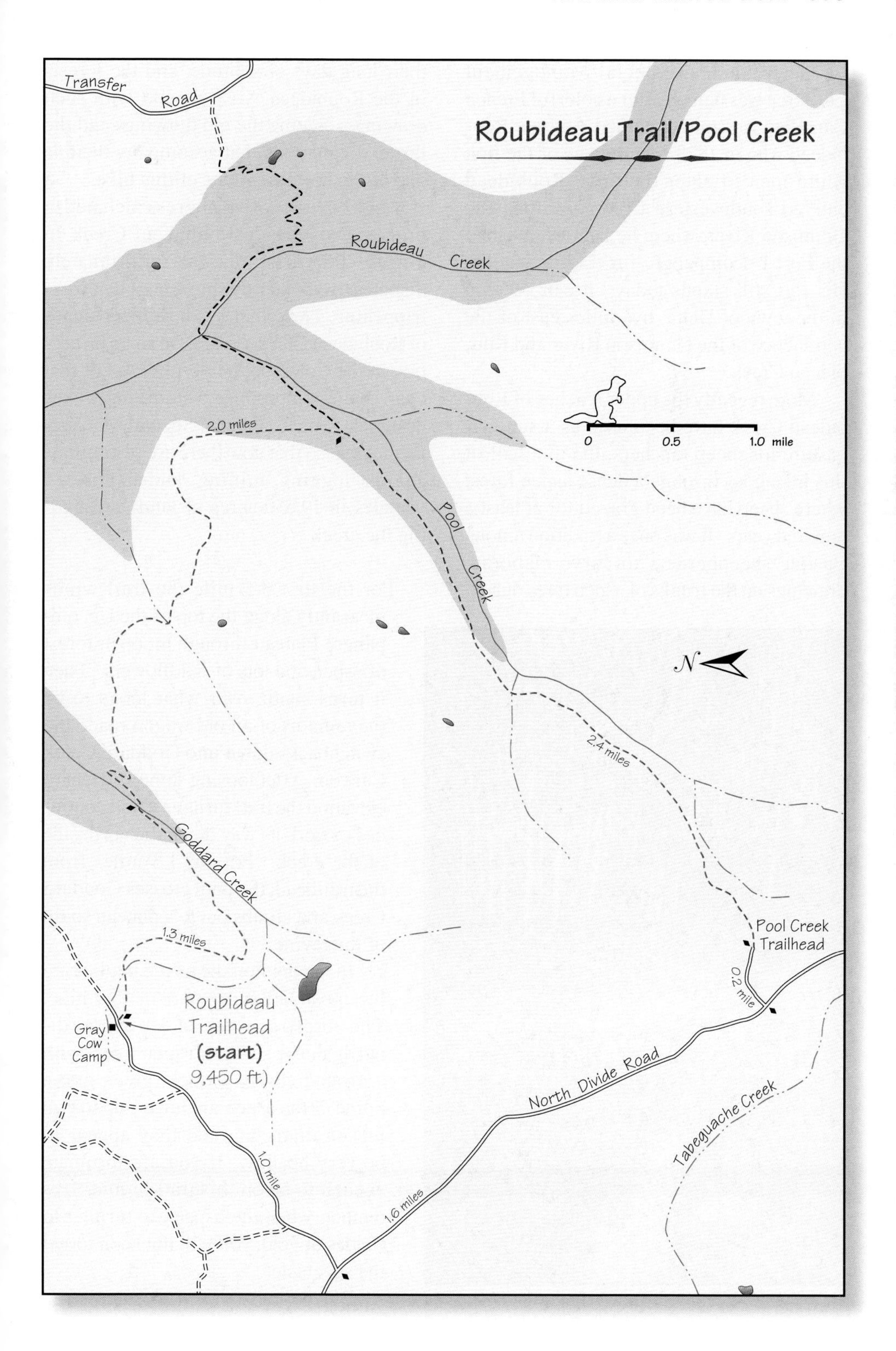

Roubideau Trail/Pool Creek
Transfer Road
Roubideau Creek
Pool Creek
Goddard Creek
2.0 miles
2.4 miles
1.3 miles
0.2 mile
1.0 mile
1.6 miles
0
0.5
1.0 mile
N
Pool Creek Trailhead
Roubideau Trailhead (start) 9,450 ft)
Gray Cow Camp
North Divide Road
Tabeguache Creek

The Roubideau Special Management Area was named after a colorful French Canadian fur trapper named Antoine Roubideau who in 1828 became one of the first white men to enter the area. Roubideau entered southwestern Colorado along the Gunnison River, where he later established the Fort Uncompahgre fur trading station. His fort still stands today. It can be seen in the town of Delta, five miles east of the confluence of the Gunnison River and Roubideau Creek.

More recently the upper reaches of Roubideau Creek have been used as a summer pasture for sheep ranchers; the first half of this hike goes through a dense aspen forest where sheep have been grazed for at least a hundred years. It was once a tradition among Basque sheepherders to carve elaborate drawings on the trunks of aspen trees during their long days of solitude, and the forests in the Roubideau Area abound with such drawings. Seeing the old drawings and the flowery signatures that accompany them is one of the key attractions of this hike.

In 1993 the US Congress debated a proposal to include Roubideau Creek in a new wilderness area, but unfortunately disputes over water use prevented that from happening. Nevertheless, the upper reaches of Roubideau Creek did receive some protection in the Colorado Wilderness Act of that year. As a compromise, the drainage was designated the Roubideau Special Management Area, so that now there are restrictions against logging, mining, and motorized vehicles in 19,650 acres of land surrounding the creek.

For the first 0.5 mile the trail winds pleasantly along the top of the Uncompahgre Plateau through an open forest of aspen and lots of wildflowers. Then it turns south, over what looks to be the remains of an old wagon road, and switchbacks down into Goddard Creek Canyon. After loosing some 200 feet of elevation the trail turns east and continues to work its way down the north side of the creek. Finally, 1.3 miles from the trailhead, the path crosses Goddard Creek and climbs out to a plateau south of the ravine.

Roubideau Trail

In my opinion the next 2.0 miles are the most satisfying part of this hike. The forest consists of an extraordinarily dense stand of aspen trees, with a ground cover of thick, green grass. Some of the aspen are huge—up to two feet in diameter—and they appear to be very healthy. If you are fortunate enough to be on this trail in mid-September, when the aspen are turning to shades of gold, you will not soon forget the spectacle.

But perhaps the most interesting

Aspen art near the Roubideau Trail

part of this aspen forest is the artwork that decorates the trees. As mentioned earlier, the plateau has long been used as a summer grazing area for sheep ranchers, and for as long as there have been sheep in Colorado there have been sheep herders carving their names and sketches into the trunks of aspen trees. Many of the drawings are so old and weathered they are difficult to interpret, but others are in surprisingly good condition. The oldest dated drawing I saw was carved in 1931.

Unfortunately the Roubideau trail begins to fade about a mile after leaving Goddard Creek. Initially the route is well marked by blaze marks on the aspens, but after the first mile the marks become scarcer and eventually they disappear altogether. The trail persists, but it is often difficult to follow in the tall grass, so it is good to carry a compass. If you loose the trail just continue in a southeasterly direction until you run into Pool Creek Canyon, an unmistakable 300-foot-deep gorge with a small creek flowing through the bottom.

According to most maps the Roubideau Trail meets the Pool Creek Trail in the bottom of the drainage 0.3 mile south of Roubideau Creek. However when I did this hike in 2001 the trail I was following met the Pool Creek Trail 150 feet above the bottom of the canyon and 0.6 mile upstream from the Roubideau Creek confluence. There is probably more than one trail in the area, but it doesn't really matter. Any secondary Roubideau Trails must end at Pool Creek, and any secondary Pool Creek Trails must follow the northwest side to the canyon to the Pool Creek Trailhead. In some ways the uncertainty of the route between Goddard Creek and Pool Creek is a bonus. The walk across the grassy plateau is so pleasant and the solitude of the aspen forest so satisfying that it is often more fun not to be on a trail at all.

Once on the Pool Creek Trail you will be heading gradually uphill for the next 2.4 miles to the Pool Creek Trailhead. Soon most of the aspen trees will be left behind, to be replaced by a forest of spruce and subalpine fir. The trail slowly improves as you continue upward and eventually becomes a well-trodden path. Finally, the path turns to the right to climb out of the top of the drainage, and 0.5 mile later you will see the trailhead signboard in front of you.

More aspen art near the Roubideau Trail

Crag Crest Trail

★★★ **day hike**

Distance:	9.0 miles (loop)
Walking time:	5 1/2 hours
Elevations:	1,160 ft. gain/loss Crag Crest East Trailhead (start): 10,130 ft. Crag Crest summit: 11,189 ft.
Trail:	This is a designated National Recreation Trail.
Season:	Midsummer through mid-fall. The upper parts of the trail are usually covered with snow from November through June.
Vicinity:	Grand Mesa, near Grand Junction
Maps:	Grand Mesa *(USGS)* Grand Mesa *(Trails Illustrated, #136)*
Information:	http://colorado.utahtrails.com/cragcrest.html http://www.fs.fed.us/r2/gmug/ *(Grand Mesa National Forest)* phone: (970) 487-3534 *(Grand Valley Ranger District)*

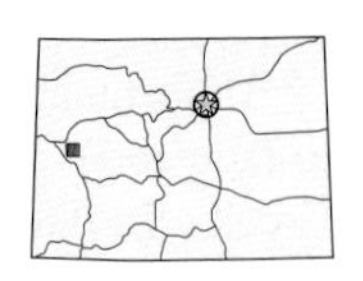

Take exit 49 from I-70 19 miles east of Grand Junction, and drive southwest on Highway 65 to Grand Mesa. 33 miles after leaving I-70 you will see a small road on the left next to a sign that says Crag Crest. This road proceeds a short distance to the Crag Crest West Trailhead. It is possible to access the Crag Crest Trail from there, but I suggest you continue driving a few more miles to the eastern trailhead.

Continue on Highway 65 for another 1.1 mile beyond the Crag Crest West Trailhead to a junction where Road 121, a paved road, departs on the left. Turn onto Road 121. As you turn you will see Cobbett Lake on your left and the Grand Mesa National Forest Visitor Center on your right. The visitor center has a nice selection of maps and books, and it is a good place to get more information about the area. It is open from 8:30-5:00 during the summer. Continue on Road 121 for another 3.4 miles past the visitor center following the signs to Crag Crest Campground. The Crag Crest East Trailhead is located just east of the entrance to the campground.

Crag Crest is a particularly scenic section of the long east-west ridge that separates western Colorado's Grand Mesa into its Gunnison and Colorado River watersheds. Some sources claim that the 50-square-mile mesa is the largest flat-topped mountain in the world. It rises abruptly from the desert environment east of Grand Junction into a lush conifer forest averaging over 10,000 feet above sea level. Dozens of deep blue lakes lie just below the crest of the mesa, making this an especially pretty hike.

About 10 million years ago a series of volcanic eruptions covered the top of the Grand Mesa with a thick layer of basaltic rock, and from all appearances Crag Crest must have been a major volcanic vent during the eruptions. Today the rocky ridge rises 500 feet above the surrounding plateau. Over the course of time the great weight of the volcanic deposits pressing down on the mesa caused the land to tilt slightly inward, forming long, narrow depressions along the top of the mesa. These depressions eventually became the jewel-like lakes that are now scattered below the ridge.

From the road the trail proceeds north for about 150 yards to a trail junction above a small clearing. As the sign at the junction indicates, the path on the left is the "lower loop trail" while the path directly in front of you leads to the Crag Crest. You should continue straight ahead toward the crest. (Disregard the third path that branches off to the right.) After another 0.4 mile the trail passes by the west side of Upper Eggleston Lake, followed by Bullfinch Reservoir 0.6 mile later. There are so many lakes on this hike you will seldom walk far without seeing one. On the northwest side of Bullfinch Reservoir there is also a short spur trail leading to Butts Lake, 0.3 mile off the main trail.

Bullfinch reservoir is situated right at the base of Crag Crest, and as you leave Bullfinch the trail begins a series of long switchbacks on its way to the top of the ridge. In the next 0.7 mile you will gain 570 feet of elevation, and the scenery starts to become dramatic as you near the top. Butts Lake lies 600 feet below the crest, a long skinny lake nestled snugly against the steeply sloping fields of volcanic rubble.

The next two miles of trail along the eastern end of Crags Crest are indeed a rare treat, even for seasoned hikers. At times the ridge is reduced to a knife-edge, barely five feet wide, with lichen-covered boulder fields plunging down precipitously on both sides. Large bunches of columbine grow all along the top of the ridge. Snowfields linger on the north facing side, often well into July, with brilliant green patches of moss and liverwort finding shade in the rocky recesses. The Cottonwood Lakes are situated on the flat

Upper Eggleston Lake

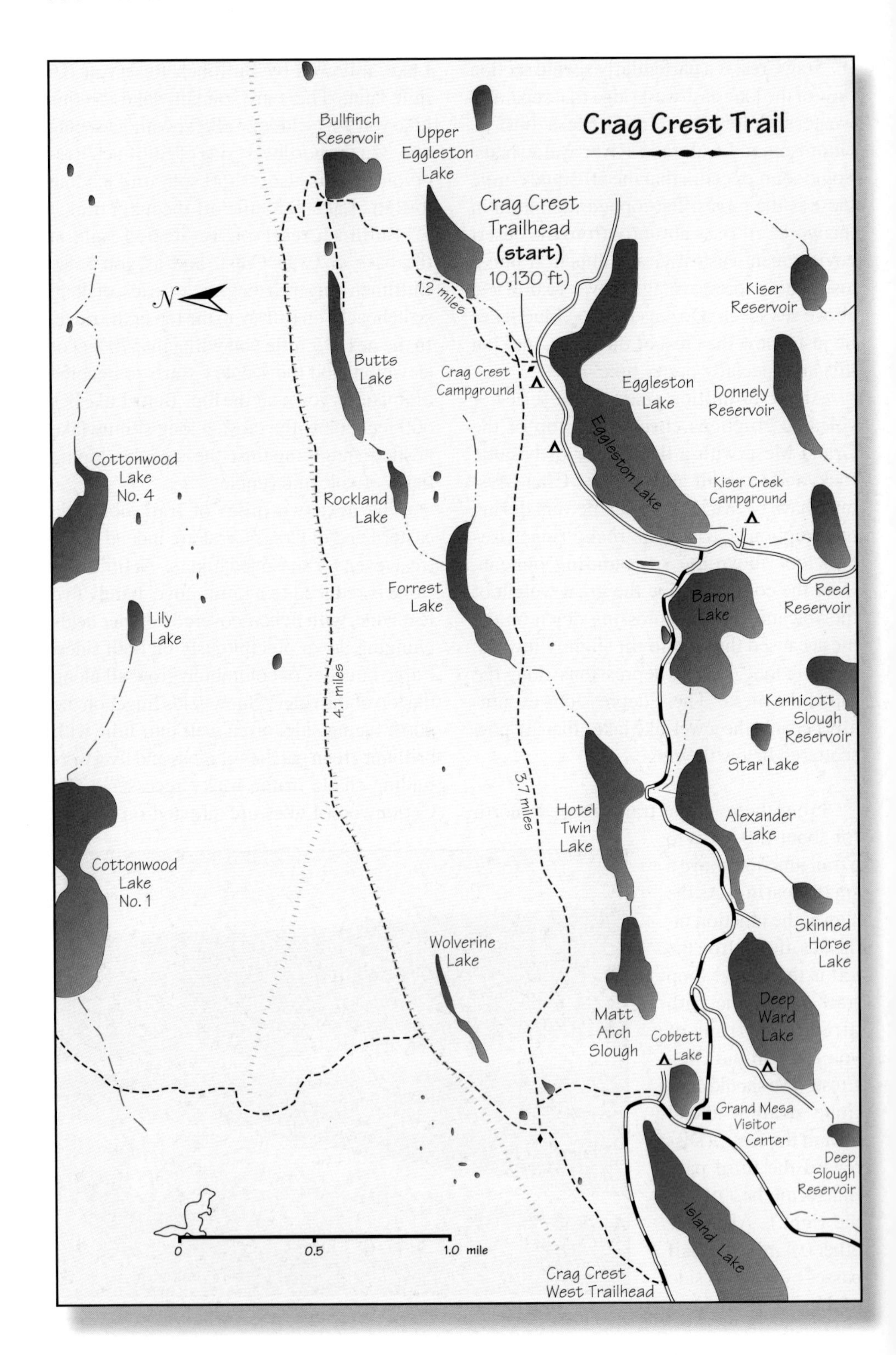

Crag Crest Trail
Bullfinch Reservoir
Upper Eggleston Lake
Crag Crest Trailhead (start) 10,130 ft)
1.2 miles
Kiser Reservoir
N
Butts Lake
Crag Crest Campground
Eggleston Lake
Donnely Reservoir
Eggleston Lake
Cottonwood Lake No. 4
Rockland Lake
Kiser Creek Campground
Forrest Lake
Baron Lake
Reed Reservoir
Lily Lake
4.1 miles
Kennicott Slough Reservoir
Star Lake
3.7 miles
Hotel Twin Lake
Alexander Lake
Cottonwood Lake No. 1
Skinned Horse Lake
Wolverine Lake
Deep Ward Lake
Matt Arch Slough
Cobbett Lake
Grand Mesa Visitor Center
Deep Slough Reservoir
0
0.5
1.0 mile
Island Lake
Crag Crest West Trailhead

plateau about a mile north of the ridgeline, and to the south there are more lakes than you can imagine. As you walk along the top of the ridge the lakes flash out through the surrounding forest of spruce and fir, and then quickly disappear again into the foliage. At least 25 lakes are visible off and on from Crag Crest. At one point on the hike I was able to see 11 of them in one sweeping panorama.

The trail crosses the highest point on the ridge above Rockland Lake, 0.9 mile after climbing up the eastern end of Crag Crest, and from there it makes a long, slow descent along the Crest to Wolverine Lake, 2.4 miles further west. Beyond Wolverine Lake the trail descends another 300 feet to meet a short spur trail leading to the Crag Crest West Trailhead. There you must turn east for the walk back along the Lower Loop Trail to East Trailhead where the hike began.

While not as spectacular as the Crest Trail, the hike along the Lower Loop is not without its rewards. The forest is much denser here and the vegetation is very different. Gone are the columbines and asters that grow along the ridge, but in their place are fields of mountain bluebells, larkspurs, and geraniums. Sadly, there is now one major distraction on the Lower Loop Trail. In 1998 a thoughtless bulldozer operator from the nearby town of Cedaredge drove his machine up the drainage on the northeast side of Hotel Twin Lake, then turned east and continued along the trail for over a mile before being halted by the Forest Service. When you reach this area you will probably be confused as to where the trail is since the bulldozer obliterated it. Just continue walking in the same direction and at the same elevation along the bulldozed path. After about 30 minutes the bulldozed path will end and you will be back on the trail again. Soon afterward the path starts dropping back down to Eggleston Lake and the end of the hike.

Near the summit of Crag Crest

Rattlesnake Arches

★★★

Black Ridge Canyons Wilderness Area
4WD vehicle useful
day hike

Distance: 12.7 miles (round trip)

Walking time: 8 hours

Elevations: 1,520 ft. gain/loss

Pollock Canyon Trailhead (start):	4,520 ft.
Rattlesnake Arches Trailhead:	5,860 ft.
Upper Arches Trail:	5,640 ft.
Lower Arches Trail:	5,440 ft.

Trail: Easy, well marked trail. At one point some minor scrambling is required to get from the Lower Arches Trail to the Upper Trail.

Season: Spring, summer, fall. This trail is very hot during the summer with no reliable water along the way. Winter hiking is feasible during years of light snowfall.

Vicinity: Near Grand Junction and Colorado National Monument

Maps: Mack *(USGS)*

Information: http://colorado.utahtrails.com/rattlesnakearches.html
http://www.blm.gov/co/st/en/fo/gjfo.html *(BLM, Grand Junction)*
phone: (970) 244-3000 *(Grand Junction Field Office)*

The hike described here begins at the Pollock Canyon Trailhead, but if you have a 4WD vehicle you can shorten the hike to 5.2 miles by starting at the Rattlesnake Arches trailhead .

To reach the Pollock Canyon Trailhead take exit 19 from I-70 at Fruita, 13 miles west of Grand Junction, and drive south on Highway 340 towards Colorado National Monument. After 1.0 mile you will cross the Colorado River, and 0.3 mile later you will see a road on the right marked by signs that say "Kings View Drive" and "Horsethief Canyon". Turn right here and drive west. After 0.6 mile you will come to a fork in the road near a gravel pit where you must bear left towards the Horsethief Canyon State Wildlife Area. 2.7 miles beyond the fork you will see a large, developed parking area on the left and a sign that says Pollock Canyon Trailhead.

In order to reach the Rattlesnake Arches Trailhead you must take exit 19 from I-70 at Fruita and drive south on Highway 340 for 2.5 miles until you see a sign marking the turnoff to

Colorado National Monument. Turn right here onto the Rimrock Road and drive 4.5 miles to the visitor center. (The Park Service will waive the entrance fee if you tell the gate attendant that you are going to Rattlesnake Arches.) Continuing south for another 6.6 miles beyond the visitor center will bring you to the Glade Park Road. Turn right here. Just 0.2 mile after leaving the Rimrock Road you will see a gravel road on your right near a sign that says "Black Ridge Road". Turn here and follow the signs for the next 13 miles to the trailhead.

Note: The Black Ridge Road follows two different routes, the upper road and the lower road, at different times of the year. Read the signs to determine which route is in use on the day of your trip. A 4WD vehicle is required for either road–particularly for the last 1.5 miles. Both roads are closed to motor vehicles from February 15 to April 15.

The hike described here starts at the Pollock Canyon Trailhead, but as mentioned above you can also begin at Rattlesnake Arches Trailhead. Unfortunately a 4WD vehicle is required to reach Rattlesnake Arches Trailhead, but if this is not a problem I suggest you begin there. The hike from Rattlesnake Arches Trailhead to all the major points of interest and back is only 5.2 miles, whereas if you begin at Pollock Canyon Trailhead your hike will be 12.7 miles long. This is a very hot hike with no reliable water along the way, and the extra 7.5 miles of walking might be stretching the limit for some people. The season is also important in choosing your trailhead. The jeep road to Rattlesnake Arches Trailhead should not be attempted during winter or early spring, or after a heavy rain. On the other hand, the hike from Pollock Canyon Trailhead can be very pleasant during the early spring when the weather is cooler.

The walk in from Pollock Canyon Trailhead passes across some interesting slickrock country, with beautiful vistas of the Grand Valley and the Colorado River. But it has to be said that the hike's major attraction is the collection of exquisite natural arches that lie along the eastern rim of Rattlesnake

View from Pollock Canyon Trail

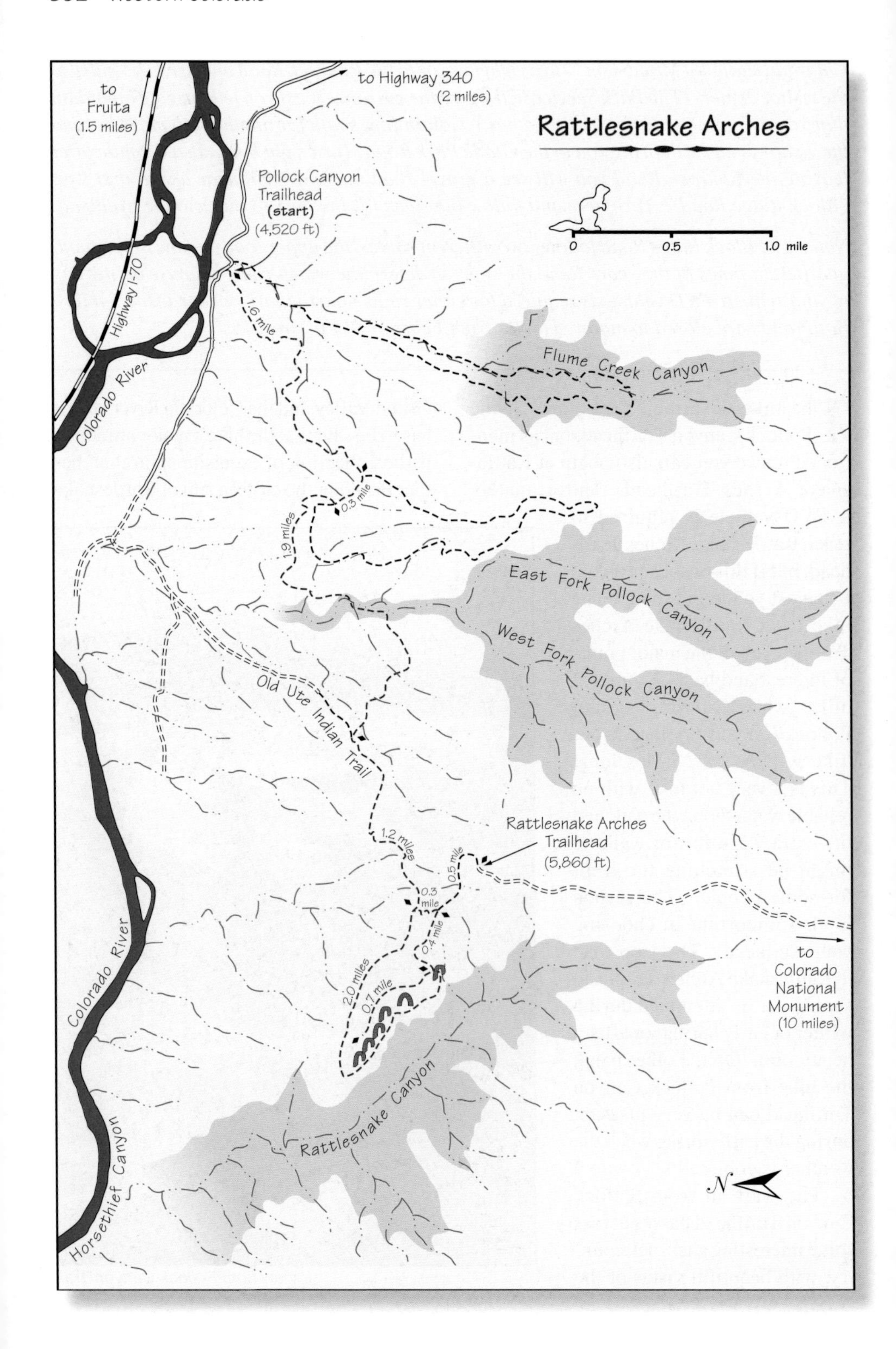
Rattlesnake Arches
0
0.5
1.0 mile
to Fruita (1.5 miles)
to Highway 340 (2 miles)
Pollock Canyon Trailhead (start) (4,520 ft)
Highway I-70
Colorado River
1.6 mile
Flume Creek Canyon
0.3 mile
1.9 miles
East Fork Pollock Canyon
West Fork Pollock Canyon
Old Ute Indian Trail
Rattlesnake Arches Trailhead (5,860 ft)
1.2 miles
0.5 mile
0.3 mile
0.4 mile
2.0 miles
0.7 mile
to Colorado National Monument (10 miles)
Rattlesnake Canyon
Colorado River
Horsethief Canyon
N

Rattlesnake Arches, second arch

Canyon at end of the trail. They are the best natural arches to be found anywhere in Colorado.

As you will soon discover, the first 1.6 miles of the Pollock Canyon Trail is also a mountain bike trail. It really is a great place to ride mountain bikes, with plenty of challenging slickrock climbs and nice views of valleys below. The bikes are prohibited from entering the Black Ridge Canyons Wilderness Area, however, so after the first 45 minutes the trail is strictly a foot path.

The bike path winds gently upward for the first half mile, then levels out on the rim of Flume Creek Canyon, a wide, flat-bottomed canyon bordered by rounded walls of pinkish sandstone. For the next half mile the trail skirts along the northern rim of the valley, offering one photographic opportunity after another. The view is especially scenic early in the morning when the valley is side-lighted by the eastern sun. Upon reaching the western side of the rim the trail begins climbing again, moving away from Flume Creek Canyon, and finally levels out onto a plateau about 400 feet higher that the trailhead. Soon you see a fork in the trail where one leg of the bicycle path begins a big loop to the south. Bear right at this point toward the Rattlesnake Arches. After another 0.3 mile the trail emerges at the upper rim of Pollock Canyon, where the foot path departs from the bicycle trail. The foot path is much less distinct than the bike path, so pay attention or you might miss it. The bicycle path turns left at

Rattlesnake Arches, third arch

Rattlesnake Arches, fourth arch

this point and follows the rim of the canyon, while the foot path veers off to the right and immediately begins descending onto Pollock Bench below.

After a very pleasant 15 minute walk across Pollock Bench you will arrive at the inner rim of Pollock Canyon, where the trail makes a sudden, steep descent to the dry stream bed below. Once you reach the canyon floor the trail turns south for 0.4 mile, and then climbs 200 feet up the other side. This is the most strenuous part of the entire hike, but fortunately it doesn't last long. 0.7 mile after leaving Pollock Canyon you will come to another trail junction, where you must turn left. You are now on the Old Ute Indian Trail, which once was the traditional route from the Colorado River to the Rattlesnake Arches. The Pollock Canyon Trail was built sometime after 1973 so that hikers would not have to cross the private land on the lower part of the Old Ute Indian Trail.

As you walk southwest on the Old Ute Indian Trail pause to look up at the horizon. Directly in front of you about a half mile away you will see a large sandstone formation that looks like the end of a butter knife protruding upward. A patch of blue sky near the base of the formation will confirm that you are looking at a natural arch. The trail climbs another 600 feet over the next 1.2 miles before arriving at another trail junction with a sign directing you left to the Upper Rattlesnake Arches trail, or right to the Lower Rattlesnake Arches trail. For reasons that will become apparent later, I suggest you turn right here onto the lower trail.

At this point you have another half hour of walking to the first of the Rattlesnake Arches. The trail proceeds along the northern base of a sandstone mesa for 1.0 mile, then swings around the western end of the mesa and starts back along its southern side to where the famous arches are located.

Geologists will immediately recognize the sandstone cliffs above the trail as a likely place to find arches. The cliffs are composed of Entrada Sandstone, a strong, homogenous layer of sedimentary rock that was deposited about 180 million years ago during the Jurassic Period. The Entrada Formation is uniformly consistent in its composition and is remarkably free of faults and cracks. It is this characteristic, along with the fact that it weathers easily, that makes it an ideal building material for natural arches. A large percentage of the Southwest's natural arches occur in the Entrada Sandstone Formation.

The first two arches will come into view soon after the trail turns east at the end of the mesa. They are located high on the sandstone cliffs about 100 yards from the end of the mesa. The first arch is just a small hole, about ten feet across, in the top of a large alcove. 200 feet to the right of the first alcove is another large alcove with a bridge spanning across the front of it. This arch is actually a double arch, since there is a small hole in the center of the bridge. Another arch is located in yet another alcove 200 feet further east. It is partially hidden, however, and it can't be seen from the trail.

Most of the arches you will see face southwest; hence early afternoon is generally the best time to photograph them. There is also some spectacular scenery on the south side of the trail, opposite the arches. The deep canyon south of the trail is Rattlesnake Canyon, one of six major canyons in the Black Ridge Canyons Wilderness Area. Notice the many alcoves in the Entrada Sandstone on the opposite rim of the gorge. There are surely many more undocumented natural arches along its southern rim waiting to be discovered by off-trail hikers.

From the first three arches to the next one is only 0.1 mile, and the rest of the arches can all be found along the following 0.9 mile stretch of trail. In all, there are six especially beautiful arches, and a few other smaller, harder-to-find ones, all located in the Entrada cliffs on the left side of the trail. The fourth arch is extremely slender and graceful, reminiscent of the Landscape Arch in Utah's Arches National Park. The fifth one is but a small hole in the top of a high sandstone alcove—like a chandelier in the top of a grand ballroom—and the sixth arch forms an almost perfect 80-foot-diameter oval against the blue Colorado sky.

There are undoubtedly more arches

Rattlesnake Arches, fifth arch

along the rim of Rattlesnake Canyon, but when you arrive at the bottom of last arch, which I will call Trail Arch, the lower trail comes to an abrupt end. Before you turn around stop and look at the slickrock above the trail and you will see a series of distinct toe holds carved into the sandstone. From there it is possible to climb up the slickrock through Trail Arch and onto the mesa above. Some hand-over-hand scrambling is necessary, but the exposure is minimal and most people shouldn't have too much trouble. After you have passed through the hole at the top bear to the right around the last obstacle, and you will soon come upon the well marked Upper Rattlesnake Arches Trail. The entire climb realizes an elevation gain of about 200 feet and should take you about ten minutes. It is easier to climb up through the arch than it is to climb down; hence my earlier suggestion to walk the Rattlesnake Arches loop in a counter-clockwise direction.

If you turn right at the top of Trail Arch it is a 15-minute walk back down to the junction between the upper and lower trails. However, if you want to lengthen the hike you can turn left on the upper trail and follow it westward along the top of the mesa to the end of Rattlesnake Point, 0.7 mile away. There are some fantastic views from the north side of the point of the Colorado River winding lazily across the bottom of Grand Valley. If you began this hike from the Rattlesnake Arches Trailhead it would definitely be worth your while to walk to the end of the upper trail, but if you began the hike at the Pollock Canyon Trailhead you have already seen many similar views of Grand Valley on your way to the arches.

Bearing right at the top of Trail Arch will take you to the Rattlesnake Arches Trailhead, 0.9 mile away, or to the Old Ute Indian Trail, 0.7 mile away, from where you can retrace your steps back to the Pollock Canyon Trailhead.

Rattlesnake Arches, Trail Arch

Monument Canyon

Colorado National Monument
shuttle car required
day hike

Distance: 5.7 miles
(plus 10.6 miles by car)

Walking time: 3 hours

Elevations: 1,450 ft. loss
Monument Canyon Trailhead (start): 6,150 ft.
base of Independence Monument: 5,300 ft.
Lower Monument Canyon Trailhead: 4,700 ft.

Trail: The trail is well marked and well maintained.

Season: Spring, summer, fall. The trail is very hot in the summer and there is no water, so be sure to carry plenty. The roads are open throughout the year, but the upper part of the trail is frequently covered with snow during the winter months.

Vicinity: Colorado National Monument, near Grand Junction

Maps: Colorado National Monument *(USGS)*
Colorado National Monument *(Trails Illustrated, #208)*

Information: http://colorado.utahtrails.com/monumentcanyon.html
http://www.nps.gov/colm/ *(Colorado National Monument)*
phone: (970) 858-3617 *(Colorado National Monument)*

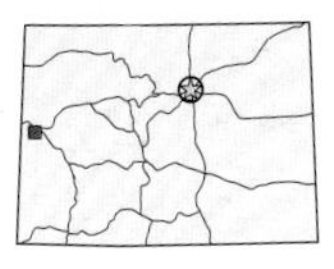

Drive west of Grand Junction on I-70 for 13 miles and turn south at exit 19 onto Highway 340. Continue south on Highway 340 for 2.5 miles until you see a sign marking the turnoff to Colorado National Monument. Turn right here onto the Rimrock Road. You will reach the visitor center after 4.5 miles and the Monument Canyon Trailhead after another 3.8 miles. This is where the hike begins.

In order to get to the lower trailhead, where you will need to leave your shuttle car, drive back down the Rimrock Road to Highway 340 and turn right. Continue east on Highway 340 for 2.1 miles where you will see a gravel road on your right and a small sign that says "Monument Canyon Trail". Turn here and drive for another 0.2 mile to the lower trailhead and parking area.

The Monument Canyon Trail is one of many trails that were built in the early 1900s by John Otto, a humble, soft-spoken, some would say eccentric man who once lived in what is now Colorado National Monument. Otto was a recluse who preferred to live alone, often seeming to enjoy the company of his horse more than any human being. Yet in spite of his quaint lifestyle his activism and his passion for the land eventually brought him widespread fame and recognition. Today John Otto is fondly remembered as the founder of Colorado National Monument, and we should be eternally grateful for what he gave us. Had it not been for Otto's efforts it is doubtful that the ruggedly beautiful Colorado National Monument would still retain the unspoiled natural grandeur it possessed at the turn of the century.

Otto first saw the redrock canyons south of the Grand Valley 1906. The following year he wrote "I came here last year and found these canyons, and they felt like the heart of the world to me. I'm going to stay...and promote this place." Stay he did, and for the next four years he undertook a one-man campaign to have the area set aside as a national park. He wrote letters to the local newspapers, he organized fund raising activities, he wrote letters to government officials in Washington, and he single-handedly built miles of tortuous trails through the canyons so that others could appreciate their beauty. Otto's enthusiasm was contagious. Soon others began to join him in his effort, and the politicians in Washington were deluged with letters and petitions supporting his proposal. Finally on May 24, 1911, President Taft signed a proclamation that made Colorado National Monument a reality, and Otto's dream was realized. Fittingly, John Otto was given the job of caretaker of the monument, a job held for 16 years until he retired in 1927.

From the trailhead on Rimrock Road the trail immediately begins descending downward through the smooth slickrock of the Entrada Sandstone Formation into a

View from the west rim of Monument Canyon

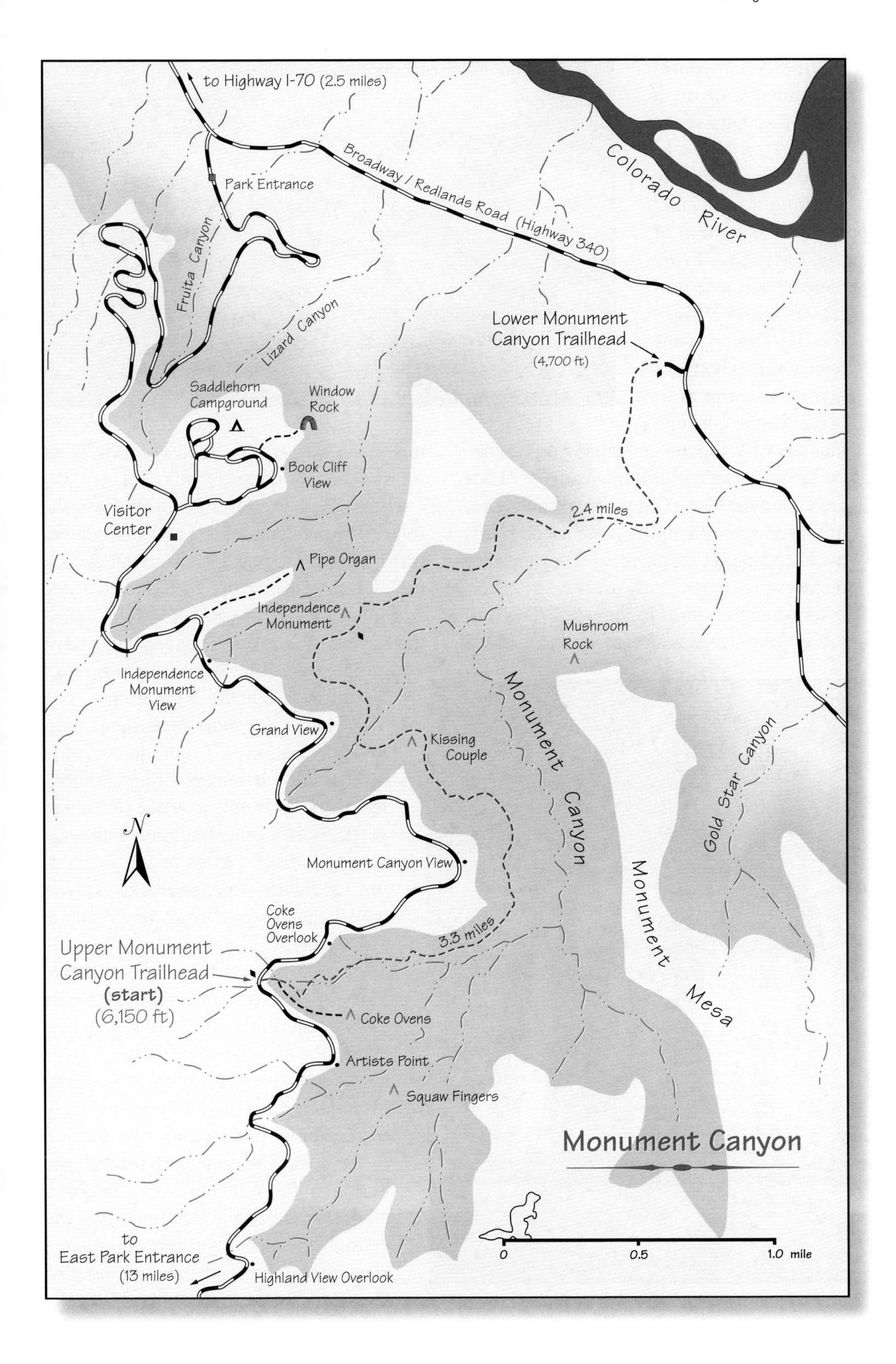
to Highway I-70 (2.5 miles)
Colorado River
Broadway / Redlands Road (Highway 340)
Park Entrance
Fruita Canyon
Lizard Canyon
Lower Monument Canyon Trailhead
(4,700 ft)
Saddlehorn Campground
Window Rock
Book Cliff View
Visitor Center
2.4 miles
Pipe Organ
Independence Monument
Mushroom Rock
Independence Monument View
Grand View
Kissing Couple
Monument Canyon
Gold Star Canyon
Monument Canyon View
Monument Mesa
Coke Ovens Overlook
3.3 miles
Upper Monument Canyon Trailhead
(start)
(6,150 ft)
Coke Ovens
Artists Point
Squaw Fingers
Monument Canyon
N
0
0.5
1.0 mile
to East Park Entrance (13 miles)
Highland View Overlook

The Coke Ovens

small side canyon of Monument Canyon. It winds through a series of short switchbacks for 0.2 mile before reaching a trail junction at the bottom of the Entrada. From there a short side trail leaves on the right for the Coke Ovens formation. The Coke Ovens are the four large dome-shaped mounds of Wingate Sandstone you can see on the south side of the side canyon. They are called the Coke Ovens because they remind some people of the large round ovens once used to prepare charcoal. They are very picturesque, particularly in the late afternoon when the sun is in the west. The trail to the Coke Ovens is an easy walk, about 0.3 miles one way, ending at an overlook point west of the first dome.

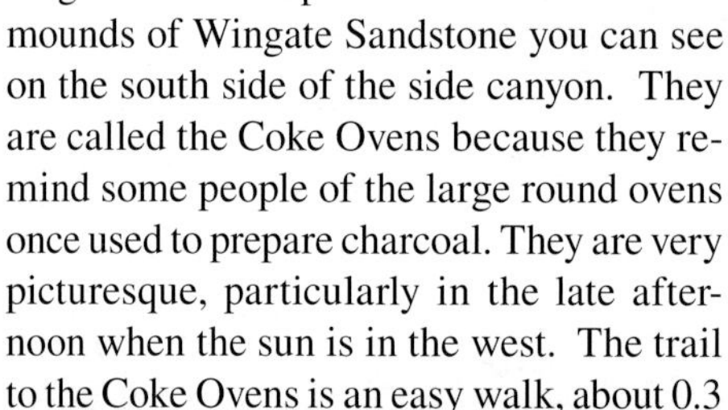

From the Coke Ovens trail junction the route to Monument Canyon continues downward, passing from the Entrada slickrock into a jumbled mixture of dark red shale and sandstone. This geologic strata, called the Kayenta Sandstone, is only a hundred or so feet thick, and beyond that the trail enters the Wingate Sandstone. The Wingate is the most prominent geologic formation in Colorado National Monument. It is about four hundred feet thick and tends to erode into sheer vertical cliffs, often fractured with long, vertical cracks. Most of the interesting landmarks in Monument Canyon have been sculpted from the Wingate Sandstone.

Wingate Cliffs above Monument Canyon

In order to get below the Wingate cliffs the trail soon turns right and heads toward an old landslide that long ago created a feasible route down. Deer also often use this route to get into Monument Canyon, and you are likely to see their tracks along this section of the trail. Once the path reaches the bottom of the Wingate cliffs it begins a long, slow descent to the bottom of the canyon, and then stays at about the same elevation for most of the remainder of the hike. The route meanders along the base of the cliffs on the west side of the canyon, first in an easterly direction and then in a northerly direction, for the next three miles.

This section of the hike is particularly scenic. The route takes you past a number of interesting spires and thumbs that have eroded away from the sandstone cliffs into unlikely shapes. The most notable of these formations is a monolith called the "Kissing Couple". It is a 300-foot-high needle of sandstone that has a vertical split near the top separating it into two seemingly intertwined columns, like two giant lovers locked in a timeless embrace. The Kissing Couple is situated 2.2 miles from the trailhead; its base is just a hundred yards west of the trail.

Independence Monument

The cliffs of Monument Canyon are also a favorite hangout for several species soaring birds, and they are a delight to watch as they glide effortlessly overhead. There are significant numbers of turkey vultures, golden eagles, several species of hawks, and even a few peregrine falcons within the monument boundaries, and if you watch the cliffs as you walk you should be able to see at least a dozen of these magnificent birds. All day long they circle lazily along the rim, taking advantage of the updrafts along the cliffs to hold them aloft as they search for food.

The Kissing Couple (right of center)

One mile from the Kissing Couple the trail veers eastward to pass by Independence Monument, a huge, isolated monolith that rises 450 feet above the valley floor. Independence Monument was named by John Otto, who once celebrated the fourth of July by climbing to the top of the pinnacle and flying an American flag from its crest. Now several hundred rock climbers complete the ascent of Independence Monument every year. The climb is a difficult one with considerable exposure, but experienced climbers can make it to the summit in about two hours. The most common route begins in a fault on the northeast side of the pinnacle. Several pairs of peregrine falcons have also chosen Independence Monument as a nesting area, and for that reason the Park Service occasionally closes the monolith to climbers.

From Independence Monument the trail continues downhill for another 1.6 miles, picking its way along the north side of Monument Canyon before it finally reaches the canyon's mouth on the western side of Grand Valley. As you descend you will occasionally see outcroppings of a black metamorphic rock, much different from the sandstone of the upper canyon. This is the basement layer—a Precambrian deposit of gneiss and schist that is 1.2 billion years older than the sedimentary rock just above it! What happened to the geologic layers in between? They must have been completely eroded away before the succeeding strata were deposited.

The lower trailhead is adjacent to a housing development, and you will probably see many more hikers on this part of the path enjoying the easy walk up to Independence Monument. Unfortunately, when the area was developed in the 1980s the public access to Monument Canyon fell on private property, so the trail had to be lengthened by a half mile and rerouted to a new trailhead. Consequently, the older maps are in error here. When you reach the mouth of the canyon you will see a fence that the Park Service has erected at the monument boundary. The new trail makes an abrupt left turn here and continues along the fence in a northerly direction for another 0.7 mile to the new trailhead and parking area.

Independence Monument, from the west rim of Monument Canyon

Liberty Cap - Ute Canyon

★

Colorado National Monument
shuttle car or bicycle required
day hike

Distance:	10.2 miles (loop) (plus 2.9 miles by car or bicycle)
Walking time:	6 hours
Elevations:	1,000 ft. loss, 950 ft. gain Liberty Cap Trailhead (start): 6,500 ft. Liberty Cap: 5,880 ft. Ute Canyon trail junction: 5,500 ft. Ute Canyon Trailhead: 6,450 ft.
Trail:	A portion of this hike is in the bottom of a canyon with no maintained trail, but the route is easy to follow.
Season:	Spring, summer, fall. The trail is very hot in the summer and there is no water, so be sure to carry plenty. The roads are open throughout the year, but the upper part of the trail is frequently covered with snow during the winter months.
Vicinity:	Colorado National Monument, near Grand Junction
Maps:	Colorado National Monument *(USGS)* Colorado National Monument *(Trails Illustrated, #208)*
Information:	http://colorado.utahtrails.com/libertycap.html http://www.nps.gov/colm/ *(Colorado National Monument)* phone: (970) 858-3617 *(Colorado National Monument)*

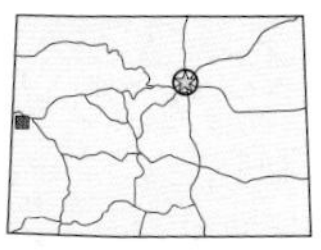

Drive west of Grand Junction on I-70 for 13 miles and turn south at exit 19 onto Highway 340. Continue south on Highway 340 for 2.5 miles until you see a sign marking the turnoff to Colorado National Monument. Turn right here onto the Rimrock Road; you will reach the visitor center after 4.5 miles. 6.3 miles beyond the Visitor Center you will come to a small, unmarked road on the left. Take this road and drive 0.1 mile to the Liberty Cap trailhead and parking area.

To get to the Ute Canyon trailhead, where the hike ends and where you should leave your bicycle or shuttle car, continue south on the Rimrock Road for 2.8 miles past the Liberty Cap Trailhead turnout until you see a Park Service sign marking the trailhead.

As explained below, this hike can be made shorter by positioning a car at the lower Liberty

Cap Trailhead and hiking only half of the loop. To get to the lower trailhead you must drive south on Rimrock Road to the southern entrance of Colorado National Monument. 0.5 mile beyond the entrance gate you will come to South Camp Road where you should turn left. Continue north on South Camp Road for 2.6 miles until the road dead-ends at South Broadway. Turn left again and drive another .5 miles to Wildwood Drive. Turn left once more onto Wildwood Drive and proceed another 0.5 mile on the paved road until you see a smaller dirt road on the right. Turn right here and drive the final 0.1 mile to the trailhead.

This hike follows two separate trails that can be combined to form an interesting loop. The first half of the loop will take you through a lush pinion-juniper forest on the top of Monument Mesa to the rim overlooking Grand Valley. The trail then passes by the Liberty Cap, a small dome-shaped sandstone formation, before dropping off the rim to join the Ute Canyon trail below. The return route winds westward through the bottom of a wide, scenic desert canyon surrounded by high cliffs of Wingate Sandstone. Before beginning the hike you may want to drive to the Ute Canyon Overlook, 1.9 miles south of Ute Canyon Trailhead on the Rimrock Road. This viewpoint offers an outstanding view of Ute Canyon. From there you will be able to see almost all of the last 4 miles of the route your hike will follow.

If you wish to shorten the hike, you can walk either the Liberty Cap Trail or the Ute Canyon Trail separately, ending your walk at the lower Liberty Cap Trailhead on Highway 340. If you do this, however, you will need a shuttle car to get back into the national monument. (From the lower trailhead it is 13.0 miles to Ute Canyon Trailhead, or 16.0 miles to Liberty Cap Trailhead.)

The loop hike can be done in either direction, but if you are starting early in the day it is probably best to start at the Liberty Cap Trailhead. The reason for this is that the second half of the hike is in the bottom of a canyon where the opportunities for good photographs are better when the sun is high.

The first half of the hike winds eastward across the Morrison Formation on an old two-track wagon road that was closed by the Park Service in the early 1970s. The remnant of the old road winds across a landscape of pinion, juniper, and sagebrush on the top of Monument Mesa for a distance of 4.3 miles before finally loosing its identity as a road. It isn't clear what the original purpose of the road was—maybe it was used by ranchers who grazed cattle on the mesa. If that is the case, it was long ago, because there is no evidence now that the land was ever used for grazing. The grass and other vegetation is lush and verdant as only ungrazed land can be.

Grand Valley, from the Liberty Cap Trail

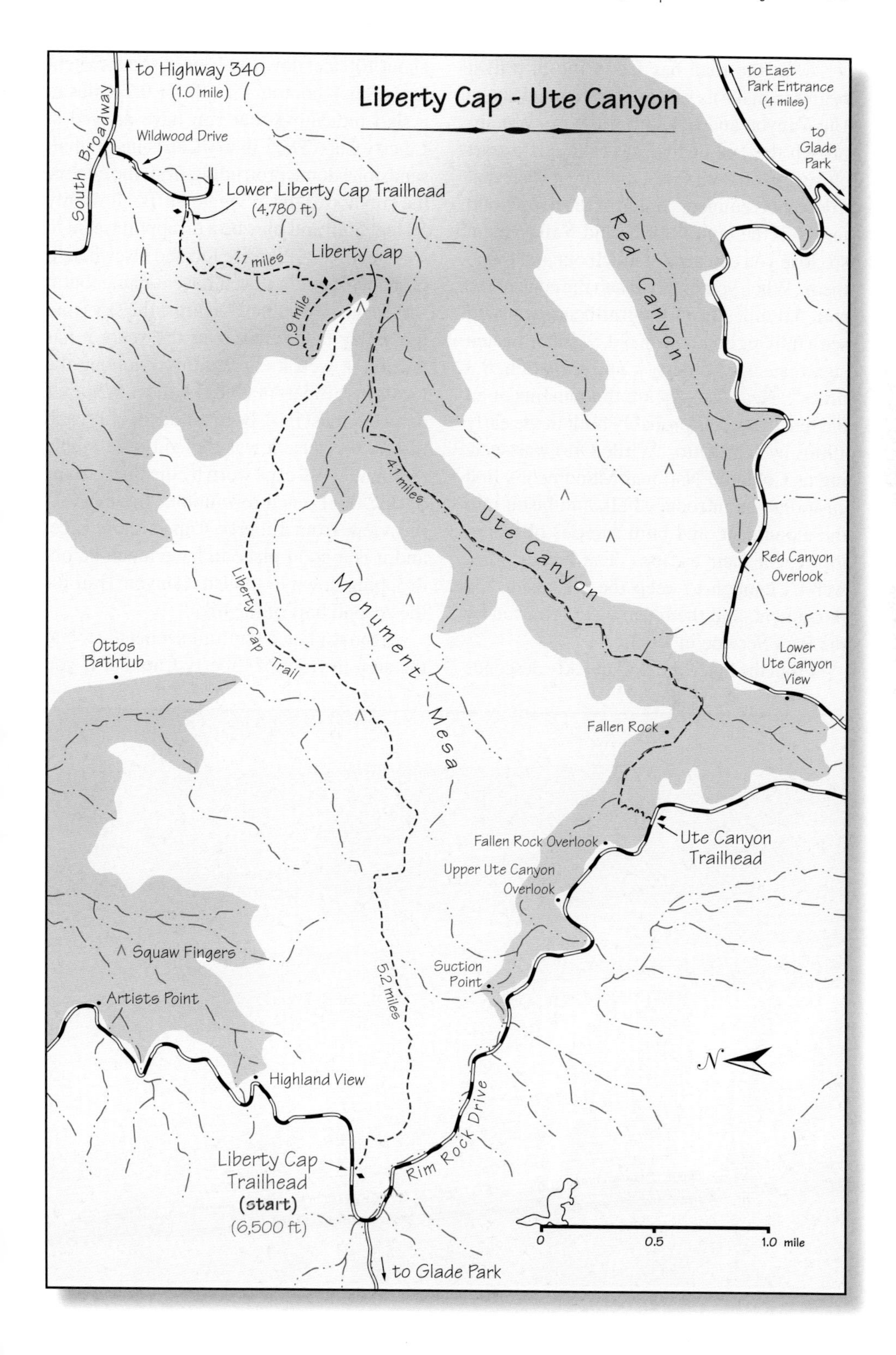
Liberty Cap - Ute Canyon
to Highway 340
(1.0 mile)
South Broadway
Wildwood Drive
Lower Liberty Cap Trailhead
(4,780 ft)
1.1 miles
Liberty Cap
0.9 mile
to East
Park Entrance
(4 miles)
to
Glade
Park
Red Canyon
4.1 miles
Ute Canyon
Red Canyon
Overlook
Lower
Ute Canyon
View
Liberty Cap Trail
Monument Mesa
Ottos
Bathtub
Fallen Rock
Fallen Rock Overlook
Ute Canyon
Trailhead
Upper Ute Canyon
Overlook
Squaw Fingers
Suction
Point
5.2 miles
Artists Point
N
Highland View
Rim Rock Drive
Liberty Cap
Trailhead
(start)
(6,500 ft)
0
0.5
1.0 mile
to Glade Park

After the road has faded into a trail it begins to make its way out onto a point above Ute Canyon and Grand Valley. As you approach the end of the mesa the cliffs start closing in on both sides, making it clear that a descent is eminent. Some of the houses and farms in the bottom of Grand Valley seem so close you can almost reach out and touch them. When you finally reach the edge of the rim, 5.0 miles from the trailhead, you will see a trail register and an old, weather-beaten sign that says "Liberty Cap Formation, 0.3 miles". Near the sign are the remains of an old fence that was probably built in the early 1900s by John Otto. While Otto was serving as Colorado National Monument's first custodian he introduced elk and bison into the monument, and built a series of fences to prevent their escape. The fences, alas, weren't enough to keep the elk inside the monument, and the bison were removed by the Park Service in 1983.

From the fence the trail quickly descends about 100 feet down a series of short switchbacks, then contours south for 0.2 miles to a sign indicating that you have arrived at Liberty Cap. The Liberty Cap is just a small sandstone dome protruding from the edge of the rim above the Wingate cliffs. It is only 50 feet high and may be a disappointment to some people. If it were located elsewhere it probably wouldn't even have a name, but it stands out so distinctly against the sky from the valley below that over the years it has become a well know landmark among the locals in this part of Grand Valley. Whoever named it must have been a student of French history, because it was thought to resemble the small cloth caps worn by the libertarians during the French revolution. In any case, the view from Liberty Cap is quite nice, and it is a good place to have lunch before dropping down to the Ute Canyon Trail for the second half of the hike.

At first glance the trail seems to stop at the sign in front of Liberty Cap, but if you

Grand Valley

Liberty Cap

look carefully you will see a small cairn on the edge of the rim about 80 feet beyond the sign. Continue walking along the rim towards Liberty Cap until you see this cairn, then turn left and you will be on the trail. The trail immediately starts downward, but then doubles back under itself to the north again. There is a break in the cliff about 0.3 mile northwest of the Liberty Cap, and after the trail reaches this break it turns downward once more, descending through a series of switchbacks to the bench below the Wingate cliffs. Finally, 0.9 mile after leaving Liberty Cap you will come to a trail junction where you must turn right onto the Ute Canyon Trail. The left fork leads to the lower Liberty Cap Trailhead, 1.1 miles from the junction.

From the junction, the Ute Canyon trail proceeds southward for about 0.3 mile, then gradually turns west into the mouth of Ute Canyon. Ute Canyon is one of many short, scenic canyons that have been etched into the eastern edge of the Uncompahgre Plateau over the last 50 million years by the forces of water and wind. It was these canyons that made John Otto fall in love with the area, and that later became the reason for the creation of Colorado National Monument. Ute Canyon is only about six miles long; nevertheless it is the longest canyon in the monument.

The trail stays in the bottom of the canyon for three miles before climbing up the south side to Rimrock Road. The route is easy to follow for the first 1.5 miles, but after that there may be come confusion in following the main trail. Don't worry if you temporarily loose the path; just stay close to the streambed in the center of the drainage and continue walking upcanyon. You will probably loose and refind the trail several times before you reach the end.

About 30 minutes from the trail junction you should start searching the left, or eastern wall of the canyon for a natural arch. The arch appears as a long slit in the wall that extends down from the top for about 200 feet like a long, narrow cup handle. The arch is 1.9 miles from the trail junction

1.2 miles beyond the arch Ute Canyon suddenly starts to get much narrower. Here you should see another drainage coming in from a smaller canyon to the south; bear to the right at the confluence of the two canyons. Ute Canyon makes an abrupt 90-degree turn at the confluence and continues in a northwesterly direction, parallel to the Rimrock Road above. If you look up from the confluence you might see other people looking down at you from the Ute Canyon Overlook, 600 feet above the canyon floor.

Within 5 minutes after leaving the confluence the streambed passes through an unusual narrows composed of black Precambrian gneiss. The gneiss is impervious to water and there are usually a few ponds in the well-shaded canyon narrows even late in the summer. Walking through this short stretch of dark metamorphic rock is an interesting diversion from the rest of the hike—the crystalline stone bears absolutely no resemblance to the surrounding sedimentary sandstone and shale.

Emerging from the narrows you will find a good trail again on the right side of the streambed. The trail winds over the sandy bottom, bypassing an obstacle in the bottom of the drainage, before crossing again to the south side of the canyon floor. When you see a sandstone finger-shaped monolith, about 40 feet high, in the bottom of the canyon you will know you are near the end. Just beyond this giant trail marker the path suddenly makes a left-hand turn and enters a series of switchbacks as it climbs up an old slide area on the south side of the canyon. After you have climbed 450 feet you will be at the Rimrock Road and the Ute Canyon Trailhead.

Ute Canyon

Big Dominguez Canyon

★★★

shuttle car required
4WD vehicle useful
day hike

Distance: 7.0 miles
(plus 31.1 miles by car)

Walking time: 3¾ hours

Elevations: 1,400 ft. loss
Cactus Park Trailhead (start): 6,120 ft.
Bridgeport Trailhead: 4,720 ft.

Trail: Unmaintained, but easy to follow

Season: Early summer through late fall. The road to Cactus Park Trailhead is impassable from late November through March.

Vicinity: South of Grand Junction

Maps: Triangle Mesa *(USGS)*

Information: http://colorado.utahtrails.com/dominguezcanyon.html
http://www.blm.gov/co/st/en/fo/gjfo.html *(BLM, Grand Junction)*
phone: (970) 244-3000 *(Grand Junction Field Office)*

Most hikes into Big Dominguez Canyon start from one of three access points: Bridgeport, Cactus Park, or Dominguez Campground.

In order to reach the Bridgeport Trailhead you must leave I-70 at Grand Junction and drive south on Highway 50 towards Montrose. 25.5 miles after leaving I-70, just a mile before leaving Mesa County, you will see a small gravel road on the right and a sign that says "Bridgeport Road". Turn right here and follow the gravel road down a small canyon for 3.2 miles to the Gunnison River. After reaching the river the road turns left and follows a set railroad tracks for 0.4 mile, then crosses the tracks and continues between the tracks and the river for another 0.6 mile to the trailhead and parking area. Dominguez Canyon is 0.6 mile downstream from the parking area, but there is an obvious problem: it is on the opposite side of the Gunnison River. A privately owned suspension bridge crosses the Gunnison near the parking area, but the bridge is in sad shape and was long ago condemned. If you ask anyone in the BLM you will be told the bridge should not be used under any circumstances. Most hiking books advise you to use a small rubber raft to cross the Gunnison; however in truth I must say that when I was last at the Bridgeport Trailhead in 1999 hikers were simply ignoring the advice and walking across the bridge.

To reach the Cactus Park Trailhead you must leave I-70 at the Highway 50 exit near Grand Junction and drive south for 14.7 miles to Highway 141. Turn west toward Gateway on Highway 141 and continue for another 8.8 miles until you see a gravel road on the left near a sign that says "Cactus Park Road". You must turn here and drive in a southerly direction for the next 4.1 miles into Cactus Park, always staying on the best-traveled road. There are two major forks in the road where it may be difficult to determine which fork is the best traveled. The first major fork occurs 1.1 miles from Highway 141. Bear left here. The second major fork occurs 3.9 miles from the highway. Bear right here. After you have driven 4.1 miles on Cactus Park Road you will come to a jeep road on the left next to a sign that says "Dominguez Canyon Access". Follow this road for the last 3.2 miles to the Cactus Park Trailhead. If you don't have a 4WD vehicle you will have to walk the last 2.0 miles to the trailhead.

To reach the Dominguez Canyon Campground and Trailhead continue south on Highway 141 for another 5.2 miles past the Cactus Park Road (or 14.0 miles from Highway 50) until you see another paved road on the left marked by a sign that says "Divide Road". Turn left here. The pavement ends after only a hundred yards, but otherwise Divide Road is a good gravel road. After driving for 6.0 miles on Divide Road you will come to another well marked dirt road on the left leading to the Dominguez Recreation Area. Again, turn left and drive south for the last 5.0 miles to the trailhead.

Several variations of the hike through Big Dominguez Canyon are possible, depending on how far you want to walk and what you want to see. If you want to walk the entire length of the canyon you can begin at the Dominguez Campground trailhead and walk to the Gunnison River at Bridgeport. The total distance of that hike is 16.6 miles, hence it is recommended as an overnighter. The trail is not maintained, but it is still generally easy to follow. It begins in a forest of pinion pine and Douglas fir, and slowly descends along the canyon bottom to the high desert environment of Bridgeport. There are plenty of good camp sites along the way, and water is normally not a problem. Alternatively, you can begin or end your hike at the Cactus Park Trailhead. A well marked spur trail leaves the bottom of Big Dominguez Canyon 5.7 miles before Bridgeport, then climbs 1.3 miles to the Cactus Park Trailhead.

The hike described here begins at the

Big Dominguez Canyon, from the Cactus Park Trailhead

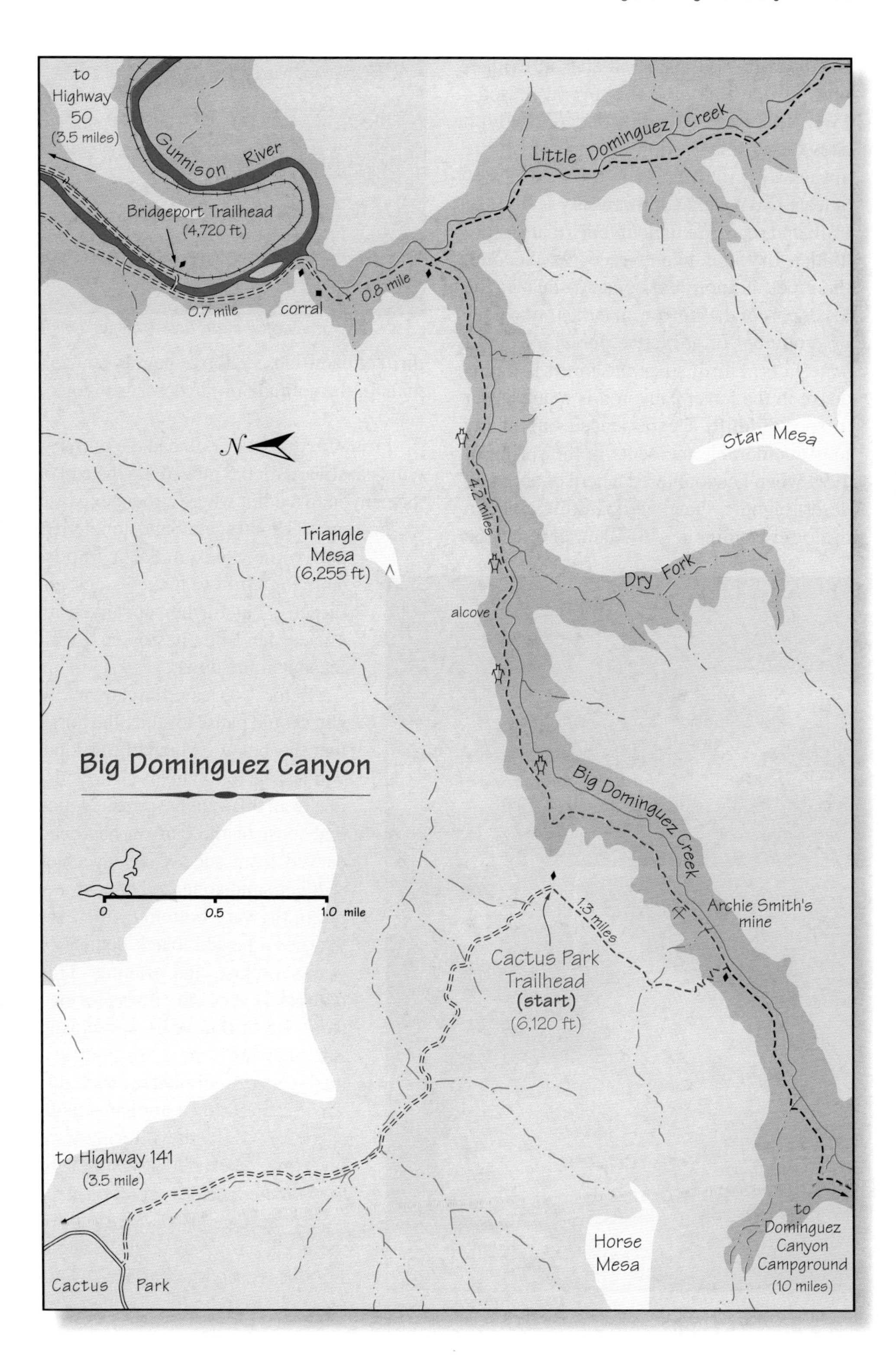

Big Dominguez Canyon
to Highway 50 (3.5 miles)
Gunnison River
Bridgeport Trailhead (4,720 ft)
0.7 mile
corral
0.8 mile
Little Dominguez Creek
Star Mesa
N
4.2 miles
Triangle Mesa (6,255 ft)
alcove
Dry Fork
Big Dominguez Creek
Archie Smith's mine
1.3 miles
Cactus Park Trailhead
(start)
(6,120 ft)
0
0.5
1.0 mile
to Highway 141 (3.5 mile)
Cactus
Park
Horse Mesa
to Dominguez Canyon Campground (10 miles)

Cactus Park Trailhead and ends at Bridgeport. I like this hike for several reasons. First, there are several good petroglyph sites along this section of trail which are always a joy to discover in the wild. I saw at least five panels within twenty feet of the trail, and there are undoubtedly many more hidden in the canyon's recesses. Second, the creek is more easily accessible in the lower part of the canyon, and the trail passes by a number of attractive pools and small waterfalls. Third, since the forest is not as dense in the lower canyon it is much easier to spot wildlife. I experienced one of my most memorable moments in the spring of 1999 when I encountered a herd of about 30 desert bighorn sheep while hiking alone in the lower Dominguez. I will never forget the thrill of being close to those magnificent animals in the solitude of the desert canyon.

Inscription near Archie Smith's mine

From Cactus Park Trailhead the trail first winds eastward for 0.6 mile along the rim of the canyon to a point where a route exists to the bottom. The Wingate Sandstone cliffs above the creek make it impossible for a trail to make its descent directly, but further upcanyon an ancient landslide has opened up a feasible route down.

Big Dominguez Creek

Before you leave the canyon rim you should pause to study the gorge that lies below. Much of the route you will be following is clearly visible from this vantage point. Notice that most of the canyon has been carved from successive layers of reddish sandstone and mudstone, but in the very bottom of the canyon lies a jagged, black deposit of gneiss, schist, and granite. This bedrock is very old; it was formed some 1.5 billion years ago during Precambrian times. In contrast, the layers of sedimentary rock just above it are little more than a tenth as old. All of the intermediate layers were eroded away before the younger rocks were deposited. Notice the large hill that rises above the north rim of the canyon about 1.5 miles east of the trailhead. This prominent landmark is called Tri-

Archie Smith's primitive stone shelter

angle Mesa. As the crow flies it lies in line with and about half way between Bridgeport Trailhead, your destination, and Cactus Park Trailhead, your starting point.

When you reach the bottom of Big Dominguez Canyon turn left towards the Gunnison River, and within 0.4 mile you will come to an old mining claim that was operated in 1907 by a man named Archie Smith. (His name is inscribed on a nearby boulder.) The mine is located about 50 feet below the trail near a few scattered pieces of old mining equipment. Above the trail is a primitive stone shelter in which Mr. Smith must have spent many a lonely night. You can still see pieces of an old iron stove inside the tiny bivouac.

There are Indian petroglyphs all along the lower part of big Dominguez Canyon, but they start becoming more frequent about 1.2 miles below Archie Smith's mine. Many are on the east side of the rocks, so be sure to look back occasionally as you walk eastward. The most likely places to find them are on the large flat vertical surfaces of sandstone—particularly those surfaces that are covered with a dark patina of desert varnish. Most of the drawings were made by chipping away the dark patina to expose the lighter underlying stone. Interestingly, many of the stone drawings are of desert bighorn sheep, an animal that must have played a major role in the lives of the Indians that occupied this canyon hundreds of years ago.

The desert bighorns became extinct in this part of Colorado soon after white settlers began frequenting the canyon country in the late 1800s. Not only was Big Dominguez occupied by miners, but until recently cattle were also grazed in the confines of the canyon. The wild sheep were easy pickings for a hungry settler armed with a rifle, and they were soon killed off. However, in the late

Petroglyphs near trail in Big Dominguez Canyon

1980s a decision was made by the BLM to reintroduce the desert bighorn to the area, and now the stately animals can occasionally be seen once again. There are currently about 250 wild sheep that range in the canyons south of the Gunnison River between Big Dominguez Canyon and Roubideau Canyon. They seem to be thriving–their population has increased six fold in the two decades since their reintroduction.

Desert Bighorn Sheep in Big Dominguez Canyon

The best petroglyph panel is probably the last one you will see on this hike. It is located 0.6 mile below the confluence with Dry Fork Canyon, or 0.9 miles upstream from the confluence with Little Dominguez Canyon. Look for a large boulder the size of a small cabin located just five feet from the trail on the north side. The panel is clearly visible from the trail, but it is on the east-facing side of the boulder so if you don't look back you will miss it. The panel contains dozens of drawings, apparently made by numerous artists over a long period of time. While you are looking at the rock art on this boulder look up at the base of the cliffs on the north side of the canyon and you will see another panel. Actually there are a number of petroglyphs in the vicinity of the Dry Fork confluence, so you should be particularly observant along this part of the trail. I must caution you that the canyon floor becomes much wider in this area, and there is more than one trail to choose from. Try to stay on the trail that stays as far above the north side of the creek bed as possible, because this is where you will see most of the petroglyphs. There is a much better trail on the south side of the creek, but you will miss a lot if you follow it.

Fifteen minutes after leaving the last petroglyph panel you will come to the confluence of Little Dominguez Canyon, after which Big Dominguez turns north and soon intersects the Gunnison River. By now you will notice that the trail is more of a jeep road than a trail. Also you will probably see other campers at the mouth of the canyon, as this is a popular overnight stop among river runners. Continuing north along the Gunnison River for another 0.6 mile will bring you to the Bridgeport Bridge, on the other side of which is the Bridgeport Trailhead and parking area.

Delores River Canyon

★ **day hike**

Distance:	5.4 miles (round trip)
Walking time:	2 3/4 hours
Elevations:	200 ft. gain/loss Delores River Trailhead (start): 4,960 ft. La Sal Creek: 5,000 ft.
Trail:	Generally well marked and easy to follow
Season:	All year round, but best in May during the spring runoff.
Vicinity:	South of Grand Junction
Maps:	Paradox *(USGS)*
Information:	http://colorado.utahtrails.com/deloresriver.html http://www.co.blm.gov/ubra/ *(BLM, Montrose)* phone: (970) 240-5300 *(Uncompahgre Field Office)*

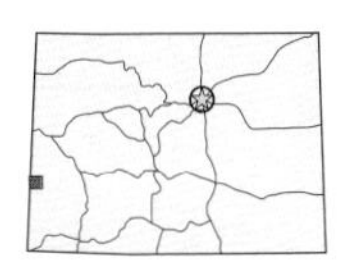

Drive south of Grand Junction on Highway 141 to the farming community of Vancorum. There you must turn west on Highway 90 and continue another 19 miles to the town of Bedrock. Turn left at the Bedrock General Store and drive on an unpaved road that follows the Delores River for the next 1.7 miles. The road ends near the water's edge at the trailhead. (Note: a 4WD vehicle is required for the last 0.6 mile of this road. You will pass a parking area for passenger cars at the boat launching area 1.1 miles from the highway, so if you don't have a 4WD vehicle you can park there and walk the last 0.6 mile to the trailhead.)

The Delores River, which drains the western side of the Uncompahgre Plateau and the San Juan Mountains, offers an often-overlooked hiking opportunity near the Utah border. The waterway is particularly scenic where it flows between the towns of Slick Rock and Bedrock, for here it has carved a winding gorge in the desert sandstone that is frequently over a thousand feet deep. This section of river, called the Delores River Canyon, has been recommended for designation as a wild river under the Wild and Scenic Rivers Act, and the surrounding terrain is also being studied by the Bureau of Land Management as a possible wilderness area.

The hike begins near the town of Bedrock, where the Delores River exits the

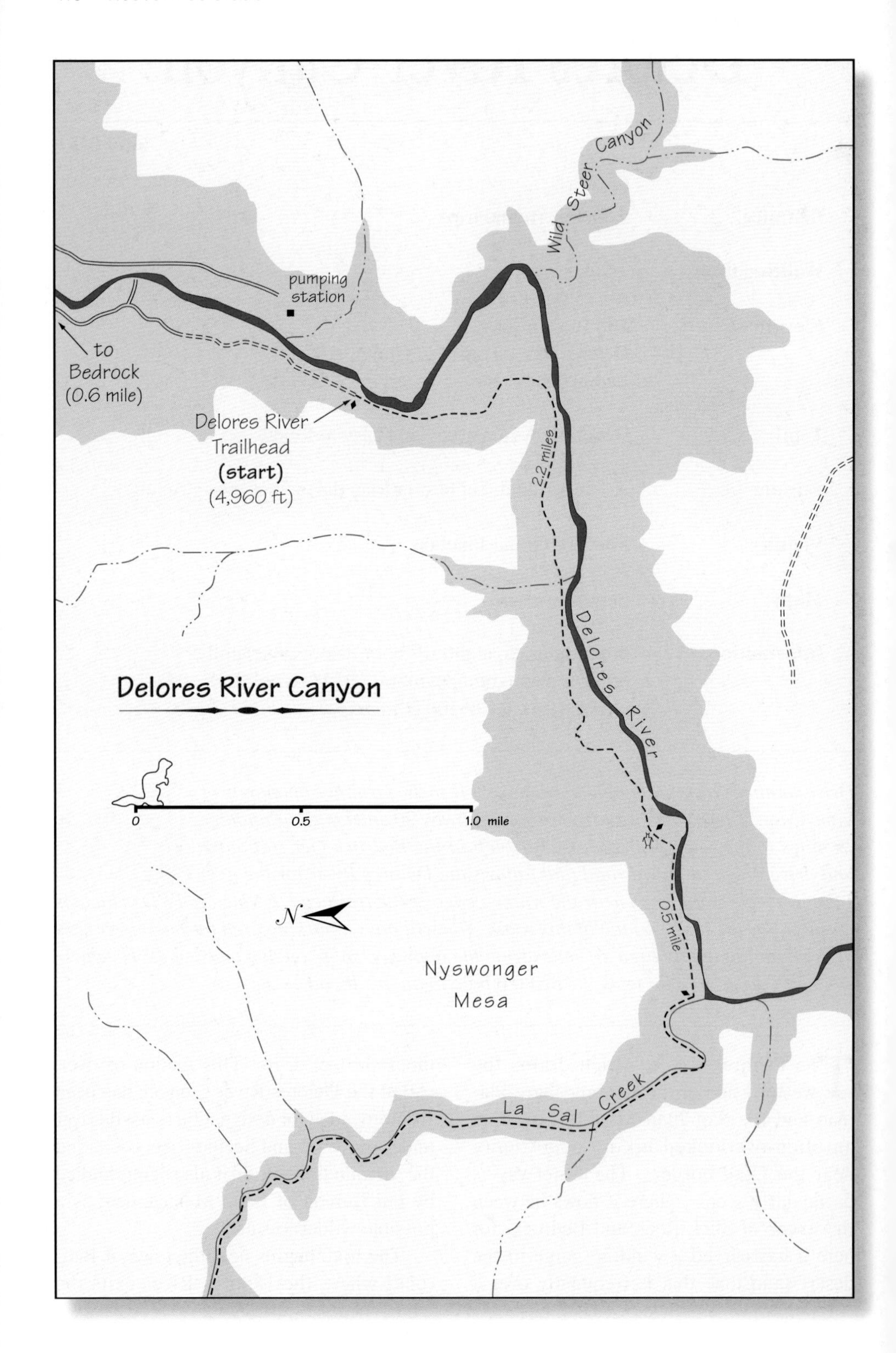
Delores River Canyon
Wild Steer Canyon
pumping station
to Bedrock (0.6 mile)
Delores River Trailhead
(start)
(4,960 ft)
2.2 miles
Delores River
0 0.5 1.0 mile
N
0.5 mile
Nyswonger Mesa
La Sal Creek

Delores River

canyon to flow across the Paradox Valley. Notice that the river does not take the easy route down the center of Paradox Valley, as one might expect, but rather flows directly across the wide, flat valley to enter another canyon on the other side. This oddity was a puzzle to early geologists, and in fact that is probably how Paradox Valley got its name. It is now known that, unlike most valleys, Paradox Valley was not formed by water. Rather it is the result of a large subterranean deposit of salt that shifted and caused the land to sink long after the Delores River channel had already been established.

For the first 0.2 mile after leaving the end of the road the trail closely parallels the west side of the river. Soon, however, the river veers away to the east toward the confluence with Wild Steer Canyon. The trail continues in a southerly direction for the next 0.5 mile, climbing 100 feet above the water. Then it descends back again to the water's edge and turns west to follow the northern shore.

The trail continues following the river in a westerly direction for the next 1.5 miles. Three times it turns north away from the water for hundred yards in order to get around miner obstacles, but for the most part it stays within a hundred feet of the water. Finally, 2.2 miles from the trailhead you will come to a small BLM sign on the right side of the path indicating that there are Indian petroglyphs in the area. The trail at this point is a few hundred feet north of the water in an area littered with large cabin-sized sandstone boulders, and it is on these boulders

Delores River Canyon Trail

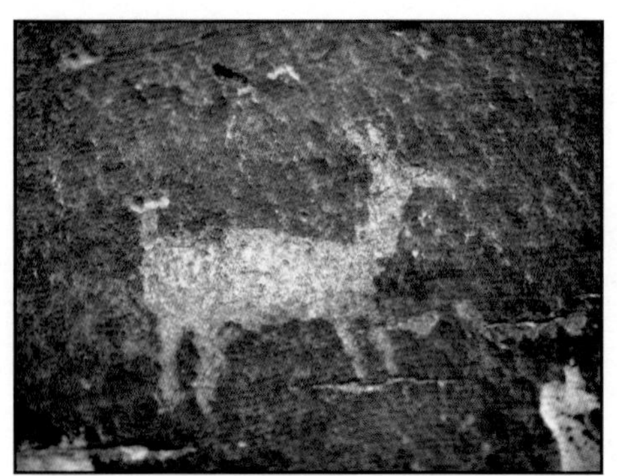
Petroglyphs near Delores River

that you will find the rock art.

The most obvious drawings are on a 15-foot-high boulder near the BLM sign about 30 feet north of the trail. The boulder has one flat side facing the trail that has a number of weathered petroglyphs chipped into its surface. This and several other nearby boulders are decorated with a variety of abstract drawings that include bear paws, spirals, snakes, several human-like figures with oversize feet and hands, and at least one antelope.

One of the boulders near the petroglyph site also contains several faint but unmistakable dinosaur tracks. Walk back down the trail about 40 feet east of the BLM sign; then turn north and walk another 40 feet north of the trail. You will come to a large boulder with a flat side that faces away from the trail toward the cliffs. Look carefully at the flat surface and you should see the fossilized tracks.

150 yards after leaving the petroglyph site the trail returns to the edge of the river, and 0.5 mile later it arrives at the mouth of La Sal Creek. Although this hike ends at the confluence of La Sal Creek and the Delores River a faint trail continues up the La Sal for another 3.0 miles, finally ending at a mine. The mine can also be reached by road from Highway 46 west of Bedrock, but numerous "no trespassing" signs have been posted in the area to let outsiders know they are not welcome.

Delores River

Sand Canyon

★★★★

Canyons of the Ancients National Monument
day hike

Distance:	6.7 miles (plus 29.6 miles by car)
Walking time:	4 1/2 hours
Elevations:	1,400 ft. gain Lower Sand Canyon Trailhead (start): 5,470 ft. Upper Sand Canyon Trailhead: 6,870 ft.
Trail:	Well maintained and easy to follow
Season:	Spring, summer, fall. The trail is very hot in the summer and there is no water, so be sure to carry plenty. The upper part of the trail is usually covered with snow from late November until mid-May.
Vicinity:	Near Cortez
Maps:	Battle Rock, Woods Canyon *(USGS)*
Information:	http://colorado.utahtrails.com/sandcanyon.html http://www.blm.gov/co/st/en/nm/canm.html *(Canyons of the Ancients National Monument)* phone: (970) 882-4811 *(Anasazi Heritage Center)*

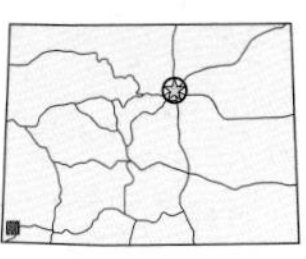

Drive to the junction of Highway 160 and 666, on the west side of Cortez, and turn south on Highway 166 towards the Four Corners area. Drive for 2.8 miles until you reach a small paved road on the right next to a sign that says "Hovenweep National Monument". Turn right here and proceed west along the south side of McElmo Creek. After 11.8 miles you will come to a bridge where the road crosses to the north side of the creek, and 0.6 mile later you will see a BLM trailhead sign and a slickrock parking area on the right. This is the lower Sand Canyon Trailhead.

To reach the upper Sand Canyon Trailhead where this hike ends you must return to Highway 666 and drive north back toward Cortez. Continue driving north for 5.1 miles beyond the junction with Highway 160 until you come to a narrow, paved county road marked by a sign that says "CR P" (County Road P). Turn left onto Road P and note the mileage on your odometer. If you have a trip meter in your car set it to zero at this point. From Highway 666 drive west on Road P for 4.6 miles, then turn south onto Road 18. At 5.1 miles Road 18 turns west again. At 6.3 miles you must turn south onto Road 17 (there is a volunteer fire station at the intersection). Bear right as Road 17 makes a turn to the west and eventually becomes Road N. Finally, at 9.3 miles you will see a small sign on the left that says "Sand Canyon Trail". The parking area for the trailhead is just behind this sign on the south side of Road N.

Sand Canyon contains one of the most interesting and accessible collections of Anasazi cliff dwellings outside Mesa Verde National Park in Colorado. There must have been tens of thousands of Anasazis living in the Four Corners area before they abandoned their settlements 700 years ago, but prior to the thirteenth century most of them lived on the mesa tops. Then in the early 1200s the Anasazis began building their houses in the sandstone cliffs of the canyon country, and it is the presence of these ancient cliff dwellings that make Sand Canyon so interesting today. The prehistoric shelters are priceless treasures from our past, waiting to be discovered by anyone willing to walk a few miles. All along the lower reaches of the canyon they lie like precious jewels set in the alcoves of the Entrada Sandstone. Some are obvious, others are hidden by the surrounding forest of pinion and juniper.

The trail passes by at least eight ruins within just the first 3.5 miles. You will not see anymore cliff dwellings once the trail begins to climb out of the canyon, but this part of the hike is interesting for two other reasons. First, the views looking back into the canyon from above are quite nice, especially since the Sleeping Ute Mountain lies just four miles south of the trailhead. Second, Sand Pueblo, a large unexcavated Anasazi ruin, is located near the upper trailhead. In fact the upper section of the trail was built in 1993 specifically to give hikers access to Sand Pueblo.

This hike can be done in either direction.

Anasazi ruins in Sand Canyon

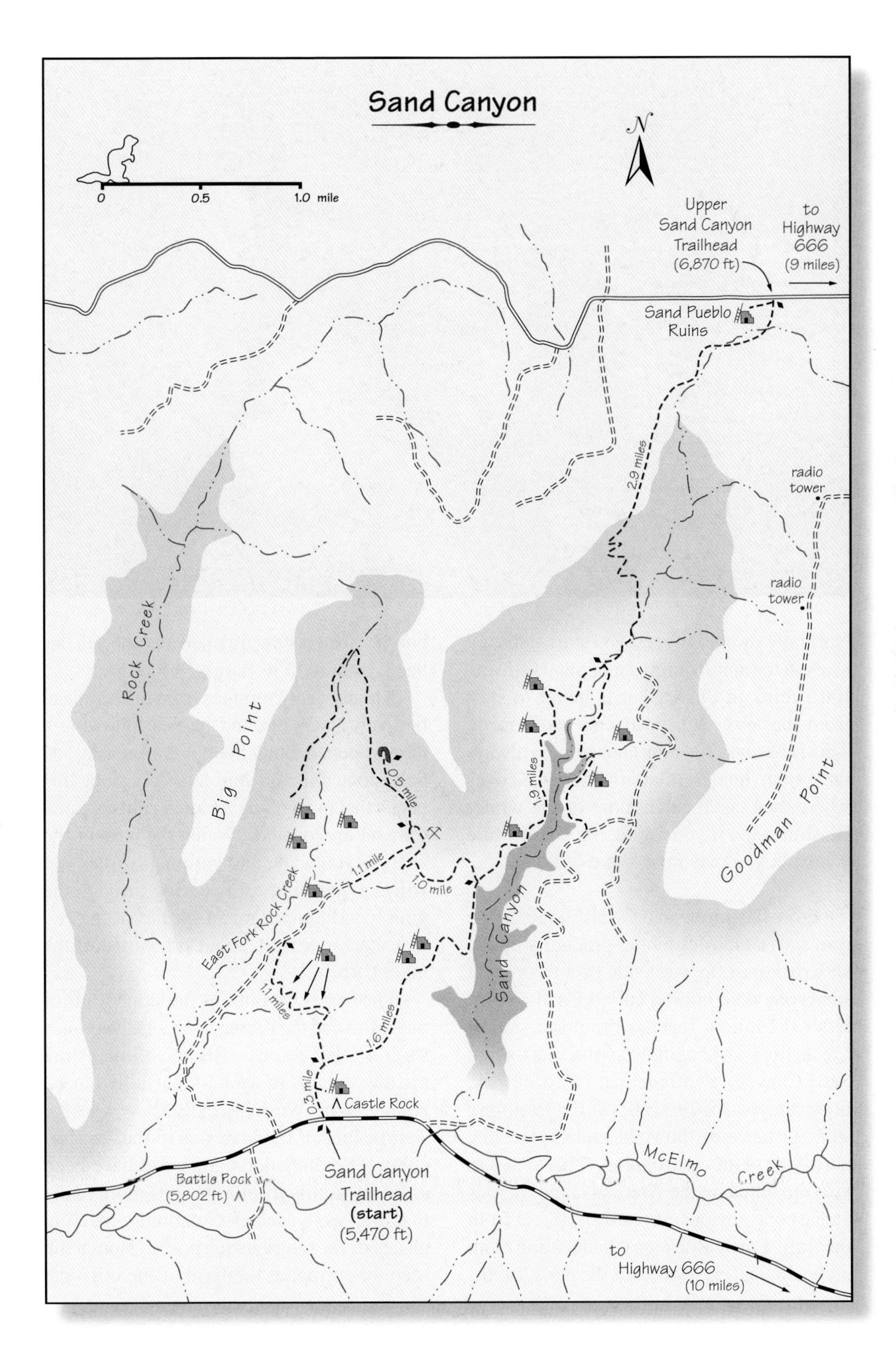
Sand Canyon
0
0.5
1.0 mile
N
Upper
Sand Canyon
Trailhead
(6,870 ft)
to
Highway
666
(9 miles)
Sand Pueblo
Ruins
2.9 miles
radio
tower
radio
tower
Rock Creek
Big Point
0.5 mile
1.9 miles
Goodman Point
1.1 mile
1.0 mile
East Fork Rock Creek
Sand Canyon
1.1 miles
1.6 miles
0.3 mile
Castle Rock
McElmo
Creek
Battle Rock
(5,802 ft)
Sand Canyon
Trailhead
(start)
(5,470 ft)
to
Highway 666
(10 miles)

Anasazi ruins in Sand Canyon

Normally I would suggest you start at the top to avoid the uphill climb out of Sand Canyon. But I think in this case it is better to start from the lower trailhead and walk north. This is because the Anasazis almost always built their homes in south-facing alcoves where they could catch more of the winter sunshine, and if you are facing south while you walk you may miss some of them.

From the trailhead on McElmo Road the trail starts out by climbing gradually up the slickrock past the west side of a prominent sandstone outcropping called Castle Rock. After 0.2 mile it reaches the north side of Castle Rock and begins to swing east toward Sand Canyon. Before leaving Castle Rock, however, you should walk off the trail for a short distance to the right and explore the north side of the outcropping. This area was also inhabited by the Anasazis, and there is at least one obvious ruin only 150 feet from the trail. Castle Rock was the location of an archeological excavation in the early 1990s, but the work is now finished and the site has been restored to its natural condition.

About twenty minutes from the trailhead the path levels out and begins following a narrow bench along the base of the Entrada Sandstone cliffs on your left. It is along this bench that most of the Anasazi ruins of Sand Canyon are located. Watch the base of the cliffs as you walk, and within 1.1 miles you will see your first ruin peering through the pinion and juniper forest. It lies at the end of a short spur trail, about 100 yards off the main path.

The first ruin contains the stone walls of one room and the rubble from what was once several other rooms. But most interesting are the remains of a small, partially buried circular kiva. We don't really know what the significance of the kiva was in the Anasazi culture, but they don't appear to have been ordinary family dwellings. It is more likely that they were used as community meeting places or for religious purposes. Notice the seep, or spring, at the base of the cliff just to the right of the ruin. This water source was undoubtedly an important factor in the choice of this particular alcove by the Indian family that once lived here.

The next ruin, a particularly picturesque one, is barely 0.1 mile beyond the first one. Notice at this ruin how the Indians filled in the floor of the alcove behind the retaining wall in order to level the floor of their dwelling. As the trail meanders northward the bench gets progressively narrower and narrower. Watch for other short trails branching off to the rim on the right, where you can look about 200 feet down into the bottom of the Sand Canyon drainage. There is seldom running water in Sand Canyon, but the streambed is almost never completely dry either. The series of springs in the bottom of the canyon would have provided a reliable source of water for the many Indians who lived here.

1.9 miles from the trailhead you will come to a junction where another well used trail comes in from the East Fork of Rock Canyon on the left. I will say more about this trail later, but for now bear right toward the bottom of Sand Canyon. Just 0.1 mile beyond the junction, you will come to point where the path drops about 100 feet into a small side canyon west of Sand Canyon. Notice the three exquisite cliff dwellings directly in front of you on the other side of the side canyon. They are probably the most photogenic of all the ruins you will pass on this hike. One of them, located in an odd onion-shaped alcove with colorful streaks of desert varnish, is particularly appealing. After dropping into the side canyon the trail bends around in front of the ruins and onto a lower bench. Take the time to climb up into one of the alcoves and you will see an impressive landscape dominated by the nearby Sleeping Ute Mountain, just as the original residents of the alcove saw it 700 years ago

Be sure also to watch the other side of the canyon for ruins as you walk. Another particularly large ruin is clearly visible on the east side of the canyon 0.4 mile upcanyon from the onion-shaped alcove. On the west side the path passes by at least two more easily accessible ruin sites before it reaches the bottom of the Sand Canyon drainage 3.8 miles from the trailhead. There is a trail junction in the bottom of the drainage with one trail staying in the bottom of the canyon and the other climbing up the other side. The trail up on the east side of Sand Canyon passes by three more ruins before joining a private road that leads back to the McElmo Road.

To reach Sand Pueblo, where your shuttle car is parked, you must bear left when the trail reaches the streambed and continue walking northeast along the bottom of the

Anasazi ruins in Sand Canyon

sandy wash. After 0.4 mile you will see a wooden trail marker, where the trail turns left to begin climbing out of the canyon. From this point on the trail becomes much steeper, as you must gain 950 feet before reaching the upper trailhead at the top of the mesa. You can monitor your progress by watching the radio towers on the other side of the canyon; they are about 200 feet higher in elevation than the upper trailhead. Most of the route out of the canyon is immersed in a forest of pinion pine and juniper, but occasionally the forest opens up to a nice view of Sleeping Ute Mountain with Sand Canyon in the foreground. You may also hear noises like motors running. Unfortunately there are several carbon dioxide wells on the east side of the canyon, and the pumps often interrupt the serenity—reminding us that ownership of Sand Canyon has already passed from the Anasazis to the white man.

About 1.0 mile after leaving the canyon bottom the trail starts to level out. Then, after another 0.7 mile it briefly reenters the upper reaches of Sand Canyon drainage once again before finally leaving the ravine near the upper trailhead.

East Fork Rock Canyon Trail

Sand Canyon Pueblo

Before leaving the upper Sand Canyon Trailhead be sure to check out the Sand Canyon Pueblo. It lies at the end of a short, well marked, 0.1 mile spur trail that departs on the west side of the Sand Canyon trailhead. This site is currently being excavated by the Crow Canyon Archeological Center, but the work is progressing very slowly and to the untrained eye the site looks more like a scattered pile of rocks than an ancient Indian pueblo. Probably the most impressive thing about the Sand Canyon Pueblo is its size. The ancient city is spread over an area of about four acres and contains some 84 kivas. During the late 1200s, at the peak of the Mesa Verde Anasazi culture, it must have been one of the largest settlements in the region. More information about the Sand Canyon Pueblo can be obtained from the Crow Canyon Archeological Center in Cortez at (970) 565-8975.

East Fork Rock Canyon

If it is inconvenient for you to place a shuttle car at the upper Sand Canyon trailhead you will be interested to know there is another trail in the lower part of Sand Canyon that can be used as a connecting trail back to the lower trailhead. This alternative route also passes by several Anasazi ruins as well as a large natural arch. The total length of the loop, including a short side trip to see the arch, is 6.4 miles.

After you have walked 1.9 miles from the lower Sand Canyon trailhead you will come to a trail junction where you must turn left on a trail leading to the East Fork of Rock Canyon. This trail proceeds in a northwesterly direction toward a large promontory of Dakota Sandstone that rises between Sand Canyon and East Fork. The trail rises slightly as it winds across the intervening layers of shale until it reaches the base of the sandstone cliffs 1.0 mile later. Near the base of the cliffs the trail passes just below an old mine that was dug a short distance into a yellowish deposit of siltstone, probably in search of uranium.

A few hundred yards beyond the mine the trail forks again. You must take the left fork to return to the trailhead, but first bear right for short side trip to see the natural arch. The arch is located at the base of the Dakota Sandstone about 0.4 mile beyond the trail junction, but you won't be able to see it until you are almost under it. After you have walked 0.3 miles you will see a fainter trail leaving on the right. This trail angles uphill, roughly parallel to the lower trail, to a point directly under the arch. If you want to get close enough to the arch to see daylight through it you will have to take this trail. The arch is about 100 feet across, but it is very close to the cliff. If you want to photograph it you should plan to be under it in the afternoon, as it is in the shade earlier in the day.

You can explore further by staying on the lower trail and continuing on past the arch. The trail arrives at the bottom of East Fork Rock Canyon after another 0.7 mile, then crosses the bottom of the drainage and turns south to follow the west side of the canyon. Otherwise, return to the trail junction near the mine and take the south fork back to the trailhead.

From the junction the trail immediately drops about 100 feet and proceeds in a southwesterly direction for 1.1 miles along a bench at the base of the Entrada Sandstone. This section of the trail is actually an old jeep road, but it doesn't appear to have been used in many years. After 1.1 miles the trail leaves the road and turns southeast, then climbs up to the base of the Entrada cliffs. Soon you will encounter the first of another four alcoves containing ruins. Most of them are very well preserved and easy to spot; the path passes just below them as it meanders along the base of the cliffs. Finally, 1.1 miles after leaving the jeep road, you will intersect the Sand Canyon trail again, and from there it is only 0.3 mile back to the trailhead.

East Fork Rock Canyon Natural Arch

Trail Maps

Most of the trails in this book can also be found on the following *Trails Illustrated* maps published by the National Geographic Society in Evergreen, Colorado.
They are available for purchase on our website:
www.colorado.utahtrails.com

Clark/Buffalo Park (map #117)
Includes Wyoming Trail (page 37)

Flat Tops NE/Trappers Lake (map #122)
Includes Lost Lakes—Devils Causeway (page 144), Hooper and Keener Lakes (page 150), Skinny Fish and McGinnis Lakes (page 154), Flat Tops (page 157)

Holy Cross/Ruedi Reservoir (map #126)
Includes Missouri Lakes/Holy Cross City (page 227), Fall Creek Pass/Tuhare Lakes (page 233)

Aspen/Independence Pass (map #127)
Includes a portion of Conundrum Creek—Gothic (page 178), Electric Pass (page 186), Lost Man Loop (page 190), La Plata Peak (page 216), Mount Massive (page 220), Mount Elbert (page 224)

Maroon Bells/Redstone/Marble (map #128)
Includes a portion of Conundrum Creek—Gothic (page 178), Maroon—Snowmass Trail (page 171)

Buena Vista/Collegiate Peaks (map #129)
Includes Kroenke Lake (page 194), Mount Yale (page 200), Lake Ann (page 203), Mount Huron (page 207), Missouri Gulch—Mount Belford (page 210)

Crested Butte/Pearl Pass (map #131)
Includes a portion of Conundrum Creek—Gothic (page 178)

Gunnison/Pitkin (map #132)
Includes Lamphier Lake/Gunsight Pass (page 167)

Kebler Pass/Paonia Reservoir (map #133)
Includes Dark Canyon (page 162)

Grand Mesa (map #136)
Includes Crag Crest Trail (page 386)

Pikes Peak/Canon City (map #137)
Includes The Crags (page 274)

Sangre De Cristo Mountains (map #138)
Incudes Brush Creek Lakes (page 277), Lakes of the Clouds (page 281), Venable and Comanche Trails (page 286), Humboldt Peak (page 290), Music Pass/Sand Creek Lakes (page 294), Willow Lake (page 299), South Zapata Lake (page 304)

La Garita/Cochetopa Hills (map #139)
Includes Powderhorn Lakes (page 325)

Weminuche Wilderness (map #140)
Includes Fourmile Creek (page 312), Rainbow Hot Springs (page 317), Highland Mary Lakes (page 340)

Telluride /Silverton /Ouray /Lake City (map #141)
Includes Uncompahgre Peak (page 329), Red Cloud and Sunshine Peaks (page 332), Handies Peak (page 336), Ice Lake Basin (page 345), Bear Creek Trail (page 350), Blue Lakes (page 355), Sneffels Highline Trail (page 361), Lizard Head Trail (page 367), Navajo Lake (page 372)

South San Juan/Del Norte (map #142)
Includes Ruybalid Lake (page 308)

Rocky Mountain National Park (map #200)
Includes Finch and Pear Lakes (page 76), Bluebird Lake (page 79), Longs Peak (page 84), Flattop Mountain/Hallett Peak (page 91), Odessa and Fern Lakes (page 95), Glacier Gorge (page 99), Loch Vale (page 102), Lulu City (page 107), East Inlet (page 112)

Colorado National Monument (map #208)
Includes Monument Canyon (page 397), Liberty Cap – Ute Canyon (page 403)

Black Canyon of the Gunnison (map #245)
Includes Black Canyon of the Gunnison (page 375), Gunnison Gorge (page 378)

Further Reading

Scott Warren, *100 Classic Hikes in Colorado, 2nd edition,* The Mountaineers Books, Seattle, 2001. A colorful compendium of hiking trails around Colorado by a notable author/photographer whose work has taken him around the world.

Mark Pearson and John Fielder, *The Complete Guide to Colorado's Wilderness Areas,* Westcliffe Publishers, Englewood, Colorado, 1994. Although this book is now 14 years old, it is still the most comprehensive book available on Colorado's Wilderness Areas.

Mark Pearson and John Fielder, *Colorado's Canyon Country,* Westcliffe Publishers, Englewood, Colorado, 2001. The definitive book on western Colorado's canyon country, written by a leading authority and activist on Colorado wilderness issues.

Gerry Roach, *Colorado's Fourteeners: From Hikes to Climbs, 2nd edition,* Fulcrum Publishing, Golden, Colorado, 1999. Roach is the undisputed authority on Colorado's celebrated fourteen-thousand-foot peaks.

Terry Root, Managing Editor, *The Colorado Trail: The Official Guide, 6th Edition,* The Colorado Mountain Club Press, Golden, Colorado, 2002. The Colorado Trail is a continuous, non-motorized recreational trail that traverses Colorado for 471 miles from Denver to Durango. This book is currently the most complete description available of this trail.

Tom Lorang Jones and John Fielder, *Colorado's Continental Divide Trail: The Official Guide,* Westcliffe Publishers, Englewood, Colorado, 2004. The Continental Divide Trail extends for some 3000 miles from Mexico to Canada. This book provides a step-by-step description of the 759-mile segment that crosses Colorado.

Ralph Lee Hopkins and Lindy Birkel Hopkins, *Hiking Colorado's Geology,* The Mountaineers Books, Seattle, 2000. 50 hikes in central and western Colorado are described from a geologist's point of view.

Halka Chronic and Felicie Williams, *Roadside Geology of Colorado, 2nd edition,* Mountain Press Publishing Company, Missoula, Montana, 2002. A revision of Halka Cronic's classic *Roadside Geology*, first published in 1980.

G. K. Guennel, *Guide to Colorado Wildflowers,* Westcliffe Publishers, Englewood, Colorado, 2005. The author, an accomplished artist and PhD botanist, has illustrated this two volume set with a stunning collection of photographs and water colors. Volume one covers Colorado's plains and foothills. Volume two describes flowers found in the mountains.

John Fielder, *John Fielder's Best of Colorado,* Westcliffe Publishers, Englewood, Colorado, 2002. A compilation of Colorado's best hiking trails, bed & breakfasts, restaurants, and scenic places, written and illustrated by Colorado's best known scenic photographer.

Public Lands Agencies

National Park Service

Black Canyon Of The Gunnison National Park
102 Elk Creek
Gunnison, CO 81230
970-641-2337

Great Sand Dunes National Park
11500 Highway 150
Mosca, CO 81146-9798
719-378-6399

Mesa Verde National Park
P.O. Box 8
Mesa Verde, CO 81330-0008
970-529-4465

Rocky Mountain National Park
1000 Highway 36
Estes Park, CO 80517-8397
970-586-1206

Colorado National Monument
Fruita, CO 81521-0001
970-858-3617

Dinosaur National Monument
4545 E. Highway 40
Dinosaur, CO 81610-9724
970-374-3000

Florissant Fossil Beds National Monument
P.O. Box 185
Florissant, CO 80816
719-748-3253

Yucca House National Monument
P.O. Box 8
Mesa Verde, Colorado 81330
970-529-4465

Curecanti National Recreation Area
102 Elk Creek
Gunnison, CO 81230
970-641-2337

National Forest Service

Arapaho & Roosevelt National Forests
www.fs.fed.us/r2/arnf/
2150 Centre Ave., Building E
Fort Collins, CO 80526
phone: 970-295-6700

Boulder Ranger District
2140 Yarmouth Ave.
Boulder, CO 80301
phone: 303-541-2500

Canyon Lakes Ranger District
2150 Centre Ave., Building E
Fort Collins, CO 80526
phone: 970-295-6700

Clear Creek Ranger District
101 Chicago Creek Road
P.O. Box 3307
Idaho Springs, CO 80452
phone: 303-567-3000

Pawnee National Grassland
660 "O" Street
Greeley, CO 80631
phone: 970-346-5000

Sulphur Ranger District
9 Ten Mile Drive
P.O. Box 10
Granby, Colorado 80446
phone: 970-887-4100

Pike & San Isabel National Forests
www.fs.fed.us/r2/psicc/coma/
2840 Kachina Drive
Pueblo, CO 81008
phone: 719-553-1400

Comanche National Grassland
Carrizo Unit
P.O. Box 127
27204 Highway 287
Springfield, CO 81073
phone: 719-523-6591

Timpas Unit
1420 East 3rd Street
La Junta, CO 81050
phone: 719-384-2181

Leadville Ranger District
810 Front Street
Leadville, CO 80461
phone: 719-486-0749

Pikes Peak Ranger District
601 South Weber
Colorado Springs, CO 80903
phone: 719-636-1602

Salida Ranger District
325 West Rainbow Blvd.
Salida, CO 81201
phone: 719-539-3591

San Carlos Ranger District
3028 East Main Street
Canon City, CO 81212
phone: 719-269-8500

South Park Ranger District
P.O. Box 219
320 Hwy 285
Fairplay, CO 80440
phone: 719-836-2031

South Platte Ranger District
19316 Goddard Ranch Court
Morrison, CO 80465
phone: 303-275-5610

Grand Mesa, Uncompahgre, and Gunnison National Forests
www.fs.fed.us/r2/gmug/
2250 Highway 50
Delta, CO 81416
phone: 970-874-6600

Grand Valley Ranger District
2777 Crossroads Blvd, Suite 1
Grand Junction, CO 81506
phone: 970-242-8211

Gunnison Ranger District
216 N. Colorado
Gunnison, CO 81230
phone: 970-641-0471

Gunnison Ranger District at Lake City
P.O. Box 89
Lake City, CO 81235
phone: 970-944-2500

Ouray Ranger District
2505 S. Townsend
Montrose, CO 81401
phone: 970-240-5300

Norwood Ranger District
P.O. Box 388
1150 Forest
Norwood, CO 81423
phone: 970-327-4261

Paonia Ranger District
P.O. Box 1030
North Rio Grande Avenue
Paonia, CO 81428
phone: 970-527-4131

Rio Grande National Forest
www.fs.fed.us/r2/riogrande/
1803 W. Highway 160
Monte Vista, CO 81144
phone: 719-852-5941

Conejos Peak Ranger District
15571 County Road T5
LaJara, CO 81140
phone: 719-274-8971

Divide Ranger District
13308 West Highway 160
Del Norte, CO 81132
phone: 719-657-3321

Divide Ranger District (Creede)
Third and Creede Avenue
Creede, CO 81130
phone: 719-658-2556

Saguache Ranger District
46525 State Highway 114
Saguache, CO 81149
phone: 719-655-2547

Medicine Bow and Routt National Forests
www.fs.fed.us/r2/mbr/
2468 Jackson Street
Laramie, WY 82070
phone: 307-745-2300

Hahns Peak/Bears Ears Ranger District
925 Weiss Drive
Steamboat Springs, CO 80487-9315
phone: 970-879-1870

Parks Ranger District at Walden
P.O. Box 158
100 Main Street
Walden, CO 80480
phone: 970-723-8204

Parks Ranger District at Kremmling
P.O. Box 1210
2103 E. Park Ave.
Kremmling, CO 80459
phone: 970-724-3000

Yampa Ranger District
P.O. Box 7
300 Roselawn Ave.
Yampa, CO 80483
phone: 970-638-4516

San Juan National Forest
www.fs.fed.us/r2/sanjuan/
15 Burnett Court
Durango, CO 81301
phone: 970-247-4874

San Juan Public Lands Center
15 Burnett Court
Durango, CO 81301
phone: 970-247-4874

Columbine Ranger District
P.O. Box 439
367 South Pearl St.
Bayfield, CO 81122
phone: 970-884-2512

San Juan Mountains Center
P.O. Box 709
1246 Blair St.
Silverton, CO 81433
phone: 970-387-5530

Dolores Ranger District
29211 Highway 184
Dolores, CO 81323
phone: 970-882-7296

Pagosa Ranger District
P.O. Box 310
180 Second St
Pagosa Springs, CO 81147
phone: 970-264-2268

White River National Forest
www.fs.fed.us/r2/whiteriver/
900 Grand Ave.
P.O. Box 948
Glenwood Springs CO 81602
phone: 970-945-2521

Aspen Ranger District
806 West Hallam
Aspen, CO 81611
phone: 970-925-3445

Blanco Ranger District
220 East Market Street
Meeker, CO 81641
phone: 970-878-4039

Dillon Ranger District
680 Blue River Parkway
Silverthorne, CO 80498
phone: 970-468-5400

Eagle Ranger District
125 West 5th Street
Eagle, CO 81631
phone: 970-328-6388

Holy Cross Ranger District
24747 Highway 24
Minturn, CO 81645
phone: 970-827-5715

Sopris Ranger District
620 Main Street
Carbondale, CO 81623
phone: 970-963-2266

Rifle Ranger District
0094 County Road 244
Rifle, CO 81650
phone: 970-625-2371

Bureau of Land Management

Canyons of the Ancients National Monument
27501 Highway 184
Dolores, CO 81323
phone: 970-882-5600

Columbine Field Office
P.O. Box 439
367 Pearl St.
Bayfield, CO 81122
phone: 970-884-2512

Dolores Public Lands Office
29211 Highway 184
Dolores, CO 81323
phone: 970-882-7296

Del Norte Field Office
13308 W. Highway 160
Del Norte, CO 81132
phone: 719-657-3321

Glenwood Springs Field Office
50629 Highway 6 & 24
Glenwood Springs, CO 81601
phone: 970-947-2800

Grand Junction Field Office
2815 H Road
Grand Junction, CO 81506
phone: 970-244-3000

Gunnison Field Office
216 N. Colorado
Gunnison, CO 81230
phone: 970-641-0471

Gunnison Gorge National Conservation Area
2465 South Townsend
Montrose, CO 81401
phone: 970-240-5300

Kremmling Field Office
P.O. Box 68
2103 E. Park Avenue
Kremmling, CO 80459
phone: 970-724-3000

La Jara Field Office
15571 County Rd T5
La Jara, CO 81140
phone: 719-274-8971

Little Snake Field Office
455 Emerson Street
Craig, CO 81625
phone: 970- 826-5000

McInnis Canyons National Conservation Area
2815 H Road
Grand Junction, CO 81506
phone: 970-244-3000

Pagosa Field Office
P.O. Box 310
Pagosa Springs, CO 81147
phone: 970-264-2268

Royal Gorge Field Office
3028 East Main Street
Canon City, CO 81212
phone: 719-269-8500

Saguache Field Office
P.O. Box 67
46525 Highway 114
Saguache, CO 81149
phone: 719-655-2547

San Juan Public Lands Center
15 Burnett Court
Durango, CO 81301
phone: 970- 247-4874

San Luis Valley Public Lands Center
1803 West Highway 160
Monte Vista, CO 81144
phone: 719-852-5941

Uncompahgre Field Office
2465 South Townsend Ave.
Montrose, CO 81401
phone: 970-240-5300

White River Field Office
220 East Market St.
Meeker, CO 81641
phone: 970-878-3800

Index

Bierstadt Willows

Brainard Lake

C

Crestone Needle

D

E

Engineer Pass

Kroenke Lake

Mitchell Lake

Pear Lake

Q

R

S

Sand Canyon

T

U

Uncompahgre Peak

V

W

Wyoming Trail

X, Y

Z

photo by Lily Day

David Day graduated in 1965 with an engineering degree from the University of Arizona. His first job after college was with the Cabin Creek Hydroelectric Project in Colorado, after which he joined the Peace Corps to teach electronics in Malaysia. He held a variety of jobs in Arizona, Nevada, Hawaii, and American Samoa before switching careers in 1977 to become a full time writer and photographer. His publications include books on Southeast Asia, Utah, and now Colorado. He currently lives with his family in Orem, Utah.

Our lives are so short, and our modern society is so filled with distractions. But it is vital that we set aside adequate time to experience the incredible wonders of our natural world. The beauty and the mystery of nature are God's gifts to mankind, and we alone have been blessed with the capacity to enjoy and appreciate His creation.